AF773831

Chase Global Data & Research

# C. David Chase

**JENNIFER PAYDOS**
Associate Editor

**Jeffrey Kooken**
Associate Analyst

**James Worthley**
Associate Analyst

# Chase Investment Performance Digest

## Performance and Rankings of the World's Major Investments

Stocks/Bonds/Currencies/Collectibles
Commodities/Metals/Insurance

## 1960 through 1995

CHASE GLOBAL DATA & RESEARCH
A DIVISION OF CHASE INVESTMENT CONSULTING GROUP, INC.

Copyright ©1996 by C. David Chase

All rights reserved.
Including the right of reproduction in whole or in part in any form.

No part of this publication may be reproduced, stored in a retrieval system, or transmitted, in any form or by any means, electronic, mechanical, photocopying, recording, scanning, facsimile, or otherwise, without the prior written permission of the copyright holder.

All Chase Global Data & Research (CGDR) products and underlying data are protected under U.S. Copyright Law. Permission requests by the customer to reprint or distribute CGDR data, graphics, or any form of software output must be submitted in advance in writing to Chase Global Data & Research. Licensing arrangements are available for CGDR products for use in seminars, sales and marketing presentations, and central data feed communication systems.

Published by: Chase Global Data and Research
A Division of Chase Investment Consulting Group, Inc.
73 Junction Square
Concord, MA 01742

Telephone (508) 371-9100 Facsimile (508) 371-9105

*InvestmentView*® is a registered trademark.

This publication is designed to provide accurate and authoritative information in regard to the subject matter covered, but it is not guaranteed. It is sold with the understanding that neither the author nor the publisher is engaged in rendering legal, accounting, or other professional service. If legal or other expert assistance is required, the services of a competent professional person should be sought.

The information contained herein is obtained from sources believed to be reliable, but neither its accuracy nor completeness is guaranteed.

From a Declaration of Principles jointly adopted by a committee of the American Bar Association and a Committee of Publishers.

1 2 3 4 5 6 7 8 9 0 6 5 4 3 2 1 0 9

Manufactured in the United States of America.

Library of Congress catalog number 90 - 660313

ISBN: 0-944822-08-8

To Barbara, Danny, and Paul

# About the author....

C. David Chase is a nationally recognized authority on dealing with the financial services industry—its services and products. Mr. Chase is a former Vice President with E.F. Hutton, having worked in the brokerage industry at Hutton and Merrill Lynch for over fifteen years. He wrote the highly acclaimed book, ***Mugged on Wall Street*** (Simon and Schuster), which *Changing Times* magazine called the best book ever written on how investors should deal with the financial system. ***Mugged on Wall Street*** was released in paperback by Fireside Press.

David Chase is founder and president of Chase Global Data & Research (CGDR), located in Concord, Massachusetts. CGDR publishes annually the ***Chase Investment Performance Digest*** (1996 edition, 404 pages). The *Digest* is the complete one-stop reference for performance results, rankings, and risk analyses on over 75 of the world's major investments. Complete annual, 3, 5, 10, 15, 20, 25, and 35 year reviews detail results on investments from 1960 through 1995. ***The Investors's Guide to Investment Performance*** (160 pages) tracks 20 investments in a manner similar to the *Digest.* CGDR also publishes a variety of ***Page Charts***, ***Wall Charts***, and ***Seminar Slide Show*** program materials.

Chase Global Data offers computer users monthly investment performance returns in its ***InvestmentView®*** **Software** series—which monitor monthly performance returns on over 300 major indices, plus additonal optional databases such as 8,000 mutual funds, 3,000 variable annuities, 7,000 stocks, and 1,200 money managers. ***InvestmentView®*** also provides definitions for all indices.

The powerful ***InvestmentView® HYPOTHETICAL*** software enables investors and financial professionals to easily compare, manipulate, and create high quality graphic presentations on over 300 major investment indices and 8,000+ *Lipper Analytical Services* mutual fund performance returns and characteristics. It comes complete with NASD reviewed disclaimers, blending options, college and retirement planners, customized cover pages, automatic page numbering, and much more.

For a catalog about our products and services please call (508)371-9100, or write:

Chase Global Data & Research, 73 Junction Square, Concord, MA, 01742.

(Please refer to the Order Information
forms on page 88, 296, and at the end of the *Digest.*)

# TABLE OF CONTENTS

# TABLE OF CONTENTS (con't.)

## TABLE OF CONTENTS (con't.)

# Introduction

"Those who do not heed the lessons of history are doomed to repeat it."

George Santayana

From early childhood we are taught that when you do your homework, you get the right answers. The *Chase Investment Performance Digest* was written with that premise in mind. The *Digest* has done your investment homework... for you. It's all about the performance results, and risks, inherent to the world's major investments. Now, once you review the *Digest* before you invest, you'll have the right answers. Then you can make the right investment moves and avoid costly mistakes, and unnecessary risks. You'll quickly appreciate how history, when it comes to investments, does repeat itself. And you will also learn how many myths about investments are just plain wrong.

Our many dedicated readers tell us the greatest strength of the *Digest* is that it's so easy to use, and is equally helpful to either an unsophisticated, or highly sophisticated investor. Over 75 subjects are reviewed in an identical, "apples to apples" manner. The *Digest* is not a textbook, and its graphs and tables are as fun and easy to use as they are important to your investment success. You needn't *guess* about your investing anymore. And remember, all subjects have identical statistical and graphic presentations, making "apples-to-apples" comparison easy!

Until the *Digest* was introduced, one key problem facing investors was there simply was no central source of information which had sought out and compiled complete historical returns, and ranked all major investments' relative performances—even though countless statistics surround the history, trading, and reporting of all investments. The absence of a complete, centralized, up-to-date historical reference to serve investors and investment professionals was incredible yet real. Because of this long standing vacuum regarding investment performance, too many myths still surround investors' decision making. This lack of knowledge has been a chief culprit in causing investors undue losses.


©1996 Chase Global Data & Research
73 Junction Square, Concord, MA 01742

Today's challenge for successful investing is to separate myth from reality, opinion from fact. The following are just a few long-held investment myths—countered with reality.

MYTH: The Swiss franc is a haven in bad times in its ability to outperform inflation.

REALITY: Inflation outperformed by over 35% the Swiss franc over the past 35 years (1961-1995) —inclusive of the period when currencies were fixed from free trading.

MYTH: Gold, Silver, and Platinum are the world's best investments during recessionary times.

REALITY: Over the past three decades, oil dramatically outperformed all major investments during recessions.

MYTH: Basic investments such as U.S. government bonds are weak performers versus more sophisticated alternatives.

REALITY: The U.S. Government 10-year bond always provided above average returns versus all other alternatives over extended time frames—15, 20, 25, and 35 year rankings. Extremely few alternative investments were as consistent or as continually above average.

No doubt, as you examine the data in the following pages, you will find your own startling "Myth versus Reality" examples.

**USING the *Chase Investment Performance Digest*.....**

When reviewing any investment in the *Digest* for more information, remember that each subject is *identically compared and reviewed* in its respective chapter by way of:

- Investment Performance Table
  (1-5-10-15-20-25-35 year performance results)
- Line Graph of Risk/Volatility Factor

©1996 Chase Global Data & Research
73 Junction Square, Concord, MA 01742

(Standard Deviation = risk quotient)

- Bar Graph Comparison of Subject vs. "Similar" Investments (5-10-15-20-25-35 yrs)

- Bar Graph Comparison of Subject vs. "Dissimilar" Investments

- Bar Graph Comparison of Subject vs. Inflation (reviewing the past decade)

**Performance Tables**

The *Digest* outlines the performance results of the modern era (1960 through 1995). Each subject's annual performance is presented in a Performance Table. In addition, all previous 5-year intervals of the past three decades (i.e. six 5-year groupings) are reviewed for their average 5-year performance results. Performance Returns are also presented for additional, longer-term time frames: 10-15-20-25 and 35-year spans.

Returns are presented two ways: 1) on a percentage basis, and 2) on the basis of how a $10,000 initial investment grew in dollars over the various time spans. That way if you don't like percentages, just review how your $10,000 investment performed instead.

**Risk (Volatility of Return) Reviews**

Each chapter's subject review contains a Line Chart, which immediately follows the Performance Table. This Line Chart not only visually outlines the way the subject gyrated during the past three decades, but it also contains the Risk/Volatility Factor (Standard Deviation data) detailing the level of volatility incurred as the investment's return was created over the period of time analyzed. (Editors Note: see page 10 for the complete definition of Risk/Volatility Factor, i.e. Standard Deviation.)

The higher the RISK/VOLATILITY FACTOR the more risky the investment. If you want a conservative investment, you want a lower figure. Yes, now you're truly doing your homework. Also note that the figure below the Risk/Volatility Factor is the "simple" annual return for the investment over the period outlined, as opposed to the "compound" return used in all other calculations in the *Digest*. (Note: simple returns are always higher than compound returns over sustained periods of time.) The compound return is, however, the better figure to use when comparing investment results.

©1996 Chase Global Data & Research
73 Junction Square, Concord, MA 01742

## Similar and Dissimilar Bar Chart Comparisons

In each chapter following the Line Chart (Risk analysis chart) are two Bar Charts. Each chart has three subjects presented versus the chapter's subject. The Bar chart comparisons review 5-10-15-20-25 and 35-year time spans.

The first Bar Chart compares "like" investments to the subject investment, i.e. a given stock index versus other stock indices. The following Bar Chart compares the subject investment to completely "dissimilar" investments. All Bar chart comparisons review and compare the growth of a $10,000 initial investment for the three detailed subjects.

## Inflation Comparisons

The final Bar Chart in each chapter details the subject investment versus Inflation. The most recent decade is reviewed, with returns during each year compared against Inflation. This Chart gives you the ability to quickly note how consistent the subject investment has been in outperforming a key benchmark (Inflation), while at the same time allowing you another manner in which to review its volatility.

Besides the Chapters on each investment subject, there are two additional key areas within the *Digest*:

## Performance Ranking Tables

All subjects in the book are ranked in the Performance Ranking Table Section (pages 11-28). For the first time, every major investment subject has been analyzed and ranked against all other major investments in an "apples to apples" head-on comparison. All figures are compound returns, over identical periods of time:

- 1 year ranking (1995)
- 3 year rankings (1993-1995)
- 5 year rankings (1991-1995)
- 10 year rankings (1986-1995)
- 15 year rankings (1981-1995)
- 20 year rankings (1976-1995)
- 25 year rankings (1971-1995)
- 35 year rankings (1961-1995)

We are confident that you will easily be able to gauge how strong any investment you are considering has truly been—over a variety of time frame comparisons—when you review this section of the *Digest*. For your convenience, we have also included additional time frames, over and above the immediate time spans preceding 1995, such

©1996 Chase Global Data & Research
73 Junction Square, Concord, MA 01742

that you can review a Ranking Table for: 1986-1990, 1981-1990, 1976-1990, 1971-1990, and so forth....

## Master Review Tables

There are a great deal of subjects, and thus many annual return figures available in the *Digest's* thirty year review. While a subject's returns for each year is obviously found within its chapter, it is nice to know there is an additional reference area. For your convenience, each subject's annual returns are located, along with all other subjects' annual returns, within an eight-page section of the *Digest* entitled Master Review Tables (pages 1-9).

Imagine, spread over eight pages (two pages for each decade) are 2,300+ returns affording you easy, at-a-glance comparisons. Just look up a year, scan for your subject, and you'll know its return for that date. And you can quickly see all other subjects' returns for that year as well. Recession years (note: there have been six recessions during the past four decades) are duly noted to help you know how investments fared during bad times, as well as good. You'll save hours of research time, and get the answers you need... fast.

You now have the single reference which places financial history at your fingertips—its patterns and its aberrations. Remember, proper use of investment history involves identifying when a pattern is highly repetitious, when an extreme is an extreme (and not merely abnormal performance), and when an investment's volatility is either a constant disadvantage, or a factor that can be turned to your advantage—there is a difference. And knowing is profiting.

Investment professionals—and all investors who care about the dollars they invest—know that accurate information is the basis for good investment results. The *Digest* enables investors to obtain a clear and proper investment prospective for any investment and its alternatives, avoid undue investment risks, debunk investment myths, and consistently profit from investment decisions. In the past, when you didn't know the facts about an investment and its alternatives, you ended up guessing first, and investing second. The *Chase Investment Performance Digest* makes guessing "history"... so investing is no longer a matter of chance.

©1996 Chase Global Data & Research
73 Junction Square, Concord, MA 01742

SECTION I

# Master Review Tables™ (1960 through 1995)

# MASTER REVIEW TABLE™ - 1990's

| | | 95 | 94 | 93 | 92 | 91* | 90* |
|---|---|---|---|---|---|---|---|
| | | % Return | | | | | |
| Major Financial Indicators | Inflation Rate | 2.5 | 2.7 | 2.8 | 2.9 | 3.1 | 6.1 |
| | GDP Change | 2.9 | 3.9 | 3.1 | 2.3 | -0.6 | 1.2 |
| | Dow Jones 30 Ind. Avg. P/E Ratio | 15.6 | 15.0 | 25.6 | 30.5 | 64.3 | 15.3 |
| | S&P 500 Composite Index P/E Ratio | 17.5 | 15.0 | 21.3 | 22.8 | 26.2 | 15.5 |
| | Dow Jones Utility Avg. P/E Ratio | 11.7 | 11.6 | 20.5 | 13.7 | 14.9 | 16.6 |
| | FHA Mortgage Rate | 8.2 | 8.7 | 7.5 | 8.5 | 9.3 | 10.2 |
| | Prime Rate | 8.8 | 7.2 | 6.0 | 6.3 | 8.4 | 10.0 |
| | U.S. Personal Disposable Income | 2.0 | 1.4 | 0.1 | 1.7 | -1.0 | 0.8 |
| | U.S. Unemployment Rate | 5.6 | 6.1 | 6.8 | 7.4 | 6.7 | 5.5 |
| U.S. Exchanges/ Indices | Dow Jones 30 Ind. Avg. with div. | 36.9 | 5.0 | 16.9 | 7.4 | 24.2 | -0.6 |
| | S&P 500 Composite Index with div. | 37.6 | 1.3 | 10.0 | 7.6 | 30.4 | -3.3 |
| | NASDAQ Index | 39.9 | -3.2 | 14.8 | 15.5 | 56.8 | -17.8 |
| | Value Line Composite Index | 19.3 | -6.0 | 10.7 | 7.0 | 27.2 | -24.3 |
| | Dow Jones Utility Avg. with div. | 32.2 | -15.1 | 9.6 | 4.0 | 15.1 | -4.5 |
| | Lipper Growth Mutual Fund Avg. with div. | 30.8 | -2.2 | 10.9 | 7.9 | 36.6 | -4.6 |
| | Lipper Income Mutual Fund Avg. with div. | 21.7 | -2.9 | 12.2 | 10.0 | 23.8 | -0.2 |
| | CDA Equity Money Manager Index | 36.0 | -0.1 | 13.4 | 9.4 | 37.1 | -6.4 |
| Foreign Exchanges/ Indices | Frankfurt Index, local currency | 7.0 | -7.1 | 46.7 | -2.1 | 12.9 | -21.9 |
| | Frankfurt Index in U.S. Dollars | 7.5 | -6.2 | 43.5 | -2.2 | 12.7 | -19.1 |
| | London Index with div., local currency | 22.3 | -5.5 | 26.7 | 19.2 | 20.1 | -8.8 |
| | London Index with div. in U.S. Dollars | 22.1 | -5.2 | 26.0 | 15.6 | 19.4 | -7.1 |
| | Tokyo Index with div., local currency | 2.0 | 9.0 | 10.9 | -22.9 | -0.5 | -39.3 |
| | Tokyo Index with div. in U.S. Dollars | 2.0 | 10.1 | 12.1 | -22.9 | -0.4 | -37.0 |
| | Morgan Stanley Europe Index with div. | 22.1 | 2.7 | 29.8 | -4.3 | 13.7 | -3.4 |
| | Morgan Stanley EAFE Index with div. | 11.6 | 8.1 | 32.9 | -11.9 | 12.5 | -23.2 |
| | Morgan Stanley North America Idx with div. | 37.1 | 1.7 | 10.5 | 6.1 | 29.9 | -2.9 |
| | Morgan Stanley Pacific Index with div. | 3.0 | 13.0 | 36.0 | -18.2 | 11.5 | -34.3 |
| | Morgan Stanley Emerging Markets Index | -10.8 | -2.4 | 65.5 | 2.6 | 29.1 | -33.0 |
| | Morgan Stanley World Index with div. | 21.3 | 5.6 | 23.1 | -4.7 | 19.0 | -16.5 |
| | Chase Balanced Global Asset Index | 22.2 | 1.5 | 15.3 | 3.5 | 19.2 | -1.1 |
| | IFC Composite Index with div. | -8.4 | -12.0 | 79.6 | 3.3 | 39.5 | -2.2 |
| | IFC Asia Index with div. | -5.5 | -12.8 | 97.6 | 18.5 | 12.4 | -19.2 |
| | IFC EMEA Index with div. | 22.5 | -27.1 | 122.4 | -32.7 | -29.2 | 13.9 |
| | IFC Latin Index with div. | -16.9 | -9.4 | 60.8 | 3.5 | 139.3 | 9.1 |
| Foreign Bond Indices | Merrill Lynch Australia Gov't Bond Indx | 19.4 | -7.4 | 17.5 | 10.2 | 24.0 | 18.4 |
| | Merrill Lynch Germany Gov't Bond Indx | 16.0 | -1.3 | 13.6 | 13.1 | 10.9 | 3.7 |
| | Merrill Lynch Global Gov't Bond Indx | 17.3 | 1.8 | 14.8 | 7.4 | 16.6 | 11.3 |
| | Merrill Lynch Japan Gov't Bond Indx | 13.5 | -2.9 | 13.4 | 11.2 | 12.4 | 2.1 |
| | Merrill Lynch U.K. Gilt Gov't Bond Indx | 16.1 | -5.7 | 21.2 | 18.5 | 17.5 | 10.3 |
| Real Estate | U.S. Single Family House Price | 2.6 | 4.0 | 2.9 | 1.9 | 0.8 | 1.5 |
| | Farmland | 6.4 | 6.3 | 3.2 | 1.4 | 2.9 | 2.3 |
| | REITs | 18.3 | 0.8 | 18.6 | 12.2 | 35.7 | -17.4 |

*Recessions: July 1990 - March 1991

©1996 Chase Global Data & Research
73 Junction Square, Concord, MA 01742

## MASTER REVIEW TABLE™ - 1990's

| Category | Index | 95 | 94 | 93 | 92 | 91* | 90* |
|---|---|---|---|---|---|---|---|
| | | % Return | | | | | |
| U.S. Income/Interest Sensitive Indices | Lipper Fixed Income Mutual Fd. Avg. with divs. | 15.2 | -3.3 | 9.7 | 7.8 | 18.1 | 5.0 |
| | Lipper General Muni. Mutual Fd. Avg. with divs. | 16.8 | -6.5 | 12.4 | 8.7 | 12.1 | 6.1 |
| | Moody's Corp. Bond Yield, Aaa | 7.6 | 8.0 | 7.5 | 8.1 | 8.8 | 9.3 |
| | Moody's Corp. Bond Yield, Baa | 8.2 | 8.6 | 7.9 | 9.0 | 9.8 | 10.4 |
| | Merrill Lynch High Yield Bond Index | 18.5 | -0.7 | 18.2 | 21.2 | 40.2 | -4.2 |
| | Lehman Bros. Govt/Corp Index | 19.3 | -3.5 | 11.0 | 7.6 | 16.1 | 8.3 |
| | Lehman Bros. Corp. Long Term Index | 28.0 | -5.8 | 13.6 | 9.3 | 21.0 | 6.5 |
| | Lehman Bros. Trsy. Long Term Index | 30.7 | -7.6 | 17.3 | 8.0 | 18.5 | 6.3 |
| | Lehman Bros. Corp. Int. Term Index | 19.0 | -2.6 | 11.1 | 8.2 | 16.6 | 7.6 |
| | Lehman Bros. Trsy. Int. Term Index | 14.4 | -1.8 | 8.2 | 7.0 | 14.1 | 9.5 |
| | Lehman Bros. Mortgage-Backed Index | 16.8 | -1.6 | 6.8 | 7.0 | 15.7 | 10.7 |
| | Lehman Bros. Long Term Municipal Inx | 23.3 | -9.1 | 14.8 | 10.2 | 13.6 | 7.2 |
| | S&P Municipal Bond Yield | 6.0 | 6.2 | 5.6 | 6.4 | 6.9 | 7.3 |
| | U.S. Treasury 10-Year Bond Yield | 6.6 | 7.1 | 5.9 | 7.0 | 7.9 | 8.6 |
| | Salomon U.S. Treasury 10-Yr. Bond Index | 15.3 | -7.8 | 11.9 | 6.5 | 17.2 | 6.8 |
| | U.S. Treasury 3-Year Bond Yield | 6.3 | 6.3 | 4.4 | 5.3 | 6.8 | 8.3 |
| | U.S. Treasury 3-Month Bill Yield | 5.6 | 4.4 | 3.1 | 3.5 | 5.5 | 7.8 |
| | Certificates of Deposit Yield, 3-Month | 5.9 | 4.6 | 3.2 | 3.7 | 5.8 | 8.2 |
| | Taxable Money Market Average | 5.5 | 3.8 | 2.7 | 3.4 | 5.7 | 7.8 |
| | Tax-Free Money Market Avg. | 3.4 | 2.4 | 2.0 | 2.6 | 4.1 | 5.5 |
| | U.S. Savings Bonds | 4.9 | 4.0 | 4.0 | 5.4 | 5.9 | 6.0 |
| | GICs 1-Year | 6.0 | 5.3 | 3.4 | 3.9 | 5.9 | 8.0 |
| | GICs 5-Year | 6.7 | 7.1 | 5.6 | 6.7 | 8.0 | 9.0 |
| Commodities | Commodity Spot Price Index | 1.1 | 16.5 | 4.3 | -1.3 | -7.7 | -1.0 |
| | Gold | 1.2 | -2.4 | 17.5 | -5.6 | -10.1 | -2.5 |
| | Silver | 4.9 | -4.1 | 38.4 | -4.7 | -7.8 | -19.4 |
| | Crude Petroleum | 9.7 | -0.4 | -15.8 | 1.9 | -22.1 | 32.3 |
| | Diamonds | 1.2 | 0.8 | 1.1 | 2.3 | 5.8 | -2.8 |
| Insurance | AM Best Universal Life Policy Avg. Yld | 7.0 | 6.6 | 7.0 | 7.7 | 8.4 | 8.8 |
| | AM Best Single Prem. Deferred Annuity | 6.0 | 5.9 | 5.8 | 6.5 | 8.0 | 8.5 |
| | Lipper General Equity Variable Annuity | 25.5 | -1.9 | 12.2 | 8.1 | 34.4 | -6.5 |
| | Lipper Gen'l Fixed Inc.Variable Annuity | 12.5 | -4.7 | 11.2 | 8.3 | 20.1 | 2.8 |
| Currencies | Australian Dollar | -4.1 | 14.2 | -1.5 | -9.3 | -1.0 | -2.5 |
| | British Pound | -1.0 | 6.1 | -2.5 | -18.9 | -3.2 | 19.6 |
| | Canadian Dollar | 2.8 | -5.7 | -3.8 | -9.1 | 0.3 | -0.1 |
| | German Mark | 7.8 | 12.2 | -6.9 | -6.1 | -1.5 | 12.7 |
| | Japanese Yen | -3.8 | 12.2 | 11.8 | 0.0 | 8.9 | 5.9 |
| | Swiss Franc | 13.3 | 13.8 | -1.5 | -7.2 | -6.1 | 20.6 |
| | U.S. Dollar | -4.6 | -8.1 | 4.7 | 10.4 | 0.4 | -10.4 |
| Stock Index Yields | Dow Jones 30 Avg. Index Div. Yield | 2.3 | 2.8 | 2.7 | 3.1 | 3.0 | 4.0 |
| | Dow Jones Utility Index Div. Yield | 5.8 | 7.2 | 5.8 | 6.1 | 6.2 | 6.8 |
| | S&P 500 Composite Index Div. Yield | 2.2 | 2.9 | 2.7 | 2.8 | 2.9 | 3.7 |
| | London Index Dividend Yield | 3.8 | 4.0 | 3.4 | 4.3 | 5.0 | 5.5 |
| | Tokyo Index Dividend Yield | 0.9 | 0.7 | 0.8 | 0.9 | 0.6 | 0.5 |
| Foreign Inflation | Australian Inflation Rate | 4.5 | 1.0 | 1.8 | 1.0 | 3.2 | 7.3 |
| | Canadian Inflation Rate | 2.1 | 0.2 | 1.8 | 1.5 | 5.6 | 4.8 |
| | German Inflation Rate | 1.8 | 2.7 | 4.5 | 5.1 | 3.6 | 2.7 |
| | Japanese Inflation Rate | -0.2 | 0.7 | 1.3 | 1.7 | 3.3 | 3.1 |
| | U.K. Inflation Rate | 2.9 | 2.5 | 1.6 | 3.7 | 5.9 | 9.5 |

*Recessions: Jan. 1980 - July 1980; July 1990 - March 1991

©1996 Chase Global Data & Research
73 Junction Square, Concord, MA 01742

# MASTER REVIEW TABLE™ - 1980's

| | 89 | 88 | 87 | 86 | 85 | 84 | 83 | 82* | 81* | 80* |
|---|---|---|---|---|---|---|---|---|---|---|
| | % Return | | | | | | | | | |
| **Major Financial Indicators** | | | | | | | | | | |
| Inflation Rate | 4.7 | 4.4 | 4.4 | 1.1 | 3.8 | 4.0 | 3.8 | 3.8 | 8.9 | 12.5 |
| GDP Change | 2.5 | 3.9 | 3.1 | 2.9 | 3.2 | 6.2 | 3.9 | -2.2 | 1.8 | -0.5 |
| Dow Jones 30 Ind. Avg. P/E Ratio | 12.4 | 10.1 | 14.6 | 16.4 | 16.1 | 10.7 | 17.4 | 114.4 | 7.7 | 7.9 |
| S&P 500 Composite Index P/E Ratio | 15.5 | 11.7 | 14.1 | 16.7 | 14.5 | 10.1 | 11.8 | 11.1 | 8.1 | 9.2 |
| Dow Jones Utility Avg. P/E Ratio | 12.7 | 15.3 | 9.4 | 14.7 | 9.6 | 7.1 | 6.7 | 6.5 | 5.9 | 7.3 |
| FHA Mortgage Rate | 10.2 | 10.5 | 10.2 | 9.9 | 12.2 | 13.8 | 13.1 | 15.3 | 16.3 | 13.4 |
| Prime Rate | 10.9 | 9.3 | 8.2 | 8.3 | 9.9 | 12.0 | 10.8 | 14.9 | 18.9 | 15.3 |
| U.S. Personal Disposable Income | 1.0 | 3.0 | 0.7 | 2.3 | 2.1 | 6.4 | 1.9 | -0.1 | 1.3 | -0.6 |
| U.S. Unemployment Rate | 5.3 | 5.5 | 6.2 | 7.0 | 7.2 | 7.5 | 9.6 | 9.7 | 7.6 | 7.1 |
| **U.S. Exchanges/ Indices** | | | | | | | | | | |
| Dow Jones 30 Ind. Avg. with div. | 32.2 | 16.1 | 5.5 | 27.1 | 33.6 | 1.3 | 26.0 | 27.1 | -3.6 | 22.2 |
| S&P 500 Composite Index with div. | 31.4 | 16.3 | 5.1 | 18.6 | 31.6 | 6.1 | 22.4 | 21.4 | -5.0 | 32.3 |
| NASDAQ Index | 19.3 | 15.4 | -5.3 | 7.4 | 31.4 | -11.2 | 19.9 | 18.7 | -3.2 | 33.9 |
| Value Line Composite Index | 11.2 | 15.4 | -10.6 | 5.0 | 20.7 | -8.4 | 22.3 | 15.3 | -4.4 | 18.3 |
| Dow Jones Utility Avg. with div. | 35.3 | 15.6 | -7.9 | 27.1 | 27.6 | 25.5 | 21.8 | 22.2 | 5.7 | 17.8 |
| Lipper Growth Mutual Fund Avg. with divs. | 26.4 | 14.2 | 3.2 | 14.2 | 28.3 | -1.8 | 20.6 | 25.3 | -2.2 | 36.8 |
| Lipper Income Mutual Fund Avg. with divs. | 13.6 | 12.1 | -0.5 | 15.0 | 24.5 | 12.4 | 14.2 | 26.9 | 6.0 | 14.0 |
| CDA Equity Money Manager Index | 28.9 | 17.8 | 2.6 | 17.2 | 32.8 | 0.7 | 20.9 | 22.5 | -5.5 | 37.3 |
| **Foreign Exchanges/ Indices** | | | | | | | | | | |
| Frankfurt Index, local currency | 34.8 | 32.8 | -30.2 | 4.8 | 66.4 | 6.1 | 40.0 | 12.7 | 2.0 | -3.4 |
| Frankfurt Index in U.S. Dollars | 36.9 | 28.8 | -23.3 | 6.2 | 85.6 | 5.2 | 35.0 | 12.0 | 1.7 | -3.8 |
| London Index with div., local currency | 34.3 | 11.2 | 8.5 | 26.4 | 19.5 | 30.4 | 27.7 | 27.3 | 13.1 | 33.2 |
| London Index with div. in U.S. Dollars | 30.6 | 10.7 | 10.8 | 27.0 | 24.4 | 24.2 | 25.0 | 23.1 | 10.5 | 35.7 |
| Tokyo Index with div., local currency | 22.7 | 37.1 | 11.5 | 49.1 | 15.8 | 25.8 | 24.6 | 5.7 | 16.9 | 9.0 |
| Tokyo Index with div. in U.S. Dollars | 19.7 | 35.9 | 15.0 | 62.6 | 19.7 | 23.8 | 25.0 | 5.3 | 15.6 | 10.6 |
| Morgan Stanley Europe Index with div. | 29.1 | 16.4 | 4.1 | 44.5 | 79.8 | 1.3 | 22.4 | 5.7 | -10.5 | 14.5 |
| Morgan Stanley EAFE Index with div. | 10.8 | 28.6 | 24.9 | 69.9 | 56.7 | 7.9 | 24.6 | -0.9 | -1.0 | 24.4 |
| Morgan Stanley North America Idx with div. | 30.9 | 16.1 | 4.6 | 17.2 | 31.5 | 5.0 | 22.9 | 19.9 | -5.1 | 29.0 |
| Morgan Stanley Pacific Index with div. | 2.7 | 35.2 | 39.9 | 93.8 | 39.4 | 13.5 | 26.4 | -6.3 | 8.3 | 36.4 |
| Morgan Stanley Emerging Markets Index | 50.6 | 75.1 | na | na | na | na | na | na | na | na |
| Morgan Stanley World Index with div. | 17.2 | 24.0 | 16.8 | 42.8 | 41.8 | 5.8 | 23.3 | 11.3 | -3.3 | 27.7 |
| Chase Balanced Global Asset Index | 17.0 | 13.9 | 10.2 | 28.0 | 33.1 | 9.9 | 17.2 | 18.7 | 1.3 | 19.1 |
| IFC Composite Index with div. | 61.5 | na | na | na | na | na | na | na | na | na |
| IFC Asia Index with div. | 54.1 | na | na | na | na | na | na | na | na | na |
| IFC EMEA Index with div. | 75.8 | na | na | na | na | na | na | na | na | na |
| IFC Latin Index with div. | 76.2 | na | na | na | na | na | na | na | na | na |
| **Foreign Bond Indices** | | | | | | | | | | |
| Merrill Lynch Australia Gov't Bond Indx | 13.7 | 9.4 | 18.5 | 19.3 | na | na | na | na | na | na |
| Merrill Lynch Germany Gov't Bond Indx | 1.8 | 4.2 | 6.3 | 8.1 | na | na | na | na | na | na |
| Merrill Lynch Global Gov't Bond Indx | 4.8 | 4.4 | 18.0 | 23.0 | na | na | na | na | na | na |
| Merrill Lynch Japan Gov't Bond Indx | -1.3 | 6.1 | 6.4 | 10.7 | na | na | na | na | na | na |
| Merrill Lynch U.K. Gilt Gov't Bond Indx | 8.0 | 6.7 | 15.5 | 12.1 | na | na | na | na | na | na |
| **Real Estate** | | | | | | | | | | |
| U.S. Single Family House Price | 3.8 | 3.6 | 5.9 | 4.8 | 2.0 | 4.4 | 2.4 | 2.5 | 8.0 | 10.4 |
| Farmland | 5.7 | 5.5 | -6.4 | -10.2 | -11.0 | 1.7 | -4.3 | 0.5 | 11.1 | 17.4 |
| REITs | -1.8 | 11.4 | -10.7 | 19.2 | 5.9 | 14.8 | 25.5 | 31.6 | 8.6 | 28.0 |

*Recessions: Jan. 1980 - July 1980; July 1981 - Nov. 1982

©1996 Chase Global Data & Research
73 Junction Square, Concord, MA 01742

# MASTER REVIEW TABLE™ - 1980's

| Category | Index | 89 | 88 | 87 | 86 | 85 | 84 | 83 | 82 | 81* | 80* |
|---|---|---|---|---|---|---|---|---|---|---|---|
| | | % Return | | | | | | | | | |
| U.S. Income/Interest Sensitive Indices | Lipper Fixed Income Mutual Fd. Avg. w/divs. | 10.1 | 8.4 | 1.5 | 13.2 | 19.9 | 11.8 | 10.3 | 30.2 | 5.8 | 2.8 |
| | Lipper General Muni. Mutual Fd. Avg. w/divs. | 9.6 | 11.5 | -1.0 | 18.7 | 20.2 | 8.7 | 10.3 | 40.1 | -7.1 | -11.5 |
| | Moody's Corp. Bond Yield, Aaa | 9.3 | 9.7 | 9.4 | 9.0 | 11.4 | 12.7 | 12.0 | 13.8 | 14.2 | 11.9 |
| | Moody's Corp. Bond Yield, Baa | 10.2 | 10.8 | 10.6 | 10.4 | 12.7 | 14.2 | 13.6 | 16.1 | 16.0 | 13.7 |
| | Merrill Lynch High Yield Bond Index | 1.1 | 14.4 | 8.1 | 13.1 | 23.7 | 7.9 | 17.5 | 33.1 | 4.7 | -1.3 |
| | Lehman Bros. Govt/Corp Index | 14.2 | 7.6 | 2.3 | 15.6 | 21.3 | 15.0 | 8.0 | 31.1 | 7.3 | 3.1 |
| | Lehman Bros. Corp. Long Term Index | 15.3 | 10.5 | 1.5 | 18.7 | 28.0 | 17.7 | 8.3 | 44.5 | -0.2 | -2.6 |
| | Lehman Bros. Trsy. Long Term Index | 18.9 | 9.2 | -2.7 | 24.1 | 31.6 | 14.8 | 2.0 | 41.8 | 0.4 | -2.9 |
| | Lehman Bros. Corp. Int. Term Index | 13.0 | 8.0 | 3.9 | 13.5 | 18.5 | 14.9 | 10.7 | 30.0 | 9.0 | 5.3 |
| | Lehman Bros. Trsy. Int. Term Index | 12.7 | 6.3 | 3.6 | 13.0 | 18.2 | 14.2 | 8.0 | 25.0 | 10.9 | 7.1 |
| | Lehman Bros. Mortgage-Backed Index | 15.4 | 8.7 | 4.3 | 13.4 | 25.2 | 15.8 | 10.1 | 43.0 | 0.1 | 0.7 |
| | Lehman Bros. Long Term Municipal Inx | 12.0 | 13.5 | 0.0 | 21.0 | 22.8 | 11.0 | 8.7 | 43.9 | -11.3 | -8.3 |
| | S&P Municipal Bond Yield | 7.2 | 7.8 | 7.7 | 7.4 | 9.2 | 10.2 | 9.5 | 11.6 | 11.2 | 8.5 |
| | U.S. Treasury 10-Year Bond Yield | 8.5 | 8.9 | 8.4 | 7.7 | 10.6 | 12.4 | 11.1 | 13.0 | 13.9 | 11.5 |
| | Salomon U.S. Treasury 10-Yr. Bond Index | 16.4 | 6.4 | -3.2 | 19.7 | 27.3 | 14.3 | 2.9 | 33.5 | 5.4 | -0.1 |
| | U.S. Treasury 3-Year Bond Yield | 8.6 | 8.3 | 7.7 | 7.1 | 9.6 | 11.9 | 10.5 | 12.9 | 14.4 | 11.6 |
| | U.S. Treasury 3-Month Bill Yield | 8.4 | 6.9 | 6.0 | 6.2 | 7.7 | 9.9 | 8.9 | 11.1 | 14.8 | 11.9 |
| | Certificates of Deposit Yield, 3-Month | 9.1 | 7.7 | 6.9 | 6.5 | 8.0 | 10.4 | 9.1 | 12.3 | 15.9 | 13.1 |
| | Taxable Money Market Average | 8.9 | 7.1 | 6.1 | 6.3 | 7.7 | 10.0 | 8.6 | 12.2 | 16.8 | 12.8 |
| | Tax-Free Money Market Avg. | 5.9 | 4.8 | 4.1 | 4.3 | 4.9 | 5.6 | 4.8 | 6.9 | 7.1 | na |
| | U.S. Savings Bonds | 6.0 | 6.0 | 6.3 | 6.9 | 7.3 | 7.0 | 7.0 | 7.4 | 7.6 | 7.8 |
| | GICs 1-Year | 8.5 | 7.5 | 7.0 | 7.0 | 8.7 | 11.1 | 10.0 | 13.2 | na | na |
| | GICs 5-Year | 9.0 | 8.8 | 8.6 | 8.3 | 10.8 | 12.8 | 12.0 | 14.4 | na | na |
| Commodities | Commodity Spot Price Index | -8.4 | 10.1 | 13.1 | -3.6 | -8.0 | -7.4 | 22.2 | -9.0 | -11.8 | -1.4 |
| | Gold | -2.0 | -15.1 | 21.9 | 20.4 | 6.9 | -19.2 | -16.5 | 13.9 | -31.6 | 14.5 |
| | Silver | -14.0 | -10.1 | 24.8 | -8.0 | -8.3 | -28.9 | -18.2 | 32.7 | -46.4 | -29.3 |
| | Crude Petroleum | 24.7 | -21.0 | 36.3 | -55.3 | -2.0 | -2.2 | -9.6 | -7.4 | -4.4 | 20.2 |
| | Diamonds | -2.8 | 0.0 | 6.9 | 13.3 | -2.2 | -6.1 | -12.7 | -30.3 | -28.8 | -9.5 |
| Insurance | AM Best Universal Life Policy Avg. Yld | 8.9 | 8.8 | 8.9 | 10.5 | 10.5 | 11.3 | 11.0 | 11.5 | 12.0 | na |
| | AM Best Single Prem. Deferred Annuity | 8.6 | 8.5 | 8.1 | 9.0 | 10.5 | 11.4 | 10.9 | 13.3 | 11.8 | na |
| | Lipper General Equity Variable Annuity | 25.7 | 1.7 | 12.9 | 27.7 | 0.1 | na | na | na | na | na |
| | Lipper Gen'l Fixed Inc.Variable Annuity | 8.0 | 0.4 | 12.7 | 20.0 | 10.8 | na | na | na | na | na |
| Currencies | Australian Dollar | -7.7 | 18.3 | 8.5 | -2.5 | -17.3 | -8.2 | -8.4 | -13.1 | -4.5 | 6.7 |
| | British Pound | -10.8 | -4.2 | 27.3 | 2.5 | 25.2 | -20.6 | -9.9 | -15.4 | -20.2 | 7.5 |
| | Canadian Dollar | 2.9 | 9.0 | 6.2 | 1.2 | -5.5 | -5.7 | -1.1 | -3.6 | 0.5 | -1.9 |
| | German Mark | 6.0 | -12.3 | 22.8 | 27.0 | 28.9 | -13.5 | -12.7 | -5.8 | -12.5 | -11.9 |
| | Japanese Yen | -13.1 | -3.2 | 30.9 | 27.6 | 24.6 | -8.0 | 1.5 | -6.7 | -7.7 | 18.2 |
| | Swiss Franc | -2.7 | -15.3 | 26.6 | 27.5 | 26.8 | -16.2 | -7.7 | -10.7 | -1.6 | -9.8 |
| | U.S. Dollar | 0.5 | 8.3 | -17.6 | -16.0 | -18.4 | 14.9 | 10.5 | 13.3 | 15.6 | 5.4 |
| Stock Index Yields | Dow Jones 30 Avg. Index Div. Yield | 3.7 | 3.7 | 3.7 | 3.5 | 4.0 | 5.0 | 4.5 | 5.2 | 6.4 | 5.6 |
| | Dow Jones Utility Index Div. Yield | 6.3 | 8.1 | 9.1 | 7.4 | 8.1 | 9.2 | 9.8 | 10.4 | 10.3 | 8.9 |
| | S&P 500 Composite Index Div. Yield | 3.3 | 3.7 | 3.6 | 3.5 | 3.9 | 4.6 | 4.3 | 4.9 | 5.7 | 4.7 |
| | London Index Dividend Yield | 4.2 | 4.7 | 4.3 | 4.0 | 4.3 | 4.4 | 4.6 | 5.3 | 5.9 | 6.1 |
| | Tokyo Index Dividend Yield | 0.5 | 0.5 | 0.6 | 0.7 | 1.0 | 1.0 | 1.3 | 1.6 | 1.5 | 1.5 |
| Foreign Inflation | Australian Inflation Rate | 7.5 | 7.3 | 8.5 | 9.1 | 6.7 | 3.9 | 10.1 | 11.2 | 9.6 | 10.2 |
| | Canadian Inflation Rate | 5.0 | 4.0 | 4.4 | 4.2 | 4.0 | 4.3 | 5.8 | 10.8 | 12.4 | 10.2 |
| | German Inflation Rate | 2.8 | 1.3 | 0.2 | -0.1 | 2.2 | 2.4 | 3.3 | 5.3 | 6.3 | 5.5 |
| | Japanese Inflation Rate | 2.3 | 0.7 | 0.1 | 0.6 | 2.0 | 2.2 | 1.9 | 2.7 | 4.9 | 7.8 |
| | U.K. Inflation Rate | 7.8 | 4.9 | 4.1 | 3.4 | 6.1 | 5.0 | 4.6 | 8.6 | 11.9 | 18.0 |

*Recessions: Jan. 1980 - July 1980; July 1990 - March 1991

©1996 Chase Global Data & Research
73 Junction Square, Concord, MA 01742

# MASTER REVIEW TABLE™ - 1970's

% Return

| Group | Indicator | 79 | 78 | 77 | 76 | 75* | 74* | 73* | 72 | 71 | 70 |
|---|---|---|---|---|---|---|---|---|---|---|---|
| Major Financial Indicators | Inflation Rate | 13.3 | 9.0 | 6.7 | 4.9 | 6.9 | 12.3 | 8.7 | 3.4 | 3.3 | 5.6 |
| | GDP Change | 2.5 | 4.8 | 4.5 | 4.9 | -0.8 | -0.6 | 5.2 | 4.8 | 3.1 | 0.0 |
| | Dow Jones 30 Ind. Avg. P/E Ratio | 6.7 | 7.1 | 9.3 | 10.4 | 11.3 | 6.2 | 9.9 | 15.2 | 16.2 | 16.4 |
| | S&P 500 Composite Index P/E Ratio | 7.3 | 7.8 | 8.7 | 10.8 | 11.3 | 7.7 | 11.9 | 18.4 | 17.9 | 18.0 |
| | Dow Jones Utility Avg. P/E Ratio | 6.9 | 6.9 | 7.8 | 8.0 | 7.2 | 5.9 | 8.3 | 10.9 | 11.6 | 12.6 |
| | FHA Mortgage Rate | 12.2 | 10.2 | 9.0 | 8.3 | 9.3 | 9.5 | 8.8 | 7.6 | 7.6 | 8.4 |
| | Prime Rate | 12.7 | 9.1 | 6.8 | 6.8 | 7.9 | 10.8 | 8.0 | 5.3 | 5.7 | 7.9 |
| | U.S. Personal Disposable Income | 1.6 | 4.0 | 2.2 | 2.9 | 0.7 | -1.7 | 6.0 | 3.4 | 2.7 | 2.7 |
| | U.S. Unemployment Rate | 5.8 | 6.1 | 7.1 | 7.7 | 8.5 | 5.6 | 4.9 | 5.6 | 5.9 | 4.9 |
| U.S. Exchanges/ Indices | Dow Jones 30 Ind. Avg. with div. | 10.6 | 2.8 | -12.8 | 22.8 | 44.8 | -23.6 | -13.3 | 18.5 | 9.8 | 9.2 |
| | S&P 500 Composite Index with div. | 18.2 | 6.4 | -7.4 | 23.6 | 37.2 | -26.4 | -14.8 | 18.9 | 14.3 | 3.9 |
| | NASDAQ Index | 28.1 | 12.3 | 7.3 | 26.1 | 29.8 | -35.1 | -31.1 | 17.2 | na | na |
| | Value Line Composite Index | 24.4 | 4.3 | 0.5 | 32.2 | 44.4 | -33.5 | -35.5 | 1.0 | 9.0 | -20.7 |
| | Dow Jones Utility Avg. with div. | 18.5 | -4.0 | 10.5 | 40.2 | 32.9 | -15.3 | -19.9 | 7.7 | 2.2 | 17.4 |
| | Lipper Growth Mutual Fund Avg. with divs. | 31.7 | 13.9 | 2.3 | 25.0 | 33.4 | -26.2 | -23.8 | 14.8 | 23.1 | -8.3 |
| | Lipper Income Mutual Fund Avg. with divs. | 12.1 | 4.0 | 4.0 | 25.4 | 24.5 | -11.1 | -10.1 | 9.3 | 17.6 | 4.2 |
| | CDA Equity Money Manager Index | na | na | na | na | na | na | na | na | na | na |
| Foreign Exchanges/ Indices | Frankfurt Index, local currency | -13.4 | 4.7 | 7.9 | -9.6 | 40.2 | 1.4 | -26.1 | 13.3 | 6.7 | -28.7 |
| | Frankfurt Index in U.S. Dollars | -12.3 | 6.0 | 7.8 | -8.7 | 37.5 | 1.5 | -20.8 | 13.6 | 7.4 | -28.4 |
| | London Index with div., local currency | 11.2 | 8.4 | 46.5 | 2.6 | 141.8 | -43.6 | -26.6 | 16.0 | 45.2 | -3.1 |
| | London Index with div. in U.S. Dollars | 12.6 | 9.0 | 51.3 | 2.1 | 123.1 | -43.4 | -26.9 | 14.8 | 47.8 | -3.1 |
| | Tokyo Index with div., local currency | 3.7 | 25.0 | -3.5 | 20.5 | 18.4 | -6.8 | -21.8 | 103.6 | 37.8 | -13.9 |
| | Tokyo Index with div. in U.S. Dollars | 3.0 | 30.7 | -2.7 | 21.3 | 18.1 | -7.2 | -20.1 | 110.1 | 42.3 | -13.9 |
| | Morgan Stanley Europe Index with div. | 14.7 | 24.3 | 23.9 | -6.4 | 43.9 | -22.8 | -7.7 | 15.6 | 28.0 | -9.4 |
| | Morgan Stanley EAFE Index with div. | 6.2 | 34.3 | 19.4 | 3.7 | 37.1 | -22.2 | -14.2 | 37.6 | 31.2 | -10.5 |
| | Morgan Stanley North America Idx with div. | 24.5 | 11.9 | -7.1 | 20.4 | 33.2 | -26.6 | -15.1 | 17.5 | 13.2 | 5.6 |
| | Morgan Stanley Pacific Index with div. | -3.5 | 48.8 | 13.7 | 21.6 | 26.7 | -20.9 | -21.0 | 107.6 | 38.8 | -12.0 |
| | Morgan Stanley Emerging Markets Index | na | na | na | na | na | na | na | na | na | na |
| | Morgan Stanley World Index with div. | 12.7 | 18.2 | 2.0 | 14.7 | 34.5 | -24.5 | -14.5 | 23.6 | 19.6 | -2.0 |
| | Chase Balanced Global Asset Index | 9.2 | 11.6 | 3.6 | 14.9 | 26.9 | -14.3 | -7.6 | na | na | na |
| | IFC Composite Index with div. | na | na | na | na | na | na | na | na | na | na |
| | IFC Asia Index with div. | na | na | na | na | na | na | na | na | na | na |
| | IFC EMEA Index with div. | na | na | na | na | na | na | na | na | na | na |
| | IFC Latin Index with div. | na | na | na | na | na | na | na | na | na | na |
| Foreign Bond Indices | Merrill Lynch Australia Gov't Bond Indx | na | na | na | na | na | na | na | na | na | na |
| | Merrill Lynch Germany Gov't Bond Indx | na | na | na | na | na | na | na | na | na | na |
| | Merrill Lynch Global Gov't Bond Indx | na | na | na | na | na | na | na | na | na | na |
| | Merrill Lynch Japan Gov't Bond Indx | na | na | na | na | na | na | na | na | na | na |
| | Merrill Lynch U.K. Gilt Gov't Bond Indx | na | na | na | na | na | na | na | na | na | na |
| Real Estate | U.S. Single Family House Price | 15.0 | 14.2 | 11.2 | 7.7 | 10.3 | 9.6 | 8.5 | 6.8 | 6.2 | 3.2 |
| | Farmland | 18.3 | 12.0 | 19.4 | 16.8 | 12.6 | 22.8 | 12.3 | 7.9 | 3.6 | 3.7 |
| | REITs | 30.5 | -1.6 | 19.1 | 49.0 | 36.3 | -42.2 | -27.2 | 11.2 | na | na |

*Recessions: Dec. 1969 - Nov. 1970; Nov. 1973 - Mar. 1975

©1996 Chase Global Data & Research
73 Junction Square, Concord, MA 01742

# MASTER REVIEW TABLE™ - 1970's

% Return

| Category | | 79 | 78 | 77 | 76 | 75* | 74* | 73* | 72 | 71 | 70* |
|---|---|---|---|---|---|---|---|---|---|---|---|
| U.S. Income/Interest Sensitive Indices | Lipper Fixed Income Mutual Fd. Avg. w/divs. | 2.8 | 1.6 | 4.4 | 20.4 | 17.6 | -7.9 | -6.4 | 8.6 | 13.8 | 4.0 |
| | Lipper General Muni. Mutual Fd. Avg. w/divs. | -1.9 | -3.8 | 6.9 | na | na | na | na | na | na | na |
| | Moody's Corp. Bond Yield, Aaa | 9.6 | 8.7 | 8.0 | 8.4 | 8.8 | 8.6 | 7.4 | 7.2 | 7.4 | 8.0 |
| | Moody's Corp. Bond Yield, Baa | 10.7 | 9.5 | 9.0 | 9.8 | 10.6 | 9.5 | 8.2 | 8.2 | 8.6 | 9.1 |
| | Merrill Lynch High Yield Bond Index | na | na | na | na | na | na | na | na | na | na |
| | Lehman Bros. Govt/Corp Index | 2.3 | 1.2 | 3.0 | 15.6 | 12.3 | 0.2 | 2.3 | na | na | na |
| | Lehman Bros. Corp. Long Term Index | -4.1 | -0.1 | 2.7 | 21.0 | 17.6 | -7.6 | 1.1 | na | na | na |
| | Lehman Bros. Trsy. Long Term Index | -0.5 | -1.4 | -0.1 | 17.1 | 8.3 | 5.0 | 1.1 | na | na | na |
| | Lehman Bros. Corp. Int. Term Index | 3.4 | 1.7 | 4.6 | 14.6 | 14.2 | 1.1 | 3.2 | na | na | na |
| | Lehman Bros. Trsy. Int. Term Index | 6.9 | 2.4 | 2.9 | 11.4 | 8.0 | 7.2 | 3.6 | na | na | na |
| | Lehman Bros. Mortgage-Backed Index | 0.1 | 2.4 | 1.9 | 16.3 | na | na | na | na | na | na |
| | Lehman Bros. Long Term Municipal Inx | na | na | na | na | na | na | na | na | na | na |
| | S&P Municipal Bond Yield | 6.4 | 5.9 | 5.6 | 6.5 | 6.9 | 6.1 | 5.2 | 5.3 | 5.7 | 6.5 |
| | U.S. Treasury 10-Year Bond Yield | 9.4 | 8.4 | 7.4 | 7.6 | 8.0 | 7.6 | 6.8 | 6.2 | 6.2 | 7.4 |
| | Salomon U.S. Treasury 10-Yr. Bond Index | na | na | na | na | na | na | na | na | na | na |
| | U.S. Treasury 3-Year Bond Yield | 9.7 | 8.3 | 6.7 | 6.8 | 7.5 | 7.8 | 7.0 | 5.7 | 5.7 | 7.3 |
| | U.S. Treasury 3-Month Bill Yield | 10.5 | 7.4 | 5.4 | 5.1 | 6.0 | 8.1 | 7.3 | 4.2 | 4.4 | 6.6 |
| | Certificates of Deposit Yield, 3-Month | 11.2 | 8.2 | 5.6 | 5.3 | 6.4 | 10.3 | 8.4 | 4.7 | 5.0 | 7.6 |
| | Taxable Money Market Average | 11.1 | 7.2 | 5.0 | 5.3 | 6.4 | na | na | na | na | na |
| | Tax-Free Money Market Avg. | na | na | na | na | na | na | na | na | na | na |
| | U.S. Savings Bonds | 7.5 | 7.2 | 7.6 | 7.6 | 7.4 | 7.3 | 7.1 | 6.9 | 6.8 | 7.2 |
| | GICs 1-Year | na | na | na | na | na | na | na | na | na | na |
| | GICs 5-Year | na | na | na | na | na | na | na | na | na | na |
| Commodities | Commodity Spot Price Index | 14.9 | 17.4 | 5.6 | 7.2 | -9.4 | 0.9 | 57.7 | 21.7 | 1.0 | -7.6 |
| | Gold | 126.6 | 37.0 | 22.4 | -4.0 | -24.9 | 66.3 | 72.2 | 48.7 | 16.5 | 6.2 |
| | Silver | 267.5 | 26.0 | 8.3 | 6.4 | -7.0 | 40.0 | 58.8 | 41.8 | -14.7 | -9.5 |
| | Crude Petroleum | 131.0 | 2.7 | 8.1 | 8.6 | -2.5 | 290.8 | 54.4 | 7.7 | 39.7 | -4.7 |
| | Diamonds | 51.5 | na | na | na | na | na | na | na | na | na |
| Insurance | AM Best Universal Life Policy Avg. Yld | na | na | na | na | na | na | na | na | na | na |
| | AM Best Single Prem. Deferred Annuity | na | na | na | na | na | na | na | na | na | na |
| | Lipper General Equity Variable Annuity | na | na | na | na | na | na | na | na | na | na |
| | Lipper Gen'l Fixed Inc.Variable Annuity | na | na | na | na | na | na | na | na | na | na |
| Currencies | Australian Dollar | -3.0 | 0.7 | 7.7 | -16.0 | -4.8 | -11.2 | 22.9 | 2.8 | 5.7 | -0.3 |
| | British Pound | 12.0 | 7.1 | 10.5 | -17.0 | -13.2 | 0.5 | -1.2 | -7.2 | 5.7 | -0.3 |
| | Canadian Dollar | 0.8 | -7.0 | -7.2 | -0.4 | -2.5 | 1.1 | -0.3 | 0.3 | 1.8 | 5.6 |
| | German Mark | 8.6 | 28.3 | -1.1 | 10.0 | -6.6 | 8.5 | 20.4 | 2.2 | 11.5 | 1.1 |
| | Japanese Yen | -18.2 | 23.0 | 22.3 | 3.7 | -1.7 | -6.7 | 7.5 | 6.2 | 11.8 | 0.0 |
| | Swiss Franc | 5.0 | 24.0 | 18.0 | 7.5 | -1.2 | 23.0 | 17.8 | 3.6 | 10.5 | -0.1 |
| | U.S. Dollar | -2.5 | -10.0 | -6.6 | 1.8 | 5.0 | -2.9 | -7.8 | -2.0 | -6.9 | -0.9 |
| Stock Index Yields | Dow Jones 30 Avg. Index Div. Yield | 6.1 | 6.0 | 5.5 | 4.1 | 4.4 | 6.1 | 4.2 | 3.2 | 3.5 | 3.8 |
| | Dow Jones Utility Index Div. Yield | 8.9 | 8.9 | 7.4 | 7.0 | 8.6 | 10.1 | 7.7 | 5.6 | 5.6 | 5.2 |
| | S&P 500 Composite Index Div. Yield | 5.6 | 5.4 | 5.1 | 3.9 | 4.1 | 5.4 | 3.6 | 2.7 | 3.0 | 3.4 |
| | London Index Dividend Yield | 6.9 | 5.8 | 5.3 | 6.4 | 5.5 | 11.7 | 4.8 | 3.2 | 3.3 | 4.4 |
| | Tokyo Index Dividend Yield | 1.4 | 1.5 | 1.7 | 1.8 | 2.2 | 2.4 | 2.0 | 2.2 | 3.4 | 3.4 |
| Foreign Inflation | Australian Inflation Rate | 9.1 | 7.9 | 12.3 | 13.5 | 15.1 | 15.1 | 9.5 | 5.8 | 6.1 | 3.9 |
| | Canadian Inflation Rate | 9.1 | 8.9 | 8.0 | 7.5 | 10.7 | 10.9 | 7.6 | 4.8 | 2.8 | 3.4 |
| | German Inflation Rate | 4.1 | 2.7 | 3.7 | 4.6 | 5.9 | 7.0 | 6.9 | 5.5 | 5.3 | 3.4 |
| | Japanese Inflation Rate | 3.7 | 4.2 | 8.2 | 9.4 | 11.8 | 24.5 | 11.7 | 4.5 | 6.1 | 7.7 |
| | U.K. Inflation Rate | 13.4 | 8.3 | 15.8 | 16.5 | 24.2 | 16.0 | 9.2 | 7.1 | 9.4 | 6.4 |

*Recessions: Dec. 1969 - Nov. 1970; Nov. 1973 - Mar. 1975

©1996 Chase Global Data & Research
73 Junction Square, Concord, MA 01742

# MASTER REVIEW TABLE™ - 1960's

% Return

| Group | | 69* | 68 | 67 | 66 | 65 | 64 | 63 | 62 | 61* | 60* |
|---|---|---|---|---|---|---|---|---|---|---|---|
| Major Financial Indicators | Inflation Rate | 6.2 | 4.7 | 3.0 | 3.5 | 1.9 | 1.0 | 1.6 | 1.3 | 0.7 | 1.4 |
| | GDP Change | 2.7 | 4.1 | 2.9 | 5.8 | 5.8 | 5.3 | 4.1 | 5.3 | 2.6 | -0.3 |
| | Dow Jones 30 Ind. Avg. P/E Ratio | 14.0 | 16.3 | 16.8 | 13.6 | 18.1 | 18.8 | 18.5 | 17.9 | 22.9 | 19.1 |
| | S&P 500 Composite Index P/E Ratio | 15.9 | 18.0 | 18.1 | 14.5 | 17.8 | 18.6 | 18.7 | 17.2 | 22.4 | 17.8 |
| | Dow Jones Utility Avg. P/E Ratio | 11.5 | 14.9 | 13.8 | 15.6 | 17.9 | 20.3 | 19.7 | 19.9 | 22.0 | 17.8 |
| | FHA Mortgage Rate | 8.6 | 7.5 | 6.8 | 6.8 | 5.6 | 5.5 | 5.5 | 5.5 | 5.7 | 6.0 |
| | Prime Rate | 8.0 | 6.3 | 5.6 | 5.6 | 4.5 | 4.5 | 4.5 | 4.5 | 4.5 | 4.8 |
| | U.S. Personal Disposable Income | 2.3 | 3.5 | 3.2 | 4.1 | 5.0 | 5.7 | 2.2 | 3.2 | 1.6 | 0.2 |
| | U.S. Unemployment Rate | 3.5 | 3.6 | 3.8 | 3.8 | 4.5 | 5.2 | 5.7 | 5.5 | 6.7 | 5.5 |
| U.S. Exchanges/ Indices | Dow Jones 30 Ind. Avg. with div. | -11.8 | 7.9 | 19.2 | -15.8 | 14.4 | 18.9 | 20.8 | -7.4 | 22.6 | -6.1 |
| | S&P 500 Composite Index with div. | -8.4 | 11.0 | 23.9 | -10.1 | 12.4 | 16.3 | 22.7 | -8.7 | 26.8 | 0.5 |
| | NASDAQ Index | na | na | na | na | na | na | na | na | na | na |
| | Value Line Composite Index | -28.7 | 19.8 | 29.1 | -12.3 | 19.0 | 13.3 | 13.6 | -16.3 | na | na |
| | Dow Jones Utility Avg. with div. | -15.4 | 12.4 | -1.8 | -6.8 | 1.7 | 15.4 | 11.6 | 2.8 | 33.9 | 18.8 |
| | Lipper Growth Mutual Fund Avg. with divs. | -12.4 | 17.1 | 44.6 | -1.9 | 28.8 | 13.7 | 21.5 | -16.9 | 26.7 | 3.1 |
| | Lipper Income Mutual Fund Avg. with divs. | -11.8 | 15.0 | 17.3 | -5.7 | 5.7 | 13.4 | 13.3 | -2.7 | 17.3 | 4.1 |
| | CDA Equity Money Manager Index | na | na | na | na | na | na | na | na | na | na |
| Foreign Exchanges/ Indices | Frankfurt Index, local currency | 12.0 | 10.4 | 50.9 | -21.1 | -11.6 | 8.9 | 13.6 | -21.1 | -8.3 | 27.8 |
| | Frankfurt Index in U.S. Dollars | 13.0 | 10.4 | 50.8 | -20.9 | -11.7 | 8.9 | 13.7 | -21.1 | -8.0 | 27.8 |
| | London Index with div., local currency | -9.3 | 43.3 | 33.3 | -3.5 | 12.0 | na | na | na | na | na |
| | London Index with div. in U.S. Dollars | -9.3 | 42.9 | 28.7 | -3.5 | 12.0 | na | na | na | na | na |
| | Tokyo Index with div., local currency | 39.9 | 34.4 | -5.1 | 9.4 | 21.7 | 2.6 | -2.7 | 2.2 | -3.6 | 40.2 |
| | Tokyo Index with div. in U.S. Dollars | 39.9 | 34.8 | -5.1 | 9.4 | 21.6 | 2.6 | -2.8 | 2.3 | -3.6 | 40.2 |
| | Morgan Stanley Europe Index with div. | na | na | na | na | na | na | na | na | na | na |
| | Morgan Stanley EAFE Index with div. | na | na | na | na | na | na | na | na | na | na |
| | Morgan Stanley North America Idx with div. | na | na | na | na | na | na | na | na | na | na |
| | Morgan Stanley Pacific Index with div. | na | na | na | na | na | na | na | na | na | na |
| | Morgan Stanley Emerging Markets Index | na | na | na | na | na | na | na | na | na | na |
| | Morgan Stanley World Index with div. | na | na | na | na | na | na | na | na | na | na |
| | Chase Balanced Global Asset Index | na | na | na | na | na | na | na | na | na | na |
| | IFC Composite Index with div. | na | na | na | na | na | na | na | na | na | na |
| | IFC Asia Index with div. | na | na | na | na | na | na | na | na | na | na |
| | IFC EMEA Index with div. | na | na | na | na | na | na | na | na | na | na |
| | IFC Latin Index with div. | na | na | na | na | na | na | na | na | na | na |
| Foreign Bond Indices | Merrill Lynch Australia Gov't Bond Indx | na | na | na | na | na | na | na | na | na | na |
| | Merrill Lynch Germany Gov't Bond Indx | na | na | na | na | na | na | na | na | na | na |
| | Merrill Lynch Global Gov't Bond Indx | na | na | na | na | na | na | na | na | na | na |
| | Merrill Lynch Japan Gov't Bond Indx | na | na | na | na | na | na | na | na | na | na |
| | Merrill Lynch U.K. Gilt Gov't Bond Indx | na | na | na | na | na | na | na | na | na | na |
| Real Estate | U.S. Single Family House Price | 7.3 | 4.8 | 2.9 | 3.9 | 2.2 | 0.0 | na | na | na | na |
| | Farmland | 5.6 | 6.6 | 6.3 | 7.5 | 6.5 | 6.2 | 4.0 | 5.0 | 1.7 | 5.4 |
| | REITs | na | na | na | na | na | na | na | na | na | na |

*Recessions: Dec. 1969 - Nov. 1970; Apr. 1960 - Feb. 1961

©1996 Chase Global Data & Research
73 Junction Square, Concord, MA 01742

# MASTER REVIEW TABLE™ - 1960's

% Return

| Category | Index | 69* | 68 | 67 | 66 | 65 | 64 | 63 | 62 | 61* | 60* |
|---|---|---|---|---|---|---|---|---|---|---|---|
| U.S. Income/Interest Sensitive Indices | Lipper Fixed Income Mutual Fd. Avg. w/divs. | -10.3 | 11.3 | 9.7 | -4.3 | 7.3 | 10.0 | 12.0 | -0.7 | 18.7 | 0.8 |
| | Lipper General Muni. Mutual Fd. Avg w/divs. | na | na | na | na | na | na | na | na | na | na |
| | Moody's Corp. Bond Yield, Aaa | 7.0 | 6.2 | 5.5 | 5.1 | 4.5 | 4.4 | 4.3 | 4.3 | 4.4 | 4.4 |
| | Moody's Corp. Bond Yield, Baa | 7.8 | 6.9 | 6.2 | 5.7 | 4.9 | 4.8 | 4.9 | 5.0 | 5.1 | 5.2 |
| | Merrill Lynch High Yield Bond Index | na | na | na | na | na | na | na | na | na | na |
| | Lehman Bros. Govt/Corp Index | na | na | na | na | na | na | na | na | na | na |
| | Lehman Bros. Corp. Long Term Index | na | na | na | na | na | na | na | na | na | na |
| | Lehman Bros. Trsy. Long Term Index | na | na | na | na | na | na | na | na | na | na |
| | Lehman Bros. Corp. Int. Term Index | na | na | na | na | na | na | na | na | na | na |
| | Lehman Bros. Trsy. Int. Term Index | na | na | na | na | na | na | na | na | na | na |
| | Lehman Bros. Mortgage-Backed Index | na | na | na | na | na | na | na | na | na | na |
| | Lehman Bros. Long Term Municipal Inx | na | na | na | na | na | na | na | na | na | na |
| | S&P Municipal Bond Yield | 5.8 | 4.5 | 4.0 | 3.8 | 3.3 | 3.2 | 3.2 | 3.2 | 3.5 | 3.7 |
| | U.S. Treasury 10-Year Bond Yield | 6.7 | 5.7 | 5.1 | 4.9 | 4.3 | 4.2 | 4.0 | 4.0 | 3.9 | 4.1 |
| | Salomon U.S. Treasury 10-Yr. Bond Index | na | na | na | na | na | na | na | na | na | na |
| | U.S. Treasury 3-Year Bond Yield | 7.0 | 5.7 | 5.0 | 5.2 | 4.2 | 4.0 | 3.7 | 3.5 | 3.6 | 4.0 |
| | U.S. Treasury 3-Month Bill Yield | 6.9 | 5.5 | 4.4 | 5.0 | 4.1 | 3.6 | 3.2 | 2.8 | 2.4 | 2.9 |
| | Certificates of Deposit Yield, 3-Month | 7.8 | 5.9 | 5.0 | 5.5 | 4.4 | 3.9 | na | na | na | na |
| | Taxable Money Market Average | na | na | na | na | na | na | na | na | na | na |
| | Tax-Free Money Market Avg. | na | na | na | na | na | na | na | na | na | na |
| | U.S. Savings Bonds | 7.0 | 6.9 | 6.6 | 6.4 | 6.3 | 6.6 | 6.5 | 6.3 | 6.2 | 6.1 |
| | GICs 1-Year | na | na | na | na | na | na | na | na | na | na |
| | GICs 5-Year | na | na | na | na | na | na | na | na | na | na |
| Commodities | Commodity Spot Price Index | 14.0 | 2.5 | -6.4 | -6.3 | 7.2 | 7.4 | 3.2 | -5.6 | 3.6 | -1.6 |
| | Gold | -15.7 | 20.1 | 0.0 | 0.0 | 0.0 | 0.0 | 0.0 | 0.0 | 0.0 | 0.0 |
| | Silver | -7.8 | -5.2 | 59.8 | 0.0 | 0.0 | 0.0 | 7.8 | 16.1 | 13.0 | 0.0 |
| | Crude Petroleum | -3.8 | -0.8 | -2.2 | -4.2 | -2.1 | -3.3 | -1.3 | -3.2 | -3.7 | -4.1 |
| | Diamonds | na | na | na | na | na | na | na | na | na | na |
| Insurance | AM Best Universal Life Policy Avg. Yld | na | na | na | na | na | na | na | na | na | na |
| | AM Best Single Prem. Deferred Annuity | na | na | na | na | na | na | na | na | na | na |
| | Lipper General Equity Variable Annuity | na | na | na | na | na | na | na | na | na | na |
| | Lipper Gen'l Fixed Inc.Variable Annuity | na | na | na | na | na | na | na | na | na | na |
| Currencies | Australian Dollar | 0.6 | -0.9 | 0.6 | -0.4 | 0.4 | -0.2 | -0.3 | -0.2 | 0.1 | 0.3 |
| | British Pound | 0.6 | -0.9 | -13.8 | -0.2 | 0.2 | -0.3 | -0.2 | -0.2 | 0.1 | 0.3 |
| | Canadian Dollar | -0.1 | 0.7 | 0.3 | -0.7 | -0.1 | 0.4 | -0.3 | -3.1 | -5.8 | -3.2 |
| | German Mark | 8.4 | -0.3 | -0.3 | 0.7 | -0.6 | -0.1 | 0.5 | 0.1 | 4.3 | 0.0 |
| | Japanese Yen | 0.1 | 1.1 | 0.2 | -0.4 | -0.5 | 1.0 | -1.2 | 1.0 | -0.7 | 0.2 |
| | Swiss Franc | -0.2 | 0.4 | 0.1 | -0.1 | 0.0 | 0.0 | 0.0 | 0.0 | -0.2 | 0.4 |
| | U.S. Dollar | -0.2 | 0.1 | na | na | na | na | na | na | na | na |
| Stock Index Yields | Dow Jones 30 Avg. Index Div. Yield | 4.2 | 3.3 | 3.3 | 4.1 | 3.0 | 3.6 | 3.1 | 3.6 | 3.1 | 3.5 |
| | Dow Jones Utility Index Div. Yield | 5.6 | 4.5 | 4.6 | 4.3 | 3.4 | 3.2 | 3.7 | 3.2 | 3.3 | 4.0 |
| | S&P 500 Composite Index Div. Yield | 3.5 | 3.0 | 3.1 | 3.6 | 3.0 | 3.0 | 3.1 | 3.4 | 2.9 | 3.4 |
| | London Index Dividend Yield | 3.9 | 3.2 | 4.3 | 5.8 | 5.2 | 5.2 | na | na | na | na |
| | Tokyo Index Dividend Yield | 3.3 | 4.3 | 4.3 | 4.0 | 5.1 | 4.9 | 4.1 | 4.2 | 3.3 | 3.7 |
| Foreign Inflation | Australian Inflation Rate | 2.9 | 2.7 | 3.2 | 2.9 | 4.0 | 2.3 | 0.6 | -0.3 | 2.5 | 3.8 |
| | Canadian Inflation Rate | 4.5 | 4.0 | 3.6 | 3.7 | 2.4 | 1.8 | 1.7 | 1.2 | 0.6 | 1.0 |
| | German Inflation Rate | 1.9 | 2.9 | 1.4 | 3.5 | 3.4 | 2.3 | 3.0 | 3.0 | 2.3 | 1.4 |
| | Japanese Inflation Rate | 5.2 | 5.3 | 4.0 | 5.1 | 6.6 | 3.9 | 8.5 | 6.8 | 5.3 | 3.6 |
| | U.K. Inflation Rate | 5.4 | 4.7 | 2.5 | 3.9 | 4.8 | 3.3 | 2.0 | 4.3 | 3.4 | 1.0 |

*Recessions: Dec. 1969 - Nov. 1970; Apr. 1960 - Feb. 1961

©1996 Chase Global Data & Research
73 Junction Square, Concord, MA 01742

# *Editor's Note:*

• **Risk/Volatility Factor,** as noted in all Line Graphs throughout the *Digest*, are terms denoting an investment's degree of risk, and represent **Standard Deviation** measurements. Standard Deviation is a measure of total risk. It is defined as the variation of an investment's returns around its average for the time period analyzed. It indicates how varied an investment's returns have been over time. Standard Deviation is usually used in a relative sense, to compare one investment's risk against another. For example, if the Standard Deviation for investment A and investment B were 10 and 5, respectively, then investment A experienced twice the variability of investment B. In the *Digest*, the Standard Deviation noted in the Line Graphs is calculated for the time period the data is available for each investment.

Risk / Volatility Factor / Standard Deviation is also reviewed in Section II's 10, 20, and 35 year Volatility Ranking tables. These tables provide a direct comparison of all subjects in the *Digest* over the past three decades.

• **Subject presentation in the *Digest* is uniform. Each subject has IDENTICAL graphic presentations: Performance Table, Volatility Line Graph, "similar subjects" Bar Chart comparison, "dissimilar subjects" Bar Chart comparison, and Inflation Bar Chart comparison.**

• **All Tables, Graphs, and Line Charts are inclusive of results of both the beginning and ending years shown.**

©1996 Chase Global Data & Research
73 Junction Square, Concord, MA 01742

SECTION II

# Investment Performance and Volatility Ranking Tables

## One - Year Performance Ranking (1995)

| Rank | | Avg. Annual Return |
|---|---|---|
| 1 | NASDAQ Composite Index | 39.92 |
| 2 | S&P 500 Composite Index, with dividends | 37.58 |
| 3 | Morgan Stanley North America Index, with dividends | 37.07 |
| 4 | Dow Jones 30 Industrials, with dividends | 36.94 |
| 5 | CDA Equity Money Manager Index | 36.03 |
| 6 | Dow Jones 15 Utilities, with dividends | 32.17 |
| 7 | Lipper Growth Mutual Fund Average | 30.79 |
| 8 | Lehman Brothers Long Term Treasury Index | 30.68 |
| 9 | Lehman Brothers Long Term Corporate Index | 27.92 |
| 10 | Lipper Equity Variable Annuity Index | 25.50 |
| 11 | Lehman Brothers Long Municipal Index | 23.28 |
| 12 | IFC EMEA Index, with dividends | 22.51 |
| 13 | London Exchange, with dividends, local currency | 22.28 |
| 14 | Chase Balanced Global Asset Index | 22.24 |
| 15 | Morgan Stanley Europe Index, with dividends | 22.13 |
| 16 | London Exchange, with dividends, in U.S. Dollars | 22.06 |
| 17 | Lipper Income Mutual Fund Average | 21.66 |
| 18 | Morgan Stanley World Index, with dividends | 21.32 |
| 19 | Merrill Lynch Australian Government Bond Index | 19.41 |
| 20 | Value Line Composite Index | 19.29 |
| 21 | Lehman Brothers Government/Corporate Index | 19.25 |
| 22 | Lehman Brothers Intermediate Corporate Index | 19.01 |
| 23 | Merrill Lynch High Yield Bond Index | 18.47 |
| 24 | Real Estate Investment Trusts | 18.28 |
| 25 | Merrill Lynch Global Government Bond Index | 17.31 |
| 26 | Lipper Municipal Bond Mutual Fund Average | 16.84 |
| 27 | Lehman Brothers Mortgage-Backed Securities Index | 16.80 |
| 28 | Merrill Lynch British Gilt Bond Index | 16.11 |
| 29 | Merrill Lynch German Government Bond Index | 16.03 |
| 30 | Salomon Brothers 10-Year U.S. Treasury Bond Index | 15.28 |
| 31 | Lipper Fixed Income Mutual Fund Average | 15.22 |
| 32 | Lehman Brothers Intermediate Treasury Index | 14.40 |
| 33 | Merrill Lynch Japanese Government Bond Index | 13.45 |
| 34 | Swiss Franc | 13.28 |
| 35 | Lipper Fixed Income Variable Annuity Index | 12.53 |
| 36 | Morgan Stanley EAFE Index, with dividends | 11.55 |
| 37 | Crude Petroleum | 9.69 |
| 38 | Prime Rate | 8.83 |
| 39 | Moody's Baa Corporate Bond Yield | 8.20 |
| 40 | FHA Mortgage Rate | 8.16 |
| 41 | German Mark | 7.82 |
| 42 | Moody's Aaa Corporate Bond Yield | 7.59 |
| 43 | Frankfurt Exchange in U.S. Dollars | 7.54 |
| 44 | Universal Life Insurance Average Rate | 7.00 |
| 45 | Frankfurt Exchange, local currency | 6.99 |
| 46 | GICs - 5 Year Market Average | 6.69 |
| 47 | U.S. Treasury Bond, 10-Year Yield | 6.57 |
| 48 | U.S. Farmland Price Index | 6.39 |
| 49 | U.S. Treasury Bond, 3-Year Yield | 6.25 |
| 50 | Single Premium Deferred Annuity Interest Rate | 6.00 |
| 51 | GICs - 1 Year Market Average | 5.97 |
| 52 | S&P Municipal Bond Yield Index | 5.95 |
| 53 | U.S. Certificate of Deposit, 3-Month Yield | 5.92 |
| 54 | U.S. Treasury Bill, 3-Month Yield | 5.64 |
| 55 | Taxable Money Market Fund | 5.47 |
| 56 | Silver | 4.93 |
| 57 | U.S. Savings Bonds - Series EE | 4.89 |
| 58 | Tax-Free Money Market Fund | 3.39 |
| 59 | Morgan Stanley Pacific Index, with dividends | 2.99 |
| 60 | Canadian Dollar | 2.79 |
| 61 | New One-Family House Price Index | 2.61 |
| 62 | Inflation | 2.54 |
| 63 | Tokyo Exchange, with dividends, local currency | 2.04 |
| 64 | Tokyo Exchange, with dividends, in U.S. Dollars | 1.97 |
| 65 | Diamonds | 1.20 |
| 66 | Gold | 1.19 |
| 67 | Commodity Spot Market Index | 1.09 |
| 68 | British Pound | -0.96 |
| 69 | Japanese Yen | -3.77 |
| 70 | Australian Dollar | -4.10 |
| 71 | U.S. Dollar | -4.59 |
| 72 | IFC Asia Index, with dividends | -5.47 |
| 73 | IFC Composite Index, with dividends | -8.42 |
| 74 | Morgan Stanley Emerging Markets Index, with dividends | -10.75 |
| 75 | IFC Latin America Index, with dividends | -16.85 |

©1996 Chase Global Data & Research
73 Junction Square, Concord, MA 01742

## Three - Year Performance Ranking
## (1993 - 1995)

| | | Avg. Annual Return |
|---|---|---|
| 1 | - IFC EMEA Index, with dividends | 25.69 |
| 2 | - Dow Jones 30 Industrials, with dividends | 18.92 |
| 3 | - IFC Asia Index, with dividends | 17.66 |
| 4 | - Morgan Stanley Europe Index, with dividends | 17.62 |
| 5 | - Morgan Stanley EAFE Index, with dividends | 17.02 |
| 6 | - Morgan Stanley Pacific Index, with dividends | 16.54 |
| 7 | - Morgan Stanley World Index, with dividends | 16.40 |
| 8 | - NASDAQ Composite Index | 15.83 |
| 9 | - CDA Equity Money Manager Index | 15.53 |
| 10 | - Morgan Stanley North America Index, with dividends | 15.51 |
| 11 | - S&P 500 Composite Index, with dividends | 15.32 |
| 12 | - London Exchange, with dividends, local currency | 13.54 |
| 13 | - Frankfurt Exchange, local currency | 13.41 |
| 14 | - London Exchange, with dividends, in U.S. Dollars | 13.40 |
| 15 | - IFC Composite Index, with dividends | 13.12 |
| 16 | - Frankfurt Exchange in U.S. Dollars | 13.12 |
| 17 | - Morgan Stanley Emerging Markets Index, with dividends | 12.96 |
| 18 | - Chase Balanced Global Asset Index | 12.65 |
| 19 | - Lipper Growth Mutual Fund Average | 12.37 |
| 20 | - Lehman Brothers Long Term Treasury Index | 12.28 |
| 21 | - Real Estate Investment Trusts | 12.23 |
| 22 | - Silver | 11.67 |
| 23 | - Merrill Lynch High Yield Bond Index | 11.63 |
| 24 | - Lipper Equity Variable Annuity Index | 11.38 |
| 25 | - Merrill Lynch Global Government Bond Index | 11.09 |
| 26 | - Lehman Brothers Long Term Corporate Index | 11.07 |
| 27 | - Merrill Lynch British Gilt Bond Index | 9.91 |
| 28 | - Lipper Income Mutual Fund Average | 9.83 |
| 29 | - Merrill Lynch German Government Bond Index | 9.19 |
| 30 | - Merrill Lynch Australian Government Bond Index | 9.12 |
| 31 | - Lehman Brothers Intermediate Corporate Index | 8.79 |
| 32 | - Lehman Brothers Long Municipal Index | 8.75 |
| 33 | - Lehman Brothers Government/Corporate Index | 8.51 |
| 34 | - Swiss Franc | 8.28 |
| 35 | - Moody's Baa Corporate Bond Yield | 8.25 |
| 36 | - FHA Mortgage Rate | 8.10 |
| 37 | - Tokyo Exchange, with dividends, in U.S. Dollars | 7.99 |
| 38 | - Moody's Aaa Corporate Bond Yield | 7.70 |
| 39 | - Merrill Lynch Japanese Government Bond Index | 7.68 |
| 40 | - Value Line Composite Index | 7.47 |
| 41 | - Prime Rate | 7.32 |
| 42 | - Tokyo Exchange, with dividends, local currency | 7.24 |
| 43 | - Dow Jones 15 Utilities, with dividends | 7.14 |
| 44 | - Commodity Spot Market Index | 7.11 |
| 45 | - Lehman Brothers Mortgage-Backed Securities Index | 7.08 |
| 46 | - Lipper Municipal Bond Mutual Fund Average | 7.06 |
| 47 | - Lipper Fixed Income Mutual Fund Average | 6.94 |
| 48 | - Universal Life Insurance Average Rate | 6.87 |
| 49 | - Lehman Brothers Intermediate Treasury Index | 6.74 |
| 50 | - IFC Latin America Index, with dividends | 6.61 |
| 51 | - U.S. Treasury Bond, 10-Year Yield | 6.51 |
| 52 | - Japanese Yen | 6.47 |
| 53 | - GICs - 5 Year Market Average | 6.47 |
| 54 | - Lipper Fixed Income Variable Annuity Index | 6.03 |
| 55 | - S&P Municipal Bond Yield Index | 5.92 |
| 56 | - Salomon Brothers 10-Year U.S. Treasury Bond Index | 5.92 |
| 57 | - Single Premium Deferred Annuity Interest Rate | 5.89 |
| 58 | - U.S. Treasury Bond, 3-Year Yield | 5.65 |
| 59 | - U.S. Farmland Price Index | 5.28 |
| 60 | - Gold | 5.10 |
| 61 | - GICs - 1 Year Market Average | 4.91 |
| 62 | - U.S. Certificate of Deposit, 3-Month Yield | 4.57 |
| 63 | - U.S. Treasury Bill, 3-Month Yield | 4.35 |
| 64 | - U.S. Savings Bonds - Series EE | 4.31 |
| 65 | - German Mark | 4.05 |
| 66 | - Taxable Money Market Fund | 3.97 |
| 67 | - New One-Family House Price Index | 3.18 |
| 68 | - Inflation | 2.65 |
| 69 | - Tax-Free Money Market Fund | 2.58 |
| 70 | - Australian Dollar | 2.56 |
| 71 | - Diamonds | 1.03 |
| 72 | - British Pound | 0.79 |
| 73 | - Canadian Dollar | -2.32 |
| 74 | - Crude Petroleum | -2.76 |
| 75 | - U.S. Dollar | -2.82 |

©1996 Chase Global Data & Research
73 Junction Square, Concord, MA 01742

## Five - Year Performance Ranking
## (1991 - 1995)

| | | | Avg. Annual Return |
|---|---|---|---|
| 1 | - | IFC Latin America Index, wih dividends | 24.56 |
| 2 | - | NASDAQ Composite Index | 22.99 |
| 3 | - | Merrill Lynch High Yield Bond Index | 18.76 |
| 4 | - | CDA Equity Money Manager Index | 18.25 |
| 5 | - | Dow Jones 30 Industrials, with dividends | 17.54 |
| 6 | - | IFC Asia Index, with dividends | 16.76 |
| 7 | - | S&P 500 Composite Index, with dividends | 16.57 |
| 8 | - | Real Estate Investment Trusts | 16.56 |
| 9 | - | Morgan Stanley North America Index, with dividends | 16.27 |
| 10 | - | London Exchange, with dividends, local currency | 15.93 |
| 11 | - | Lipper Growth Mutual Fund Average | 15.90 |
| 12 | - | IFC Composite Index, with dividends | 15.84 |
| 13 | - | London Exchange, with dividends, in U.S. Dollars | 15.02 |
| 14 | - | Lipper Equity Variable Annuity Index | 14.94 |
| 15 | - | Morgan Stanley Emerging Markets Index, with dividends | 13.81 |
| 16 | - | Merrill Lynch British Gilt Bond Index | 13.09 |
| 17 | - | Lehman Brothers Long Term Corporate Index | 12.63 |
| 18 | - | Lehman Brothers Long Term Treasury Index | 12.61 |
| 19 | - | Lipper Income Mutual Fund Average | 12.53 |
| 20 | - | Morgan Stanley World Index, with dividends | 12.33 |
| 21 | - | Merrill Lynch Australian Government Bond Index | 12.18 |
| 22 | - | Morgan Stanley Europe Index, with dividends | 12.11 |
| 23 | - | Chase Balanced Global Asset Index | 12.02 |
| 24 | - | Merrill Lynch Global Government Bond Index | 11.42 |
| 25 | - | Value Line Composite Index | 11.05 |
| 26 | - | Merrill Lynch German Government Bond Index | 10.31 |
| 27 | - | Lehman Brothers Intermediate Corporate Index | 10.19 |
| 28 | - | Frankfurt Exchange, local currency | 10.02 |
| 29 | - | Lehman Brothers Long Municipal Index | 9.99 |
| 30 | - | Lehman Brothers Government/Corporate Index | 9.80 |
| 31 | - | Frankfurt Exchange in U.S. Dollars | 9.78 |
| 32 | - | Morgan Stanley EAFE Index, with dividends | 9.71 |
| 33 | - | Merrill Lynch Japanese Government Bond Index | 9.31 |
| 34 | - | Lipper Fixed Income Mutual Fund Average | 9.25 |
| 35 | - | Lipper Fixed Income Variable Annuity Index | 9.16 |
| 36 | - | Lehman Brothers Mortgage-Backed Securities Index | 8.73 |
| 37 | - | Moody's Baa Corporate Bond Yield | 8.71 |
| 38 | - | FHA Mortgage Rate | 8.40 |
| 39 | - | Lipper Municipal Bond Mutual Fund Average | 8.37 |
| 40 | - | Lehman Brothers Intermediate Treasury Index | 8.21 |
| 41 | - | Salomon Brothers 10-Year U.S. Treasury Bond Index | 8.20 |
| 42 | - | Dow Jones 15 Utilities, with dividends | 8.05 |
| 43 | - | Moody's Aaa Corporate Bond Yield | 8.00 |
| 44 | - | Morgan Stanley Pacific Index, with dividends | 7.63 |
| 45 | - | Universal Life Insurance Average Rate | 7.34 |
| 46 | - | Prime Rate | 7.33 |
| 47 | - | U.S. Treasury Bond, 10-Year Yield | 6.88 |
| 48 | - | GICs - 5 Year Market Average | 6.82 |
| 49 | - | Single Premium Deferred Annuity Interest Rate | 6.44 |
| 50 | - | S&P Municipal Bond Yield Index | 6.21 |
| 51 | - | U.S. Treasury Bond, 3-Year Yield | 5.81 |
| 52 | - | Japanese Yen | 5.62 |
| 53 | - | GICs - 1 Year Market Average | 4.89 |
| 54 | - | U.S. Savings Bonds - Series EE | 4.84 |
| 55 | - | U.S. Certificate of Deposit, 3-Month Yield | 4.64 |
| 56 | - | U.S. Treasury Bill, 3-Month Yield | 4.42 |
| 57 | - | Taxable Money Market Fund | 4.19 |
| 58 | - | Silver | 4.12 |
| 59 | - | U.S. Farmland Price Index | 4.03 |
| 60 | - | Tax-Free Money Market Fund | 2.88 |
| 61 | - | Inflation | 2.79 |
| 62 | - | New One-Family House Price Index | 2.45 |
| 63 | - | Commodity Spot Market Index | 2.29 |
| 64 | - | Diamonds | 2.22 |
| 65 | - | Swiss Franc | 2.05 |
| 66 | - | German Mark | 0.83 |
| 67 | - | U.S. Dollar | 0.33 |
| 68 | - | Gold | -0.30 |
| 69 | - | Australian Dollar | -0.65 |
| 70 | - | Tokyo Exchange, with dividends, in U.S. Dollars | -0.67 |
| 71 | - | Tokyo Exchange, with dividends, local currency | -1.09 |
| 72 | - | IFC EMEA Index, with dividends | -1.10 |
| 73 | - | Canadian Dollar | -3.19 |
| 74 | - | British Pound | -4.26 |
| 75 | - | Crude Petroleum | -6.10 |

©1996 Chase Global Data & Research
73 Junction Square, Concord, MA 01742

## Five - Year Performance Ranking
## (1986 - 1990)

| Rank | | | Avg. Annual Return |
|---|---|---|---|
| 1 | - | Morgan Stanley Pacific Index, with dividends | 19.84 |
| 2 | - | Morgan Stanley EAFE Index, with dividends | 18.36 |
| 3 | - | Morgan Stanley Europe Index, with dividends | 16.89 |
| 4 | - | Merrill Lynch Australian Government Bond Index | 15.80 |
| 5 | - | Dow Jones 30 Industrials, with dividends | 15.40 |
| 6 | - | Morgan Stanley World Index, with dividends | 15.12 |
| 7 | - | Tokyo Exchange, with dividends, in U.S. Dollars | 13.89 |
| 8 | - | London Exchange, with dividends, in U.S. Dollars | 13.58 |
| 9 | - | London Exchange, with dividends, local currency | 13.29 |
| 10 | - | Chase Balanced Global Asset Index | 13.21 |
| 11 | - | S&P 500 Composite Index, with dividends | 12.99 |
| 12 | - | Morgan Stanley North America Index, with dividends | 12.58 |
| 13 | - | Merrill Lynch Global Government Bond Index | 12.07 |
| 14 | - | Dow Jones 15 Utilities, with dividends | 11.83 |
| 15 | - | Lipper Equity Variable Annuity Index | 11.51 |
| 16 | - | CDA Equity Money Manager Index | 11.31 |
| 17 | - | Tokyo Exchange, with dividends, local currency | 11.14 |
| 18 | - | Lehman Brothers Long Term Treasury Index | 10.77 |
| 19 | - | Lehman Brothers Long Municipal Index | 10.51 |
| 20 | - | Moody's Baa Corporate Bond Yield | 10.47 |
| 21 | - | Merrill Lynch British Gilt Bond Index | 10.45 |
| 22 | - | Lehman Brothers Mortgage-Backed Securities Index | 10.43 |
| 23 | - | German Mark | 10.32 |
| 24 | - | Lehman Brothers Long Term Corporate Index | 10.32 |
| 25 | - | FHA Mortgage Rate | 10.19 |
| 26 | - | Lipper Growth Mutual Fund Average | 10.15 |
| 27 | - | Swiss Franc | 9.91 |
| 28 | - | Lehman Brothers Government/Corporate Index | 9.49 |
| 29 | - | Moody's Aaa Corporate Bond Yield | 9.34 |
| 30 | - | Prime Rate | 9.34 |
| 31 | - | Universal Life Insurance Average Rate | 9.17 |
| 32 | - | Lehman Brothers Intermediate Corporate Index | 9.14 |
| 33 | - | Lehman Brothers Intermediate Treasury Index | 8.95 |
| 34 | - | Salomon Brothers 10-Year U.S. Treasury Bond Index | 8.93 |
| 35 | - | Lipper Municipal Bond Mutual Fund Average | 8.78 |
| 36 | - | GICs - 5 Year Market Average | 8.74 |
| 37 | - | Single Premium Deferred Annuity Interest Rate | 8.55 |
| 38 | - | Lipper Fixed Income Variable Annuity Index | 8.54 |
| 39 | - | U.S. Treasury Bond, 10-Year Yield | 8.39 |
| 40 | - | Japanese Yen | 8.26 |
| 41 | - | U.S. Treasury Bond, 3-Year Yield | 7.96 |
| 42 | - | Lipper Income Mutual Fund Average | 7.77 |
| 43 | - | U.S. Certificate of Deposit, 3-Month Yield | 7.67 |
| 44 | - | GICs - 1 Year Market Average | 7.55 |
| 45 | - | Lipper Fixed Income Mutual Fund Average | 7.54 |
| 46 | - | S&P Municipal Bond Yield Index | 7.47 |
| 47 | - | Taxable Money Market Fund | 7.23 |
| 48 | - | U.S. Treasury Bill, 3-Month Yield | 7.02 |
| 49 | - | Merrill Lynch High Yield Bond Index | 6.27 |
| 50 | - | U.S. Savings Bonds - Series EE | 6.23 |
| 51 | - | British Pound | 5.92 |
| 52 | - | Tax-Free Money Market Fund | 4.92 |
| 53 | - | Merrill Lynch German Government Bond Index | 4.78 |
| 54 | - | Merrill Lynch Japanese Government Bond Index | 4.74 |
| 55 | - | Inflation | 4.13 |
| 56 | - | New One-Family House Price Index | 3.90 |
| 57 | - | Canadian Dollar | 3.82 |
| 58 | - | Gold | 3.56 |
| 59 | - | Frankfurt Exchange in U.S. Dollars | 3.03 |
| 60 | - | NASDAQ Composite Index | 2.84 |
| 61 | - | Diamonds | 2.74 |
| 62 | - | Australian Dollar | 2.40 |
| 63 | - | Commodity Spot Market Index | 1.75 |
| 64 | - | Frankfurt Exchange, local currency | 0.46 |
| 65 | - | Real Estate Investment Trusts | -0.77 |
| 66 | - | U.S. Farmland Price Index | -0.86 |
| 67 | - | Value Line Composite Index | -1.82 |
| 68 | - | Crude Petroleum | -4.51 |
| 69 | - | Silver | -6.46 |
| 70 | - | U.S. Dollar | -7.57 |

©1996 Chase Global Data & Research
73 Junction Square, Concord, MA 01742

## Ten-Year Performance Ranking
## (1986 - 1995)

| Rank | | | Avg. Annual Return |
|---|---|---|---|
| 1 | - | Dow Jones 30 Industrials, with dividends | 16.46 |
| 2 | - | S&P 500 Composite Index, with dividends | 14.77 |
| 3 | - | CDA Equity Money Manager Index | 14.73 |
| 4 | - | London Exchange, with dividends, local currency | 14.60 |
| 5 | - | Morgan Stanley Europe Index, with dividends | 14.48 |
| 6 | - | Morgan Stanley North America Index; with dividends | 14.41 |
| 7 | - | London Exchange, with dividends, in U.S. Dollars | 14.29 |
| 8 | - | Merrill Lynch Australian Government Bond Index | 13.98 |
| 9 | - | Morgan Stanley EAFE Index, with dividends | 13.95 |
| 10 | - | Morgan Stanley World Index, with dividends | 13.72 |
| 11 | - | Morgan Stanley Pacific Index, with dividends | 13.57 |
| 12 | - | Lipper Equity Variable Annuity Index | 13.21 |
| 13 | - | Lipper Growth Mutual Fund Average | 12.99 |
| 14 | - | Chase Balanced Global Asset Index | 12.61 |
| 15 | - | NASDAQ Composite Index | 12.47 |
| 16 | - | Merrill Lynch High Yield Bond Index | 12.34 |
| 17 | - | Merrill Lynch British Gilt Bond Index | 11.76 |
| 18 | - | Merrill Lynch Global Government Bond Index | 11.75 |
| 19 | - | Lehman Brothers Long Term Treasury Index | 11.68 |
| 20 | - | Lehman Brothers Long Term Corporate Index | 11.47 |
| 21 | - | Lehman Brothers Long Municipal Index | 10.25 |
| 22 | - | Lipper Income Mutual Fund Average | 10.12 |
| 23 | - | Dow Jones 15 Utilities, with dividends | 9.92 |
| 24 | - | Lehman Brothers Intermediate Corporate Index | 9.66 |
| 25 | - | Lehman Brothers Government/Corporate Index | 9.65 |
| 26 | - | Lehman Brothers Mortgage-Backed Securities Index | 9.58 |
| 27 | - | Moody's Baa Corporate Bond Yield | 9.58 |
| 28 | - | FHA Mortgage Rate | 9.29 |
| 29 | - | Lipper Fixed Income Variable Annuity Index | 8.85 |
| 30 | - | Moody's Aaa Corporate Bond Yield | 8.67 |
| 31 | - | Lehman Brothers Intermediate Treasury Index | 8.58 |
| 32 | - | Lipper Municipal Bond Mutual Fund Average | 8.57 |
| 33 | - | Salomon Brothers 10-Year U.S. Treasury Bond Index | 8.56 |
| 34 | - | Lipper Fixed Income Mutual Fund Average | 8.39 |
| 35 | - | Prime Rate | 8.33 |
| 36 | - | Universal Life Insurance Average Rate | 8.25 |
| 37 | - | GICs - 5 Year Market Average | 7.78 |
| 38 | - | U.S. Treasury Bond, 10-Year Yield | 7.63 |
| 39 | - | Real Estate Investment Trusts | 7.55 |
| 40 | - | Merrill Lynch German Government Bond Index | 7.51 |
| 41 | - | Single Premium Deferred Annuity Interest Rate | 7.49 |
| 42 | - | Merrill Lynch Japanese Government Bond Index | 7.00 |
| 43 | - | Japanese Yen | 6.93 |
| 44 | - | U.S. Treasury Bond, 3-Year Yield | 6.88 |
| 45 | - | S&P Municipal Bond Yield Index | 6.84 |
| 46 | - | Tokyo Exchange, with dividends, in U.S. Dollars | 6.36 |
| 47 | - | Frankfurt Exchange in U.S. Dollars | 6.35 |
| 48 | - | GICs - 1 Year Market Average | 6.21 |
| 49 | - | U.S. Certificate of Deposit, 3-Month Yield | 6.14 |
| 50 | - | Swiss Franc | 5.91 |
| 51 | - | U.S. Treasury Bill, 3-Month Yield | 5.71 |
| 52 | - | Taxable Money Market Fund | 5.70 |
| 53 | - | U.S. Savings Bonds - Series EE | 5.53 |
| 54 | - | German Mark | 5.47 |
| 55 | - | Frankfurt Exchange, local currency | 5.13 |
| 56 | - | Tokyo Exchange, with dividends, local currency | 4.85 |
| 57 | - | Value Line Composite Index | 4.42 |
| 58 | - | Tax-Free Money Market Fund | 3.89 |
| 59 | - | Inflation | 3.45 |
| 60 | - | New One-Family House Price Index | 3.17 |
| 61 | - | Diamonds | 2.48 |
| 62 | - | Commodity Spot Market Index | 2.02 |
| 63 | - | Gold | 1.61 |
| 64 | - | U.S. Farmland Price Index | 1.56 |
| 65 | - | Australian Dollar | 0.86 |
| 66 | - | British Pound | 0.70 |
| 67 | - | Canadian Dollar | 0.25 |
| 68 | - | Silver | -1.31 |
| 69 | - | U.S. Dollar | -3.70 |
| 70 | - | Crude Petroleum | -5.31 |

©1996 Chase Global Data & Research
73 Junction Square, Concord, MA 01742

## Ten-Year Performance Ranking
## (1981 - 1990)

| | | Avg. Annual Return |
|---|---|---|
| 1 | - London Exchange, with dividends, local currency | 18.26 |
| 2 | - Morgan Stanley Pacific Index, with dividends | 17.51 |
| 3 | - London Exchange, with dividends, in U.S. Dollars | 17.38 |
| 4 | - Morgan Stanley EAFE Index, with dividends | 16.99 |
| 5 | - Morgan Stanley Europe Index, with dividends | 16.49 |
| 6 | - Dow Jones 15 Utilities, with dividends | 15.98 |
| 7 | - Tokyo Exchange, with dividends, in U.S. Dollars | 15.75 |
| 8 | - Dow Jones 30 Industrials, with dividends | 15.64 |
| 9 | - Morgan Stanley World Index, with dividends | 14.93 |
| 10 | - Lehman Brothers Long Term Corporate Index | 14.42 |
| 11 | - Chase Balanced Global Asset Index | 14.37 |
| 12 | - Tokyo Exchange, with dividends, local currency | 14.29 |
| 13 | - Lehman Brothers Mortgage-Backed Securities Index | 14.14 |
| 14 | - Lehman Brothers Long Term Treasury Index | 13.84 |
| 15 | - S&P 500 Composite Index, with dividends | 13.76 |
| 16 | - Morgan Stanley North America Index, with dividends | 13.32 |
| 17 | - Frankfurt Exchange in U.S. Dollars | 13.30 |
| 18 | - Lehman Brothers Government/Corporate Index | 12.80 |
| 19 | - Lehman Brothers Intermediate Corporate Index | 12.69 |
| 20 | - Moody's Baa Corporate Bond Yield | 12.47 |
| 21 | - Salomon Brothers 10-Year U.S. Treasury Bond Index | 12.44 |
| 22 | - CDA Equity Money Manager Index | 12.33 |
| 23 | - FHA Mortgage Rate | 12.15 |
| 24 | - Lipper Income Mutual Fund Average | 12.07 |
| 25 | - Lehman Brothers Long Municipal Index | 12.04 |
| 26 | - Lehman Brothers Intermediate Treasury Index | 11.99 |
| 27 | - Lipper Growth Mutual Fund Average | 11.68 |
| 28 | - Merrill Lynch High Yield Bond Index | 11.48 |
| 29 | - Lipper Fixed Income Mutual Fund Average | 11.34 |
| 30 | - Prime Rate | 11.28 |
| 31 | - Frankfurt Exchange, local currency | 11.26 |
| 32 | - Lipper Municipal Bond Mutual Fund Average | 11.06 |
| 33 | - Moody's Aaa Corporate Bond Yield | 11.06 |
| 34 | - U.S. Treasury Bond, 10-Year Yield | 10.28 |
| 35 | - Universal Life Insurance Average Rate | 10.20 |
| 36 | - Single Premium Deferred Annuity Interest Rate | 10.05 |
| 37 | - U.S. Treasury Bond, 3-Year Yield | 9.89 |
| 38 | - U.S. Certificate of Deposit, 3-Month Yield | 9.37 |
| 39 | - Taxable Money Market Fund | 9.11 |
| 40 | - S&P Municipal Bond Yield Index | 8.88 |
| 41 | - U.S. Treasury Bill, 3-Month Yield | 8.72 |
| 42 | - Real Estate Investment Trusts | 7.69 |
| 43 | - U.S. Savings Bonds - Series EE | 6.74 |
| 44 | - NASDAQ Composite Index | 6.33 |
| 45 | - Tax-Free Money Market Fund | 5.38 |
| 46 | - Inflation | 4.48 |
| 47 | - Japanese Yen | 4.07 |
| 48 | - New One-Family House Price Index | 3.87 |
| 49 | - Swiss Franc | 3.30 |
| 50 | - Value Line Composite Index | 3.12 |
| 51 | - German Mark | 2.75 |
| 52 | - Canadian Dollar | 0.29 |
| 53 | - U.S. Farmland Price Index | -0.76 |
| 54 | - U.S. Dollar | -0.87 |
| 55 | - Commodity Spot Market Index | -0.93 |
| 56 | - British Pound | -2.13 |
| 57 | - Gold | -3.92 |
| 58 | - Australian Dollar | -4.22 |
| 59 | - Crude Petroleum | -4.83 |
| 60 | - Diamonds | -7.57 |
| 61 | - Silver | -12.24 |

©1996 Chase Global Data & Research
73 Junction Square, Concord, MA 01742

## Fifteen-Year Performance Ranking
## (1981 - 1995)

| Rank | | Avg. Annual Return |
|---|---|---|
| 1 - | London Exchange, with dividends, local currency | 17.48 |
| 2 - | London Exchange, with dividends, in U.S. Dollars | 16.58 |
| 3 - | Dow Jones 30 Industrials, with dividends | 16.27 |
| 4 - | Morgan Stanley Europe Index, with dividends | 15.01 |
| 5 - | S&P 500 Composite Index, with dividends | 14.69 |
| 6 - | Morgan Stanley EAFE Index, with dividends | 14.51 |
| 7 - | Morgan Stanley North America Index, with dividends | 14.29 |
| 8 - | CDA Equity Money Manager Index | 14.27 |
| 9 - | Morgan Stanley Pacific Index, with dividends | 14.12 |
| 10 - | Morgan Stanley World Index, with dividends | 14.06 |
| 11 - | Merrill Lynch High Yield Bond Index | 13.86 |
| 12 - | Lehman Brothers Long Term Corporate Index | 13.82 |
| 13 - | Chase Balanced Global Asset Index | 13.58 |
| 14 - | Lehman Brothers Long Term Treasury Index | 13.42 |
| 15 - | Dow Jones 15 Utilities, with dividends | 13.28 |
| 16 - | Lipper Growth Mutual Fund Average | 13.07 |
| 17 - | Lehman Brothers Mortgage-Backed Securities Index | 12.31 |
| 18 - | Lipper Income Mutual Fund Average | 12.22 |
| 19 - | Frankfurt Exchange in U.S. Dollars | 12.12 |
| 20 - | Lehman Brothers Intermediate Corporate Index | 11.85 |
| 21 - | Lehman Brothers Government/Corporate Index | 11.79 |
| 22 - | NASDAQ Composite Index | 11.62 |
| 23 - | Lehman Brothers Long Municipal Index | 11.35 |
| 24 - | Moody's Baa Corporate Bond Yield | 11.20 |
| 25 - | Salomon Brothers 10-Year U.S. Treasury Bond Index | 11.01 |
| 26 - | FHA Mortgage Rate | 10.88 |
| 27 - | Frankfurt Exchange, local currency | 10.85 |
| 28 - | Lehman Brothers Intermediate Treasury Index | 10.72 |
| 29 - | Lipper Fixed Income Mutual Fund Average | 10.64 |
| 30 - | Real Estate Investment Trusts | 10.57 |
| 31 - | Lipper Municipal Bond Mutual Fund Average | 10.16 |
| 32 - | Moody's Aaa Corporate Bond Yield | 10.03 |
| 33 - | Tokyo Exchange, with dividends, in U.S. Dollars | 10.00 |
| 34 - | Prime Rate | 9.95 |
| 35 - | Universal Life Insurance Average Rate | 9.24 |
| 36 - | U.S. Treasury Bond, 10-Year Yield | 9.14 |
| 37 - | Tokyo Exchange, with dividends, local currency | 8.91 |
| 38 - | Single Premium Deferred Annuity Interest Rate | 8.83 |
| 39 - | U.S. Treasury Bond, 3-Year Yield | 8.51 |
| 40 - | S&P Municipal Bond Yield Index | 7.99 |
| 41 - | U.S. Certificate of Deposit, 3-Month Yield | 7.77 |
| 42 - | Taxable Money Market Fund | 7.45 |
| 43 - | U.S. Treasury Bill, 3-Month Yield | 7.27 |
| 44 - | U.S. Savings Bonds - Series EE | 6.10 |
| 45 - | Value Line Composite Index | 5.70 |
| 46 - | Japanese Yen | 4.59 |
| 47 - | Tax-Free Money Market Fund | 4.54 |
| 48 - | Inflation | 3.91 |
| 49 - | New One-Family House Price Index | 3.40 |
| 50 - | Swiss Franc | 2.88 |
| 51 - | German Mark | 2.11 |
| 52 - | U.S. Farmland Price Index | 0.81 |
| 53 - | Commodity Spot Market Index | 0.13 |
| 54 - | U.S. Dollar | -0.47 |
| 55 - | Canadian Dollar | -0.88 |
| 56 - | Gold | -2.73 |
| 57 - | British Pound | -2.85 |
| 58 - | Australian Dollar | -3.04 |
| 59 - | Diamonds | -4.41 |
| 60 - | Crude Petroleum | -5.25 |
| 61 - | Silver | -7.09 |

©1996 Chase Global Data & Research
73 Junction Square, Concord, MA 01742

## Fifteen-Year Performance Ranking (1976 - 1990)

| Rank | | | Avg. Annual Return |
|---|---|---|---|
| 1 | - | Morgan Stanley Pacific Index, with dividends | 19.00 |
| 2 | - | London Exchange, with dividends, local currency | 18.59 |
| 3 | - | London Exchange, with dividends, in U.S. Dollars | 18.51 |
| 4 | - | Morgan Stanley EAFE Index, with dividends | 17.01 |
| 5 | - | Dow Jones 15 Utilities, with dividends | 15.90 |
| 6 | - | Morgan Stanley Europe Index, with dividends | 15.53 |
| 7 | - | Morgan Stanley World Index, with dividends | 14.88 |
| 8 | - | Lipper Growth Mutual Fund Average | 14.78 |
| 9 | - | Tokyo Exchange, with dividends, in U.S. Dollars | 14.46 |
| 10 | - | Morgan Stanley North America Index, with dividends | 13.87 |
| 11 | - | S&P 500 Composite Index, with dividends | 13.75 |
| 12 | - | Chase Balanced Global Asset Index | 13.43 |
| 13 | - | Dow Jones 30 Industrials, with dividends | 13.12 |
| 14 | - | Tokyo Exchange, with dividends, local currency | 12.98 |
| 15 | - | Real Estate Investment Trusts | 12.83 |
| 16 | - | Lipper Income Mutual Fund Average | 11.92 |
| 17 | - | Moody's Baa Corporate Bond Yield | 11.81 |
| 18 | - | FHA Mortgage Rate | 11.63 |
| 19 | - | NASDAQ Composite Index | 11.05 |
| 20 | - | Prime Rate | 10.88 |
| 21 | - | Lehman Brothers Mortgage-Backed Securities Index | 10.70 |
| 22 | - | Lehman Brothers Long Term Corporate Index | 10.48 |
| 23 | - | Moody's Aaa Corporate Bond Yield | 10.48 |
| 24 | - | Lehman Brothers Intermediate Corporate Index | 10.35 |
| 25 | - | Lehman Brothers Government/Corporate Index | 10.10 |
| 26 | - | Lehman Brothers Intermediate Treasury Index | 9.99 |
| 27 | - | Lehman Brothers Long Term Treasury Index | 9.81 |
| 28 | - | U.S. Treasury Bond, 10-Year Yield | 9.81 |
| 29 | - | Lipper Fixed Income Mutual Fund Average | 9.59 |
| 30 | - | U.S. Treasury Bond, 3-Year Yield | 9.45 |
| 31 | - | U.S. Certificate of Deposit, 3-Month Yield | 9.12 |
| 32 | - | Taxable Money Market Fund | 8.82 |
| 33 | - | U.S. Treasury Bill, 3-Month Yield | 8.49 |
| 34 | - | S&P Municipal Bond Yield Index | 8.11 |
| 35 | - | Frankfurt Exchange in U.S. Dollars | 7.77 |
| 36 | - | Gold | 7.10 |
| 37 | - | Value Line Composite Index | 7.03 |
| 38 | - | U.S. Savings Bonds - Series EE | 7.01 |
| 39 | - | New One-Family House Price Index | 6.40 |
| 40 | - | Frankfurt Exchange, local currency | 6.25 |
| 41 | - | Inflation | 6.04 |
| 42 | - | Japanese Yen | 5.55 |
| 43 | - | Swiss Franc | 4.94 |
| 44 | - | Crude Petroleum | 4.87 |
| 45 | - | U.S. Farmland Price Index | 4.76 |
| 46 | - | German Mark | 3.80 |
| 47 | - | Commodity Spot Market Index | 2.13 |
| 48 | - | Silver | 0.15 |
| 49 | - | British Pound | -0.32 |
| 50 | - | Canadian Dollar | -0.89 |
| 51 | - | U.S. Dollar | -1.43 |
| 52 | - | Australian Dollar | -3.21 |

©1996 Chase Global Data & Research
73 Junction Square, Concord, MA 01742

## Twenty-Year Performance Ranking (1976 - 1995)

| Rank | | Investment | Avg. Annual Return |
|---|---|---|---|
| 1 | - | London Exchange, with dividends, local currency | 17.92 |
| 2 | - | London Exchange, with dividends, in U.S. Dollars | 17.63 |
| 3 | - | Morgan Stanley Pacific Index, with dividends | 16.05 |
| 4 | - | Morgan Stanley EAFE Index, with dividends | 15.14 |
| 5 | - | Lipper Growth Mutual Fund Average | 15.06 |
| 6 | - | Morgan Stanley Europe Index, with dividends | 14.66 |
| 7 | - | Morgan Stanley North America Index, with dividends | 14.47 |
| 8 | - | S&P 500 Composite Index, with dividends | 14.45 |
| 9 | - | Morgan Stanley World Index, with dividends | 14.23 |
| 10 | - | Dow Jones 30 Industrials, with dividends | 14.21 |
| 11 | - | NASDAQ Composite Index | 13.92 |
| 12 | - | Dow Jones 15 Utilities, with dividends | 13.89 |
| 13 | - | Real Estate Investment Trusts | 13.75 |
| 14 | - | Chase Balanced Global Asset Index | 13.07 |
| 15 | - | Lipper Income Mutual Fund Average | 12.07 |
| 16 | - | Moody's Baa Corporate Bond Yield | 11.03 |
| 17 | - | Lehman Brothers Long Term Corporate Index | 11.01 |
| 18 | - | FHA Mortgage Rate | 10.82 |
| 19 | - | Lehman Brothers Long Term Treasury Index | 10.50 |
| 20 | - | Tokyo Exchange, with dividends, in U.S. Dollars | 10.48 |
| 21 | - | Lehman Brothers Intermediate Corporate Index | 10.31 |
| 22 | - | Lehman Brothers Mortgage-Backed Securities Index | 10.20 |
| 23 | - | Lehman Brothers Government/Corporate Index | 10.03 |
| 24 | - | Prime Rate | 9.98 |
| 25 | - | Moody's Aaa Corporate Bond Yield | 9.86 |
| 26 | - | Lehman Brothers Intermediate Treasury Index | 9.54 |
| 27 | - | Lipper Fixed Income Mutual Fund Average | 9.50 |
| 28 | - | Tokyo Exchange, with dividends, local currency | 9.29 |
| 29 | - | U.S. Treasury Bond, 10-Year Yield | 9.07 |
| 30 | - | U.S. Treasury Bond, 3-Year Yield | 8.53 |
| 31 | - | Frankfurt Exchange in U.S. Dollars | 8.27 |
| 32 | - | Value Line Composite Index | 8.03 |
| 33 | - | U.S. Certificate of Deposit, 3-Month Yield | 7.98 |
| 34 | - | Taxable Money Market Fund | 7.64 |
| 35 | - | S&P Municipal Bond Yield Index | 7.63 |
| 36 | - | U.S. Treasury Bill, 3-Month Yield | 7.46 |
| 37 | - | Frankfurt Exchange, local currency | 7.18 |
| 38 | - | U.S. Savings Bonds - Series EE | 6.46 |
| 39 | - | Japanese Yen | 5.57 |
| 40 | - | New One-Family House Price Index | 5.40 |
| 41 | - | Inflation | 5.22 |
| 42 | - | Gold | 5.20 |
| 43 | - | U.S. Farmland Price Index | 4.58 |
| 44 | - | Swiss Franc | 4.21 |
| 45 | - | German Mark | 3.05 |
| 46 | - | Commodity Spot Market Index | 2.17 |
| 47 | - | Crude Petroleum | 2.01 |
| 48 | - | Silver | 1.13 |
| 49 | - | U.S. Dollar | -0.99 |
| 50 | - | British Pound | -1.32 |
| 51 | - | Canadian Dollar | -1.47 |
| 52 | - | Australian Dollar | -2.58 |

©1996 Chase Global Data & Research
73 Junction Square, Concord, MA 01742

## Twenty-Year Performance Ranking (1971 - 1990)

| | | Avg. Annual Return |
|---|---|---|
| 1 | - Morgan Stanley Pacific Index, with dividends | 18.73 |
| 2 | - London Exchange, with dividends, local currency | 16.65 |
| 3 | - London Exchange, with dividends, in U.S. Dollars | 16.16 |
| 4 | - Tokyo Exchange, with dividends, in U.S. Dollars | 16.11 |
| 5 | - Crude Petroleum | 15.57 |
| 6 | - Morgan Stanley EAFE Index, with dividends | 15.37 |
| 7 | - Tokyo Exchange, with dividends, local currency | 14.55 |
| 8 | - Morgan Stanley Europe Index, with dividends | 13.78 |
| 9 | - Gold | 12.44 |
| 10 | - Morgan Stanley World Index, with dividends | 12.35 |
| 11 | - Dow Jones 15 Utilities, with dividends | 11.66 |
| 12 | - Lipper Growth Mutual Fund Average | 11.22 |
| 13 | - Moody's Baa Corporate Bond Yield | 11.10 |
| 14 | - S&P 500 Composite Index, with dividends | 11.01 |
| 15 | - Dow Jones 30 Industrials, with dividends | 10.91 |
| 16 | - FHA Mortgage Rate | 10.85 |
| 17 | - Morgan Stanley North America Index, with dividends | 10.78 |
| 18 | - Lipper Income Mutual Fund Average | 10.16 |
| 19 | - Prime Rate | 10.03 |
| 20 | - Moody's Aaa Corporate Bond Yield | 9.83 |
| 21 | - U.S. Treasury Bond, 10-Year Yield | 9.08 |
| 22 | - U.S. Treasury Bond, 3-Year Yield | 8.76 |
| 23 | - U.S. Certificate of Deposit, 3-Month Yield | 8.57 |
| 24 | - Lipper Fixed Income Mutual Fund Average | 8.32 |
| 25 | - U.S. Treasury Bill, 3-Month Yield | 7.85 |
| 26 | - S&P Municipal Bond Yield Index | 7.53 |
| 27 | - Frankfurt Exchange in U.S. Dollars | 7.37 |
| 28 | - U.S. Savings Bonds - Series EE | 7.03 |
| 29 | - New One-Family House Price Index | 6.87 |
| 30 | - U.S. Farmland Price Index | 6.44 |
| 31 | - Swiss Franc | 6.27 |
| 32 | - Inflation | 6.25 |
| 33 | - Frankfurt Exchange, local currency | 5.90 |
| 34 | - Japanese Yen | 4.96 |
| 35 | - Silver | 4.80 |
| 36 | - German Mark | 4.55 |
| 37 | - Commodity Spot Market Index | 4.54 |
| 38 | - Value Line Composite Index | 3.24 |
| 39 | - Canadian Dollar | -0.65 |
| 40 | - British Pound | -1.07 |
| 41 | - Australian Dollar | -1.83 |
| 42 | - U.S. Dollar | -1.83 |

©1996 Chase Global Data & Research
73 Junction Square, Concord, MA 01742

## Twenty Five - Year Performance Ranking
## (1971 - 1995)

| | | Avg. Annual Return |
|---|---|---|
| 1 | London Exchange, with dividends, local currency | 16.50 |
| 2 | Morgan Stanley Pacific Index, with dividends | 16.42 |
| 3 | London Exchange, with dividends, in U.S. Dollars | 15.93 |
| 4 | Morgan Stanley EAFE Index, with dividends | 14.22 |
| 5 | Morgan Stanley Europe Index, with dividends | 13.45 |
| 6 | Tokyo Exchange, with dividends, in U.S. Dollars | 12.54 |
| 7 | Morgan Stanley World Index, with dividends | 12.35 |
| 8 | Dow Jones 30 Industrials, with dividends | 12.20 |
| 9 | Lipper Growth Mutual Fund Average | 12.14 |
| 10 | S&P 500 Composite Index, with dividends | 12.10 |
| 11 | Morgan Stanley North America Index, with dividends | 11.86 |
| 12 | Tokyo Exchange, with dividends, local currency | 11.24 |
| 13 | Dow Jones 15 Utilities, with dividends | 10.93 |
| 14 | Crude Petroleum | 10.87 |
| 15 | Lipper Income Mutual Fund Average | 10.63 |
| 16 | Moody's Baa Corporate Bond Yield | 10.62 |
| 17 | FHA Mortgage Rate | 10.36 |
| 18 | Gold | 9.77 |
| 19 | Prime Rate | 9.48 |
| 20 | Moody's Aaa Corporate Bond Yield | 9.46 |
| 21 | U.S. Treasury Bond, 10-Year Yield | 8.64 |
| 22 | Lipper Fixed Income Mutual Fund Average | 8.51 |
| 23 | U.S. Treasury Bond, 3-Year Yield | 8.17 |
| 24 | Frankfurt Exchange in U.S. Dollars | 7.85 |
| 25 | U.S. Certificate of Deposit, 3-Month Yield | 7.77 |
| 26 | S&P Municipal Bond Yield Index | 7.27 |
| 27 | U.S. Treasury Bill, 3-Month Yield | 7.16 |
| 28 | Frankfurt Exchange, local currency | 6.72 |
| 29 | U.S. Savings Bonds - Series EE | 6.59 |
| 30 | New One-Family House Price Index | 5.97 |
| 31 | U.S. Farmland Price Index | 5.95 |
| 32 | Inflation | 5.55 |
| 33 | Swiss Franc | 5.41 |
| 34 | Japanese Yen | 5.09 |
| 35 | Value Line Composite Index | 4.76 |
| 36 | Silver | 4.66 |
| 37 | Commodity Spot Market Index | 4.09 |
| 38 | German Mark | 3.79 |
| 39 | Canadian Dollar | -1.16 |
| 40 | U.S. Dollar | -1.40 |
| 41 | Australian Dollar | -1.59 |
| 42 | British Pound | -1.72 |

©1996 Chase Global Data & Research
73 Junction Square, Concord, MA 01742

## Twenty Five - Year Performance Ranking (1966 - 1990)

| | | Avg. Annual Return |
|---|---|---|
| 1 | - London Exchange, with dividends, local currency | 15.31 |
| 2 | - Tokyo Exchange, with dividends, in U.S. Dollars | 15.07 |
| 3 | - London Exchange, with dividends, in U.S. Dollars | 14.75 |
| 4 | - Tokyo Exchange, with dividends, local currency | 13.82 |
| 5 | - Crude Petroleum | 11.55 |
| 6 | - Moody's Baa Corporate Bond Yield | 10.30 |
| 7 | - FHA Mortgage Rate | 10.20 |
| 8 | - Gold | 10.15 |
| 9 | - Lipper Growth Mutual Fund Average | 10.14 |
| 10 | - S&P 500 Composite Index, with dividends | 9.42 |
| 11 | - Prime Rate | 9.35 |
| 12 | - Dow Jones 15 Utilities, with dividends | 9.31 |
| 13 | - Moody's Aaa Corporate Bond Yield | 9.13 |
| 14 | - Dow Jones 30 Industrials, with dividends | 8.82 |
| 15 | - Lipper Income Mutual Fund Average | 8.73 |
| 16 | - U.S. Treasury Bond, 10-Year Yield | 8.45 |
| 17 | - U.S. Treasury Bond, 3-Year Yield | 8.22 |
| 18 | - U.S. Certificate of Deposit, 3-Month Yield | 8.12 |
| 19 | - U.S. Treasury Bill, 3-Month Yield | 7.41 |
| 20 | - S&P Municipal Bond Yield Index | 7.00 |
| 21 | - U.S. Savings Bonds - Series EE | 6.99 |
| 22 | - Lipper Fixed Income Mutual Fund Average | 6.97 |
| 23 | - New One-Family House Price Index | 6.37 |
| 24 | - U.S. Farmland Price Index | 6.34 |
| 25 | - Frankfurt Exchange in U.S. Dollars | 6.12 |
| 26 | - Inflation | 5.92 |
| 27 | - Swiss Franc | 4.99 |
| 28 | - Frankfurt Exchange, local currency | 4.90 |
| 29 | - Silver | 4.80 |
| 30 | - German Mark | 4.01 |
| 31 | - Japanese Yen | 3.99 |
| 32 | - Commodity Spot Market Index | 3.40 |
| 33 | - Value Line Composite Index | 1.50 |
| 34 | - Canadian Dollar | -0.30 |
| 35 | - Australian Dollar | -1.48 |
| 36 | - British Pound | -1.48 |

©1996 Chase Global Data & Research
73 Junction Square, Concord, MA 01742

## Thirty Five - Year Performance Ranking
## (1961 - 1995)

| Rank | | Avg. Annual Return |
|---|---|---|
| 1 | Lipper Growth Mutual Fund Average | 11.40 |
| 2 | Tokyo Exchange, with dividends, in U.S. Dollars | 11.01 |
| 3 | S&P 500 Composite Index, with dividends | 10.95 |
| 4 | Dow Jones 30 Industrials, with dividends | 10.66 |
| 5 | Tokyo Exchange, with dividends, local currency | 10.08 |
| 6 | Dow Jones 15 Utilities, with dividends | 9.58 |
| 7 | Lipper Income Mutual Fund Average | 9.32 |
| 8 | Moody's Baa Corporate Bond Yield | 9.29 |
| 9 | FHA Mortgage Rate | 9.26 |
| 10 | Prime Rate | 8.35 |
| 11 | Moody's Aaa Corporate Bond Yield | 8.27 |
| 12 | Lipper Fixed Income Mutual Fund Average | 7.62 |
| 13 | U.S. Treasury Bond, 10-Year Yield | 7.58 |
| 14 | U.S. Treasury Bond, 3-Year Yield | 7.23 |
| 15 | Gold | 7.11 |
| 16 | Crude Petroleum | 6.73 |
| 17 | U.S. Savings Bonds -Series EE | 6.59 |
| 18 | U.S. Treasury Bill, 3-Month Yield | 6.37 |
| 19 | S&P Municipal Bond Yield Index | 6.35 |
| 20 | U.S. Farmland Price Index | 5.76 |
| 21 | Silver | 5.04 |
| 22 | Frankfurt Exchange in U.S. Dollars | 5.04 |
| 23 | Inflation | 4.79 |
| 24 | Frankfurt Exchange, local currency | 4.20 |
| 25 | Swiss Franc | 3.83 |
| 26 | Japanese Yen | 3.63 |
| 27 | Commodity Spot Market Index | 3.19 |
| 28 | German Mark | 3.09 |
| 29 | Canadian Dollar | -0.93 |
| 30 | Australian Dollar | -1.16 |
| 31 | British Pound | -1.68 |

©1996 Chase Global Data & Research
73 Junction Square, Concord, MA 01742

# Volatility Rankings: Ten, Twenty, and Thirty-Five Years

## Ten-Year Volatility Ranking
## (1986 - 1995)

| | | Return's Volatility | Avg. Annual Return |
|---|---|---|---|
| 1 - | Morgan Stanley Pacific Index, with dividends | 33.78 | 13.57 |
| 2 - | Crude Petroleum | 27.03 | -5.31 |
| 3 - | Tokyo Exchange, with dividends, in U.S. Dollars | 26.50 | 6.36 |
| 4 - | Tokyo Exchange, with dividends, local currency | 24.63 | 4.85 |
| 5 - | Morgan Stanley EAFE Index, with dividends | 24.22 | 13.95 |
| 6 - | Frankfurt Exchange, local currency | 23.55 | 5.13 |
| 7 - | Frankfurt Exchange in U.S. Dollars | 21.38 | 6.35 |
| 8 - | NASDAQ Composite Index | 20.64 | 12.47 |
| 9 - | Silver | 17.18 | -1.31 |
| 10 - | Dow Jones 15 Utilities, with dividends | 16.33 | 9.92 |
| 11 - | Morgan Stanley World Index, with dividends | 15.66 | 13.72 |
| 12 - | Morgan Stanley Europe Index, with dividends | 15.22 | 14.48 |
| 13 - | Real Estate Investment Trusts | 15.07 | 7.55 |
| 14 - | Swiss Franc | 14.53 | 5.91 |
| 15 - | Value Line Composite Index | 14.50 | 4.42 |
| 16 - | CDA Equity Money Manager Index | 14.16 | 14.73 |
| 17 - | London Exchange, with dividends, local currency | 13.33 | 14.60 |
| 18 - | Lipper Equity Variable Annuity Index | 13.19 | 13.21 |
| 19 - | S&P 500 Composite Index, with dividends | 13.14 | 14.77 |
| 20 - | Japanese Yen | 13.12 | 6.93 |
| 21 - | Lipper Growth Mutual Fund Average | 13.10 | 12.99 |
| 22 - | Morgan Stanley North America Index, with dividends | 12.93 | 14.41 |
| 23 - | British Pound | 12.87 | 0.70 |
| 24 - | Gold | 12.37 | 1.61 |
| 25 - | Merrill Lynch High Yield Bond Index | 12.31 | 12.34 |
| 26 - | German Mark | 12.31 | 5.47 |
| 27 - | London Exchange, with dividends, in U.S. Dollars | 12.29 | 14.29 |
| 28 - | Dow Jones 30 Industrials, with dividends | 12.08 | 16.46 |
| 29 - | Lehman Brothers Long Term Treasury Index | 11.27 | 11.68 |
| 30 - | Lehman Brothers Long Term Corporate Index | 9.26 | 11.47 |
| 31 - | U.S. Dollar | 9.25 | -3.70 |
| 32 - | Lehman Brothers Long Municipal Index | 9.04 | 10.25 |
| 33 - | Chase Balanced Global Asset Index | 8.95 | 12.61 |
| 34 - | Australian Dollar | 8.79 | 0.86 |
| 35 - | Lipper Income Mutual Fund Average | 8.67 | 10.12 |
| 36 - | Salomon Brothers 10-Year U.S. Treasury Bond Index | 8.57 | 8.56 |
| 37 - | Merrill Lynch Australian Government Bond Index | 8.38 | 13.98 |
| 38 - | Commodity Spot Market Index | 8.10 | 2.02 |
| 39 - | Lipper Fixed Income Variable Annuity Index | 7.60 | 8.85 |
| 40 - | Merrill Lynch British Gilt Bond Index | 7.39 | 11.76 |
| 41 - | Lipper Municipal Bond Mutual Fund Average | 7.29 | 8.57 |
| 42 - | Merrill Lynch Global Government Bond Index | 6.69 | 11.75 |
| 43 - | Lehman Brothers Government/Corporate Index | 6.56 | 9.65 |
| 44 - | Lipper Fixed Income Mutual Fund Average | 6.03 | 8.39 |
| 45 - | Lehman Brothers Intermediate Corporate Index | 5.97 | 9.66 |
| 46 - | Merrill Lynch Japanese Government Bond Index | 5.78 | 7.00 |
| 47 - | Lehman Brothers Mortgage Backed Securities Index | 5.54 | 9.58 |
| 48 - | Merrill Lynch German Government Bond Index | 5.39 | 7.51 |
| 49 - | U.S. Farmland Price Index | 5.34 | 1.56 |
| 50 - | Canadian Dollar | 5.16 | 0.25 |
| 51 - | Lehman Brothers Intermediate Treasury Index | 4.92 | 8.58 |
| 52 - | Diamonds | 4.65 | 2.48 |
| 53 - | Taxable Money Market Fund | 1.88 | 5.70 |
| 54 - | U.S. Certificate of Deposit, 3-Month Yield | 1.82 | 6.14 |
| 55 - | U.S. Treasury Bill, 3-Month Yield | 1.63 | 5.71 |
| 56 - | GICs - 1 Year Market Average | 1.58 | 6.21 |
| 57 - | New One-Family House Price Index | 1.47 | 3.17 |
| 58 - | Prime Rate | 1.47 | 8.33 |
| 59 - | Inflation | 1.35 | 3.45 |
| 60 - | U.S. Treasury Bond, 3-Year Yield | 1.28 | 6.88 |
| 61 - | Tax-Free Money Market Fund | 1.24 | 3.89 |
| 62 - | Single Premium Deferred Annuity Interest Rate | 1.23 | 7.49 |
| 63 - | Universal Life Insurance Average Rate | 1.13 | 8.25 |
| 64 - | GICs - 5 Year Market Average | 1.11 | 7.78 |
| 65 - | Moody's Baa Corporate Bond Yield | 1.01 | 9.58 |
| 66 - | FHA Mortgage Rate | 1.00 | 9.29 |
| 67 - | U.S. Treasury Bond, 10-Year Yield | 0.93 | 7.63 |
| 68 - | U.S. Savings Bond - Series EE | 0.90 | 5.53 |
| 69 - | Moody's Aaa Corporate Bond Yield | 0.74 | 8.67 |
| 70 - | S&P Municipal Bond Yield Index | 0.72 | 6.84 |

©1996 Chase Global Data & Research
73 Junction Square, Concord, MA 01742

## Twenty - Year Volatility Ranking
## (1976 - 1995)

| | Return's Volatility | Avg. Annual Return |
|---|---|---|
| 1 - Silver | **62.61** | 1.13 |
| 2 - Crude Petroleum | **34.85** | 2.01 |
| 3 - Gold | **31.68** | 5.20 |
| 4 - Morgan Stanley Pacific Index, with dividends | **26.83** | 16.05 |
| 5 - Frankfurt Exchange in U.S. Dollars | **24.58** | 8.27 |
| 6 - Frankfurt Exchange, local currency | **23.36** | 7.18 |
| 7 - Morgan Stanley EAFE Index, with dividends | **21.08** | 15.14 |
| 8 - Tokyo Exchange, with dividends, in U.S. Dollars | **20.28** | 10.48 |
| 9 - Morgan Stanley Europe Index, with dividends | **20.11** | 14.66 |
| 10 - Tokyo Exchange, with dividends, local currency | **18.98** | 9.29 |
| 11 - NASDAQ Composite Index | **17.76** | 13.92 |
| 12 - Real Estate Investment Trusts | **15.89** | 13.75 |
| 13 - Dow Jones 15 Utilities, with dividends | **14.67** | 13.89 |
| 14 - Swiss Franc | **14.62** | 4.21 |
| 15 - British Pound | **14.37** | -1.32 |
| 16 - German Mark | **14.25** | 3.05 |
| 17 - Value Line Composite Index | **14.18** | 8.03 |
| 18 - Morgan Stanley World Index, with dividends | **14.17** | 14.23 |
| 19 - Japanese Yen | **14.05** | 5.57 |
| 20 - Dow Jones 30 Industrials, with dividends | **13.61** | 14.21 |
| 21 - Lipper Growth Mutual Fund Average | **13.46** | 15.06 |
| 22 - London Exchange, with dividends, local currency | **13.44** | 17.92 |
| 23 - London Exchange, with dividends, in U.S. Dollars | **13.30** | 14.45 |
| 24 - S&P 500 Composite Index, with dividends | **13.40** | 17.63 |
| 25 - Lehman Brothers Long Term Treasury Index | **13.23** | 10.50 |
| 26 - Morgan Stanley North America Index, with dividends | **12.93** | 14.47 |
| 27 - Lehman Brothers Long Term Corporate Index | **12.55** | 11.01 |
| 28 - U.S. Dollar | **10.57** | -0.99 |
| 29 - Lehman Brothers Mortgage-Backed Securities Index | **10.25** | 10.20 |
| 30 - Commodity Spot Market Index | **10.03** | 2.17 |
| 31 - Australian Dollar | **9.20** | -2.58 |
| 32 - Chase Balanced Global Asset Index | **8.78** | 13.07 |
| 33 - U.S. Farmland Price Index | **8.74** | 4.58 |
| 34 - Lipper Income Mutual Fund Average | **8.67** | 12.07 |
| 35 - Lehman Brothers Government/Corporate Index | **8.07** | 10.03 |
| 36 - Lipper Fixed Income Mutual Fund Average | **7.82** | 9.50 |
| 37 - Lehman Brothers Intermediate Corporate Index | **7.19** | 10.31 |
| 38 - Lehman Brothers Intermediate Treasury Index | **5.91** | 9.54 |
| 39 - Canadian Dollar | **4.55** | -1.47 |
| 40 - New One-Family House Price Index | **4.12** | 5.40 |
| 41 - Taxable Money Market Fund | **3.43** | 7.64 |
| 42 - Prime Rate | **3.26** | 9.98 |
| 43 - Inflation | **3.21** | 5.22 |
| 44 - U.S. Certificate of Deposit, 3-Month Yield | **3.20** | 7.98 |
| 45 - U.S. Treasury Bill, 3-Month Yield | **2.91** | 7.46 |
| 46 - U.S. Treasury Bond, 3-Year Yield | **2.56** | 8.53 |
| 47 - FHA Mortgage Rate | **2.43** | 10.82 |
| 48 - Moody's Baa Corporate Bond Yield | **2.41** | 11.03 |
| 49 - U.S. Treasury Bond, 10-Year Yield | **2.20** | 9.07 |
| 50 - Moody's Aaa Corporate Bond Yield | **1.99** | 9.86 |
| 51 - S&P Municipal Bond Yield Index | **1.77** | 7.63 |
| 52 - U.S. Savings Bond - Series EE | **1.15** | 6.46 |

©1996 Chase Global Data & Research
73 Junction Square, Concord, MA 01742

## Thirty Five - Year Volatility Ranking
## (1961 - 1995)

| | Return's Volatility | Avg. Annual Return |
|---|---|---|
| 1 - Crude Petroleum | 55.39 | 6.73 |
| 2 - Silver | 49.93 | 5.04 |
| 3 - Gold | 29.94 | 7.11 |
| 4 - Tokyo Exchange, with dividends, in U.S. Dollars | 25.70 | 11.01 |
| 5 - Tokyo Exchange, with dividends, local currency | 24.37 | 10.08 |
| 6 - Frankfurt Exchange, with dividends, in U.S. Dollars | 23.62 | 5.04 |
| 7 - Frankfurt Exchange, local currency | 23.15 | 4.20 |
| 8 - Lipper Growth Mutual Fund Average | 17.68 | 11.40 |
| 9 - Dow Jones 30 Industrials, with dividends | 15.99 | 10.66 |
| 10 - Dow Jones 15 Utilities, with dividends | 15.80 | 9.58 |
| 11 - S&P 500 Composite Index, with dividends | 15.59 | 10.95 |
| 12 - Commodity Spot Market Index | 13.10 | 3.19 |
| 13 - Swiss Franc | 12.05 | 3.83 |
| 14 - German Mark | 11.54 | 3.09 |
| 15 - British Pound | 11.39 | -1.68 |
| 16 - Japanese Yen | 11.28 | 3.63 |
| 17 - Lipper Income Mutual Fund Average | 10.45 | 9.32 |
| 18 - Lipper Fixed Income Mutual Fund Average | 8.62 | 7.62 |
| 19 - Australian Dollar | 8.41 | -1.16 |
| 20 - U.S. Farmland Price Index | 7.48 | 5.76 |
| 21 - Canadian Dollar | 3.83 | -0.93 |
| 22 - Prime Rate | 3.32 | 8.35 |
| 23 - Inflation | 3.21 | 4.79 |
| 24 - Moody's Baa Corporate Bond Yield | 2.97 | 9.29 |
| 25 - U.S. Treasury Bill, 3-Month Yield | 2.76 | 6.37 |
| 26 - FHA Mortgage Rate | 2.73 | 9.26 |
| 27 - U.S. Treasury Bond, 3-Year Yield | 2.63 | 7.23 |
| 28 - Moody's Aaa Corporate Bond Yield | 2.59 | 8.27 |
| 29 - U.S. Treasury Bond, 10-Year Yield | 2.55 | 7.58 |
| 30 - S&P Municipal Bond Yield Index | 2.16 | 6.35 |
| 31 - U.S. Savings Bond - Series EE | 0.91 | 6.59 |

©1996 Chase Global Data & Research
73 Junction Square, Concord, MA 01742

SECTION III

# General Financial Indicators

Chapter One

# Inflation

Experts agree that inflation is the rate of increase of prices. Another way to understand inflation is to say that it is the exact opposite of deflation—a decline in the price level that causes the purchasing power of money to rise. Inflation causes the purchasing power of money to fall. The debate over inflation begins, however, when one tries to define its causes and effects. For example, some economists maintain that inflation occurs when the means of payment, i.e. dollars, is in the hands of people willing to spend faster than production can produce.

The U.S. has a lengthy history of inflation. In fact, inflation is one of the pieces of economic data that has been collected for the longest period of time. Data on wholesale prices is available as far back as 1720, and on consumer prices starting in 1800.

Overall, prices in the U.S. have tended to rise consistently since the beginning of the Republic—and, hence, the value of the dollar has declined. By 1990, after two hundred years, the value of the dollar was ten times less than in 1790—in other words, the dollar was worth only 10% of what it was worth in 1790. Prices rise most during war time—for example, 1812, 1861, 1916, 1942, 1950, and 1966. During the Civil War inflation was over 25%; during World War I and the Korean War it was over 15%. Up until World War II prices declined after each war. One study has shown that if war periods were excluded from inflation statistics, inflation would have been no higher in 1960 than it was in 1800.

Ironically, immediately after the Federal Reserve Act of 1913, which mandated that (1) banks were to be overseen by the Federal Reserve, and (2) the initial levying of Federal income taxes, wholesale prices skyrocketed. The wholesale price index went from 33 in 1914 to 80 in 1920. Throughout the 1920's wholesale prices began to drop, and plummeted even more after the stock market crash of '29. Recently, there was another tremendous acceleration of wholesale prices from


©1996 Chase Global Data & Research
73 Junction Square, Concord, MA 01742

120 on the wholesale price index in 1974 to approximately 290 in 1985.

From 1900 to 1980, the average annual rate of price increase in the U.S.—inflation—was about 2.5%. However, since 1970 the rate has been approximately 5.6%. If you project this inflation rate over an extended period of time—say 50 years—an hourly wage of $5.00 in 1990 would have to increase to $92.00 an hour in the year 2040 to be an equivalent wage. A $10,000 annual income would rise to $184,000 to remain parallel to the half century earlier level. The Sunday newspaper would cost $55, a pair of blue jeans would cost $920, and a stripped down Mercedes Benz $1.4 million. The average single family house in the U.S. will cost $2.4 million. Inflation may grow or even decrease, but even if it maintains the same pace as the last quarter century, life could prove more difficult in the future.

An analysis of U.S. inflation shows that since 1955 there has been a distinct change in inflationary pressures. Prices have risen consistently from 1955 to 1990, a period of 35 years. Such a consistent level of price increase over a sustained period of time has not happened so dramatically in more than 120 years. In fact, since 1950 the levels of price increases in the U.S. are greater than the total level of price increases in the U.S. in the preceding 100 years.

The real level of inflation that we worry about today began not in the 1950's but in the 1960's—and was not a result of war. (During the Vietnam War inflation was not much above 6%, but during the 1970's oil shock, inflation reached 13%.) Since World War II, the rate of inflation has been over 8% only three times: in the early 1950's, in the mid-1970's, and in the early 1980's. The only good news is that there seems to be a distinct relationship (an inverse one) between the inflation rate and the unemployment rate. Since 1960, the higher the rate of inflation, the lower the level of unemployment.

The historical precedent of hyperinflation runs the gamut. In George Washington's days of the Revolutionary War, it took a wagonload of Continental currency to buy a wagonload of provisions. Napoleon Bonaparte was contemptuous of paper money as a result of the ravages of inflation in France from 1790 to 1796. More recently, South American countries have experienced annual inflation rates over 75% for many years. In 1989 Argentina's rate was 5,000%, and in 1993 Brazil's rate was over 1000%!

A classic example of hyperinflation occurred in Germany between 1921 and 1924. Germany was a financially advanced nation

©1996 Chase Global Data & Research
73 Junction Square, Concord, MA 01742

with a modern credit system. Its problem originated when the government financed its budget deficits directly through the central bank, instead of using its Treasury to finance the nation's deficits in the open market. In 1921, expenditures for the German government were 145 billion marks. By 1923, expenditures totaled 8 trillion marks and by 1924 had reached 49 quadrillion marks. Currency in circulation in Germany in August 1922 was 252 billion marks; five months later it increased 8 fold to 2 trillion marks; eight months later it increased another 14 fold to 28 quadrillion marks; and finally by the end of 1923 the total reached 497 quintillion marks. The gold value of the mark on foreign currency exchanges dropped from 23.82 cents to 3 trillionths of a cent in two years. Children were playing with piles of marks as if they were toys.

Although the parallels are not exact, the United States has similar budget deficit problems. In the U.S., direct financing by the Treasury through the Federal Reserve is authorized by Congress for renewable periods of time and limited in amount. Yet persistent federal budget deficits can only monetize the debt by increasing the money supply through the issuance of additional dollars—which could lead to greater inflationary pressures. And 1995's deficit was $164 billion.

Another key indicator for renewed inflation is labor expense. Why? Because labor costs make up two-thirds of the Gross Domestic Product. When wages go up price increases are inevitable. With relatively stable wages, price increases follow a more ordinary pattern. Today most experts feel commodity prices are not likely to spiral because of the abundance of industrial raw materials throughout the world. Yet shortages in major raw materials, like those of copper and aluminum in 1988 and oil in 1990 have played a major role in the level of inflation worldwide.

Inflation in the 1990's has moderated, with this decade's readings reminiscent of the 1960's. What constitutes high and low levels of Inflation? As a general benchmark, based on statistics for the past quarter century and three decade spans most economists would agree that levels under 3% are low—from 3% to 5% is moderate—and readings above that level are above average.

©1996 Chase Global Data & Research
73 Junction Square, Concord, MA 01742

**INFLATION**

| Year | CPI Change* | Compound return on a five year $10,000 investment | Annual compound rate of return |
|---|---|---|---|
| 1995 | 2.54% | 1991 - 1995 | |
| 1994 | 2.67% | | 2.79% |
| 1993 | 2.75% | ... $11,472 | |
| 1992 | 2.90% | | |
| 1991 | 3.06% | | |
| 1990 | 6.11% | 1986 - 1990 | |
| 1989 | 4.65% | | 4.13% |
| 1988 | 4.42% | ... $12,242 | |
| 1987 | 4.43% | | |
| 1986 | 1.10% | | |
| 1985 | 3.80% | 1981 - 1985 | |
| 1984 | 3.95% | | 4.84% |
| 1983 | 3.79% | ... $12,665 | |
| 1982 | 3.83% | | |
| 1981 | 8.92% | | |
| 1980 | 12.52% | 1976 - 1980 | |
| 1979 | 13.29% | | 9.23% |
| 1978 | 9.02% | ... $15,550 | |
| 1977 | 6.70% | | |
| 1976 | 4.86% | | |
| 1975 | 6.94% | 1971 - 1975 | |
| 1974 | 12.34% | | 6.88% |
| 1973 | 8.71% | ... $13,945 | |
| 1972 | 3.41% | | |
| 1971 | 3.27% | | |
| 1970 | 5.57% | 1966 - 1970 | |
| 1969 | 6.20% | | 4.59% |
| 1968 | 4.72% | ... $12,516 | |
| 1967 | 3.04% | | |
| 1966 | 3.46% | | |
| 1965 | 1.92% | 1961 -1965 | |
| 1964 | 0.97% | | 1.31% |
| 1963 | 1.64% | ... $10,671 | |
| 1962 | 1.33% | | |
| 1961 | 0.67% | | |
| 1960 | 1.36% | | |

How a $10,000 investment performed over

| 5 years | 10 years | 15 years | 20 years | 25 years | 35 years |
|---|---|---|---|---|---|
| 1991 - 1995 | | | | | |
| $11,472 (2.79%)^ | 1986 - 1995 | | | | |
| | $14,044 (3.45%) | 1981 - 1995 | | | |
| | | $17,787 (3.91%) | 1976 - 1995 | | |
| | | | $27,658 (5.22%) | 1971 - 1995 | |
| | | | | $38,568 (5.55%) | 1961 - 1995 |
| | | | | | $51,510 (4.79%) |

^ annual compound rate of return for that period
* Source: U.S. Bureau of Labor Statistics

©1996 Chase Global Data & Research
73 Junction Square, Concord, MA 01742

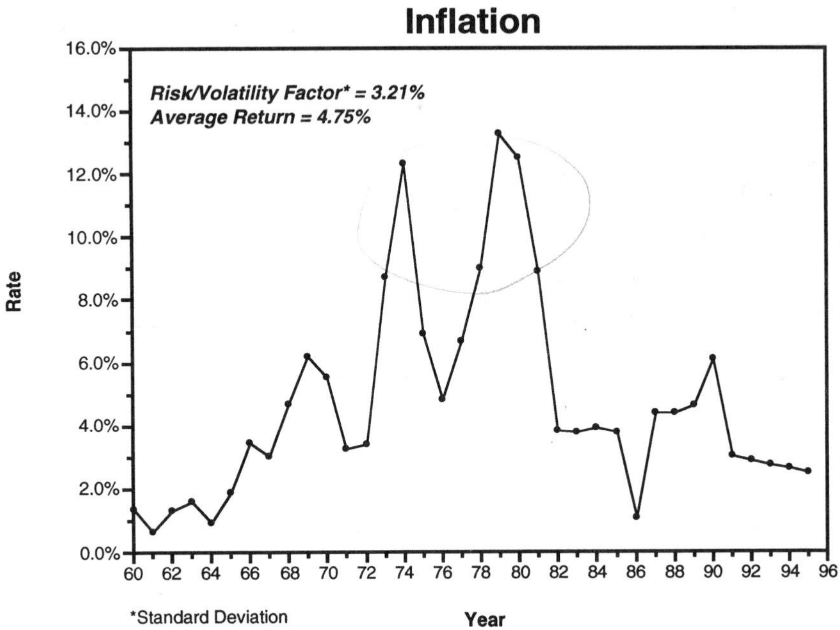


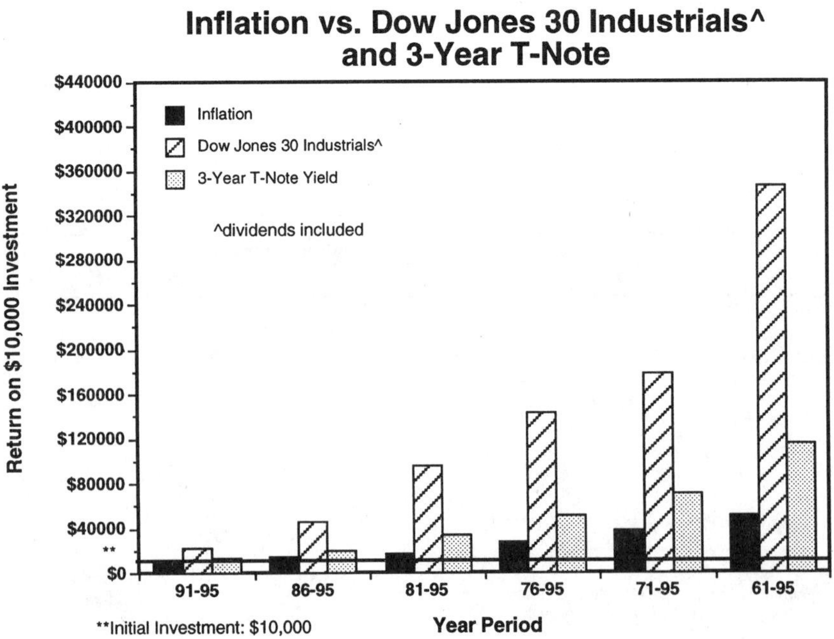


©1996 Chase Global Data & Research
73 Junction Square, Concord, MA 01742

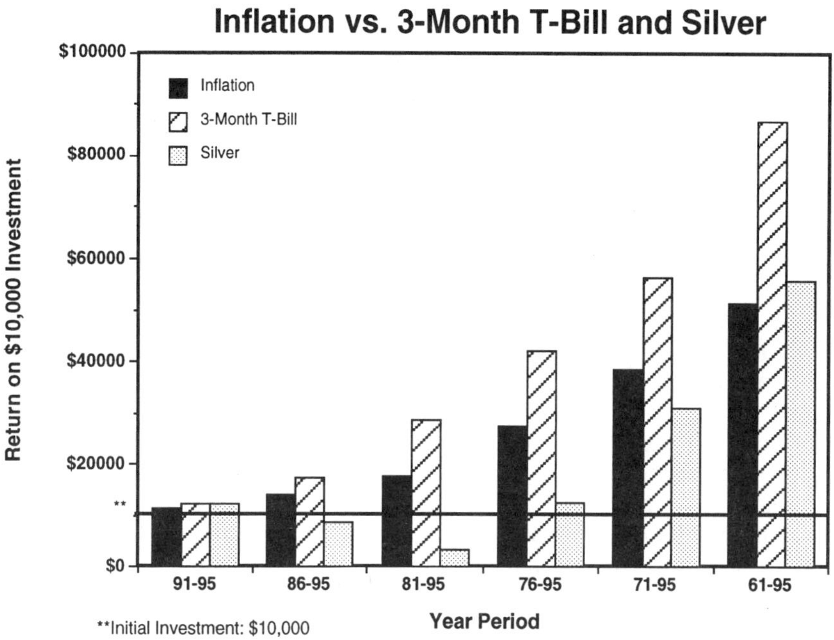


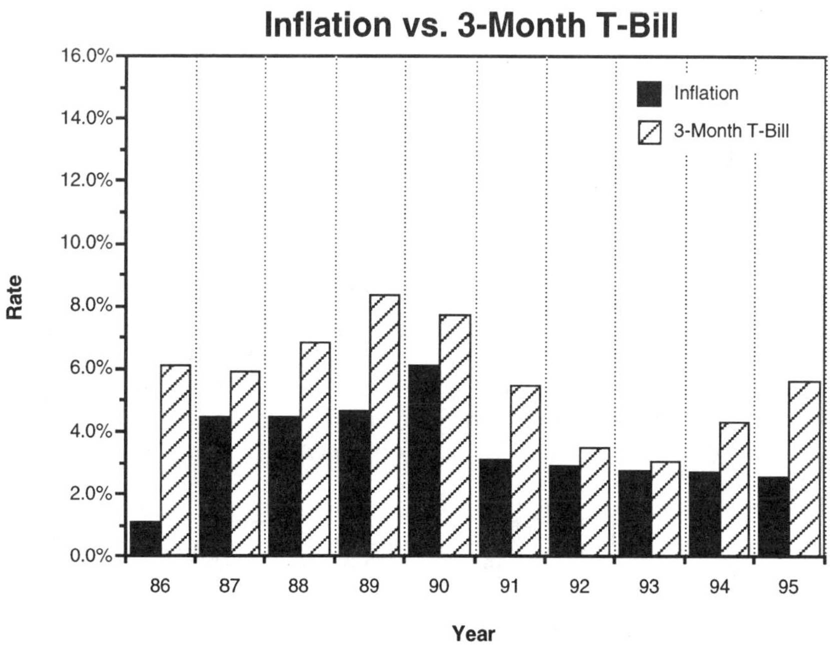


©1996 Chase Global Data & Research
73 Junction Square, Concord, MA 01742

# Chapter Two

# U.S. Disposable Personal Income

Personal income is defined as income received by individuals from all sources—participation in production, government and business transfer payments, and government interest. Personal income is the total of private and government wages and salary disbursements, other labor income, farm and non-farm proprietor's income, rental income of persons, personal dividend income, personal interest income, and transfer payments, less personal contributions for Social Security insurance. The final tally is measured before the deduction of personal income taxes and other forms of taxes and is reported in current dollars, without adjustment for inflation.

The U.S. Department of Commerce has been tracking U.S. per capita personal income since 1929. Annual statistics are compiled as of July 1st each year and reflect the reported total annual personal income of legal residents divided by the resident population.

In addition to national analysis, the government also conducts regional studies. Over the half-century span from 1929 to 1979 the most profound regional income changes took place. Differences in regional per capita income, formerly significant, began to narrow. For example, in 1929 the mid-East and New England regions were tracking at 25% to 38% above the U.S. average income—while the Southeast and Southwest sectors were 47% and 32% below average, respectively. By 1979, New England was only 17% above the national average and the mid-East 13% above, whereas the Southeast was only 13% below the norm and the Southwest 10% below. Nevertheless, the narrowing trend from 1929 to 1979 reversed after 1979—partly due to major disruptions in the economy. Another major regional change factor is not simply income earned, but the movement of populations between regions.

Since World War II there have been marked changes in size and composition of the U.S. population. The baby boom, which followed low birth rates of the 1930's and early 1940's, in combination with changes in health care, elongated life spans, and major shifts in


©1996 Chase Global Data & Research
73 Junction Square, Concord, MA 01742

immigration patterns have all contributed to a new profile for the U.S. population—especially since 1950.

When analyzing population as well as income per capita, on the supply side the size of the working age population is a key factor in determining the number of people who work toward production of goods and services. Changes in population composition affect productivity, growth, labor force participation rates, and even the length of work weeks. On the demand side population growth directly influences consumer expenditures both in total as well in composition. (Of note, housing is one business segment especially sensitive to demographic changes.) These factors all ultimately impact personal income, because they are forces creating demand for wage earners.

Population growth is determined by 3 forces: (1) number of births; (2) number of deaths; and (3) total net immigration. In 1995 the U.S. population was 262 million people. That figure represents an increase of over 100 million people, or 70%, since 1950. Population growth accelerated in the 1950's and by the 1960's averaged 1.5% growth per year. But since the early 1960's population growth has markedly decreased, to under 1% annually. Only very recently has the population boom shown any signs of reawakening. Experts anticipate the population will grow 2 million annually in the 1990's.

The greatest change in population growth in the U.S. came from the baby booms of the late 1940's and early 1960's—which caused the percentage of children in the population to reach one-third of the total. Today the patterns of income and growth in population are dramatically changing again because those baby boomers are now middle-aged, and have either formed families or are continuing to do so. And major advances in health care have extended the average individual's life expectancy more than a decade from the 1940 levels. In fact, the average life expectancy has increased over 60% since the turn of the century. In 1900 the average person lived 47 years, today the average citizen lives 76 years. Death rates have decreased in a similar manner, from about fifteen deaths per thousand to five.

Immigration patterns have also changed. The post-World War II immigration level of growth averaged 0.2% annually—substantially below the levels of the 19th and early 20th centuries. But by the 1970's net immigration was rising to 0.25% of the population annually—or a 25% increase over the pace of the previous two decades. Yet these statistics do not take into account the influx of illegal aliens entering the country—a number estimated at 1.5 million people per year, 40% of the legal immigrant total.

©1996 Chase Global Data & Research
73 Junction Square, Concord, MA 01742

Household formation also impacts population and per capita income. There have been major changes in age composition, marital status, and living arrangements in the population. One-person households, which accounted for less than 10% in 1950, have become commonplace and now account for nearly one-fourth of all households. The number of single parents has doubled since 1970 to 15 million households, or about 10% overall. Reflecting this change was a 1993 government report which detailed that 31% of *all* births in the U.S. were by unwed mothers—double the rate of 1970. Approximately 90% of U.S. teenagers giving birth are unmarried.

The population's tendency toward independent living arrangements, and birth rate has caused the average size of a U.S. household to shrink from 3.7 persons per household in 1960 to 2.7 persons in 1990. Likewise, the average number of children per family has dropped from 1.11 in 1960, to 0.99 in 1990.

The working-age population has also changed. The increase in the working-age population (age 16 and over) rose from an annual 1% rate of increase in the 1950's to 1.75% per year in the next two decades. The pace of growth in the labor force has doubled since the 1950's—a result of the increase in the overall population and because more working-age women are entering the labor market.

In the 1990's an abundant youth labor force is a thing of the past as we face shortages of workers at the low end of the skilled labor force. Lack of skills is a critical reason for much of the unemployment rate today. The situation is weak for the "second tier" baby boomers, too. The first baby boom wave took advantage of many of the labor opportunities that the second wave found filled. This sad state of affairs is reflected in the following statistics. In 1975 heads of households aged 25 to 34 earned 79.4% of what the 45 to 54 year-old heads of households earned. But by 1990 heads of households aged 25 to 34 only earned only 75% of the 45 to 54 year-old group's level. Thus today's younger earning group finds a smaller share of the pie available.

By contrast, per capita income of the elderly is improving. In 1959, 35% of the elderly were living at the poverty level, while approximately 15% did so in 1990. In 1967 heads of households aged 65+ had income at 30% of the level of persons aged 45 to 54. However, by 1990 heads of households aged 65+ earned income approximating 40% of that of persons aged 45 to 54. Relatively speaking, today their lot is one-third better than in 1967. A key reason for the change is that since the early 1970's Social Security has been mandated by law to keep pace with inflation. Reductions in social security, and/or delaying benefits from

©1996 Chase Global Data & Research
73 Junction Square, Concord, MA 01742

aged 62 to 70, could swing the pendulum back towards the status of the 1970's however.

However, some economists and sociologists would argue that the elderly's wealth increase is due to the small portion of elderly who have unusually high income which is consistently increasing, while an increasing number of older Americans live in near poverty. According to the Senate Committee on Aging, while as many elderly as nonelderly are deemed poor, a greater portion of elderly are living in "near poverty" status. And what is happening to our elderly is demographically very important, given the U.S. population is aging so quickly. The nation's median age in 1992 was 33. Today it is 36. By the year 2030 it will be 42. The average American will live 10% longer in 2050, reaching 83. In fact, by the end of a baby boomer's natural lifetime, there could be two retirees for every teenager. All of these statistics will strain both personal and federal retirement plans and safety nets.

To be sure, U.S. Per Capita Income statistics convey that the U.S. is a wealthy nation among the family of nations. Another issue, not addressed by average national statistics is how the wealth in income is distributed per capita. Overall income throughout the globe is surprisingly broad. 1991 data showed non-inflation adjusted annual per capita income in Austria: $8,714, Canada: $13,783, China: $251, France: $9,275, Hong Kong: $6290, Germany: $10,224, Japan: $11,025, Spain: $4,265, Switzerland: $14,306, Thailand: $734, and the United Kingdom: $8,111. The United States was *highest* among these major nations at $16,662 per capita. Of note, the average U.S. college graduate aged 45 to 54 earned $49,900 today.

But in 1994 the average American manufacturing employee made 20% less wages on an hourly basis ($16) than his/her counterpart in Germany ($25), Switzerland ($22), Canada ($18), and Japan ($17). And American managers made on average 20% less than those in Italy, France, and Japan. But perhaps the most startling statistic regarding American's incomes is the fact that 15% of the population lives at or below the poverty level—defined in 1995 as a family of four earning less than $15,500 or individuals earning $7,800.

Lastly, personal income statistics are being shadowed in importance by income stability, i.e. job security. Major corporations announce large layoffs on a frequent basis, despite their strong profitability. In fact, the corporate downsizing of the present economic recovery has generated 6.5 million less jobs than preceding expansions—a further sign of wage instability in the 1990's.

©1996 Chase Global Data & Research
73 Junction Square, Concord, MA 01742

## U.S. DISPOSABLE PERSONAL INCOME

[per capita, in 1992 dollars; annual average]

| Year | Income* | Income Growth | Average Annual Income Growth |
|---|---|---|---|
| 1995 | $18,687 | 2.00% | 1991 - 1995 |
| 1994 | $18,320 | 1.36% | |
| 1993 | $18,075 | 0.07% | 0.82% |
| 1992 | $18,062 | 1.73% | |
| 1991 | $17,755 | -1.04% | |
| 1990 | $17,942 | 0.79% | 1986 - 1990 |
| 1989 | $17,801 | 1.02% | |
| 1988 | $17,621 | 3.01% | 1.57% |
| 1987 | $17,106 | 0.74% | |
| 1986 | $16,981 | 2.31% | |
| 1985 | $16,597 | 2.12% | 1981 - 1985 |
| 1984 | $16,252 | 6.38% | |
| 1983 | $15,277 | 1.85% | 2.30% |
| 1982 | $14,999 | -0.07% | |
| 1981 | $15,009 | 1.32% | |
| 1980 | $14,813 | -0.58% | 1976 - 1980 |
| 1979 | $14,899 | 1.62% | |
| 1978 | $14,662 | 4.02% | 2.02% |
| 1977 | $14,095 | 2.19% | |
| 1976 | $13,793 | 2.90% | |
| 1975 | $13,404 | 0.71% | 1971 - 1975 |
| 1974 | $13,310 | -1.69% | |
| 1973 | $13,539 | 6.02% | 2.20% |
| 1972 | $12,770 | 3.44% | |
| 1971 | $12,345 | 2.69% | |
| 1970 | $12,022 | 2.68% | 1966 - 1970 |
| 1969 | $11,708 | 2.27% | |
| 1968 | $11,448 | 3.50% | 3.16% |
| 1967 | $11,061 | 3.23% | |
| 1966 | $10,715 | 4.11% | |
| 1965 | $10,292 | 4.97% | 1961 - 1965 |
| 1964 | $9,805 | 5.73% | |
| 1963 | $9,274 | 2.17% | 3.51% |
| 1962 | $9,077 | 3.22% | |
| 1961 | $8,794 | 1.55% | |
| 1960 | $8,660 | 0.22% | |

Average Annual Personal Income Growth over

| 5 years | 10 years | 15 years | 20 years | 25 years | 35 years |
|---|---|---|---|---|---|
| 1991 - 1995 | | | | | |
| 0.82% | 1986 - 1995 | | | | |
| | 1.19% | 1981 - 1995 | | | |
| | | 1.56% | 1976 - 1995 | | |
| | | | 1.68% | 1971 - 1995 | |
| | | | | 1.78% | 1961 - 1995 |
| | | | | | 2.22% |

^ annual compound rate of return for that period; 1995 4Q estimated.
* Source: Bureau of Economic Analysis; Bureau of Census.

©1996 Chase Global Data & Research
73 Junction Square, Concord, MA 01742

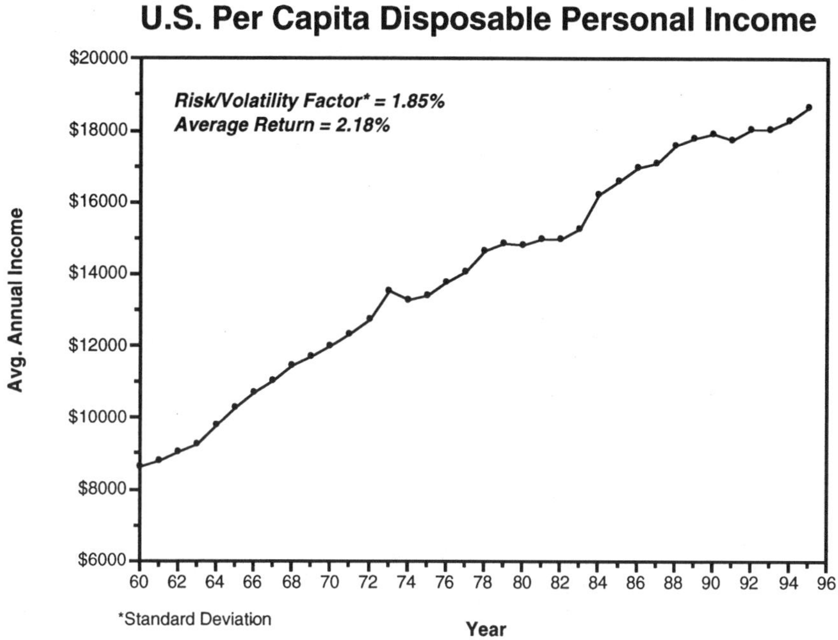


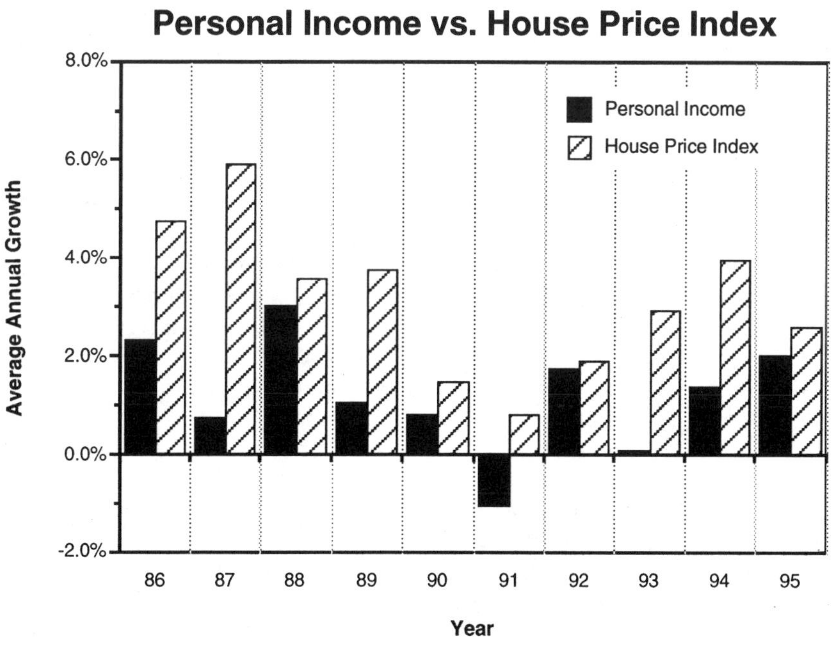


©1996 Chase Global Data & Research
73 Junction Square, Concord, MA 01742

# Chapter Three

# Prime Rate

The prime rate is a major financial icon, quoted in newspapers and magazines as the best indicator of where interest rates are—at a given moment in time. The prime rate is the interest rate banks charge to their most credit worthy customers, deemed riskless in their ability to repay a loan. Thus the prime rate is an interest rate quoted for the pure use of money, not for the use of money with additional burdens of risk incurred by the lender. One way to analyze differences between riskless and almost riskless lending is to review yields of U.S. Government securities (generally considered a riskless form of debt) versus yields of Aaa corporate paper. Such an analysis is a partial avenue banks use to begin to price the prime rate. The prime rate is also impacted by market forces affecting the banks' cost of funds, as well as by borrowers acceptance of such charges.

The prime rate's movements tend to be uniform across the nation's banking industry. It is rare to find banks out of step with the general prime rate quoted nationwide. Typically, when a bank digresses from the quoted prime rate, it is for a period of one to two weeks and to a maximum level of 0.50%. However, there is much debate over the true meaning of the prime rate. For example, much borrowing is done at a level of prime rate plus 2% by businesses that are small or less well established. Major banks will loan funds at levels below the quoted prime for their best customers (in effect altering the definition) when such banks are in competition to make loans to blue chip companies. Even small companies with top credit standings borrow at levels below prime rate. So the prime rate is a reflection of the level at which a bank can readily and profitably lend money to its better customers given its operating expenses and cost of funds. A bank's cost of funds derives from its expense in garnering deposits and borrowing funds from the federal government—"fed funds." However, funds borrowed from the federal government come and go quickly—due to the nature of these short term borrowings and market pressures dictated by the Federal Reserve System. Thus banks aim to keep their prime rate at a stable level that reflects not only today's cost of funds but also anticipated


©1996 Chase Global Data & Research
73 Junction Square, Concord, MA 01742

near-term cost of funds.

The prime rate is also based on other factors besides the cost of a bank's borrowings from the Federal Reserve. These include such sensitive instruments as Treasury bills, commercial paper, and money market fund interest levels. Even the Eurodollar marketplace affects the quoted interest rate of the prime. This was especially apparent in the 1970's when a shortage of lendable funds caused U.S. banks to ration credit. The Eurodollar marketplace began to grow, and with that growth it began to dictate certain levels of interest. Because of the past volatility of the prime rate and the general growing complexity of the lending marketplace, the prime rate has retained its notoriety—but is now only one of many pricing formulas used by banks to price loans to corporate and foreign borrowers.

The history of the prime rate and its evolution into a highly visible financial icon begins in 1929. In that year the prime rate ranged between 5.5% and 6%. The all-time low for the prime rate was 1.5%—where it stayed from 1933 to 1947, fourteen years. In 1948 the prime rate went over 2%. By April, 1968 it passed 6% for the first time. The lowest level for the prime in the 1970's was 4.75% in January 1972. The prime touched 10% for the first time in September 1973. In the 15 years from 1973 to 1987, the lowest level of the prime was 6.25% in December, 1976. The prime reached the dizzying level of 20% for the first time on April 2, 1980. Reflecting the increased volatility of the past two decades, the prime went from 20% in April, 1980 to 11% ninety days later in July, only to later reach its all-time high of 21.5% in December of that same year—almost doubling its level of five months earlier.

A further analysis of the growth in prime rate volatility is both fascinating and alarming. From 1934 to November 1947 the prime rate never changed—not once. Between 1947 and 1978—a period of 31 years—the prime rate changed 143 times. From 1978 to 1984—6 years—the rate changed 112 times.

From 1985 to 1987 we had a respite from the prime's volatility. It is worth noting that at the same time, overall, we had a moderate level of inflation. But by 1988 the prime inched up four times, to 10.5%. From 1986 through 1995 the prime rate averaged 8.33%. In the past three years the prime rate has averaged 7.33%. Overall during the past quarter century the prime rate has averaged 9.48%, and for the past 35 years 8.35%. Given the dramatic changes recently in our financial history, if the U.S. were to incur a higher level of inflation one could

©1996 Chase Global Data & Research
73 Junction Square, Concord, MA 01742

expect a return to volatility and rising levels for the prime rate. 1993's rate of 6.00% was the lowest average annual rate since the late 1960's and early 1970's. But 1995's rate of 8.83% was almost double the five year period from 1960 through 1964, when it average 4.56%.

When analyzing the prime, one should remember that it is first and foremost a financial icon that closely follows levels of inflation. It is an "artificial" indicator of interest rates, but not as clear an indicator as others—such as a Treasury bill, which truly does exist. Over time the Prime Rate has proved itself a strong investment performer versus alternative safe fixed income investments. Quite obviously its performance clearly demonstrates that banks are getting a sufficient return on their prime rate loans.

Until recently banks were the only beneficiary of the generous interest levels of the Prime Rate. However, today some mutual funds offer funds which invest in the loans banks have made at the prime rate. These funds, when properly managed for accepting only loans which are credit worthy and thus low risk, can provide investors a solid yield which for the most part parallels the Prime Rate's yield—while attempting to sustain stability in the principal invested. It is worthy to note that in *each* of the past 10, 20 and 35 year Volatility Rankings the Prime Rate optimally placed in the quartile of lowest volatility.

©1996 Chase Global Data & Research
73 Junction Square, Concord, MA 01742

**PRIME RATE**
[average annual bank rate]

| Year | Rate* | Compound return on a five year $10,000 investment | Annual compound rate of return |
|---|---|---|---|
| 1995 | 8.83% | 1991 - 1995 | |
| 1994 | 7.15% | | 7.33% |
| 1993 | 6.00% | ... $14,240 | |
| 1992 | 6.25% | | |
| 1991 | 8.43% | | |
| 1990 | 10.01% | 1986 - 1990 | |
| 1989 | 10.87% | | 9.34% |
| 1988 | 9.32% | ... $15,630 | |
| 1987 | 8.21% | | |
| 1986 | 8.33% | | |
| 1985 | 9.93% | 1981 - 1985 | |
| 1984 | 12.04% | | 13.25% |
| 1983 | 10.79% | ... $18,631 | |
| 1982 | 14.86% | | |
| 1981 | 18.87% | | |
| 1980 | 15.27% | 1976 - 1980 | |
| 1979 | 12.67% | | 10.08% |
| 1978 | 9.06% | ... $16,165 | |
| 1977 | 6.82% | | |
| 1976 | 6.84% | | |
| 1975 | 7.86% | 1971 - 1975 | |
| 1974 | 10.80% | | 7.51% |
| 1973 | 8.02% | ... $14,362 | |
| 1972 | 5.25% | | |
| 1971 | 5.70% | | |
| 1970 | 7.91% | 1966 - 1970 | |
| 1969 | 7.95% | | 6.67% |
| 1968 | 6.28% | ... $13,812 | |
| 1967 | 5.63% | | |
| 1966 | 5.62% | | |
| 1965 | 4.54% | 1961 - 1965 | |
| 1964 | 4.50% | | 4.51% |
| 1963 | 4.50% | ... $12,467 | |
| 1962 | 4.50% | | |
| 1961 | 4.50% | | |
| 1960 | 4.82% | | |

How a $10,000 investment performed over

| 5 years | 10 years | 15 years | 20 years | 25 years | 35 years |
|---|---|---|---|---|---|
| 1991 - 1995 | | | | | |
| $14,240 (7.33%)^ | 1986 - 1995 | | | | |
| | $22,258 (8.33%) | 1981 - 1995 | | | |
| | | $41,468 (9.95%) | 1976 - 1995 | | |
| | | | $67,034 (9.98%) | 1971 - 1995 | |
| | | | | $96,271 (9.48%) | 1961 - 1995 |
| | | | | | $165,773 (8.35%) |

^ annual compound rate of return for that period
* Source: U.S. Department of Commerce.

©1996 Chase Global Data & Research
73 Junction Square, Concord, MA 01742

## Prime Rate

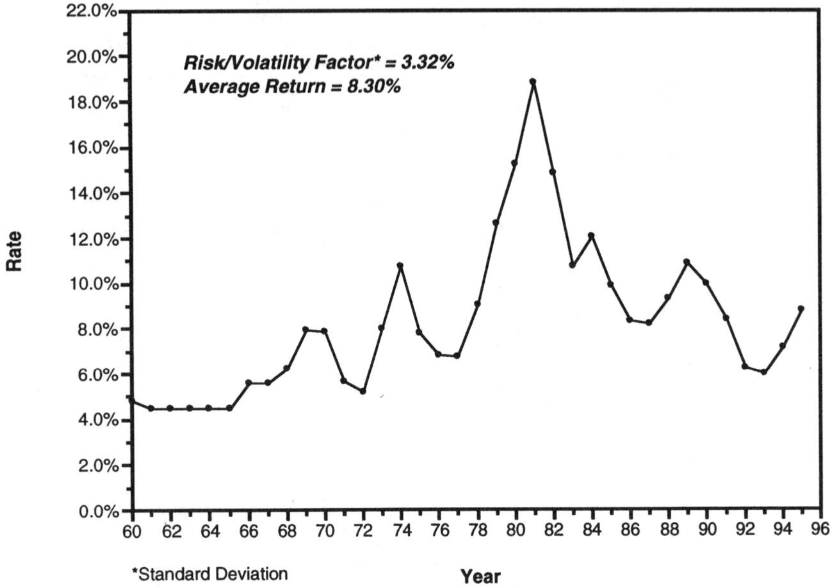


## Prime Rate vs. Inflation

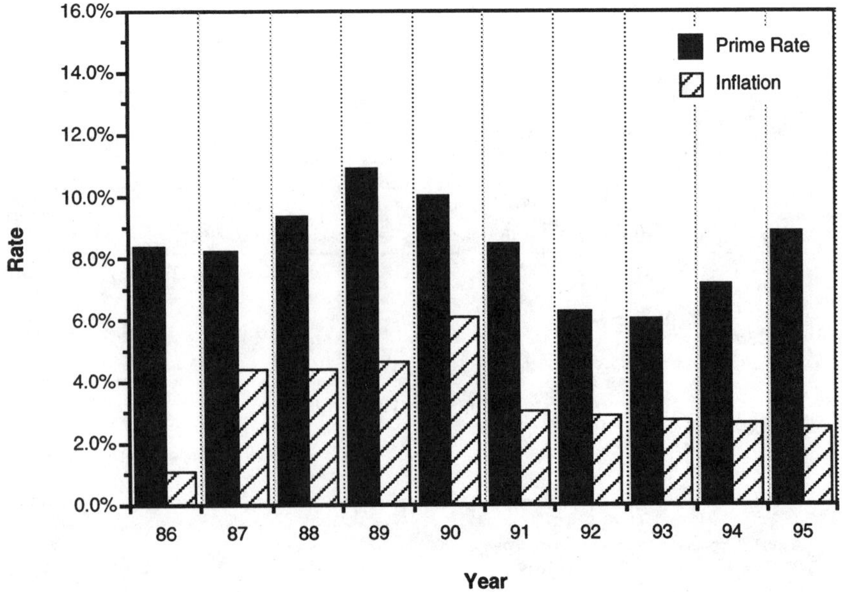


©1996 Chase Global Data & Research
73 Junction Square, Concord, MA 01742

# Chapter Four

# FHA Mortgage Rate

The Federal Housing Administration (FHA) is a U.S. Government agency whose primary role is to insure residential mortgages, thereby stimulating residential construction. The role of the Federal government in housing finance came about as a result of the Great Depression. In 1932, the first housing organization created by the government was the Federal Home Loan Bank, which loaned funds to mortgage lenders. The FHLB was an important aid to the housing industry because, after the crash of 1929, mortgage credit had been effectively frozen. Residential construction had stopped in its tracks. Production of homes in 1933 had dropped to 93,000 units, down from over one million units built in 1925. In a nation whose population was over 100 million, the construction industry—a major industry—was only employing 150,000 people. This caused a tremendous loss of production of materials and equipment for home construction.

After the Federal Home Loan Bank, the FHA was created on June 27, 1934. Initially, the FHA's goal was to help unemployment by creating more jobs in construction. Through the National Housing Act, the FHA was to provide insurance for long-term mortgages used for the construction and sale of housing and commercial properties. The FHA also insured lenders against loss on short-term loans made for repairs and improvements.

The FHA's long-term goal was to provide more and better housing through overseeing mortgage lending practices and general construction practices. The FHA established building and minimum property standards that had to be met before a construction loan could be granted. The FHA also established appraisal procedures that had to be followed before any loans were approved. In addition, the FHA, as well as Veterans Administration loans, required builders receiving loans to warrant construction for any house built for a period of one year from purchase date. In general, FHA lending requirements significantly educated lenders about better loan approval practices.

©1996 Chase Global Data & Research
73 Junction Square, Concord, MA 01742

Essentially the FHA provided banks, and later other forms of lenders such as insurance companies and private individuals, an ability to make loans that they might not have made by providing mortgage insurance guaranteed by the Federal government. The fee charged by the FHA for insuring a mortgage was passed along to the borrower. In the past six decades, it has ranged from 0.5% to as high as 1%. Initially, the interest rate on FHA mortgages could not exceed 5%. Today a typical FHA loan requires a 20% equity deposit and provides loan maturities of 20 to 30 years.

FHA loans are available for construction, purchase, or refinancing of one to 4-family homes. The FHA also provides loan insurance for improvements to existing homes and other small buildings. The FHA is authorized to insure mortgages on housing projects of both federal and state governments and for private corporations building for persons of low income—if the rents and operation of such projects are regulated.

FHA mortgages benefit the borrower in many ways. The rate on FHA mortgages has historically been low, ranging from approximately 5.5% to a high of over 15% during the past 36 years. It is well known that the FHA is liberal in its forbearance procedures on potential foreclosures on defaulting loans. Changes in FHA procedures over the years—such as through the Housing and Urban Development Act of 1965—give "moratorium" relief to distressed mortgagers. The FHA has also provided, through its maximum interest rates ceilings, a way of limiting potential excessive rate changes and abuses which otherwise could be made by some lenders. When FHA rates are very competitive because of its maximum caps on rates, it is more difficult for other lenders to raise fees and overcharge. Unfortunately when interest rates skyrocket during times of severe credit shortages lenders on FHA mortgages have resorted to charging substantial additional fees over and above the lower interest rate. These fees typically end up being translated into higher housing prices. The FHA was also the first lending organization, through President Kennedy's 1962 Executive Order, to provide Equal Opportunity in housing by mandating mortgages be provided to all races and creeds without discrimination.

The FHA has had serious problems over the years. Because of its insurance policy and its loans made during good and hard economic times, the FHA has had high levels of mortgage foreclosures—and as a result has acquired weak properties. Much of the time such acquisitions result in losses to the FHA. As recently as 1986, because of weaknesses in regional sectors of U.S. housing the FHA faced the cessation of its insurance guarantees for its popular mortgages. It needed a

©1996 Chase Global Data & Research
73 Junction Square, Concord, MA 01742

Congressional bailout of additional funds in order to keep operating.

Since its inception, the FHA has always been a major player in mortgages in the U.S. In the 1930's approximately one-fourth of all 1 to 4-family housing units had an FHA mortgage. The percentage of FHA housing units in the U.S. rose to 45% between 1940 and 1944, but dropped to only 14% by 1970. By the 1980's total FHA insured housing loans in the U.S. were over $40 billion. Nevertheless, the reason for the FHA's gradual decline in U.S. housing was the ongoing rise in the issuance of Veterans Administration's guaranteed mortgage loans, which began after World War II. By 1960 VA guaranteed mortgages represented 30% of 1-4 family mortgage activity. Today other major players in the mortgage lending marketplace are life insurance companies with an approximate 20% market share, S&L institutions at 30%, mutual savings banks at 15%, commercial banks at 15%, and the growing segment of independent lending organizations which now account for 10% of the overall marketplace.

Over the past half century the FHA and its mortgages have provided loans that are both consistently available and more competitive than standard mortgages offered by other U.S. lenders. More important, the FHA proved to be the forerunner of a group of government agencies responsible for the expansion in the secondary market for mortgages, such as the Government National Mortgage Association (Ginnie Mae) and the Federal National Mortgage Association (Fannie Mae). The FHA and its mortgage insurance have also aided in the improvement of housing standards through the establishment of minimum property standards, architectural analysis, construction inspection, and the establishment of methods of locating, planning, and developing subdivisions. The FHA has also provided analysis which has helped deter over-building in certain areas and in certain price ranges. Through both its ability to change required down payment levels and its granting of mortgages with maximum interest rate levels, the FHA has been able to successfully exercise a major positive influence on housing lending activity throughout the U.S. over the past seven decades.

1995's average FHA Mortgage rate remained slightly above the classic year of 1993 (7.46%), when rates were the lowest in over twenty years. In 1995 the FHA Mortgage Rate averaged 8.16%—a 0.5% from 1994 level. Over the past thirty five years FHA Mortgage Rates have averaged 9.26%. Over the past 15, 20, and 25 year spans the FHA Mortgage Rate stood over 10%, proving that FHA Mortgages as an investment are an above average performer.

©1996 Chase Global Data & Research
73 Junction Square, Concord, MA 01742

## FHA MORTGAGE RATE

[Average annual yield; secondary market; 30 yr. maturity]

| Year | Yield* | Compound return on a five year $10,000 investment | Annual compound rate of return |
|---|---|---|---|
| 1995 | 8.16% | 1991 - 1995 | |
| 1994 | 8.67% | | 8.40% |
| 1993 | 7.46% | ... $14,968 | |
| 1992 | 8.45% | | |
| 1991 | 9.27% | | |
| 1990 | 10.15% | 1986 - 1990 | |
| 1989 | 10.23% | | 10.19% |
| 1988 | 10.49% | ... $16,246 | |
| 1987 | 10.18% | | |
| 1986 | 9.91% | | |
| 1985 | 12.23% | 1981 - 1985 | |
| 1984 | 13.80% | | 14.14% |
| 1983 | 13.10% | ... $19,371 | |
| 1982 | 15.29% | | |
| 1981 | 16.32% | | |
| 1980 | 13.43% | 1976 - 1980 | |
| 1979 | 12.24% | | 10.61% |
| 1978 | 10.23% | ... $16,557 | |
| 1977 | 8.96% | | |
| 1976 | 8.28% | | |
| 1975 | 9.32% | 1971 - 1975 | |
| 1974 | 9.51% | | 8.55% |
| 1973 | 8.78% | ... $15,070 | |
| 1972 | 7.56% | | |
| 1971 | 7.59% | | |
| 1970 | 8.40% | 1966 - 1970 | |
| 1969 | 8.62% | | 7.62% |
| 1968 | 7.50% | ... $14,435 | |
| 1967 | 6.81% | | |
| 1966 | 6.77% | | |
| 1965 | 5.62% | 1961 -1965 | |
| 1964 | 5.45% | | 5.55% |
| 1963 | 5.45% | ... $13,099 | |
| 1962 | 5.53% | | |
| 1961 | 5.69% | | |
| 1960 | 6.04% | | |

How a $10,000 investment performed over

| 5 years | 10 years | 15 years | 20 years | 25 years | 35 years |
|---|---|---|---|---|---|
| 1991 - 1995 | | | | | |
| $14,968 (8.40%)^ | 1986 - 1995 | | | | |
| | $24,316 (9.29%) | 1981 - 1995 | | | |
| | | $47,104 (10.88%) | 1976 - 1995 | | |
| | | | $77,992 (10.82%) | 1971 - 1995 | |
| | | | | $117,538 (10.36%) | 1961 - 1995 |
| | | | | | $222,246 (9.26%) |

^ annual compound rate of return for that period
* Source: U.S. Department of Commerce.

©1996 Chase Global Data & Research
73 Junction Square, Concord, MA 01742

## FHA Mortgage Rate

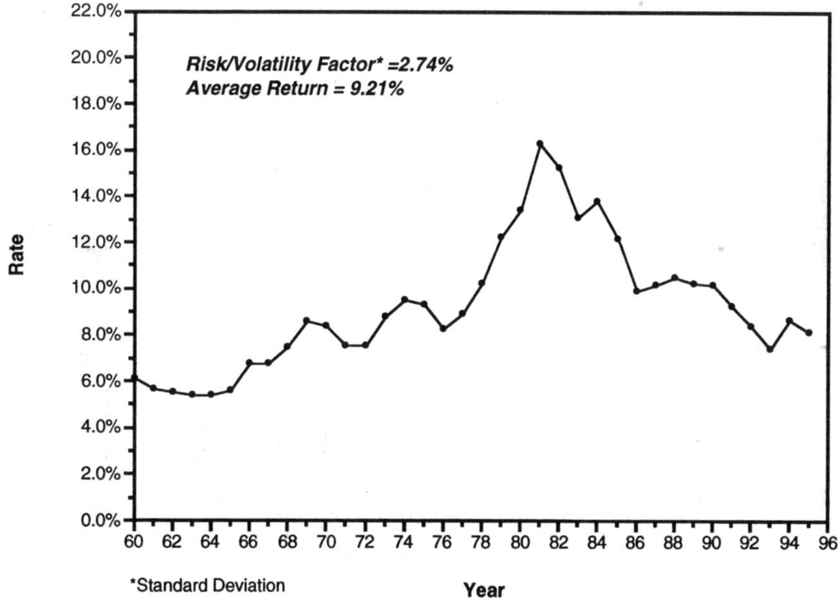


*Standard Deviation

## FHA Mortgage Rate vs. Prime Rate and 10-Year T-Bond

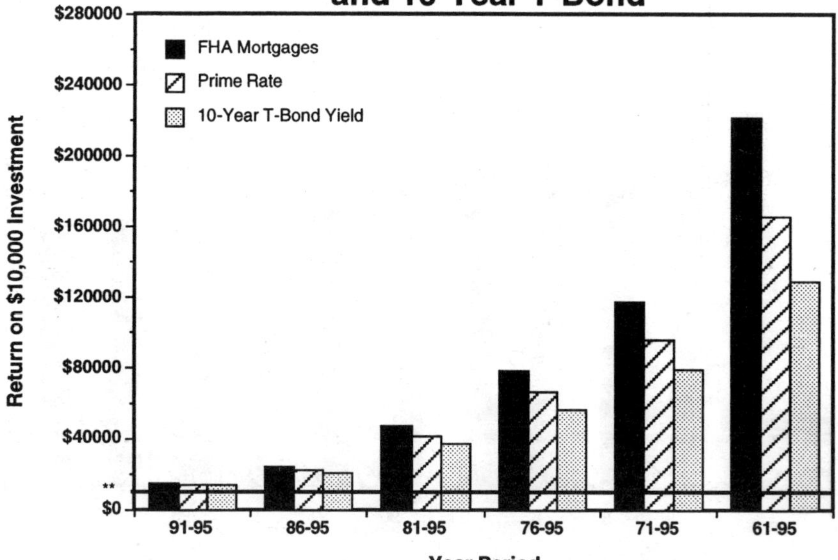


**Initial Investment: $10,000

©1996 Chase Global Data & Research
73 Junction Square, Concord, MA 01742

## FHA Mortgage Rate vs. Dow Jones 30 Industrials^ and Commodity Spot Price Index

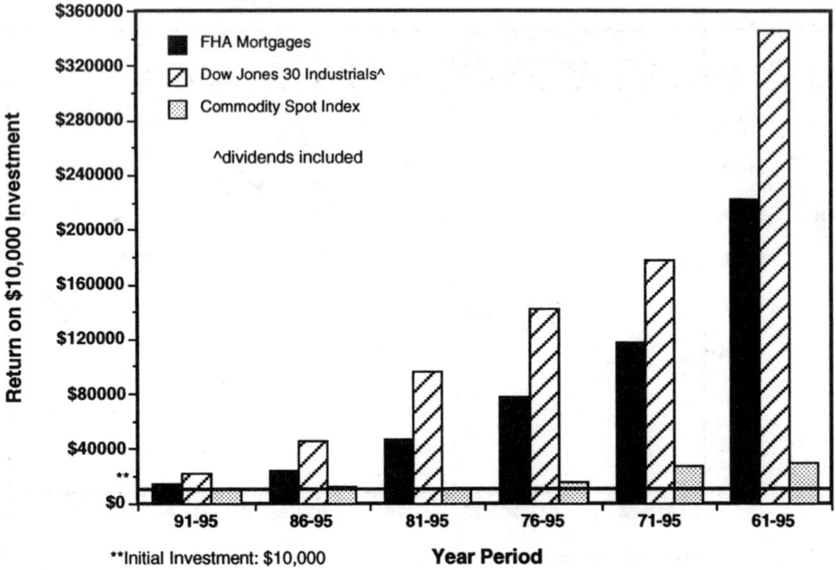


## FHA Mortgage Rate vs. Inflation

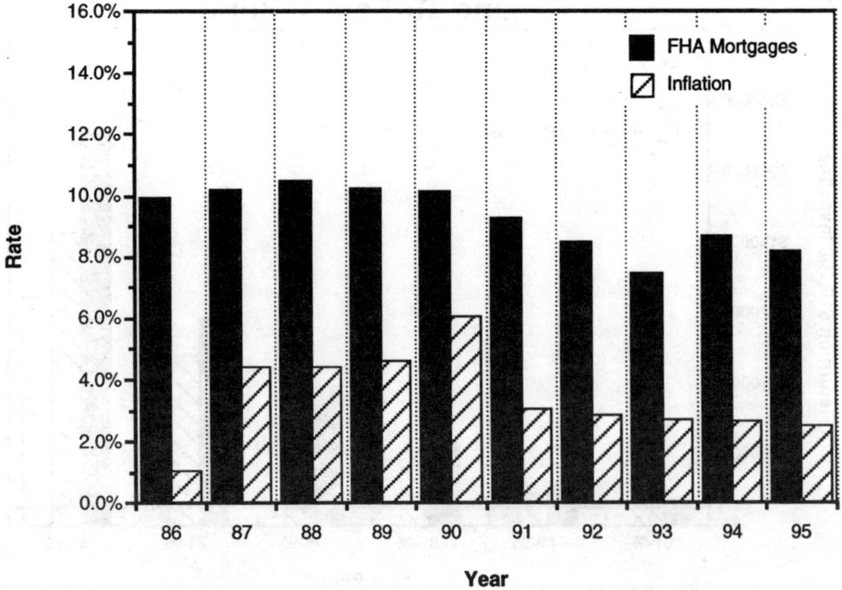


©1996 Chase Global Data & Research
73 Junction Square, Concord, MA 01742

SECTION IV

# U.S. Equity Markets and Indicators

Chapter Five

# Dow Jones Averages

Charles Dow and Edward Jones were two New Englanders. Charles grew up on a farm and had no significant educational background. Edward was a college drop-out. In 1882, they formed Dow Jones & Company, determined to write unbiased, honest news stories about business. Their original headquarters with six employees was in a small back room in the basement of a candy store on Wall Street.

The Dow Jones stock average, which appeared in 1884, was primarily a transportation average. It was made up of nine railroads, one steamship line and the Western Union Company. The Dow Jones Industrial Average first appeared in 1896. A year later, Dow Jones formed the Dow Jones News Service and used tickers to print pages of news releases. The ticker, which had to be wound, weighed 96 pounds and was enclosed in a tall wooden case. Eventually it was replaced by a 4-volt battery machine ticker, which in turn was replaced by a motor driven model in 1926. By October 1928, the Dow Jones Industrial Average had evolved into the 30 stock index it remains today.

The Dow Jones Average rose over 200 for the first time in 1928 and had almost reached 400 prior to the Crash of 1929. But it did not go over the 200 mark again until 1950, and managed to go up only 100 points (from 300 to 400) over the 26 years from 1928 to 1954. By 1987 however, the DJIA was moving over 100 points an hour. It took 60 years to make the first 500 point move. Then the Dow Jones lost over 500 points in one day—October 19, 1987.

In recent times, the Dow Jones Average traded, each year, at or through the 800 level for 18 consecutive years. Then, in 1986, it managed to go up a chilling 500 points—with essentially no earnings growth within the stocks of the Average. Ever since the Dow Jones closed over 2000 on January 8, 1986, it has increasingly become the most talked about stock index of them all. When the Dow passed 2000 for the first time, it showed an appreciation of 154% over four and one half years from August of 1982. But of the 30 components of the Dow


©1996 Chase Global Data & Research
73 Junction Square, Concord, MA 01742

Jones Average, only 11 of the 30 appreciated at a level above 154%, while 19 out of the 30 failed to match the average appreciation of the Dow. In fact IBM, the bluest of blue chips, was unable to make a net advance over the period from 1982 through 1992 while the Dow Jones Average rose over 450%. In 1990 the Dow almost crossed 3,000—missing by the smallest of margins in reaching 2,999.75. Finally in 1991 the 3000 level was reached. Four years later in 1995, the Dow crossed two thousand intervals—4,000 and 5,000—all in one year.

The Dow Jones 30 Industrial Average makes the evening news five days a week, gets analyzed in Barron's on Saturday, and occasionally rests on Sunday. However, the Dow Jones Industrial Average quoted each day is the Dow Jones without dividends. The Dow Jones 30 Industrial Average does not recognize the dividends paid by the 30 different stocks—although dividends are a critical measure of the overall return in a stock investment. Therefore, it's only fair to analyze the dividend return in addition to the stock performance of the 30 Dow Jones stocks. The *Chase Investment Performance Digest* provides in the Performance Tables which follow the total return of the Dow Jones Industrial Average. For your convenience the Dow Jones Dividend Yield Table is included in the Addendum section, on page 386.

The thirty stocks within the Dow Jones Average are the bluest of the blue chips. Today's examples are: American Telephone, General Motors, IBM, and General Electric. All of these companies pay a regular dividend and rarely run into severe financial problems. However, occasionally Dow Jones Industrial companies have had financial difficulties that have affected the performance of the overall Average. Thus there are times when even this ultimate blue chip average is impacted by a member's significantly less than blue chip corporate performance.

Over the past quarter century, the Dow Jones Industrials of 30 stocks has performed similarly to the Standard & Poor's 500 stocks, although the S&P's stocks have outperformed the Dow Jones. And when the Dow Jones, excluding dividends, is adjusted for inflation all the positive numbers turn negative. For example, during the quarter century from 1965 to 1990, after being adjusted for inflation the Dow Jones Industrial Average was worth only three-quarters of its 1965 value.

Today, futures contracts help investors parallel an investment in the Dow Jones Average by investing in the Major Market Index—which has 20 of the 30 Dow Jones stocks in its index. Many institutions presently use these option contracts to hedge their positions in the stock

©1996 Chase Global Data & Research
73 Junction Square, Concord, MA 01742

market—and especially in the individual securities that are reflected in the option index. Many experts feel that such financial contracts are one of the reasons for the higher volatility in the marketplace, and would like to see their usage either curtailed or eliminated.

The yield of the Dow Jones Average has been surprisingly consistent, around the 3.0—3.5% level per year. As far back as 1926, the yield of the Dow was 3.22%. From 1926 to 1986, it fell below 3% only twice—in 1927 and 1965. Before the Crash of 1987, the yield based on 1987 and 1988 estimated earnings was 2.7% and 2.9% respectively—the lowest yield levels since 1920. Conventional wisdom says that the Dow's yielding less than 3% spells big trouble for the Average—that it is overpriced at such levels compared to normal historical precedents. Conventional wisdom was very right in October, 1987. In fact, the yield for the Dow Jones Industrial Average has been below 3% for only 19 weeks during the 30 year period between World War II and 1975. Norman Fosback, in his book *Stock Market Logic*, states that when the yield of the Dow Jones Averages is below 3% "in every case the ensuing one year market return was sharply negative." For example, the Dow did not yield less than 3% until it soared over 2300 in the first quarter of 1987, and we all know what happed in October of 1987. However, more recently in 1991 and 1993, and 1994 Fosback's "under 3%" warning has proven false. In December 1991 the Dow's yield was 2.8%—yet in 1992 the Dow rose 7.41%; in 1993 the Dow's year-end yield was 2.65%—yet in 1994 the Dow rose 5.02%. In 1994 the Dow's yield was but 2.79%—followed by the explosive 36.94 in 1995. Of obvious note, in December 1995 the Dow Jones' yield was the lowest in recent memory, 2.30%.

Many people feel that because of the tremendous rise in the Dow Jones Average, the Average itself should be split. But others point out that the Japanese Nikkei Average trades at the 20,000 level—which even after it precipitous decline is four times the Dow Jones Average. As long as the public understands the impact of 30, 50, and 100 point days versus the old-fashioned 5 and 10 point moves, there is likely no need to split the Dow.

There is a dramatic difference between the Average With Dividends versus the Average Without Dividends. Over the past three decades the With-Dividend return is four times greater than the Without-Dividend results. In fact the Dow Jones Without Dividends is a mediocre performer. Nevertheless, as quoted without dividends, it continues to be the most frequently discussed Index—but a continual misleading and consistent understatement of the true total return of the 30 Dow Jones stocks.

©1996 Chase Global Data & Research
73 Junction Square, Concord, MA 01742

Despite the occasional setbacks by a few stocks within the Dow over the past quarter century (for example, International Harvester, US Steel, and Union Carbide) the Dow Jones Average With Dividends has been an excellent performer. It has also been somewhat of a rocky performer. For a better perspective, try to remember that the 30 Dow Jones Industrials' stocks represent 1.2% (30/2570) of all listed NYSE securities. So while the Dow is not a large cross section, it's the most popular average nonetheless.

The *Chase Investment Performance Digest* also includes a review of the Dow Jones Utility Average. While it is a second cousin to the more famous Industrial Average, its consistently high yield and overall solid performance over the past thirty five years is certainly worthy of note. The Dow Jones Utility Average is made up of 15 major utility companies, representing all regions of the United States. The Utility Average is sometimes likened to a fixed income investment, but as one can see from its overall returns over the past thirty years, that is not an altogether fair characterization. During the past quarter century and thirty five year spans the Utility Average has lost to the Industrials by a margin of about 1% annually. After the fourth best rise since World War II, the Dow Jones Industrials celebrates its 100th anniversary in 1996.

©1996 Chase Global Data & Research
73 Junction Square, Concord, MA 01742

**DOW JONES INDUSTRIAL AVERAGE®**
**TOTAL RETURN (with dividends)**

| Year | Total Return* | Compound return on a five year $10,000 investment | Annual compound rate of return |
|---|---|---|---|
| 1995 | 36.94% | 1991 - 1995 | |
| 1994 | 5.02% | | 17.54% |
| 1993 | 16.94% | ... $22,433 | |
| 1992 | 7.41% | | |
| 1991 | 24.19% | | |
| 1990 | -0.56% | 1986 - 1990 | |
| 1989 | 32.19% | | 15.40% |
| 1988 | 16.14% | ... $20,467 | |
| 1987 | 5.48% | | |
| 1986 | 27.10% | | |
| 1985 | 33.55% | 1981 - 1985 | |
| 1984 | 1.31% | | 15.87% |
| 1983 | 25.97% | ... $20,889 | |
| 1982 | 27.11% | | |
| 1981 | -3.57% | | |
| 1980 | 22.17% | 1976 - 1980 | |
| 1979 | 10.55% | | 8.24% |
| 1978 | 2.79% | ... $14,859 | |
| 1977 | -12.84% | | |
| 1976 | 22.82% | | |
| 1975 | 44.75% | 1971 - 1975 | |
| 1974 | -23.58% | | 4.54% |
| 1973 | -13.28% | ... $12,483 | |
| 1972 | 18.48% | | |
| 1971 | 9.83% | | |
| 1970 | 9.21% | 1966 - 1970 | |
| 1969 | -11.78% | | 0.86% |
| 1968 | 7.93% | ... $10,436 | |
| 1967 | 19.16% | | |
| 1966 | -15.78% | | |
| 1965 | 14.39% | 1961 - 1965 | |
| 1964 | 18.85% | | 13.27% |
| 1963 | 20.83% | ... $18,644 | |
| 1962 | -7.43% | | |
| 1961 | 22.60% | | |
| 1960 | -6.13% | | |

How a $10,000 investment performed over

| 5 years | 10 years | 15 years | 20 years | 25 years | 35 years |
|---|---|---|---|---|---|
| 1991 - 1995 | | | | | |
| $22,433 (17.54%)^ | 1986 - 1995 | | | | |
| | $45,914 (16.46%) | 1981 - 1995 | | | |
| | | $95,909 (16.27%) | 1976 - 1995 | | |
| | | | $142,506 (14.21%) | 1971 - 1995 | |
| | | | | $177,895 (12.20%) | 1961 - 1995 |
| | | | | | $346,122 (10.66%) |

^ annual compound rate of return for that period
*Source: "Barron's National Business and Financial Weekly".
includes index growth and reinvestment of dividends.

©1996 Chase Global Data & Research
73 Junction Square, Concord, MA 01742

## Dow Jones 30 Industrials Average with Dividends

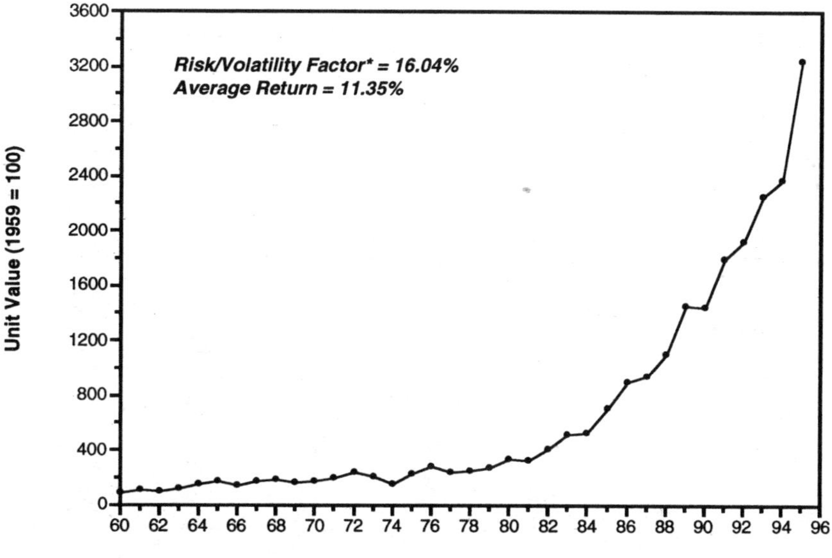


*Standard Deviation

## Dow Jones 30 Industrials^ vs. Dow Jones 15 Utilities^ and S&P Composite Index^

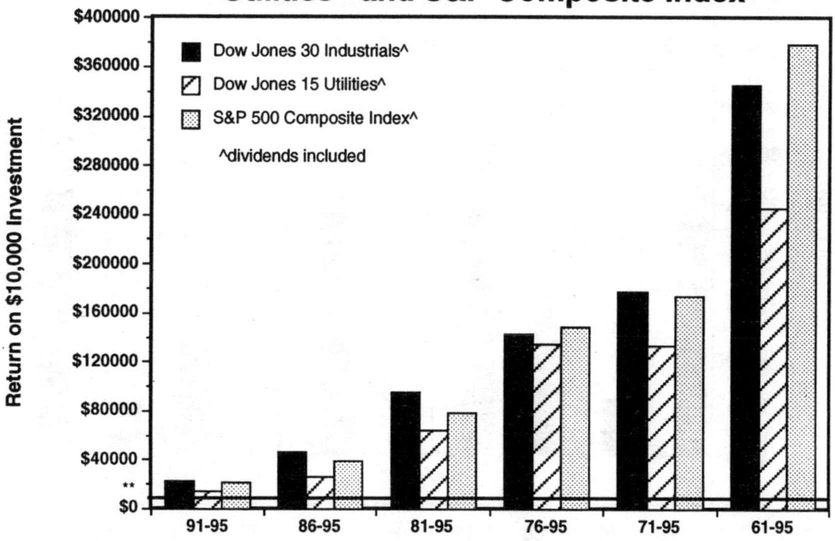


**Initial Investment: $10,000

©1996 Chase Global Data & Research
73 Junction Square, Concord, MA 01742

## Dow Jones 30 Industrials^ vs. 3-Month T-Bill and Gold

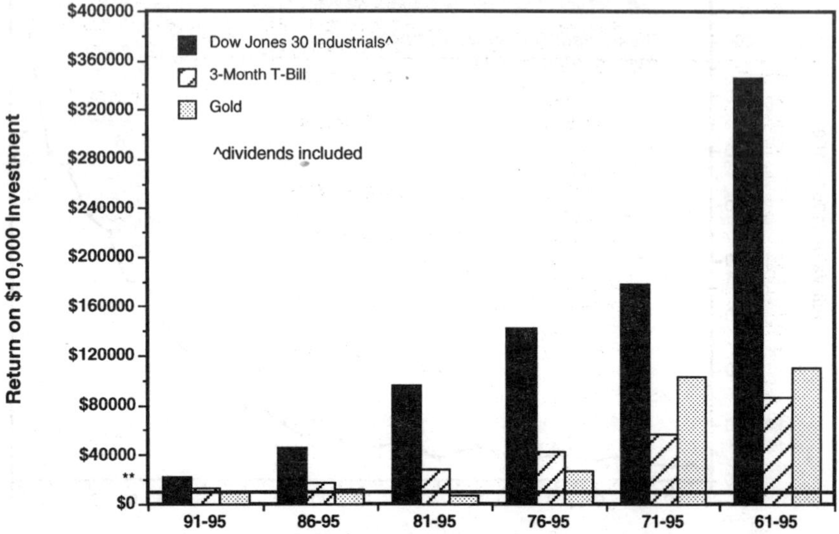


**Initial Investment: $10,000

## Dow Jones 30 Industrials^ vs. Inflation

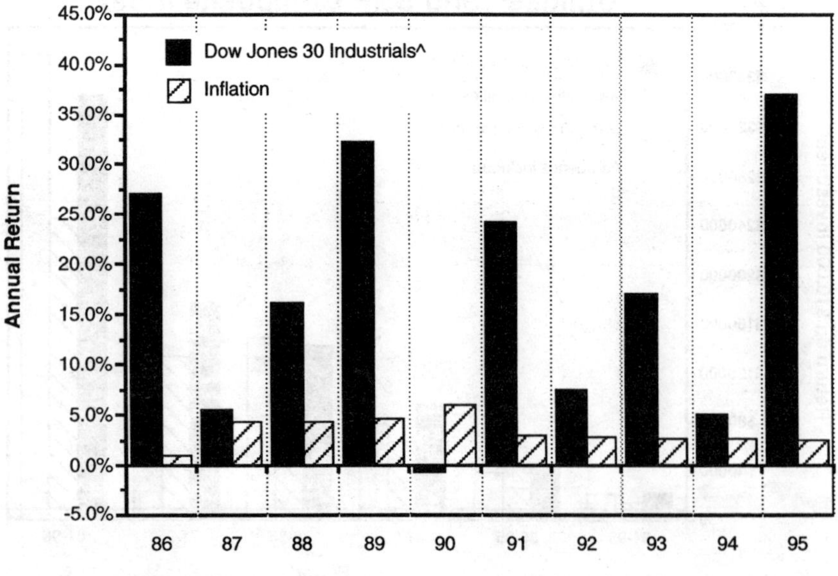


^dividends included

©1996 Chase Global Data & Research
73 Junction Square, Concord, MA 01742

**DOW JONES 15 UTILITY AVERAGE®**
**TOTAL RETURN (with dividends)**

| Year | Total Return* | Compound return on a five year $10,000 investment | Annual compound rate of return |
|---|---|---|---|
| 1995 | 32.17% | 1991 - 1995 | |
| 1994 | -15.08% | | 8.05% |
| 1993 | 9.59% | ... $14,724 | |
| 1992 | 4.01% | | |
| 1991 | 15.09% | | |
| 1990 | -4.52% | 1986 - 1990 | |
| 1989 | 35.33% | | 11.83% |
| 1988 | 15.64% | ... $17,491 | |
| 1987 | -7.92% | | |
| 1986 | 27.12% | | |
| 1985 | 27.58% | 1981 - 1985 | |
| 1984 | 25.52% | | 20.29% |
| 1983 | 21.82% | ... $25,188 | |
| 1982 | 22.17% | | |
| 1981 | 5.68% | | |
| 1980 | 17.81% | 1976 - 1980 | |
| 1979 | 18.52% | | 15.74% |
| 1978 | -3.99% | ... $20,768 | |
| 1977 | 10.48% | | |
| 1976 | 40.21% | | |
| 1975 | 32.87% | 1971 - 1975 | |
| 1974 | -15.28% | | -0.15% |
| 1973 | -19.91% | ... $ 9,923 | |
| 1972 | 7.72% | | |
| 1971 | 2.18% | | |
| 1970 | 17.37% | 1966 - 1970 | |
| 1969 | -15.43% | | 0.41% |
| 1968 | 12.36% | ... $10,206 | |
| 1967 | -1.81% | | |
| 1966 | -6.80% | | |
| 1965 | 1.67% | 1961 - 1965 | |
| 1964 | 15.44% | | 12.51% |
| 1963 | 11.59% | ... $18,028 | |
| 1962 | 2.80% | | |
| 1961 | 33.91% | | |
| 1960 | 18.81% | | |

How a $10,000 investment performed over

| 5 years | 10 years | 15 years | 20 years | 25 years | 35 years |
|---|---|---|---|---|---|
| 1991 - 1995 | | | | | |
| $14,724 (8.05%)^ | 1986 - 1995 | | | | |
| | $25,753 (9.92%) | 1981 - 1995 | | | |
| | | $64,866 (13.28%) | 1976 - 1995 | | |
| | | | $134,712 (13.89%) | 1971 - 1995 | |
| | | | | $133,675 (10.93%) | 1961 - 1995 |
| | | | | | $245,966 (9.58%) |

^ annual compound rate of return for that period
*Source: "Barron's National Business and Financial Weekly". includes index growth and reinvestment of dividends.

©1996 Chase Global Data & Research
73 Junction Square, Concord, MA 01742

## Dow Jones 15 Utilities with Dividends

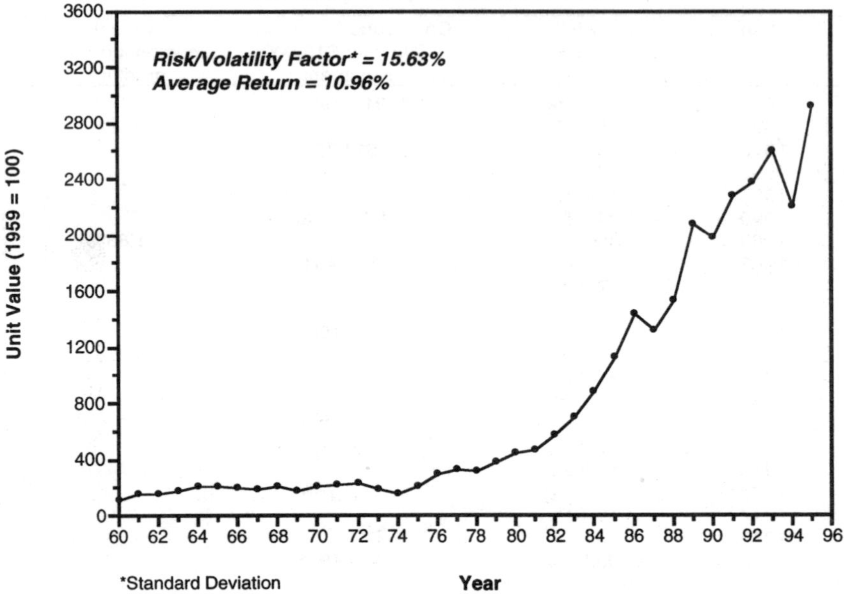


## Dow Jones 15 Utilities^ vs. 10-Year T-Bond and Lipper Income Fund Average^

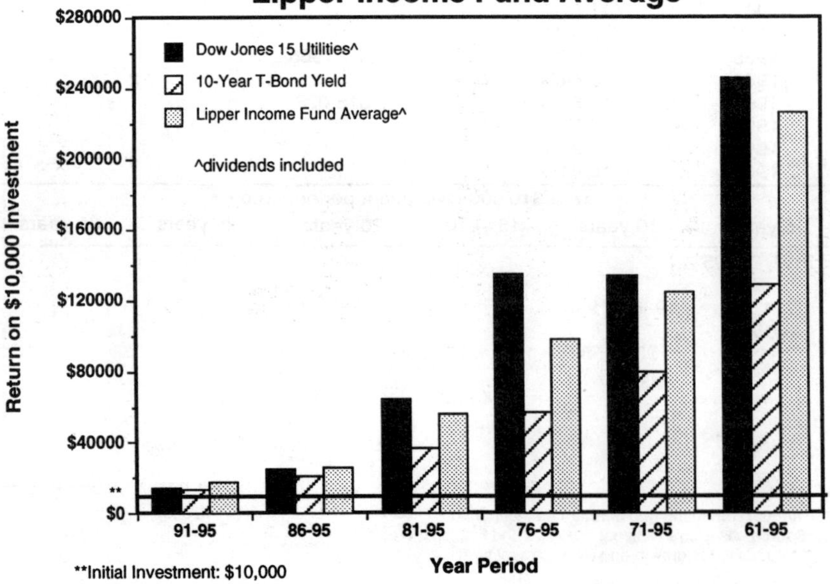


©1996 Chase Global Data & Research
73 Junction Square, Concord, MA 01742

## Dow Jones 15 Utilities^ vs. Tokyo Stock Exchange Index^ and British Pound

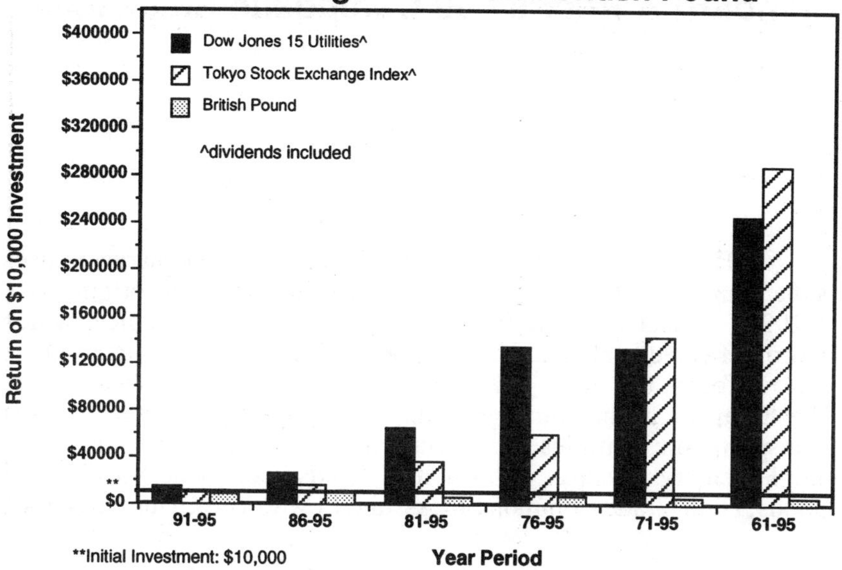


## Dow Jones 15 Utilities^ vs. Inflation

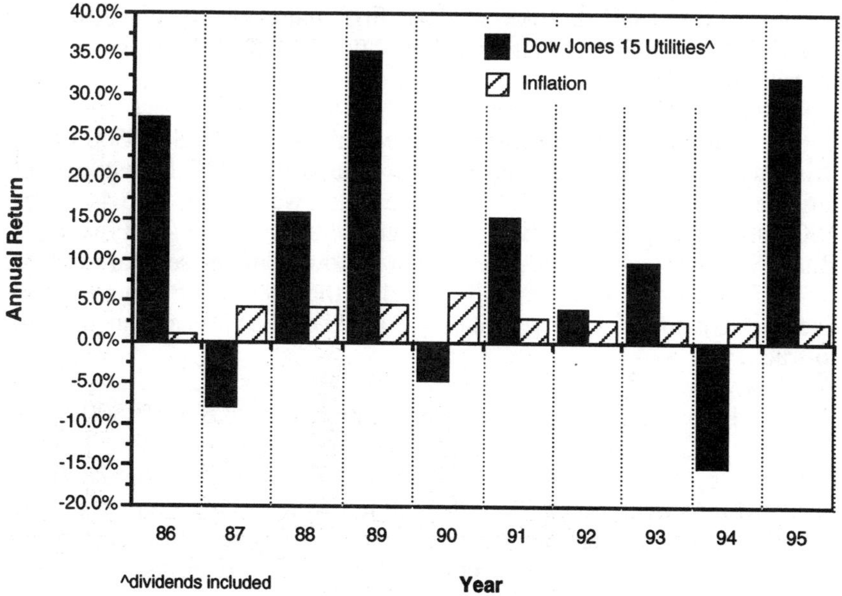


©1996 Chase Global Data & Research
73 Junction Square, Concord, MA 01742

# Chapter Six

# Standard & Poor's 500 Composite Stock Index

The most popular of the all-inclusive U.S. stock market indices is the Standard & Poor's 500 Stock Index, which traces its origins back to 1923. At that time, the Index reflected 26 sub-group indices which in turn reflected leading industrial groups. There were 233 stocks in the Index. Today, the Index covers 500 stocks from 83 industrial groups. The 83 areas are broken down into five primary groups: Industrials; Transportation; Utilities; Financial; the 500 Composite; and four supplementary groups: the Capital Goods Companies; Consumer Goods; High Grade Common Stocks, and Low Priced Common Stocks.

The S&P Index is based on the aggregate market value of all shares of the common stocks of companies in the Index, unlike the Dow Jones, which reflects only the price of shares within the Index—not the overall value of the total shares of the 30 companies in the Dow Jones. In March 1957, the base of 10 (which equaled the 1941-1943 period) was adopted. The 1957 revision was the first major change since the late 1920's. Today the total market value of the S&P 500 securities is about $5 trillion.

Another major change took place in 1976 in the S&P 500 Index. Prior to 1976, the S&P had 3 main groups, the 425 Industrials; 60 Utilities; and 15 Rails. As of 1976 the Index was enlarged to 4 groups: 400 Industrials; 40 Utilities; 20 Transportations; and 40 Financials. Bank and insurance stocks have been followed under separate indices by S&P and have never been included in the S&P's 500 Index, in part because so many of those securities are traded on the OTC and are difficult to track.

In order to make accurate comparisons, the S&P 500 Index slowly changed its basic formula over the years, reflecting gradual changes in the stock market. Up until 1954, the data for the Index reflected mid-week figures, which S&P felt were the most representative. Monthly averages were based on the 4 or 5 weekly readings each month. Up to 1954 the year's closing price was the last Wednesday of the year;


©1996 Chase Global Data & Research
73 Junction Square, Concord, MA 01742

after 1954 it was the last trading day of the year. In addition, because of changes within the market due to mergers, acquisitions, etc., the S&P 500 Committee must choose stocks to replace those that have left the exchanges, and thus the Index itself. And changes can indeed be frequent. In the two year period between 1984 and 1986, 59 stocks—more than 10%—were added to the S&P Index. Of note, one study reported that the average security added to the S&P 500 index experienced a 3.1% additional gain over and above the averages of the marketplace.

There is no doubt that the S&P 500 Index changes when new securities are added to the Index. Nowadays the newer securities are not only smaller in size, they also often do not reflect the same industry as the departing security. Frequently replacements are half the size of the company being replaced. One member of the S&P Selection Committee said, "We're being forced to reach out to smaller and smaller companies for the Index." Today portfolio managers cite security "downsizing" as a key reason why the S&P 500 Index has become more difficult to beat.

The impact of individual securities on the pricing of the Index varies widely. For example, massive IBM's market value (and thus its impact) on the S&P 500 is about 3%, while various other securities' market value, and relative impact on the Index, is only 0.1%. But IBM's failure to advance over the past decade had a much greater negative impact on the Dow Jones than the S&P 500. Another example of differences between the two major indices was shown in 1984 when Union Carbide stock fell dramatically after the infamous toxic gas leak in India. Union Carbide was a part of both the Dow Jones and S&P Indices. The Dow Jones fell 25 points (4.7%) when the leak was announced, with Union Carbide's stock responsible for 41% of the decline. Yet Union Carbide impacted the S&P 500 only 0.8% that day.

The most popular commodity futures contracts reflecting overall stock market activity is unquestionably the S&P 500 futures contract. And the S&P 100 "OEX" option is the most popular of all stock options. The OEX 100 reflects the hundred largest companies of the S&P 500. The S&P 500 futures contract trades on the Chicago Mercantile Exchange. The S&P 100 OEX stock option contract is traded on the Chicago Board Options Exchange.

A key ratio that sophisticated investors watch in analyzing the stock market is the cumulative price/earnings multiple of the companies in the S&P 500 Index versus historical precedent. (A P/E ratio of between 12 and 14 is considered normal for the S&P 500, with numbers either

©1996 Chase Global Data & Research
73 Junction Square, Concord, MA 01742

below or above such levels deemed out of the norm.) Prior to the "Crash of 1987" the P/E ratio for the S&P 500 was 18. Several individual industry components within the S&P 500 were well into the 20's. In modern times the highest P/E—and the only time the P/E went over 20—was in 1961 when it averaged 20.4. That is, until late 1991, when the P/E reached 22.7. It then made a new record of 24.1 in late 1992. At the end of 1995 the reading was 17.7. The lowest all time P/E level of 7.0 came in 1979.

About 80% of the total market value of the NYSE is represented by the S&P 500, reflecting the fact that over 90% of the S&P 500's securities hail from the NYSE. Only a fraction of the S&P 500 is listed on the AMEX and OTC. To date, the S&P 500's all-time high came in 1995, when it reached 621.69. The all-time record low came over sixty years earlier, when it bottomed at 4.40 on June 1, 1932. During the past two decades the S&P 500's low was 62.68 on October 3, 1974. Since then the Index has gone up over seven fold. And amazingly over the past 60 years it's up over *150 fold!*

As a reflection of the widespread impact of the S&P 500 Index on investors and market watchers everywhere, it has been selected as one of the 12 leading Economic Indicators (representing stock market activity) used by the U.S. Commerce Department. It was also used in a study by the University of Michigan regarding whether investors should "Buy and Hold" when investing in the equity marketplace. Michigan studied the major Bull Market of the mid-80's from August 12, 1982 (beginning) to August 25, 1987 (peak). U of M calculated the average return over the period and then analyzed returns if the best 10, 20, 30, and 40 trading days were *deleted* from the 1,276 potential days stocks could have been held by an investor. The report showed that if investors missed these days—even though they represented only 1% to 3% of the total period—results were dramatically reduced:

1982 - 1987 Bull Market

| Period Investment | % of Time Investment Maintained | S&P 500 Avg. Annual Return |
|---|---|---|
| Full 1,276 Trading Days | 100% | 26.3% |
| minus the 10 Best Days | 99% | 18.3% |
| minus the 20 Best Days | 98% | 13.1% |
| minus the 30 Best Days | 98% | 8.5% |
| minus the 40 Best Days | 97% | 4.3% |

Source: University of Michigan

©1996 Chase Global Data & Research
73 Junction Square, Concord, MA 01742

**S&P 500 COMPOSITE INDEX**
**TOTAL RETURN (with dividends)**

| Year | Total Return* | Compound return on a five year $10,000 investment | Annual compound rate of return |
|---|---|---|---|
| 1995 | 37.58% | 1991 - 1995 | |
| 1994 | 1.32% | | 16.57% |
| 1993 | 10.02% | ... $21,522 | |
| 1992 | 7.61% | | |
| 1991 | 30.41% | | |
| 1990 | -3.27% | 1986 - 1990 | |
| 1989 | 31.37% | | 12.99% |
| 1988 | 16.33% | ... $18,420 | |
| 1987 | 5.10% | | |
| 1986 | 18.56% | | |
| 1985 | 31.57% | 1981 - 1985 | |
| 1984 | 6.10% | | 14.53% |
| 1983 | 22.39% | ... $19,707 | |
| 1982 | 21.44% | | |
| 1981 | -5.01% | | |
| 1980 | 32.27% | 1976 - 1980 | |
| 1979 | 18.20% | | 13.73% |
| 1978 | 6.39% | ... $19,030 | |
| 1977 | -7.41% | | |
| 1976 | 23.57% | | |
| 1975 | 37.16% | 1971 - 1975 | |
| 1974 | -26.39% | | 3.17% |
| 1973 | -14.77% | ... $ 11,690 | |
| 1972 | 18.90% | | |
| 1971 | 14.25% | | |
| 1970 | 3.93% | 1966 - 1970 | |
| 1969 | -8.43% | | 3.31% |
| 1968 | 10.98% | ... $11,768 | |
| 1967 | 23.88% | | |
| 1966 | -10.05% | | |
| 1965 | 12.36% | 1961 - 1965 | |
| 1964 | 16.31% | | 13.15% |
| 1963 | 22.66% | ... $18,547 | |
| 1962 | -8.73% | | |
| 1961 | 26.78% | | |
| 1960 | 0.45% | | |

How a $10,000 investment performed over

| 5 years | 10 years | 15 years | 20 years | 25 years | 35 years |
|---|---|---|---|---|---|
| 1991 - 1995 | | | | | |
| $21,522 (16.57%)^ | 1986 - 1995 | | | | |
| | $39,644 (14.77%) | 1981 - 1995 | | | |
| | | $78,126 (14.69%) | 1976 - 1995 | | |
| | | | $148,671 (14.45%) | 1971 - 1995 | |
| | | | | $173,795 (12.10%) | 1961 - 1995 |
| | | | | | $379,342 (10.95%) |

^ annual compound rate of return for that period
*Source: Standard & Poor's Corp.
includes index growth and reinvestment of dividends.

©1996 Chase Global Data & Research
73 Junction Square, Concord, MA 01742

## S&P 500 Composite Index with Dividends

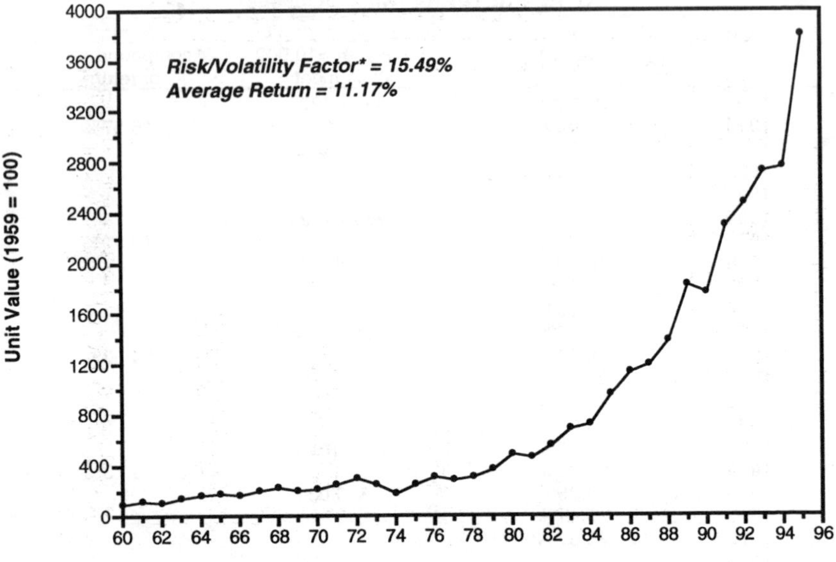


*Standard Deviation

## S&P 500 Composite Index^ vs. Tokyo Stock Exchange Index^ and Lipper Growth Fund Average^

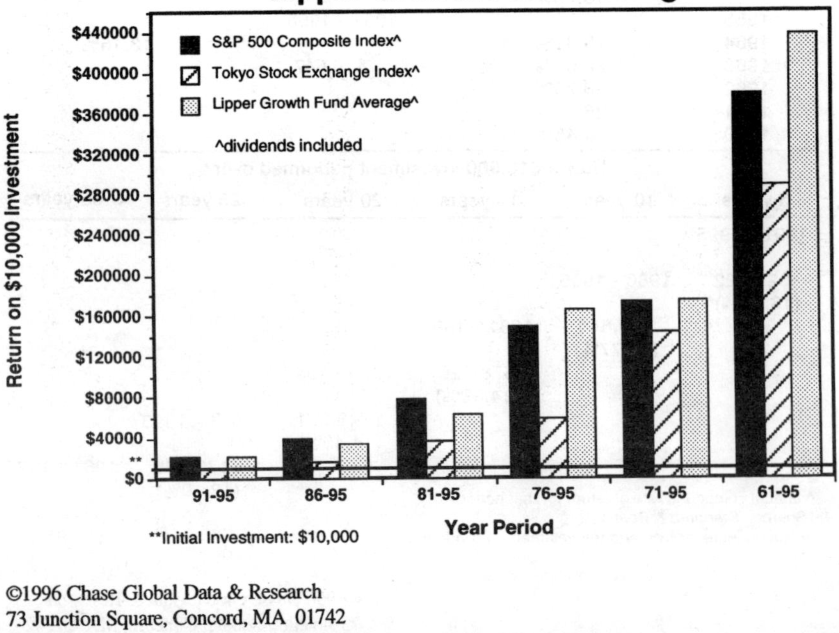


**Initial Investment: $10,000

©1996 Chase Global Data & Research
73 Junction Square, Concord, MA 01742

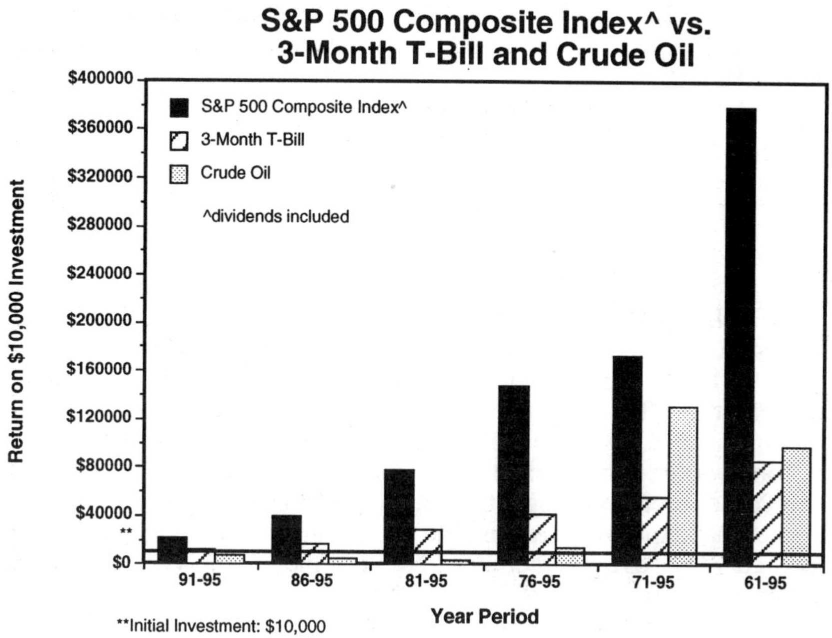


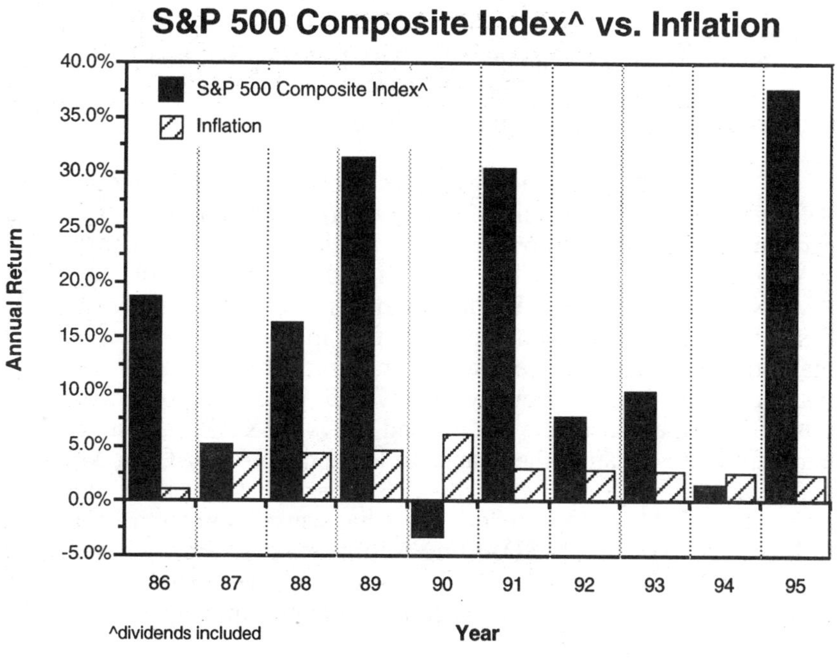


©1996 Chase Global Data & Research
73 Junction Square, Concord, MA 01742

Chapter Seven

# OTC Market

NASDAQ stands for the National Association of Securities Dealers Automated Quotation System. In U.S. stock trading today, the NASDAQ is the modern, automated version of the old Over-the-Counter market. The OTC marketplace was the first marketplace for securities trading in the U.S. After all, before two dozen brokers met under a Buttonwood tree in Manhattan and formally created what is now the New York Stock Exchange, they all were OTC dealers in an over-the-counter marketplace. In addition to its informal history spanning several hundred years, over-the-counter trading in the U.S. has a more formal history dating from the 1930's.

The NASD (National Association of Securities Dealers) is a self-regulatory organization of securities industry companies organized to regulate the over-the-counter marketplace. The NASD was established by the 1938 Maloney Act—a series of amendments to the 1934 Securities and Exchange Act. The 1938 act required a voluntary cooperative association of broker dealers to regulate themselves and their trading—while being overseen by the SEC.

The method of trading on the over-the counter-markets (both before and after the SEC and Maloney Acts) is different from that of the exchanges. There are no specialists trading securities on the OTC/NASDAQ markets as is the case with the regional exchanges, the AMEX, and the NYSE. Rather, market makers survive and prosper based on their ability to compete in a free marketplace. Because their marketplace is less stringent and formalized, there are usually many market makers in each security. Many U.S. public corporations prefer this trading method to the NYSE and the AMEX. As a result, many companies are resisting the chance to leave the NASDAQ marketplace and relocate on a formal exchange. But the debate over trading practices on the NASDAQ in recent years has caused some marketmakers to leave. As a result NASDAQ marketmakers per security have fallen from past levels, especially during 1995. On the NYSE the average number of common stocks per specialist is approximately 25—with the


©1996 Chase Global Data & Research
73 Junction Square, Concord, MA 01742

highest number for one specialist being over 40. On the NASDAQ the average number of market makers per security today is 10 (down 7% in 1995), with over 400 securities having an average of over 17 market makers each.

The NYSE is the largest equity marketplace in the world, in which resides 70% of all equities listed on U.S. exchanges. But the NASDAQ is the second largest securities marketplace in the U.S.—and the third largest in the world. It is second largest in the world based on dollar trading volume. Since 1982 the number of issues trading on the NASDAQ has more than doubled, while the total of companies trading on the NYSE and AMEX has remained relatively static. By the end of 1995 the aggregate NASDAQ market value is reached a record $1.15 trillion, up over 30% from 1994.

There are 5,761 domestic and foreign securities traded on the NASDAQ (double the amount on the NYSE) representing over 4,900 companies. Over the past decade NASDAQ's trading volume increased more than 700%. For 1995 the average daily volume reached the incredible level of 400 million shares (although some experts believe the NASDAQ is guilty of double-counting trades). In 1995 annual trading volume was a record 100 billion shares—exceeding the NYSE. A growing institutional and foreign marketplace, over half of all NASDAQ/National Market System (NMS) volume can be attributed to institutions (trades of 10,000 shares or more) with the average trade exceeding 20,000 shares. 20% of all NASDAQ institutions are foreign.

The dramatic growth of NASDAQ is partly due to the fact that it is represented by over 400,000 sales representatives and over 6,600 principal member securities organizations—which in turn are represented by about 500 dealers who make markets in the more than 5,000 securities of the NASDAQ. Another prime reason for the expansion of the NASDAQ marketplace came as a result of the formation of the NASDAQ National Market System (NMS) which began in April, 1982. The NMS was mandated by Congress in 1975 to increase competition and efficiency in the securities markets. A follow-up to the 1975 mandate was the SEC ruling that required not only listed securities but also some securities quoted on the NASDAQ system be included in the NMS.

That ruling was to cause a profound change in both the perception and the manner of trading in the NASDAQ markets. One of the major SEC requirements was that securities allowed into the NMS have their transactions reported in real-time (immediate) transaction quote form. The SEC did not require any changes in the method of operation of the

©1996 Chase Global Data & Research
73 Junction Square, Concord, MA 01742

NASDAQ—such as using specialists, but it did require up-to-date reporting of transactions. Today NASDAQ/NMS had expanded so dramatically that the market value of the securities traded in the NMS represent over 90% of total NASDAQ market value. In addition, over 40% of the NMS securities are held by institutions. Today over 200,000 terminals in 52 nations throughout the globe track NASDAQ pricing on an up to the minute basis.

In the past few years, NASDAQ has made major strides in many areas. It has the capacity to monitor securities transactions on the most advanced computerized systems, capable of handling the 300+ million share standard trading days anticipated in the future. NASDAQ maintains a 110,000 square foot facility to support anticipated increases in trading. However, in late 1987 its entire system fell prey to a wayward squirrel which literally cut out its power for about two hours.

Another major addition is NASDAQ's market link with the London Stock Exchange, representing the first intercontinental link of major world markets. The linkage allows the two marketplaces to trade via satellite with real-time quotations in over 550 issues. Presently, the NASDAQ/NMS offers domestically an ability for the public to buy and sell over 100 ADRs (American Depository Receipts) and 221 foreign securities. The aggregate market value of the ADRs is $35 billion, with NASDAQ trading reflecting 20% of all U.S. ADR trading.

The increased international activity in the NASDAQ marketplace is due in part to the 30,000 quotation terminals in 52 foreign lands. In London 200 major U.S. companies and ADRs of 70 non-British firms are carried by NASDAQ. NASDAQ terminals carry quotes on over 400 stocks from London including the 100 issues of the Financial Times Stock Index and 300 other international issues traded in the London marketplace. In 1992 NASDAQ began NASDAQ International, the closest move to date to a 24 hour marketplace in the United States—with market hours from 3:30 PM to 9 AM.

Any dealer who meets certain net capital requirements can make a market in a NASDAQ security simply by registering through a NASDAQ electronic terminal. All market makers are governed by the "firm" quote rule requiring any market maker to buy or sell at least 100 shares at their quoted price. (That rule may soon be changed to 1,000 shares.) There are over 50,000 market making stock positions for all the securities of the NASDAQ marketplace. The market maker may be a major retail national brokerage firm, an institutional firm, or a local trading firm—from one of 38 states and the District of Columbia.

©1996 Chase Global Data & Research
73 Junction Square, Concord, MA 01742

Whenever a bid and an offer are displayed on a NASDAQ terminal, the identity of the market maker is also displayed with that quote.

As with any major system, some weaknesses are inherent in the structure. First, NASDAQ's trading figures are inflated by at least 10% due to inter dealer trades—because while they are not trades with the public they are nevertheless reflected in the trading totals. Also, during the havoc of the Crash of 1987, many institutions and individual investors were disappointed that communications of both traders and brokers with the marketmakers were not handled well, often because phones were not answered. The result was that transactions that should or could have been completed never were done at all. The inability to communicate by telephone—nipping transactions in the bud—produced a situation far different from one in which a stock trader stands in front of a live specialist on the floor of the NYSE and screams to get his trade completed. While the specialists have been accused of making less than a perfect market during the Crash of 1987, they can't be accused of not even answering their phones and hence failing to complete a transaction.

The competitive climate between the NYSE, the AMEX, and the NASDAQ markets is increasing each year. By most accounts, the NASDAQ is winning the race. One reason is that small companies can easily join the NASDAQ. In 1995, NASDAQ accounted for over 400 initial public offerings, worth a total of $41 billion. NASDAQ's regular segment has been renamed NASDAQ SmallCap Market, with almost 2,000 securities now trading with real time quotes. A second difficulty facing the exchanges is that major companies are being purchased through leveraged buy-outs and mergers. In one recent year alone the NYSE lost 157 listings to buy-outs. With many major companies choosing not to jump to the Big Board (hardly the case prior to 1980) the Big Board has reason to worry. In fact, in 1995 NASDAQ's daily volume of 400 million exceeded the NYSE's by 20% (although that statistic is tainted by alledged double-counting practices). On several days recently the NYSE and AMEX volume *combined* was less than NASDAQ's. But since 1994 federal scrutiny of NASDAQ trading practices has made headlines. It is likely a harbinger of changes coming in NASDAQ business practices and recordkeeping, especially in regards to its treatment of the small investor. In 1996 the AMEX publicly accused the NASDAQ of costing investors billions through wide trading spreads being maintained by marketmakers.

Overall performance of NASDAQ stocks has been solid recently. After skyrocketing almost 60% to an all time high in 1991, the NASDAQ Composite reached a new record high in 1995 at 1069.79 (+39.92%).

©1996 Chase Global Data & Research
73 Junction Square, Concord, MA 01742

## NASDAQ COMPOSITE STOCK INDEX

[without dividends; year-end]

| Year | Index Value* | Index Growth | Compound return on a five year $10,000 investment | Annual compound rate of return |
|---|---|---|---|---|
| 1995 | 1052.13 | 39.92% | 1991 - 1995 | |
| 1994 | 751.96 | -3.20% | | 22.99% |
| 1993 | 776.80 | 14.75% | ... $28,144 | |
| 1992 | 676.95 | 15.45% | | |
| 1991 | 586.34 | 56.84% | | |
| 1990 | 373.84 | -17.80% | 1986 - 1990 | |
| 1989 | 454.82 | 19.26% | | 2.84% |
| 1988 | 381.38 | 15.41% | ... $11,505 | |
| 1987 | 330.47 | -5.26% | | |
| 1986 | 348.83 | 7.36% | | |
| 1985 | 324.93 | 31.36% | 1981 - 1985 | |
| 1984 | 247.35 | -11.22% | | 9.94% |
| 1983 | 278.60 | 19.87% | ... $16,059 | |
| 1982 | 232.41 | 18.67% | | |
| 1981 | 195.84 | -3.21% | | |
| 1980 | 202.34 | 33.88% | 1976 - 1980 | |
| 1979 | 151.14 | 28.11% | | 21.12% |
| 1978 | 117.98 | 12.31% | ... $26,068 | |
| 1977 | 105.05 | 7.33% | | |
| 1976 | 97.88 | 26.10% | | |
| 1975 | 77.62 | 29.76% | | |
| 1974 | 59.82 | -35.11% | | |
| 1973 | 92.19 | -31.06% | | |
| 1972 | 133.73 | 17.18% | | |
| 1971 | 114.12 | | | |

How a $10,000 investment performed over

| 5 years | 10 years | 15 years | 20 years |
|---|---|---|---|
| 1991 - 1995 | | | |
| $28,144 (22.99%)^ | 1986 - 1995 | | |
| | $32,380 (12.47%) | 1981 - 1995 | |
| | | $51,998 (11.62%) | 1976 - 1995 |
| | | | $135,549 (13.92%) |

^ annual compound rate of return for that period

* Source: National Association of Securities Dealers, Inc.

©1996 Chase Global Data & Research
73 Junction Square, Concord, MA 01742

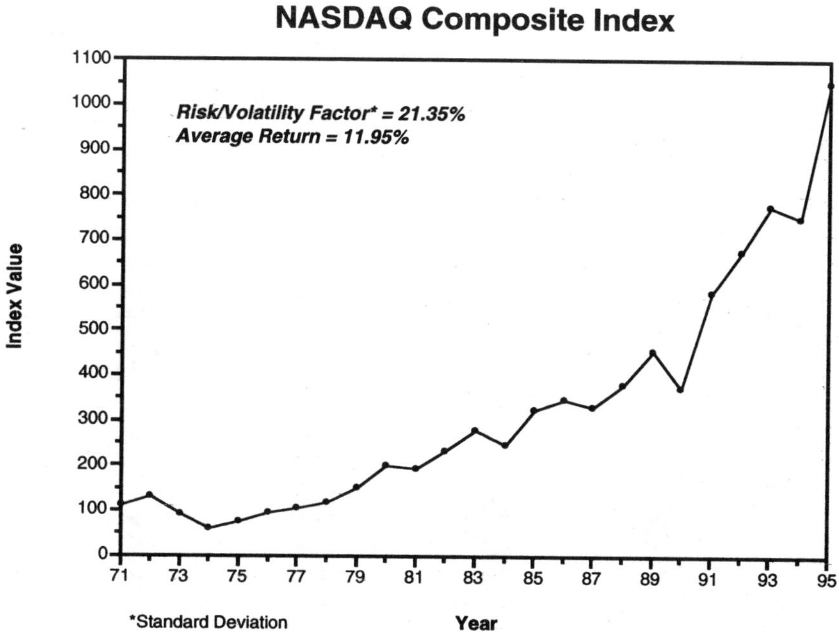


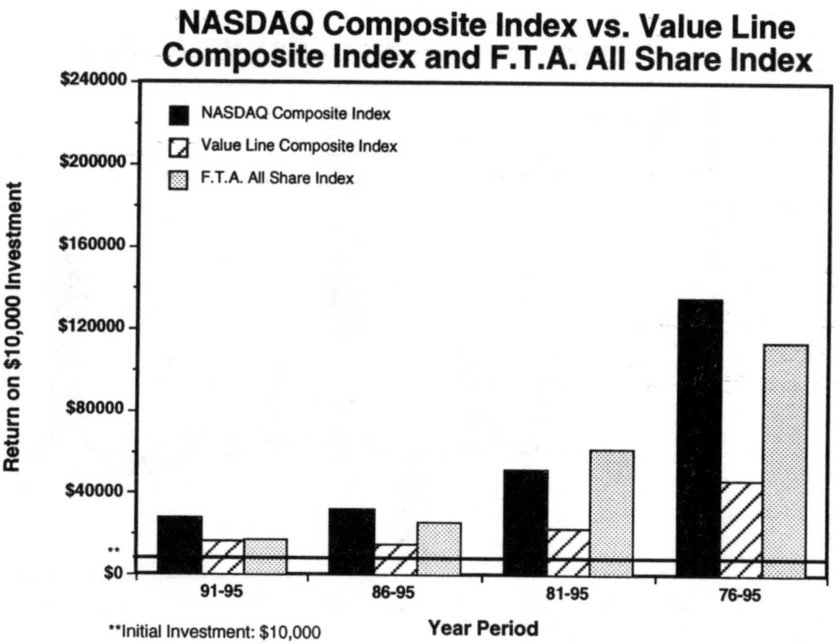


©1996 Chase Global Data & Research
73 Junction Square, Concord, MA 01742

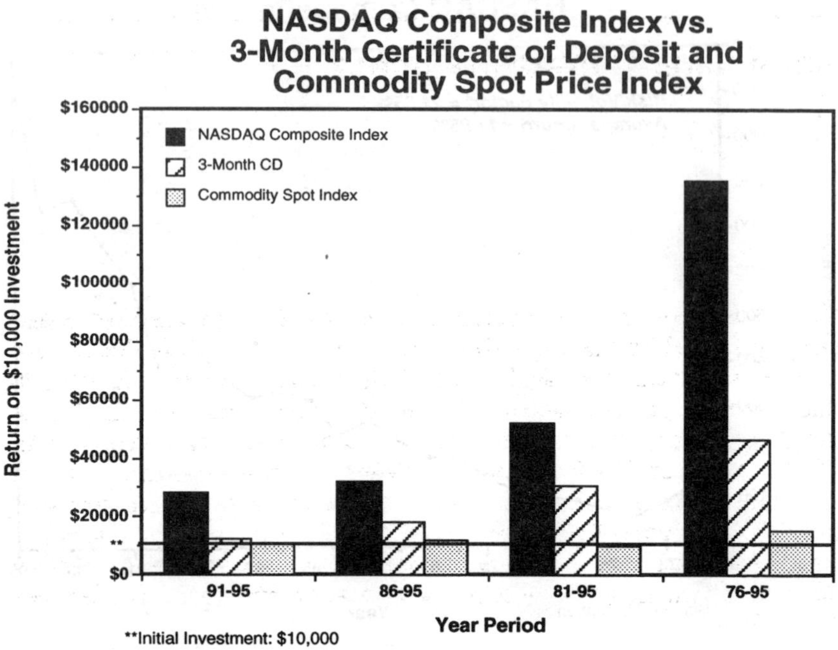


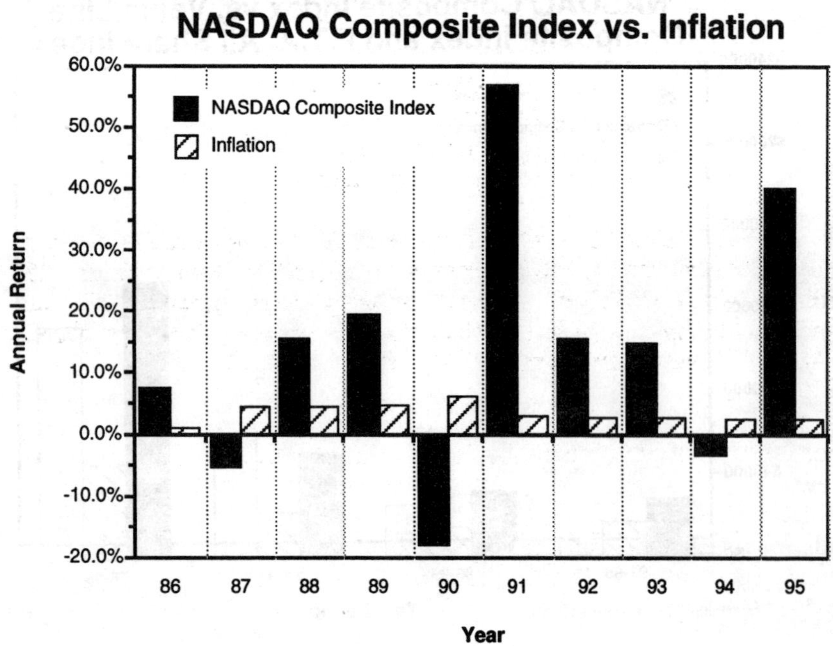


©1996 Chase Global Data & Research
73 Junction Square, Concord, MA 01742

# Chapter Eight

# Value Line Composite Index

Perhaps the best indicator reflecting the movement of equity portfolios held by the proverbial "average" investor is the Value Line Composite Index. John and Jane Doe do not typically hold only the 30 blue chips securities represented by the Dow Jones Industrials. Nor do they exclusively purchase the nation's 500 largest companies (S&P 500) when over 7,000 remain from which to choose—among which could be the next IBM or Xerox. In reality investors hold a generous mix of stocks from the NYSE, AMEX, and OTC markets. The Value Line Composite is the key index market watchers turn to when seeking out a clear, unweighted reflection of how the broad equity marketplace is performing.

Such a broad market index is accomplished through a mix of over 1,600 common stocks. As of late 1995 the Value Line Composite Index was represented by the following marketplaces:

| | |
|---|---|
| 74.1% | New York Stock Exchange |
| 20.2% | NASDAQ (OTC) |
| 3.2% | American Stock Exchange |
| 2.5% | Canadian Exchanges |

The Value Line Index represents 96 industry groups. At year end 1995 the Index was composed of 1,458 industrial firms, 164 utilities, and 10 railroads. The Index composition varies slightly over time in a manner similar to other major indices such as the NYSE, NASDAQ, and AMEX market indices.

The Value Line Composite Index is produced by Value Line, Inc.—a diversified financial publishing and services company based in New York. Value Line publishes several financial publications, provides computer support systems and software programs to individuals and institutions, and manages over $5 billion through its mutual fund and asset management divisions. Value Line was founded by the late Arnold Bernhard during the Depression. He had been an

©1996 Chase Global Data & Research
73 Junction Square, Concord, MA 01742

analyst with Moody's Investors Service, but was sued by a client irate about his Depression era losses. Upon his dismissal he began formulating at his kitchen table the discipline carried on even today by Value Line, which rates stocks for Timeliness™ (price-appreciation potential) on a basis of 1 (highest) to 5 (lowest).

*The Value Line Investment Survey*, the nation's leading investment-related periodical, founded in 1931 by Value Line, Inc., presents these rankings to investors on a weekly basis. Almost 1,700 securities are tracked in *The Value Line Investment Survey*. Group rating breakdowns are approximately as follows:

| | |
|---|---|
| 6% | Rating 1 |
| 18% | Rating 2 |
| 52% | Rating 3 |
| 18% | Rating 4 |
| 6% | Rating 5 |

The results over sustained time periods in using the ratings methodology are surprisingly strong, and would put those who believe the market is efficient and difficult to beat over long periods of time to shame. For the 30 year period from 1965 through 1995 stocks in the top ranking (Ranking 1) gained 36,370%—while those ranked #5 *lost* 97%. Over the same time period the S&P 500 rose 2,298%. The formula used to differentiate securities and rank them from 1 through 5 is based on five components: long term earnings, long term prices, recent price performance, earnings momentum, and earnings surprise.

The Value Line Composite Index was initiated on June 30, 1961. Now in its fourth decade, it is a geometrically averaged index. It is not market weighted, i.e. the index price movement is impacted by share-price movement, not per-share price movement in conjunction with total shares outstanding of each security in the index. The Value Line Composite Index has reflected the true movement of a broad cross section of stocks, which are likely additions to many investors' portfolios. While it has underperformed the S&P 500 and Dow Jones Industrials, it accurately reflects what the average investor's portfolio has accomplished over the years, unless an investor has exclusively held positions in only the small cross section of larger and more mature U.S. corporations—a situation deemed unlikely by most observers of investor activity.

©1996 Chase Global Data & Research
73 Junction Square, Concord, MA 01742

**VALUE LINE COMPOSITE INDEX**
[without dividends; year-end]

| Year | Index Value* | Index Growth | Compound return on a five year $10,000 investment | Annual compound rate of return |
|---|---|---|---|---|
| 1995 | 331.04 | 19.29% | 1991 - 1995 | |
| 1994 | 277.52 | -6.01% | | 11.05% |
| 1993 | 295.28 | 10.72% | ... $16,891 | |
| 1992 | 266.68 | 6.95% | | |
| 1991 | 249.34 | 27.22% | | |
| 1990 | 195.99 | -24.26% | 1986 - 1990 | |
| 1989 | 258.78 | 11.22% | | -1.82% |
| 1988 | 232.68 | 15.41% | ... $ 9,122 | |
| 1987 | 201.62 | -10.64% | | |
| 1986 | 225.62 | 5.01% | | |
| 1985 | 214.86 | 20.72% | 1981 - 1985 | |
| 1984 | 177.98 | -8.42% | | 8.30% |
| 1983 | 194.35 | 22.28% | ... $14,900 | |
| 1982 | 158.94 | 15.33% | | |
| 1981 | 137.81 | -4.43% | | |
| 1980 | 144.20 | 18.28% | 1976 - 1980 | |
| 1979 | 121.91 | 24.44% | | 15.32% |
| 1978 | 97.97 | 4.31% | ... $20,399 | |
| 1977 | 93.92 | 0.48% | | |
| 1976 | 93.47 | 32.23% | | |
| 1975 | 70.69 | 44.35% | 1971 - 1975 | |
| 1974 | 48.97 | -33.47% | | -7.36% |
| 1973 | 73.61 | -35.46% | ... $ 6,823 | |
| 1972 | 114.05 | 0.98% | | |
| 1971 | 112.94 | 9.02% | | |
| 1970 | 103.60 | -20.65% | 1966 - 1970 | |
| 1969 | 130.56 | -28.73% | | -5.17% |
| 1968 | 183.18 | 19.81% | ... $ 7,668 | |
| 1967 | 152.89 | 29.08% | | |
| 1966 | 118.45 | -12.33% | | |
| 1965 | 135.11 | 18.99% | | |
| 1964 | 113.55 | 13.31% | | |
| 1963 | 100.21 | 13.62% | | |
| 1962 | 88.20 | -16.26% | | |
| 1961 | 105.33 | n.a. | | |
| 1960 | n.a. | n.a. | | |

How a $10,000 investment performed over

| 5 years | 10 years | 15 years | 20 years | 25 years | 30 years |
|---|---|---|---|---|---|
| 1991 - 1995 | | | | | |
| $16,891 (11.05%)^ | 1986 - 1995 | | | | |
| | $15,407 (4.42%) | 1981 - 1995 | | | |
| | | $22,957 (5.70%) | 1976 - 1995 | | |
| | | | $46,830 (8.03%) | 1971 - 1995 | |
| | | | | $31,954 (4.76%) | 1966 - 1995 |
| | | | | | $24,502 (3.03%) |

^ annual compound rate of return for that period
* Source: ©1995 Value Line, Inc.
n.a. = data not available

©1996 Chase Global Data & Research
73 Junction Square, Concord, MA 01742

## Value Line Composite Index

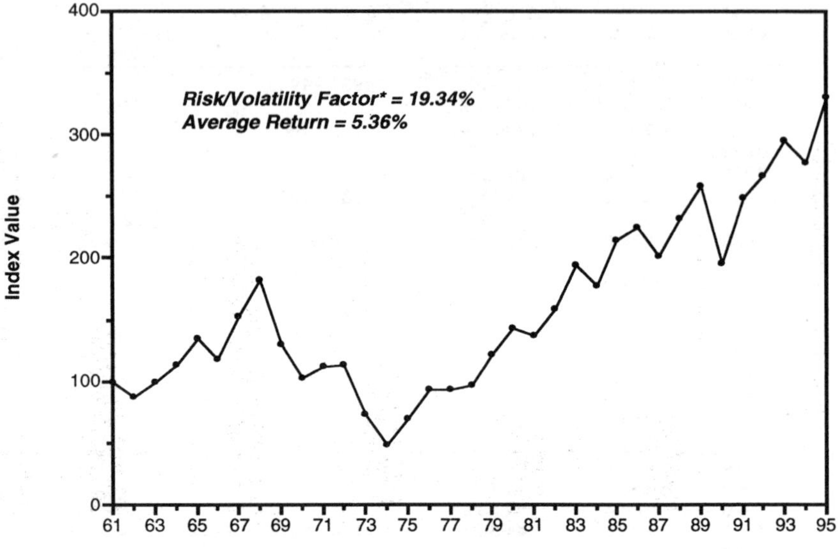


*Standard Deviation

## Value Line Composite Index vs. 3-Month T-Bill and Farmland

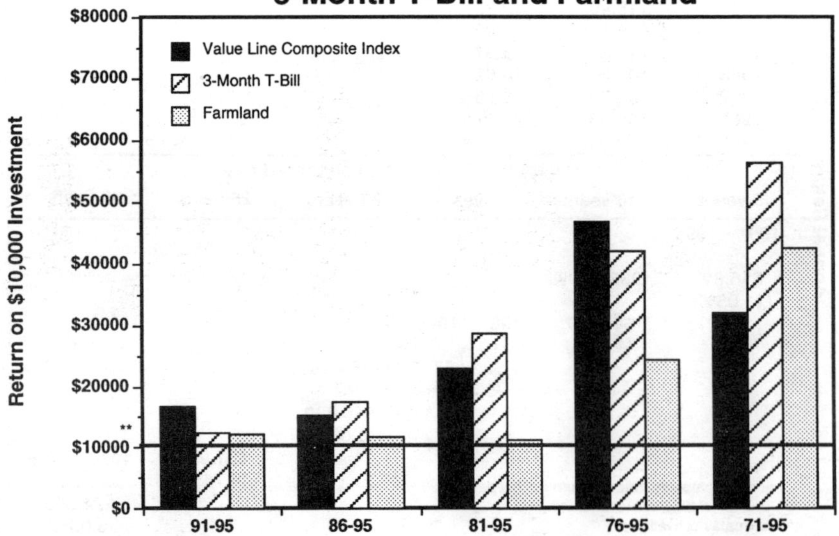


**Initial Investment: $10,000

©1996 Chase Global Data & Research
73 Junction Square, Concord, MA 01742

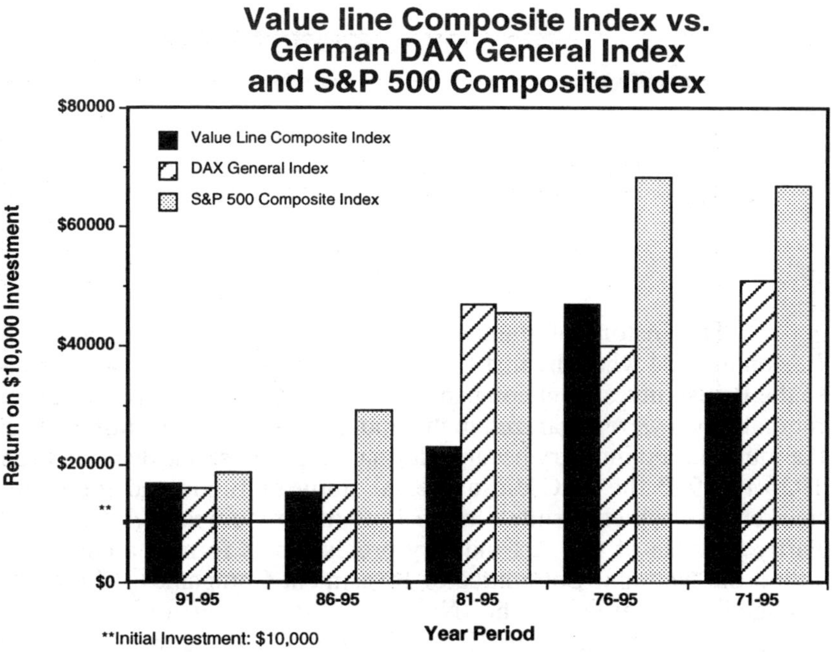


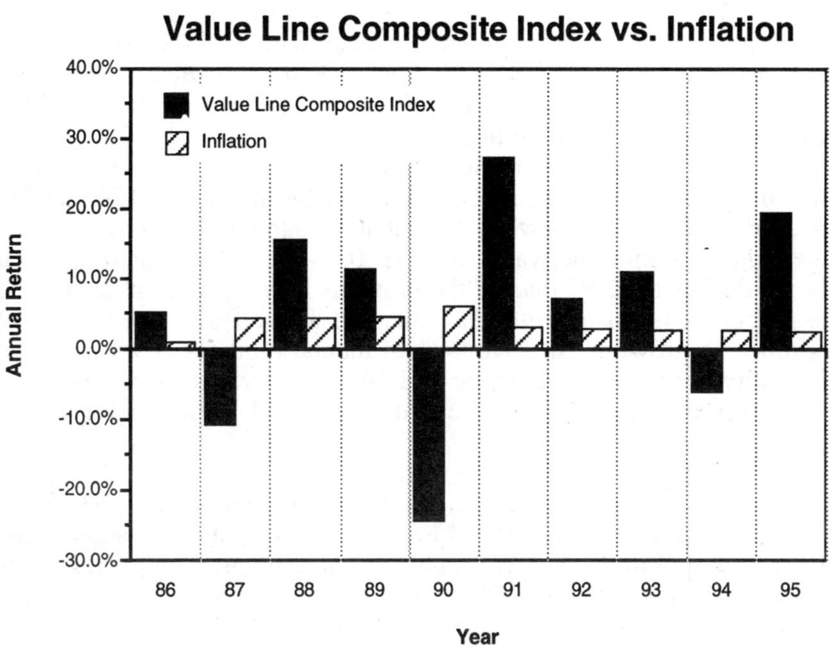


©1996 Chase Global Data & Research
73 Junction Square, Concord, MA 01742

Chapter Nine

# Mutual Funds

The history of mutual funds in the United States begins in Boston in 1924 when the first fund was organized. The style was similar to the British investment companies that formed "trusts." While several mutual funds were organized in the mid-1920's, after the Crash of 1929 the mutual fund industry became dormant for almost one decade. From 1936 to 1940 the SEC did a special study of funds and the equity marketplace which resulted in the Investment Company Act of 1940. Partly because of this Act industry professionals formed a committee called the National Committee of Investment Companies, which later changed its name to the National Association of Investment Companies, and finally, in 1961 it became the Investment Company Institute.

The Investment Company Institute, operating from Washington, D.C., gathers an enormous amount of information on the industry and each year issues the *Mutual Fund Fact Book*. There is a lot of activity to oversee as the number of shareholders has risen from 296,000 in 1940 to 37 million in 1994. In the early 1970's industry assets were a mere $40 billion. By 1990 the total had reached $1 trillion, in 1993 it crossed $2 trillion, and by the end of 1995 totaled $2.6 trillion. In 1993, new investment alone into mutual funds exceeded the industry's entire net value as of 1980. More money entered mutual funds during 1992-93 than in the previous fifty years combined. The asset composition of funds has changed as well over the years—in addition to growing. In 1973 94% of mutual fund assets was invested in equity funds, but by the year-end 1995 the percentage had fallen to 30% (representing $750 billion) despite $118 billion being added during the year.

Four major organizations track mutual funds. They are Lipper Analytical Services, Morningstar Corporation, Standard and Poor's Corporation, and Wiesenberger Investment Companies. The data that follows in the *Chase Investment Performance Digest* on Growth, Income, Fixed Income, and Municipal Bond mutual funds


©1996 Chase Global Data & Research
73 Junction Square, Concord, MA 01742

comes from Lipper Analytical Services. Lipper maintains data on mutual funds from December 31, 1959. (Of note, Chase Global Data & Research's ***InvestmentView® Hypothetical*** software contains over 8,000 Lipper Analytical Services mutual fund performance and characteristics data—in addition to over 300 Chase indices.)

Beyond a doubt, mutual funds are Wall Street's most popular product. Investors have many types of funds to choose from, and their initial investment can be as low as $25. A primary fund choice is the money market fund. Thirty percent of all first time mutual fund investors buy a money market fund. Money market funds were created in 1972, Municipal Bond funds followed in 1976, Option Income funds began in 1977, and Government funds and Ginnie Mae funds started in the early 1980's. More recently sector funds joined the list of mutual funds. Mutual funds have experienced explosive growth since the 1980's. At the present time there are over 8,000 mutual funds—triple the number of stocks on the NYSE. Over 6,000 funds have been introduced since 1970. For every dollar of value in NYSE stocks, there is sixty cents invested in mutual funds!

In the 1990's funds are growing sharply in popularity with institutions, pension funds, and 37 million individuals investing in stock, bond, and money market funds. Mutual funds sales experienced bad times throughout the 1970's, but it was in the decade of the 1980's where the remarkable growth trend began. By 1993 mutual fund companies passed insurance companies in total assets—and quickly approached banks as the U.S. industry leader in total assets under control. As to the expansion of mutual funds, Michael Lipper of Lipper Analytical was once asked if there were too many funds. His answer, "There are not enough successful funds."

There clearly *is* a group of cream-of-the-crop mutual funds within the industry, but alas, also a large group of mediocre to poor performers. The consistently stellar funds have truly remarkable performance histories. The most famous example, and the fund with the best long term record, is Fidelity Magellan Fund. Magellan earned its shareholders from 1979 to 1995 over 45 times their original investment. Amazingly, during the past 20 years there have been hundreds of funds which have made investors between 1000% to 2000+% gains. The trick, obviously, is to choose the good mutual funds from among the growing myriad of choices—not an easy task. And the ever expanding list of fund alternatives can only increase the difficulty in finding the better mutual funds.

One of the problems in evaluating and choosing a fund is trying

©1996 Chase Global Data & Research
73 Junction Square, Concord, MA 01742

to understand a fund's performance numbers and its overall cost to investors. Today advisory fees can be 0.7% or more, with additional expenses raising the total annual expense for some funds to as high as over 2% annually. A 2% fee greatly affects the performance of a fund, especially when levied over several years. The Lipper Growth Mutual Fund Average which follows acknowledges the problem of varying fees and sales charges in its qualifying statement, "Any fund charges not reflected in net asset value or gross income and any tax consequences incurred by the shareholder are not taken into consideration."

In the late 1980's the SEC acknowledged that it had become extremely difficult to ascertain a mutual fund's true rate of return. The SEC then mandated changes in the method of presentation of fees and performance results in mutual fund prospectuses. The SEC required changes in how returns were calculated and presented to investors—in order to promote better public understanding and simplify comparisons of net returns. Investors can now identify total returns, not just yields or stated returns. Today's prospectuses now fully address front-end sales charges and back-end fees, as well as annual and other maintenance fees.

Another significant evolutionary trend in mutual funds is the growth of Sector funds. Sector funds allow investors to diversify their assets in several distinct investment areas, always knowing that no matter where they have diversified, their assets are being managed by professionals who are acutely aware of that particular segment of the marketplace. Allocation changes from one area to a new area may be made by investors through "switches" within the fund family's portfolio. The "switches" are executed at either no charge or a minimal one, unlike a stock transaction, and can be done by telephone. At times Sector fund performance has been exceptional. In 1991 and 1995 several Small Capitalization and Biotechnology Sector funds recorded gains of 60% to 100% for the one year period. Even a sector fund investing exclusively in Russian securities was created in 1994.

Another change is that some mutual funds are becoming non-mutual funds. Management groups are creating limited partnerships which are similar to mutual funds in that they manage portfolios of stocks and bonds. The difference is that the partnerships can buy unregistered securities, deal in the options market, and eliminate stocks from their portfolios entirely to create total cash positions. In addition, they can use margin to leverage their investments in a more aggressive manner.

©1996 Chase Global Data & Research
73 Junction Square, Concord, MA 01742

In today's marketplace individual managers are overseeing $50+ billion funds (each with millions of shareholders) whereas even seven years ago managing more than $1 billion was unheard of. Peter Lynch, who until 1990 managed the world's largest mutual fund—the Fidelity Magellan Fund—left the then $12 billion fund after he oversaw its rise from only $147 million in assets eight years earlier. Peter Lynch believes in mutual funds, stating "I think the public is not well served by its own investing. People tend to go to the library and do research, talk to friends, and buy the right microwave oven for $700. Then they put $5000 in a stock on somebody's tip on the bus." Lynch is often right, of course.

But a greater issue is that in order for an investor to make good choices among mutual funds—as well as microwave ovens—he or she needs accurate research materials. Among other things, investors must be able to compare mutual funds' total net returns and do some modicum of homework before they invest. Otherwise, they are throwing darts at a product line that has thousands more choices than today's New York Stock Exchange has stocks.

It should be emphasized that the following Performance Tables on Mutual Funds (as reflected by the Lipper Averages) show exceptional performance. In fact, the **Lipper Growth Mutual Fund Average** ***RANKS 1st AMONG ALL INVESTMENTS*** *in the Chase Investment Performance Digest in the thirty-five year ranking period from 1961 through 1995.* The Lipper Income Mutual Fund Average ranks 7th. Important, too, is the fact that the Lipper Income Mutual Fund Average displayed relatively low risk/volatility in all major time frames, thus displaying key positive investment characteristics over sustained periods of time (see Volatility Ranking Tables on pages 25-28). Simply put, over the long haul mutual funds have proven themselves excellent investments—beyond any shadow of a doubt.

©1996 Chase Global Data & Research
73 Junction Square, Concord, MA 01742

## LIPPER GROWTH MUTUAL FUND AVERAGE

[dividends included; year-end]

| Year | Index Value* | Index Growth | Compound return on a five year $10,000 investment | Annual compound rate of return |
|---|---|---|---|---|
| 1995 | 4512.89 | 30.79% | 1991 - 1995 | |
| 1994 | 3450.49 | -2.15% | | 15.90% |
| 1993 | 3526.30 | 10.88% | ... $20,916 | |
| 1992 | 3180.24 | 7.90% | | |
| 1991 | 2947.46 | 36.61% | | |
| 1990 | 2157.62 | -4.58% | 1986 - 1990 | |
| 1989 | 2261.07 | 26.36% | | 10.15% |
| 1988 | 1789.40 | 14.15% | ... $16,215 | |
| 1987 | 1567.63 | 3.18% | | |
| 1986 | 1519.30 | 14.18% | | |
| 1985 | 1330.66 | 28.28% | 1981 - 1985 | |
| 1984 | 1037.31 | -1.75% | | 13.24% |
| 1983 | 1055.74 | 20.58% | ... $18,617 | |
| 1982 | 875.53 | 25.26% | | |
| 1981 | 698.95 | -2.21% | | |
| 1980 | 714.75 | 36.80% | 1976 - 1980 | |
| 1979 | 522.49 | 31.70% | | 21.25% |
| 1978 | 396.72 | 13.85% | ... $26,208 | |
| 1977 | 348.45 | 2.25% | | |
| 1976 | 340.80 | 24.96% | | |
| 1975 | 272.72 | 33.36% | 1971 - 1975 | |
| 1974 | 204.50 | -26.23% | | 1.16% |
| 1973 | 277.23 | -23.83% | ... $10,595 | |
| 1972 | 363.96 | 14.83% | | |
| 1971 | 316.95 | 23.13% | | |
| 1970 | 257.42 | -8.31% | 1966 - 1970 | |
| 1969 | 280.75 | -12.43% | | 5.93% |
| 1968 | 320.58 | 17.13% | ... $13,339 | |
| 1967 | 273.70 | 44.59% | | |
| 1966 | 189.29 | -1.91% | | |
| 1965 | 192.98 | 28.76% | 1961 - 1965 | |
| 1964 | 149.88 | 13.65% | | 13.37% |
| 1963 | 131.87 | 21.54% | ... $18,727 | |
| 1962 | 108.50 | -16.88% | | |
| 1961 | 130.53 | 26.67% | | |
| 1960 | 103.05 | 3.05% | | |

How a $10,000 investment performed over

| 5 years | 10 years | 15 years | 20 years | 25 years | 35 years |
|---|---|---|---|---|---|
| 1991 - 1995 | | | | | |
| $20,916 (15.90%)^ | 1986 - 1995 | | | | |
| | $33,915 (12.99%) | 1981 - 1995 | | | |
| | | $63,140 (13.07%) | 1976 - 1995 | | |
| | | | $165,476 (15.06%) | 1971 - 1995 | |
| | | | | $175,315 (12.14%) | 1961 - 1995 |
| | | | | | $437,953 (11.40%) |

^ annual compound rate of return for that period
* Source: Lipper Analytical Services.

©1996 Chase Global Data & Research
73 Junction Square, Concord, MA 01742

## Lipper Growth Fund Average^

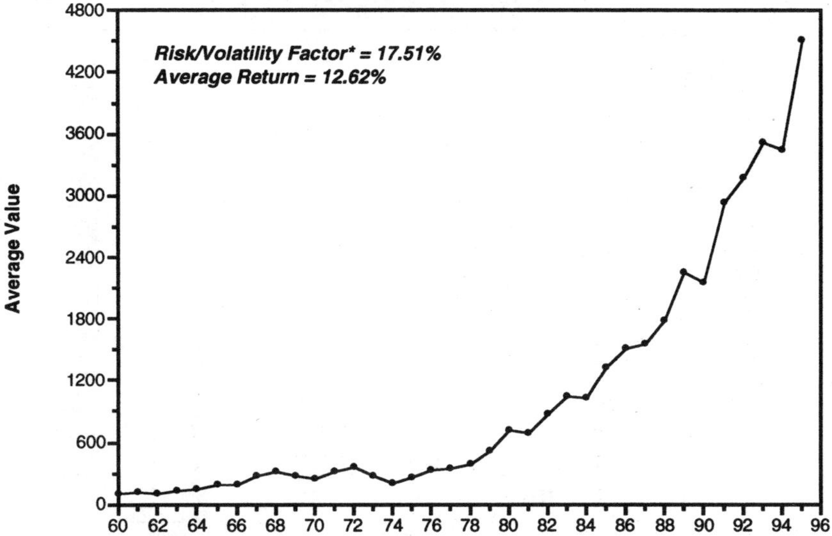


*Standard Deviation
^dividends included

## Lipper Growth Fund Average^ vs. S&P 500 Composite Index^ and Lipper Income Fund Average^

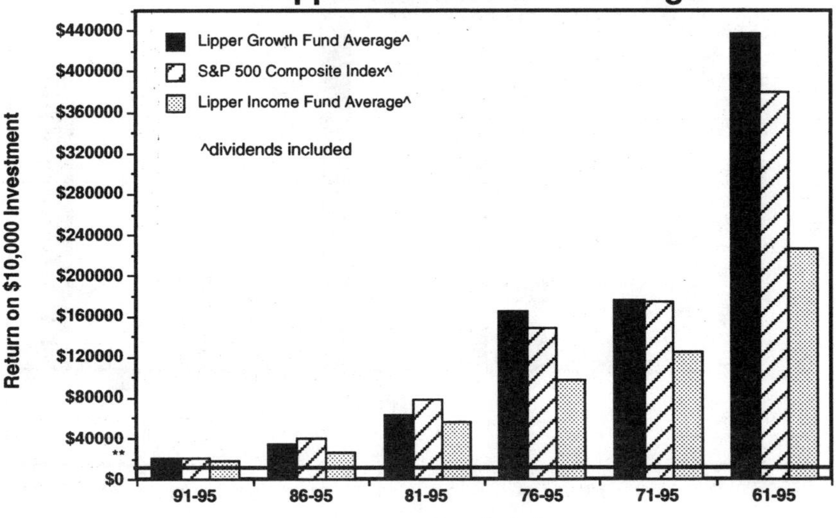


**Initial Investment: $10,000

©1996 Chase Global Data & Research
73 Junction Square, Concord, MA 01742

## Lipper Growth Fund Average^ vs. 3-Month T-Bill and Crude Oil

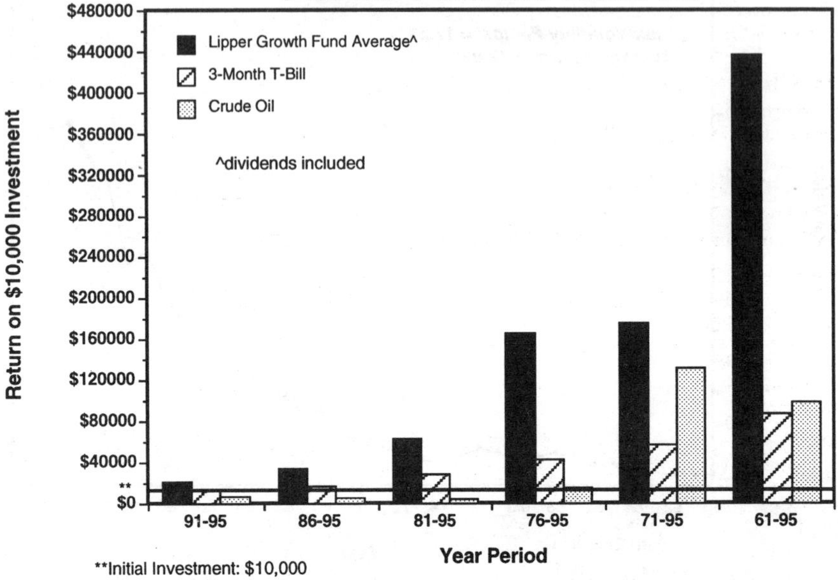


## Lipper Growth Fund Average^ vs. Inflation

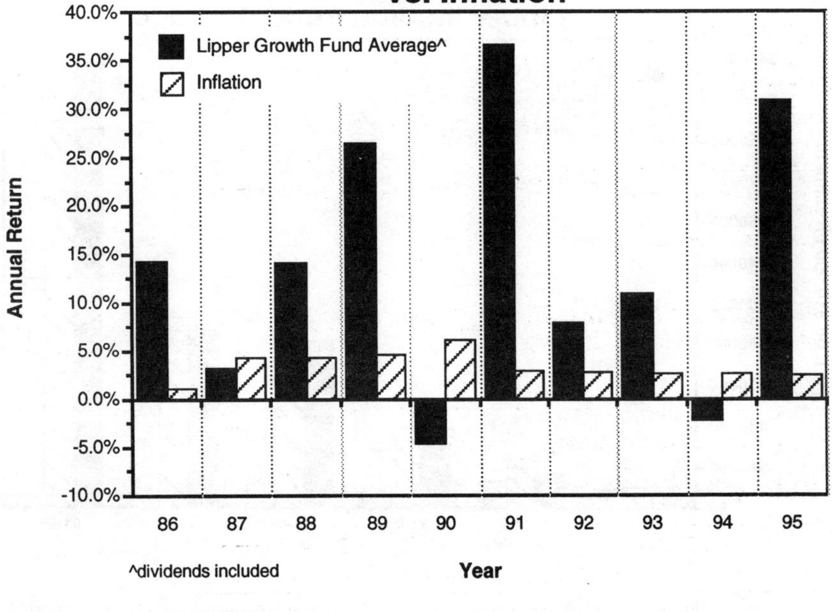


©1996 Chase Global Data & Research
73 Junction Square, Concord, MA 01742

# ORDER FORM

| Product | Quantity | Price |
|---|---|---|
| **1996 Chase Investment Performance Digest**<br>Reviewing over 80 investment subjects covering 1960 thru 1995.<br>400 pages @ **$23.95, plus $4** shipping and handling. | ______ | $ ________ |
| **1996 Chase Guide to Investment Performance**<br>Reviewing over 20 investment subjects covering 1960 thru 1995.<br>160 pages @ **$11.95, plus $4** shipping and handling. | ______ | $ ________ |
| **1996 Chase Page Charts**<br>6 Major Investments. 1960 thru 1995.<br>8.5" x 11", full-color, laminated. @ **$9.95**. Please indicate quantities: | ______ | $ ________ |

_______ Mutual Fund Investing _______ Global Investing

_______ Equity Investing _______ Balanced Investing

_______ Risk: Stocks vs. Bonds _______ Risk: Global Investing

| | | |
|---|---|---|
| **1996 Chase WALL Charts**<br>***Mutual Fund Investing in the Modern Era***<br>6 Major Investments. 1960 thru 1995.<br>37" x 24", full-color, laminated. @ **$23.95.** | ______ | $ ________ |
| ***InvestmentView*® Software**<br>Easy to use, Powerful graphics, with performance and risk data from 1960 to present on 300+ indices. Windows 3.1. 4 MB RAM and 5 MB in hard drive required. Monthly data. | ______ | $ ________ |

**Quarterly Shipments** **$295/year** _______

**Monthly Shipments** **$425/year** _______

| | | |
|---|---|---|
| ***InvestmentView*® Hypothetical Software**<br>All features of ***InvestmentView*®** plus 8,000+ Lipper Mutal Funds with returns and characteristics. College & Retirement Planning (with college tuition database). Disclaimers for printouts, more.<br>Windows 3.1. 4 MB RAM. 60 MB hard disk. Monthly data shipped quarterly. @ **$495** | ______ | $ ________ |
| **SINGLE Edition *InvestmentView*® Version**<br>Indicate Monthly Edition (__________) **@ $129** | ______ | $ ________ |
| **SINGLE Edition *InvestmentView*® Hypothetical Version**<br>Indicate Quarterly Edition (_____Q) **@ $225** | ______ | $ ________ |
| **College and Retirement Planning**<br>(combined programs) **@ $69**<br>(with College Tuition database and Social Security data) | ______ | $ ________ |
| **FREE DEMO DISK** (30 day working copy) **@ FREE** | ______ | $ N/A |

**CALL FOR INFO on 5000+ Stocks, 2,700+ Variable Annuities, and 1200+ Money Managers Databases.**

**Please see continuation of product listing on reverse side ☞**

**Phone – (800) 639-9494 or (508) 371-9100 FAX – (508) 371-9105**

| Product | Quantity | Price |
|---|---|---|
| **Seminar Slide Show Presentation**<br>***Risks and Returns: Investment Options in the Modern Era***<br>(1960 through 1995) 30 slides with script and audiotape. Please check format(s): | _____ | $ ________ |

SLIDES @ $295_____ OVERHEADS @ $350 ____

DISK @ $150 ____ (WINDOWS ___ or MAC ___)

Individual Slide @ $35 Please identify: ________________

5 Slides @ $100 Please identify: ____________________________

______________________________________________________________

**Subtotal** $ ____________

(Massachusetts residents include 5% tax) $ ____________

## Method of Payment:

_____Check or money order _____VISA _____MasterCard

Card Account Number ______________________________________

Card Expires ______________________________________

Signature ______________________________________

## Ship To:

Name ______________________________________

Title ______________________________________

Company ______________________________________

Address ______________________________________

______________________________________

City________________________ State__________ Zip__________

Business Telephone ( ) ______________________

## Shipping and Handling Charges

**Chase Investment Performance Digest and the The Investor's Guide to Investment Performance**

| | |
|---|---|
| 1-3 | $4 each |
| 4-24 | $3 each |
| 25-99 | $2 each |
| 100+ | Call |

Next day shipping – $18 each

UPS 2nd Day – $9 each

**FREE SHIPPING on these products:**

- InvestmentView® Software
- InvestmentView® Hypothetical Software
- College and Retirement Planning Software
- Chase Page and Wall Charts
- Chase Seminar Slide Show and/or Individual Slides

**To order, please call (800) 639-9494 or (508) 371-9100**

**For fastest service, credit card orders may be faxed to us at (508) 371-9105**

**❑ Please send me your catalog!**

## LIPPER INCOME MUTUAL FUND AVERAGE

[dividends included; year-end]

| Year | Index Value* | Index Growth | Compound return on a five year $10,000 investment | Annual compound rate of return |
|---|---|---|---|---|
| 1995 | 2355.43 | 21.66% | 1991 - 1995 | |
| 1994 | 1936.07 | -2.92% | | 12.53% |
| 1993 | 1994.31 | 12.17% | ... $18,042 | |
| 1992 | 1777.93 | 10.03% | | |
| 1991 | 1615.86 | 23.77% | | |
| 1990 | 1305.54 | -0.24% | 1986 - 1990 | |
| 1989 | 1308.68 | 13.62% | | 7.77% |
| 1988 | 1151.80 | 12.12% | ... $14,539 | |
| 1987 | 1027.29 | -0.50% | | |
| 1986 | 1032.46 | 14.98% | | |
| 1985 | 897.94 | 24.52% | 1981 - 1985 | |
| 1984 | 721.12 | 12.41% | | 16.53% |
| 1983 | 641.51 | 14.17% | ... $21,489 | |
| 1982 | 561.89 | 26.89% | | |
| 1981 | 442.82 | 5.97% | | |
| 1980 | 417.87 | 13.97% | 1976 - 1980 | |
| 1979 | 366.65 | 12.11% | | 11.62% |
| 1978 | 327.05 | 4.03% | ... $17,324 | |
| 1977 | 314.38 | 3.95% | | |
| 1976 | 302.43 | 25.38% | | |
| 1975 | 241.21 | 24.52% | 1971 - 1975 | |
| 1974 | 193.71 | -11.09% | | 5.05% |
| 1973 | 217.88 | -10.05% | ... $12,796 | |
| 1972 | 242.22 | 9.27% | | |
| 1971 | 221.67 | 17.59% | | |
| 1970 | 188.51 | 4.19% | 1966 - 1970 | |
| 1969 | 180.93 | -11.76% | | 3.18% |
| 1968 | 205.04 | 15.00% | ... $11,696 | |
| 1967 | 178.30 | 17.27% | | |
| 1966 | 152.04 | -5.67% | | |
| 1965 | 161.18 | 5.65% | 1961 - 1965 | |
| 1964 | 152.56 | 13.40% | | 9.15% |
| 1963 | 134.53 | 13.31% | ... $15,491 | |
| 1962 | 118.73 | -2.68% | | |
| 1961 | 122.00 | 17.25% | | |
| 1960 | 104.05 | 4.05% | | |

How a $10,000 investment performed over

| 5 years | 10 years | 15 years | 20 years | 25 years | 35 years |
|---|---|---|---|---|---|
| 1991 - 1995 | | | | | |
| $18,042 (12.53%)^ | 1986 - 1995 | | | | |
| | $26,231 (10.12%) | 1981 - 1995 | | | |
| | | $56,367 (12.22%) | 1976 - 1995 | | |
| | | | $97,650 (12.07%) | 1971 - 1995 | |
| | | | | $124,950 (10.63%) | 1961 - 1995 |
| | | | | | $226,374 (9.32%) |

^ annual compound rate of return for that period
* Source: Lipper Analytical Services.

©1996 Chase Global Data & Research
73 Junction Square, Concord, MA 01742

## Lipper Income Fund Average^

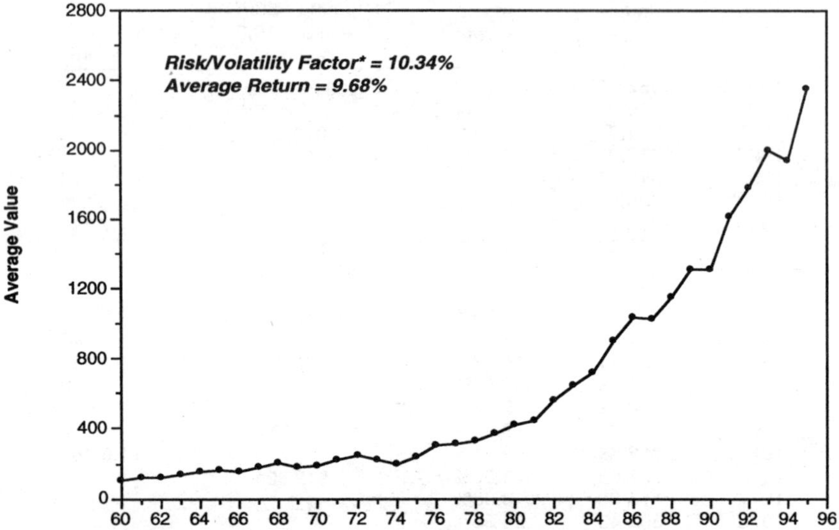


*Standard Deviation
^dividends included

## Lipper Income Fund Average^ vs. 3-Month T-Bill and 3-Year T-Note

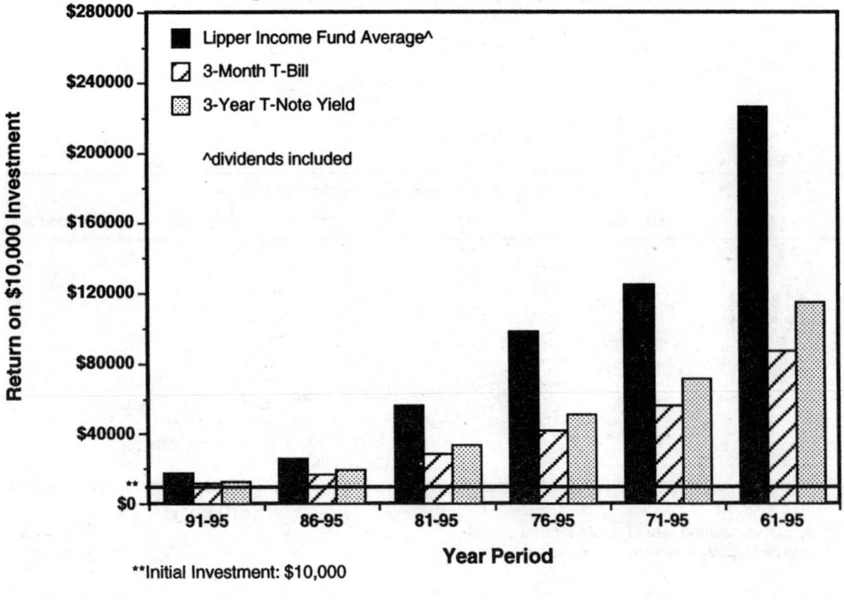


**Initial Investment: $10,000

©1996 Chase Global Data & Research
73 Junction Square, Concord, MA 01742

## Lipper Income Fund Average^ vs. Silver and Farmland

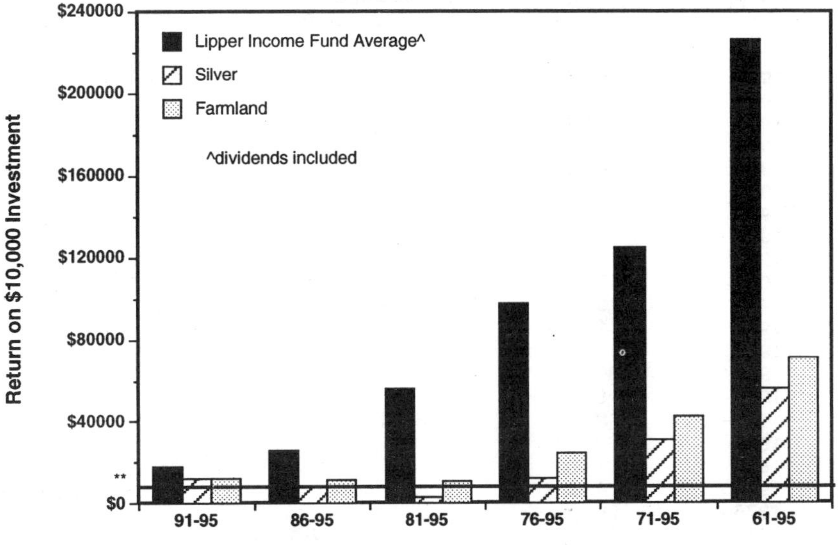


**Initial Investment: $10,000

## Lipper Income Fund Average^ vs. Inflation

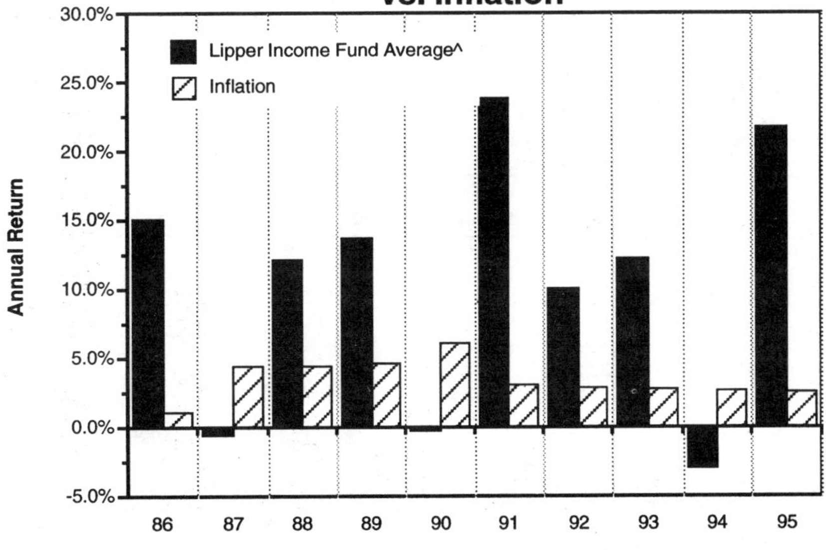


^dividends included

©1996 Chase Global Data & Research
73 Junction Square, Concord, MA 01742

## LIPPER FIXED INCOME MUTUAL FUND AVERAGE

[dividends included]

| Year | Index Growth* | Compound return on a five year $10,000 investment | Annual compound rate of return |
|---|---|---|---|
| 1995 | 15.22% | 1991 - 1995 | |
| 1994 | -3.28% | | 9.25% |
| 1993 | 9.73% | ... $15,563 | |
| 1992 | 7.78% | | |
| 1991 | 18.08% | | |
| 1990 | 4.95% | 1986 - 1990 | |
| 1989 | 10.05% | | 7.54% |
| 1988 | 8.42% | ... $14,384 | |
| 1987 | 1.51% | | |
| 1986 | 13.16% | | |
| 1985 | 19.93% | 1981 - 1985 | |
| 1984 | 11.76% | | 15.27% |
| 1983 | 10.28% | ... $20,351 | |
| 1982 | 30.18% | | |
| 1981 | 5.76% | | |
| 1980 | 2.79% | 1976 - 1980 | |
| 1979 | 2.77% | | 6.16% |
| 1978 | 1.60% | ... $13,485 | |
| 1977 | 4.40% | | |
| 1976 | 20.35% | | |
| 1975 | 17.63% | 1971 - 1975 | |
| 1974 | -7.90% | | 4.62% |
| 1973 | -6.37% | ... $12,534 | |
| 1972 | 8.59% | | |
| 1971 | 13.79% | | |
| 1970 | 3.98% | 1966 - 1970 | |
| 1969 | -10.27% | | 1.73% |
| 1968 | 11.29% | ... $10,896 | |
| 1967 | 9.67% | | |
| 1966 | -4.32% | | |
| 1965 | 7.25% | 1961 - 1965 | |
| 1964 | 9.97% | | 9.27% |
| 1963 | 12.00% | ... $15,575 | |
| 1962 | -0.70% | | |
| 1961 | 18.74% | | |
| 1960 | 0.80% | | |

How a $10,000 investment performed over

| 5 years | 10 years | 15 years | 20 years | 25 years | 35 years |
|---|---|---|---|---|---|
| 1991 - 1995 | | | | | |
| $15,563 (9.25%)^ | 1986 - 1995 | | | | |
| | $22,386 (8.39%) | 1981 - 1995 | | | |
| | | $45,556 (10.64%) | 1976 - 1995 | | |
| | | | $61,433 (9.50%) | 1971 - 1995 | |
| | | | | $77,000 (8.51%) | 1961 - 1995 |
| | | | | | $130,670 (7.62%) |

^ annual compound rate of return for that period

* Source: Lipper Analytical Services.

©1996 Chase Global Data & Research
73 Junction Square, Concord, MA 01742

## Lipper Fixed Income Fund Average^

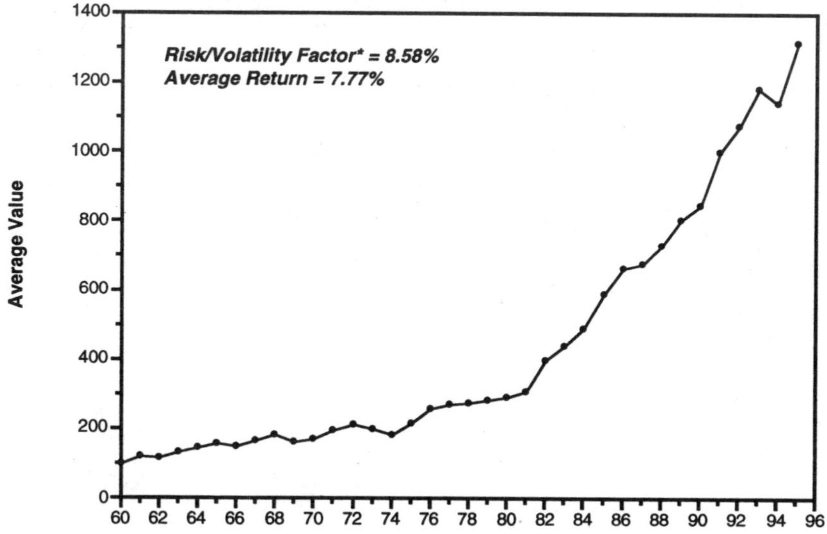


*Standard Deviation
^dividends included

## Lipper Fixed Income Fund Average^ vs. 3-Month Certificate of Deposit and Lipper Income Fund Average^

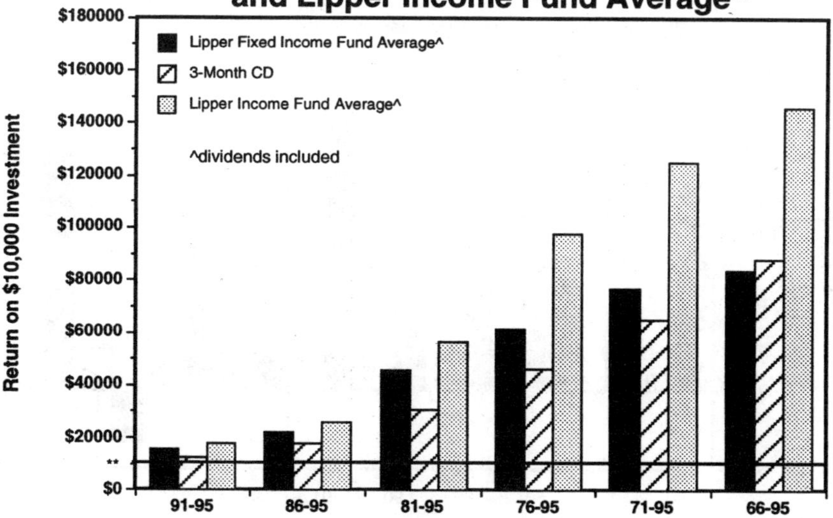


**Initial Investment: $10,000

©1996 Chase Global Data & Research
73 Junction Square, Concord, MA 01742

## Lipper Fixed Income Fund Average^ vs. REITs and Morgan Stanley World Equity Index^

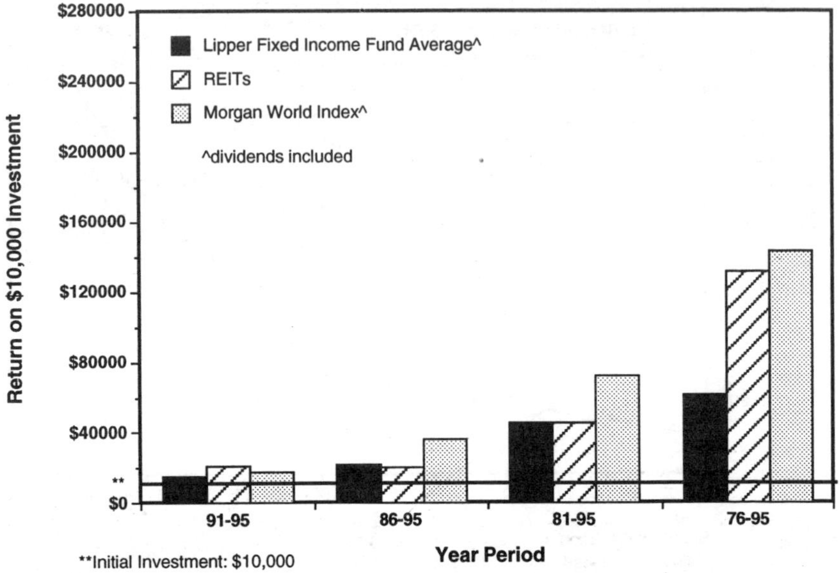


## Lipper Fixed Income Fund Average^ vs. Inflation

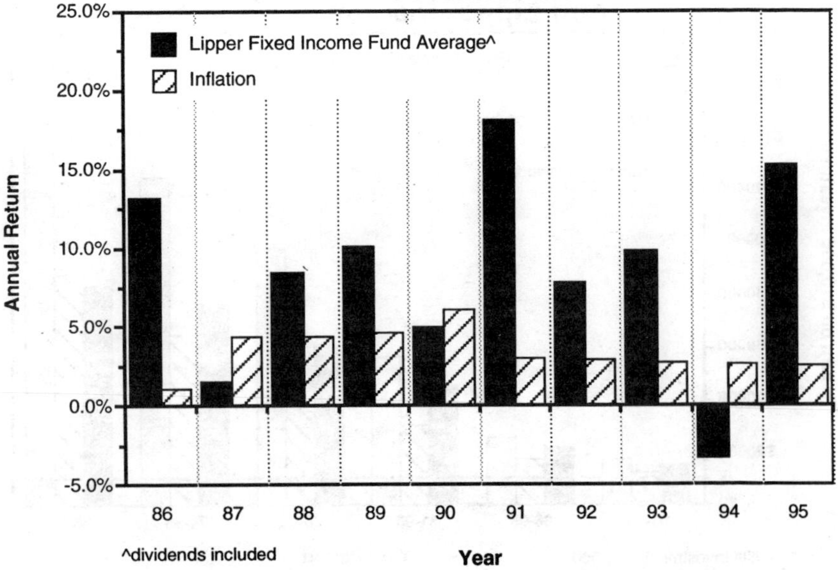


©1996 Chase Global Data & Research
73 Junction Square, Concord, MA 01742

## LIPPER GENERAL MUNICIPAL BOND MUTUAL FUND AVERAGE

[dividends included]

| Year | Index Growth* | Compound return on a five year $10,000 investment | Annual compound rate of return |
|---|---|---|---|
| 1995 | 16.84% | 1991 - 1995 | |
| 1994 | -6.53% | | 8.37% |
| 1993 | 12.35% | ... $14,950 | |
| 1992 | 8.74% | | |
| 1991 | 12.05% | | |
| 1990 | 6.07% | 1986 - 1990 | |
| 1989 | 9.62% | | 8.78% |
| 1988 | 11.47% | ... $15,228 | |
| 1987 | -1.01% | | |
| 1986 | 18.69% | | |
| 1985 | 20.17% | 1981 - 1985 | |
| 1984 | 8.69% | | 13.39% |
| 1983 | 10.29% | ... $18,742 | |
| 1982 | 40.11% | | |
| 1981 | -7.14% | | |
| 1980 | -11.51% | | |
| 1979 | -1.87% | | |
| 1978 | -3.84% | | |
| 1977 | 6.89% | | |

How a $10,000 investment performed over

| 5 years | 10 years | 15 years |
|---|---|---|
| 1991 - 1995<br>$14,950<br>(8.37%)^ | 1986 - 1995<br>$22,766<br>(8.57%) | 1981 - 1995<br>$42,668<br>(10.16%) |

^ annual compound rate of return for that period
* Source: Lipper Analytical Services.

©1996 Chase Global Data & Research
73 Junction Square, Concord, MA 01742

## Lipper General Municipal Bond Fund Average^

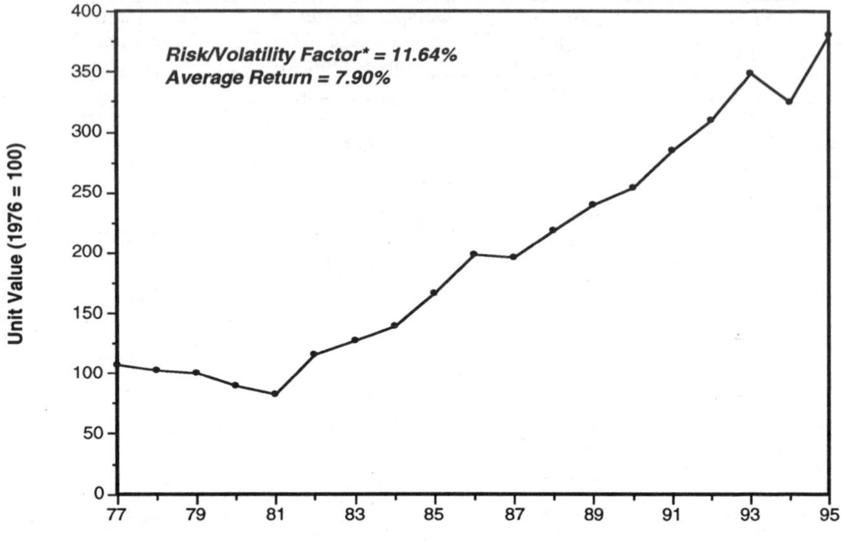


*Standard Deviation
^dividends included

## Lipper General Municipal Bond Fund Average^ vs. S&P Municipal Bond Yield, Lehman Intermediate Treasury Bond Index, and 3-Month T-Bill

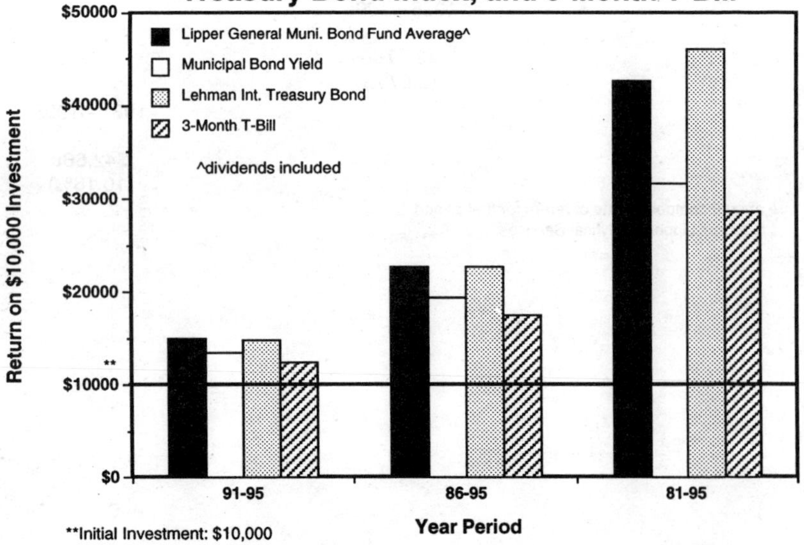


**Initial Investment: $10,000

©1996 Chase Global Data & Research
73 Junction Square, Concord, MA 01742

## Lipper General Municipal Bond Fund Average^ vs. U.S. Dollar Index, Value Line Composite Index, and Gold

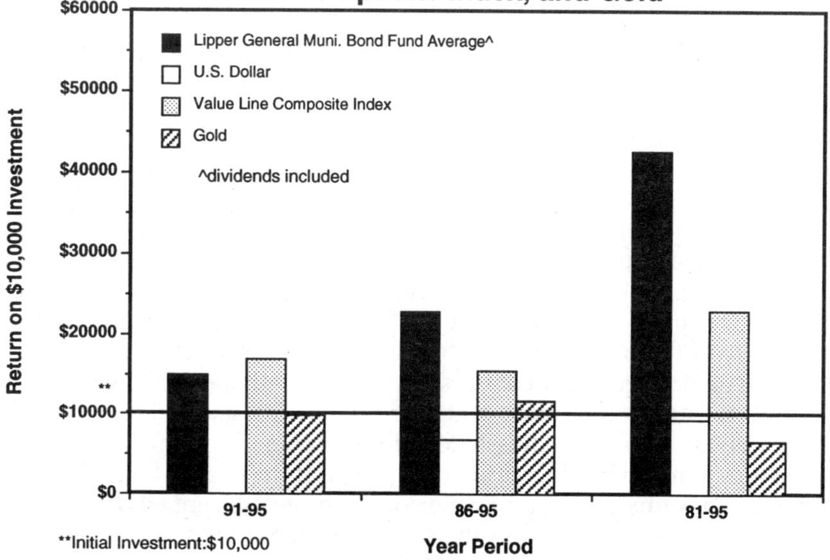


## Lipper General Muni. Bond Fund Average^ vs. Inflation

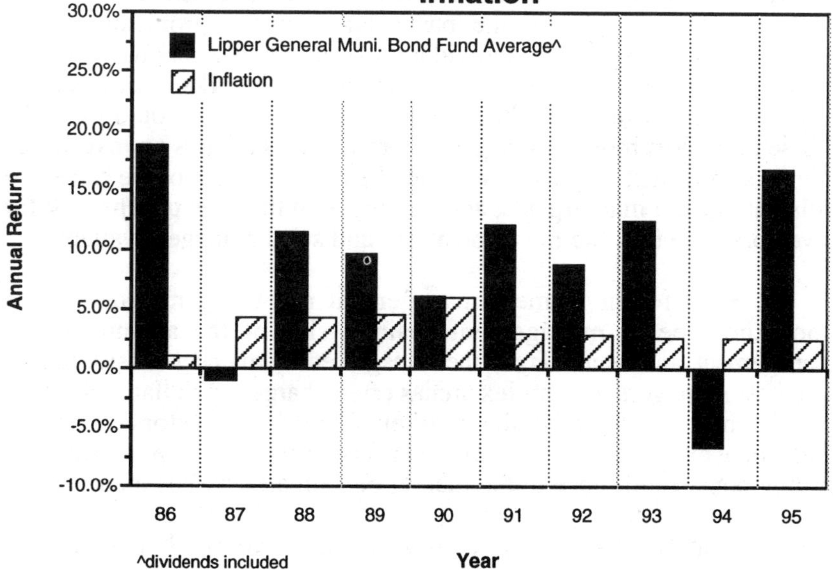


©1996 Chase Global Data & Research
73 Junction Square, Concord, MA 01742

Chapter Ten

# Equity Money Managers

In the United States today over $4 trillion is managed by investment advisors, or professional money managers. The amount of assets under management has exploded more than twelve fold since 1980. Independent investment advisors and mutual fund managers initiate over three fourths of all transactions on the stock exchanges. A quarter century ago the situation was reversed, with the public generating over 80% of all transactions and institutions initiating the minority. In 1950 private pension funds held only 0.8% of all U.S. equities, but today the number has increased over twenty fold to about 20%. Given the massive sums placed under the control of investment advisors, there is a growing need to monitor their performance results.

While investment management can take many forms, the key strength of the investment advisor/money manager is that they provide a customized approach versus the mutual fund alternative for pools of capital ranging from minimum account sizes of $50,000 to over $100 million—depending upon the particular advisor. Ironically, many mutual fund managers and individual investment advisors have consistently underperformed the major market benchmarks. But equally important, many investors know that their own results would likely be worse than most money managers. Fortunately, statistics on investment advisors show that they usually shield clients from much of the excessive volatility of the marketplace, and thereby earn their keep. The task for investors is to find the most consistent and solid manager available.

Fees for investment management run the gamut depending upon the type of management desired, size of the account under management, and desirability of the management team under consideration. The best managers in complex arenas often charge top dollar, but if they consistently outperform the marketplace few investors mind the additional expense. Low cost managers can turn out to be very expensive if they consistently lose to the market benchmarks and/or their peers.

Generally speaking, equity managers charge between 0.5%


©1996 Chase Global Data & Research
73 Junction Square, Concord, MA 01742

and 1.2% for accounts under management in the range of $250,000 to $10 million. Accounts over $25 million may see fees as low as 0.20%. Fixed income investment advisor management fees are usually lower than equity managers, and international money managers are today's most expensive form of investment advisor—with the notable exception of commodity asset managers. Investment advisor accounts may begin at $50,000 in assets, but today truly individualized service to accounts of that size is rare. Typical minimums today are $250,000 to $1 million and more. But whatever the minimum, the marketplace requires the buyer beware—for even high priced, high minimum account investment advisors don't always provide the best results. And one should also always remember that past performance is by no means a perfect indicator of future results.

CDA Investment Technologies is one of several firms monitoring the results of investment advisors. CDA monitors over 3,000 professional money managers in the equity, fixed income, and balanced investment arenas. The CDA Equity Investment Advisor Performance Index which follows reflects results gathered by CDA Investment Technologies based on reports filed under Section 13(f) of the 1975 Securities Acts Amendments. All institutions managing $100 million or more are required to report their common stock holdings to the SEC as of each quarter. CDA then assumes the securities held are not sold for the quarter, and calculates weighted average returns inclusive of dividends on that basis. The index is weighted with managers having substantial pools of capital under management impacting the Index to a greater degree. While the practice of intra-quarter transaction deletion may seem suspect, over time quarter to quarter returns appear to fairly reflect performance.

There are several characteristics inherent to performance data derived from 13(f) filings. It allows for all accounts and positions of each manager to be monitored—which is not always the case with results presented by the investment advisors. And the computation of each manager's results is done in a uniform manner, not subject to variance in methodology of computation. Lastly, there is a sufficient universe within the the CDA Equity Investment Advisor Index from which one can draw a reasonable conclusion as to how managers are performing.

The following Performance Table shows the average Equity Investment Advisor has performed in a positive manner. Overall the Index beats growth mutual funds over the past 3, 5, 10, and 15 years. Of note, its volatility is above average and greater than mutual funds. The Index should serve as an excellent benchmark by which an investor can locate and evaluate an investment advisor.

©1996 Chase Global Data & Research
73 Junction Square, Concord, MA 01742

## CDA EQUITY MONEY MANAGER PERFORMANCE INDEX

[year-end]

| Year | Total* Return | Compound return on a five year $10,000 investment | Annual compound rate of return |
|---|---|---|---|
| 1995 | 36.03% | 1991 - 1995 | |
| 1994 | -0.05% | | 18.25% |
| 1993 | 13.40% | ... $23,125 | |
| 1992 | 9.40% | | |
| 1991 | 37.10% | | |
| 1990 | -6.40% | 1986 - 1990 | |
| 1989 | 28.90% | | 11.31% |
| 1988 | 17.80% | ... $17,090 | |
| 1987 | 2.60% | | |
| 1986 | 17.20% | | |
| 1985 | 32.80% | 1981 - 1985 | |
| 1984 | 0.70% | | 13.36% |
| 1983 | 20.90% | ... $18,716 | |
| 1982 | 22.50% | | |
| 1981 | -5.50% | | |
| 1980 | 37.30% | | |

How a $10,000 investment performed over

| 5 years | 10 years | 15 years |
|---|---|---|
| 1991 - 1995 | 1986 - 1995 | 1981 - 1995 |
| $23,125 | $39,522 | $73,970 |
| (18.25%)^ | (14.73%) | (14.27%) |

^ annual compound rate of return for that period
* Source: ©1995 CDA Investment Technologies, Inc.

©1996 Chase Global Data & Research
73 Junction Square, Concord, MA 01742

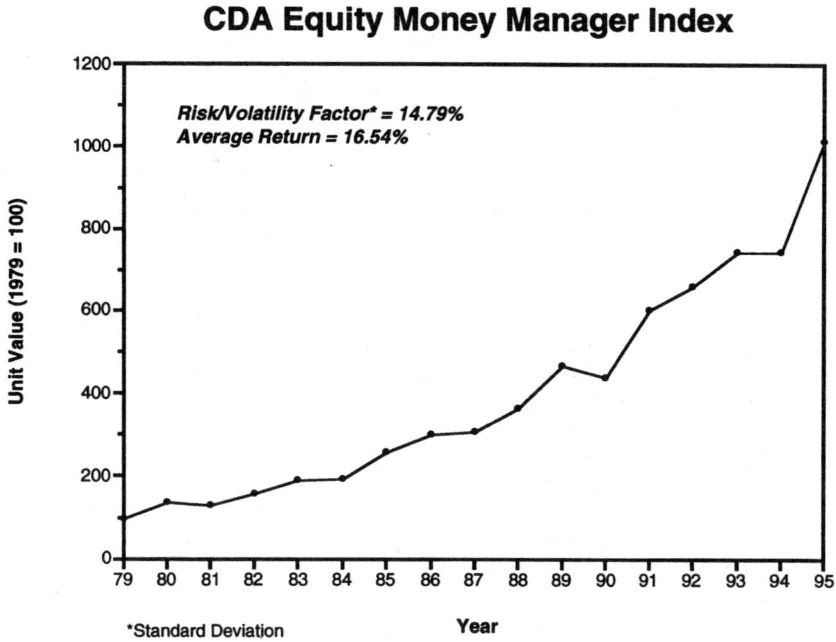


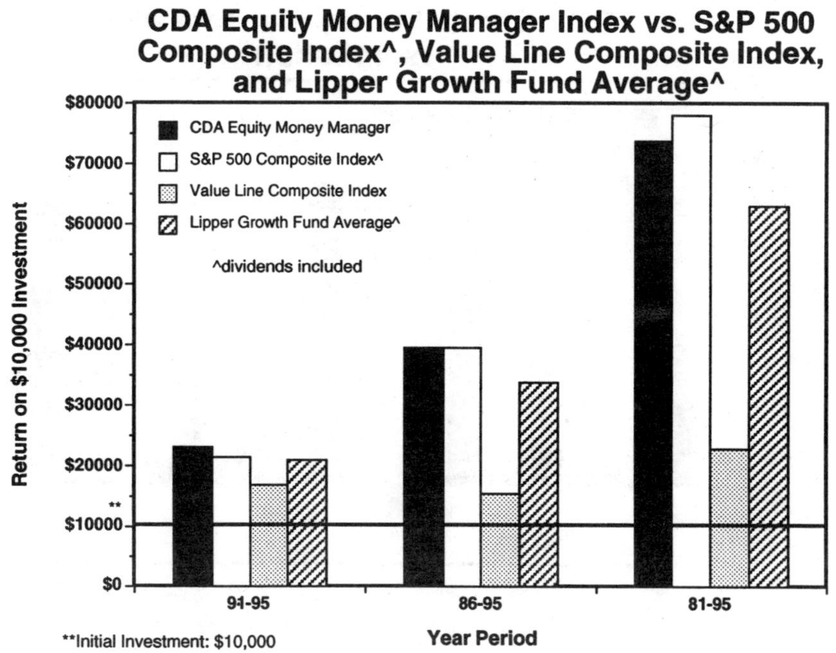


©1996 Chase Global Data & Research
73 Junction Square, Concord, MA 01742

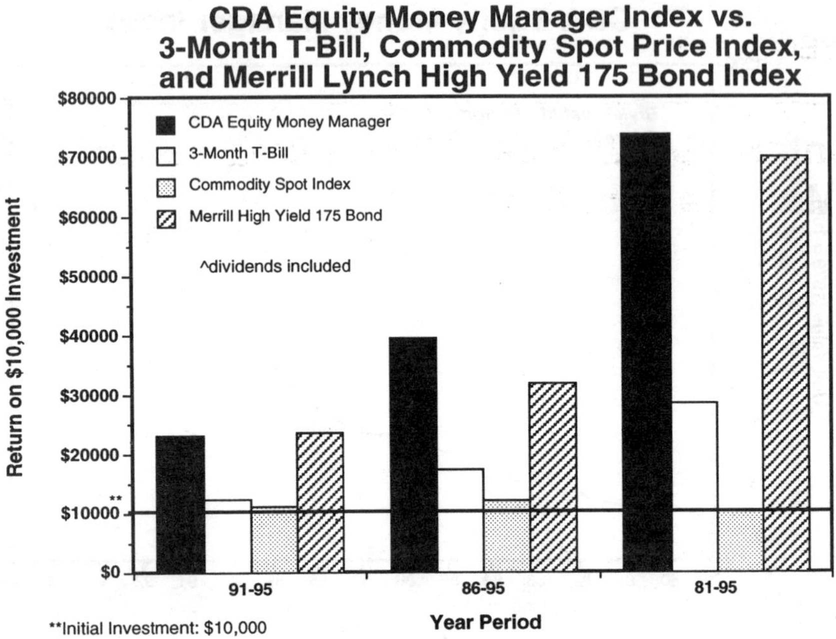


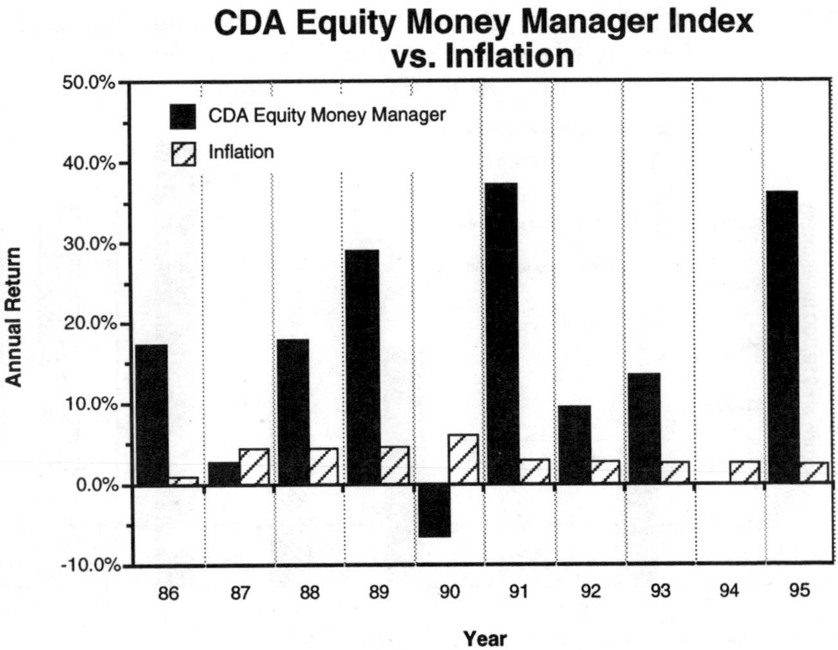


©1996 Chase Global Data & Research
73 Junction Square, Concord, MA 01742

SECTION V

# International Equity and Fixed Income Markets & Indices

Chapter Eleven

# International Stock Markets

The first exchanges did not trade stocks; instead they traded agricultural and commodity products, although other forms of assets were traded shortly after the exchanges became involved with commodities. By the Middle Ages, exchanges were familiar with the use of credit, purchasing and selling, and required in most cases supporting documents, drafts, notes, and bills of exchange.

The first stock exchange is thought to have been initiated in France sometime in the 12th century—the Paris Exchange, called La Bourse, started in 1138. That exchange traded in commercial bills of exchange and duly labeled its traders as agents, the forerunners of stockbrokers. Many more exchanges appeared in the 16th and 17th centuries in Europe, primarily in Amsterdam, Great Britain, Denmark and Germany. (Amsterdam's Effectenbeurs, which began in 1602, is officially the oldest Stock Exchange in the world.) The most famous stock traded in the early years of the exchanges was the Dutch East India Company, traded as early as the 1600's. By 1773, London stock dealers who had previously met in coffee houses set up their own formal location. By the 19th century securities were traded on a formal basis in almost all industrialized countries.

Even from early times some exchanges believed in formal regulation of their transactions while others regulated little and let the marketplace accept the consequences. That is still true today with a large number of exchanges throughout the world—some are quite tightly regulated like those in the U.S., Canada, and Australia, while others in Japan, Mexico, and Hong Kong are considered less so.

The saying "the world is getting smaller" is nowhere more applicable than to the international stock exchanges. Americans are investing more and more each year in foreign exchanges. At the same time, foreigners, especially Japanese and Europeans, have been investing huge sums in the American marketplace. A primary reason for foreigners' investment in the U.S. is the huge trade surpluses they run in the United

 ©1996 Chase Global Data & Research
73 Junction Square, Concord, MA 01742

States. Money flowing into the U.S. stock market from Japan alone exceeded $5 billion per month in the late 1980's. And the major political changes which have taken place in Eastern Europe have enticed much investment toward Europe—and especially Germany.

Foreign investment in the U.S. marketplace is growing. By 1995, foreigners accounted for over $400 billion in ownership of stocks on the NYSE, a ten fold increase in one decade. Foreigners own almost 10% of all stocks on the NYSE, or $1 of every $10 owned by all stockholders of the NYSE. Overall foreign holdings of U.S. financial assets now total over $1 trillion. Yet Americans hold only about $650 billion in foreign assets, with slightly more than half of that total in securities. Such statistics parallel the fact that in 1985 the U.S. crossed a major threshold. It became worldwide a "net debtor" of several hundred billion dollars—despite having formerly been a "net creditor". The U.S. net credit position of several hundred billion dollars in 1983 was erased in only two years. The net debtor condition begun in 1985 has expanded to the present with no signs of abating.

U.S. investors are expanding their investment in international markets, primarily through mutual funds. The number of U.S. mutual funds devoted to foreign securities has grown more than ten fold since 1986. Today there are over 300 such funds, with over equity based from which investors may choose. However there are over 2,500 equity mutual funds, such that global equity mutual funds represent only 15% of the equity funds marketed in the United States. Sales of global bond and global equity mutual funds have doubled since 1991 to over $30 billion in 1995.

There is about $16 trillion in foreign equity marketplaces worldwide, most of it tracked by Morgan Stanley & Co. through the Morgan Stanley Capital International Perspective. Morgan Stanley's World Index grew over 300% during the past decade, and about 1800% over the past quarter century. International investment has a proven appeal, and capital continues to flow in that direction. Private pension funds have increased their foreign investments from $20 billion in 1980 to over $300 billion by 1995. In late 1995 U.S. investors reversed a long term trend and tallied holdings of $350 billion in foreign shares—exceeding the total foreigners held in U.S. shares.

In the U.S., investing through the actual exchanges of foreign lands might seem unnecessary because there are presently about 300 foreign equities trading American Depository receipts (ADRs) on exchanges in the U.S. The ADRs and foreign securities are extremely

©1996 Chase Global Data & Research
73 Junction Square, Concord, MA 01742

popular, with annual total volume setting a record in 1995 at over $275 billion on 10 billion shares traded.

Americans have a diverse ADR menu from which to purchase. Today they are over 170 from Australia; over 140 from Japan; and over 130 stocks from the United Kingdom. These totals represent a sizeable percentage of the total listings of companies at the ADR's home exchange. Also, mutual funds are investing in international marketplaces, having increased those holdings fifty fold from the 1985 level of $1.9 billion to over $100 billion today, representing hundreds of mutual funds of all types.

Addressing both currency changes and stock exchange performance gives one a total return in an international investment. And currency fluctuation is a major factor in final returns. In 1992-1994 turmoil ruled the international currency markets, and investors gained a greater appreciation of the importance of currency movement in overall performance return. History gives us additional examples as well, for in 1986 over half the total return gained from Canadian, French, Swiss, British, Australian, and Norwegian stock markets derived from movements in the dollar. One must remember that a strong performance in the U.S. dollar (for Americans) negatively impacts international investments, unless currency movements are hedged in some manner. Conversely, from 1985-1987 and in 1994 alone, several major foreign markets received additional boosts in return of over 15% per annum due to the weak U.S. dollar, when calculated versus a purely domestic investment. The U.S. dollar made a post World War II low falling under 90 yen in 1994, aiding global investments by its decline.

It is also important to note that exchanges have different characteristics, some of which are major. P/E ratios (price/earnings) throughout the globe can differ widely. For example, at year-end 1995 Tokyo's P/E (price/earnings) average was 105 versus a 17 P/E for the NYSE. Tokyo's stock exchange is considered extremely volatile and less regulated, with four major brokerage firms controlling much of the action. For example, in the not too distant past (1987) Japan's stock market was the world's largest, but then came its crash. In that same year a single Japanese security, Nippon Telephone and Telegraph, had a market capitalization of over $300 billion, making it alone worth more than 6 major world stock exchanges. Since then the stock has lost about 75% of its value, but it is still mammoth nevertheless. In another unusual note, bank stocks in Japan make up over 25% of overall equity value. But in another display of foreign market volatility those bank stocks tripled in value in six months during 1987. Today, however,

©1996 Chase Global Data & Research
73 Junction Square, Concord, MA 01742

many question their true financial worth given the depreciation of the Japanese stock market and weakening real estate values.

Before you consider investing internationally keep in mind that both accounting and reporting procedures are different for foreign companies on the foreign exchanges. For example, in Japan annual reports are very brief and do not consider finances of subsidiaries. Administration of the paperwork is also much more difficult. Michael Lipper, President of Lipper Analytical Services says, "Just getting hold of the shares is hard—and then there's getting the dividends and getting the reports." In addition, spreads between bid and ask may be much wider in foreign securities, quotes are not always available or necessarily reliable, and political and economic developments are oftentimes less clearly reported, understandable, or predictable.

On the other hand there are always the sleeper investment arenas that are worth considering, and make international investing so interesting. One such example was the Swiss market of 1987. The Swiss passed legislation late that year which for the first time allowed Swiss pension funds to put 30% of their assets into stocks—up from the former 10% limitation. This obviously caused a sharp increase in demand for Swiss securities. After a weak 1987 (-24.4%), the Swiss market reversed direction and rose almost 50% from 1988 to 1990. And in 1991 Mexico, Argentina, and Chile all more than doubled over a 12 month period.

Given all the activity occurring worldwide, there is an obvious need to improve communications between the marketplaces of the world. One step in that direction began in the late 1980's with the initiation of night trading at the Chicago Board of Trade, the first U.S. attempt to bring foreigners into our marketplace on a 24 hour basis. In 1990 Globex, an electronic global trading system linking North America, Europe, and Asia began operations. In 1992 NASDAQ International was introduced. It offers trading in global markets from 3:30 PM to 9 AM, which inclusive of the foreign markets own trading hours equates to a 24 hour marketplace. There is no longer any doubt that all of the world's financial capitols see a need to link exchanges—and better understand and follow each other's markets. The investment world is truly shrinking, and business will never be the same again.

©1996 Chase Global Data & Research
73 Junction Square, Concord, MA 01742

Chapter Twelve

# British Stock Market

After the Tokyo and NYSE, London's International Stock Exchange is the third largest stock exchange in the world. One of six exchanges in the United Kingdom, it is about 20% the size of the NYSE. Approximately seventy percent of its aggregate market value derives from foreign stocks. However, when those foreign stocks are added to the U.K. listings the overall market value of the Exchange is about half of the NYSE. The International Stock Exchange, with over 2,700 listings has even more equities listed for trading than the New York Stock Exchange. Unknown to many, London's International Exchange has been truly a spectacular investment performer, ranking at the top over the long term among all subjects tracked by Chase Global Data & Research.

London's International Stock Exchange bears a close resemblance to American exchanges in regulation and structure. Started in 1773, the Exchange has been at its present site since 1802. It recently revised its operating system which had been established in 1908 and survived unchanged for 78 years. But recent changes in world trading required it to bend with the forces of the marketplace. In 1986, for the first time, foreigners were allowed to own 100% of Exchange member firms, a change dubbed the "Big Bang." As a result of Big Bang changes, the former London Stock Exchange renamed itself the International Stock Exchange. During that same year the International Stock Exchange phased out fixed commissions, a move which has greatly contributed to growing competition.

In terms of size and capitalization, United States firms far outweigh British brokerage houses, moreso than their population differences of 260 million people versus 65 million as of 1995. For example, the major London securities firms have about 1,000 employees—yet Merrill Lynch has over 25,000. Why? The Chairman of Credit Suisse First Boston said "there is a popular saying that an Englishman who makes $5 million retires to the country, but an American tries to make another $5 million." Presently, there are scores of brokerage


©1996 Chase Global Data & Research
73 Junction Square, Concord, MA 01742

firms on the International Stock Exchange, but it is expected that by the end of the decade about one dozen major brokerage firms will remain, controlling over 70% of business.

Today's format of the former London Stock Exchange is similar to the U.S.'s NASDAQ automated quotation system of market makers. On the International Exchange there are many market makers for each security who provide competing bids/asks—in contrast to the NYSE where a single "specialist" exclusively provides the bid/ask. Today, brokerage firms are also now making markets in stocks and have their own trading floors, which cost as much as $50 million each. Changes to date have been successful, in that equity volume in British securities has more than tripled since 1988 due to the inter-dealer trading.

The British have regulations for the Exchange, but for the most part the major institutions are expected to safeguard and police themselves. The International Exchange is overseen by the Securities and Investment Board which is a compromise between industry self-regulation and an SEC type of regulatory body. Where there are problems, complaints are directed to the Secretary of the Council of the Stock Exchange.

Although the British exchange is becoming quite modern, the individual members still follow old practices such as hunting deer and fox. But while the Exchange members are hunting four-legged prey on country estates, they themselves have become a popular two-legged prey of international brokerage houses. Major British brokerage houses have been purchased over the past several years by Japanese, Chinese, and American firms, among others. British banks have also acquired brokerage houses because they are now permitted to perform brokerage services. (But in 1995 there also came the infamous self-destruction of Britain's oldest bank, Barings PLC, due to over $1 billion in losses caused by unauthorized Japanese futures trading by a trader based in Singapore.)

The International Stock Exchange has many listings, more than any other exchange in the world. Most are foreign companies. The U.S. has the greatest representation—about 200 companies—followed by South Africa's 100 firms. As the International Exchange moves towards its goal of being a 24-hour global securities market, its average daily volume exceeds 100 million shares. In addition to trading securities on the main exchange, there is an off-floor market in stocks (an electronic trading system by Reuters Ltd.), and an unlisted securities market (USM) similar to the AMEX/OTC in the U.S.

©1996 Chase Global Data & Research
73 Junction Square, Concord, MA 01742

Government bonds are the most widely traded financial instrument in Britain and constitute a very large and liquid market. They are issued by the Bank of England and their interest and principal are guaranteed by the British government. British government bonds are called "gilts." Gilts represent 90% of fixed interest securities and 80% of the value of all the securities in Britain. However, gilts are less frequently traded and account for only 20% of the volume of all securities traded in Britain. Mutual funds, sold as "unit trusts," are becoming extremely popular. Over 12 million Britons (18% of the population) own shares directly in British corporations, compared to 21% of the U.S. population.

The major index for the International Stock Exchange is the Financial Times Industrial Ordinary Share Index, called the Financial Times Index. Begun in 1935 by the Financial Times of London, it consists of 30 Industrial stocks and is comparable to the Dow Jones Industrial Average. There is another index called the Financial Times All Share Index, which is the broadest of all International Exchange Indexes and consists of 750 securities. A more recent index, the Financial Times 100 (based on the 100 largest companies by market capitalization and updated each minute) has also become popular.

The British "export" much of the trading in their securities. The ADR trading of several major British companies' shares is a high percentage of the overall activity in those corporations' securities. For example, half of the total trading of the International Exchange's perennial volume leader, Jaguar, was done in its ADRs worldwide—before Jaguar was acquired by Ford Motor. One reason the British enjoy expanding ADR trading is because their brokerage firms arbitrage the prices of British securities being traded on other worldwide exchanges. Plus ADR trading increases demand for British securities overall.

Of importance, the British are increasingly investing in American business. In 1987 alone over 150 American enterprises were acquired by British companies, representing an investment of over $25 billion. By 1990 British investment in the U.S. had increased 30 fold from the 1970 level, and over eight fold since 1980. Today the British have surpassed the Japanese in investing in U.S. assets. Britain made over one-third of all investments by foreigners in the U.S. in 1994-95. As the Japanese reduce their investments in the U.S. due to real estate losses in California and at home, the British increase theirs. Today U.S. businesses own over $50 billion of British enterprises, while the British control over $100 billion of corporate America.

©1996 Chase Global Data & Research
73 Junction Square, Concord, MA 01742

In the 1990's the major foreign players on the British Exchange are Merrill Lynch, Morgan Stanley, Goldman Sachs, Citicorp, First Boston, and Nomura Securities. The Japanese have also made their presence known. Nomura Securities, Daiwa Securities, and Yamaichi Securities have been number one, two, and three in Eurobond underwriting—a $600+ billion industry for which London is the primary marketplace.

Overall, the performance of the International Stock Exchange's Index (with dividends) over the past quarter century has been quite extraordinary—and largely unnoticed. For a nation whose Gross Domestic Product (GDP) has grown such that it presently is only slightly more than half the size of Germany's, less than France's, and one-third the size of Japan's.... it ranked ***#1 in performance over the past 15, 20, and 25 year periods*** among ALL subjects tracked by Chase Global Data & Research. It is rarely lower than in the top 10% in any time period reviewed. Also a positive, it has shown only moderate levels of risk in our ten and twenty years Volatility Ranking Tables. Thus London's International Stock Exchange continues to be a rarity—a stellar performer largely unnoticed by the vast majority of investors.

©1996 Chase Global Data & Research
73 Junction Square, Concord, MA 01742

## LONDON F.T.A. ALL SHARE PRICE INDEX
## TOTAL RETURN (in local currency; with dividends)

| Year | Total Return* (in local currency) | Compound return on a five year $10,000 investment | Annual compound rate of return |
|---|---|---|---|
| 1995 | 22.28% | 1991 - 1995 | |
| 1994 | -5.54% | | 15.93% |
| 1993 | 26.72% | ... $20,942 | |
| 1992 | 19.17% | | |
| 1991 | 20.08% | | |
| 1990 | -8.81% | 1986 - 1990 | |
| 1989 | 34.25% | | 13.29% |
| 1988 | 11.19% | ... $18,660 | |
| 1987 | 8.48% | | |
| 1986 | 26.38% | | |
| 1985 | 19.51% | 1981 - 1985 | |
| 1984 | 30.44% | | 23.46% |
| 1983 | 27.72% | ... $28,679 | |
| 1982 | 27.33% | | |
| 1981 | 13.13% | | |
| 1980 | 33.17% | 1976 - 1980 | |
| 1979 | 11.22% | | 19.26% |
| 1978 | 8.44% | ... $24,121 | |
| 1977 | 46.46% | | |
| 1976 | 2.55% | | |
| 1975 | 141.80% | 1971 - 1975 | |
| 1974 | -43.63% | | 11.00% |
| 1973 | -26.59% | ... $16,848 | |
| 1972 | 15.97% | | |
| 1971 | 45.18% | | |
| 1970 | -3.13% | 1966 - 1970 | |
| 1969 | -9.33% | | 10.11% |
| 1968 | 43.28% | ... $16,183 | |
| 1967 | 33.28% | | |
| 1966 | -3.52% | | |
| 1965 | 11.96% | | |
| 1964 | n.a. | | |
| 1963 | n.a. | | |
| 1962 | n.a. | | |
| 1961 | n.a. | | |
| 1960 | n.a. | | |

How a $10,000 investment performed over

| 5 years | 10 years | 15 years | 20 years | 25 years | 30 years |
|---|---|---|---|---|---|
| 1991 - 1995 | | | | | |
| $20,942 (15.93%)^ | 1986 - 1995 | | | | |
| | $39,078 (14.60%) | 1981 - 1995 | | | |
| | | $112,071 (17.48%) | 1976 - 1995 | | |
| | | | $270,330 (17.92%) | 1971 - 1995 | |
| | | | | $455,439 (16.50%) | 1966 - 1995 |
| | | | | | $737,018 (15.41%) |

^ annual compound rate of return for that period
* Source: Financial Times, London; sum of index growth and dividend yield.
n.a. = data not available

©1996 Chase Global Data & Research
73 Junction Square, Concord, MA 01742

## F.T.A. All Share Index with Dividends

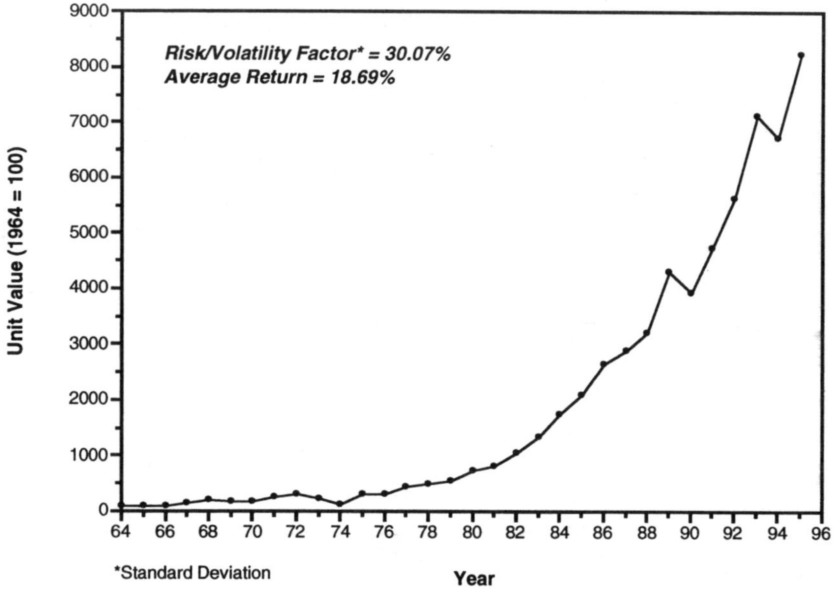


## F.T.A. All Share Index^ vs. Inflation

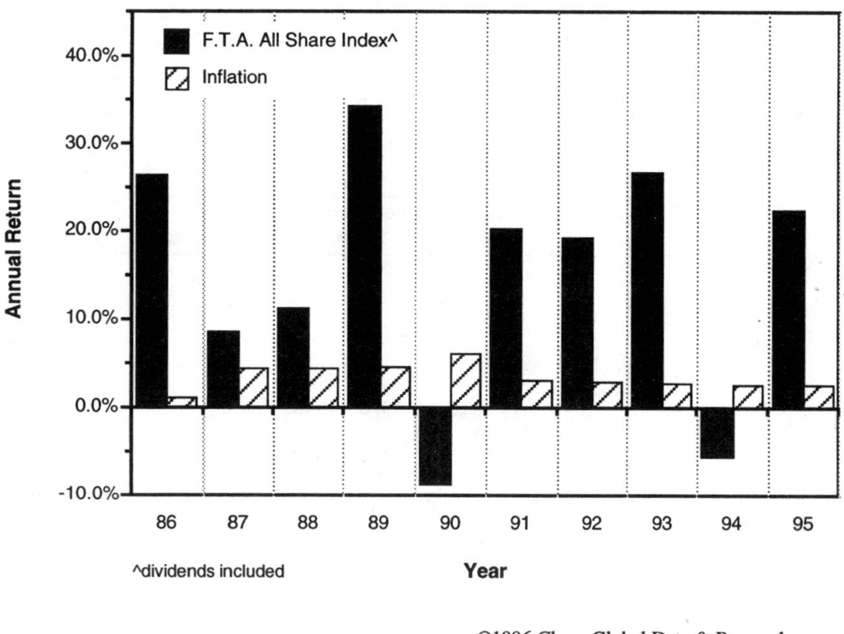


©1996 Chase Global Data & Research
73 Junction Square, Concord, MA 01742

## LONDON F.T.A. ALL SHARE PRICE INDEX
## TOTAL RETURN IN U.S. DOLLARS (with dividends)

| Year | Total Return* (in U.S. Dollars) | Compound return on a five year $10,000 investment | Annual compound rate of return |
|---|---|---|---|
| 1995 | 22.06% | 1991 - 1995 | |
| 1994 | -5.21% | | 15.02% |
| 1993 | 26.04% | ... $20,128 | |
| 1992 | 15.55% | | |
| 1991 | 19.44% | | |
| 1990 | -7.08% | 1986 - 1990 | |
| 1989 | 30.55% | | 13.58% |
| 1988 | 10.72% | ... $18,900 | |
| 1987 | 10.79% | | |
| 1986 | 27.02% | | |
| 1985 | 24.42% | 1981 - 1985 | |
| 1984 | 24.19% | | 21.30% |
| 1983 | 24.96% | ... $26,263 | |
| 1982 | 23.13% | | |
| 1981 | 10.47% | | |
| 1980 | 35.66% | 1976 - 1980 | |
| 1979 | 12.56% | | 20.81% |
| 1978 | 9.04% | ... $25,731 | |
| 1977 | 51.33% | | |
| 1976 | 2.12% | | |
| 1975 | 123.10% | 1971 - 1975 | |
| 1974 | -43.40% | | 9.38% |
| 1973 | -26.90% | ... $15,659 | |
| 1972 | 14.82% | | |
| 1971 | 47.75% | | |
| 1970 | -3.14% | 1966 - 1970 | |
| 1969 | -9.27% | | 9.29% |
| 1968 | 42.88% | ... $15,590 | |
| 1967 | 28.71% | | |
| 1966 | -3.53% | | |
| 1965 | 11.98% | | |
| 1964 | n.a. | | |
| 1963 | n.a. | | |
| 1962 | n.a. | | |
| 1961 | n.a. | | |
| 1960 | n.a. | | |

How a $10,000 investment performed over

| 5 years | 10 years | 15 years | 20 years | 25 years | 30 years |
|---|---|---|---|---|---|
| 1991 - 1995 | 1986 - 1995 | 1981 - 1995 | 1976 - 1995 | 1971 - 1995 | 1966 - 1995 |
| $20,128 (15.02%)^ | $38,042 (14.29%) | $99,910 (16.58%) | $257,081 (17.63%) | $402,568 (15.93%) | $627,586 (14.79%) |

^ annual compound rate of return for that period
* Source: Financial Times, London; sum of index growth and dividend yield.
n.a. = data not available

©1996 Chase Global Data & Research
73 Junction Square, Concord, MA 01742

## F.T.A. All Share Index in U.S. Dollars^

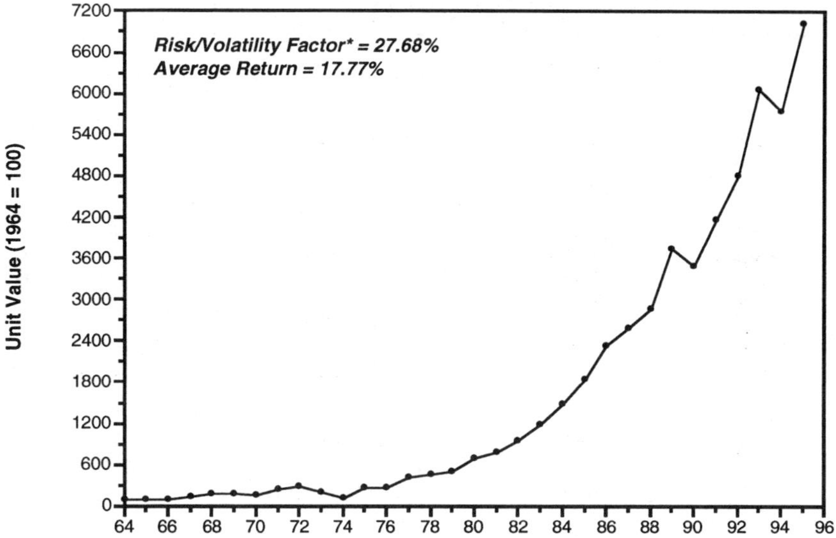


*Standard Deviation
^dividends included

## F.T.A. All Share Index^** vs. Inflation

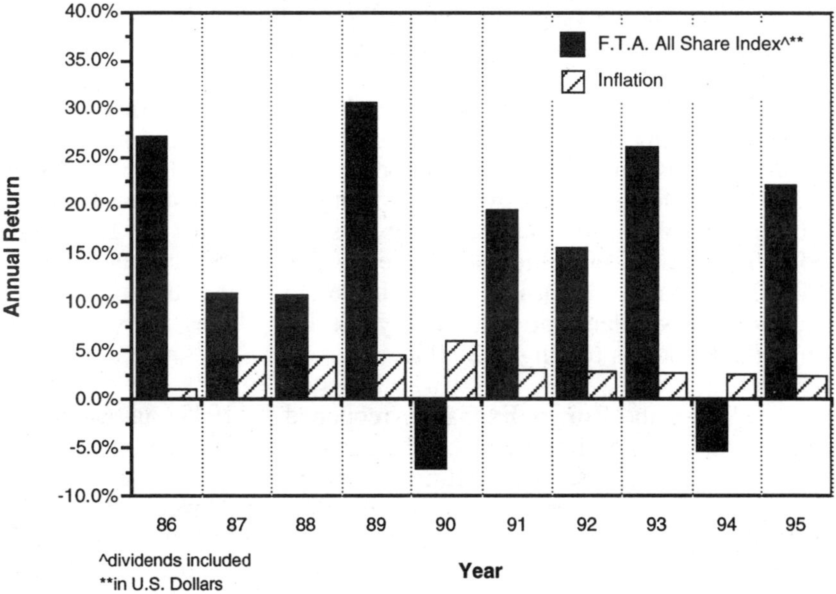


^dividends included
**in U.S. Dollars

©1996 Chase Global Data & Research
73 Junction Square, Concord, MA 01742

# Chapter Thirteen

# Japanese Stock Market

Japan has 8 exchanges—7 regional exchanges plus the powerful Tokyo Exchange, which is the world's second largest and does 85% of all business transacted in Japan. The value of Japanese equities today is estimated to be about $2.5 trillion, second only to the New York Stock Exchange's $6 trillion. The value of a seat on the Tokyo Exchange is second to none, having escalated more rapidly than the securities listed there. In 1989 a membership on the Tokyo Exchange sold for a record $9.2 million—the most expensive stock exchange seat ever sold in the world, and a price much greater than the record $1.25 million paid in early 1996 for a seat on the NYSE.

Japan, with its 140 million people is the world's fastest growing industrialized nation. While it presently has a per capita income level 25% less than the U.S., it is expected to match the U.S. standard by the year 2000. With the age of its average citizen approaching 50, Japanese pension assets now exceed one-half trillion dollars—a sum larger than several of the world's major stock exchanges.

The Tokyo Exchange was founded in 1878 as a marketplace primarily dealing in the sale of bonds, rather than stocks. In 1945 its trading was suspended by American occupiers at the end of World War II, but the Exchange was allowed to reopen in 1949. That year it traded 256 million shares. It continued to grow so rapidly that the Exchange today trades over 300 billion shares versus the still expanding NYSE's 700 billion shares. Back in 1949 both the Dow Jones and the Nikkei indices were similarly priced. Today the Dow Jones is over 5,000, while the Nikkei is trading at 20,000.

When the Tokyo Exchange reopened in 1949, an American style of trading was imprinted on the exchange. For example, active floor traders, specialists, and trading booths cover the Exchange's floor. To a Westerner however, or more specifically to an American, the two exchanges differ as much as eating a McDonald's hamburger and sushi. The Japanese have essentially no over-the-counter market. What little


©1996 Chase Global Data & Research
73 Junction Square, Concord, MA 01742

OTC market they have trades almost exclusively in government bonds. Therefore their primary exchange is extremely busy.

At the start of the day, 2000 Japanese traders are crammed onto the floor of the Exchange trading the Exchange's 1,200+ issues. Much like the U.S.'s American Stock Exchange, the Japanese use hand signals to execute buy and sell orders. The congestion is so extreme that brokerage houses hire the tallest and most athletic males so they will be more visible, and also more aggressive in pushing away competitors. There are no female traders on the floor.

It is important to note that almost 60% of all shares listed on the Exchange are never traded, primarily because corporations hold onto them rather than trade them. Trading by individuals accounts for less than one-third of all transactions—much like in the U.S. where institutions do most of the stock trading. As of 1995, about 20% of each country's population own stock—27 million in Japan and 52 million in the United States. Major Japanese insurance companies, banks, and manufacturing corporations invest a portion of their profits in the equity marketplace. Yet 70% of all transactions are initiated by the public, whereas the inverse is the case in the U.S. where 85% of all transactions are institutionally based.

One of the reasons some Japanese choose not to hold shares is the questionable practices exercised on their exchanges—the Japanese do not have an equivalent of the U.S.'s SEC. Price earnings multiples are uncommonly high, at 30 to 100 times earnings. The Morgan Stanley Japan Index had a P/E of 97 as of December 1994. Dividends are extremely low (about one-half percent) because they are based on par values, not stock price values. However, Japanese companies sometimes underplay their financial situations. For example, real estate values, which have gyrated recently but have increased over time in Japan are carried by corporations at their *original* purchase price rather than at present market value—which in many cases greatly understates the value of some corporations' assets. Some corporations' securities have gyrated in value irrespective of their earnings based on general real estate price movement.

Professionals commonly cite the high P/E multiples of Japanese securities, yet it is not so straightforward an exercise. For example, major Japanese corporations do not reflect financial results of subsidiary corporations. If earnings were consolidated and included all the assets of the company and its subsidiaries, in many cases the P/E multiple would be lower.

©1996 Chase Global Data & Research
73 Junction Square, Concord, MA 01742

Required reports to the investing public are thin and bear little resemblance to those done in the U.S. or Britain. In fact, it is considered impolite for research reports or even financial newsletters to report on negative conditions in a corporation. In some cases, those who do write negative commentaries have become victims of beatings by gangsters hired to change their minds—and their faces. Another unusual custom is that Japanese firms first "push" buy recommendations to clients who have lost money in recent transactions—so they may possibly recoup some of their losses. The stocks recommended are called "ambulance stocks."

Four major brokerage firms called "The Big Four" (Nomura, Yamaichi, Daiwa Securities Company, Ltd. and Nikko Securities Company, Ltd.) account for 70% of all Japanese brokerage business and produce the majority of in-depth research material for investors. However, sometimes these reports sound very similar—and often recommend the same securities. Nomura is perceived as the most aggressive firm in pushing stocks, and is the largest Japanese securities firm. Before Tokyo's stock crash, Nomura's 1991 total assets were estimated at over $47 billion—a value equal to the total of *all* securities firms in the U.S. Of late, however, Nomura and other major Japanese brokerage firms have made headlines for alleged scandalous sales and operational practices, and reduced profitability.

Nomura's giant size is understandable. One reason it has grown is foreign competitors have found it difficult to penetrate Japanese securities markets. And as noted earlier it is also a very expensive exercise. There are only 83 seats available on the Tokyo Exchange versus over 1300 on the NYSE. Until 1985 none were available to foreigners. Finally, five years later there were four U.S. firms with Tokyo Exchange seats—Merrill Lynch, Morgan Stanley, Goldman Sachs, and Vickers DaCosta, an affiliate of Citicorp. Ironically, at the same time over 150 Japanese companies were trading their ADRs on the U.S. OTC and major exchanges being the most popular of foreign investments to U.S. investors. Another drawback to foreigners owning assets in Japan is the fact that Japan does not allow stock ownership by non-citizens of more than 10% of a Japanese corporation without permission from the Minister of Finance.

To understand how the Japanese invest, consider the Japanese saying, "If we all cross on the red light together, there's no need to be afraid." They follow the crowd. One general manager of a major Japanese securities company was quoted as saying "Japanese investors move like a buffalo herd." But that doesn't make them herds of

©1996 Chase Global Data & Research
73 Junction Square, Concord, MA 01742

gamblers. In fact, the majority of Japanese are good savers and heavily invest their yen in banks. The average Japanese household saves 15% of his disposable income, three times the rate in the U.S. Diversifying their investments into mutual funds is somewhat difficult, however, in that only a few dozen mutual fund companies are licensed in Japan. In 1991 Fidelity Investments became the first U.S. mutual fund firm permitted to sell in Japan.

Despite Japan's huge trade surpluses, the Japanese do not live in luxury. A typical Japanese upper middle class worker who earns $50,000 lives on a 2100 square foot plot of land which was bought for $60,000 over a decade ago and is now worth $300,000. (For several years during the 1980's Tokyo real estate prices rose over 50% annually.) His daily commute to work is two hours. Beef is $20 per pound. Incredibly, golf club memberships can cost $1 million—and those memberships trade on the Tokyo Stock Exchange! Golfing can be very expensive—one round in Japan can cost $300 per person. Today newly built 600 square foot apartments in Tokyo cost $500,000—over ten times the average resident's income. A parcel of land in Tokyo's financial district the size of a newspaper page is worth $50,000. Japan also has begun experiencing a rise in unemployment. The current rate of 4% is up from 3% in 1988. Companies began employee layoffs for the first time in 1994. Employment in Japan had been considered a life-long tenure until then.

Ominously, there are several indications that real estate prices may be artificially high. Vast amounts of farmlands which are taxed at minimal rates by the government are not being freed up for housing and general development. One reason is that while it would be a financial windfall for farmers, it could be a disaster for those who paid high prices for real estate when it was perceived as very scarce. At present, the farmland is unavailable. However, should this false supply and demand system change, prices could come down sharply. The enormous rise in real estate prices over the years allowed the Japanese equivalent of home equity loan assets to flow into the stock market, pushing it higher. But times changed and the weakness in real estate coupled with a shaken and leveraged equity marketplace fueled Japan's collapse in the early 1990's.

There are two major stock indexes reflecting the trading of stocks in Japan. The Nikkei Dow Jones Average was designed by the Dow Jones Company and is an unweighted arithmetic average based on 225 securities. Although the Average is susceptible to the volatility of thinly traded and high-priced securities, it is the most popular average

©1996 Chase Global Data & Research
73 Junction Square, Concord, MA 01742

for the Tokyo Stock Exchange. The other major average, broader in scope, is the TSE Index. It was established in 1968 and is based on 1000 securities. There are about 1700 securities on the TSE. About 10% of stocks on the Tokyo Stock Exchange have ADRs trading in the United States.

There are a variety of unusual aspects to the Tokyo Exchange. One example is that forty percent of the Tokyo Exchange is represented by bank securities. Another is the fact that 5% of the Exchange's total capitalization is due to one security, Nippon Telephone and Telegraph (NT&T), which has a market value in excess of $75 billion. In 1989 NT&T was selling at over $25,000/share and sported a 270 P/E multiple. By 1990 it was listed on the NYSE, as part of a plan to boost its shares through greater worldwide visibility. Another victim of the stock market crash, by 1993 the NT&T had fallen 75% from its 1989 high.

The Japanese bond market is second only in size to that of the U.S. with over 600 separate issues listed, including government bonds. It has a market value of over $2 trillion. Japanese stock exchanges simultaneously trade bonds and stocks. In Japan, if a bond is secured by only general assets of a corporation it is called a debenture. If it is specifically insured by a certain asset it is called a bond. Short term government bonds issued in Japan mature in as little as two months whereas long term bonds run from 1 to 10 years. Bonds sold with maturities of less than 5 years are sold at a discount and thus do not pay interest until redeemed at maturity. Corporate bonds, also called industrial bonds, make up only 5% of the overall bond market and primarily reflect the issues of nine electric power companies.

Although Japanese stocks have crashed in the 1990's, the strong performance of the Tokyo Stock Exchange is well known. Over the past several years—for the longer term periods of twenty-five and thirty-five years—the Tokyo Exchange (TSE Index) has frequently ranked #1 among all subjects tracked by Chase Global Data & Research. (Recently it was replaced as #1 by the Average Growth Mutual Fund.) Despite recent losses in the 1990's, a $10,000 investment in the Japanese stock market 35 years ago would have grown over *twenty-five fold* to $288,175. Its volatility has been significant—a noteworthy example being the Nikkei average dropped from 36,000 in 1989 to a low of 14,309 by 1992. Overall, Japanese securities ranked 4th in volatility within the CGDR universe over the past 35 years, being about 50% more volatile than the average U.S. Growth Mutual Fund.

©1996 Chase Global Data & Research
73 Junction Square, Concord, MA 01742

**TOKYO STOCK EXCHANGE INDEX**
**TOTAL RETURN (in local currency; with dividends)**

| Year | Total Return* (in local currency) | Compound return on a five year $10,000 investment | Annual compound rate of return |
|---|---|---|---|
| 1995 | 2.04% | 1991 - 1995 | |
| 1994 | 9.03% | | -1.09% |
| 1993 | 10.86% | ... $ 9,469 | |
| 1992 | -22.86% | | |
| 1991 | -0.48% | | |
| 1990 | -39.34% | 1986 - 1990 | |
| 1989 | 22.70% | | 11.14% |
| 1988 | 37.08% | ... $16,954 | |
| 1987 | 11.48% | | |
| 1986 | 49.05% | | |
| 1985 | 15.81% | 1981 - 1985 | |
| 1984 | 25.83% | | 17.53% |
| 1983 | 24.57% | ... $22,424 | |
| 1982 | 5.68% | | |
| 1981 | 16.88% | | |
| 1980 | 8.98% | 1976 - 1980 | |
| 1979 | 3.66% | | 10.42% |
| 1978 | 24.96% | ... $16,417 | |
| 1977 | -3.48% | | |
| 1976 | 20.49% | | |
| 1975 | 18.44% | 1971 - 1975 | |
| 1974 | -6.76% | | 19.38% |
| 1973 | -21.75% | ... $24,247 | |
| 1972 | 103.61% | | |
| 1971 | 37.82% | | |
| 1970 | -13.89% | 1966 - 1970 | |
| 1969 | 39.85% | | 10.93% |
| 1968 | 34.41% | ... $16,799 | |
| 1967 | -5.12% | | |
| 1966 | 9.39% | | |
| 1965 | 21.67% | 1961 - 1965 | |
| 1964 | 2.57% | | 3.66% |
| 1963 | -2.73% | ... $11,971 | |
| 1962 | 2.24% | | |
| 1961 | -3.55% | | |
| 1960 | 40.15% | | |

How a $10,000 investment performed over

| 5 years | 10 years | 15 years | 20 years | 25 years | 35 years |
|---|---|---|---|---|---|
| 1991 - 1995 | | | | | |
| $9,469 (-1.09%)^ | 1986 - 1995 | | | | |
| | $16,053 (4.85%) | 1981 - 1995 | | | |
| | | $35,998 (8.91%) | 1976 - 1995 | | |
| | | | $59,098 (9.29%) | 1971 - 1995 | |
| | | | | $143,299 (11.24%) | 1961 - 1995 |
| | | | | | $288,175 (10.08%) |

^ annual compound rate of return for that period
*Source: Tokyo Stock Exchange.
sum of index growth and dividend yield.

©1996 Chase Global Data & Research
73 Junction Square, Concord, MA 01742

## Tokyo Stock Exchange Index with Dividends

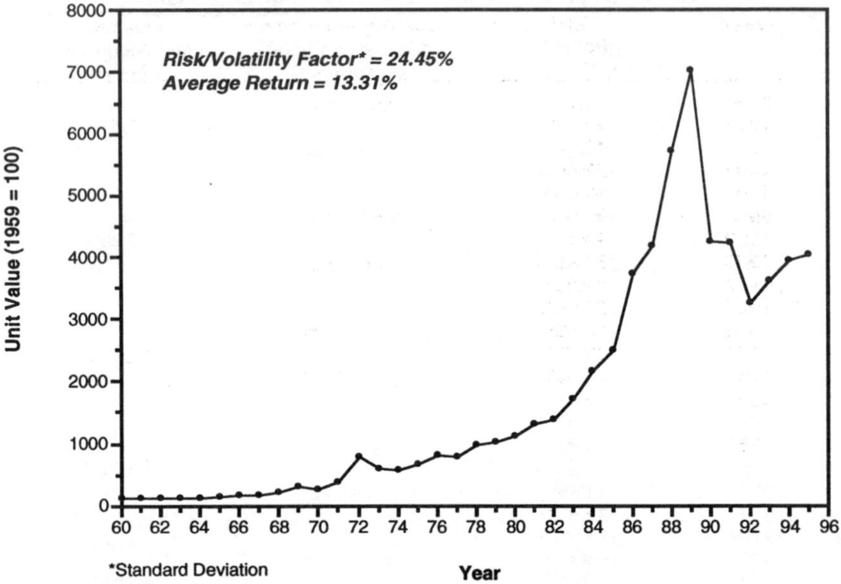


*Standard Deviation

## Tokyo Stock Exchange Index^ vs. Inflation

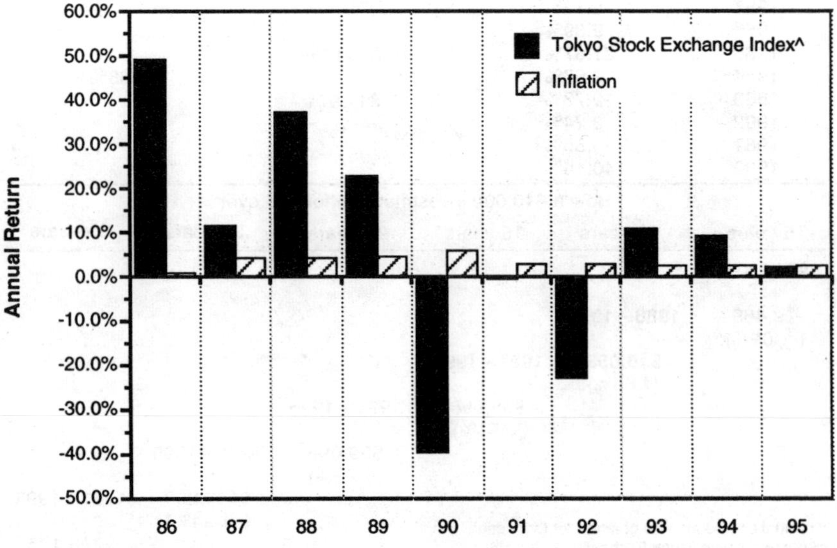


^dividends included

©1996 Chase Global Data & Research
73 Junction Square, Concord, MA 01742

**TOKYO STOCK EXCHANGE INDEX**
**TOTAL RETURN IN U.S. DOLLARS (with dividends)**

| Year | Total Return* (in U.S. Dollars) | Compound return on a five year $10,000 investment | Annual compound rate of return |
|---|---|---|---|
| 1995 | 1.97% | 1991 - 1995 | |
| 1994 | 10.13% | | -0.67% |
| 1993 | 12.14% | ... $ 9,672 | |
| 1992 | -22.86% | | |
| 1991 | -0.44% | | |
| 1990 | -37.02% | 1986 - 1990 | |
| 1989 | 19.17% | | 13.89% |
| 1988 | 35.90% | ... $19,163 | |
| 1987 | 15.03% | | |
| 1986 | 62.59% | | |
| 1985 | 19.69% | 1981 - 1985 | |
| 1984 | 23.76% | | 17.64% |
| 1983 | 24.94% | ... $22,528 | |
| 1982 | 5.31% | | |
| 1981 | 15.58% | | |
| 1980 | 10.62% | 1976 - 1980 | |
| 1979 | 2.99% | | 11.93% |
| 1978 | 30.70% | ... $17,567 | |
| 1977 | -2.70% | | |
| 1976 | 21.25% | | |
| 1975 | 18.12% | 1971 - 1975 | |
| 1974 | -7.22% | | 21.21% |
| 1973 | -20.12% | ... $26,165 | |
| 1972 | 110.07% | | |
| 1971 | 42.27% | | |
| 1970 | -13.89% | 1966 - 1970 | |
| 1969 | 39.87% | | 10.99% |
| 1968 | 34.79% | ... $16,846 | |
| 1967 | -5.11% | | |
| 1966 | 9.35% | | |
| 1965 | 21.56% | 1961 - 1965 | |
| 1964 | 2.60% | | 3.64% |
| 1963 | -2.77% | ... $11,958 | |
| 1962 | 2.26% | | |
| 1961 | -3.57% | | |
| 1960 | 40.22% | | |

How a $10,000 investment performed over

| 5 years | 10 years | 15 years | 20 years | 25 years | 35 years |
|---|---|---|---|---|---|
| 1991 - 1995 | | | | | |
| $9,672 (-0.67%)^ | 1986 - 1995 | | | | |
| | $18,534 (6.36%) | 1981 - 1995 | | | |
| | | $41,753 (10.00%) | 1976 - 1995 | | |
| | | | $73,349 (10.48%) | 1971 - 1995 | |
| | | | | $191,915 (12.54%) | 1961 - 1995 |
| | | | | | $386,602 (11.01%) |

^ annual compound rate of return for that period
*Source: Tokyo Stock Exchange.
sum of index growth and dividend yield.

©1996 Chase Global Data & Research
73 Junction Square, Concord, MA 01742

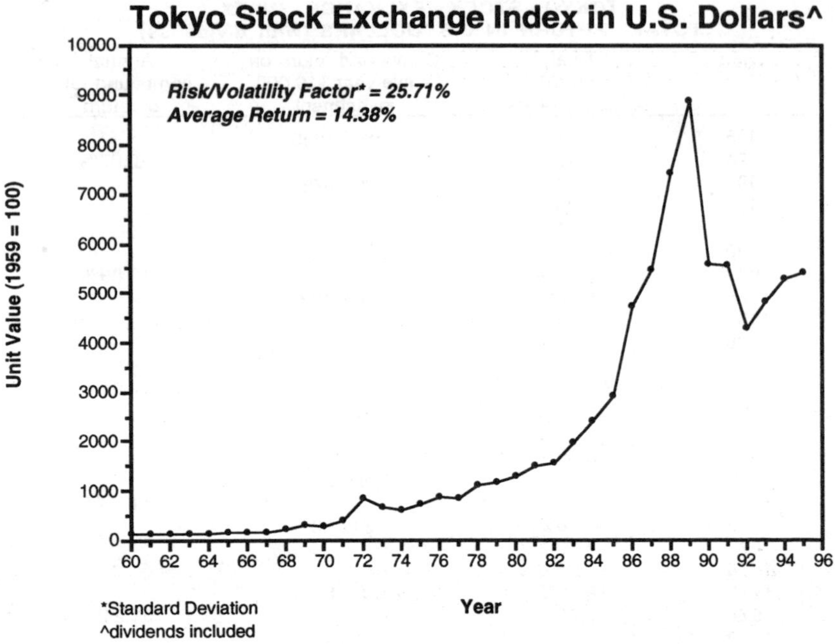


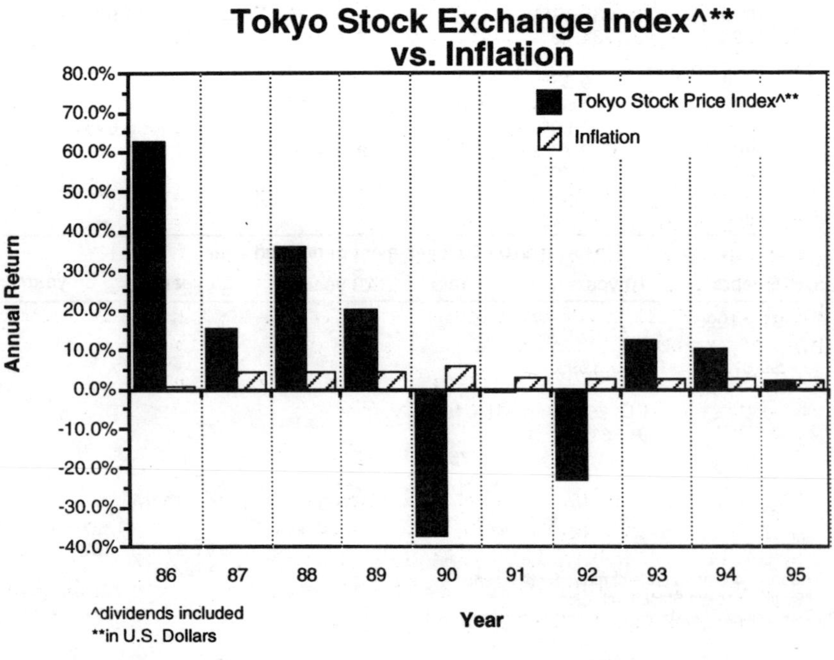


©1996 Chase Global Data & Research
73 Junction Square, Concord, MA 01742

# Chapter Fourteen

# German Stock Market

Today, given the collapse of the Berlin Wall and communism throughout Europe and the world, the German stock market is at the eye of a financial storm. With the joining of the two German nations after their separation fifty years ago, many experts believe that the German stock market will receive the greatest positive impact during the decade of the 1990's.

The Frankfurt Stock Exchange is the fourth largest stock exchange in the world with a total market value of over one-quarter trillion dollars. It is also the largest exchange in Germany, handling 50% of all security transactions. Germany has seven other exchanges. Together they are called the Association of German Stock Exchanges. While the Frankfurt Exchange's overall market capitalization is high, it has fewer listed issues listed than one would expect. The Exchange lists only 350 domestic stocks, and approximately 5000 bonds. In addition, 200 foreign shares are listed and over 600 foreign bonds. There are no restrictions to foreigners owning German stock, and proceeds from the sale of securities can be easily transferred out of Germany.

German stock exchanges have their inception in the Middle Ages when each major city, such as Frankfurt, had a trade fair. There were fairs for every type of German industry such as farming, heavy and light machinery, and clothing materials. Even in the early fairs a lot of paperwork revolved around various financial obligations, such as bills of exchange which were settled at the close of the fairs. By the 15th century Germans began to trade in currencies. Stocks were latecomers to the German exchanges and did not formally appear until the 1800's.

The Frankfurt Exchange was first held outdoors in 1558. The Exchange moved indoors when the "Old Exchange" was opened in 1843 to be later followed by the "New Stock Exchange" in 1879. It is still used in trading today. The Frankfurt Exchange has dominated the German Exchanges. Its zenith internationally was prior to World War

©1996 Chase Global Data & Research
73 Junction Square, Concord, MA 01742

I when it had 1500 securities, among them over 50 foreign stocks and 388 foreign bonds. At the outset of the War, however, the government confiscated all foreign securities and eliminated any further international trading.

The World Depression affected the German exchanges as well, and during 1930 and 1931 the Exchange was closed. The Frankfurt Exchange was almost destroyed during a World War II air raid. By then trading had fled to small rooms in the basement of the Exchange. When World War II ended the Exchange was closed for six months. It reopened in September, 1945. The trading floor was rebuilt in 1957, and a bond floor was added in 1966.

The German Stock Exchange has no stockbrokers. Instead, bankers act as brokers and only banks are allowed to be members of the stock exchanges. German banks underwrite new issues of stock—whereas in the U.S. such underwriting by banks is illegal.

There are three forms of broker on the floor of the Frankfurt Exchange. The transactions of foreign brokerage houses are represented on the Exchange by bank members who are called Enterprise members. There are also floorbrokers called Kursmakler members who help set official prices for securities and execute transactions between members, for which the banks pay them a commission. The third form of broker are the Frei Makler members who arrange transactions only between members. They cannot set official prices. Unofficial dealing, often by telephone, exclusively reflects trading that is not limited to the Exchange or Exchange hours and occurs between banks and floor members who publish the prices themselves, rather than depend on the Exchange.

German banks are more profitable than American banks, with lending a more common fiscal exercise employed by Germans than equity raising through stock sales. In fact, the equity market in Germany is quite secondary to the debt marketplace. This is also reflected in statistics which show that equity capital in the average German company is only about one fifth of corporate assets, the lowest ratio among all major economic powers—and about half the level of United States business.

There are two key indices which follow German stocks. The first is the Frankfurt Stock Exchange Share Price Index, or FAZ Index. Initiated in 1968, it is a broad base index calculated from a base of 100 securities. Today the FAZ Index is giving way to a more popular index,

©1996 Chase Global Data & Research
73 Junction Square, Concord, MA 01742

the DAX Index. The reason for the growing popularity of the 30 stock DAX Index is that it changes in price each minute during the trading day, while the FAZ Index is priced once each day at noon. The FAZ Index also reflects some stocks which are not as liquid as those in the DAX Index. The DAX Index was formally introduced in the spring of 1988, but its past history of trading prices has been calculated to afford a clear historical pricing range. (The DAX Index is represented in the Performance Table which follows.) Regarding ADRs, there are so few German securities being traded on the German exchanges that it is not surprising to find only a few German ADRs traded in the United States. Only one (Daimler Benz) is traded on the NYSE, with only a few more traded on the OTC.

The German market has several unusual characteristics. It is only open for trading a few hours per day, from 11:30 to 1:30 P.M., Monday through Friday. These sessions are supervised by a member of the Board of Governors whose role is limited to intervening only when there is a severe imbalance in trading of a security. The illiquid securities are priced at the outset of the day's trading and in the majority of cases their price does not change. This is because the Exchange operates on the principle that the initial orders on the more illiquid shares reflect a fair price for the day. However, many more liquid stocks do continue to be traded during the day. If they move sharply one way or the other trading limits then apply. Stocks are not allowed to rise or fall in a given day by more than 5% of their value, and bonds are limited to 1.5% movements. When these limits are reached, the member from the Board of Governors can be called upon to allow further trading.

Transactions on the German Exchange are charged turnover taxes on both the buy and sell for stocks and bonds. If you are a foreigner purchasing a German security you will be quoted a marked-up price which reflects the commission charged by the German broker—and your domestic broker will charge you an additional commission.

The specialist trading on the floor of the Frankfurt Exchange is similar to the NYSE specialist. The Frankfurt specialist fixes the price and on occasion steps in and purchases or sells securities through his own account. Foreign securities do reflect their ongoing price changes on other foreign exchanges where they are being traded. Thus, such securities prove more volatile than the domestic issues of the Frankfurt Exchange.

In Germany, a bank can immediately complete an OTC

©1996 Chase Global Data & Research
73 Junction Square, Concord, MA 01742

transaction for cash or give the client a bearer's certificate for his stock or bond—whichever the customer chooses. Even high quality corporations' shares can be traded this way if the client wishes to have a bearer's certificate quickly.

Banks in Germany truly are financial powerhouses, more so than in most other nations. The three largest commercial banks in Germany (Deutsche Bank, Commerzbank, and Dresdner Bank) are major shareholders in German business. Experts estimate they control over one third of all shares in the 75 largest corporations in Germany. German banks also offer mutual funds, which for the most part are conservatively managed and primarily hold blue chip securities in their portfolios. The mutual fund industry in Germany is growing robustly, similar to the United States.

With its GDP 40% larger than France and Great Britain, and per capita income over 25% higher as well, the now united Germany is truly the financial powerhouse of Europe. Of note, the German manufacturing industry pays the highest wages in the world ($25/hour), over 50% higher than the United States. There is little doubt that the German stock market is the key European marketplace today and into the foreseeable future. Much of the economic changes in Eastern Europe are expected to be reflected in German corporate growth and lending transactions initiated by major German banks. For Germany's geographic location, history, and financial status are underlying powerful forces which should propel her forward in the 1990's.

©1996 Chase Global Data & Research
73 Junction Square, Concord, MA 01742

**DAX GENERAL INDEX**
[Frankfurt; in local currency; without dividends; year-end]

| Year | Index Value* (in local currency) | Index Growth | Compound return on a five year $10,000 investment | Annual compound rate of return |
|---|---|---|---|---|
| 1995 | 2253.88 | 6.99% | 1991 - 1995 | |
| 1994 | 2106.58 | -7.06% | | 10.02% |
| 1993 | 2266.68 | 46.71% | ... $16,120 | |
| 1992 | 1545.05 | -2.09% | | |
| 1991 | 1577.98 | 12.86% | | |
| 1990 | 1398.23 | -21.90% | 1986 - 1990 | |
| 1989 | 1790.37 | 34.83% | | 0.46% |
| 1988 | 1327.87 | 32.79% | ... $10,234 | |
| 1987 | 1000.00 | -30.18% | | |
| 1986 | 1432.30 | 4.84% | | |
| 1985 | 1366.20 | 66.43% | 1981 - 1985 | |
| 1984 | 820.90 | 6.06% | | 23.22% |
| 1983 | 774.00 | 40.01% | ... $28,409 | |
| 1982 | 552.80 | 12.72% | | |
| 1981 | 490.40 | 1.98% | | |
| 1980 | 480.90 | -3.39% | 1976 - 1980 | |
| 1979 | 497.80 | -13.44% | | -3.11% |
| 1978 | 575.10 | 4.70% | ... $ 8,539 | |
| 1977 | 549.30 | 7.92% | | |
| 1976 | 509.00 | -9.62% | | |
| 1975 | 563.20 | 40.17% | 1971 - 1975 | |
| 1974 | 401.80 | 1.39% | | 4.88% |
| 1973 | 396.30 | -26.12% | ... $12,688 | |
| 1972 | 536.40 | 13.28% | | |
| 1971 | 473.50 | 6.67% | | |
| 1970 | 443.90 | -28.68% | 1966 - 1970 | |
| 1969 | 622.40 | 12.02% | | 1.00% |
| 1968 | 555.60 | 10.41% | ... $10,509 | |
| 1967 | 503.20 | 50.93% | | |
| 1966 | 333.40 | -21.07% | | |
| 1965 | 422.40 | -11.61% | 1961 - 1965 | |
| 1964 | 477.90 | 8.89% | | -4.58% |
| 1963 | 438.90 | 13.62% | ... $ 7,909 | |
| 1962 | 386.30 | -21.13% | | |
| 1961 | 489.80 | -8.29% | | |
| 1960 | 534.10 | 27.84% | | |

How a $10,000 investment performed over

| 5 years | 10 years | 15 years | 20 years | 25 years | 35 years |
|---|---|---|---|---|---|
| 1991 - 1995 | | | | | |
| $16,120 (10.02%)^ | 1986 - 1995 | | | | |
| | $16,497 (5.13%) | 1981 - 1995 | | | |
| | | $46,868 (10.85%) | 1976 - 1995 | | |
| | | | $40,019 (7.18%) | 1971 - 1995 | |
| | | | | $50,774 (6.72%) | 1961 - 1995 |
| | | | | | $42,200 (4.20%) |

^ annual compound rate of return for that period
* Source: Frankfurt Stock Exchange.

©1996 Chase Global Data & Research
73 Junction Square, Concord, MA 01742

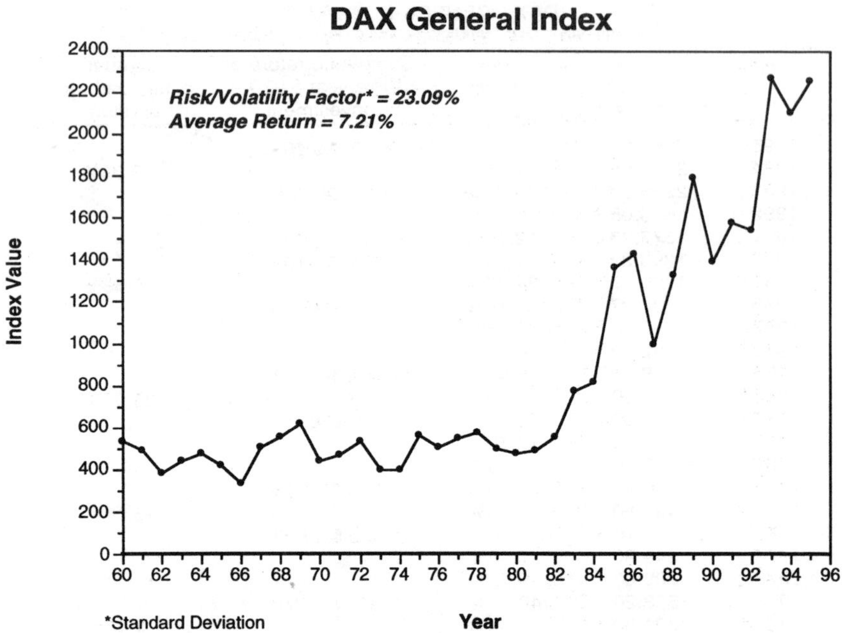


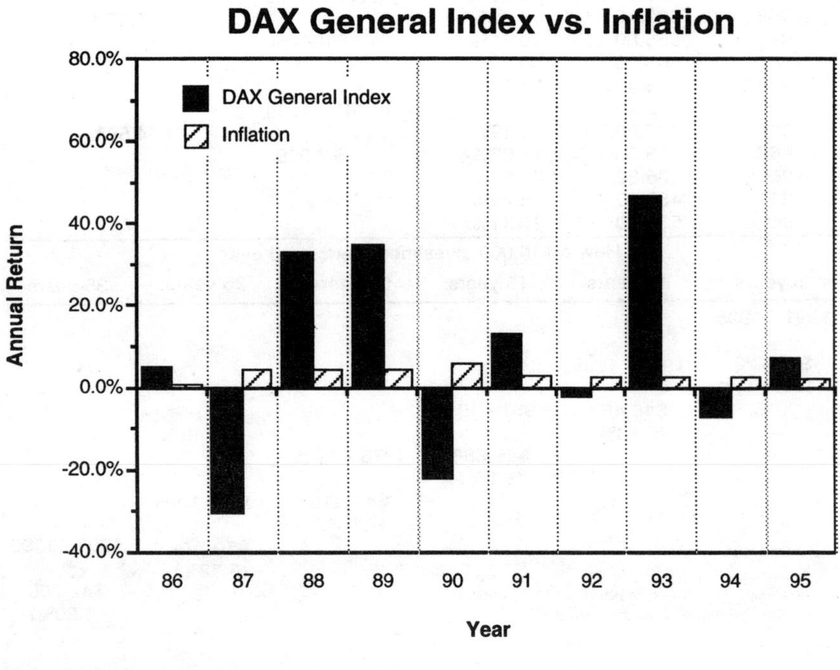


©1996 Chase Global Data & Research
73 Junction Square, Concord, MA 01742

**DAX GENERAL INDEX**
**TOTAL RETURN IN U.S. DOLLARS**

| Year | Total Return* (in U.S. Dollars) | Compound return on a five year $10,000 investment | Annual compound rate of return |
|---|---|---|---|
| 1995 | 7.54% | 1991 - 1995 | |
| 1994 | -6.20% | | 9.78% |
| 1993 | 43.49% | ... $15,946 | |
| 1992 | -2.21% | | |
| 1991 | 12.66% | | |
| 1990 | -19.13% | 1986 - 1990 | |
| 1989 | 36.92% | | 3.03% |
| 1988 | 28.76% | ... $11,608 | |
| 1987 | -23.29% | | |
| 1986 | 6.15% | | |
| 1985 | 85.64% | 1981 - 1985 | |
| 1984 | 5.24% | | 24.60% |
| 1983 | 34.95% | ... $30,036 | |
| 1982 | 11.99% | | |
| 1981 | 1.73% | | |
| 1980 | -3.80% | 1976 - 1980 | |
| 1979 | -12.28% | | -2.50% |
| 1978 | 6.02% | ... $ 8,812 | |
| 1977 | 7.83% | | |
| 1976 | -8.66% | | |
| 1975 | 37.54% | 1971 - 1975 | |
| 1974 | 1.51% | | 6.17% |
| 1973 | -20.80% | ... $13,492 | |
| 1972 | 13.57% | | |
| 1971 | 7.44% | | |
| 1970 | -28.36% | 1966 - 1970 | |
| 1969 | 13.03% | | 1.28% |
| 1968 | 10.39% | ... $10,659 | |
| 1967 | 50.78% | | |
| 1966 | -20.92% | | |
| 1965 | -11.69% | 1961 - 1965 | |
| 1964 | 8.88% | | -4.51% |
| 1963 | 13.69% | ... $ 7,940 | |
| 1962 | -21.11% | | |
| 1961 | -7.94% | | |
| 1960 | 27.84% | | |

How a $10,000 investment performed over

| 5 years | 10 years | 15 years | 20 years | 25 years | 35 years |
|---|---|---|---|---|---|
| 1991 - 1995 | | | | | |
| $15,946 (9.78%)^ | 1986 - 1995 | | | | |
| | $18,509 (6.35%) | 1981 - 1995 | | | |
| | | $55,594 (12.12%) | 1976 - 1995 | | |
| | | | $48,988 (8.27%) | 1971 - 1995 | |
| | | | | $66,095 (7.85%) | 1961 - 1995 |
| | | | | | $55,934 (5.04%) |

^ annual compound rate of return for that period
*Source: Frankfurt Stock Exchange

©1996 Chase Global Data & Research
73 Junction Square, Concord, MA 01742

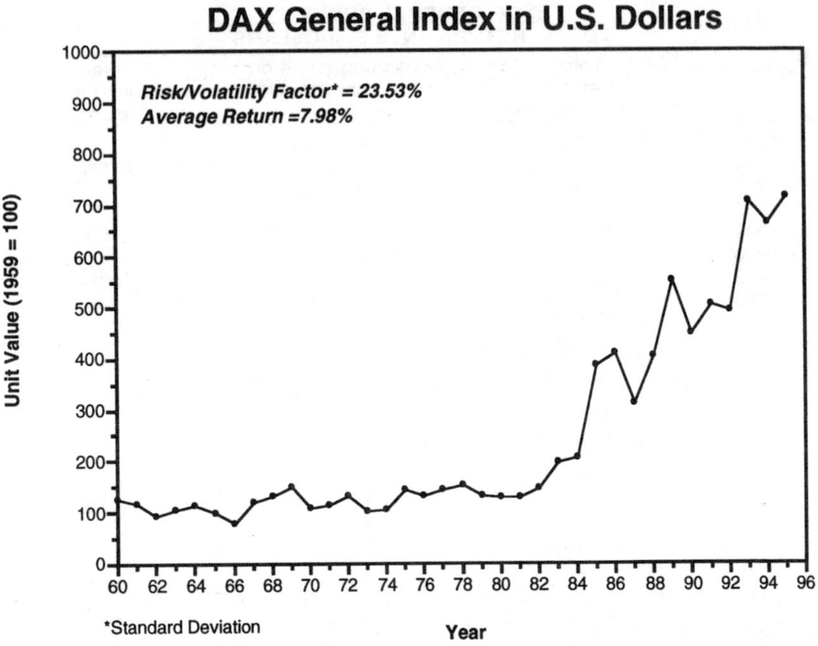


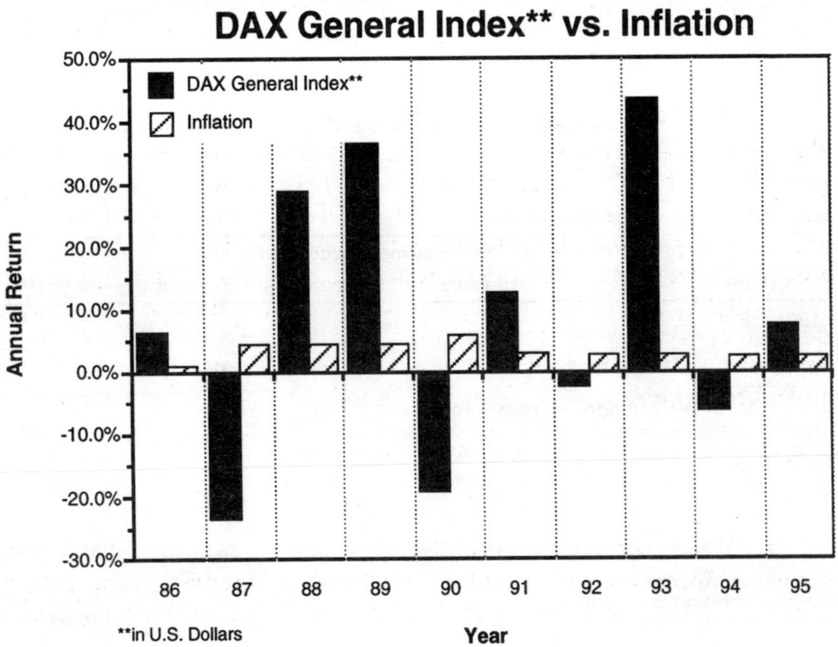


©1996 Chase Global Data & Research
73 Junction Square, Concord, MA 01742

# Chapter Fifteen

# Morgan Stanley Capital International Indices

- The World Index
- Emerging Market Index
- Europe/Australasia/Far East Index (EAFE)
- Europe Index
- North America Index
- Pacific Index

The Morgan Stanley Capital International Indices are the premier indices in the growing field of monitoring equity performance on a global scale. Morgan Stanley, the international investment banking and brokerage firm, has extensive proprietary data on the world's global equity markets since 1969. Now in their third decade, Morgan Stanley has expanded their market universe to directly monitor equities with a combined US$ market value of 16.6 *trillion*.

The Morgan Stanley Capital International (MSCI) Indices deserve their highly respected reputation, if not simply for the tremendous penetration their indices represent of the world's overall equity marketplace. In the U.S. alone, over 98% of international assets are measured against MSCI benchmarks. Major institutional money managers in over forty countries subscribe to MSCI's flagship publication, the Morgan Stanley Capital International Perspective. Morgan Stanley's goal is to create stock market indices which accurately represent various marketplace securities which can be purchased by investors anywhere. MSCI has "Free" indices which accommodate the global and domestic investor by excluding those shares in nations which do not readily allow foreign investors access to their securities. Such variables are addressed by Morgan Stanley's country specialists.

On a daily basis MSCI country specialists, based in Geneva Switzerland, monitor each index's securities for pricing, rights issues, stock dividends, and splits. Indices are calculated without dividends,

©1996 Chase Global Data & Research
73 Junction Square, Concord, MA 01742

with gross dividends, and with net dividends reinvested. National indices are tracked both in local currency and in US dollar equivalents. From time to time MSCI adjusts indices to maintain their consistency and representativeness.

MSCI's World Index is based on share prices of about 1600 companies in the world's 22 primary national marketplaces. Measured in the primary national indices are the stock markets in the United States, Europe, Canada, Australia, New Zealand, and the Far East. Also monitored are twenty-three Emerging Markets—Argentina, Brazil, Chile, China, Colombia, Greece, India, Indonesia, Israel, Jordan, Korea, Malaysia, Mexico, Pakistan, Peru, Philippines, Poland, Portugal, South Africa, Sri Lanka, Taiwan, Thailand, Turkey, and Venezuela. The combined capitalization of the firms in these indices represent approximately 60% of the aggregate market value of the above 45 countries. MSCI tracks 4100 companies, with 2600 corporations directly represented in their indices. Put another way, MSCI monitors 80% of the total market value of the world's stock markets.

So much of the popularity of MSCI Indices comes from the obvious fact that the world is growing smaller, and that events within a nation's domestic marketplace are by no means subject only to the economic and market factors within that nation's borders. Recognizing such needs, Morgan Stanley has instituted indices in global "sub-group sectors"—which are especially growing in importance to both institutional and individual investors as we head into the 1990's. Several of MSCI's global Regional Indices, fifteen in all, are becoming as popular today with investors as the Dow Jones Transportation and Utility averages were just a few short years ago. In addition to the preceding indices, Morgan Stanley also tracks 38 international Industry Groups, 8 Economic Sectors, 22 "Free" Indices, 15 Hedged regions, and 37 Hedged Indices (EAFE and 22 countries).

MSCI Indices seek to include 60% of the total market capitalization for each equity marketplace indexed. In general, companies included in their indices replicate the industrial composition of the respective marketplace represented. Companies included mirror small, medium, and large capitalization companies of each marketplace. Importantly, only securities deemed sufficiently liquid for trading by interested investors are included in MSCI Indices. MSCI "Free" Indices appropriately address the restrictions facing foreign investors in those "Free" markets, but investors able to invest in those restricted markets (locals) may use the standard MSCI International and National Indices. Ironically, only 11 securities, or 0.4% of the total MSCI universe

©1996 Chase Global Data & Research
73 Junction Square, Concord, MA 01742

for developed markets are removed from standard indices to make up the "Free" Indices.

For investors who wish greater diversification in countries which are less developed but nevertheless increasing their pace of expansion, MSCI's Emerging Market Global Index covers a sizeable portion of the world's emerging equity markets. 977 companies are represented in the Index. The average size of the corporations within the index is about 16% of those of the companies in MSCI's World Index ($914 million vs. $5.8 billion capitalization). The companies' small size is inverse to their expected potential for growth over the long term.

The Emerging Market "Free" Index is comprised of 22 nations open to foreign investment. Foreign investors seeking out Taiwan markets must use mutual funds. Because of investment restrictions, Morgan Stanley provides Free and Global versions of its Mexico and Philippines indices. All Emerging Market Indices are calculated without dividends and with dividends reinvested—both in local currency and US dollars terms.

MSCI also offers customized indices tailored to the specific requirements of the client. Customized indices allow clients to better compare their individual portfolios and better review on an ongoing basis a particular strategy or portfolio. Customization may be a combination of indices, deletion of certain securities or groups within a marketplace, or simply using a different weighing basis for creating a portfolio.

Experts debate the importance of the wide disparity in P/E (share price to earnings per share) ratios as reflected in various exchanges throughout the world. Differences in accounting methods for earnings, assets, and debts statistics are many, such that it is incorrect to perceive items such as P/Es in similar ways for different countries. As a point of reference, the following are the P/E ratios representative of some Morgan Stanley Regional and National Indices (as of December 31, 1995):

| | |
|---|---|
| EAFE | 26.0 P/E |
| Europe | 17.0 P/E |
| Japan | 105.2 P/E |
| United Kingdom | 15.1 P/E |
| United States | 17.2 P/E |
| World | 21.3 P/E |

©1996 Chase Global Data & Research
73 Junction Square, Concord, MA 01742

The following MSCI Indices have been included in the statistical review which follows: World Index, Europe-Australasia-Far East (EAFE), Europe, North America, Pacific. A listing of the countries and the market capitalization of each index as of December 31, 1995 is also provided to afford you a better overview of the composition of each index.

*World Index:* 22 Countries. 1579 companies. Total capitalization is $9.2 trillion. Average company capitalization is $5.8 billion.
Countries: Australia, Austria, Belgium, Canada, Denmark, Finland, France, Germany, Hong Kong, Ireland, Italy, Japan, Malaysia, Netherlands, New Zealand, Norway, Singapore, Spain, Sweden, Switzerland, United Kingdom, and the United States.

*EAFE:* 20 Countries. 1112 companies. Total capitalization is $5.3 trillion. Average company capitalization is $4.7 billion.
Countries: Australia, Austria, Belgium, Denmark, Finland, France, Germany, Hong Kong, Ireland, Italy, Japan, Malaysia, Netherlands, New Zealand, Norway, Singapore, Spain, Sweden, Switzerland, and United Kingdom.

*Europe:* 14 Countries. 591 companies. Total capitalization is $2.6 trillion. Average company capitalization is $4.4 billion.
Countries: Austria, Belgium, Denmark, Finland, France, Germany, Ireland, Italy, Netherlands, Norway, Spain, Sweden, Switzerland, and the United Kingdom.

*North America:* 2 Countries. 467 Companies. Total capitalization is $3.9 trillion. Average company capitalization is $8.5 billion.
Countries: Canada and the United States.

*Pacific:* 6 Countries. 521 companies. Total capitalization is $2.6 trillion. Average company capitalization is $5.1 billion.
Countries: Australia, Hong Kong, Japan, Malaysia, New Zealand, and Singapore.

*Emerging Markets (Global):* 23 countries. 977 companies. Total capitalization is $893 billion. Average company capitalization is $914 million.
Countries: Argentina, Brazil, Chile, Colombia, Greece, India, Indonesia, Israel, Jordan, Korea, Malaysia, Mexico, Pakistan, Peru, Philippines, Poland, Portugal, South Africa, Sri Lanka, Taiwan, Thailand, Turkey, and Venezuela.

©1996 Chase Global Data & Research
73 Junction Square, Concord, MA 01742

## MORGAN STANLEY WORLD EQUITY MARKETS INDEX

[with dividends; year-end; in U.S. dollars]

| Year | Index Value* | Index Growth | Compound return on a five year $10,000 investment | Annual compound rate of return |
|---|---|---|---|---|
| 1995 | 1800.55 | 21.32% | 1991 - 1995 | |
| 1994 | 1484.18 | 5.58% | | 12.33% |
| 1993 | 1405.71 | 23.13% | ... $17,888 | |
| 1992 | 1141.66 | -4.66% | | |
| 1991 | 1197.46 | 18.97% | | |
| 1990 | 1006.55 | -16.52% | 1986 - 1990 | |
| 1989 | 1205.70 | 17.19% | | 15.12% |
| 1988 | 1028.81 | 23.95% | ... $20,220 | |
| 1987 | 830.02 | 16.76% | | |
| 1986 | 710.85 | 42.80% | | |
| 1985 | 497.80 | 41.77% | 1981 - 1985 | |
| 1984 | 351.13 | 5.77% | | |
| 1983 | 331.96 | 23.28% | ... $19,891 | 14.74% |
| 1982 | 269.28 | 11.27% | | |
| 1981 | 242.00 | -3.30% | | |
| 1980 | 250.27 | 27.72% | 1976 - 1980 | |
| 1979 | 195.95 | 12.67% | | 14.76% |
| 1978 | 173.91 | 18.22% | ... $19,905 | |
| 1977 | 147.12 | 2.00% | | |
| 1976 | 144.23 | 14.71% | | |
| 1975 | 125.73 | 34.50% | 1971 - 1975 | |
| 1974 | 93.48 | -24.48% | | 5.11% |
| 1973 | 123.79 | -14.51% | ... $12,828 | |
| 1972 | 144.79 | 23.55% | | |
| 1971 | 117.19 | 19.56% | | |
| 1970 | 98.02 | -1.98% | | |
| 1969 | 100.00 | n.a. | | |
| 1968 | n.a. | n.a. | | |
| 1967 | n.a. | n.a. | | |
| 1966 | n.a. | n.a. | | |
| 1965 | n.a. | n.a. | | |
| 1964 | n.a. | n.a. | | |
| 1963 | n.a. | n.a. | | |
| 1962 | n.a. | n.a. | | |
| 1961 | n.a. | n.a. | | |
| 1960 | n.a. | n.a. | | |

How a $10,000 investment performed over

| 5 years | 10 years | 15 years | 20 years | 25 years |
|---|---|---|---|---|
| 1991 - 1995 | 1986 - 1995 | 1981 - 1995 | 1976 - 1995 | 1971 - 1995 |
| $17,888 (12.33%)^ | $36,170 (13.72%) | $71,945 (14.06%) | $143,206 (14.23%) | $183,698 (12.35%) |

^ annual compound rate of return for that period
* Source: ©1995 Morgan Stanley Capital International.
n.a. = data not available

©1996 Chase Global Data & Research
73 Junction Square, Concord, MA 01742

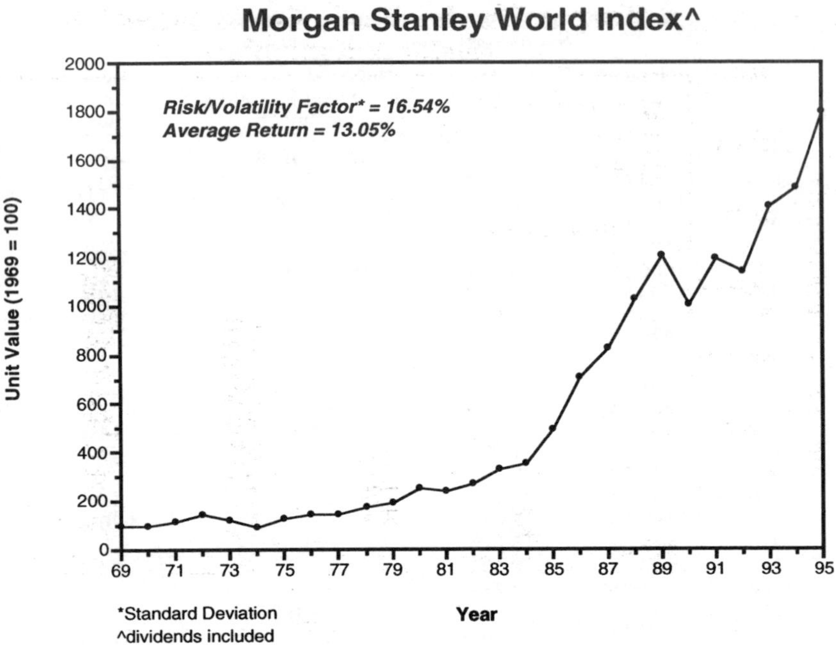


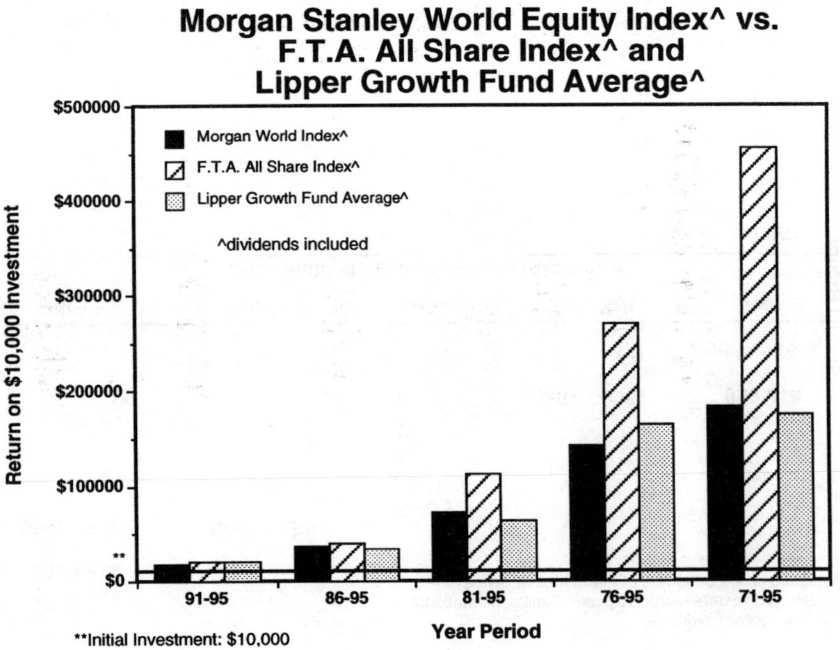


©1996 Chase Global Data & Research
73 Junction Square, Concord, MA 01742

## Morgan Stanley World Equity Index^ vs. Silver and Inflation

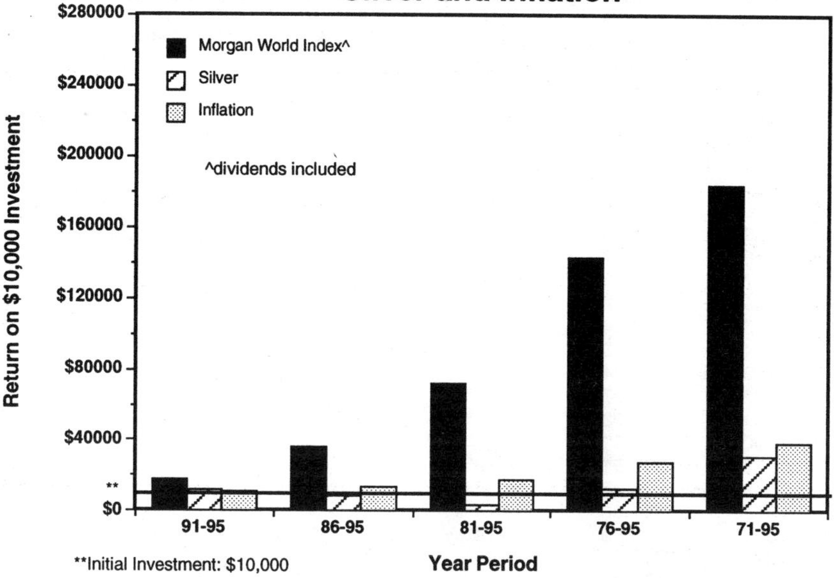


## Morgan Stanley World Equity Index^ vs. Inflation

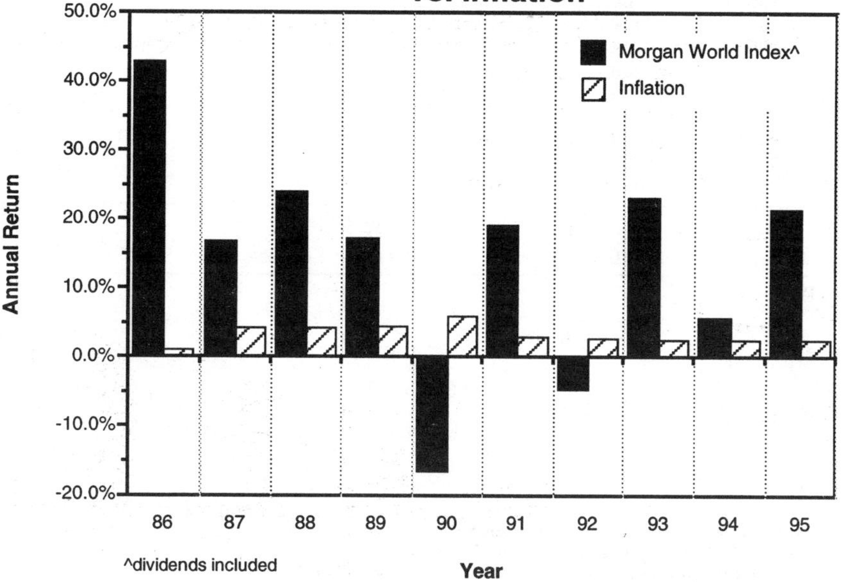


©1996 Chase Global Data & Research
73 Junction Square, Concord, MA 01742

## MORGAN STANLEY EAFE INDEX

[EAFE = Europe, Australia, New Zealand, Far East; with dividends; year-end; in U.S. dollars]

| Year | Index Value* | Index Growth | Compound return on a five year $10,000 investment | Annual compound rate of return |
|---|---|---|---|---|
| 1995 | 2483.07 | 11.55% | 1991 - 1995 | |
| 1994 | 2225.95 | 8.06% | | 9.71% |
| 1993 | 2059.89 | 32.94% | ... $15,892 | |
| 1992 | 1549.43 | -11.85% | | |
| 1991 | 1757.71 | 12.50% | | |
| 1990 | 1562.45 | -23.20% | 1986 - 1990 | |
| 1989 | 2034.33 | 10.80% | | 18.36% |
| 1988 | 1836.07 | 28.59% | ... $23,232 | |
| 1987 | 1427.88 | 24.93% | | |
| 1986 | 1142.92 | 69.94% | | |
| 1985 | 672.54 | 56.72% | | |
| 1984 | 429.13 | 7.86% | 1981 - 1985 | |
| 1983 | 397.84 | 24.61% | | 15.63% |
| 1982 | 319.27 | -0.86% | ... $20,669 | |
| 1981 | 322.03 | -1.03% | | |
| 1980 | 325.39 | 24.43% | | |
| 1979 | 261.51 | 6.18% | | |
| 1978 | 246.28 | 34.30% | 1976 - 1980 | |
| 1977 | 183.38 | 19.42% | | 17.06% |
| 1976 | 153.55 | 3.74% | ... $21,983 | |
| 1975 | 148.02 | 37.10% | | |
| 1974 | 107.96 | -22.15% | | |
| 1973 | 138.67 | -14.17% | | |
| 1972 | 161.56 | 37.60% | 1971 - 1975 | |
| 1971 | 117.42 | 31.21% | | 10.59% |
| 1970 | 89.49 | -10.51% | ... $16,540 | |
| 1969 | 100.00 | n.a. | | |
| 1968 | n.a. | n.a. | | |
| 1967 | n.a. | n.a. | | |
| 1966 | n.a. | n.a. | | |
| 1965 | n.a. | n.a. | | |
| 1964 | n.a. | n.a. | | |
| 1963 | n.a. | n.a. | | |
| 1962 | n.a. | n.a. | | |
| 1961 | n.a. | n.a. | | |
| 1960 | n.a. | n.a. | | |

How a $10,000 investment performed over

| 5 years | 10 years | 15 years | 20 years | 25 years |
|---|---|---|---|---|
| 1991 - 1995 | 1986 - 1995 | 1981 - 1995 | 1976 - 1995 | 1971 - 1995 |
| $15,892 (9.71%)^ | $36,921 (13.95%) | $76,311 (14.51%) | $167,757 (15.14%) | $277,475 (14.22%) |

^ annual compound rate of return for that period
* Source: ©1995 Morgan Stanley Capital International.
n.a. = data not available

©1996 Chase Global Data & Research
73 Junction Square, Concord, MA 01742

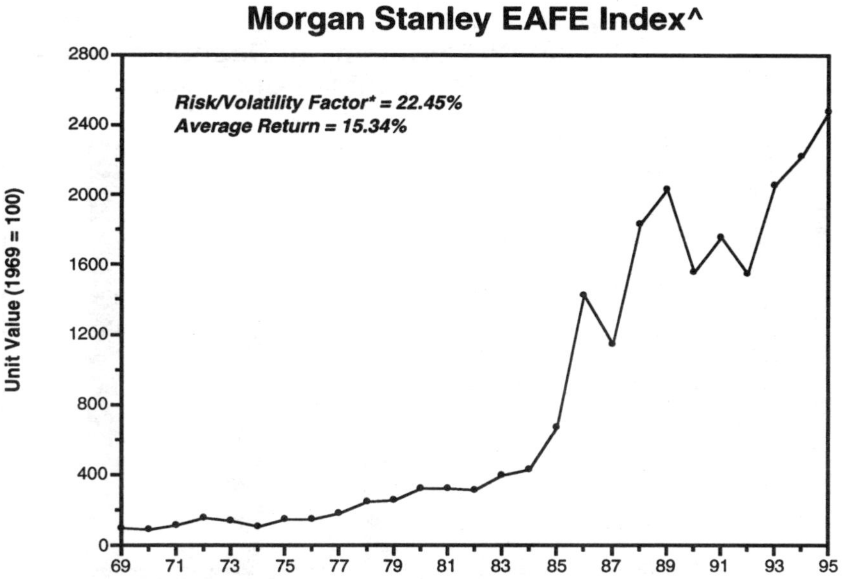


*Standard Deviation
^dividends included

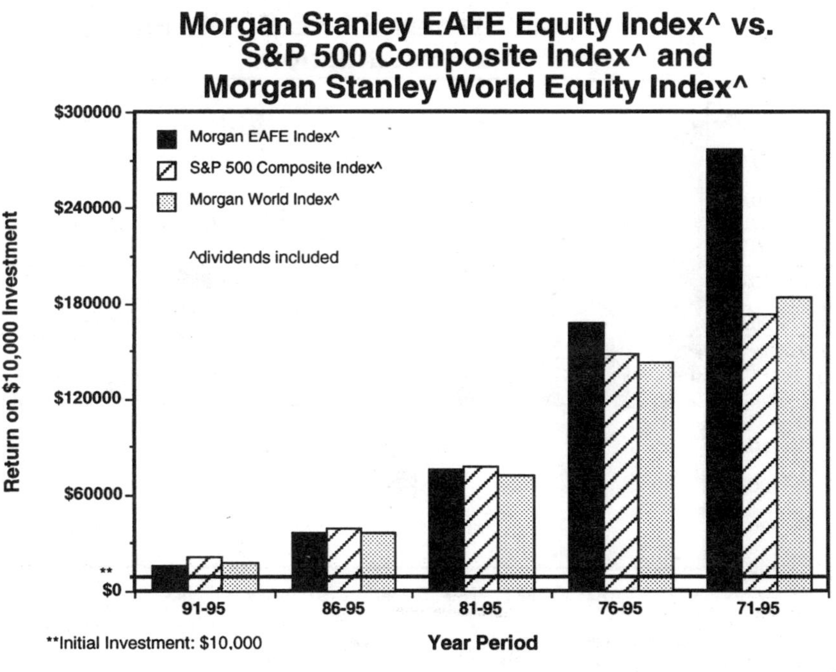


**Initial Investment: $10,000

©1996 Chase Global Data & Research
73 Junction Square, Concord, MA 01742

## Morgan Stanley EAFE Equity Index^ vs. 3-Month Certificate of Deposit and Lipper Fixed Income Fund Average^

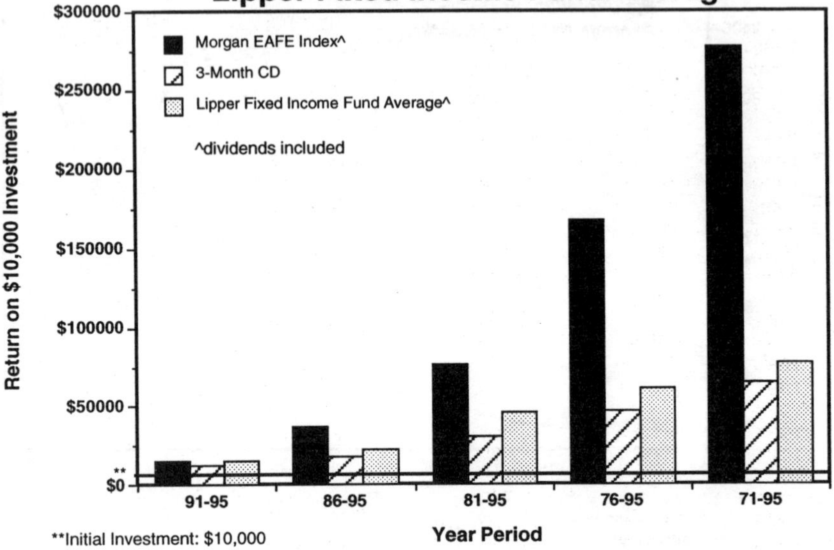


**Initial Investment: $10,000

## Morgan Stanley EAFE Equity Index^ vs. Inflation

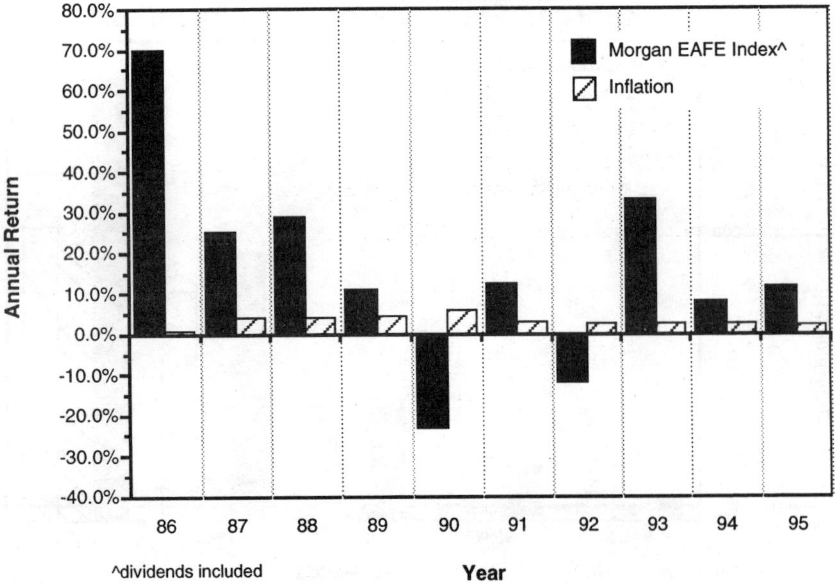


^dividends included

©1996 Chase Global Data & Research
73 Junction Square, Concord, MA 01742

## MORGAN STANLEY EUROPE INDEX

[with dividends; year-end; in U.S. dollars]

| Year | Index Value* | Index Growth | Compound return on a five year $10,000 investment | Annual compound rate of return |
|---|---|---|---|---|
| 1995 | 2123.98 | 22.13% | 1991 - 1995 | |
| 1994 | 1739.11 | 2.66% | | 12.11% |
| 1993 | 1694.01 | 29.79% | ... $17,712 | |
| 1992 | 1305.15 | -4.25% | | |
| 1991 | 1363.02 | 13.66% | | |
| 1990 | 1199.20 | -3.37% | 1986 - 1990 | |
| 1989 | 1241.01 | 29.06% | | 16.89% |
| 1988 | 961.58 | 16.35% | ... $21,820 | |
| 1987 | 826.44 | 4.10% | | |
| 1986 | 793.92 | 44.46% | | |
| 1985 | 549.58 | 79.79% | 1981 - 1985 | |
| 1984 | 305.68 | 1.26% | | 16.09% |
| 1983 | 301.87 | 22.38% | ... $21,088 | |
| 1982 | 246.67 | 5.69% | | |
| 1981 | 233.38 | -10.45% | | |
| 1980 | 260.61 | 14.53% | 1976 - 1980 | |
| 1979 | 227.56 | 14.67% | | 13.63% |
| 1978 | 198.44 | 24.30% | ... $18,940 | |
| 1977 | 159.65 | 23.92% | | |
| 1976 | 128.83 | -6.37% | | |
| 1975 | 137.60 | 43.90% | 1971 - 1975 | |
| 1974 | 95.62 | -22.78% | | 8.71% |
| 1973 | 123.82 | -7.73% | ... $15,180 | |
| 1972 | 134.19 | 15.62% | | |
| 1971 | 116.06 | 28.04% | | |
| 1970 | 90.65 | -9.36% | | |
| 1969 | 100.00 | n.a. | | |
| 1968 | n.a. | n.a. | | |
| 1967 | n.a. | n.a. | | |
| 1966 | n.a. | n.a. | | |
| 1965 | n.a. | n.a. | | |
| 1964 | n.a. | n.a. | | |
| 1963 | n.a. | n.a. | | |
| 1962 | n.a. | n.a. | | |
| 1961 | n.a. | n.a. | | |
| 1960 | n.a. | n.a. | | |

How a $10,000 investment performed over

| 5 years | 10 years | 15 years | 20 years | 25 years |
|---|---|---|---|---|
| 1991 - 1995 | | | | |
| $17,712 (12.11%)^ | 1986 - 1995 | | | |
| | $38,648 (14.48%) | 1981 - 1995 | | |
| | | $81,500 (15.01%) | 1976 - 1995 | |
| | | | $154,357 (14.66%) | 1971 - 1995 |
| | | | | $234,319 (13.45%) |

^ annual compound rate of return for that period
* Source: ©1995 Morgan Stanley Capital International.
n.a. = data not available

©1996 Chase Global Data & Research
73 Junction Square, Concord, MA 01742

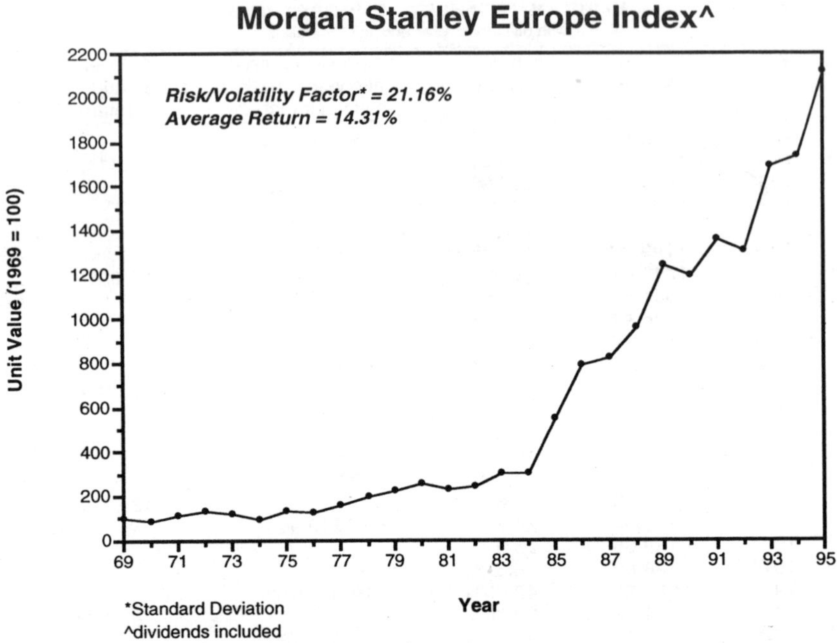


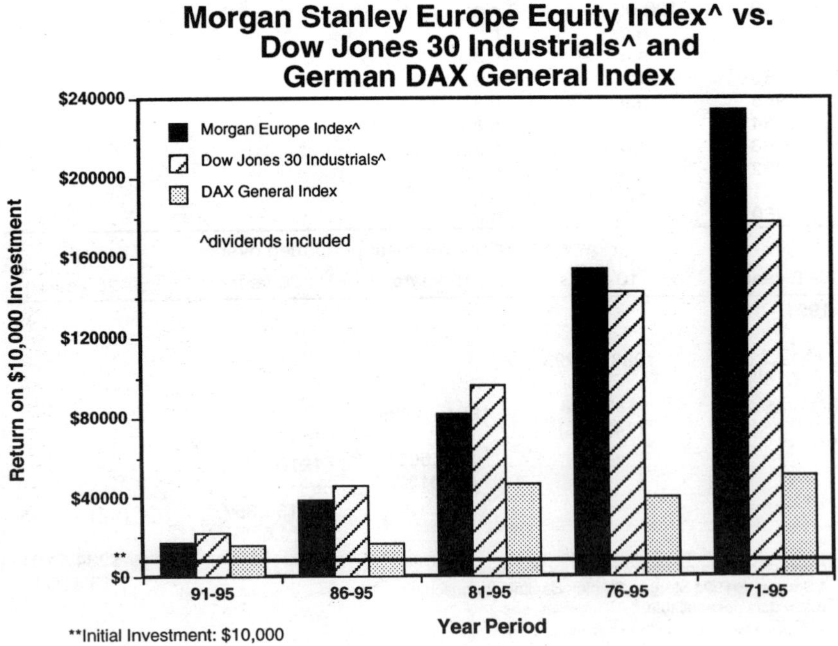


©1996 Chase Global Data & Research
73 Junction Square, Concord, MA 01742

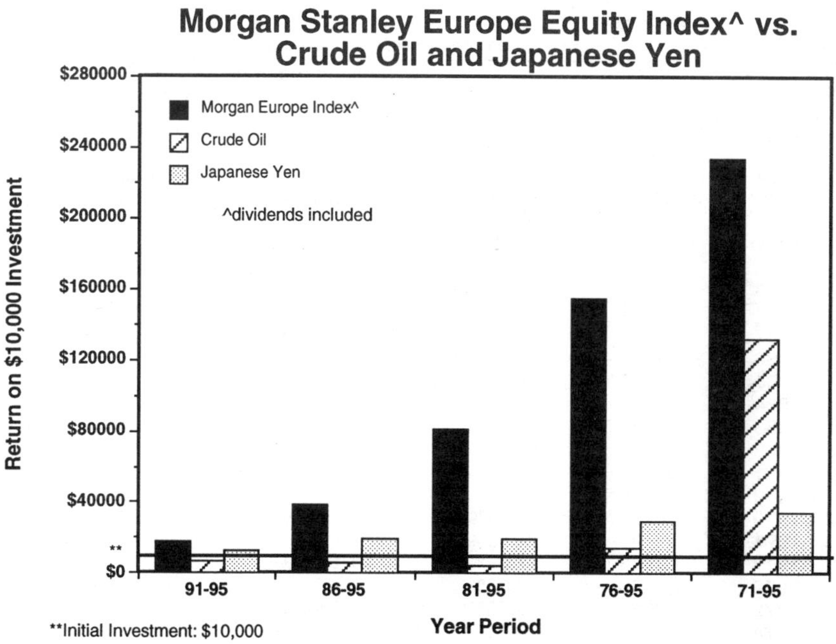


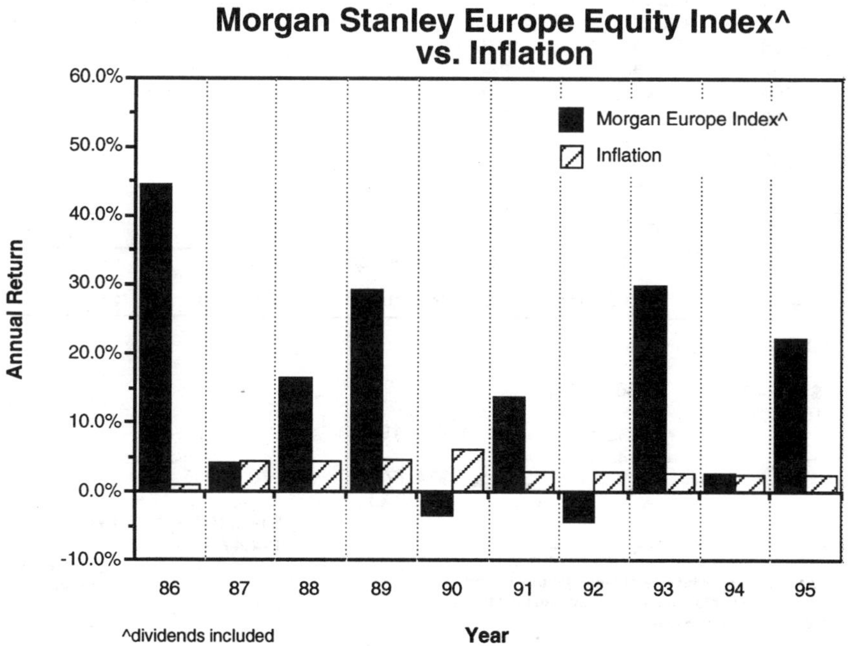


©1996 Chase Global Data & Research
73 Junction Square, Concord, MA 01742

## MORGAN STANLEY NORTH AMERICA INDEX

[with dividends; year-end; in U.S. dollars]

| Year | Index Value* | Index Growth | Compound return on a five year $10,000 investment | Annual compound rate of return |
|---|---|---|---|---|
| 1995 | 1738.58 | 37.07% | 1991 - 1995 | |
| 1994 | 1268.36 | 1.73% | | 16.27% |
| 1993 | 1246.76 | 10.53% | ... $21,249 | |
| 1992 | 1127.94 | 6.14% | | |
| 1991 | 1062.72 | 29.89% | | |
| 1990 | 818.19 | -2.91% | | |
| 1989 | 842.71 | 30.89% | 1986 - 1990 | |
| 1988 | 643.84 | 16.06% | | 12.58% |
| 1987 | 554.75 | 4.59% | ... $18,084 | |
| 1986 | 530.42 | 17.24% | | |
| 1985 | 452.43 | 31.50% | | |
| 1984 | 344.05 | 4.96% | | |
| 1983 | 327.80 | 22.90% | 1981 - 1985 | |
| 1982 | 266.72 | 19.88% | | 14.06% |
| 1981 | 222.48 | -5.08% | ... $19,303 | |
| 1980 | 234.39 | 28.97% | | |
| 1979 | 181.74 | 24.54% | | |
| 1978 | 145.93 | 11.89% | | |
| 1977 | 130.43 | -7.08% | 1976 - 1980 | |
| 1976 | 140.36 | 20.38% | | 14.99% |
| 1975 | 116.60 | 33.23% | ... $20,102 | |
| 1974 | 87.52 | -26.62% | | |
| 1973 | 119.26 | -15.07% | | |
| 1972 | 140.42 | 17.49% | | |
| 1971 | 119.52 | 13.22% | 1971 -1975 | |
| 1970 | 105.57 | 5.57% | | 2.01% |
| 1969 | 100.00 | n.a. | ... $11,045 | |
| 1968 | n.a. | n.a. | | |
| 1967 | n.a. | n.a. | | |
| 1966 | n.a. | n.a. | | |
| 1965 | n.a. | n.a. | | |
| 1964 | n.a. | n.a. | | |
| 1963 | n.a. | n.a. | | |
| 1962 | n.a. | n.a. | | |
| 1961 | n.a. | n.a. | | |
| 1960 | n.a. | n.a. | | |

How a $10,000 investment performed over

| 5 years | 10 years | 15 years | 20 years | 25 years |
|---|---|---|---|---|
| 1991 - 1995 | 1986 - 1995 | 1981 - 1995 | 1976 - 1995 | 1971 - 1995 |
| $21,249 (16.27%)^ | $38,427 (14.41%) | $74,176 (14.29%) | $149,106 (14.47%) | $164,693 (11.86%) |

^ annual compound rate of return for that period

* Source: ©1995 Morgan Stanley Capital International.

n.a. = data not available

©1996 Chase Global Data & Research
73 Junction Square, Concord, MA 01742

## Morgan Stanley North America Index^

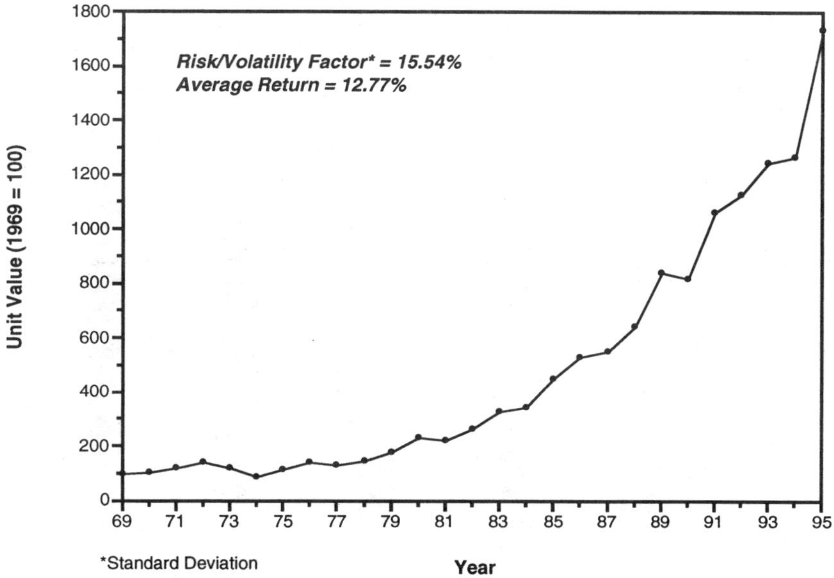


*Standard Deviation
^dividends included

## Morgan Stanley North America Index^ vs. Morgan Stanley Europe Equity Index^ and Morgan Stanley Pacific Equity Index^

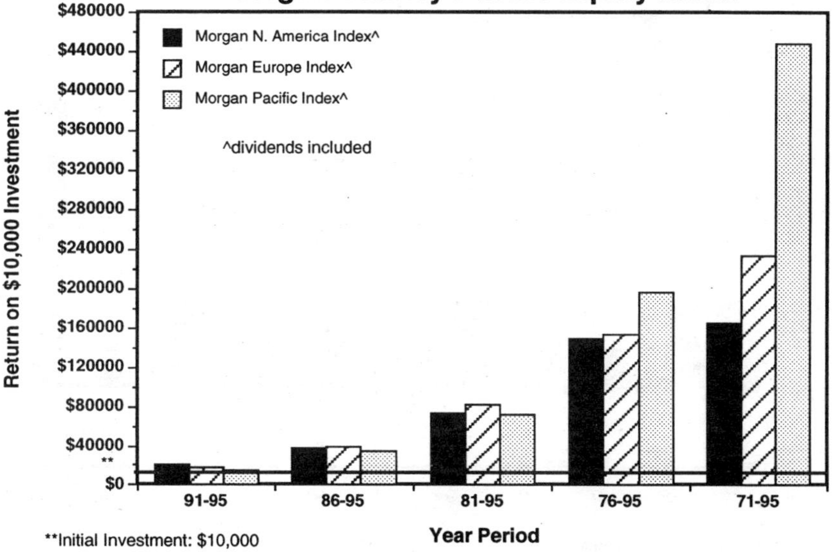


**Initial Investment: $10,000

©1996 Chase Global Data & Research
73 Junction Square, Concord, MA 01742

## Morgan Stanley North America Equity Index^ vs. 3-Month T-Bill and Swiss Franc

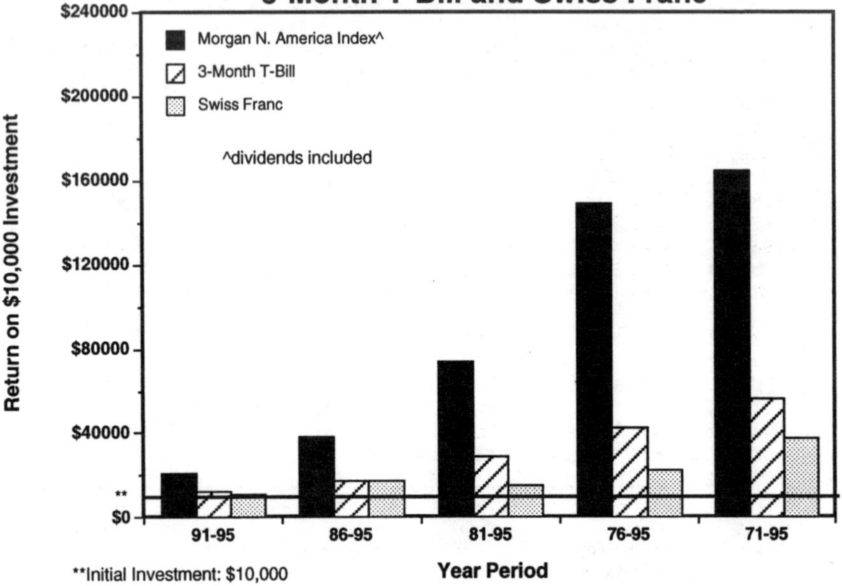


## Morgan Stanley N. America Equity Index^ vs. Inflation

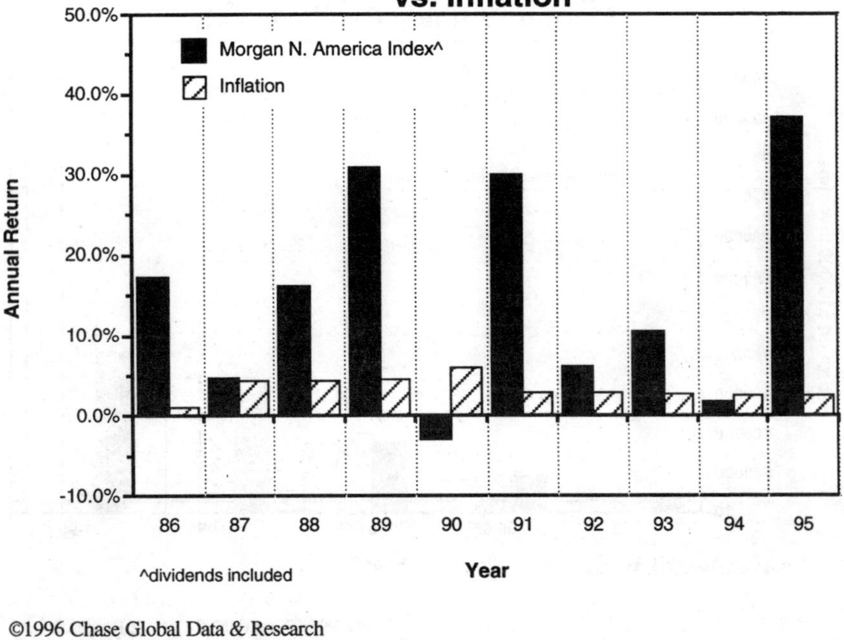


©1996 Chase Global Data & Research
73 Junction Square, Concord, MA 01742

## MORGAN STANLEY PACIFIC INDEX

[with dividends; year-end; in U.S. dollars]

| Year | Index Value* | Index Growth | Compound return on a five year $10,000 investment | Annual compound rate of return |
|---|---|---|---|---|
| 1995 | 3940.51 | 2.99% | 1991 - 1995 | |
| 1994 | 3826.04 | 13.03% | | 7.63% |
| 1993 | 3385.03 | 35.97% | ... $14,442 | |
| 1992 | 2489.56 | -18.20% | | |
| 1991 | 3043.39 | 11.54% | | |
| 1990 | 2728.59 | -34.29% | | |
| 1989 | 4152.31 | 2.68% | 1986 - 1990 | |
| 1988 | 4044.11 | 35.19% | | 19.84% |
| 1987 | 2991.50 | 39.85% | ... $24,723 | |
| 1986 | 2139.13 | 93.82% | | |
| 1985 | 1103.68 | 39.39% | | |
| 1984 | 791.80 | 13.48% | | |
| 1983 | 697.74 | 26.42% | 1981 - 1985 | |
| 1982 | 551.94 | -6.26% | | 15.22% |
| 1981 | 588.78 | 8.31% | ... $20,303 | |
| 1980 | 543.60 | 36.38% | | |
| 1979 | 398.59 | -3.48% | | |
| 1978 | 412.95 | 48.77% | | |
| 1977 | 277.58 | 13.69% | 1976 - 1980 | |
| 1976 | 244.16 | 21.64% | | 22.05% |
| 1975 | 200.73 | 26.72% | ... $27,081 | |
| 1974 | 158.40 | -20.94% | | |
| 1973 | 200.35 | -20.95% | | |
| 1972 | 253.45 | 107.55% | | |
| 1971 | 122.12 | 38.76% | 1971 - 1975 | |
| 1970 | 88.01 | -11.99% | | 17.93% |
| 1969 | 100.00 | n.a. | ... $22,808 | |
| 1968 | n.a. | n.a. | | |
| 1967 | n.a. | n.a. | | |
| 1966 | n.a. | n.a. | | |
| 1965 | n.a. | n.a. | | |
| 1964 | n.a. | n.a. | | |
| 1963 | n.a. | n.a. | | |
| 1962 | n.a. | n.a. | | |
| 1961 | n.a. | n.a. | | |
| 1960 | n.a. | n.a. | | |

How a $10,000 investment performed over

| 5 years | 10 years | 15 years | 20 years | 25 years |
|---|---|---|---|---|
| 1991 - 1995 | | | | |
| $14,442 (7.63%)^ | 1986 - 1995 | | | |
| | $35,703 (13.57%) | 1981 - 1995 | | |
| | | $72,490 (14.12%) | 1976 - 1995 | |
| | | | $196,311 (16.05%) | 1971 - 1995 |
| | | | | $447,745 (16.42%) |

^ annual compound rate of return for that period
* Source: ©1995 Morgan Stanley Capital International.
n.a. = data not available

©1996 Chase Global Data & Research
73 Junction Square, Concord, MA 01742

## Morgan Stanley Pacific Index^

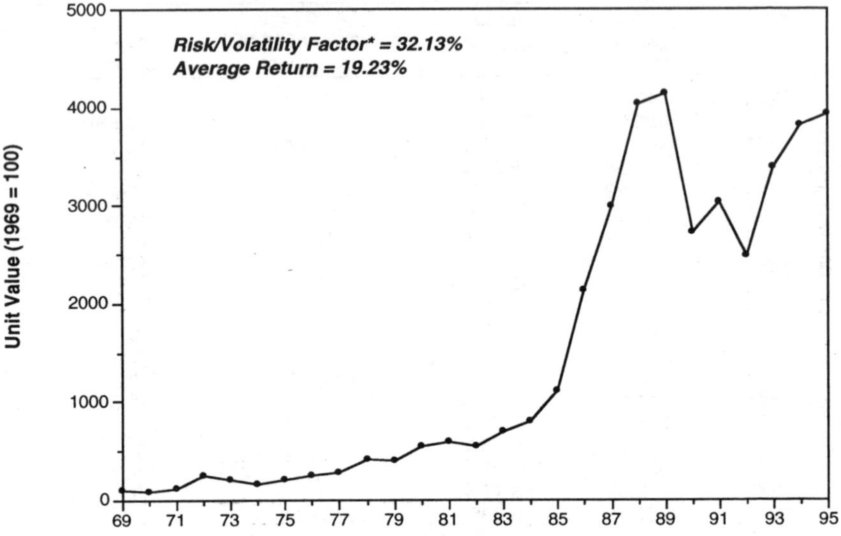


*Standard Deviation
^dividends included

## Morgan Stanley Pacific Equity Index^ vs. Value Line Composite Index and Tokyo Stock Exchange Index^

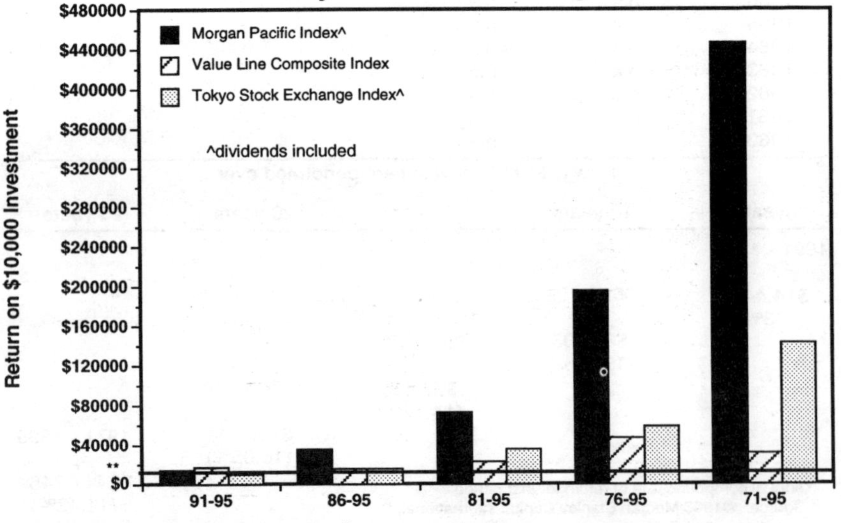


**Initial Investment: $10,000

©1996 Chase Global Data & Research
73 Junction Square, Concord, MA 01742

## Morgan Stanley Pacific Equity Index^ vs. 3-Year T-Note and REITs

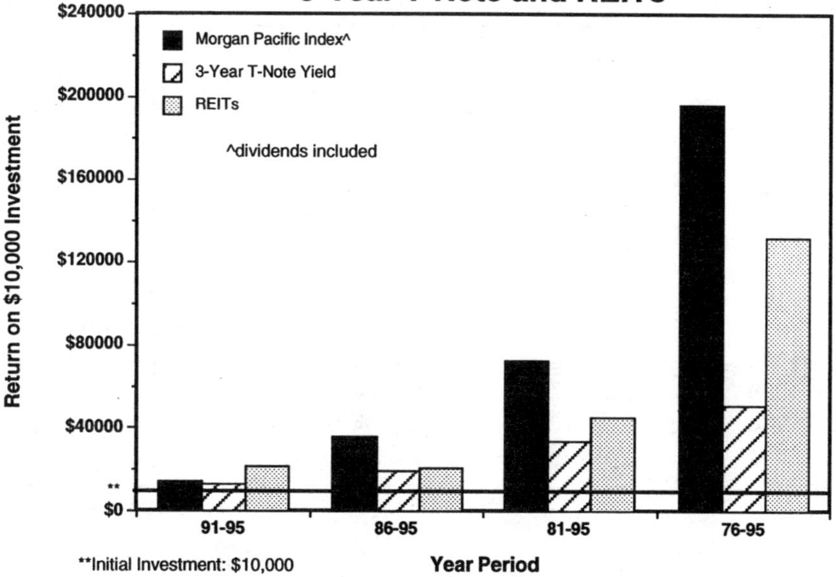


## Morgan Stanley Pacific Equity Index^ vs. Inflation

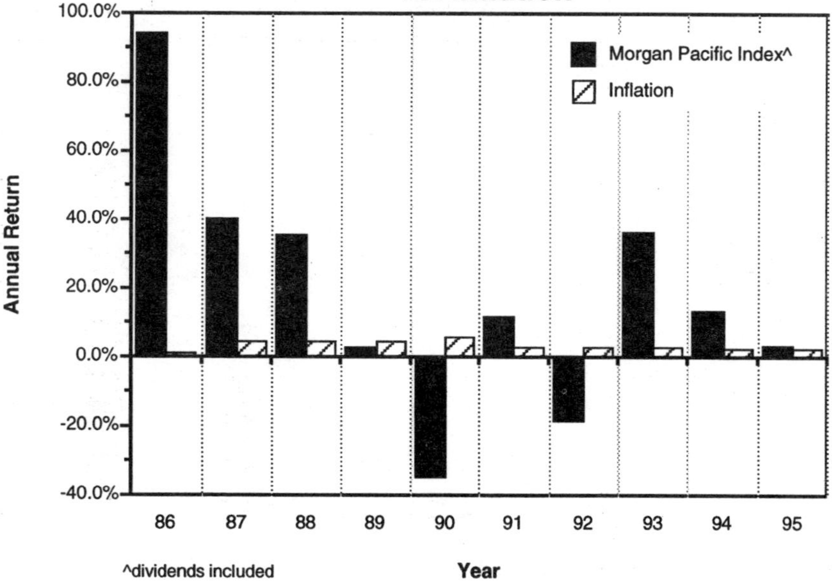


©1996 Chase Global Data & Research
73 Junction Square, Concord, MA 01742

## MORGAN STANLEY EMERGING MARKETS GLOBAL INDEX

[Global Index; without dividends; year-end; in U.S. dollars]

| Year | Index Value* | Total Return | Compound return on a five year $10,000 investment |
|---|---|---|---|
| 1995 | 337.258 | -10.75% | 1991 - 1995 |
| 1994 | 377.901 | -2.41% | |
| 1993 | 387.250 | 65.50% | ... $19,094 |
| 1992 | 233.989 | 2.61% | (13.81%) |
| 1991 | 228.048 | 29.11% | |
| 1990 | 176.632 | -33.02% | |
| 1989 | 263.717 | 50.60% | |
| 1988 | 175.110 | 75.11% | |
| 1987 | 100.000 | | |

* Source: ©1995 Morgan Stanley Capital International.

©1996 Chase Global Data & Research
73 Junction Square, Concord, MA 01742

## Morgan Stanley Emerging Markets Global Index

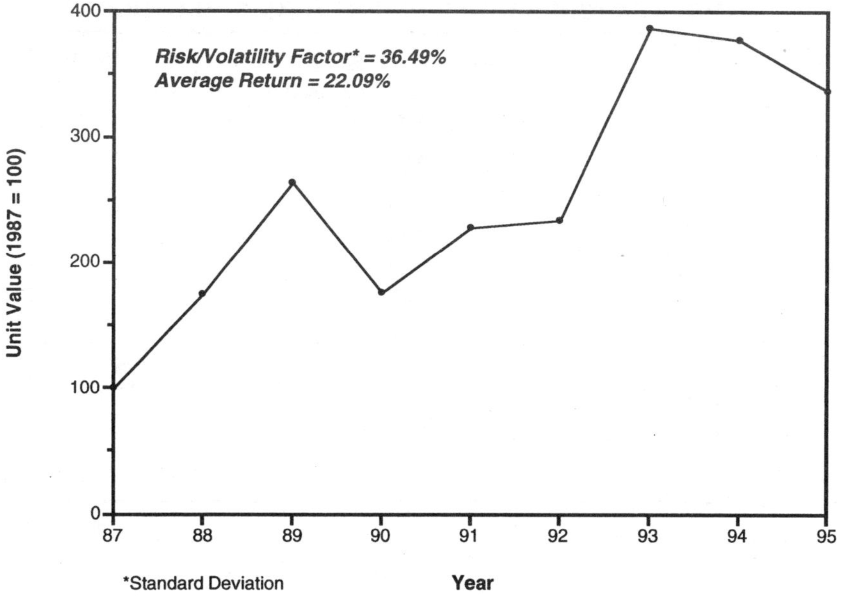


## Morgan Stanley Emerging Markets Global Index vs. Morgan Stanley World Equity Index^ and Morgan Stanley Pacific Equity Index^

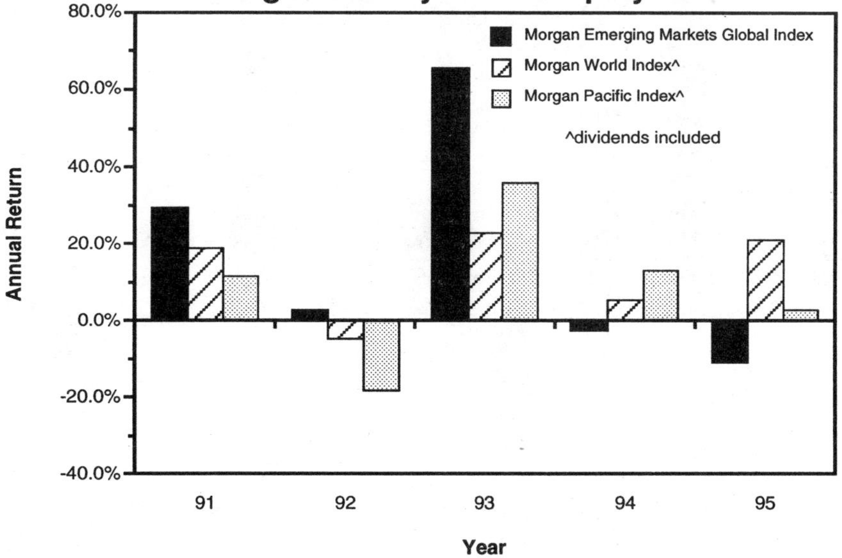


©1996 Chase Global Data & Research
73 Junction Square, Concord, MA 01742

## Morgan Stanley Emerging Markets Global Index vs. Taxable Money Market Avg. and Crude Oil

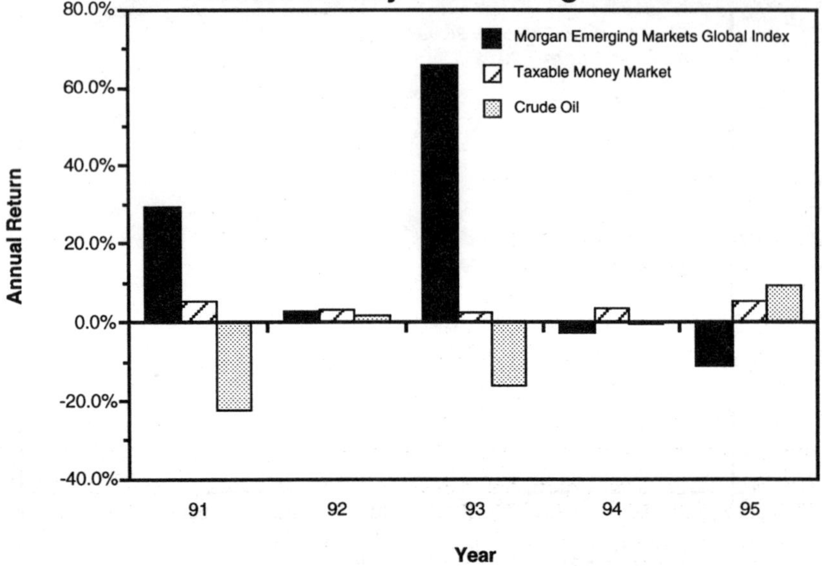


## Morgan Stanley Emerging Markets Global Index vs. Inflation

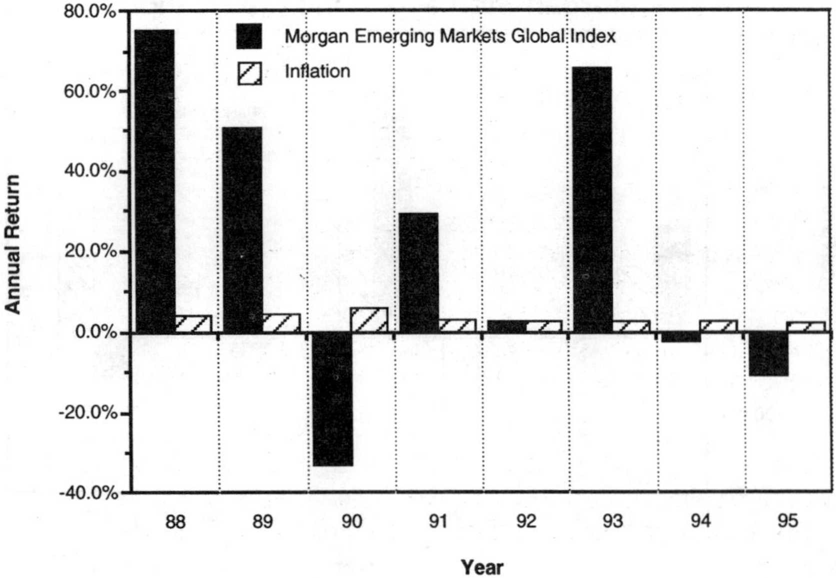


©1996 Chase Global Data & Research
73 Junction Square, Concord, MA 01742

# Chapter Sixteen

# IFC Emerging Markets Indices

IFC Composite
IFC Asia
IFC Europe/MidEast/Africa (EMEA)
IFC Latin America

Emerging Markets are arguably the world's fastest growing investment segment. The percentage growth in assets invested in the world's youngest equity marketplaces is staggering. In 1980 foreigners had invested only several million dollars in Emerging Markets, yet today there is well over $50 billion. Individual markets where a decade ago investors didn't even know, or care, they existed now have mutual funds exclusively devoted to investing in them. The reasons for this past explosive growth are strong, but the evidence for even greater growth in the future is stronger still.

Tracking the movement of equity exchanges in the Emerging Markets is a complex task. The International Finance Corporation (IFC), established in 1956, has followed Emerging Markets since the 1975. IFC is a member of the World Bank Group, and is owned by the over 150 member countries. IFC's mandate is to promote the growth of profitable and productive private enterprises in developing member countries. To date IFC has invested US$11 billion in over 1,500 businesses in over 100 developing countries. Today the IFC is the world's largest source of financial assistance to developing countries. Monitoring the equities and exchanges of the various developing countries in the world is an important function of the IFC. Its detailed information helps educate foreigners as to the performance of the investment arena known as the world's emerging marketplaces.

As stated earlier, the growth of emerging markets has been enormous. In 1982 the 32 developing countries followed by IFC had a market capitalization of $67 billion. One decade later those same 32 marketplaces had grown 11 fold to $740 billion. Trading volume in the

©1996 Chase Global Data & Research
73 Junction Square, Concord, MA 01742

Emerging Markets has increased 25 fold, and today the total listings in the Emerging Markets represents 40% of the world's total listings of 30,000 securities.

The popularity and potential growth of Emerging Markets derives from very compelling reasons. Simply stated, Emerging Markets reflect countries which have not advanced to the mature status of developed countries and their markets. Companies which dwell domestically within the borders of emerging nations—whose expansion potential seems likely to go nowhere but upward—tend to advance albeit with risks. Who will be the ultimate business "winners" and which companies will fail or at least not live up to expectations is part of the complexity involving Emerging Markets investing.

While it is difficult to predict the *when* and *who* will ultimately create great gains, it is not hard to understand that, for example, communications will expand in the markets of Africa where there is one telephone for every 30,000 people. Or that communications will expand sharply in South America—where in some nations selected apartments and condos command significant premiums for sale or rent simply because a telephone line is connected to the residence. And what about the need for computers firms to help those markets' small emerging companies join the 20th century via technology—and thus compete better in the world. And remember, too, that labor is much cheaper in the Emerging Markets.

Ten or fifteen years ago the majority of leaders in South America and in other emerging nations were dictators or non-democratic leaders with little interest in what was outside their borders. Today many of those same nations' leaders are well educated business people who seek interaction with the global economic community as they sharply expand their nation's GDP. To be sure, those new leaders are succeeding admirably where their predecessors had failed.

Today's new leadership in Emerging Markets often privatize state owned businesses. As this process evolves, the markets reflecting those new major securities gain depth and breadth and become much more attractive to sophisticated global institutions—which may then look for even more opportunities within those markets. Success is also reflected in the corporate earnings for Emerging Markets, for they expanded 50% more than developed countries during the quarter century from 1965 through 1989. The International Monetary Fund estimated in 1992 that output growth was over 3.5 times greater in Emerging Markets than developed ones.

©1996 Chase Global Data & Research
73 Junction Square, Concord, MA 01742

The IFC Indices as reflected in the Performance Tables which follow require some explanation. The original IFC indexes, still used but now known as IFC Global Indices, do not take into consideration certain restrictions on ownership of shares by foreigners—which would in reality limit ownership of the assets reflected in the indexes. Examples of restrictions on foreign ownership are: special classes of shares, market sector restrictions (no banking stocks open for investment etc.), single foreign shareholder limits on share classes, restrictions allowing "Authorized Investors" (only fund managers of certain size etc.), individual company statutes restricting ownership, and national limits on total foreign investment capital. Thus the IFC Global Indices' primary function was to enable investors to compare and gauge local market price movement and relative market size.

But in 1992 the IFC *Investable* (I) indexes were created. These indexes accurately reflect Emerging Market assets which could in fact be owned by foreigners without restriction. Of note, both the IFCI (Investable) and Global (original) indices use the same methodology and reflect total return with dividends reinvested. A stock must qualify for IFC Global Index status before it can be admitted to IFCI security status. In order for a security to qualify for IFC "I" status, it must qualify for an IFC Global Index, be an openly traded security in an open market, have a market capitalization of US$25 million or more, and have annual trading volume of at least US$10 million. (Note: Certain exemption rules may apply in some cases.)

For an individual stock market/exchange to qualify for Emerging Market status the exchange must be located in a developing country as defined by the World Bank's GNP per capita criteria. The latest available data (as of 1993) defines a developing country GNP per capita as either 1) Low-Income Economy (US$695 or less) or 2) Middle Income Economy (US$696 to US$8,625).

The IFC Investable indexes in the Performance Tables which follow show dollar adjusted growth which overall has been outstanding. The returns reflect, however, the risks of investing in these markets as well—for they have been quite volatile. For example, while the IFCI EMEA market ranked #1 among all subjects in the *Digest* for the past three years, both the IFCI Composite and IFCI Asia indexes were very close to last in overall performance in 1995. As developing countries GDPs expand and contract in increments of 5%-15% per year, they also display improvements in inflation down from 1000% per annum to 30%. But 30% inflation still mirrors a risky financial environment nonetheless, and Emerging Markets returns reflect such uncertainty in

©1996 Chase Global Data & Research
73 Junction Square, Concord, MA 01742

their volaility. However, over the long term there should be ample room for rewards commensurate with the risks.

The IFC analyzes over 1000 stocks (about half the number on the NYSE) in 20 markets and creates indices reflecting various groups' investment performance. Information is compiled in both local currency and in U.S. dollar equivalents. The indices are weighted by market capitalization. The key indices IFC tracks—which are thus included in the *Chase Investment Performance Digest* in U.S. dollar terms—are the IFCI Composite (the "I" standing for Investable), IFCI Asia, IFCI Europe/Mideast/Africa, and IFCI Latin America. The component details of these indices as of July 1995 are as follows:

*IFCI Composite:* 24 countries. 1,446 companies. Total capitalization: $1.1 trillion.
Countries: Argentina, Brazil, Chile, China (Mainland), Colombia, Greece, Hungary, India, Indonesia, Jordan, Korea, Malaysia, Mexico, Nigeria, Pakistan, Peru, Philippines, Poland, Portugal, South Africa, Sri Lanka, Taiwan (China), Thailand, Turkey, Venezuela, Zimbabwe.

*IFCI Asia:* 10 Countries. 784 countries. Total capitalization: $653 billion.
Countries: China (Mainland), India, Indonesia, Korea, Malaysia, Pakistan, Philippines, Sri Lanka, Taiwan (China), Thailand.

*IFCI Europe/Mideast/Africa (EMEA):* 7 Countries. 335 companies. Total Capitalization: $199 billion.
Countries: Greece, Hungary, Jordan, Nigeria, Poland, Portugal, South Africa, Turkey, Zimbabwe.

*IFCI Latin America:* 7 Countries. 327 companies. Total Capitalization: $263 billion.
Countries: Argentina, Brazil, Chile, Colombia, Mexico, Peru, Venezuela.

©1996 Chase Global Data & Research
73 Junction Square, Concord, MA 01742

## IFC Composite Index

[Investable for foreigners; Global Index; with dividends; year-end; in U.S. dollars]

| Year | Index Value* | Total Return | Compound return on a five year $10,000 investment |
|---|---|---|---|
| 1995 | 329.530 | -8.42% | 1991 - 1995 |
| 1994 | 359.840 | -12.00% | |
| 1993 | 408.890 | 79.61% | ... $20,863 |
| 1992 | 227.650 | 3.28% | (15.84%) |
| 1991 | 220.410 | 39.54% | |
| 1990 | 157.950 | -2.20% | |
| 1989 | 161.510 | 61.51% | |
| 1988 | 100.00 | | |

* Source: ©1995 International Finance Corporation

©1996 Chase Global Data & Research
73 Junction Square, Concord, MA 01742

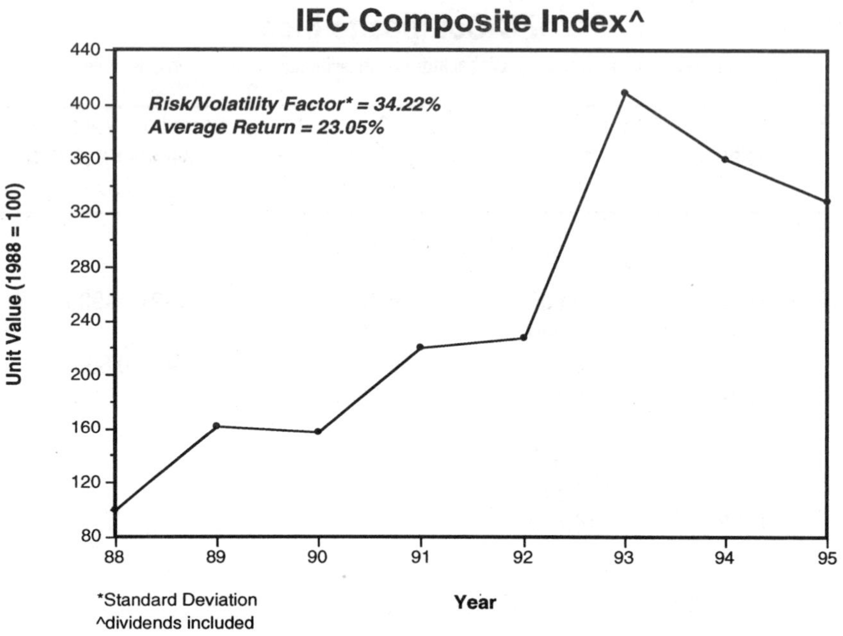


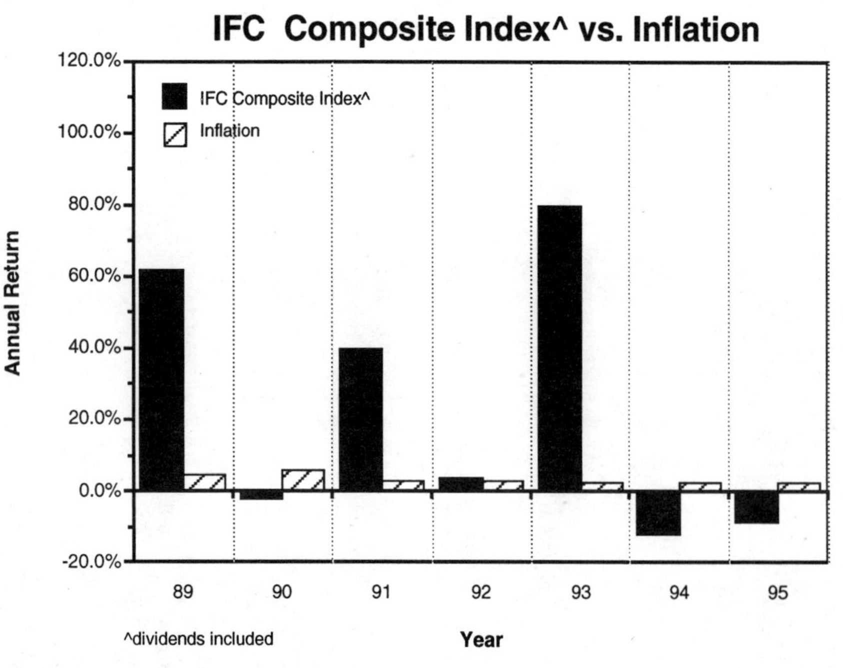


©1996 Chase Global Data & Research
73 Junction Square, Concord, MA 01742

## IFC Asia Index

[Investable for foreigners; Global Index; with dividends; year-end; in U.S. dollars]

| Year | Index Value* | Total Return | Compound return on a five year $10,000 investment |
|---|---|---|---|
| 1995 | 270.130 | -5.47% | 1991 - 1995 |
| 1994 | 285.760 | -12.80% | |
| 1993 | 327.710 | 97.62% | ... $21,697 |
| 1992 | 165.830 | 18.53% | (16.76%) |
| 1991 | 139.900 | 12.37% | |
| 1990 | 124.500 | -19.22% | |
| 1989 | 154.120 | 54.12% | |
| 1988 | 100.00 | | |

* Source: ©1995 International Finance Corporation

©1996 Chase Global Data & Research
73 Junction Square, Concord, MA 01742

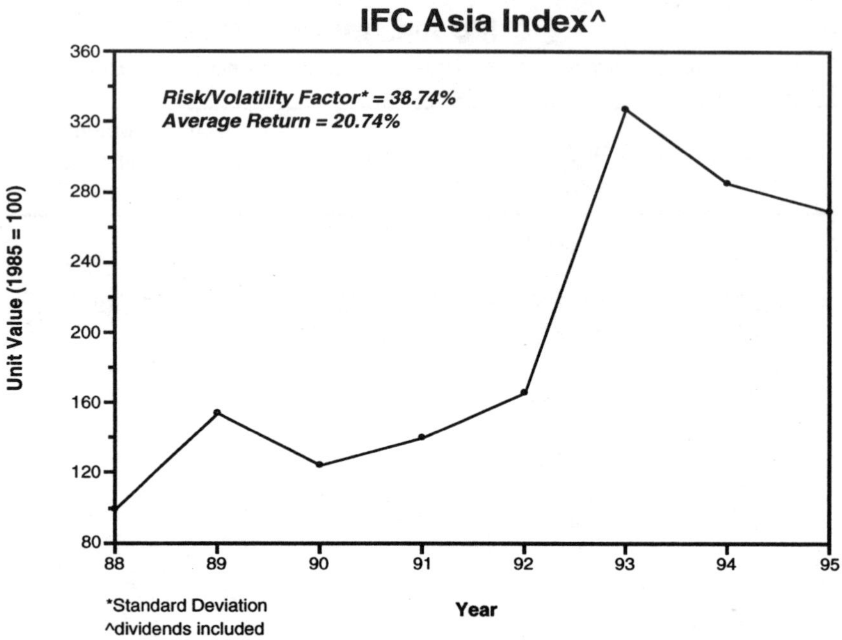


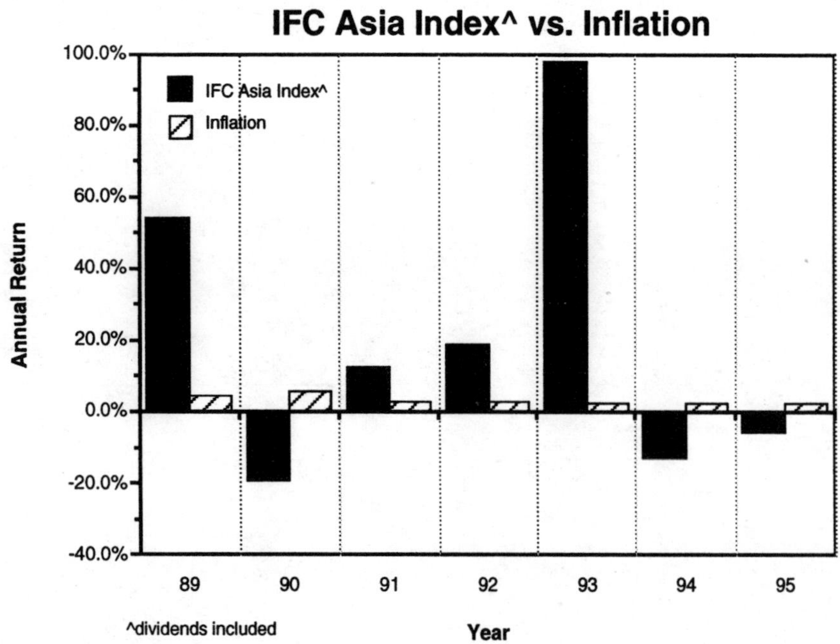


©1996 Chase Global Data & Research
73 Junction Square, Concord, MA 01742

## IFC EUROPE/MIDEAST/AFRICA Index

[Investable for foreigners; Global Index; with dividends; year-end; in U.S. dollars]

| Year | Index Value* | Total Return | Compound return on a five year $10,000 investment |
|---|---|---|---|
| 1995 | 189.430 | 22.51% | 1991 - 1995 |
| 1994 | 154.620 | -27.12% | |
| 1993 | 212.160 | 122.41% | ... $9,460 |
| 1992 | 95.390 | -32.69% | (-1.10%) |
| 1991 | 141.720 | -29.22% | |
| 1990 | 200.240 | 13.90% | |
| 1989 | 175.800 | 75.80% | |
| 1988 | 100.00 | | |

* Source: ©1995 International Finance Corporation

©1996 Chase Global Data & Research
73 Junction Square, Concord, MA 01742

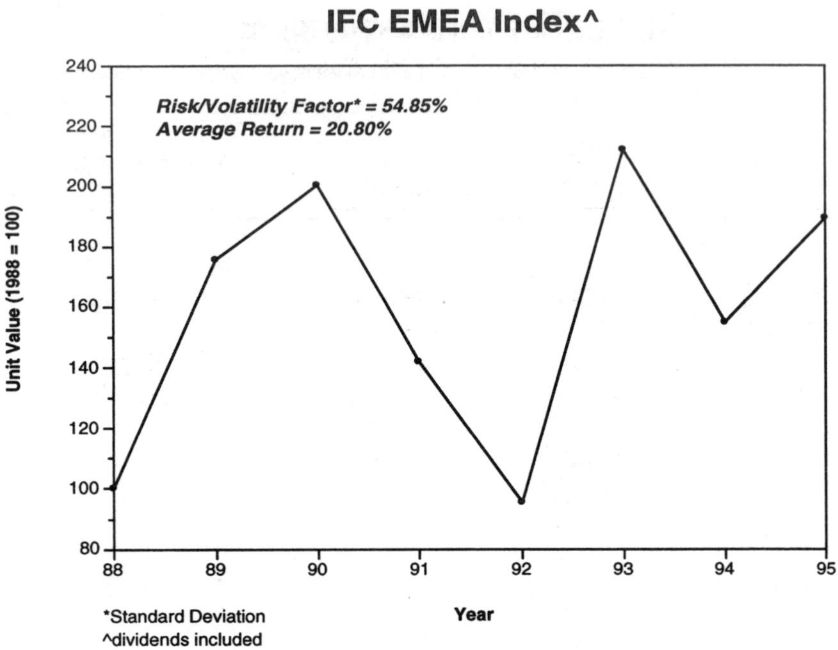


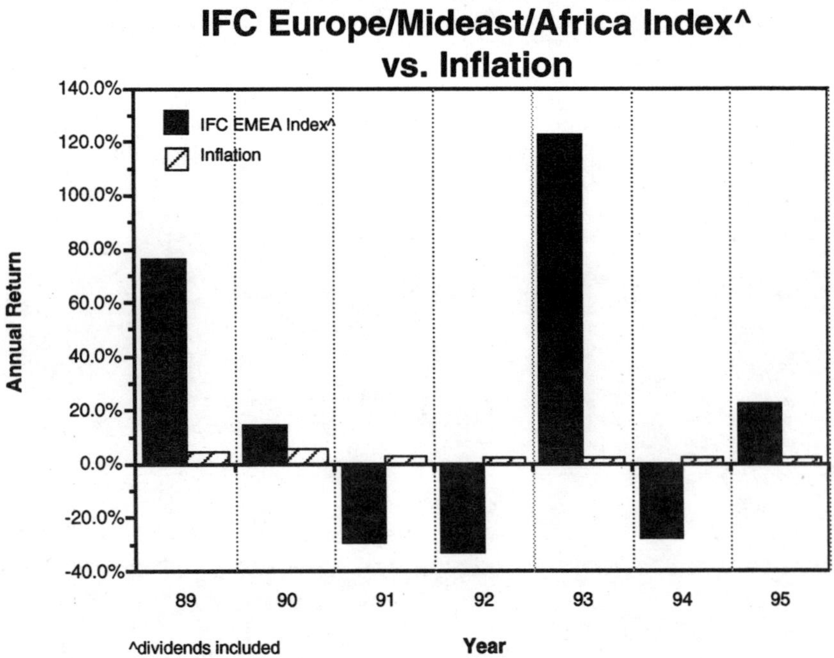


©1996 Chase Global Data & Research
73 Junction Square, Concord, MA 01742

## IFC Latin America Index

[Investable for foreigners; Global Index; with dividends; year-end; in U.S. dollars]

| Year | Index Value* | Total Return | Compound return on a five year $10,000 investment |
|---|---|---|---|
| 1995 | 576.470 | -16.85% | 1991 - 1995 |
| 1994 | 693.290 | -9.36% | |
| 1993 | 764.880 | 60.75% | ... $29,985 |
| 1992 | 475.820 | 3.45% | (24.56%) |
| 1991 | 459.950 | 139.25% | |
| 1990 | 192.250 | 9.14% | |
| 1989 | 176.150 | 76.15% | |
| 1988 | 100.00 | | |

* Source: ©1995 International Finance Corporation

©1996 Chase Global Data & Research
73 Junction Square, Concord, MA 01742

## IFC Latin America Index^

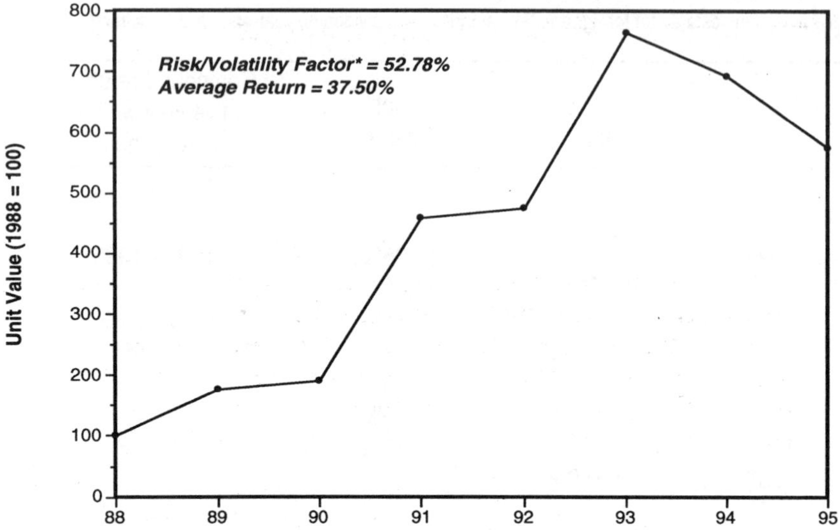


*Standard Deviation
^dividends included

## IFC Latin America Index^ vs. Inflation

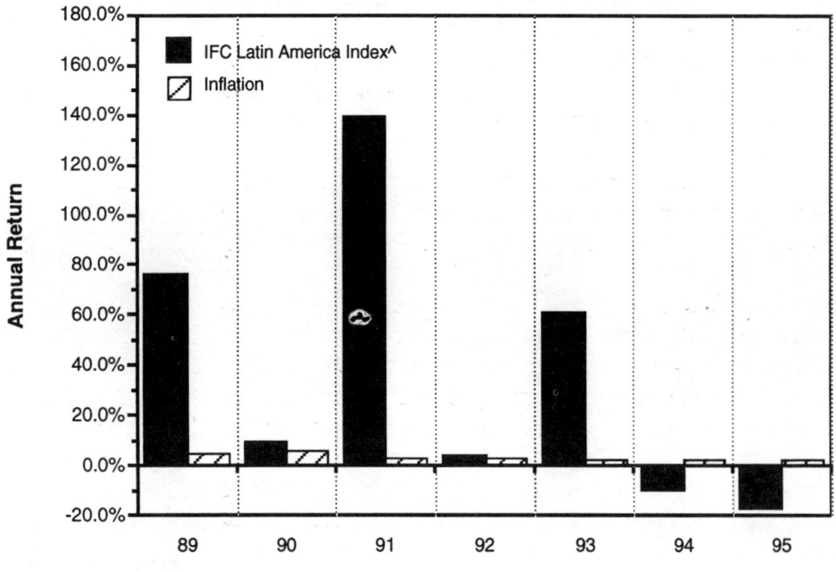


^dividends included

©1996 Chase Global Data & Research
73 Junction Square, Concord, MA 01742

# Chapter Seventeen

# Merrill Lynch Global Bond Indices

Merrill Lynch Global Government Bond Index
Merrill Lynch Australia Government Bond Index
Merrill Lynch Japan Government Bond Index
Merrill Lynch United Kingdom Government Bond Index
Merrill Lynch Germany Government Bond Index

By year-end 1995 the world's major bond markets exceeded \$19 *trillion* in market value. Today global bond markets assets exceed the value of the world's equity markets by \$2.5 trillion. Even United States investors, both sophisticated and non-sophisticated, have recently begun to recognize the upside potential of investing in fixed income assets abroad—rather than exclusively using domestic markets. Over the past several years U.S. investors have exercised their initial global investment forays into equity markets. However, today global bond investing both in the U.S. and abroad is markedly on the increase. And there is no turning back. For as the world grows smaller each day, fixed income and equity trading continues on all continents around the clock.

The enormous task of tracking the global bond markets was undertaken in earnest in the mid-1980's by Merrill Lynch—the nation's largest brokerage firm. The Merrill Lynch International Fixed Income Research Department initiated dozens of worldwide, regional, Eurodollar, and government issue indices in December 1985. Merrill Lynch's indices are recognized as the premier performance gauges for analyzing fixed income markets around the globe. Merrill's Global Bond Indices are cited frequently in major national and international publications, not the least of which are daily and weekly listings in the *Wall Street Journal*. Until the Merrill Lynch Global Bond Indices gained prominence, accurate gauging of global bond markets was extremely difficult. The indices have filled a major void in global investing.

©1996 Chase Global Data & Research
73 Junction Square, Concord, MA 01742

The Merrill Lynch Global Bond Indices address three major bond market groups—all U.S. domestic and Eurodollar bonds, foreign government bonds, and non-U.S. dollar Eurobonds. In all, Merrill Lynch Domestic and Global bond indices cover over half of the total bond debt outstanding in the world's major markets. Merrill assists qualified clients such as pension plans, money managers, and wealthy individuals who seek to diversify their assets through investing in various global bond markets. Some investors seek to maximize their overall returns by actively investing in many areas, while others desire Merrill Lynch's assistance in creating customized passive index funds which mirror returns found outside domestic markets.

Merrill Lynch tracks over 11,000 bonds with a total value exceeding US$9 trillion. Their all-inclusive Global Bond Index contains all U.S. dollar denominated debt issues and 25 non-dollar market indices. Merrill's index system comprises more than 1,900 master and sub-indices. The overall basic structure of the Merrill Lynch global bond indices is by necessity a consistent one. The average maturity of the foreign bonds followed is 9.9 years. Merrill Lynch indices require all bonds have a fixed coupon and maturity. Floating rate, index-linked, and zero coupon bonds are excluded. The exception is a specific zero coupon U.S. Treasury index. Bonds must have a maturity of at least one year and have an investment grade rating of at least BBB; however, some indices may include foreign issues which have not been rated by major U.S. rating services. While U.S. dollar denominated convertibles issues are included in the Merrill Lynch Convertible Index, all other convertibles and bonds issued with equity warrants are excluded.

All Merrill Lynch bond indices reflect total return performance and are available in local currency and U.S. dollar terms, as well as any of 23 alternative currencies. The composite indices are market weighted by their components after all currency adjustments. The Merrill Lynch Eurobond indices encompass eleven markets and currencies. By the end of 1995, Merrill Lynch's Government/Eurobond Index included 2,139 issues, both dollar and non-dollar with a market value of US$6.4 trillion. The Merrill Lynch Non-U.S. Dollar Bond Index contains all non-U.S. dollar market indices reflecting 16 foreign government markets. The Non-U.S. Dollar Index holds 2,035 issues valued at $4 trillion.

In the latter part of the 1980's the world's bond markets grew over 20%, reflecting an ever increasing propensity for business enterprises and governments everywhere to increase their debts. Of

©1996 Chase Global Data & Research
73 Junction Square, Concord, MA 01742

note, central government borrowings and corporate debts share the overall debt structure about equally, 48% versus 52% respectively. By the end of 1995, the nations with the greatest overall piece of the Global Government debt pie were the United States (44%), Japan (29%), and Germany (8%). Ever rising, the United States' bond market share increased one trillion dollars since 1990 The global top ten overall government debt markets as of December 31, 1995 were:

| | |
|---|---|
| United States | $2.260 trillion |
| Japan | $1.190 trillion |
| Germany | $0.451 trillion |
| France | $0.411 trillion |
| United Kingdom | $0.319 trillion |
| Italy | $0.295 trillion |
| Belgium | $0.182 trillion |
| Canada | $0.175 trillion |
| Netherlands | $0.152 trillion |
| Sweden | $0.104 trillion |

Several studies have shown that prudent diversification of fixed income assets into foreign bonds does reap dual rewards. Through comparing the returns of the InterSec Research Non-North American bond index (a composite of total returns of German, French, Swiss, Dutch, Japanese, and British bonds) versus the Merrill Lynch U.S. Corporate and Government Master Index, the foreign bond index wins. The InterSec Index returned 12.0% per annum during the fifteen year period from 1973 to 1988, while the Merrill Lynch domestic index returned 9.0%. In addition, the non-dollar index was less volatile than the U.S. domestic bond index, with 7.4% and 12.4% standard deviations respectively (a lower standard deviation reflects a lower volatility of return).

Currency risk is beyond question the greatest negative inherent to investing in global bond markets. But properly managed, currency fluctuations can be an additional avenue toward greater overall return, i.e. one can make money in currency management, too. Overall the additional variable of currency fluctuations negates about half of the markets' reduced volatility—through adding another aspect of ownership bearing additional risk. However, currency considerations are by no means the overwhelming force in portfolio performance. For

©1996 Chase Global Data & Research
73 Junction Square, Concord, MA 01742

example, during the three consecutive losing years from 1977-1979 currency changes accounted for less than half of the total return in foreign bonds—the markets contributed 53% of total return while dollar movement accounted for 47%.

Investment in fixed income vehicles on a global scale need not be limited to medium and long term maturities. Sophisticated management of yield differentials promises gains for shorter term maturities as well. For example, when funds were invested exclusively in foreign money markets and currency fluctuations were not hedged, returns were about 2% higher in the foreign money funds for the six year period from 1983 through 1988. Volatility was 25 times higher than a domestic money market fund, however. Nevertheless, past studies have shown that if only 20% of a money market fund is invested in foreign short term paper and currency fluctuations are managed, volatility is only 2.5 times greater than a domestic money market fund and the overall yield increases 1.7%. On an annual basis over the six year period studied the yield of the foreign money market fund outpaced the domestic fund three times, underperformed twice, and was identical once.

Investment in foreign bonds today is a compelling choice for several reasons. One is that foreign bond markets in general are about half as volatile as the U.S. bond market. Also of importance is the fact that historically domestic bond money managers have lost to the U.S. bond benchmark performance indices almost two-thirds of the time. Results have been so poor that several institutions have given up trying to beat the indices and instead seek only to match their returns through indexing. It follows that domestic bond money managers are now seeking to actively invest in foreign bonds to improve their returns, sometimes investing in global bond markets by way of indexing the global markets as well. Several studies show this strategy as a worthwhile exercise, especially if employed when the manager believes the U.S. dollar is vulnerable to decline and as a result places about 20% of his/her portfolio in foreign bonds. Here again the strategy has obvious potential rewards if the currency play is on target. It also has the added advantage of reducing the portfolio's overall volatility.

Of significance is the fact that a graduated mix of foreign bonds and domestic U.S. bonds has proven to increase return, while reducing risk. Studies in global bond diversification in relation to U.S. domestic bond portfolios show that the replacement of 10% to 30% of domestic bonds with major foreign market bonds tends to increase returns while reducing overall volatility. The best of both worlds. But investing sums exceeding the 30% level does not seem as

©1996 Chase Global Data & Research
73 Junction Square, Concord, MA 01742

productive an exercise. However, as global bond market investments increase there is little doubt the sophistication and success levels in managing these portfolios will increase, too.

In that vein, for the year 1990 Global Income Bond funds were second only to health care funds as the top performing mutual fund investment group. The Merrill Lynch Global Government Bond Index has been an above average performer. It ranked in the top third of all subjects tracked by Chase Global Data & Research for the past decade. And many investors are taking notice. By 1995 Global Bond Mutual Funds saw their assets triple since 1990 level to over $35 billion. While many investment discussions have ample room for debate, there is no doubt that global bond investing is an arena which will experience sustained and dramatic growth now and into the future.

©1996 Chase Global Data & Research
73 Junction Square, Concord, MA 01742

## MERRILL LYNCH GLOBAL GOVERNMENT BOND INDEX

[in U.S. dollars]

| Year | Total* Return | Compound return on a five year $10,000 investment | Annual compound rate of return |
|---|---|---|---|
| 1995 | 17.31% | 1991 - 1995 | |
| 1994 | 1.84% | | 11.42% |
| 1993 | 14.76% | ... $17,174 | |
| 1992 | 7.42% | | |
| 1991 | 16.61% | | |
| 1990 | 11.31% | | |
| 1989 | 4.80% | | |
| 1988 | 4.42% | 1986 - 1990 | |
| 1987 | 18.00% | | 12.07% |
| 1986 | 23.00% | ... $17,679 | |

How a $10,000 investment performed over

| 5 years | 10 years |
|---|---|
| 1991 - 1995<br>$17,174<br>(11.42%)^ | |
| | 1986 - 1995<br>$30,362<br>(11.75%) |

^ annual compound rate of return for that period

*Source: Copyright ©1995 Merrill Lynch, Pierce, Fenner & Smith Incorporated.

©1996 Chase Global Data & Research
73 Junction Square, Concord, MA 01742

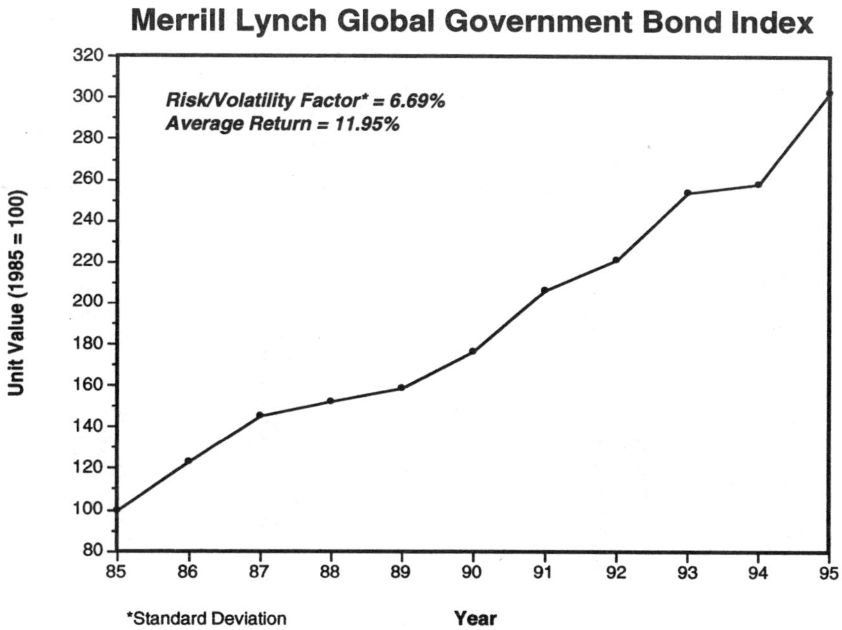


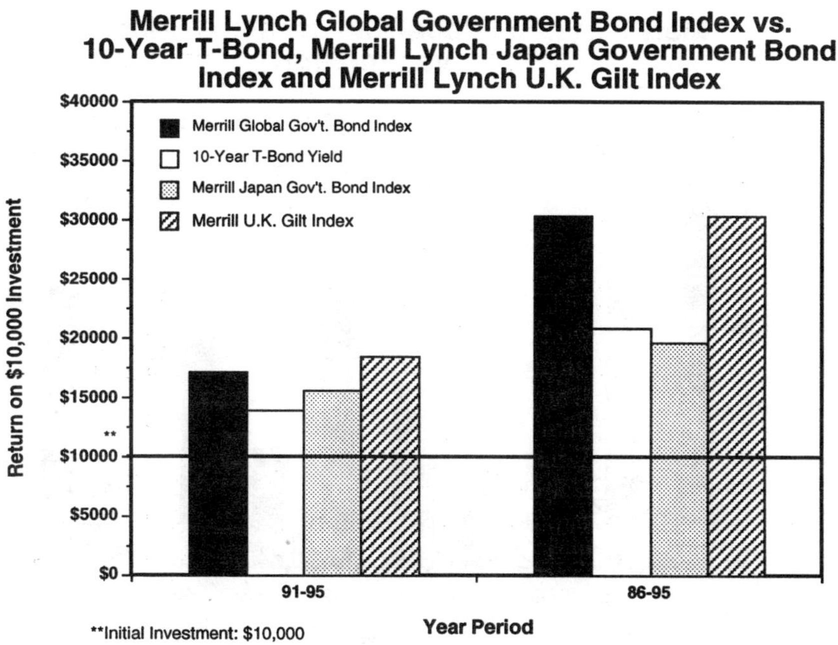


©1996 Chase Global Data & Research
73 Junction Square, Concord, MA 01742

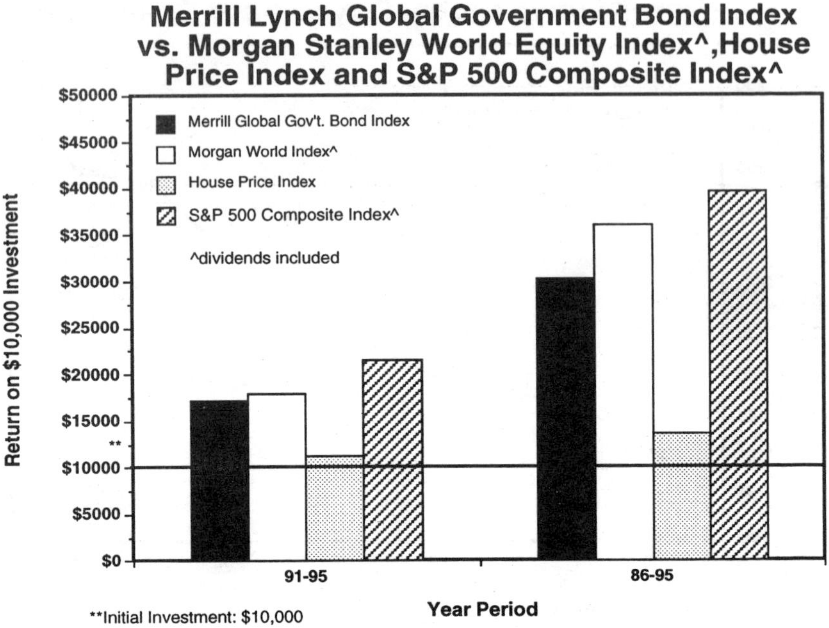


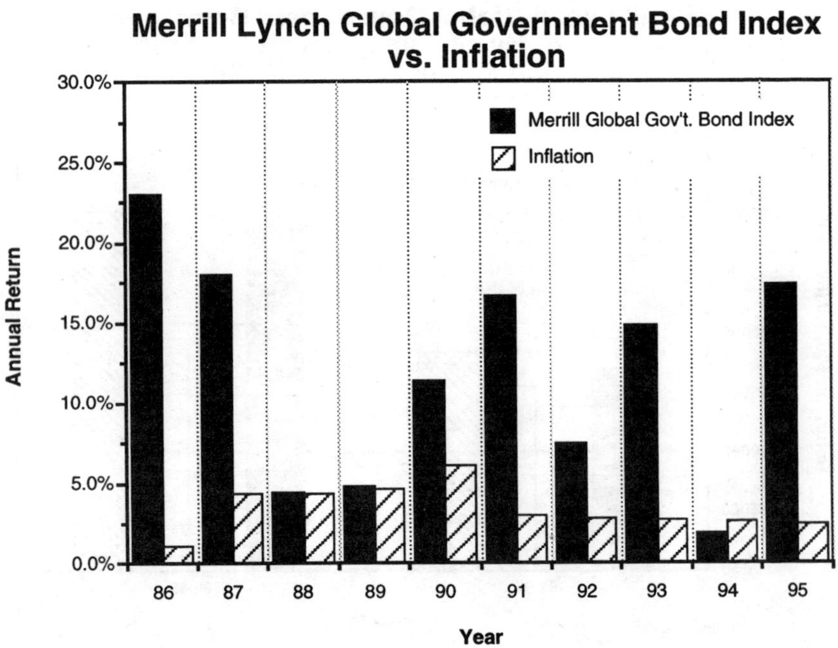


©1996 Chase Global Data & Research
73 Junction Square, Concord, MA 01742

## MERRILL LYNCH AUSTRALIA GOVERNMENT BOND INDEX

[in local currency]

| Year | Total* Return | Compound return on a five year $10,000 investment | Annual compound rate of return |
|---|---|---|---|
| 1995 | 19.41% | 1991 - 1995 | |
| 1994 | -7.40% | | 12.18% |
| 1993 | 17.50% | ... $17,764 | |
| 1992 | 10.23% | | |
| 1991 | 24.04% | | |
| 1990 | 18.36% | | |
| 1989 | 13.67% | | |
| 1988 | 9.43% | 1986 - 1990 | |
| 1987 | 18.53% | | 15.80% |
| 1986 | 19.34% | ... $20,825 | |

How a $10,000 investment performed over

| 5 years | 10 years |
|---|---|
| 1991 - 1995<br>$17,764<br>(12.18%)^ | |
| | 1986 - 1995<br>$36,994<br>(13.98%) |

^ annual compound rate of return for that period

*Source: Copyright ©1995 Merrill Lynch, Pierce, Fenner & Smith Incorporated.

©1996 Chase Global Data & Research
73 Junction Square, Concord, MA 01742

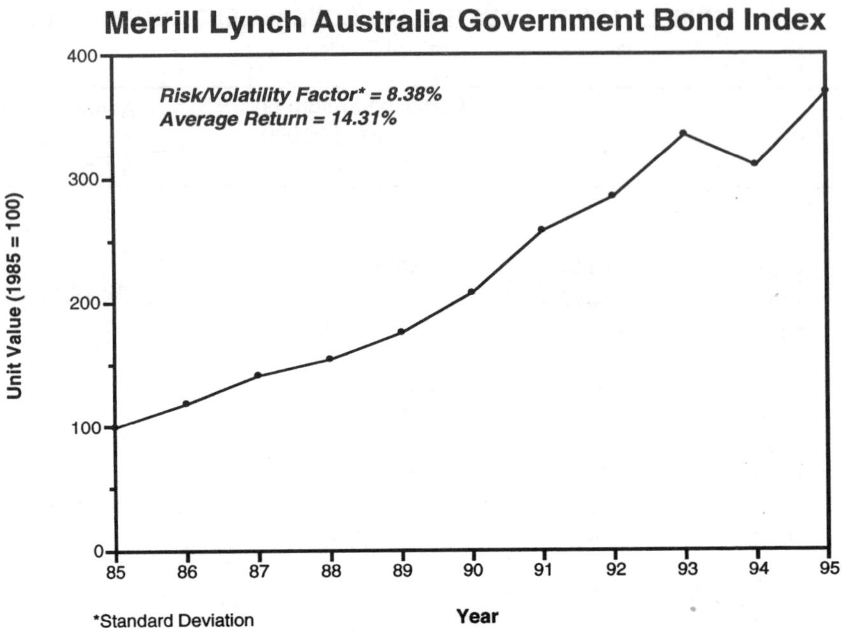


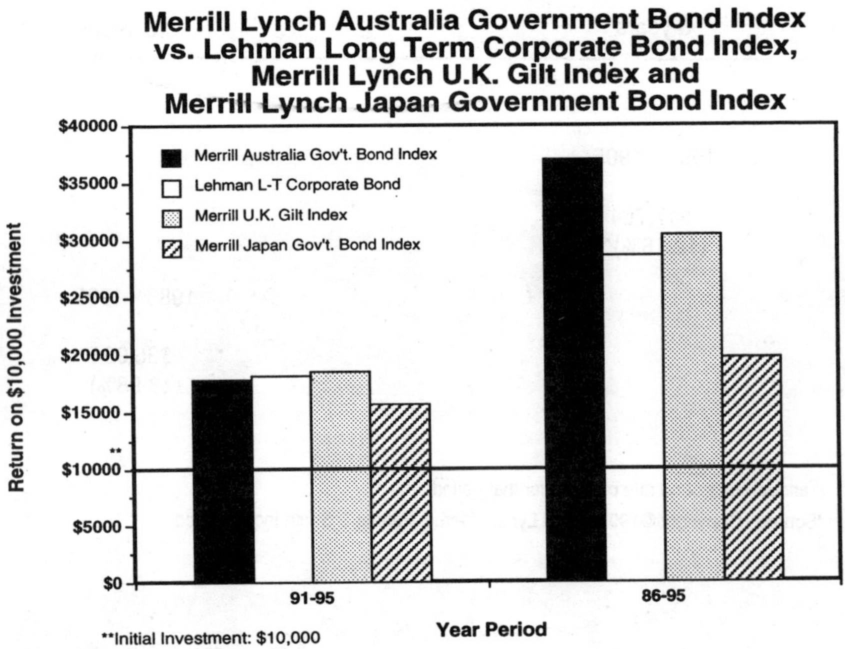


©1996 Chase Global Data & Research
73 Junction Square, Concord, MA 01742

## Merrill Lynch Australia Government Bond Index vs. Morgan Stanley North America Equity Index^, Australian Dollar and S&P 500 Composite Index^

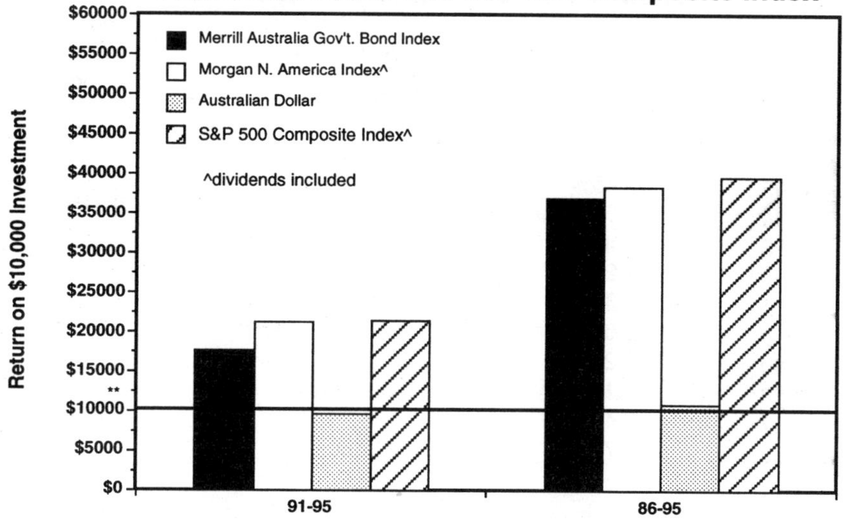


**Initial Investment: $10,000

## Merrill Lynch Australia Government Bond Index vs. Inflation

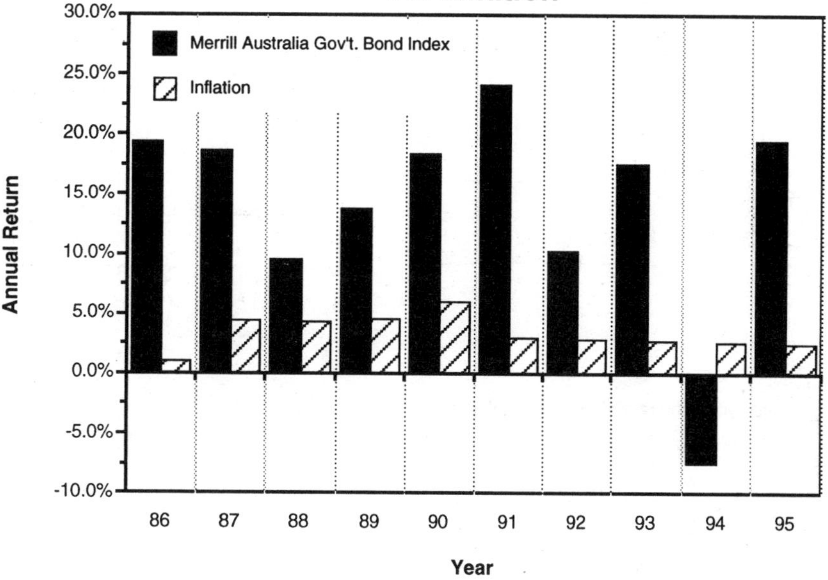


©1996 Chase Global Data & Research
73 Junction Square, Concord, MA 01742

## MERRILL LYNCH JAPAN GOVERNMENT BOND INDEX

[in local currency]

| Year | Total* Return | Compound return on a five year $10,000 investment | Annual compound rate of return |
|---|---|---|---|
| 1995 | 13.45% | 1991 - 1995 | 9.31% |
| 1994 | -2.92% | | |
| 1993 | 13.36% | ... $15,606 | |
| 1992 | 11.23% | | |
| 1991 | 12.38% | | |
| 1990 | 2.09% | | |
| 1989 | -1.25% | | |
| 1988 | 6.14% | 1986 - 1990 | 4.74% |
| 1987 | 6.41% | | |
| 1986 | 10.72% | ... $12,607 | |

How a $10,000 investment performed over

| 5 years | 10 years |
|---|---|
| 1991 - 1995 | 1986 - 1995 |
| $15,606 | $19,675 |
| (9.31%)^ | (7.00%) |

^ annual compound rate of return for that period

*Source: Copyright ©1995 Merrill Lynch, Pierce, Fenner & Smith Incorporated.

©1996 Chase Global Data & Research
73 Junction Square, Concord, MA 01742

## Merrill Lynch Japan Government Bond Index

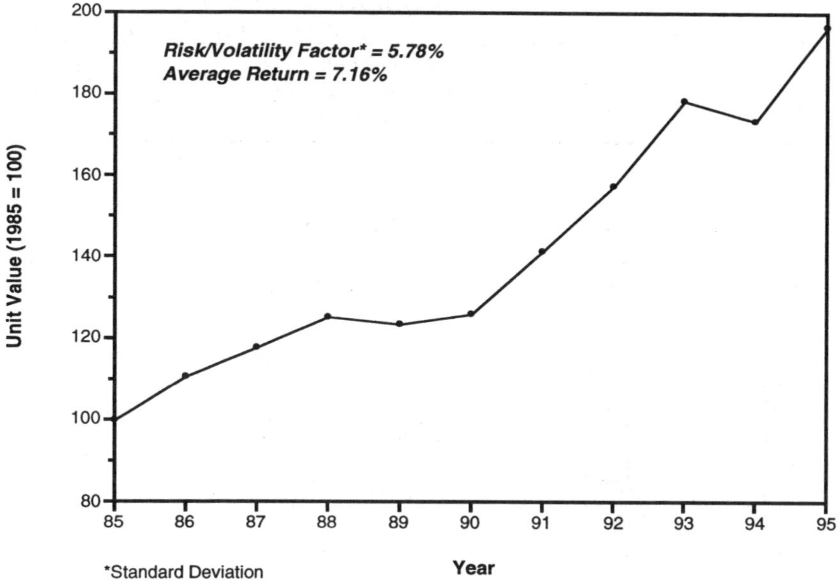


*Standard Deviation

## Merrill Lynch Japan Government Bond Index vs. Lehman Long Term Treasury Bond Index, Merrill Lynch Germany Government Bond Index, and Merrill Lynch U.K. Gilt Index

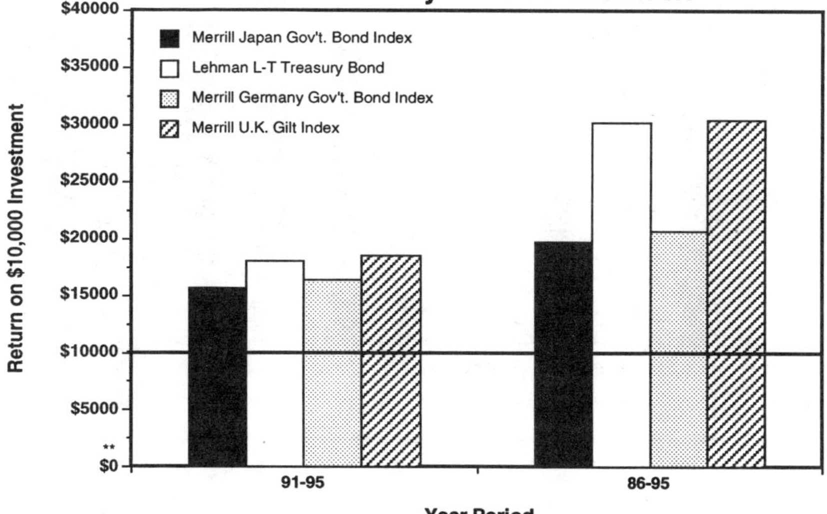


**Initial Investment: $10,000

©1996 Chase Global Data & Research
73 Junction Square, Concord, MA 01742

## Merrill Lynch Japan Government Bond Index vs. S&P 500 Composite Index^, Gold, Merrill Germany Government Bond Index and Japanese Yen

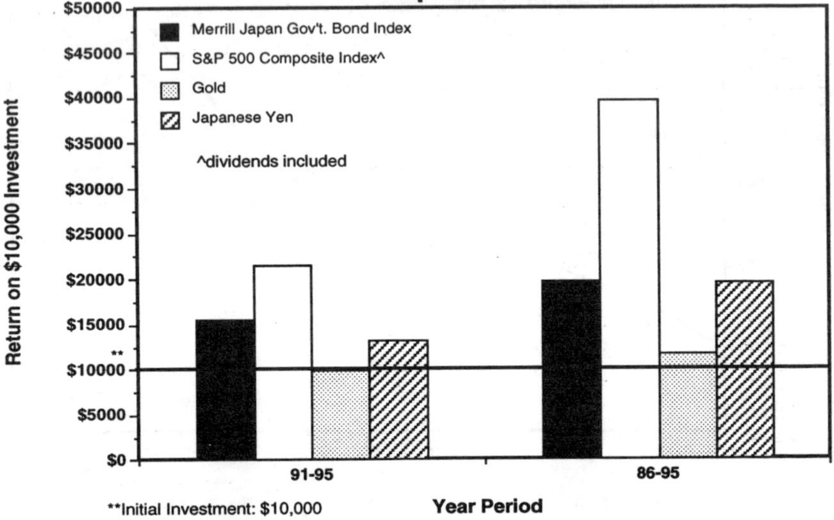


## Merrill Lynch Japan Government Bond Index vs. Inflation

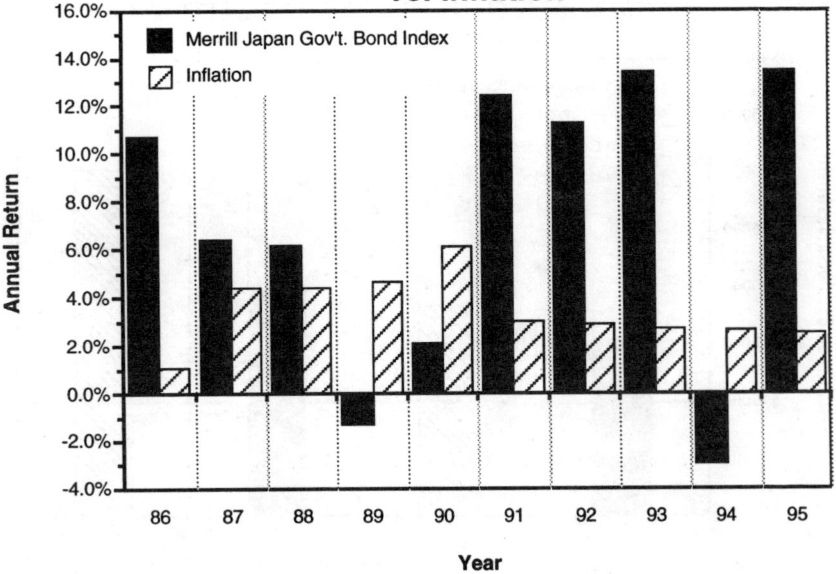


©1996 Chase Global Data & Research
73 Junction Square, Concord, MA 01742

## MERRILL LYNCH U.K. GILT BOND INDEX

[in local currency]

| Year | Total* Return | Compound return on a five year $10,000 investment | Annual compound rate of return |
|---|---|---|---|
| 1995 | 16.11% | 1991 - 1995 | |
| 1994 | -5.65% | | 13.09% |
| 1993 | 21.20% | ... $18,496 | |
| 1992 | 18.53% | | |
| 1991 | 17.53% | | |
| 1990 | 10.25% | | |
| 1989 | 7.99% | | |
| 1988 | 6.67% | 1986 - 1990 | |
| 1987 | 15.46% | | 10.45% |
| 1986 | 12.11% | ... $16,439 | |

How a $10,000 investment performed over

| 5 years | 10 years |
|---|---|
| 1991 - 1995 | |
| $18,496 | |
| (13.09%)^ | |
| | 1986 - 1995 |
| | $30,405 |
| | (11.76%) |

^ annual compound rate of return for that period

*Source: Copyright ©1995 Merrill Lynch, Pierce, Fenner & Smith Incorporated.

©1996 Chase Global Data & Research
73 Junction Square, Concord, MA 01742

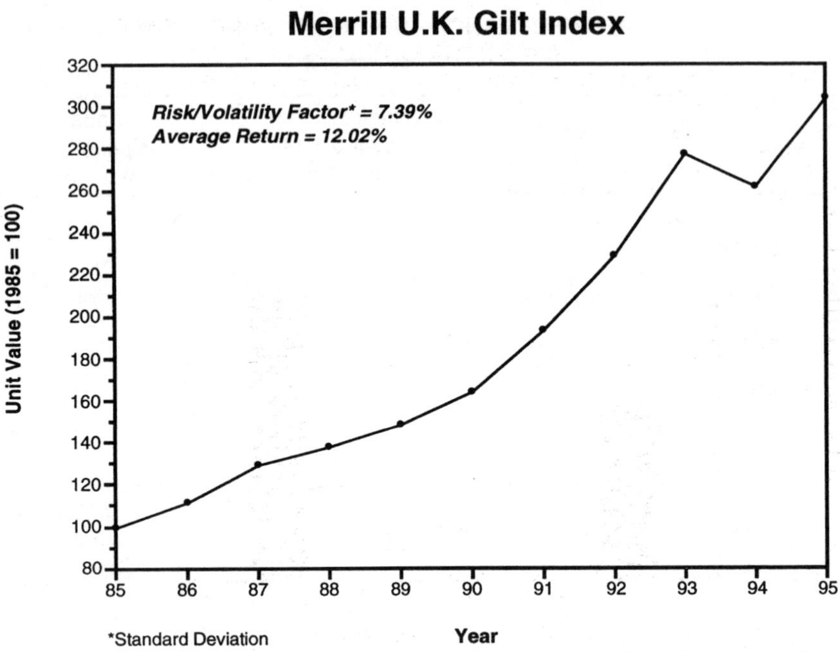


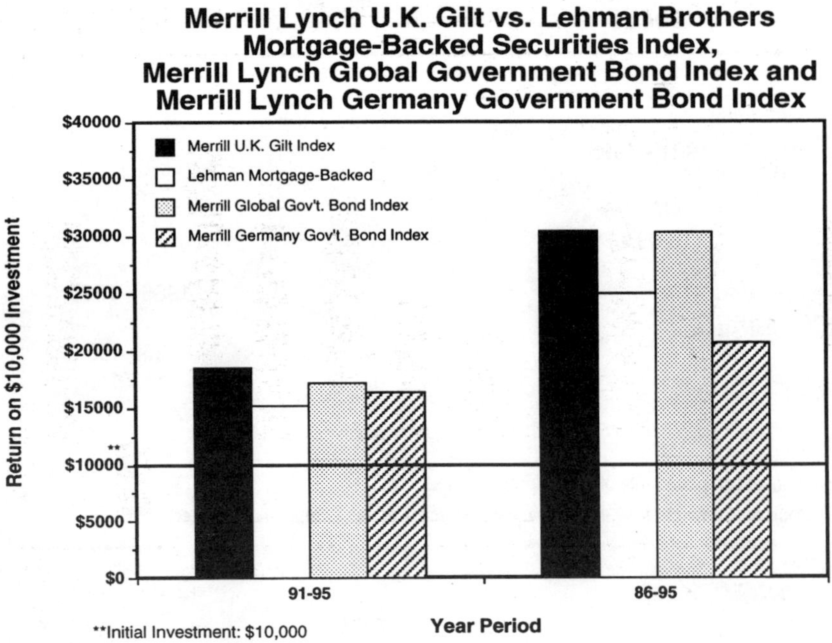


©1996 Chase Global Data & Research
73 Junction Square, Concord, MA 01742

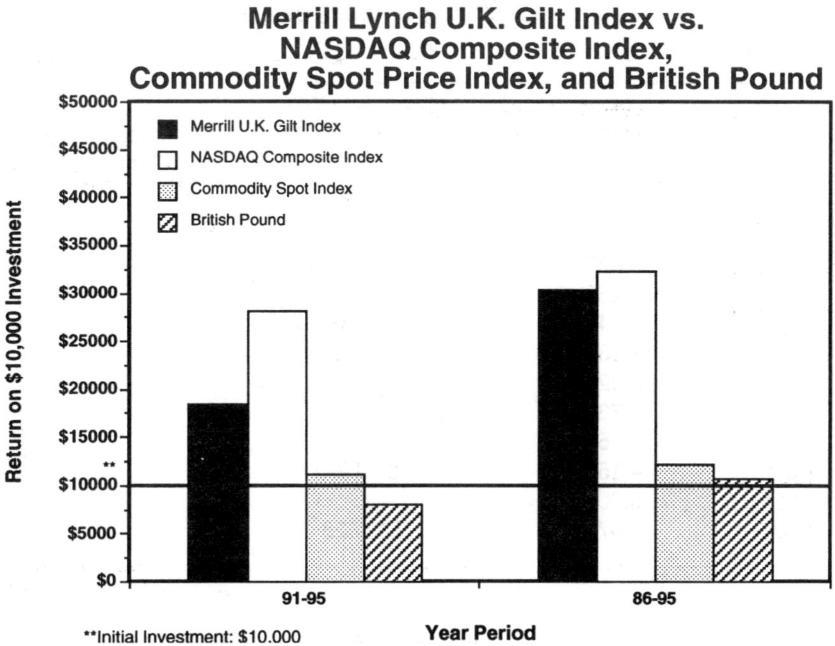


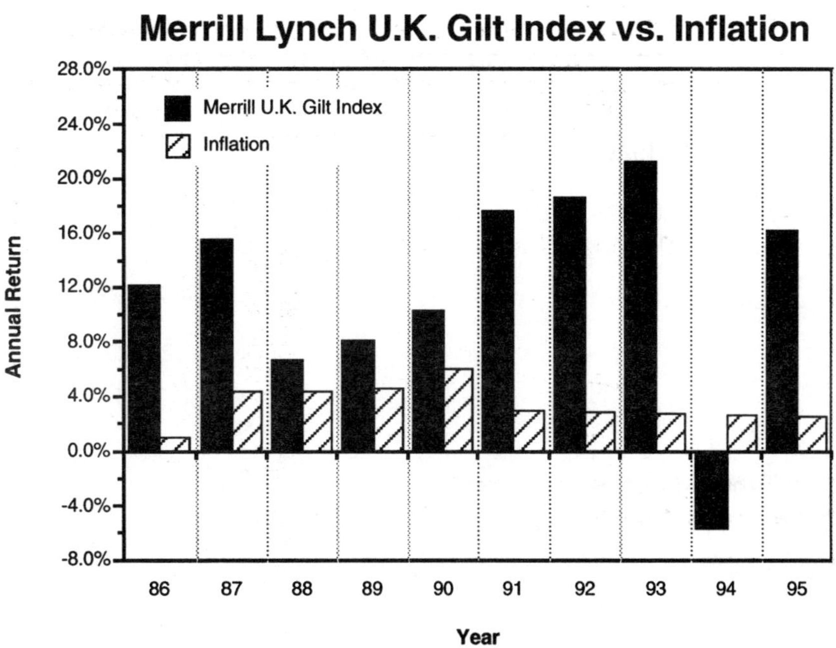


©1996 Chase Global Data & Research
73 Junction Square, Concord, MA 01742

## MERRILL LYNCH GERMANY GOVERMENT BOND INDEX

[in local currency]

| Year | Total* Return | Compound return on a five year $10,000 investment | Annual compound rate of return |
|---|---|---|---|
| 1995 | 16.03% | 1991 - 1995 | |
| 1994 | -1.26% | | 10.31% |
| 1993 | 13.64% | ... $16,337 | |
| 1992 | 13.13% | | |
| 1991 | 10.92% | | |
| 1990 | 3.73% | | |
| 1989 | 1.75% | | |
| 1988 | 4.15% | 1986 - 1990 | |
| 1987 | 6.30% | | 4.78% |
| 1986 | 8.07% | ... $12,628 | |

How a $10,000 investment performed over

| 5 years | 10 years |
|---|---|
| 1991 - 1995<br>$16,337<br>(10.31%)^ | |
| | 1986 - 1995<br>$20,629<br>(7.51%) |

^ annual compound rate of return for that period

*Source: Copyright ©1995 Merrill Lynch, Pierce, Fenner & Smith Incorporated.

©1996 Chase Global Data & Research
73 Junction Square, Concord, MA 01742

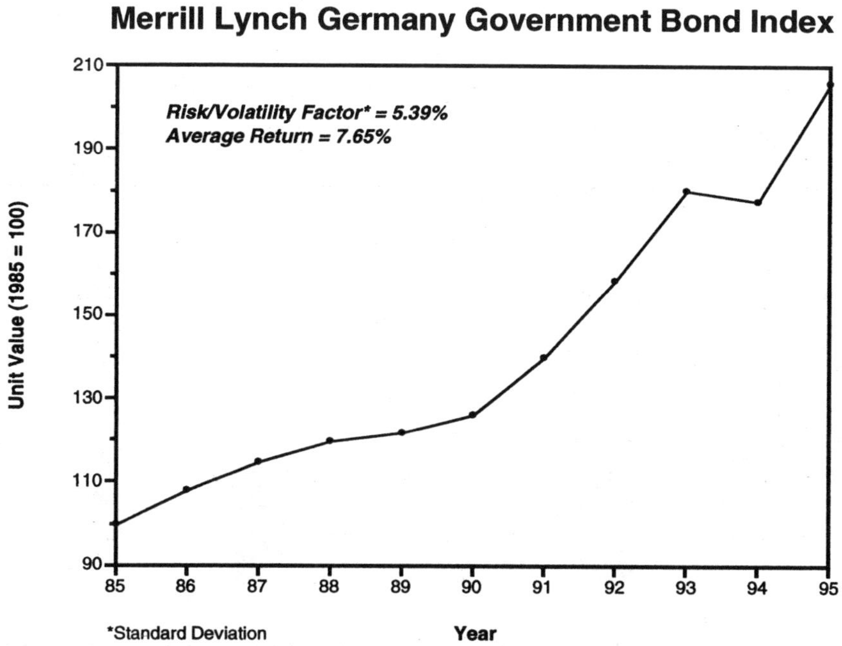


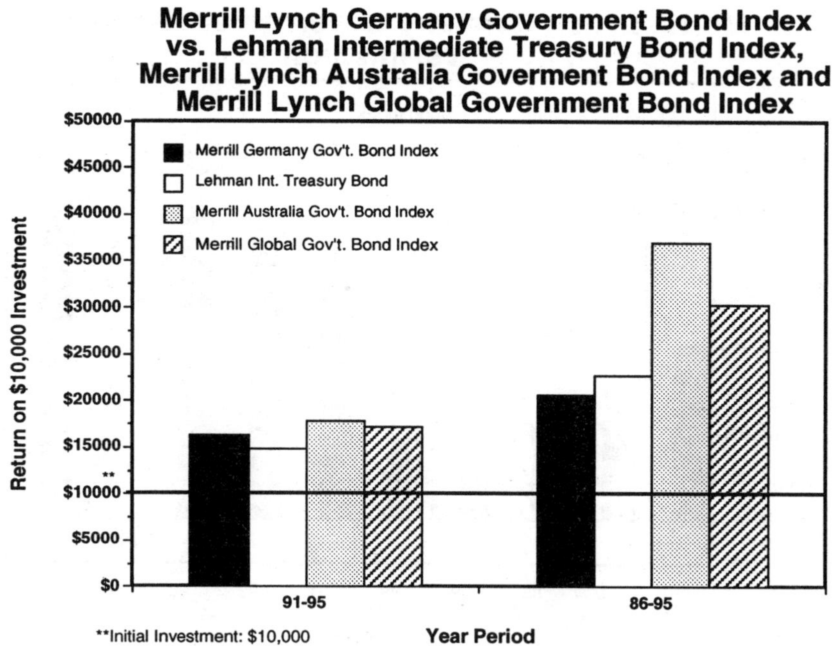


©1996 Chase Global Data & Research
73 Junction Square, Concord, MA 01742

## Merrill Lynch Germany Government Bond Index vs. Germany DAX General Index, German Mark and S&P 500 Composite Index^

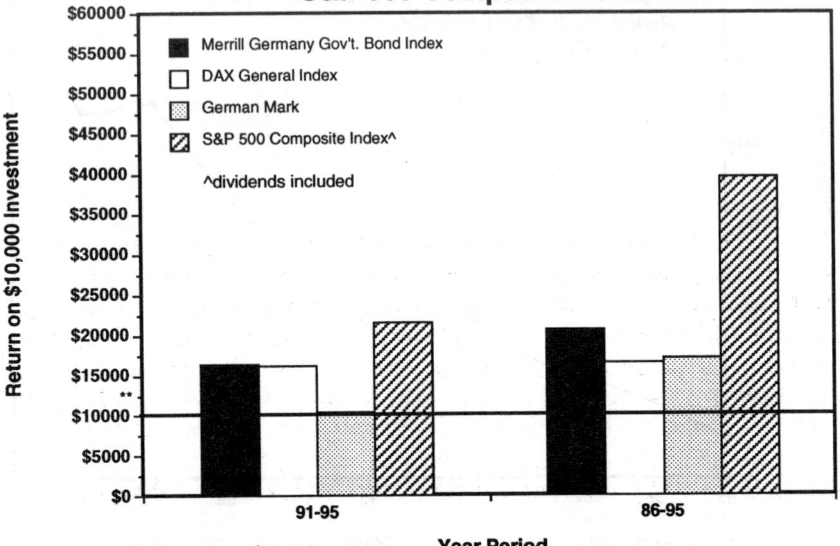


**Initial Investment: $10,000

## Merrill Lynch Germany Governement Bond Index vs. Inflation

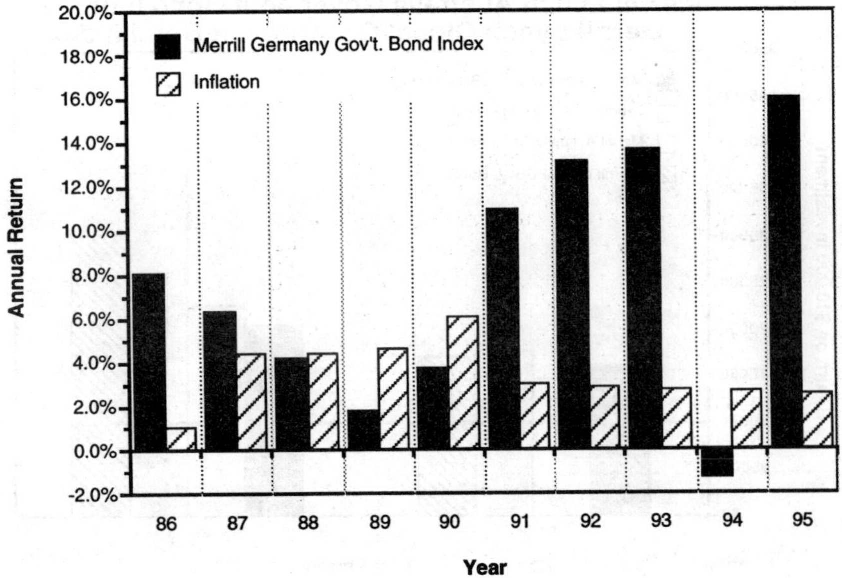


©1996 Chase Global Data & Research
73 Junction Square, Concord, MA 01742

Chapter Eighteen

# Chase Balanced Global Asset Index

Diversifying one's investment portfolio has been a basic axiom for investors since money was first invented. For no one knows what the future will bear, and no single investment performs optimally at all times. Riskless investments provide the least reward. Risky investments have the dual potential of either a large gain or loss. It is readily apparent that marketplaces have efficiently evolved such that investments which carry great risk normally do provide greater rewards over time. But the rewards can come in varying ways—in spurts, without warning, and then suddenly the investment can reverse direction and cause losses.

Asset allocation is an investment term, and philosophy, that has grown dramatically in popularity over the past decade. Part of the reason is that today more and more investment alternatives exist from which investors may choose than was the case twenty years ago. And many of the new investment alternatives harbor sizeable risks in addition to their rewards. Given these changes in the marketplace, the need to allocate assets is an obvious one. Today asset allocation is practiced by sophisticated pension fund managers, "prudent man" trustees, and ordinary unsophisticated investors. The trend is here to stay.

An obvious question to ask in regards to diversifying/allocating one's assets is what are the proven rewards? If one had executed a program of asset allocation over the years, how would he have fared versus his peers? This line of thinking led to the creation of the Chase Balanced Global Asset Index. The Index is a reflection of how a broad based, diversified portfolio performed over the past two decades. The Index incorporates a generally accepted and sophisticated degree of portfolio diversification. The Index's Performance Tables which follow reveal important information on how diversification works over time, and how it impacts the degree of risk encountered while investing.

The Chase Balanced Global Asset Index (CBGA) assumes a modern day portfolio is to be invested in equities, bonds, and cash equivalents. The Index portfolio is global in nature, with a moderate

©1996 Chase Global Data & Research
73 Junction Square, Concord, MA 01742

risk/reward posture. We have developed the Index using well known components. Equities represent one half of the Index. Bonds and cash equivalents comprise the other half. A constant 5% cash position (T-bills) is maintained within the fixed income segment. The Index is composed as follows:

| | |
|---|---|
| 30% | S&P 500 Composite Index |
| 20% | Morgan Stanley EAFE Index |
| 30% | Lehman Brothers Government/Corporate Index |
| 15% | Merrill Lynch Global Government Bond Index |
| 5% | 90 day Treasury Bills |

The CBGA's "Equity component" reflects the two best known and broad based domestic and international indices. The S&P 500's 60% share represents domestic equities, while the international EAFE component reflects 40% of the Equity component. The "Fixed Income" portion is 60% Lehman Brothers Government/Corporate Index, while 30% of the Fixed component is composed of the Merrill Lynch Global Government Bond Index. 10% of the Fixed Income segment (or 5% of the overall Chase Balanced Global Asset Index) is Cash, represented by 90 day T-bills.

A review of the CBGA Index performance exceeding five years is impacted by the fact that Merrill Lynch has no data prior to 1986 for its Global Government Bond Index. Hence the Index has been modified in an attempt to afford a long term overview for years prior to 1986. The net 15% component as represented by the Merrill Global Government Bond Index has been prorated among the three remaining components—the S&P 500 (35%), EAFE (25%), and Lehman Brothers Government Corporate (35%). While international fixed income cannot be analyzed for the full period because data was not available, the minor modification allows for a unique 20 year overview of an asset allocation index made up of well known components.

The 30% fixed income component represented by the Merrill Lynch Global Government Bond Index also reflects a degree thought by many international fixed income management experts to be near optimum. As detailed in Chapter 17 (page 170) several studies have shown a domestic bond portfolio is strengthened by an international bond mix, with a 30% international mix considered the best ratio for attaining optimum appreciation without undue volatility. Hence the Chase Balanced Global Asset Index's Fixed Income segment is comprised of 30% global bonds.

©1996 Chase Global Data & Research
73 Junction Square, Concord, MA 01742

Upon close review of the results of the CBGA Index Performance Tables which follow, one no doubt will gain a greater respect for asset allocation and global investment diversification. Simply put, over both the long and short run the diversified CBGA Index performed better than the more conservative domestic bond portfolio, and almost equaled in return several more volatile domestic equity indices—yet with less volatility. It was in the top quartile (25%) for key periods of its existence—the past 10, 15, and 20 year time frames. In conclusion, the Chase Balanced Global Asset Index proved itself a very solid performer providing a handsome return within the confines of decidedly reduced risk.

©1996 Chase Global Data & Research
73 Junction Square, Concord, MA 01742

## CHASE BALANCED GLOBAL ASSET INDEX

| Year | Total Return* | Compound return on a five year $10,000 investment | Annual compound rate of return |
|---|---|---|---|
| 1995 | 22.24% | 1991 - 1995 | |
| 1994 | 1.45% | | 12.02% |
| 1993 | 15.27% | ... $17,637 | |
| 1992 | 3.48% | | |
| 1991 | 19.23% | | |
| 1990 | -1.05% | 1986 - 1990 | |
| 1989 | 16.98% | | 13.21% |
| 1988 | 13.90% | ... $18,597 | |
| 1987 | 10.20% | | |
| 1986 | 28.00% | | |
| 1985 | 33.07% | 1981 - 1985 | |
| 1984 | 9.85% | | 15.55% |
| 1983 | 17.23% | ... $20,603 | |
| 1982 | 18.72% | | |
| 1981 | 1.27% | | |
| 1980 | 19.07% | 1976 - 1980 | |
| 1979 | 9.24% | | 11.55% |
| 1978 | 11.60% | ... $17,273 | |
| 1977 | 3.57% | | |
| 1976 | 14.89% | | |
| 1975 | 26.88% | | |
| 1974 | -14.31% | | |
| 1973 | -7.55% | | |

How a $10,000 investment performed over

| 5 years | 10 years | 15 years | 20 years |
|---|---|---|---|
| 1991 - 1995 | 1986 - 1995 | 1981 - 1995 | 1976 - 1995 |
| $17,637 (12.02%)^ | $32,799 (12.61%) | $67,576 (13.58%) | $116,722 (13.07%) |

^ annual compound rate of return for that period
* includes index growth and reinvestment of dividends.
Index composition: <u>1973-1985:</u> 25% EAFE, 35% S&P 500, 35% Lehman Govt/Corp, and 5% T-Bill. <u>1986-1995:</u> 20% EAFE, 30% S&P 500, 30% Lehman Govt/Corp,15% Merrill Global Government Bond, and 5% T-Bill.

©1996 Chase Global Data & Research
73 Junction Square, Concord, MA 01742

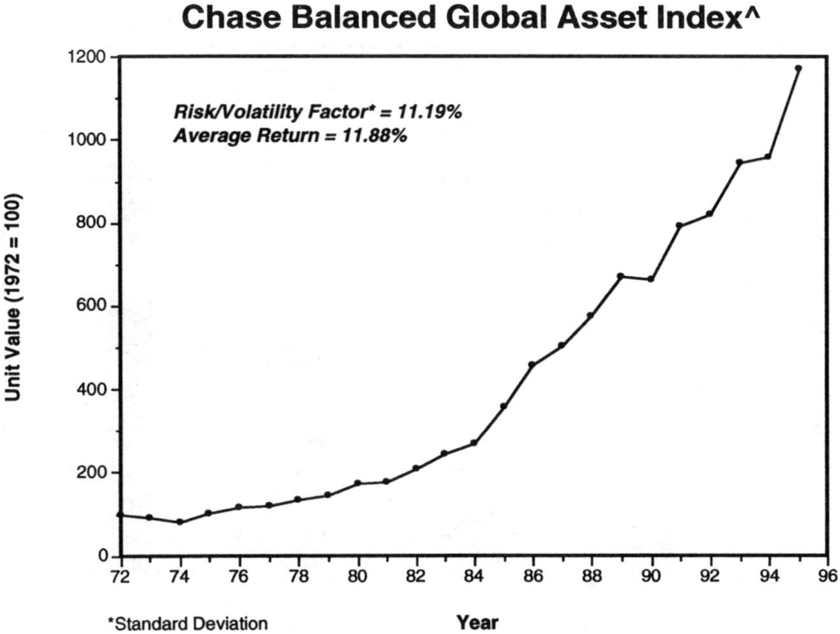


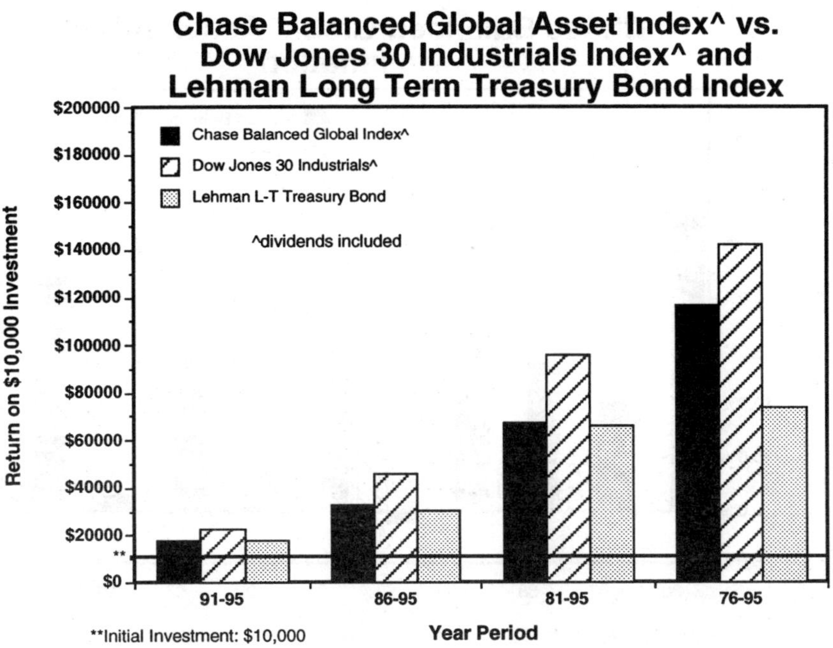


©1996 Chase Global Data & Research
73 Junction Square, Concord, MA 01742

## Chase Balanced Global Asset Index^ vs. Gold and Inflation

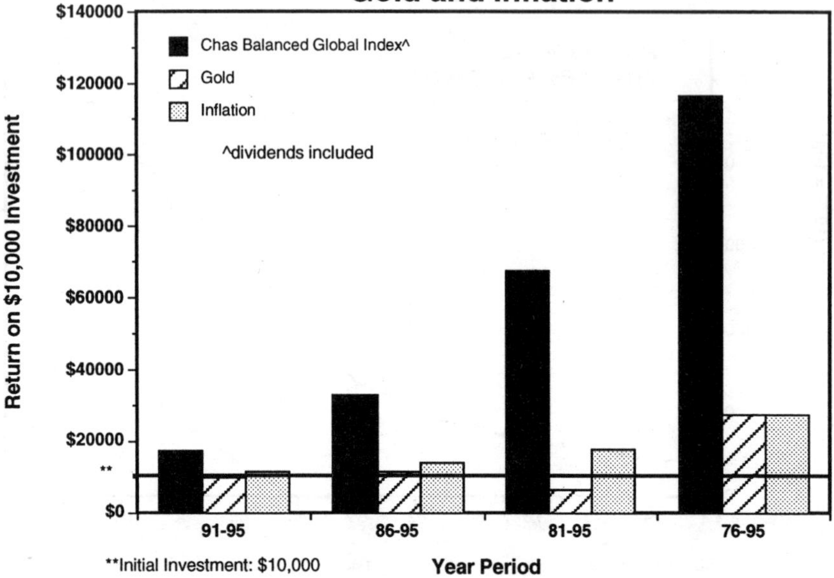


## Chase Balanced Global Asset Index^ vs. Inflation

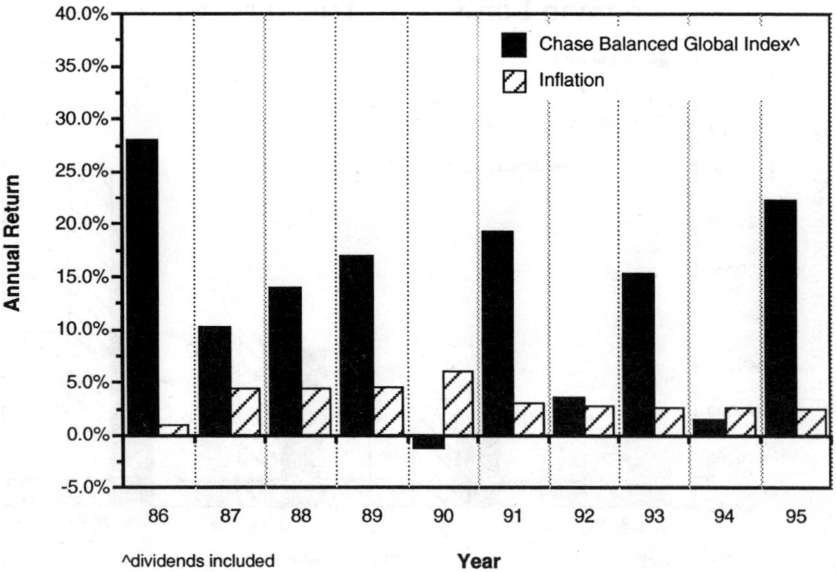


©1996 Chase Global Data & Research
73 Junction Square, Concord, MA 01742

SECTION VI

# U.S. Fixed Income Markets and Interest Sensitive Indices

# Chapter Nineteen

# U.S. Government Obligations

U.S. Government Obligations are the ultimate safe investment. The size and liquidity of the government bond market is immense. In fact, more securities have been issued under the name of U.S. Government Bonds and Notes than any other investment. In world government bond debt rankings, the total of the U.S. government's bond debt outstanding is almost twice that of the second ranked nation. Uncle Sam's total then dwarfs the combined total of the next eight nations in the top ten rankings. But to be sure, it is a first place ranking status any nation could well do without.

Bonds represent an I.O.U. They come in various sizes, maturities, and pay different levels of interest depending on the circumstances at the time of their issuance. A U.S. Government Bond is considered unequaled in terms of safety because of the stability of the U.S. government and its ability to tax its citizens. However in recent times the government has begun to create a large level of debt which has affected the quality of some of its bonds. At the end of 1995 total U.S. government liabilities, the majority represented by its bond issues, exceeded $4.9 trillion. An eerie indicator of how well nations directly back their debts is reflected in the fact that the U.S. total indebtedness is backed by reserves of $100 billion in gold—or about 2%. There is obviously much faith in the government's unlimited ability to tax its citizens, given the solid stature U.S. government bonds hold in the marketplace.

The U. S. government issues either short term Treasury bills or notes, or long term government bonds in order to pays its bills. It also issues bonds to cover previous bond obligations that are maturing. U.S. government bonds are issued at auction. Short term bonds of under one year in maturity are auctioned either weekly or monthly. Two year notes are also auctioned monthly. Three, four, five, seven, ten, twenty, and thirty year bonds and notes are issued on a quarterly basis each year. Today the average duration of debt issued by the federal government and held by private investors is five years to maturity. Ten-year bonds represent fifteen percent of government debt whereas 2 to 10 year notes represent about half. Maturities of one year or less account for one


©1996 Chase Global Data & Research
73 Junction Square, Concord, MA 01742

third. Most government bonds are issued in denominations of $1000 or more and interest is paid at maturity or by coupon on a periodic basis—typically at maturity for short term 90 day T-bills, and by way of semi-annual coupons with longer term paper. While bonds are generally issued a rating of Aaa, Aa, etc. U.S. government bonds are given no rating because their quality is considered the highest of all.

As a nation, the United States has a history of being fiscally responsible. In the past, its primary reason for going into debt was war—and after a war there was usually a rapid retirement of that debt. The U.S. government carried no appreciable debt from its inception in the late 1700's through the 1800's—with the exception of the debt incurred during the Civil War. The War of 1812 and the Civil War were financed 85% through federal government borrowing. Nevertheless, overall debt was steadily reduced until the outbreak of World War I. The huge debt incurred during World War I was financed 72% through government borrowings, but again was gradually reduced during the 1930's. World War II brought new debt, as the War was 58% financed through government bonds. Our overall debt level did not grow appreciably until the Vietnam War. After Vietnam, in spite of weak economies and oil embargoes, the national debt did not explode until the early 1980's. Unfortunately, it has continued its meteoric rise ever since.

Although there have been very few problems with any form of U.S. government obligations in the past, many experts fear that the U.S. government is in financial trouble. Although most U.S. government bonds are direct obligations of the federal government, others are indirect obligations of certain agencies that are not as secure. In part this is due to our changing status in the world economy. In 1980 the rest of the world owed the U.S. Government over $100 billion. By the end of 1986, the United States owed other countries $264 billion, a number which doubled from 1985. By 1994 total U.S. debt held by foreigners was over $650 billion with approximately one of every six dollars of U.S. debt in foreign hands. Then in 1995 foreigners purchased a record $99 billion in U.S. government bonds. The U.S. government owes the world more than Mexico, Brazil, and Argentina combined—the three former largest world debtors. In addition, foreigners now hold more in U.S. investments than Americans own in foreign investments, something that has not happened since 1914. And the ratio has quickly grown to over two to one.

If for a moment you think of the government as a corporation, a review of the 1980's shows that from 1981 to 1986 the corporation/government increased its outlays by 50%—while increasing its net

©1996 Chase Global Data & Research
73 Junction Square, Concord, MA 01742

revenues by only 20%. At that rate most companies would have gone bankrupt long ago. Worse, the government's then 210 year old total debt more than *doubled* during that same five year span. From 1981 to 1985, only once did total revenues match levels anticipated, whereas total outlays exceeded budget projections in 3 of those 5 years—an exercise in poor planning indeed. Also, for the first time U.S. debt significantly increased without the usual reason—a major war—a significant break with historical precedent. Since 1986 debt levels have accelerated at a rate of $200 to $300 billion per year. Most ominously, the U.S. government's total deficit will increase to $8 trillion by the year 2000—*even if it succeeds in balancing its deficit immediately*, with the lone exception being the interest costs on today's debt load.

Another cause for concern is the huge amount of U.S Government debt *not* on the balance sheets. As of late 1995, obligations on the balance sheet and carried within the federal budget totaled $4.9 trillion. There are other debts, however, that are held through government agencies that are not on the books and those debts also total over $3 trillion. We are thus failing to acknowledge about 40% of our overall debt, known as "off-balance-sheet" debt. Perennial budget squeezes on direct spending seems to trigger more loan guarantees/off-budget maneuvering. Because of the continuing weakness in the FDIC, the Farm Credit system, the Pension Benefit Guarantee Corporation, and other organizations, it is estimated that over $100 billion in government guarantees are presently total losses.

It is true that Congress has placed a ceiling on the level of federal debt. However, the ceiling inexorably rises to match the debt that is being created by the operation of the federal government. The government is essentially operating with a blank check-writing posture. When the checkbook runs dry and is in danger of being overdrawn, new bonds are issued to cover shortfalls. New bonds are also issued to replace maturing old bonds, and to pay interest owed on the many bonds outstanding.

Experts now believe that over half of all government bond auctions taking place in the 1990's will simply be exercises in refinancing—rolling over previous obligations. These auctions will have no impact, or be actually counterproductive to the raising of new capital should the government need more funds to finance its future deficits. Such exercises merely pay off old bonds that have reached maturity. In 1776, Adam Smith warned that government borrowing is "ruinous" and "the practice of funding has gradually enfeebled every state which has adopted it." However, Alexander Hamilton in 1781 said he considered federal borrowing "a national blessing." He

©1996 Chase Global Data & Research
73 Junction Square, Concord, MA 01742

thought it wise to build up the country's credit standing, internally and externally. Yet what would he say if he were told that our country has gone from a net creditor to a net debtor status in such a short period of time—and to such a large degree?

Perhaps the best measure of past debt held by the government versus our present debt situation is U.S. per capita federal debt figures. In 1790 per capita debt was $19; in 1814 it was $12; in 1870 it was $78; in 1920 it was $240; and in 1946 it was $1720; in 1984 it grew to $6640. Amazingly in the four years from 1984 to 1988 total federal debt grew 60%! Since then we have added over $1 trillion in debt during the past 4 years. Per capita U.S. government debt today is $19,000 and per household debt is $67,000. Per taxpayer debt is even higher at $45,000. In 1995, the $4.9 trillion U.S. government debt was greater than the total of all loans made by banks in the United States. The interest charge on that debt exceeds $39 million per hour, and represents over 15% of all federal expense—versus only 3% in 1950. Put another way, interest expense is $11,000 per *second.* Of note, total U.S. debt from *all* sources (business, consumer, and government) in 1995 was over $14 trillion, exceeding $50,000 per capita.

Ironically, the same tradition holds true on a global basis regarding debt. Internationally, debt retirement has never been in vogue. Many foreign governments have made only slight efforts to retire war debts and have actually added to them through peacetime borrowing for internal improvements. As a result of excessive borrowing over time, the currencies of some countries have become virtually worthless, leading to political instability.

If you are considering investing in government bonds, you should recognize that in the past larger and larger amounts of debt have created higher interest rates through the need to re-issue more debt to pay off previous debt. When interest rates rise, older bonds (with lower rates) look worse in comparison and therefore drop in value. However, as shown by the Performance Tables that follow on short and long term government bonds, interest rates tend to go in cycles. So far in the 1990's interest rates have been at the low end of the historical cycle.

In recent years government debt creation has changed in two significant ways, size and manner of distribution. In the near future there will be over $1 trillion of U.S. government debt in foreign hands. For example, by 1993 foreign central banks held 22% of all short term T-bills, or over $120 billion. These changing trends cause much concern to professionals. If in the future sizable amounts of government bonds are sold, prices could drop and illiquidity might become a

©1996 Chase Global Data & Research
73 Junction Square, Concord, MA 01742

problem for bonds for the first time in years. U.S. bond markets could see price movements dictated by events and investors located outside its borders. The $120 billion per day trading of U.S. governments has been volatile for many reasons. For example, during 1990 the Japanese reduced their U.S. government bond purchases from 50% to 30% of their overall foreign bond investment—yet Japanese purchases totaled $30 billion nevertheless.

Another area impacted by federal debt creation is our currency. More than ever, the value of a country's currency is tied to its burden of debt. The larger the level of a country's debt, the weaker its currency may become and the faster its devalued bonds will be sold. But despite spiraling debt, bonds do have their strong points. The security inherent in government bonds, the choices of maturity which provide liquidity if needed, plus their ability to pay interest at a level of 5% to 12% during various times in their cycles show them to be a good, secure, and logical investment.

Ironically in 1994, safe and staid U.S. government bonds became the root cause for the debacle and infamous municipal bankruptcy of Orange County, California. The county lost almost $2 billion of its $7.5 billion fund. It had invested in derivatives—risky and leveraged financial contracts which were based on U.S. government bond holdings. While U.S. government bonds are truly safe, investment methods which can change a straightforward investment exercise into a complex and inherently riskier one by employing derivatives are obviously not.

It is important to note in the following Performance Tables and Charts that the 3-year government note over extended time periods has a yield approximately 0.50% less than a 10-year government bond, but it obviously provides greater liquidity and the likelihood of less fluctuation in its underlying principal value. Also of note, a one-year government bond is minimally higher in yield than the 90-day T-bill or the 6-month Certificate of Deposit. Thus an investor should consider 6 month CD's (up to $100,000 per insured lending institution) as an indirect way to invest with government guarantees and still obtain a higher yield. Also consider 3-year notes instead of one-year notes or 10-year notes—especially if liquidity is an issue. However, 10-year government bonds have performed admirably over extended time periods versus a variety of investments. The *Digest* includes the Salomon Brothers 10-Year Treasury Index Table for total return analysis, as well as the U.S. Government Bond 10-Year Yield Table. Please also refer to the Long Term and Intermediate Term Tables of the Lehman Brothers Bond Indices of Chapter 22 for additional total return performance data.

©1996 Chase Global Data & Research
73 Junction Square, Concord, MA 01742

**U.S. 10-YEAR TREASURY BOND YIELD**
[Average annual yield]

| Year | Yield* | Compound return on a five year $10,000 investment | Annual compound rate of return |
|---|---|---|---|
| 1995 | 6.57% | 1991 - 1995 | |
| 1994 | 7.09% | | 6.88% |
| 1993 | 5.87% | ... $13,946 | |
| 1992 | 7.01% | | |
| 1991 | 7.86% | | |
| 1990 | 8.55% | 1986 - 1990 | |
| 1989 | 8.49% | | 8.39% |
| 1988 | 8.85% | ... $14,960 | |
| 1987 | 8.39% | | |
| 1986 | 7.67% | | |
| 1985 | 10.62% | 1981 - 1985 | |
| 1984 | 12.44% | | 12.21% |
| 1983 | 11.10% | ... $17,787 | |
| 1982 | 13.00% | | |
| 1981 | 13.91% | | |
| 1980 | 11.46% | 1976 - 1980 | |
| 1979 | 9.44% | | 8.86% |
| 1978 | 8.41% | ... $15,286 | |
| 1977 | 7.42% | | |
| 1976 | 7.61% | | |
| 1975 | 7.99% | 1971 - 1975 | |
| 1974 | 7.56% | | 6.95% |
| 1973 | 6.84% | ... $13,992 | |
| 1972 | 6.21% | | |
| 1971 | 6.16% | | |
| 1970 | 7.35% | 1966 - 1970 | |
| 1969 | 6.67% | | 5.93% |
| 1968 | 5.65% | ... $13,337 | |
| 1967 | 5.07% | | |
| 1966 | 4.92% | | |
| 1965 | 4.28% | 1961 - 1965 | |
| 1964 | 4.19% | | 4.06% |
| 1963 | 4.00% | ... $12,203 | |
| 1962 | 3.95% | | |
| 1961 | 3.89% | | |
| 1960 | 4.13% | | |

How a $10,000 investment performed over

| 5 years | 10 years | 15 years | 20 years | 25 years | 35 years |
|---|---|---|---|---|---|
| 1991 - 1995 | 1986 - 1995 | 1981 - 1995 | 1976 - 1995 | 1971 - 1995 | 1961 - 1995 |
| $13,946 (6.88%)^ | $20,863 (7.63%) | $37,109 (9.14%) | $56,726 (9.07%) | $79,374 (8.64%) | $129,178 (7.58%) |

^ annual compound rate of return for that period
* Source: Board of Governors, Federal Reserve System.

©1996 Chase Global Data & Research
73 Junction Square, Concord, MA 01742

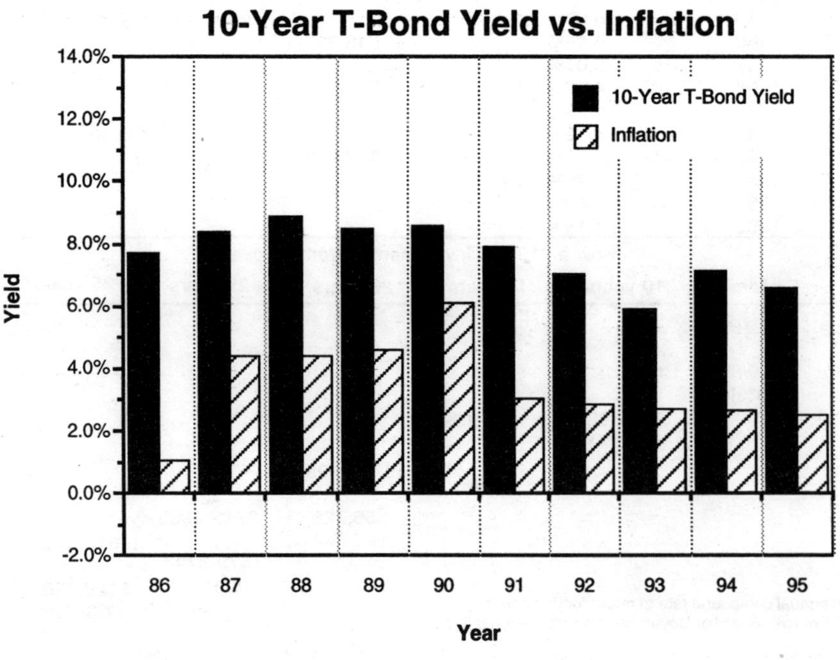


©1996 Chase Global Data & Research
73 Junction Square, Concord, MA 01742

## SALOMON BROTHERS U.S. 10-YEAR TREASURY BOND INDEX

(Total Return Index)

| Year | Total Return* | Compound return on a five year $10,000 investment | Annual compound rate of return |
|---|---|---|---|
| 1995 | 15.28% | 1991 - 1995 | |
| 1994 | -7.84% | | 8.20% |
| 1993 | 11.85% | ... $14,832 | |
| 1992 | 6.50% | | |
| 1991 | 17.20% | | |
| 1990 | 6.80% | 1986 - 1990 | |
| 1989 | 16.39% | | 8.93% |
| 1988 | 6.43% | ... $15,333 | |
| 1987 | -3.19% | | |
| 1986 | 19.72% | | |
| 1985 | 27.29% | 1981 - 1985 | |
| 1984 | 14.32% | | 16.06% |
| 1983 | 2.91% | ... $21,062 | |
| 1982 | 33.45% | | |
| 1981 | 5.39% | | |
| 1980 | -0.07% | | |

How a $10,000 investment performed over

| 5 years | 10 years | 15 years |
|---|---|---|
| 1991 - 1995<br>$14,832<br>(8.20%)^ | 1986 - 1995<br>$22,743<br>(8.56%) | 1981 - 1995<br>$47,900<br>(11.01%) |

^ annual compound rate of return for that period

* Source: Salomon Brothers.

©1996 Chase Global Data & Research
73 Junction Square, Concord, MA 01742

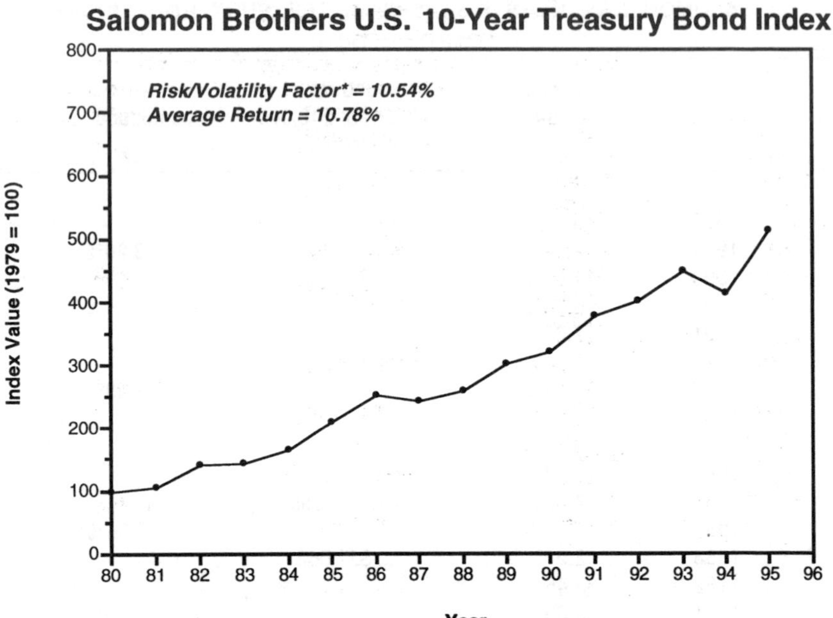


*Standard Deviation

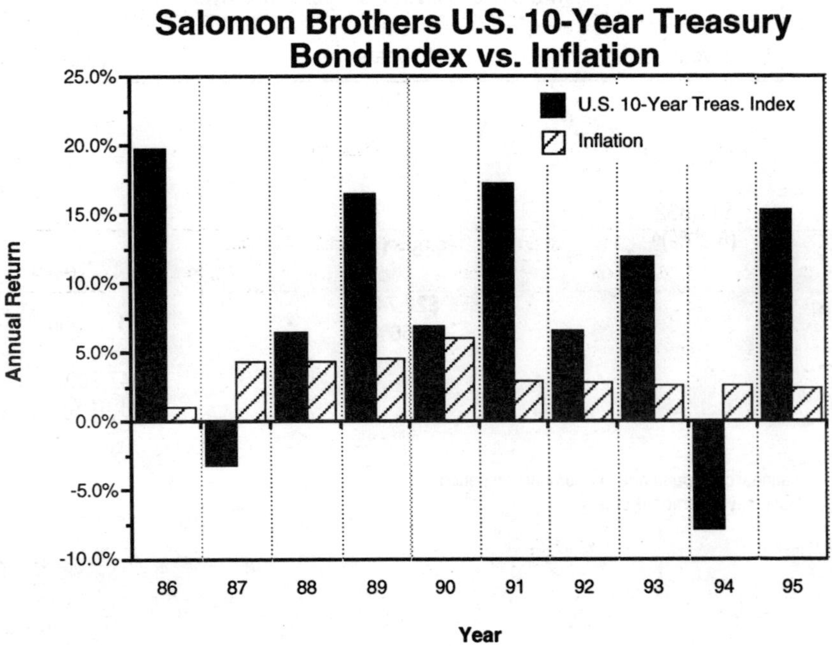


©1996 Chase Global Data & Research
73 Junction Square, Concord, MA 01742

## U.S. 3-YEAR TREASURY NOTE

[Average annual yield]

| Year | Yield* | Compound return on a five year $10,000 investment | Annual compound rate of return |
|---|---|---|---|
| 1995 | 6.25% | 1991 - 1995 | |
| 1994 | 6.27% | | 5.81% |
| 1993 | 4.44% | ... $13,264 | |
| 1992 | 5.30% | | |
| 1991 | 6.82% | | |
| 1990 | 8.26% | 1986 - 1990 | |
| 1989 | 8.55% | | 7.96% |
| 1988 | 8.26% | ... $14,667 | |
| 1987 | 7.68% | | |
| 1986 | 7.06% | | |
| 1985 | 9.64% | 1981 - 1985 | |
| 1984 | 11.89% | | 11.85% |
| 1983 | 10.45% | ... $17,510 | |
| 1982 | 12.92% | | |
| 1981 | 14.44% | | |
| 1980 | 11.55% | 1976 - 1980 | |
| 1979 | 9.71% | | 8.59% |
| 1978 | 8.29% | ... $15,097 | |
| 1977 | 6.69% | | |
| 1976 | 6.77% | | |
| 1975 | 7.49% | 1971 - 1975 | |
| 1974 | 7.82% | | 6.72% |
| 1973 | 6.95% | ... $13,844 | |
| 1972 | 5.72% | | |
| 1971 | 5.65% | | |
| 1970 | 7.29% | 1966 - 1970 | |
| 1969 | 7.02% | | 6.05% |
| 1968 | 5.68% | ... $13,411 | |
| 1967 | 5.03% | | |
| 1966 | 5.23% | | |
| 1965 | 4.22% | 1961 - 1965 | |
| 1964 | 4.03% | | 3.80% |
| 1963 | 3.67% | ... $12,050 | |
| 1962 | 3.47% | | |
| 1961 | 3.61% | | |
| 1960 | 4.00% | | |

How a $10,000 investment performed over

| 5 years | 10 years | 15 years | 20 years | 25 years | 35 years |
|---|---|---|---|---|---|
| 1991 - 1995 | | | | | |
| $13,264 (5.81%)^ | 1986 - 1995 | | | | |
| | $19,454 (6.88%) | 1981 - 1995 | | | |
| | | $34,064 (8.51%) | 1976 - 1995 | | |
| | | | $51,424 (8.53%) | 1971 - 1995 | |
| | | | | $71,194 (8.17%) | 1961 - 1995 |
| | | | | | $115,051 (7.23%) |

^ annual compound rate of return for that period

* Source: Board of Governors, Federal Reserve System.

©1996 Chase Global Data & Research
73 Junction Square, Concord, MA 01742

## 3-Year Treasury Note Yield

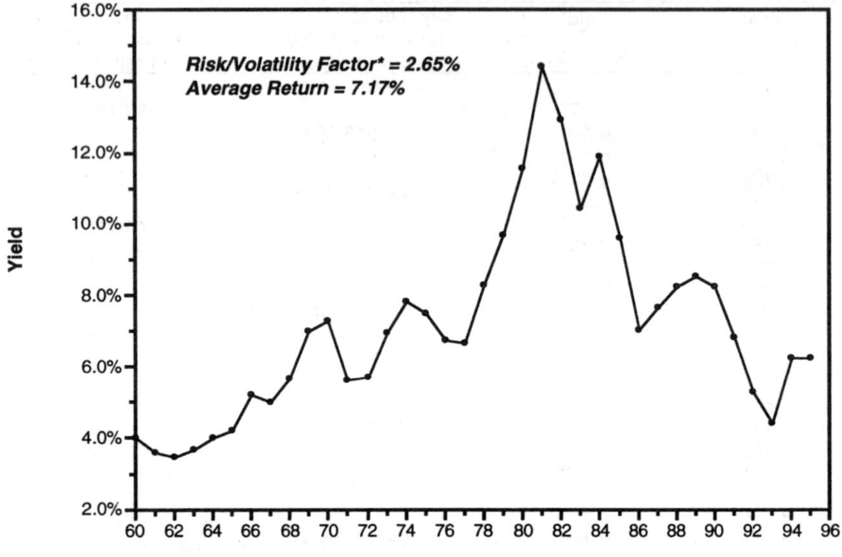


*Standard Deviation

## 3-Year T-Note Yield vs. Inflation

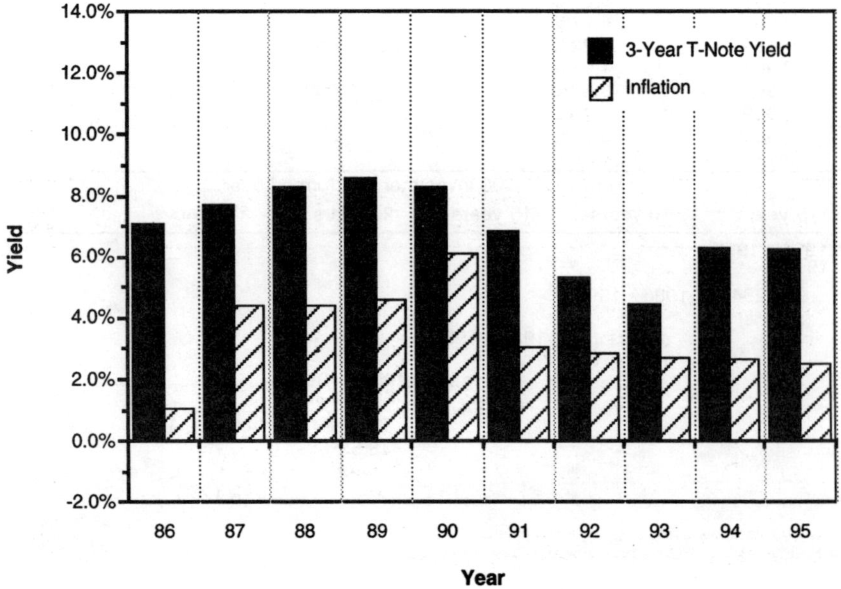


©1996 Chase Global Data & Research
73 Junction Square, Concord, MA 01742

## U.S. 3-MONTH TREASURY BILL

[Average annual yield]

| Year | Yield* | Compound return on a five year $10,000 investment | Annual compound rate of return |
|---|---|---|---|
| 1995 | 5.64% | 1991 - 1995 | |
| 1994 | 4.36% | | 4.42% |
| 1993 | 3.06% | ... $12,412 | |
| 1992 | 3.51% | | |
| 1991 | 5.53% | | |
| 1990 | 7.75% | 1986 - 1990 | |
| 1989 | 8.39% | | 7.02% |
| 1988 | 6.88% | ... $14,040 | |
| 1987 | 5.95% | | |
| 1986 | 6.16% | | |
| 1985 | 7.73% | 1981 - 1985 | |
| 1984 | 9.89% | | 10.44% |
| 1983 | 8.92% | ... $16,432 | |
| 1982 | 11.05% | | |
| 1981 | 14.75% | | |
| 1980 | 11.93% | 1976 - 1980 | |
| 1979 | 10.48% | | 8.04% |
| 1978 | 7.42% | ... $14,718 | |
| 1977 | 5.42% | | |
| 1976 | 5.10% | | |
| 1975 | 5.94% | 1971 - 1975 | |
| 1974 | 8.10% | | 5.97% |
| 1973 | 7.26% | ... $13,363 | |
| 1972 | 4.17% | | |
| 1971 | 4.44% | | |
| 1970 | 6.59% | 1966 - 1970 | |
| 1969 | 6.88% | | 5.66% |
| 1968 | 5.49% | ... $13,171 | |
| 1967 | 4.40% | | |
| 1966 | 4.99% | | |
| 1965 | 4.05% | 1961 - 1965 | |
| 1964 | 3.62% | | 3.22% |
| 1963 | 3.23% | ... $11,720 | |
| 1962 | 2.83% | | |
| 1961 | 2.41% | | |
| 1960 | 2.93% | | |

How a $10,000 investment performed over

| 5 years | 10 years | 15 years | 20 years | 25 years | 35 years |
|---|---|---|---|---|---|
| 1991 - 1995 | | | | | |
| $12,412 (4.42%)^ | 1986 - 1995 | | | | |
| | $17,425 (5.71%) | 1981 - 1995 | | | |
| | | $28,634 (7.27%) | 1976 - 1995 | | |
| | | | $42,144 (7.46%) | 1971 - 1995 | |
| | | | | $56,315 (7.16%) | 1961 - 1995 |
| | | | | | $86,930 (6.37%) |

^ annual compound rate of return for that period
* Source: Board of Governors, Federal Reserve System.

©1996 Chase Global Data & Research
73 Junction Square, Concord, MA 01742

## 3-Month Treasury Bill

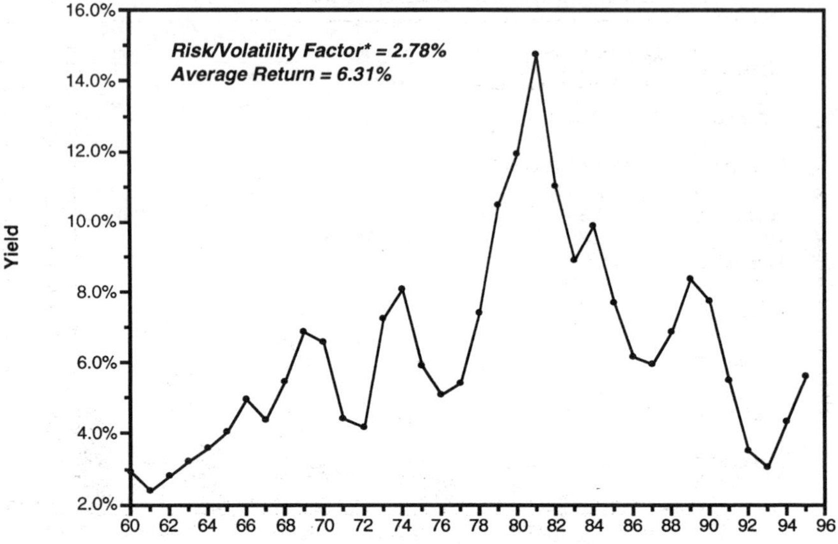


*Standard Deviation

## 3-Month T-Bill vs. 3-Year T-Note and Inflation

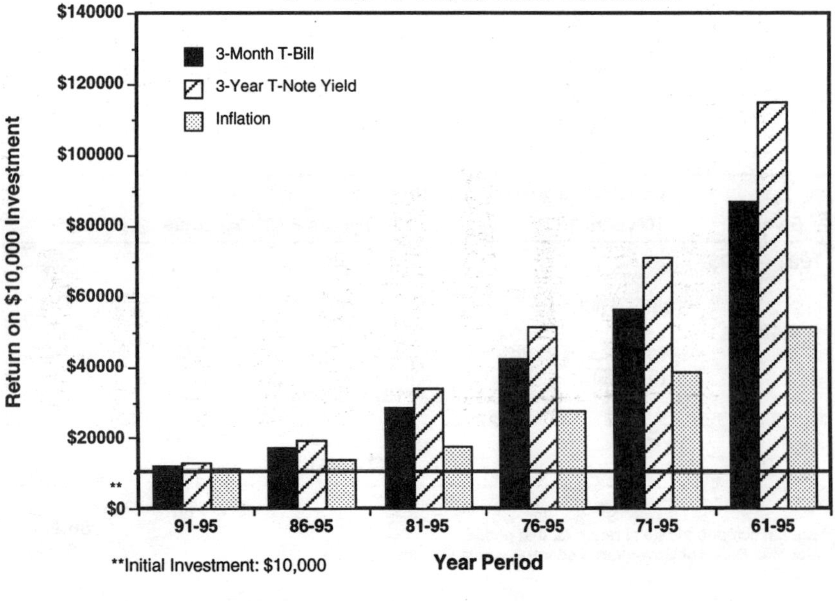


**Initial Investment: $10,000

©1996 Chase Global Data & Research
73 Junction Square, Concord, MA 01742

## 3-Month T-Bill vs. S&P 500 Composite Index^ and Farmland

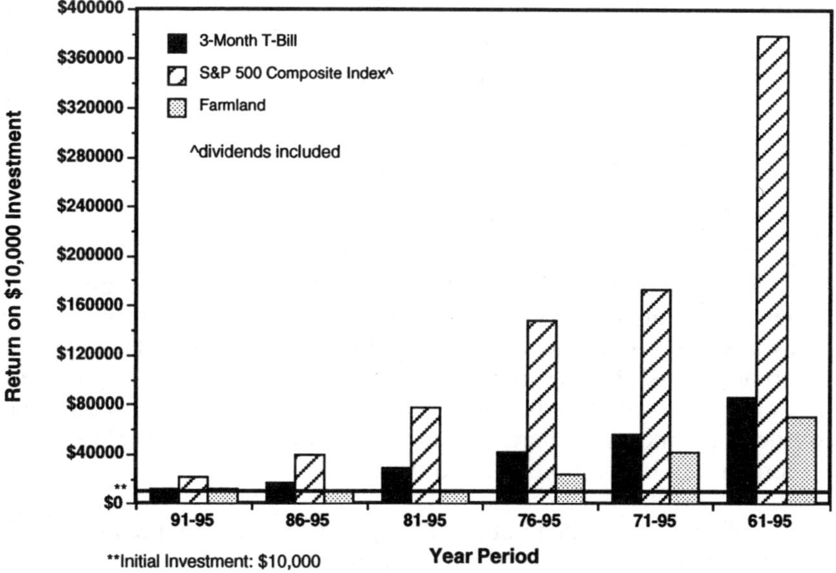


## 3-Month T-Bill Yield vs. Inflation

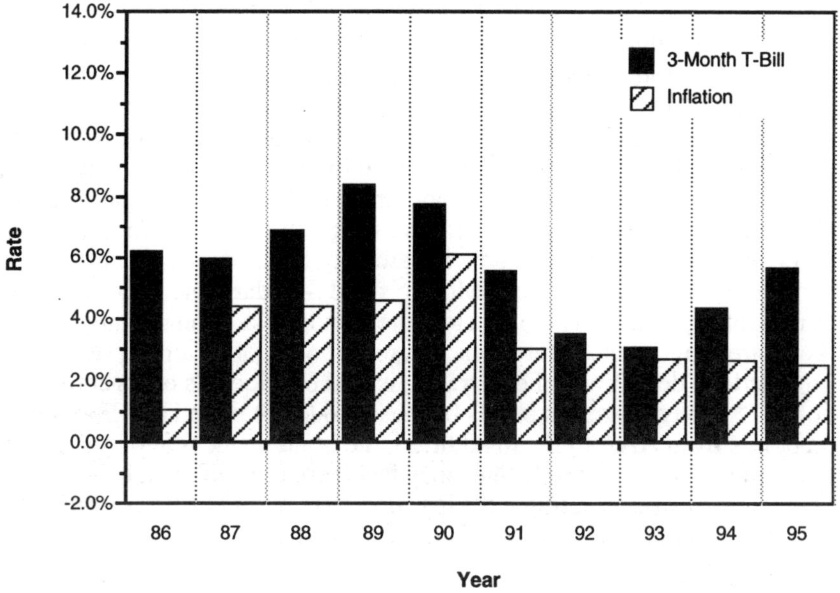


©1996 Chase Global Data & Research
73 Junction Square, Concord, MA 01742

# Chapter Twenty

# Corporate Bonds

A bond is a security which promises its holder periodic payments of interest and/or principal, financed from a first claim on the issuer's earnings or assets. Bonds are typically less secure than bank loans made to corporations that issue bonds (unless they attach specific corporate assets), but are more secure than stocks issued to shareholders by said corporations. It is one thing for a corporation to suspend dividend payments to shareholders. It is quite another to declare it can no longer pay interest on its bond debt.

Bonds are issued in three primary forms: corporate, municipal, and federal government issue. A detailed explanation of U.S. Government bonds is provided in the U.S. Government Obligations chapter. Federal government obligations represent the largest sector of all bonds. However, the corporate and municipal sectors of the bond marketplace are growing each year both in size and diversity of issues.

Other than government obligations, all bonds carry some form of risk. Therefore it is important to determine the level of risk associated with each bond. In order to do this a system of rating securities was originated by John Moody in 1909. Moody wanted to provide investors with a simple rating system for evaluating the relative investment qualities of bonds. In the U.S. today three key bond rating organizations ascertain the levels of risk and assign ratings on bonds—both municipal and corporate. The rating agencies are Moody's, Standard and Poor's, and Fitch Financial Services. Moody's and Standard and Poor's are the dominant agencies. The agencies rate bonds in a similar manner, but there are important differences. For purposes of example, we have provided the definitions of each rating issued by Moody's on its corporate bonds. Moody's rates its bonds from Aaa to C. Standard and Poor rates its bonds from AAA to D. In addition, the bond services at times assign the rating "NR" (no rating), when they feel there is insufficient information on which to base a rating. S&P's also uses a "+" or "-" to reflect a relative standing between major rating categories.


©1996 Chase Global Data & Research
73 Junction Square, Concord, MA 01742

## Bond Rating Definitions

Aaa. (AAA = S&P). Bonds rated Aaa are generally referred to as gilt-edge—the best bonds. Interest payments are protected by a large or an exceptionally stable margin and principal is secure. The issuing entity is considered so stable that any changes by the issuer are thought unlikely to impair its strong position for the foreseeable future.

Aa. (AA = S&P). Bonds rated Aa are high quality bonds by all standards. Combined with the Aaa group, they comprise the group generally known as high grade bonds. Aa are rated lower than Aaa bonds because their margins for protection are not quite as large and their potential for fluctuation may be greater.

A. (A = S&P). Bonds rated A possess many favorable investment attributes and are considered upper-medium grade obligations. The security for both payback of principal and interest is considered adequate but certain factors, such as consistent profitability, suggest a susceptibility to impairment sometime in the future.

Baa. (BBB = S&P). Bonds rated Baa are considered medium-grade obligations, neither highly protected nor poorly secured. Principal and interest payments appear secure but cannot be projected for a substantial period of time. The bonds also lack outstanding investment characteristics and have the flavor of speculation about them. Bonds rated Baa or higher are considered "prudent-man" investments under rules of law. Such a legal axiom is important when investments are made for retirement plans using funds which by law must be safely invested for the long term.

Ba. (BB = S&P). Bonds rated Ba have speculative elements and their future cannot be considered well assured. Protection of interest and principal may be moderate, and therefore not well safeguarded during bad times. Uncertainty characterizes bonds in this class. Bonds rated Ba or lower are not considered "prudent-man" investments.

B. (B= S&P). Bonds rated B generally lack characteristics of desirable investments. The assurance of interest and principal payments or maintenance of other terms of the bond's contract over any sustained period of time is small.

Caa. (CCC = S&P). Bonds rated Caa have a poor standing. Such issues may be in default, or may have elements of danger in terms of paying interest or principal.

©1996 Chase Global Data & Research
73 Junction Square, Concord, MA 01742

Ca. (CC = S&P). Bonds rated Ca represent obligations which are highly speculative. Such issues are often in default or have other marked shortcomings.

C. (C = S&P). C bonds are Moody's lowest rated class of bonds. Issues rated C are considered poor prospects for any real investment standing. (S&P also has a rating of CI for income bonds which are paying no interest at the present time.)

D. S&P uses the rating of D for bonds in default in payment of interest and/or repayment of principal is in arrears.

These ratings have many limitations. The main limitation is that the quality of most bonds is not fixed or steady and tends to change over a period of time. Thus one cannot assume that any rating, even the highest rating of Aaa, can be sustained without potential for change in risk. For example, there have been instances of highly rated bonds suspending interest payments, defaulting, and being subject to bankruptcy proceedings. Also, bonds carrying the same rating are not necessarily of equal quality. By necessity, ratings are defined in a broad sense because there are a limited number of rating classes and there are thousands of bonds, each with many variables. Keep in mind that highly rated bonds, as well as low rated bonds, suffer similar fates in very weak bond markets and bad times—they all go down noticeably.

Perhaps the biggest question regarding bond ratings is the rating system itself. One economist from the Federal Reserve Bank said, "Ratings provide information, albeit with a lag, to investors who don't have the resources to investigate the firm, but there are questions about their usefulness." Recently several studies have shown that ratings provide a valuable service distinguishing between investment grade bonds and low grade junk bonds, but beyond that their ability to adequately separate bonds of one investment grade versus another is questionable. (Bonds are considered junk bonds when their rating is below Baa/Moody's or BBB/S&P.) Such a qualification is important when one considers that the difference between Aaa bonds and A bonds may be over 1% in yield for long term bonds.

There certainly is a lot of confusion regarding bond ratings. One Oklahoma State University professor commented, "ratings aren't predictors of the future likelihood of bonds to default, or an indicator of the way they perform in the market." The profits for giving credit appraisals on the smallest municipal borrowing, as well as corporate analyses, are increasing because many issues are employing insurance

©1996 Chase Global Data & Research
73 Junction Square, Concord, MA 01742

guarantees from major insurance corporations in order to raise their bond rating and thus make the bonds more easily rateable and saleable. The process lowers the costs of issuance, makes the rating process simpler, and of course lowers the yields for "safer" bonds that are insured.

Today many traders detect a potential loosening of standards as rating agencies compete with each other to judge the credit quality of new securities which have no history. Issuers now play the game of "rent-a-rating." It is based on the premise that many low grade issues are instantly improved in rating by purchasing a term guarantee for timely payment of interest and principal by an insurance company. The credit analyst simply looks to the quality of the guarantor and, if the firm is of high quality, issues an investment grade rating. Yet a senior vice president of a major U.S. insurance company said, "You can't blindly rely on any single rating....God knows, the rating agencies can be wrong." For example, Ticor Mortgage Insurance Co. was forced into rehabilitation in the 80's due to its guarantee of the Equity Protections Investment Corp. (EPIC), which defaulted on its interest and principal payments. Prior to its being thrown into rehabilitation due to an estimated $200 million loss, Ticor was the darling of many rating agencies. After EPIC's demise, approximately 15 Ticor insured bonds worth $475 million were downgraded by rating agencies.

Moody's and Standard and Poor's evaluate over 90% of the new issue corporate and municipal marketplace each year. The rating companies receive a few thousand dollars to over $50,000 per issue (depending on the size and complexity of the issue) for providing their service. 1990 was an unusual year, with the rating agencies seemingly being paid to break the annual downgrade record. Standard and Poor's Rating Group had a record 768 downgradings in 1990—almost double the 419 of 1989. The value of the downgrades was $510 billion, of which $14 billion went into default. Downgrades for 1990 were four times the number of upgrades, which were represented by 189 issues valued at $113 billion. During the previous year the Campeau Corporation defaulted, causing the greatest default to date in the corporate junk bond market. It entered bankruptcy proceedings only two years after its bonds were offered to the public.

The United States corporate bond market today is huge, valued at over $2 *trillion*, and growing in popularity. New corporate bond sales reached a record $301 billion in 1992, equal to the combined totals for 1990 and 1991. Bonds are traded both on the OTC marketplace and on the NYSE Bond Exchange. The OTC market is by far the most

©1996 Chase Global Data & Research
73 Junction Square, Concord, MA 01742

active marketplace, trading $46 billion daily. However, little is reported to the public regarding pricing on the OTC. The NYSE Bond Exchange, while smaller, fills the void for the public regarding bond pricing and information as relates to its own domain.

NYSE bond trading is done through the Automated Bond System (ABS) which uses an advanced computer system for fast and accurate order entry, execution, and confirmation. The NYSE fixed income market has a wide selection of 2,100 corporate and government bonds. Included are U.S. government, corporate obligations, bonds guaranteed by foreign governments, foreign corporate debt, and international bank bonds. In 1994 the total volume of NYSE bond trading was over $7 billion, a volume level double that of 1980. Average daily NYSE bond volume for 1994 was $50 million. Corporate debt issues listed on the Exchange had a total par value exceeding $2 billion.

Despite the popularity of the bond markets and the ease in which orders can be executed, over the past few years there have been some problems—staggering losses incurred in the marketplace. Most of the losses were taken by professional traders of major U.S. brokerage houses. The greatest bond loss in U.S. history was suffered in 1987 by Merrill Lynch and Co., which lost $377 million trading in mortgage securities during one month. During the spring 1987 bond market crash, several Wall Street firms each lost $20 to $50 million trading debt securities. After the dust settles on the derivative debacle of 1994 in Orange County, California that record may well be broken.

The quickest, most sustained drop that occurred during the first three quarters of 1987 represented the worst collapse in U.S. debt markets since World War II. Thirty-year Treasury bonds bought in January and sold in September lost over 20%. In the first nine months of 1987 the U.S. bond market lost $360 billion. In September 1987, during one precipitous drop in the bond market, some corporate issues of high rating lost as much as 15% of their value in two days. During this collapse, foreigners trading in the U.S. bond market that year were severely impacted by both the drop in the bond markets and the U.S. dollar. Japanese investors who held long-term U.S. Treasury bonds lost over 30% of their investment during the first nine months of 1987. However overall, bond markets have experienced strong solid gains, due to rebounds from bad periods and the constancy of interest payments adding to overall cumulative returns.

©1996 Chase Global Data & Research
73 Junction Square, Concord, MA 01742

## Bond Index Funds

Given the complexity and risks in today's bond marketplace, many investors and pension funds are turning to Bond Index funds—funds managed primarily by computer. "Active" portfolio management is being replaced by "passive" portfolio management. Managing $100 million in an active bond portfolio can require two dozen managers. That's one reason why some experts estimate that active management is about ten times more expensive than passive.

The Lehman Brothers Corporate/Government Bond Index is a key index that Bond Index funds attempt to mirror. Lehman Brothers has estimated that over $175 billion of the $700+ billion in fixed income pension fund assets is invested in portfolios modeled after their index. Why? Because investors, especially large pension funds, are growing impatient with sub-par performances by bond portfolio managers. In recent years the management by active bond portfolio managers has lagged the major bond market averages. Sadly, about two-thirds of active fixed income bond managers have lost to the averages over the past decade. And active bond manager's fees are greater than those of the Bond Index funds.

Of note, Bond Index fund managers have begun to customize their portfolios to mature at a pace that matches various pension fund liabilities on an individual corporate basis. Lehman Brothers, Merrill Lynch, Salomon Brothers, and other major players in the fixed income marketplace create customized indices which match their client's needs through the creation of bond portfolios with the appropriate mix of maturities and bond rating quality. In addition, they may invest a client's assets into a personalized portfolio which matches one or more of their own indices. Companies with young employees and thus long-term pension fund liabilities track indices of long-term bonds, while companies with a more mature census of employees use a shorter term index fund for their pension management. Most Bond Index portfolios, such as those used by Wells Fargo Investment Advisors (the nation's largest Bond Index fund manager), have 450 to 500 different issues in each Bond Index fund. But deciding on how to go with a Bond Index fund is becoming complex. More index funds are being introduced each year—representing different forms of bonds with different maturities. With the majority of active professional bond portfolio managers losing to the basic averages, the popularity of Bond Index funds will no doubt continue to grow.

©1996 Chase Global Data & Research
73 Junction Square, Concord, MA 01742

## High Yield/Junk Bond Markets

The $300 billion junk bond/high yield marketplace (Ba rating or less) collapsed in 1990. During the same year the key figures behind the growth of the junk bond market—Michael Milken and his firm Drexel Burnham & Lambert—also fell. Milken was convicted of securities violations, fined $600 million, and sentenced to ten years in jail (he was paroled after two years). Drexel went bankrupt. The degree of collapse in the junk bond market in 1990 was truly unparalleled. Many experts called the selloff a year of panic. Prior to 1990 the spread between quality and junk bonds was about 3%, but by the end of 1990 the spread exceeded 12%. During one phase of the selloff the largest junk bond issue (RJR Nabisco) saw its bonds topple 10% in one day due to a rating decrease. But in 1991 prices reversed and moved sharply higher. Investors who remained with this volatile segment of the bond marketplace were rewarded with substantial gains. Yet 1991 sales of new junk bonds fell to $10 billion from $31 billion in 1986. However, by 1992 the junk bond market new issues sales sharply reversed direction, breaking the 1986 record level with total sales of $38 billion.

The movement of junk bonds, or high yield bonds, is tracked by Merrill Lynch and other Wall Street firms through High Yield Bond indices. Merrill Lynch's High Yield Index Performance Table follows, outlining the movement and results of a segment of the bond market which was as popular in the 1980's as it has been volatile in the 1990's. As noted above, 1991-1993 saw a major turnaround in High Yield Bonds. 1995 again saw a rebound, moving up 18.47%.

Remember 1994? It was the worst bond market year since the Great Depression. For example, the Lehman Government/Corporate Index suffered its first losing year since its inception in 1973. Caused in large degree by six consecutive increases in the Prime Rate over one year, rates rose sharply and bond prices lost more in principal value than they generated in interest—netting losses for most investors. But as the *Chase Investment Performance Digest* noted in early 1995 (in its 1995 Edition) investors should remember that during the bond market declines in the past 35 years sharp declines were *consistently* followed by major gains within 24 months. True to form, the very bad 1994 bond year was followed by a banner 1995 year — with the overall bond market up approximately 20%.

©1996 Chase Global Data & Research
73 Junction Square, Concord, MA 01742

## MOODY'S Aaa CORPORATE BOND YIELD

[Average annual yield]

| Year | Yield* | Compound return on a five year $10,000 investment | Annual compound rate of return |
|---|---|---|---|
| 1995 | 7.59% | 1991 - 1995 | |
| 1994 | 7.97% | | 8.00% |
| 1993 | 7.54% | ... $14,694 | |
| 1992 | 8.14% | | |
| 1991 | 8.77% | | |
| 1990 | 9.32% | 1986 - 1990 | |
| 1989 | 9.26% | | 9.34% |
| 1988 | 9.71% | ... $15,626 | |
| 1987 | 9.38% | | |
| 1986 | 9.02% | | |
| 1985 | 11.37% | 1981 - 1985 | |
| 1984 | 12.71% | | 12.81% |
| 1983 | 12.04% | ... $18,271 | |
| 1982 | 13.79% | | |
| 1981 | 14.17% | | |
| 1980 | 11.94% | 1976 - 1980 | |
| 1979 | 9.63% | | 9.34% |
| 1978 | 8.73% | ... $15,629 | |
| 1977 | 8.02% | | |
| 1976 | 8.43% | | |
| 1975 | 8.83% | 1971 - 1975 | |
| 1974 | 8.57% | | 7.89% |
| 1973 | 7.44% | ... $14,616 | |
| 1972 | 7.21% | | |
| 1971 | 7.39% | | |
| 1970 | 8.04% | 1966 - 1970 | |
| 1969 | 7.03% | | 6.37% |
| 1968 | 6.18% | ... $13,619 | |
| 1967 | 5.51% | | |
| 1966 | 5.13% | | |
| 1965 | 4.49% | 1961 - 1965 | |
| 1964 | 4.40% | | 4.37% |
| 1963 | 4.26% | ... $12,382 | |
| 1962 | 4.33% | | |
| 1961 | 4.35% | | |
| 1960 | 4.41% | | |

How a $10,000 investment performed over

| 5 years | 10 years | 15 years | 20 years | 25 years | 35 years |
|---|---|---|---|---|---|
| 1991 - 1995 | | | | | |
| $14,694 (8.00%)^ | 1986 - 1995 | | | | |
| | $22,961 (8.67%) | 1981 - 1995 | | | |
| | | $41,952 (10.03%) | 1976 - 1995 | | |
| | | | $65,565 (9.86%) | 1971 - 1995 | |
| | | | | $95,828 (9.46%) | 1961 - 1995 |
| | | | | | $161,600 (8.27%) |

^ annual compound rate of return for that period
* Source: Moody's Investors Services.

©1996 Chase Global Data & Research
73 Junction Square, Concord, MA 01742

## Aaa Corporate Bond Yield

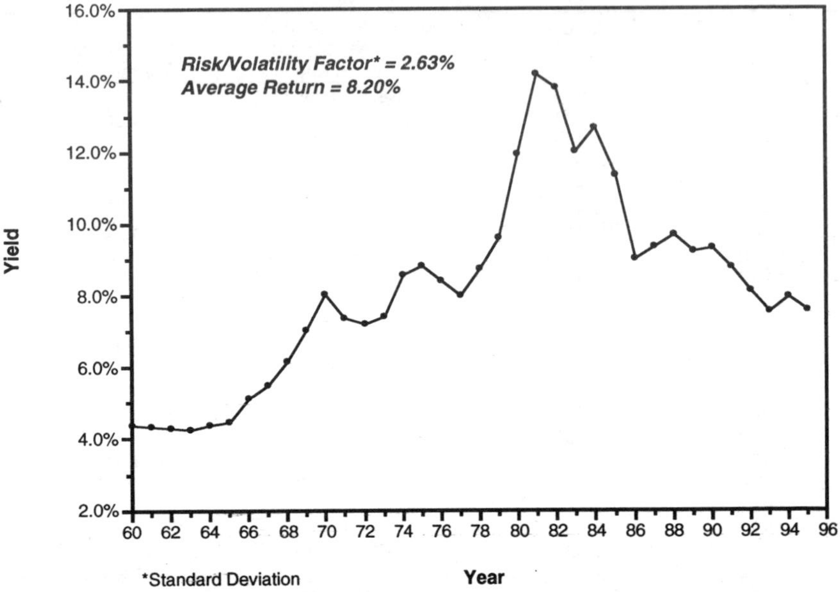


*Standard Deviation

## Aaa Corporate Bond Yield vs. Inflation

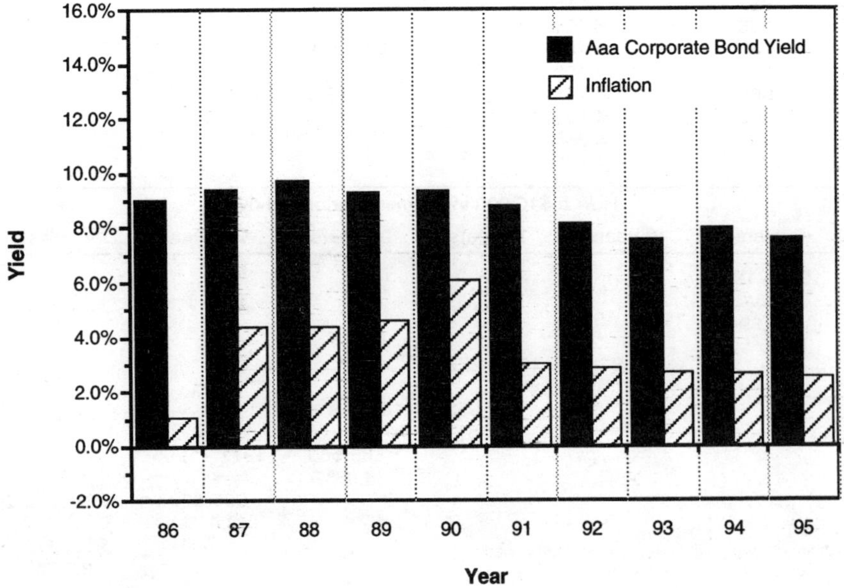


©1996 Chase Global Data & Research
73 Junction Square, Concord, MA 01742

## MOODY'S Baa CORPORATE BOND YIELD

[Average annual yield]

| Year | Yield* | Compound return on a five year $10,000 investment | Annual compound rate of return |
|---|---|---|---|
| 1995 | 8.20% | 1991 - 1995 | |
| 1994 | 8.63% | | 8.71% |
| 1993 | 7.93% | ... $15,180 | |
| 1992 | 8.98% | | |
| 1991 | 9.80% | | |
| 1990 | 10.36% | 1986 - 1990 | |
| 1989 | 10.18% | | 10.47% |
| 1988 | 10.83% | ... $16,450 | |
| 1987 | 10.58% | | |
| 1986 | 10.39% | | |
| 1985 | 12.72% | 1981 - 1985 | |
| 1984 | 14.19% | | 14.51% |
| 1983 | 13.55% | ... $19,692 | |
| 1982 | 16.11% | | |
| 1981 | 16.04% | | |
| 1980 | 13.67% | 1976 - 1980 | |
| 1979 | 10.69% | | 10.49% |
| 1978 | 9.45% | ... $16,470 | |
| 1977 | 8.97% | | |
| 1976 | 9.75% | | |
| 1975 | 10.61% | 1971 - 1975 | |
| 1974 | 9.50% | | 9.01% |
| 1973 | 8.24% | ... $15,392 | |
| 1972 | 8.15% | | |
| 1971 | 8.56% | | |
| 1970 | 9.10% | 1966 - 1970 | |
| 1969 | 7.81% | | 7.14% |
| 1968 | 6.94% | ... $14,120 | |
| 1967 | 6.23% | | |
| 1966 | 5.67% | | |
| 1965 | 4.87% | 1961 - 1965 | |
| 1964 | 4.83% | | 4.93% |
| 1963 | 4.86% | ... $12,722 | |
| 1962 | 5.02% | | |
| 1961 | 5.08% | | |
| 1960 | 5.19% | | |

How a $10,000 investment performed over

| 5 years | 10 years | 15 years | 20 years | 25 years | 35 years |
|---|---|---|---|---|---|
| 1991 - 1995 | | | | | |
| $15,180 (8.71%)^ | 1986 - 1995 | | | | |
| | $24,972 (9.58%) | 1981 - 1995 | | | |
| | | $49,175 (11.20%) | 1976 - 1995 | | |
| | | | $80,988 (11.03%) | 1971 - 1995 | |
| | | | | $124,656 (10.62%) | 1961 - 1995 |
| | | | | | $223,911 (9.29%) |

^ annual compound rate of return for that period
* Source: Moody's Investors Services.

©1996 Chase Global Data & Research
73 Junction Square, Concord, MA 01742

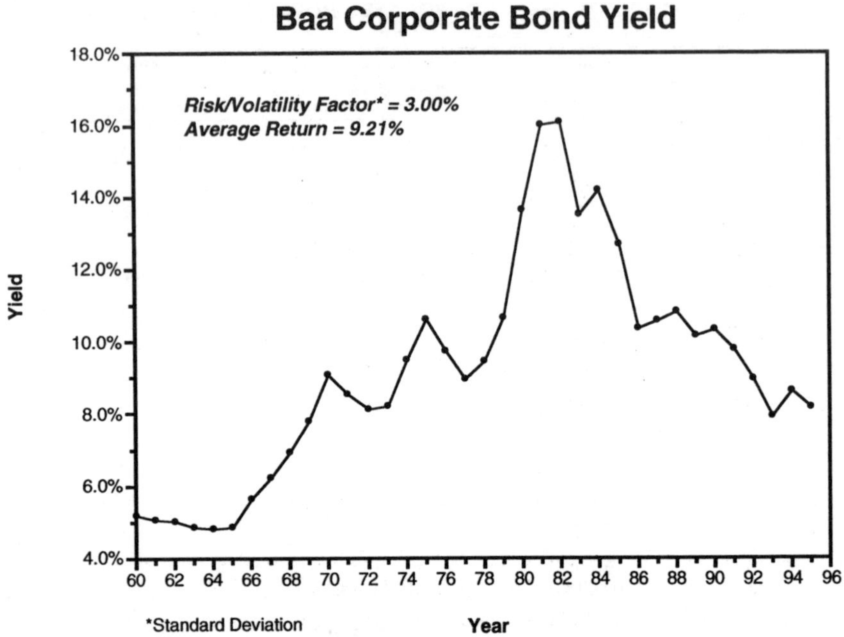


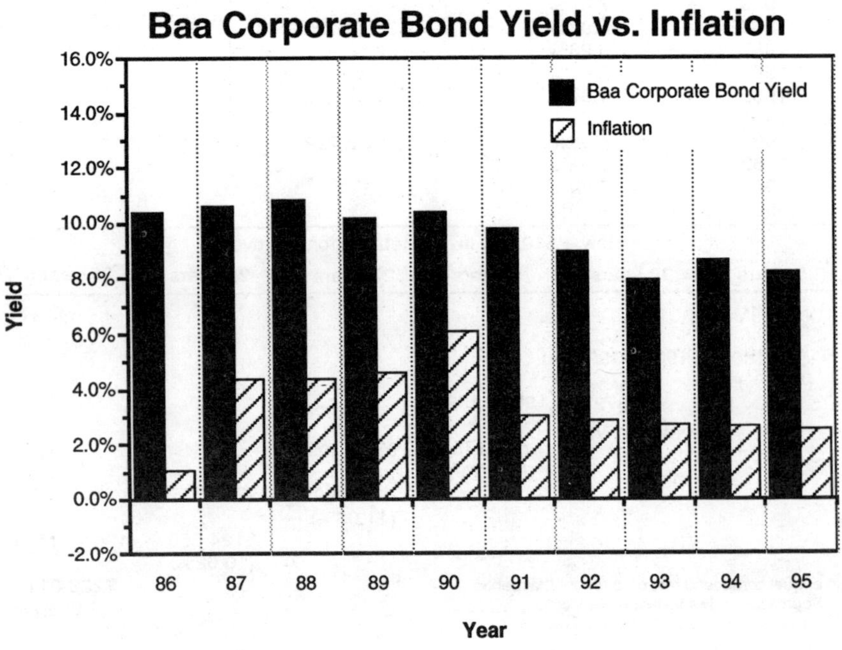


©1996 Chase Global Data & Research
73 Junction Square, Concord, MA 01742

**MERRILL LYNCH HIGH YIELD 175 CORPORATE BOND INDEX**

| Year | Total Return* | Compound return on a five year $10,000 investment | Annual compound rate of return |
|---|---|---|---|
| 1995 | 18.47% | 1991 - 1995 | |
| 1994 | -0.69% | | 18.76% |
| 1993 | 18.22% | ... $23,628 | |
| 1992 | 21.15% | | |
| 1991 | 40.22% | | |
| 1990 | -4.24% | 1986 - 1990 | |
| 1989 | 1.14% | | 6.27% |
| 1988 | 14.42% | ... $13,553 | |
| 1987 | 8.09% | | |
| 1986 | 13.14% | | |
| 1985 | 23.73% | 1981 - 1985 | |
| 1984 | 7.92% | | 16.95% |
| 1983 | 17.53% | ....$21,879 | |
| 1982 | 33.10% | | |
| 1981 | 4.74% | | |
| 1980 | -1.34% | | |

How a $10,000 investment performed over

| 5 years | 10 years | 15 years |
|---|---|---|
| 1991 - 1995<br>$23,628<br>(18.76%)^ | 1986 - 1995<br>$32,022<br>(12.34%) | 1981 - 1995<br>$70,060<br>(13.86%) |

^ annual compound rate of return for that period
*Source: Copyright ©1995 Merrill Lynch, Pierce, Fenner & Smith Incorporated.

©1996 Chase Global Data & Research
73 Junction Square, Concord, MA 01742

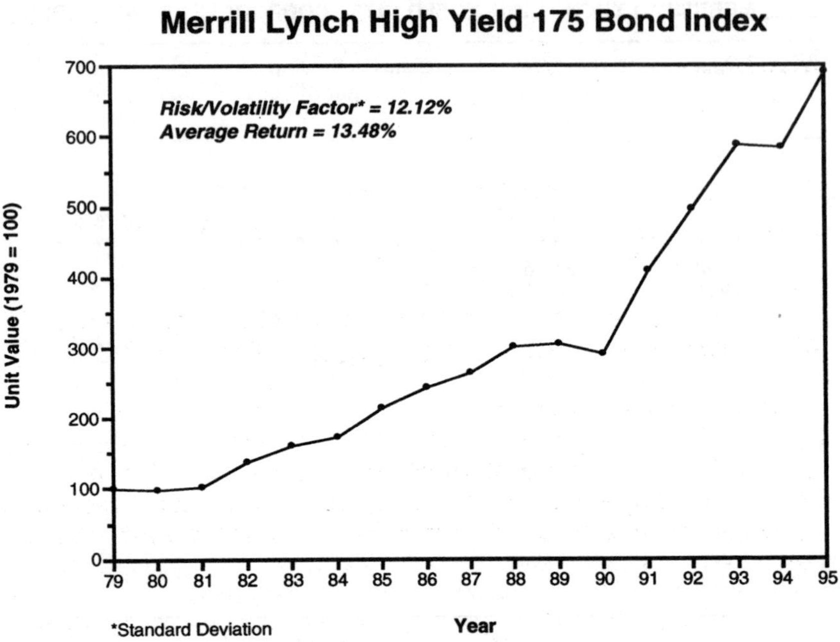


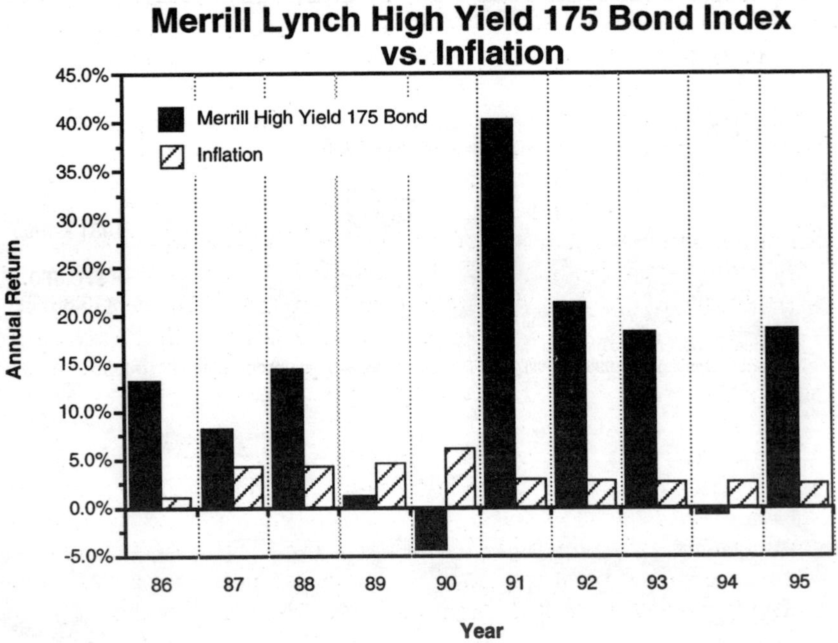


©1996 Chase Global Data & Research
73 Junction Square, Concord, MA 01742

# Chapter Twenty One

# Municipal Bonds

A municipal bond, or "muni," is a debt obligation of a U.S. state or political subdivision (county, city, town, village or other authority), which is exempt from federal income taxes. Usually a municipal security's interest payments are exempt from state and local income taxes as well. Being exempt from federal income taxation is a major strength of municipal bonds. However, their interest yields are always lower than comparable taxable bonds (government and corporate) of equivalent rating and maturity. Individual investors own an estimated 60% of all municipal bonds issued.

Municipal bonds come in two primary categories. The first are general obligation notes and bonds that are backed by the full faith and credit (and taxing power) of the issuer. Sometimes the issuer is additionally backed by federal and state aid. The second form is the revenue obligation municipal bond, which is used in financing specific projects such as bridges and sewer systems, with revenues from the facilities earmarked toward interest and principal repayment. Examples are housing bonds, utility revenue bonds, hospital revenue bonds and industrial development bonds.

Municipal bonds are normally issued in $5,000 minimum denominations, with each bond having a $1,000 par value. Maturities vary from notes ranging from 90 days to 5 years, to bonds which typically have 5 to 30 year durations until maturity. In the U.S. today over 100 different brokerage houses, banks, and other investment companies are underwriters for corporate, municipal and government bond issues.

The rating of municipal bonds is similar to that of corporate bonds (discussed in the preceding section). Municipals are rated by Standard and Poor's, Moody's, and Fitch Rating Services. In addition, municipal notes have another form of rating that addresses the concerns of the short term bond marketplace. Standard and Poor's rates notes maturing in 3 years or less by rating them SP-1, SP-2, and SP-3. This

©1996 Chase Global Data & Research
73 Junction Square, Concord, MA 01742

note rating system analyzes the amortization schedule of the short-term notes and the source of payment for interest and principal. SP-1 reflects a strong capacity to pay interest and principal. SP-1+ reflects overwhelming safety characteristics. SP-2 notes are considered to have satisfactory capacity to pay principal and interest. SP-3 notes are deemed to have a speculative capacity to pay principal and interest. Moody's has a similar note rating system ranging from MIG-1 (highest) to MIG-4 (lowest).

The municipal bond marketplace is huge, valued at over $1.5 trillion as of 1995. New long-term issues in 1993 were a record $323 billion. Today's market is more sophisticated as evidenced by the initiation of Municipal Bond Futures trading in 1985, later followed by the introduction of Treasury Bond futures. Although municipal bonds are considered very safe, there have been isolated instances of default. But municipal bond issues can even be insured for default by insurance companies. Insuring municipal bonds has been a practice for over 15 years since AMBAC Indemnity Corporation began offering such insurance. And the practice is growing. In 1980 only 3% of all bonds issued were insured—compared to over 30% by 1990. The cost of insurance for municipal bonds amounts to a reduced yield of about 0.5%. Of note, AMBAC insured Washington Public Power Systems Bonds (WPPS), paying $23.5 million in claims resulting from the largest municipal bond failure in U.S. history. With the bankruptcy of Orange County in 1994 due to losses incurred from derivatives, the WPPS failure may soon be surpassed.

The WPPS story is a sad one, but worth telling. The bonds were assigned A+ and A-1 ratings by Moody's and S&P when they were introduced in the late 1970's and early 1980's. By May 1981 several analysts forecast the WPPS nuclear power plants would never be built. Soon after the rating agencies downgraded WPPS debt, but the debt was still rated investment grade. Only after the plants were canceled did Moody's and S&P assign "junk" status to the bonds. The bonds went into default in June 1982, representing the biggest default in the history of the U.S. municipal bond market to date. The default took place less than two years after some WPPS bonds were sold as investment grade.

In the 1990's professionals and investors alike remain concerned that municipal bonds could have their own junk bond segment, potentially causing losses for investors in the future. Over $9 billion of municipals defaulted in 1990, and Standard and Poor's downgraded over $40 billion of municipals versus only $12 billion in upgrades. But

©1996 Chase Global Data & Research
73 Junction Square, Concord, MA 01742

it should be noted, however, that today's municipal bond market is valued at over $1 trillion, and the defaults represent less than 1% of outstanding municipals. For a better perspective, during the Great Depression 10% of all municipals defaulted.

The municipal bond markets have recently been in flux due to tax law revisions. When federal tax brackets are at high levels municipal bonds are attractive because their exclusion of interest from taxation provides greater "after-tax" yields for investors. However when tax brackets are lower, savings after tax considerations are less—due to the lower effect of federal taxes on the equation.

Municipal bonds are growing more popular with investors because experts feel the federal bracket reductions of the 1980's will prove to be the exception, not the rule. Tax laws passed in 1990 raised brackets, as did the Tax Act of 1993. From a long term perspective, experts estimate that in 1948 2% of salaries went toward paying federal taxes, versus 20% in 1995. Today joint filers with $147,700 income are in the 36% bracket, and the top bracket of 39.6% impacts earners of $263,750+. (Editor's note: For a complete review of past federal tax brackets since 1960 please turn to the Addendum section's pages 392-393.)

In 1996, a taxpayer filing jointly with income of $96,900 is in the 31% federal bracket. If state taxation of the taxpayer is at 5%, a 6% municipal is equal to a 9.4% corporate bond yield—after taxes are considered. And generally speaking the risks are lower with a municipal bond. Thus upon closer examination, municipal bonds are an attractive alternative for high tax bracket investors. That is, until a lower level flat tax is passed in Congress—a favorite campaign issue in 1996.

Finally, bear in mind that the Tables that follows cover the two aspects of municipal bond investment—yield and total return on investment. The Standard and Poor's Municipal Bond Yield Index reflects the average annual yield of 15 high grade municipal bonds which S&P's tracks. It is not a review of net returns after consideration of both principal fluctuation and interest income received. The Lehman Brothers Long Municipal Bond Index is a total return index, and reflects coupon interest and gain/loss on principal as it occurred on an annual basis. There are over 29,000 issues in the Lehman Long Municipal Bond Index, having maturities exceeding twenty-two years. The Index's bonds are a combination of both revenue and general obligation issue, have at least $100 million in principal outstanding, and carry a rating of Baa or higher.

©1996 Chase Global Data & Research
73 Junction Square, Concord, MA 01742

# MUNICIPAL BOND YIELD TAXABLE EQUIVALENT TABLE

| | ---- Income Tax Bracket ---- | | | | |
|---|---|---|---|---|---|
| | 15% | 28% | 31% | 36% | 39.6% |
| Joint Return Taxable Income* | $0-40,100 | $40,101-96,900 | $96,901-147,700 | $147,701-263,750 | Over $263,750 |
| Single Return Taxable Income* | $0-24,000 | $24,001-58,150 | $58,151-121,300 | $121,301-263,750 | Over $263,750 |
| **TAX-EXEMPT YIELD** % | **TAXABLE EQUIVALENT YIELD** % | | | | |
| 2.5 | 2.94 | 3.47 | 3.62 | 3.91 | 4.14 |
| 3.0 | 3.53 | 4.17 | 4.35 | 4.69 | 4.97 |
| 3.5 | 4.12 | 4.86 | 5.07 | 5.47 | 5.79 |
| 4.0 | 4.71 | 5.56 | 5.80 | 6.25 | 6.62 |
| 4.5 | 5.29 | 6.25 | 6.52 | 7.03 | 7.45 |
| 5.0 | 5.88 | 6.94 | 7.25 | 7.81 | 8.28 |
| 5.5 | 6.47 | 7.64 | 7.97 | 8.59 | 9.11 |
| 6.0 | 7.06 | 8.33 | 8.70 | 9.38 | 9.93 |
| 6.5 | 7.65 | 9.03 | 9.42 | 10.16 | 10.76 |
| 7.0 | 8.24 | 9.72 | 10.14 | 10.94 | 11.59 |
| 7.5 | 8.82 | 10.42 | 10.87 | 11.72 | 12.42 |
| 8.0 | 9.41 | 11.11 | 11.59 | 12.50 | 13.24 |
| 8.5 | 10.00 | 11.81 | 12.31 | 13.28 | 14.07 |
| 9.0 | 10.59 | 12.50 | 13.04 | 14.06 | 14.90 |

* Net amount subject to federal income tax after deductions and exemptions. Tax year 1996.

Source: Chase Global Data & Research.

©1996 Chase Global Data & Research
73 Junction Square, Concord, MA 01742

**MUNICIPAL BOND YIELD**

[high grade S&P 15 bonds; average annual yield]

| Year | Yield* | Compound return on a five year $10,000 investment | Annual compound rate of return |
|---|---|---|---|
| 1995 | 5.95% | 1991 - 1995 | |
| 1994 | 6.19% | | 6.21% |
| 1993 | 5.63% | ... $13,517 | |
| 1992 | 6.41% | | |
| 1991 | 6.89% | | |
| 1990 | 7.25% | 1986 - 1990 | |
| 1989 | 7.24% | | 7.47% |
| 1988 | 7.76% | ... $14,337 | |
| 1987 | 7.73% | | |
| 1986 | 7.38% | | |
| 1985 | 9.18% | 1981 - 1985 | |
| 1984 | 10.15% | | 10.32% |
| 1983 | 9.47% | ... $16,338 | |
| 1982 | 11.57% | | |
| 1981 | 11.23% | | |
| 1980 | 8.51% | 1976 - 1980 | |
| 1979 | 6.39% | | 6.57% |
| 1978 | 5.90% | ... $13,743 | |
| 1977 | 5.56% | | |
| 1976 | 6.49% | | |
| 1975 | 6.89% | 1971 - 1975 | |
| 1974 | 6.09% | | 5.82% |
| 1973 | 5.18% | ... $13,272 | |
| 1972 | 5.27% | | |
| 1971 | 5.70% | | |
| 1970 | 6.51% | 1966 - 1970 | |
| 1969 | 5.81% | | 4.92% |
| 1968 | 4.51% | ... $12,715 | |
| 1967 | 3.98% | | |
| 1966 | 3.82% | | |
| 1965 | 3.27% | 1961 - 1965 | |
| 1964 | 3.22% | | 3.27% |
| 1963 | 3.23% | ... $11,747 | |
| 1962 | 3.18% | | |
| 1961 | 3.46% | | |
| 1960 | 3.73% | | |

How a $10,000 investment performed over

| 5 years | 10 years | 15 years | 20 years | 25 years | 35 years |
|---|---|---|---|---|---|
| 1991 - 1995 | | | | | |
| $13,517 (6.21%)^ | 1986 - 1995 | | | | |
| | $19,380 (6.84%) | 1981 - 1995 | | | |
| | | $31,663 (7.99%) | 1976 - 1995 | | |
| | | | $43,514 (7.63%) | 1971 - 1995 | |
| | | | | $57,750 (7.27%) | 1961 - 1995 |
| | | | | | $86,253 (6.35%) |

^ annual compound rate of return for that period

* Source: Standard & Poor's Corp.

©1996 Chase Global Data & Research
73 Junction Square, Concord, MA 01742

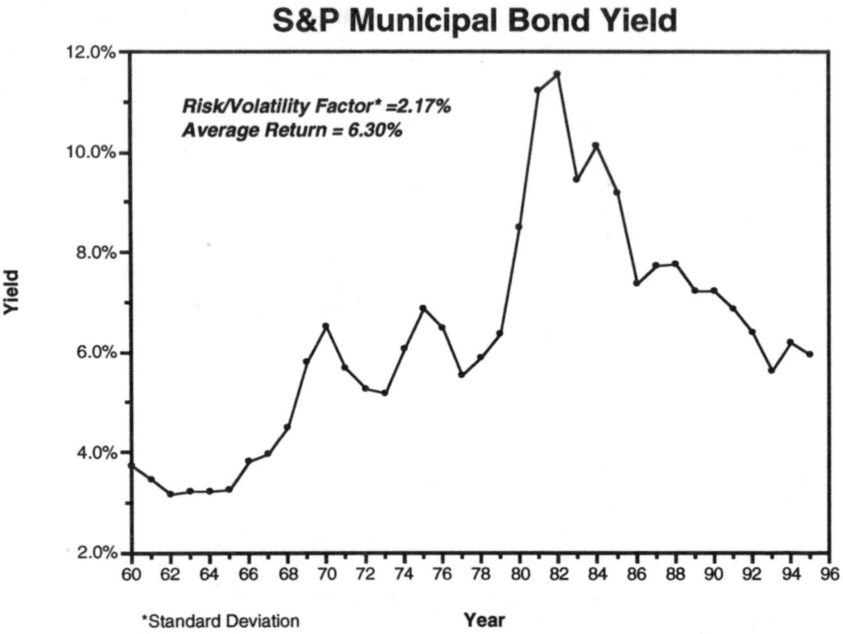


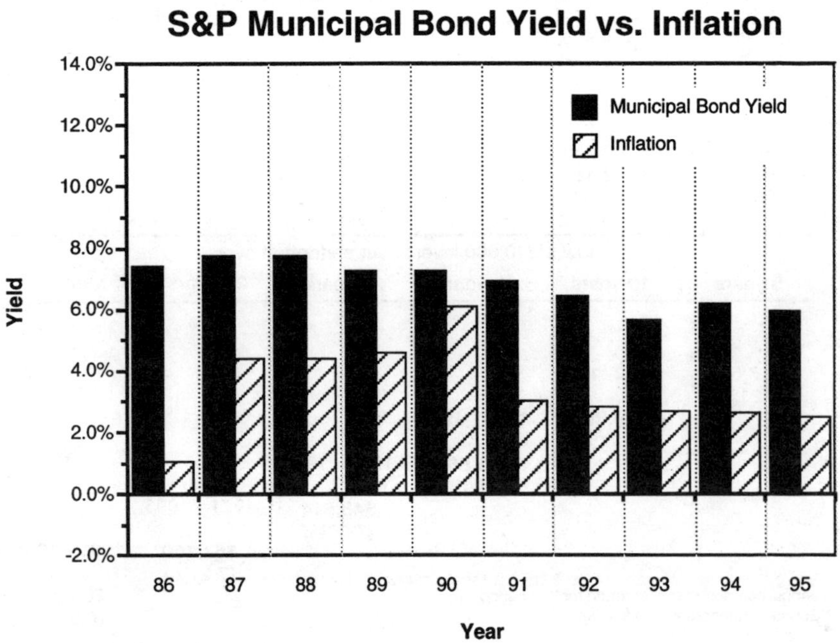


©1996 Chase Global Data & Research
73 Junction Square, Concord, MA 01742

## LEHMAN BROTHERS TOTAL RETURN MUNICIPAL BOND INDEX

[long term, 22+ yrs]

| Year | Total Return* | Compound return on a five year $10,000 investment | Annual compound rate of return |
|---|---|---|---|
| 1995 | 23.28% | 1991 - 1995 | |
| 1994 | -9.10% | | 9.99% |
| 1993 | 14.76% | ... $16,097 | |
| 1992 | 10.23% | | |
| 1991 | 13.55% | | |
| 1990 | 7.21% | | |
| 1989 | 11.98% | 1986 - 1990 | |
| 1988 | 13.50% | | 10.51% |
| 1987 | -0.02% | ... $16,485 | |
| 1986 | 21.00% | | |
| 1985 | 22.79% | | |
| 1984 | 10.99% | | |
| 1983 | 8.67% | 1981 - 1985 | |
| 1982 | 43.92% | | 13.59% |
| 1981 | -11.28% | ... $18,912 | |
| 1980 | -8.33% | | |

How a $10,000 investment performed over

| 5 years | 10 years | 15 years |
|---|---|---|
| 1991 - 1995 | | |
| $16,097 (9.99%)^ | 1986 - 1995 | |
| | $26,535 (10.25%) | 1981 - 1995 |
| | | $50,185 (11.35%) |

^ annual compound rate of return for that period
* Source: Lehman Brothers.

©1996 Chase Global Data & Research
73 Junction Square, Concord, MA 01742

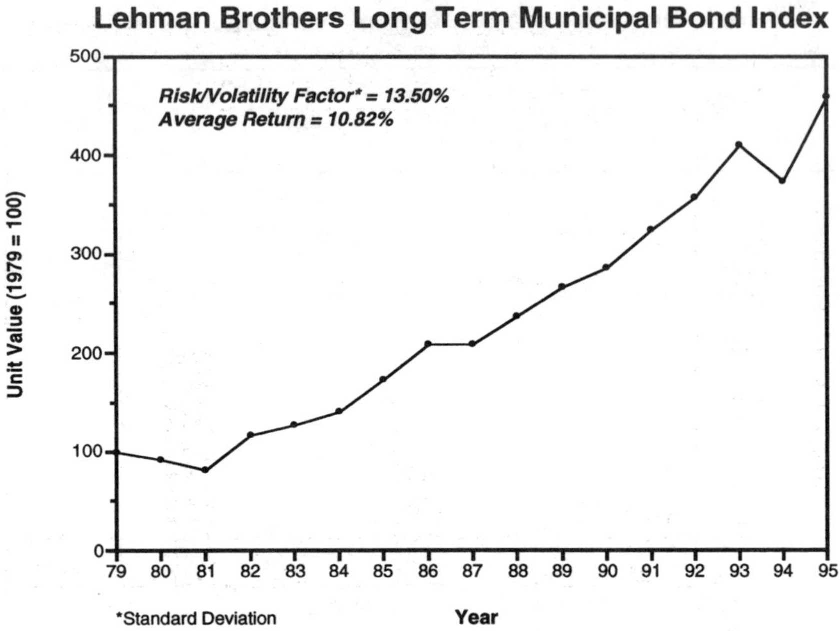


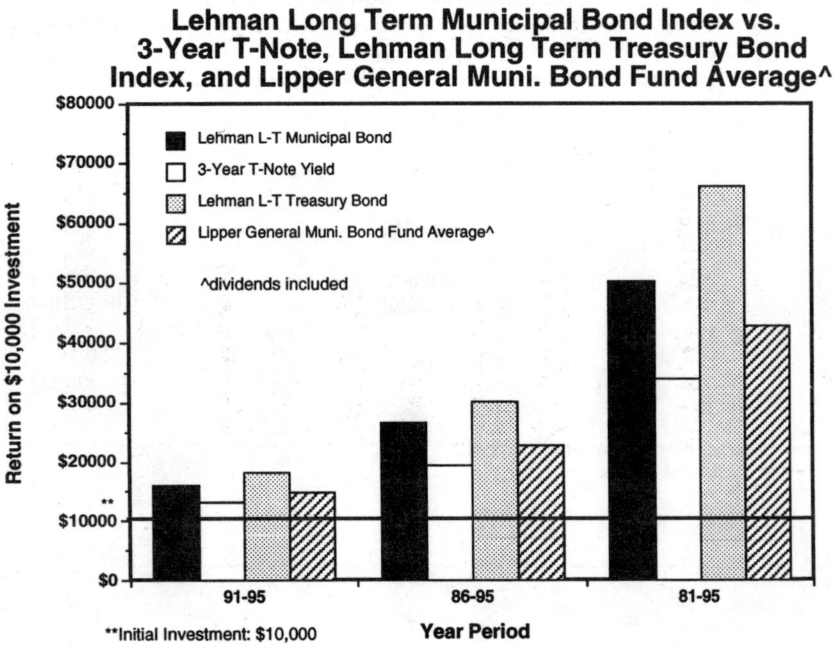


©1996 Chase Global Data & Research
73 Junction Square, Concord, MA 01742

## Lehman Brothers Long Term Municipal Bond Index vs. Morgan Stanley Europe Equity Index^, Silver, and Farmland

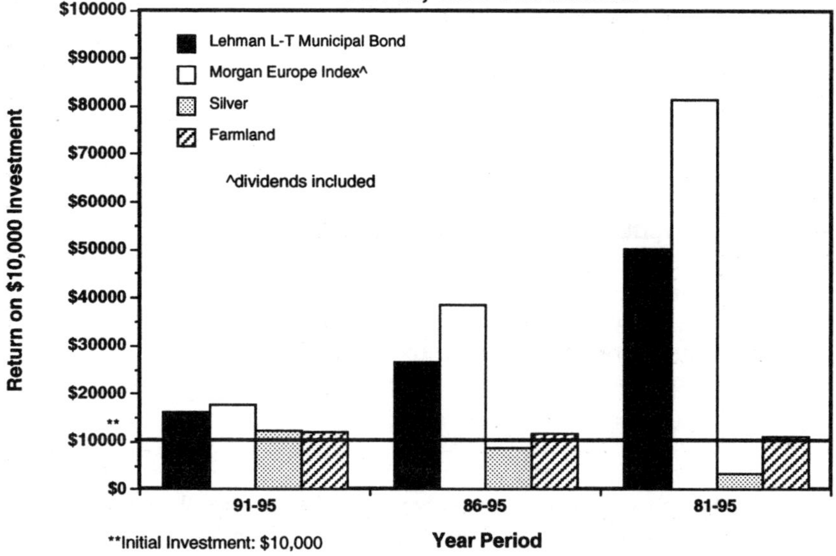


## Lehman Brothers Long Term Municipal Bond Index vs. Inflation

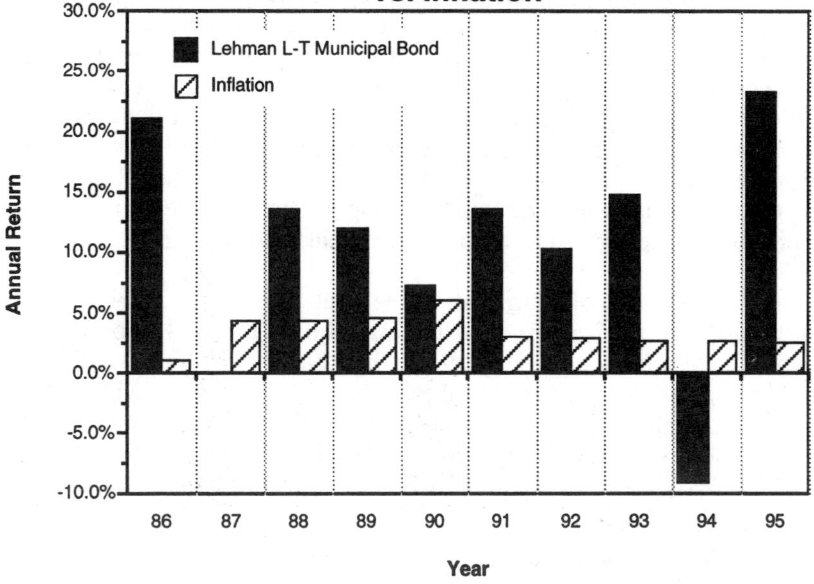


©1996 Chase Global Data & Research
73 Junction Square, Concord, MA 01742

Chapter Twenty Two

# Lehman Brothers Bond Indices

- Government/Corporate Bond Index
- Long Term Treasury Bond Index
- Long Term Corporate Bond Index
- Intermediate Term Treasury Bond Index
- Intermediate Term Corporate Bond Index
- Mortgage-Backed Securities Index

The most widely used benchmarks of bond market "total return" performance are the Lehman Brothers Bond Indices. Lehman Brothers began publishing the Indices on a monthly basis on December 31, 1972. The Indices reflect total return as price appreciation/depreciation on bond investments plus any income earned, expressed as a percentage of the initial investment. Therefore the standard components for the total return are: price return plus coupon return. For periods greater than one month, coupon return also includes the reinvestment component. Reinvestment is considered to be done monthly on a market-weighted proportionate basis. The Index portfolios are evaluated on a month-end to month-end basis. The Lehman Brothers Indices reflect bonds 99% of which are market value priced by Lehman Brothers' trading desk, with 1% being priced via proprietary pricing (a necessity for the illiquid and low-capitalized issues). The Indices, being market-weighted, give greater emphasis to issues which have more bonds outstanding.

As a point of clarification, several other bond Tables in the *Chase Investment Performance Digest* such as the U.S. Government bonds, Corporate Bond averages, and the Aaa and Baa Tables reflect an assumption that bonds purchased will be held to maturity with no loss on the principal. In those Tables the chief variable annually is the new coupon yield. Thus we consider the Tables exclusively yield-related bond Tables. Such is not the case with the Lehman Brothers Bond Tables in this chapter.


©1996 Chase Global Data & Research
73 Junction Square, Concord, MA 01742

Only notes and bonds with a minimum outstanding par value of $100 million and with minimum maturities of one year are included in the Lehman Brothers Corporate and Treasury Indices. The Treasury Bond Indices include all public obligations of the U.S. Treasury with the exception of flower bonds and foreign targeted issues, which are excluded. The Lehman Brothers Corporate Bond Indices reflect all public, fixed rate, non-convertible domestic corporate debts which are rated at least investment grade (Baa3 or higher). Over time, the cumulative performance of the Indices reflect all major market trends in the bond marketplace. The Aggregate Index, for example, reflects returns for bond portfolios worth $4.5 trillion and 5,343 individual issues. For the preceding reasons, the Lehman Brothers Indices are considered the major benchmark for the U.S. bond marketplace. The Indices can be replicated. They therefore are a popular benchmark for Bond Index portfolio passive management accounts. And as stated earlier in the Corporate Bond section, Bond Index portfolios have been outperforming actively managed bond portfolios with some frequency.

The Lehman Brothers Government/Corporate Bond Index included in this chapter is the grandfather of all Lehman Brothers Indices, and is a combination of the Government and Corporate Bond Indices. No asset-backed securities are included in the Government/Corporate Index. However, Lehman Brothers now tracks the Aggregate Bond Index, a combination of the Government/Corporate, Mortgage-Backed, and Asset-Backed Indices. At year-end 1995, the Aggregate Index's total value was approximately $4.5 trillion, and the Government/Corporate Index was comprised of 4,616 bonds.

The Mortgage-Backed Securities Index covers all fixed rate bonds backed by mortgage pools of the Government National Mortgage Association (GNMA), the Federal Home Loan Mortgage Corporation (FHLMC), and the Federal National Mortgage Association (FNMA). The Index includes Graduated Payment Mortgages and excludes Graduated Equity Mortgages. In total there are 603 issues in the Mortgage-Backed Securities Index. The major groupings within the Index are FHLMC 30 year original issues and FNMA 30 year original issues. Mortgage-backed securities have been steadily growing in popularity within the fixed income arena.

The Lehman Brothers Corporate Bond Indices for both intermediate and long term are made up of four major corporate classifications: industrial, utility, finance, and yankee. Lehman Brothers Intermediate Term Bond Indices (Corporate and Treasury) are comprised of bonds which have maturities from 1 to 9.99 years. Thus

©1996 Chase Global Data & Research
73 Junction Square, Concord, MA 01742

the Intermediate Treasury Index is primarily made up of treasury notes. Long Term Bond Indices reflect bonds with maturities from 10 to 30 years.

Lehman Brothers also customizes client portfolios to mature at a pace that matches various pension fund liabilities on a corporate basis. The firm also provides clients custom portfolios which meet the need for an appropriate mix of maturities in tandem with proper bond rating quality. Lehman Brothers relies on the various attributes of their many indices as a guideline toward the customization process. For example, companies with young employees and thus long-term pension fund liabilities may track indices of long-term bonds, while companies with a more mature census of employees might use a shorter term Index Fund for their pension management.

Not included in the *Chase Investment Performance Digest* but also tracked by Lehman Brothers are a variety of specialized indices. The AAA Corporate Bonds and BAA Corporate Bonds, for example, are extremely valuable in their ability to accurately reflect the returns made in specific areas of the overall bond marketplace. Other Lehman fixed income indices include global, high yield, municipal, Eurobond, ARMs, emerging Americas, AA, A, utility, finance, industrial, asset-backed, and more.

As of year end 1995, the Lehman Brothers indices examined in the *Chase Investment Performance Digest* held the following number of issues:

| | |
|---|---|
| Government/Corporate Bond Index | 4616 issues |
| Long Term Treasury Bond Index | 43 issues |
| Long Term Corporate Bond Index | 1251 issues |
| Intermediate Term Treasury Bond Index | 128 issues |
| Intermediate Term Corporate Bond Index | 2136 issues |
| Mortgage-Backed Securities Index | 603 issues |
| Municipal Bond Index (see Municipal Bond Chapter) | 29334 issues |

(*Editors note:* From time to time the makeup of the Lehman Brothers Indices may change slightly in regards to maturity and composition.)

©1996 Chase Global Data & Research
73 Junction Square, Concord, MA 01742

## LEHMAN BROTHERS GOVERNMENT / CORPORATE BOND INDEX

| Year | Total Return* | Compound return on a five year $10,000 investment | Annual compound rate of return |
|---|---|---|---|
| 1995 | 19.25% | 1991 - 1995 | |
| 1994 | -3.51% | | 9.80% |
| 1993 | 11.03% | ... $15,961 | |
| 1992 | 7.58% | | |
| 1991 | 16.13% | | |
| 1990 | 8.28% | 1986 - 1990 | |
| 1989 | 14.24% | | 9.49% |
| 1988 | 7.58% | ... $15,739 | |
| 1987 | 2.29% | | |
| 1986 | 15.62% | | |
| 1985 | 21.30% | 1981 - 1985 | |
| 1984 | 15.02% | | 16.20% |
| 1983 | 8.00% | ... $21,187 | |
| 1982 | 31.09% | | |
| 1981 | 7.26% | | |
| 1980 | 3.06% | 1976 - 1980 | |
| 1979 | 2.30% | | 4.90% |
| 1978 | 1.19% | ... $12,699 | |
| 1977 | 2.98% | | |
| 1976 | 15.59% | | |
| 1975 | 12.29% | | |
| 1974 | 0.17% | | |
| 1973 | 2.28% | | |

How a $10,000 investment performed over

| 5 years | 10 years | 15 years | 20 years |
|---|---|---|---|
| 1991 - 1995 | | | |
| $15,961 (9.80%)^ | 1986 - 1995 | | |
| | $25,120 (9.65%) | 1981 - 1995 | |
| | | $53,221 (11.79%) | 1976 - 1995 |
| | | | $67,587 (10.03%) |

^ annual compound rate of return for that period

* Source: Lehman Brothers.

©1996 Chase Global Data & Research
73 Junction Square, Concord, MA 01742

## Lehman Brothers Government/Corporate Bond Index

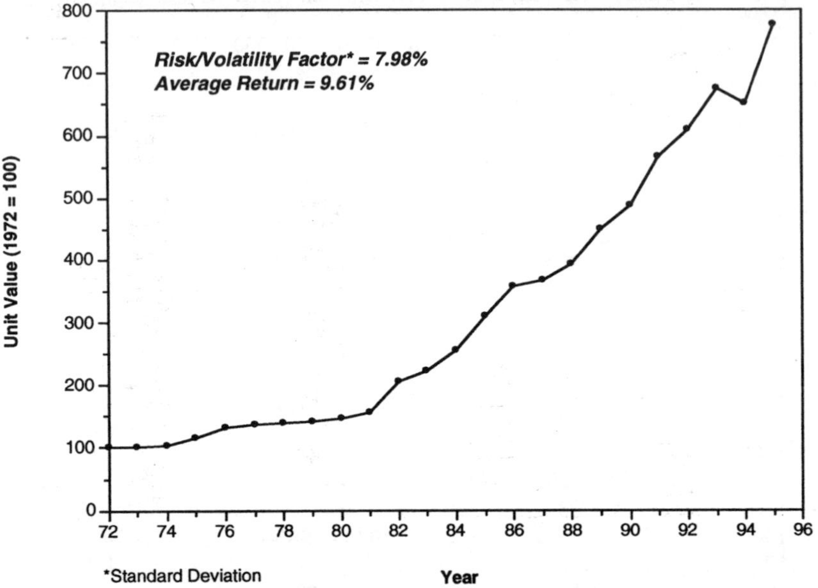


## Lehman Brothers Government/Corporate Bond Index vs. 3-Month T-Bill and Lehman Brothers Long Term Corporate Bond Index

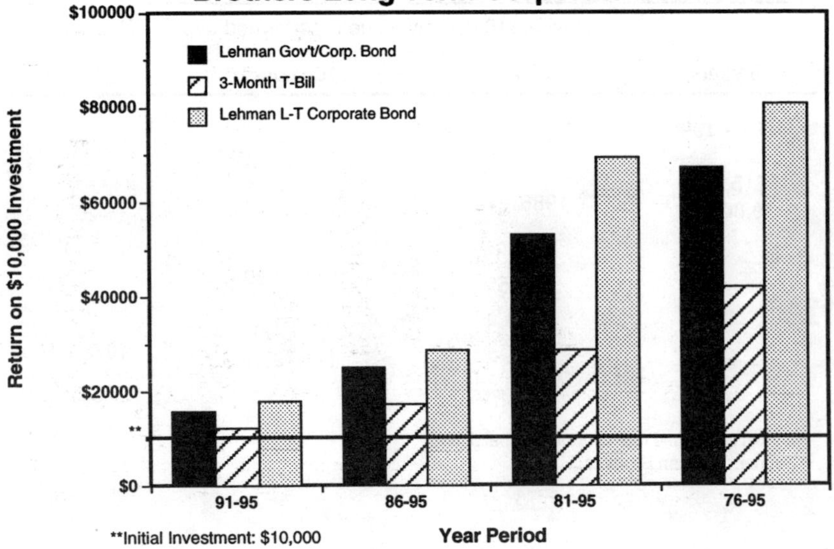


©1996 Chase Global Data & Research
73 Junction Square, Concord, MA 01742

## Lehman Brothers Government/Corporate Bond Index vs. Value Line Composite Index and Silver

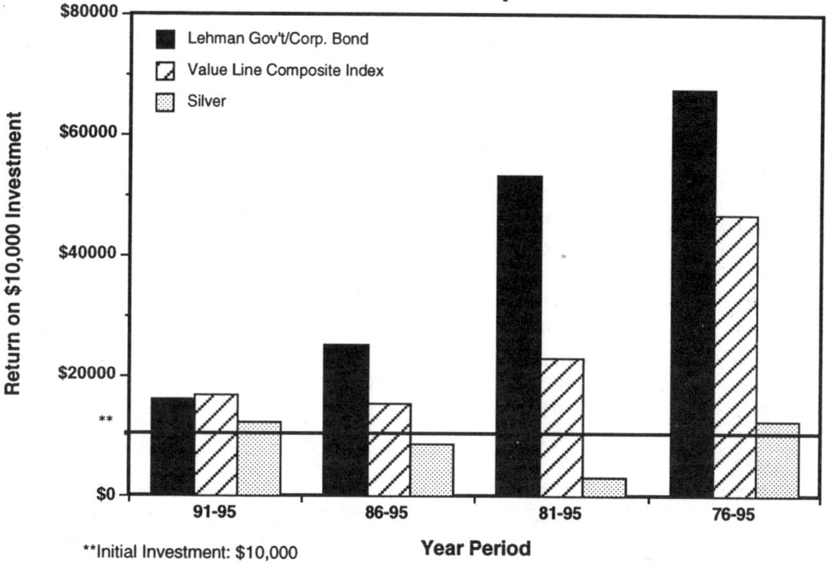


## Lehman Brothers Government/Corporate Bond Index vs. Inflation

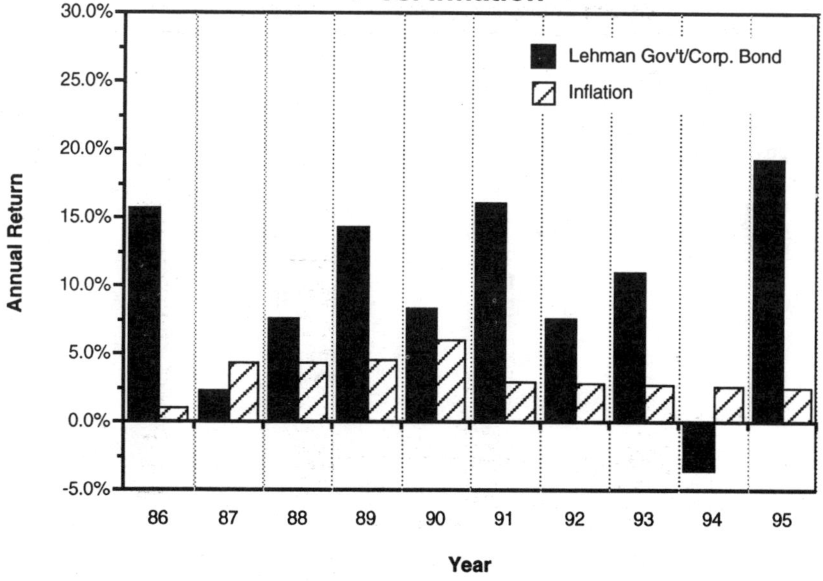


©1996 Chase Global Data & Research
73 Junction Square, Concord, MA 01742

## LEHMAN BROTHERS LONG TERM TREASURY BOND INDEX

[long term, 10+ yrs]

| Year | Total Return* | Compound return on a five year $10,000 investment | Annual compound rate of return |
|---|---|---|---|
| 1995 | 30.68% | 1991 - 1995 | |
| 1994 | -7.63% | | 12.61% |
| 1993 | 17.25% | ... $18,105 | |
| 1992 | 7.96% | | |
| 1991 | 18.49% | | |
| 1990 | 6.30% | 1986 - 1990 | |
| 1989 | 18.94% | | 10.77% |
| 1988 | 9.19% | ... $16,675 | |
| 1987 | -2.67% | | |
| 1986 | 24.10% | | |
| 1985 | 31.56% | 1981 - 1985 | |
| 1984 | 14.79% | | 16.99% |
| 1983 | 1.98% | ... $21,913 | |
| 1982 | 41.76% | | |
| 1981 | 0.37% | | |
| 1980 | -2.94% | 1976 - 1980 | |
| 1979 | -0.53% | | 2.18% |
| 1978 | -1.44% | ... $11,137 | |
| 1977 | -0.05% | | |
| 1976 | 17.10% | | |
| 1975 | 8.34% | | |
| 1974 | 5.02% | | |
| 1973 | 1.14% | | |

How a $10,000 investment performed over

| 5 years | 10 years | 15 years | 20 years |
|---|---|---|---|
| 1991 - 1995<br>$18,105<br>(12.61%)^ | 1986 - 1995<br>$30,190<br>(11.68%) | 1981 - 1995<br>$66,155<br>(13.42%) | 1976 - 1995<br>$73,677<br>(10.50%) |

^ annual compound rate of return for that period

* Source: Lehman Brothers.

©1996 Chase Global Data & Research
73 Junction Square, Concord, MA 01742

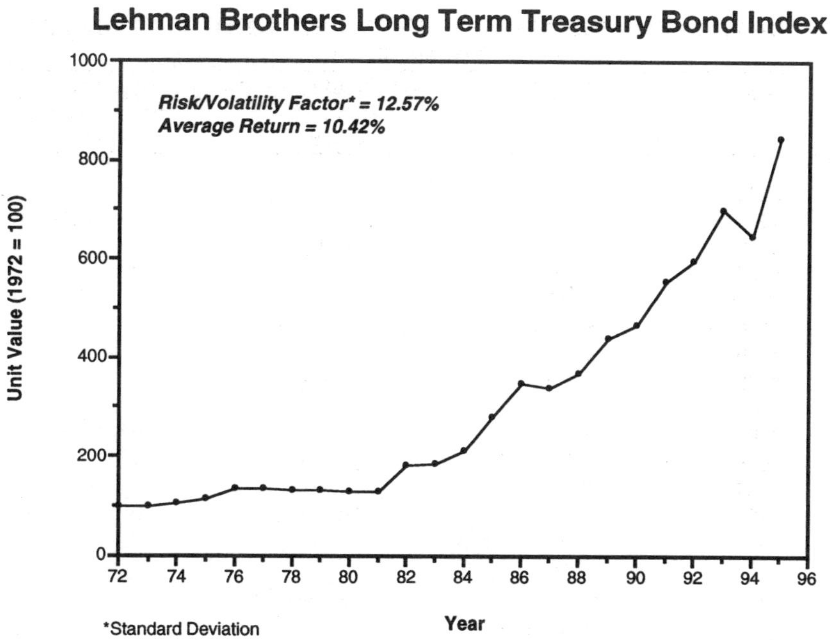


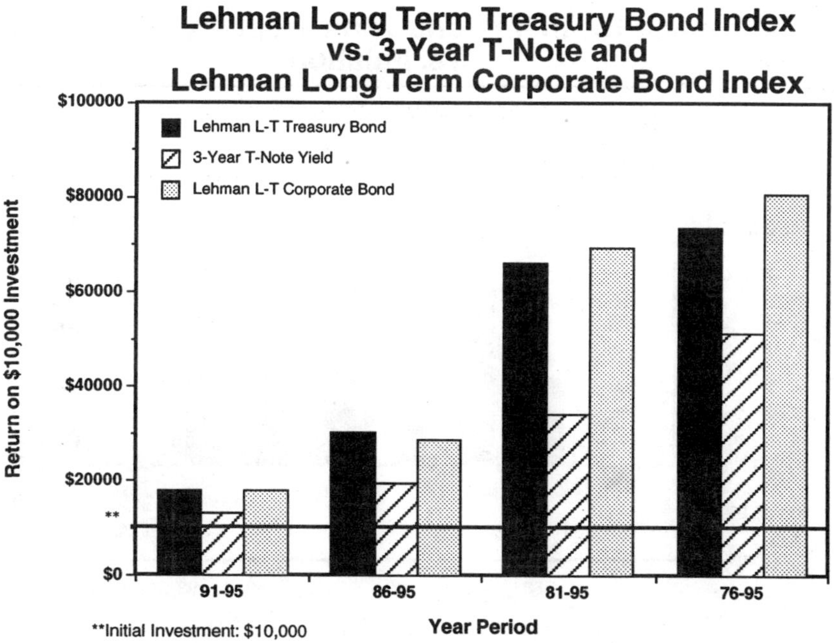


©1996 Chase Global Data & Research
73 Junction Square, Concord, MA 01742

## Lehman Brothers Long Term Treasury Bond Index vs. Gold and Morgan Stanley EAFE Equity Index^

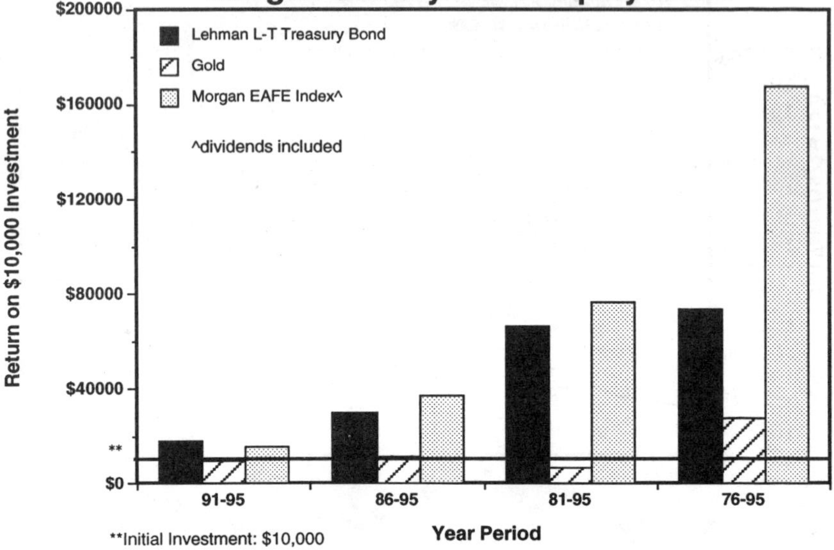


## Lehman Brothers Long Term Treasury Bond Index vs. Inflation

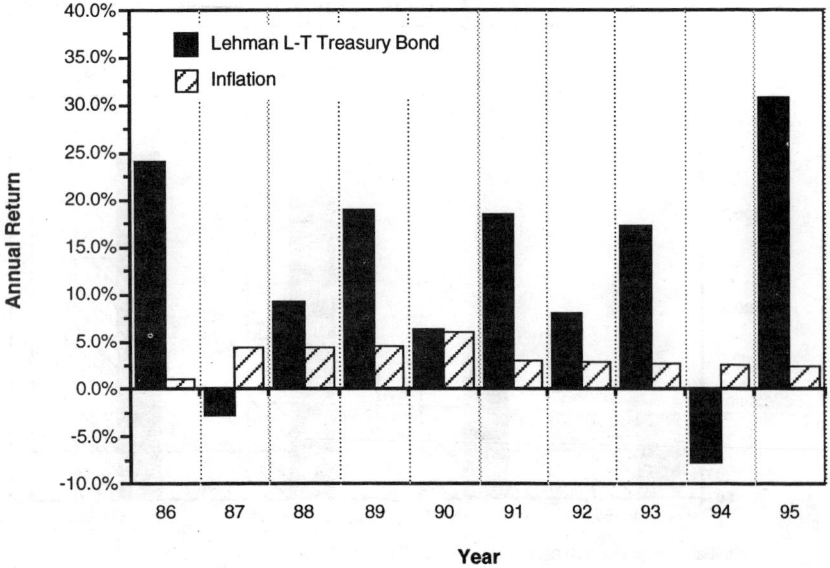


©1996 Chase Global Data & Research
73 Junction Square, Concord, MA 01742

## LEHMAN BROTHERS LONG TERM CORPORATE BOND INDEX

[long term, 10+ yrs]

| Year | Total Return* | Compound return on a five year $10,000 investment | Annual compound rate of return |
|---|---|---|---|
| 1995 | 27.92% | 1991 - 1995 | |
| 1994 | -5.75% | | 12.63% |
| 1993 | 13.64% | ... $18,124 | |
| 1992 | 9.34% | | |
| 1991 | 20.98% | | |
| 1990 | 6.48% | 1986 - 1990 | |
| 1989 | 15.29% | | 10.32% |
| 1988 | 10.49% | ... $16,338 | |
| 1987 | 1.47% | | |
| 1986 | 18.71% | | |
| 1985 | 27.99% | 1981 - 1985 | |
| 1984 | 17.66% | | 18.67% |
| 1983 | 8.32% | ... $23,537 | |
| 1982 | 44.52% | | |
| 1981 | -0.16% | | |
| 1980 | -2.60% | 1976 - 1980 | |
| 1979 | -4.08% | | 3.01% |
| 1978 | -0.10% | ... $11,598 | |
| 1977 | 2.67% | | |
| 1976 | 21.03% | | |
| 1975 | 17.56% | | |
| 1974 | -7.61% | | |
| 1973 | 1.09% | | |

How a $10,000 investment performed over

| 5 years | 10 years | 15 years | 20 years |
|---|---|---|---|
| 1991 - 1995<br>$18,124<br>(12.63%)^ | 1986 - 1995<br>$29,611<br>(11.47%) | 1981 - 1995<br>$69,694<br>(13.82%) | 1976 - 1995<br>$80,829<br>(11.01%) |

^ annual compound rate of return for that period

* Source: Lehman Brothers.

©1996 Chase Global Data & Research
73 Junction Square, Concord, MA 01742

## Lehman Brothers Long Term Corporate Bond Index

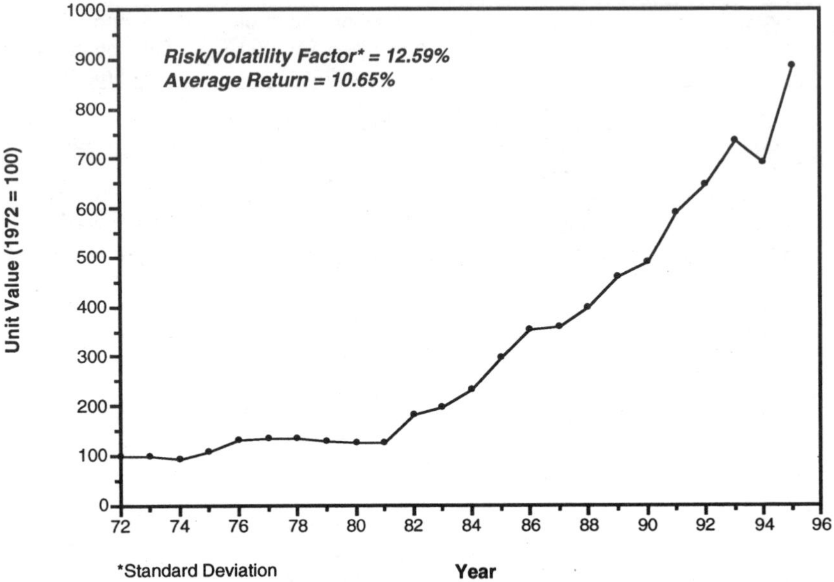


*Standard Deviation

## Lehman Brothers Long Term Corporate Bond Index vs. 10-Year T-Bond and Lipper Fixed Income Fund Average^

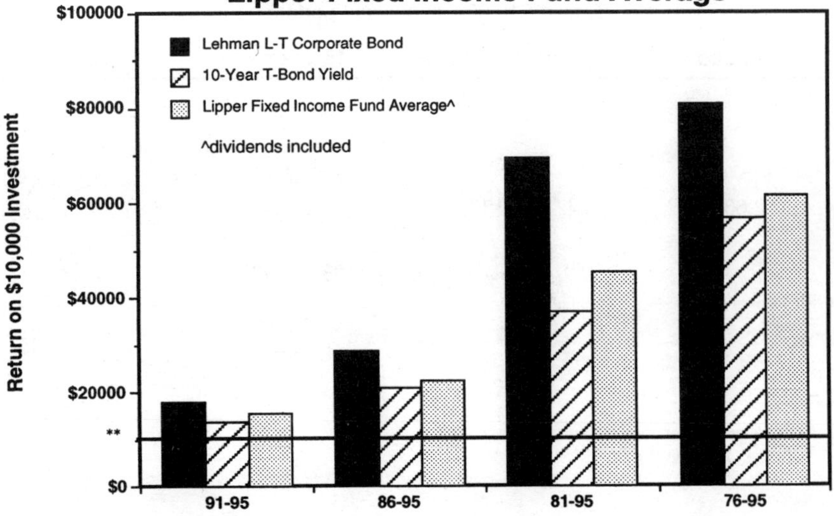


**Initial Investment: $10,000

©1996 Chase Global Data & Research
73 Junction Square, Concord, MA 01742

## Lehman Brothers Long Term Corporate Bond Index vs. Dow Jones 30 Industrials^ and House Price Index

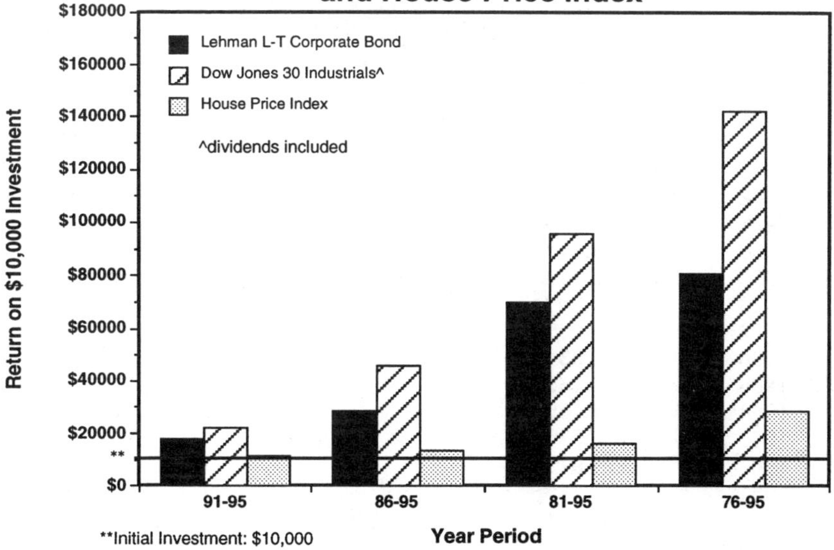


## Lehman Brothers Long Term Corporate Bond Index vs. Inflation

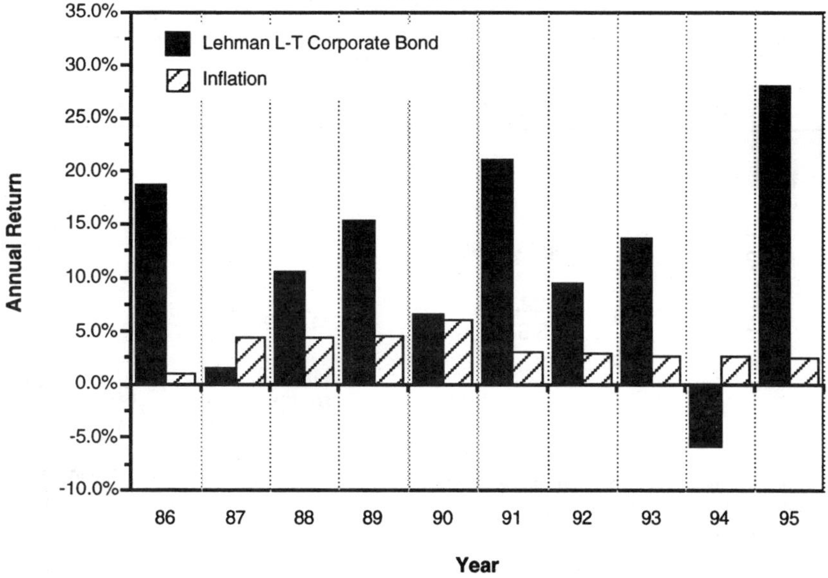


©1996 Chase Global Data & Research
73 Junction Square, Concord, MA 01742

## LEHMAN BROTHERS INTERMEDIATE TREASURY BOND INDEX

[intermediate term, 1-10 yrs.]

| Year | Total Return* | Compound return on a five year $10,000 investment | Annual compound rate of return |
|---|---|---|---|
| 1995 | 14.40% | 1991 - 1995 | |
| 1994 | -1.78% | | 8.21% |
| 1993 | 8.22% | ... $14,839 | |
| 1992 | 6.95% | | |
| 1991 | 14.10% | | |
| 1990 | 9.45% | 1986 - 1990 | |
| 1989 | 12.70% | | 8.95% |
| 1988 | 6.26% | ... $15,348 | |
| 1987 | 3.60% | | |
| 1986 | 13.03% | | |
| 1985 | 18.15% | 1981 - 1985 | |
| 1984 | 14.23% | | 15.11% |
| 1983 | 8.03% | ... $20,214 | |
| 1982 | 24.97% | | |
| 1981 | 10.94% | | |
| 1980 | 7.12% | 1976 - 1980 | |
| 1979 | 6.92% | | 6.10% |
| 1978 | 2.44% | ... $13,448 | |
| 1977 | 2.90% | | |
| 1976 | 11.39% | | |
| 1975 | 8.03% | | |
| 1974 | 7.18% | | |
| 1973 | 3.61% | | |

How a $10,000 investment performed over

| 5 years | 10 years | 15 years | 20 years |
|---|---|---|---|
| 1991 - 1995 | 1986 - 1995 | 1981 - 1995 | 1976 - 1995 |
| $14,839 (8.21%)^ | $22,775 (8.58%) | $46,038 (10.72%) | $61,912 (9.54%) |

^ annual compound rate of return for that period

* Source: Lehman Brothers.

©1996 Chase Global Data & Research
73 Junction Square, Concord, MA 01742

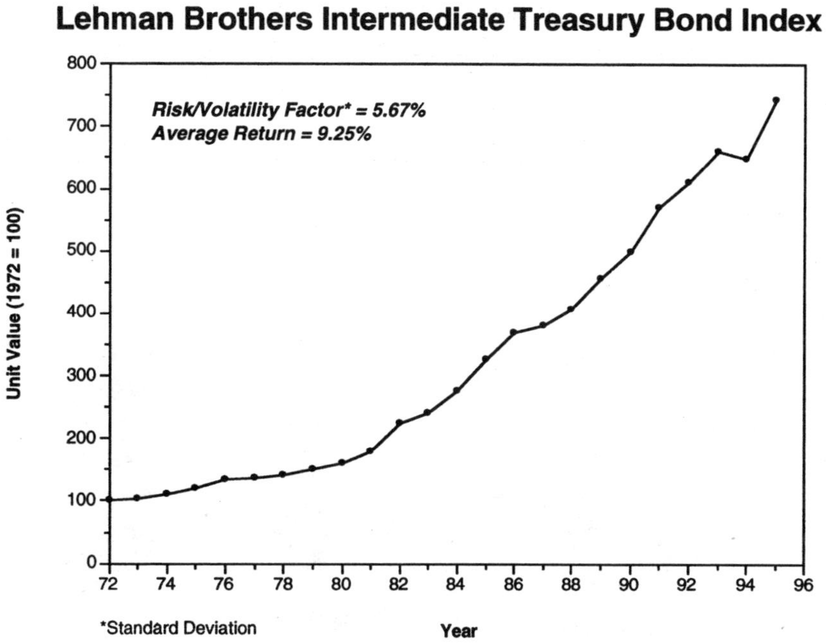


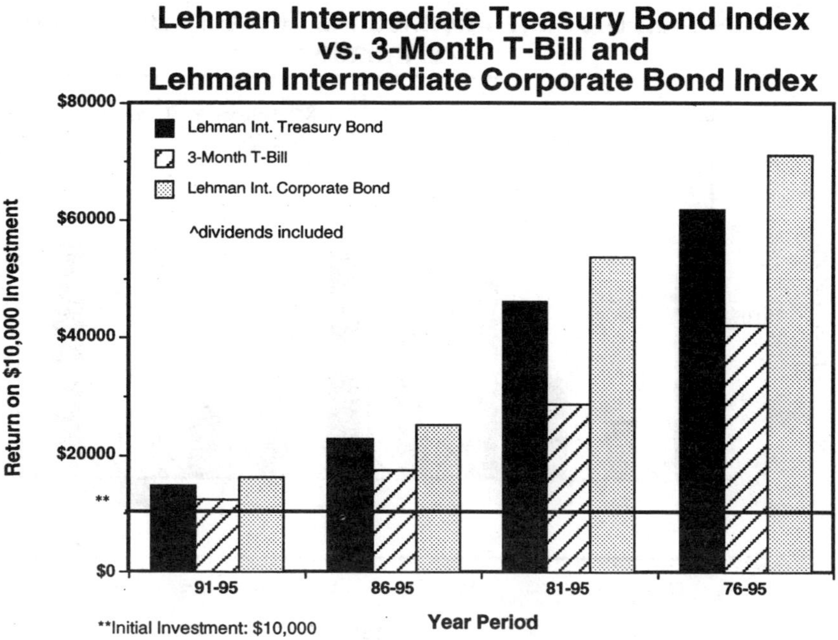


©1996 Chase Global Data & Research
73 Junction Square, Concord, MA 01742

## Lehman Brothers Intermediate Treasury Bond Index vs. NASDAQ Composite Index and REITs

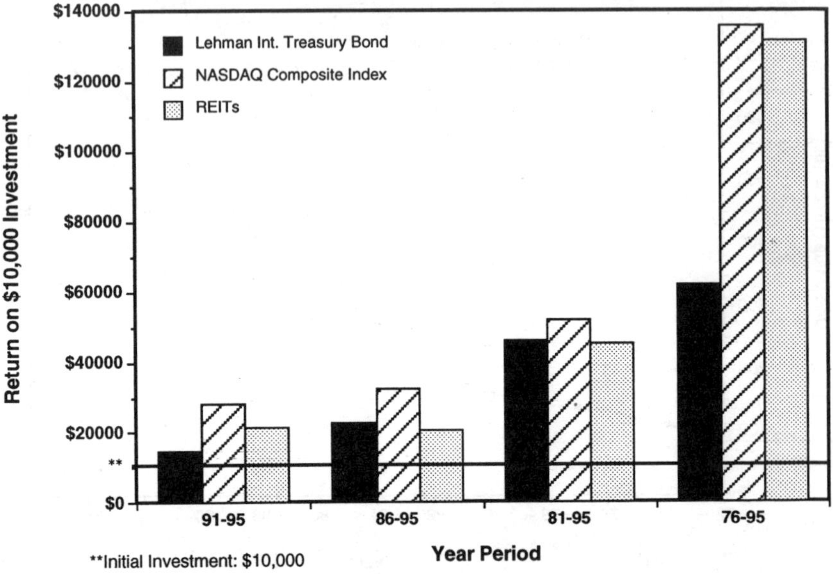


## Lehman Brothers Intermediate Treasury Bond Index vs. Inflation

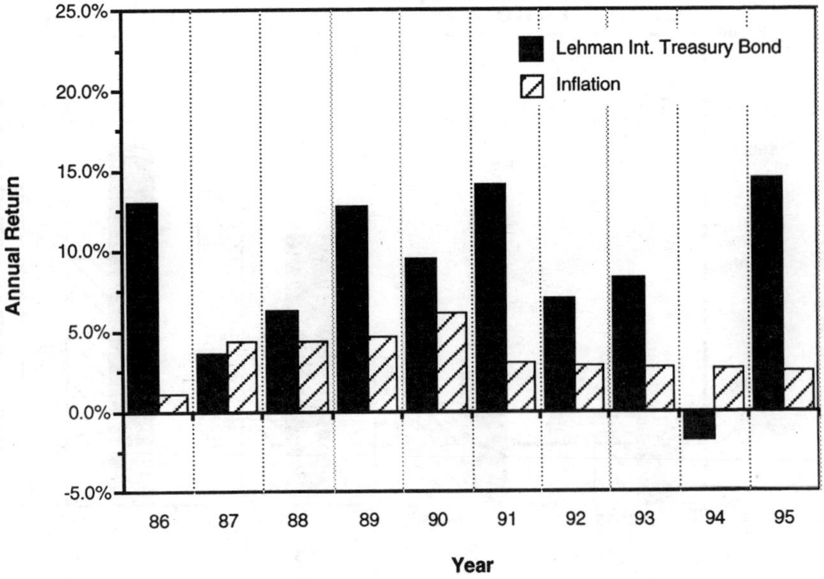


©1996 Chase Global Data & Research
73 Junction Square, Concord, MA 01742

## LEHMAN BROTHERS INTERMEDIATE CORPORATE BOND INDEX

[intermediate term, 1-10 yrs.]

| Year | Total Return* | Compound return on a five year $10,000 investment | Annual compound rate of return |
|---|---|---|---|
| 1995 | 19.01% | 1991 - 1995 | |
| 1994 | -2.64% | | 10.19% |
| 1993 | 11.13% | ... $16,246 | |
| 1992 | 8.20% | | |
| 1991 | 16.61% | | |
| 1990 | 7.64% | 1986 - 1990 | |
| 1989 | 12.95% | | 9.14% |
| 1988 | 7.97% | ... $15,483 | |
| 1987 | 3.94% | | |
| 1986 | 13.48% | | |
| 1985 | 18.46% | 1981 - 1985 | |
| 1984 | 14.87% | | 16.36% |
| 1983 | 10.65% | ... $21,335 | |
| 1982 | 30.02% | | |
| 1981 | 8.98% | | |
| 1980 | 5.34% | 1976 - 1980 | |
| 1979 | 3.35% | | 5.82% |
| 1978 | 1.65% | ... $13,269 | |
| 1977 | 4.60% | | |
| 1976 | 14.63% | | |
| 1975 | 14.15% | | |
| 1974 | 1.06% | | |
| 1973 | 3.19% | | |

How a $10,000 investment performed over

| 5 years | 10 years | 15 years | 20 years |
|---|---|---|---|
| 1991 - 1995<br>$16,246<br>(10.19%)^ | 1986 - 1995<br>$25,155<br>(9.66%) | 1981 - 1995<br>$53,667<br>(11.85%) | 1976 - 1995<br>$71,212<br>(10.31%) |

^ annual compound rate of return for that period
* Source: Lehman Brothers.

©1996 Chase Global Data & Research
73 Junction Square, Concord, MA 01742

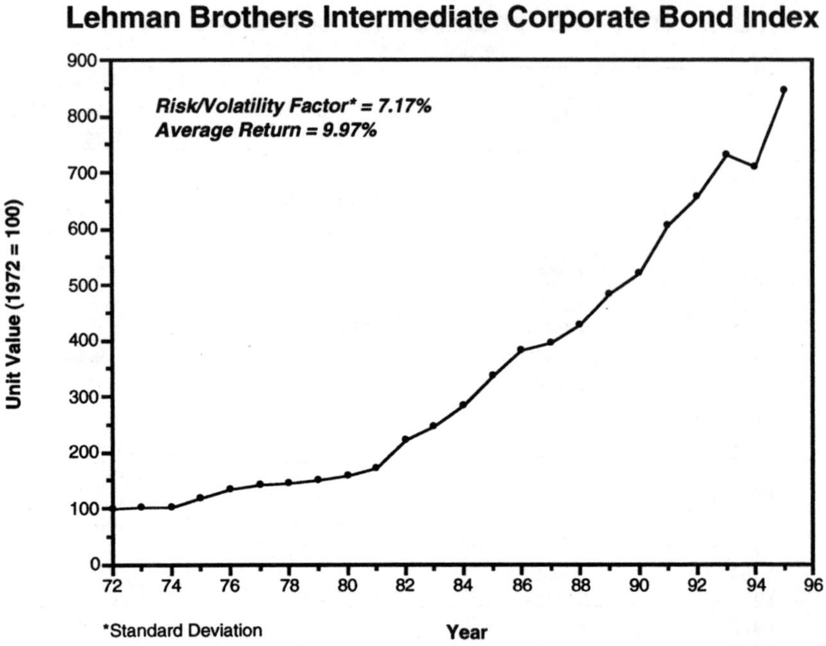


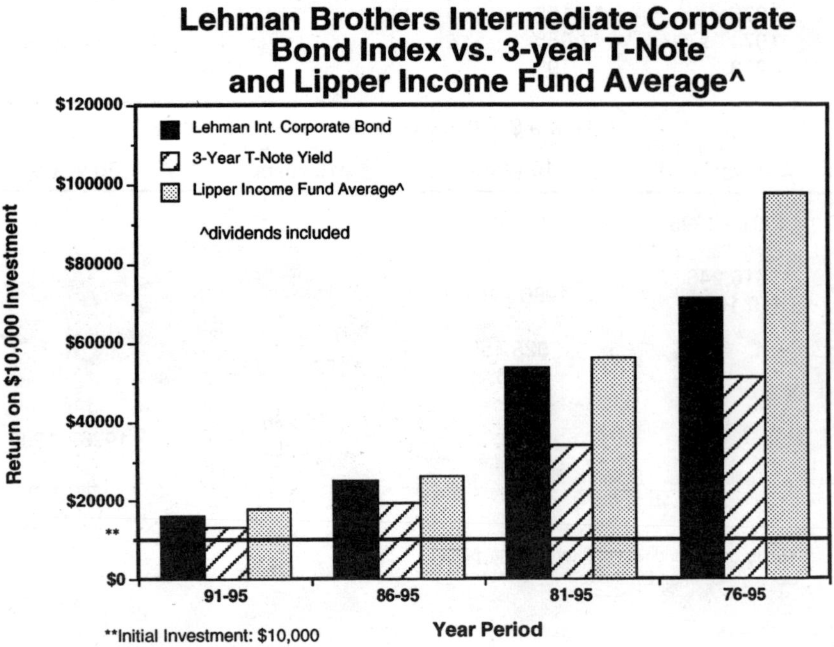


©1996 Chase Global Data & Research
73 Junction Square, Concord, MA 01742

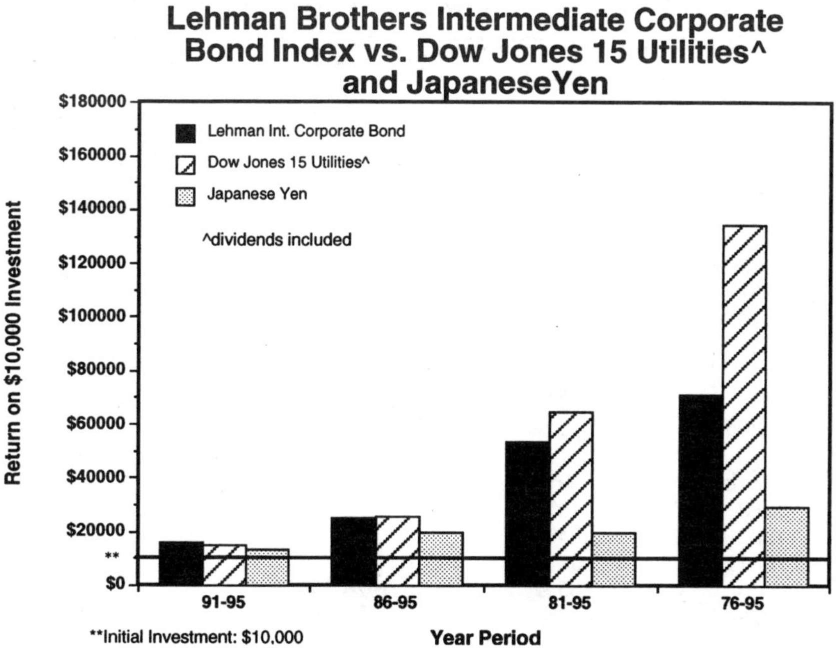


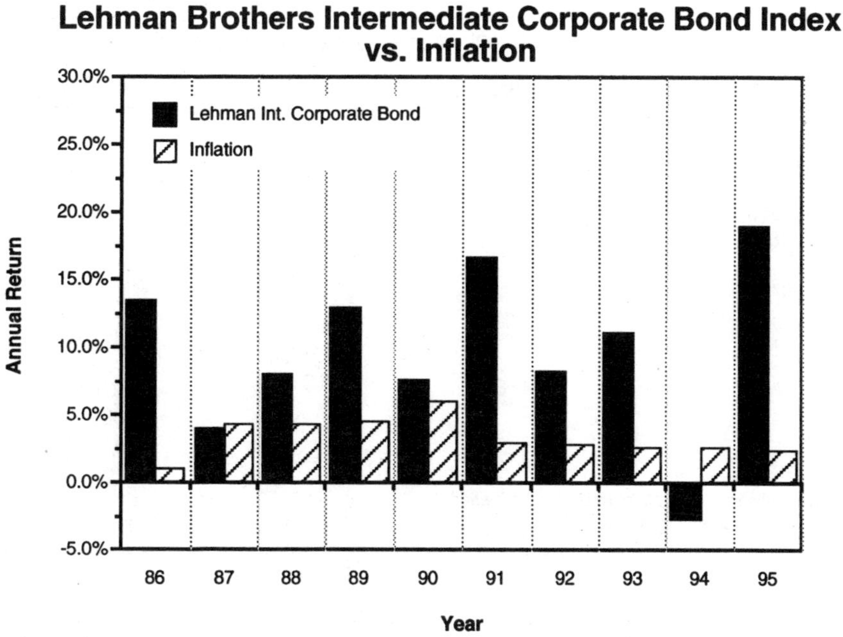


©1996 Chase Global Data & Research
73 Junction Square, Concord, MA 01742

## LEHMAN BROTHERS MORTGAGE-BACKED SECURITIES INDEX

| Year | Total Return* | Compound return on a five year $10,000 investment | Annual compound rate of return |
|---|---|---|---|
| 1995 | 16.80% | 1991 - 1995 | |
| 1994 | -1.61% | | 8.73% |
| 1993 | 6.84% | ... $15,198 | |
| 1992 | 6.97% | | |
| 1991 | 15.72% | | |
| 1990 | 10.72% | 1986 - 1990 | |
| 1989 | 15.35% | | 10.43% |
| 1988 | 8.72% | ... $16,424 | |
| 1987 | 4.28% | | |
| 1986 | 13.43% | | |
| 1985 | 25.21% | 1981 - 1985 | |
| 1984 | 15.79% | | 17.98% |
| 1983 | 10.13% | ... $22,855 | |
| 1982 | 43.04% | | |
| 1981 | 0.07% | | |
| 1980 | 0.65% | 1976 - 1980 | |
| 1979 | 0.13% | | 4.11% |
| 1978 | 2.41% | ... $12,232 | |
| 1977 | 1.90% | | |
| 1976 | 16.31% | | |

How a $10,000 investment performed over

| 5 years | 10 years | 15 years | 20 years |
|---|---|---|---|
| 1991 - 1995<br>$15,198<br>(8.73%)^ | 1986 - 1995<br>$24,962<br>(9.58%) | 1981 - 1995<br>$57,050<br>(12.31%) | 1976 - 1995<br>$69,786<br>(10.20%) |

^ annual compound rate of return for that period
* Source: Lehman Brothers.

©1996 Chase Global Data & Research
73 Junction Square, Concord, MA 01742

## Lehman Brothers Mortgage-Backed Securities Index

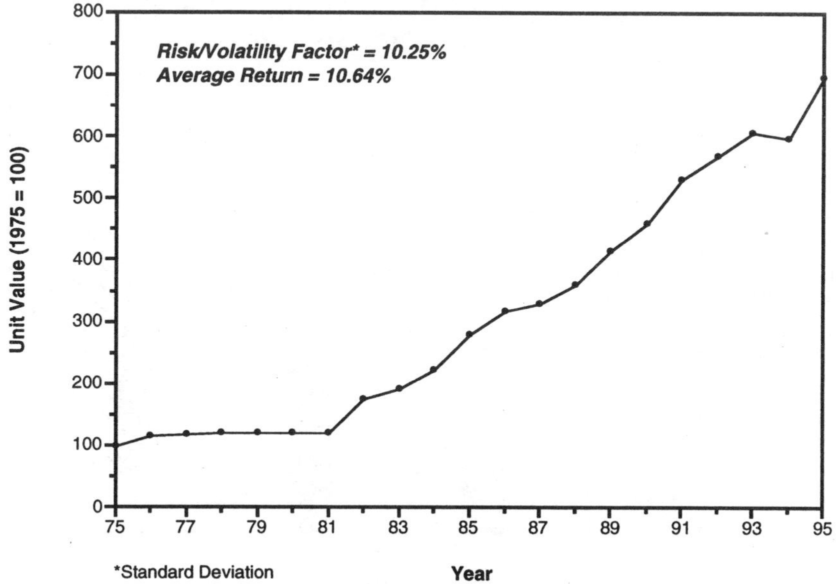


## Lehman Brothers Mortgage-Backed Securities Index vs. 10-Year T-Bond and Lehman Brothers Long Term Treasury Bond Index

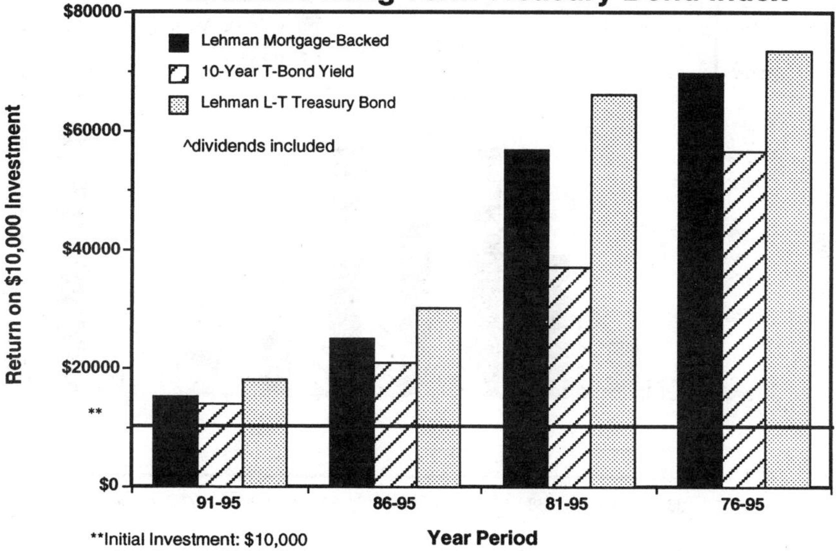


©1996 Chase Global Data & Research
73 Junction Square, Concord, MA 01742

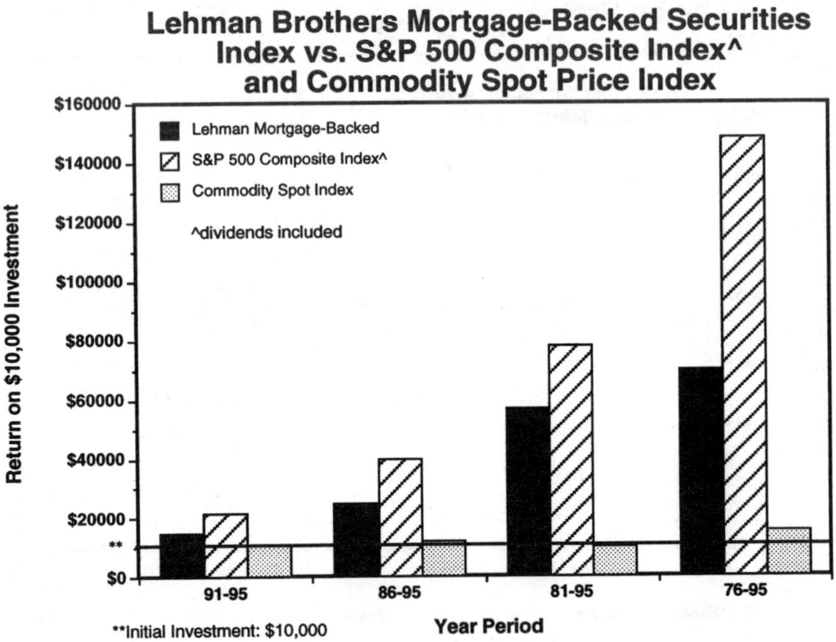


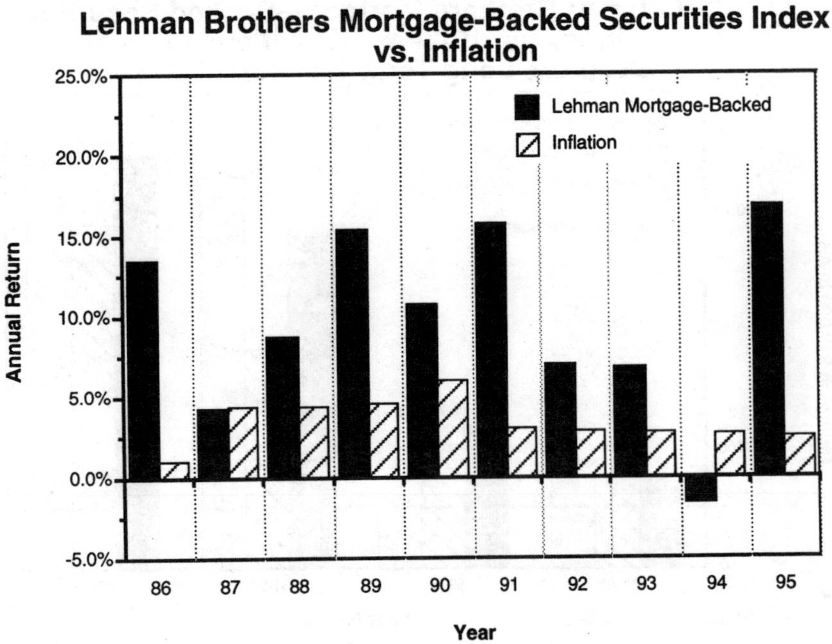


©1996 Chase Global Data & Research
73 Junction Square, Concord, MA 01742

# Chapter Twenty Three

# Certificates of Deposit

The Certificate of Deposit is a relatively new arrival to the investment world. Although banks issued a form of CD immediately after World War II, it had to be held to maturity—a minimum of thirty days. As a result, the CD was much less popular than T-bills and commercial paper.

The modern CDs were first created in 1961, although even they bear little resemblance to today's CD. The original CDs were issued in minimum sizes of $1 million and their primary benefit was liquidity. They were purchased by large institutions and gained their improved liquidity by means of a secondary market. Institutions could receive funds simply by selling their CD to another buyer. Citibank was the first financial organization to develop the large denomination CD as a legally negotiable certificate. Citibank arranged for the First Boston Corporation to initiate the secondary market for CDs, which allowed the CDs to be negotiable. (The bank could not legally make a market in its own CD because that would be the equivalent of redeeming a time deposit before its scheduled maturity date.)

The CDs offered yields slightly higher than T-bills—and soon became very popular. By 1963 the CD market had grown to $10 billion, 30% higher than the dollar volume in commercial paper, and eight times greater than banker's acceptances. By the mid 1980's, the CD marketplace was over one-third trillion dollars—the largest money market instrument in existence other than Treasury bills. Historically, CDs have been competitive with U.S. government Treasury bills because CDs purchased in less than $100,000 denominations offer equal security and thus are a logical choice.

CDs have been modified over the years although the fixed coupon interest rate CD still exists. By 1977 Morgan Guaranty introduced the first Variable Rate CD. By 1981, the first Zero Coupon CD was created. Today CDs obviously come in denominations well below $1 million, with jumbo CDs issued at $100,000 face value. CDs

©1996 Chase Global Data & Research
73 Junction Square, Concord, MA 01742

are normally issued in $500 minimum denominations, but some banks offer $100 CDs. CDs can be purchased from a bank, a savings institution, or other financial institutions such as brokerage firms. The quality of a CD is based on the rating of the issuing institution. Some banks are healthier than others and their ratings and interest rates reflect this. In the secondary market a CD fluctuates in value similarly to a bond, depending on where interest rates are and the maturity of the CD.

Although maturity dates for CDs range from 30 days to 10 years, the majority are issued between six-month and three-year denominations. CDs bought through a broker can be sold in a secondary market. CDs purchased through a bank should be held to maturity, otherwise you will be charged substantial penalties for early withdrawal. In addition, CDs can be subject to a refusal to honor withdrawal requests, except in cases of hardship. In March 1986, the Federal Reserve Board voted to impose a penalty of 7 days interest on amounts withdrawn within the first week from a bank CD. For a CD that is within one year of maturity, a common penalty is forfeiture of 3 months interest (that's a reduction of 25% of your annual rate of interest). On longer term CDs, the penalty can be up to 6 months forfeited interest. Obviously these withdrawal penalties are severe, normally more than the withering withdrawal penalties (back-end sales charges) on mutual funds. And banks have the right to charge even greater penalties than those already cited.

CDs are permissible as an investment for IRA's. Their strengths are safety and a fixed level of interest. CDs are taxed by state governments, but the interest earned from T-bills and other forms of government bonds cannot be taxed by a state. Depending on taxation issues in your state, this can be a major factor in analyzing CD after-tax net returns. While today's lower federal brackets (see Addendum pages 392-393) make CD investments more palatable, some experts fear higher brackets triggered by larger federal deficits during the '90s will make such investments less attractive over time.

Note that when the bond market becomes extremely volatile penalties imposed on CDs can be less than the potential loss of principal on a bond. However, interest rates would have to rise significantly for the price of bonds to drop substantially in value. And if interest rates drop, the value of a bond would increase. The CD, however, does not fluctuate unless it is purchased with a longer term maturity and done so through a brokerage house, allowing the CD to trade on the secondary market. In CD secondary trading the CD can be sold for either a gain or a loss in its principal, but not have the early withdrawal penalty.

©1996 Chase Global Data & Research
73 Junction Square, Concord, MA 01742

In 1987, in order to capture some of the money investors and savers were putting into the stock market, Chase Manhattan initiated CD accounts tiered to the performance of the S&P 500 Index. The strength of their CD is that unlike a falling stock market, the CD would not lose money—but also would not pay interest. Chase offered two forms of tiered S&P CDs: a 40% option or level of participation in the appreciation of the S&P 500 Index over 3, 6, or 12 months, and a 70% option. The 40% CD option offered a minimum level of interest of 4% per annum. The 70% option offered no minimum level of interest but did offer a greater participation in the stock market. If the market took a loss the investor gained nothing, but also did not lose. Here's what this can mean: had this form of CD been cumulatively purchased over the prior 10 year period from 1977 to 1987, it would not have been advantageous. A 1-year T-bill grew 158% over the 10 year period, while the 40% option CD tiered against the S&P grew only 103%. The 70% option grew 178%—not much better than the 1-year T-bill. However, the S&P grew 266% over the 10 years. Should the stock market do extremely well, the CD program would be a positive investment, but as we all know the market has risks.

The trick to investing in CDs is to pick the level of maturity you need and attain an optimum level of interest versus other alternatives. Generally, the longer the maturity the higher the level of interest. However, if you "marry" a long term CD you may regret it in a few years—if rates go higher. There is now a new breed of CD which could be more attractive than the old version. Some banks are now addressing the "marriage" problem by offering "bump and run" CDs which allow the purchaser to switch out of his present CD and go into another CD once during the contract period. Typically the initial rates of interest for this form of CD are below normal market rates, but the flexibility may prove more important than the slightly lower interest rate.

During the late 1980's and early 1990's almost 1,000 banks and S&Ls have failed in the United States. The estimated cost of the federal S&L bailout is over $550 billion—or more than a dozen times the cost of the Vietnam War. By 1991 the FDIC fund had so rapidly diminished, it required emergency funding. During that same year Rhode Island authorities closed 45 independent credit unions.

Today the FDIC fund is healthy again, in fact so healthy that insurance premiums paid by banks have been waived for 1996. The Resolution Trust Corporation (RTC) closed its last bank in early 1995, effectively ending the banking crisis begun in 1989. Overall 744 banks were closed or sold, reflecting 25 million depositors and $219 billion in

©1996 Chase Global Data & Research
73 Junction Square, Concord, MA 01742

assets which were at risk. Nevertheless, one should also remember that today about 10% of the 1,400 credit unions in the U.S. have insurance coverage independent of the FDIC, and thus may be placing their depositors at greater risk than would otherwise be the case, i.e. in the case of Rhode Island in 1991.

Newly implemented rules of the FDIC regarding insurance coverage for depositors compels CD investors to strictly stay within the guidelines of the $100,000 maximum coverage limitation, for the safety of banks in the U.S. will remain an issue for depositors for years to come. Know how your bank is insured. And for the over one million depositors holding $100,000 or more in deposits in banks throughout the nation, remain acutely aware of the financial health of the institutions holding your CDs and cash deposits.

©1996 Chase Global Data & Research
73 Junction Square, Concord, MA 01742

## U.S. 3-MONTH CERTIFICATE OF DEPOSIT

[Average annual yield; secondary market]

| Year | Yield* | Compound return on a five year $10,000 investment | Annual compound rate of return |
|---|---|---|---|
| 1995 | 5.92% | 1991 - 1995 | |
| 1994 | 4.63% | | 4.64% |
| 1993 | 3.17% | ... $12,546 | |
| 1992 | 3.68% | | |
| 1991 | 5.83% | | |
| 1990 | 8.15% | 1986 - 1990 | |
| 1989 | 9.09% | | 7.67% |
| 1988 | 7.73% | ... $14,468 | |
| 1987 | 6.87% | | |
| 1986 | 6.51% | | |
| 1985 | 8.04% | 1981 - 1985 | |
| 1984 | 10.37% | | 11.10% |
| 1983 | 9.07% | ... $16,925 | |
| 1982 | 12.27% | | |
| 1981 | 15.91% | | |
| 1980 | 13.07% | 1976 - 1980 | |
| 1979 | 11.22% | | 8.63% |
| 1978 | 8.22% | ... $15,125 | |
| 1977 | 5.58% | | |
| 1976 | 5.26% | | |
| 1975 | 6.43% | 1971 - 1975 | |
| 1974 | 10.27% | | 6.94% |
| 1973 | 8.41% | ... $13,983 | |
| 1972 | 4.67% | | |
| 1971 | 5.00% | | |
| 1970 | 7.57% | 1966 - 1970 | |
| 1969 | 7.77% | | 6.33% |
| 1968 | 5.86% | ... $13,593 | |
| 1967 | 5.02% | | |
| 1966 | 5.47% | | |
| 1965 | 4.35% | | |
| 1964 | 3.91% | | |
| 1963 | n.a. | | |
| 1962 | n.a. | | |
| 1961 | n.a. | | |
| 1960 | n.a. | | |

How a $10,000 investment performed over

| 5 years | 10 years | 15 years | 20 years | 25 years | 30 years |
|---|---|---|---|---|---|
| 1991 - 1995 | | | | | |
| $12,564 (4.64%)^ | 1986 - 1995 | | | | |
| | $18,150 (6.14%) | 1981 - 1995 | | | |
| | | $30,719 (7.77%) | 1976 - 1995 | | |
| | | | $46,462 (7.98%) | 1971 - 1995 | |
| | | | | $64,968 (7.77%) | 1966 - 1995 |
| | | | | | $88,312 (7.53%) |

^ annual compound rate of return for that period
* Source: Board of Governors, Federal Reserve System.
n.a. = data not available

©1996 Chase Global Data & Research
73 Junction Square, Concord, MA 01742

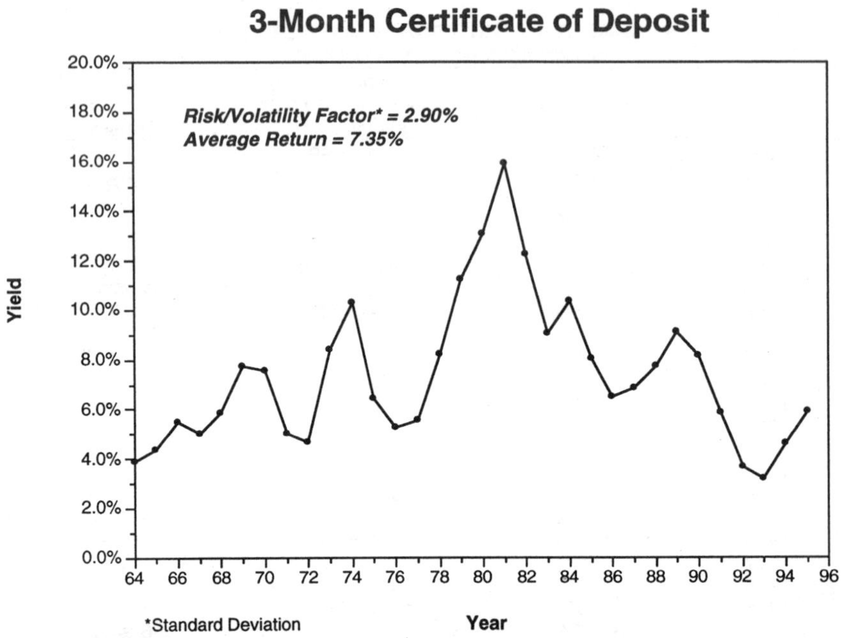


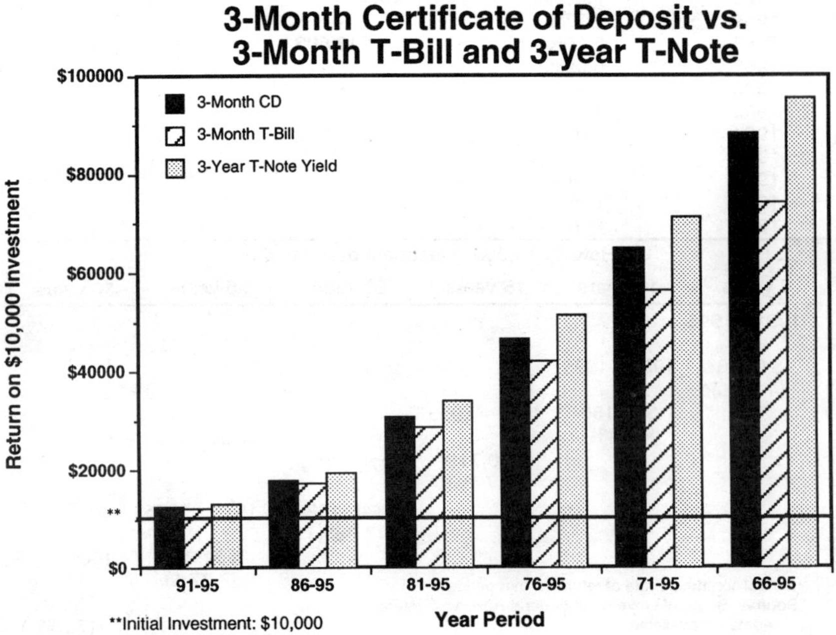


©1996 Chase Global Data & Research
73 Junction Square, Concord, MA 01742

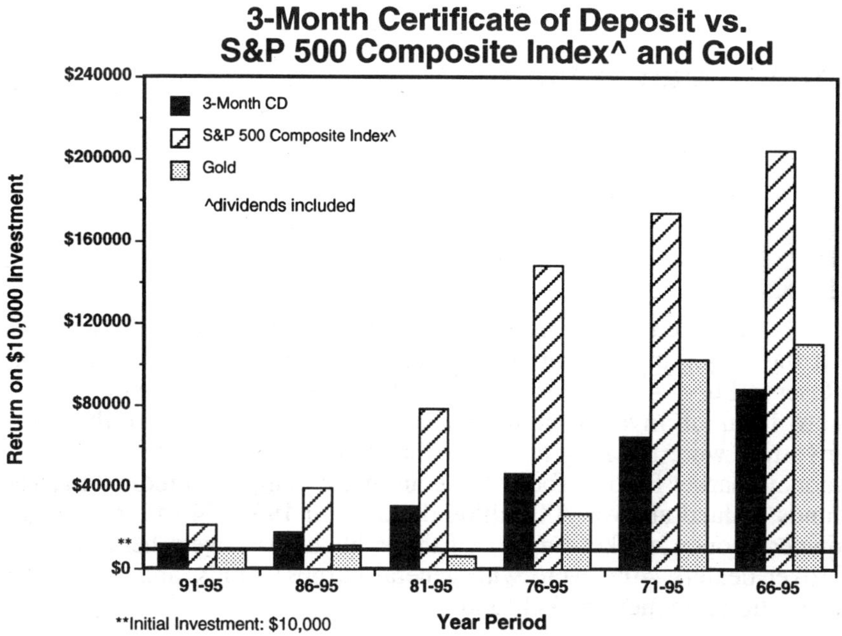


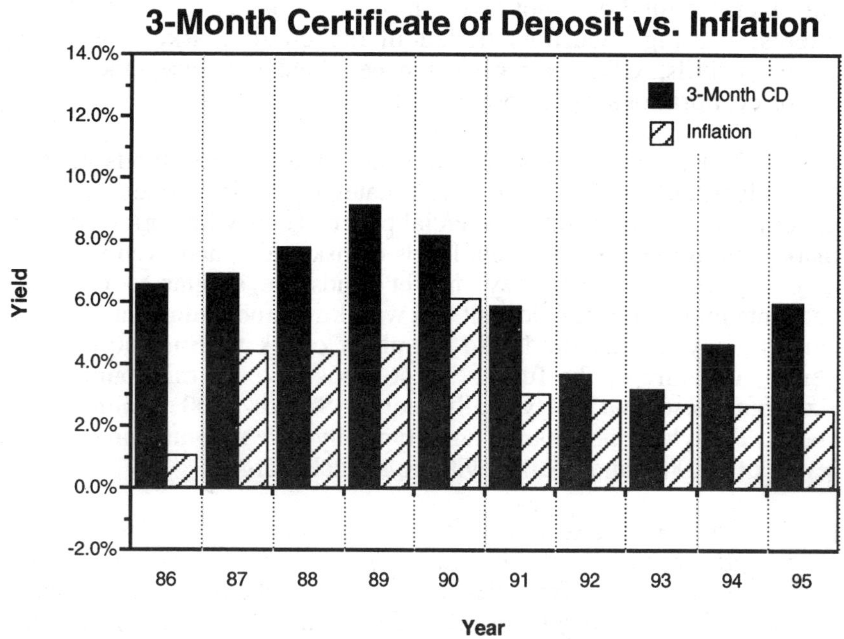


©1996 Chase Global Data & Research
73 Junction Square, Concord, MA 01742

Chapter Twenty Four

# Money Market Funds

In recent times, money market funds have become the new kid on the major investment block. The first money market fund—the Reserve Fund—was invented in 1972. It took several months for the new form of investment to become popular, but soon millions of investors were flocking to it. By the end of 1972 there were over 50 money market funds. Today there are more than 1,000 money market funds, valued at over 700 billion dollars. In 1995, 24 million people owned money market funds. Of these, about 30% were held through broker dealers, 40% were with general purpose funds, and 30% were institutional money market funds.

A money market fund is a mutual fund that gathers a pool of money from investors and manages those assets for its shareholders. However, the fund does not invest in stocks or bonds, but in short term interest bearing securities traded in the credit markets—such as Treasury bills, CDs, commercial paper, banker's acceptances, and major corporations' short term paper.

Not all money market funds are alike. Some funds confine themselves exclusively to a certain category of investment such as government securities or commercial paper. Thus, with various money market funds there are different levels of risk, yield, and even volatility in changing yields. Money market funds are similar to checking accounts in that you can deposit and withdraw funds immediately. The early money market funds did not allow check writing; now it is a common feature of the funds. Most funds have no minimum check size, but those that do typically require $25 to $100 minimum per check. Today's money market funds typically have minimum investment levels of $1,000, and operate with no annual charges.

Share prices of money market funds are managed so that the share's price remains static at exactly $1.00 per share. Sometimes there is a slight fluctuation from that level, but any change is readjusted to $1.00 by either taking from or adding to the interest rate, or yield.

 ©1996 Chase Global Data & Research
73 Junction Square, Concord, MA 01742

Money market funds are not rated in the same manner as bonds and stocks, but they are differentiated through the types of securities they invest in—such as exclusively corporate and bank short-term paper versus exclusively U.S. government short term-paper.

The typical manager's fee for overseeing a money market fund's assets is 0.6% per year, but some funds charge over 1% per year. (A low-fee form of money market fund which guarantees annual charges under 0.4% was recently introduced by several major mutual fund groups.) Income earned from a money market fund is credited into new shares of the fund automatically. Interest is usually credited monthly. The levels of interest paid by the funds are quoted in past 7-day average yield and past 30-day average yield. Some money market funds are tax exempt at the federal level through their exclusive investment in short-term municipal securities. In order to increase yields some money market funds invest in Eurodollar CDs, as well as in medium-term notes and even foreign debt short-term securities.

As already pointed out, the growth in money market funds has been enormous. By the early 1980's, the two largest money market funds operated by Merrill Lynch had total assets greater than the fifth largest commercial bank in the U.S., and greater than any thrift institution in the U.S. During the 1980s money market fund assets increased seven fold. Thanks to a surge in 1994-95, taxable money market funds assets now are over $750 billion, almost equaling the $800 billion of small-saver CDs (under $100,000). Money market fund assets have had substantial drops in total investment, however, as in 1983 when assets dropped 30% ($60 billion) because dollars left money market funds to enter IRAs and Keoghs. Until 1994, 1990's lower yields caused investors to leave money market funds in favor of equity and fixed income funds. Such money tends to leave money market funds but return to a large degree at a later time. Traditionally, money market funds have proven to be a good investment for IRA and Keogh accounts as well.

A major group of money market funds that has grown rapidly is the tax-exempt money market fund. When this form of fund was first introduced in 1979, assets totaled only $300 million. By 1995 they controlled well over $100 billion in assets, or three times the 1985 level. Today 2 million people invest in tax-exempt money market funds. Most tax-exempt funds are federal tax-exempt funds, but taxable by individual states. About 30% of tax-free money market funds provide both state and federal tax-free interest income. The latter form of money fund does so by investing in the given state's short term

©1996 Chase Global Data & Research
73 Junction Square, Concord, MA 01742

obligations. The following Performance Tables cover yields of both the average taxable and tax-free money market funds since 1977.

Since their inception, the safety of money market funds has been exemplary; however, their history does not cover a long enough period to assume that these funds are totally safe at all times. In 1990 there were two defaults totaling $1.2 billion in commercial paper holdings which could have potentially caused losses to investors. But the parent companies of the money market funds involved stepped in and covered the losses. Therefore no investors suffered losses. In 1994 the first money market fund failed—due to investments in risky derivative products. As a result of the defaults, the SEC has formulated higher standards for portfolios of money markets funds. Of note, there is no federal insurance program covering money market funds. However, brokerage firms do have Securities Investors Protection Corporation insurance for their money market funds. Also, some money market funds are covered by private insurers.

There are some tax disadvantages with the average money market fund. Some state governments will not tax in-state bank interest, but will tax dividends—and money market funds pay dividends. And some "single state" tax-free funds are not 100% state tax free because in a few instances they do not exclusively hold debt tax-exempt from a given state—usually for credit quality reasons. Growing in popularity, there were approximately 150 single-state funds with $75 billion in assets as of 1995. Lastly, there remains a debate involving U.S. government money market funds being taxed by state governments. While an individual government security cannot be taxed by state governments, some states are attempting to tax money market funds which invest in government securities.

©1996 Chase Global Data & Research
73 Junction Square, Concord, MA 01742

## TAXABLE MONEY MARKET FUND AVERAGE

[Average annual yield]

| Year | Yield* | Compound return on a five year $10,000 investment | Annual compound rate of return |
|---|---|---|---|
| 1995 | 5.47% | 1991 - 1995 | |
| 1994 | 3.75% | | 4.19% |
| 1993 | 2.70% | ... $12,280 | |
| 1992 | 3.37% | | |
| 1991 | 5.71% | | |
| 1990 | 7.82% | 1986 - 1990 | |
| 1989 | 8.87% | | 7.23% |
| 1988 | 7.11% | ... $14,178 | |
| 1987 | 6.12% | | |
| 1986 | 6.26% | | |
| 1985 | 7.71% | 1981 - 1985 | |
| 1984 | 10.04% | | 11.03% |
| 1983 | 8.58% | ... $16,873 | |
| 1982 | 12.23% | | |
| 1981 | 16.82% | | |
| 1980 | 12.78% | 1976 - 1980 | |
| 1979 | 11.08% | | 8.22% |
| 1978 | 7.22% | ... $14,847 | |
| 1977 | 4.98% | | |
| 1976 | 5.29% | | |
| 1975 | 6.36% | | |

How a $10,000 investment performed over

| 5 years | 10 years | 15 years | 20 years |
|---|---|---|---|
| 1991 - 1995 | | | |
| $12,280 (4.19%)^ | 1986 - 1995 | | |
| | $17,410 (5.70%) | 1981 - 1995 | |
| | | $29,376 (7.45%) | 1976 - 1995 |
| | | | $43,614 (7.64%) |

^ annual compound rate of return for that period

* Source: "Barron's National Business and Financial Weekly"; Donoghue's MONEY FUND REPORT® of Ashland, MA 01721.

©1996 Chase Global Data & Research
73 Junction Square, Concord, MA 01742

## Taxable Money Market Fund Average

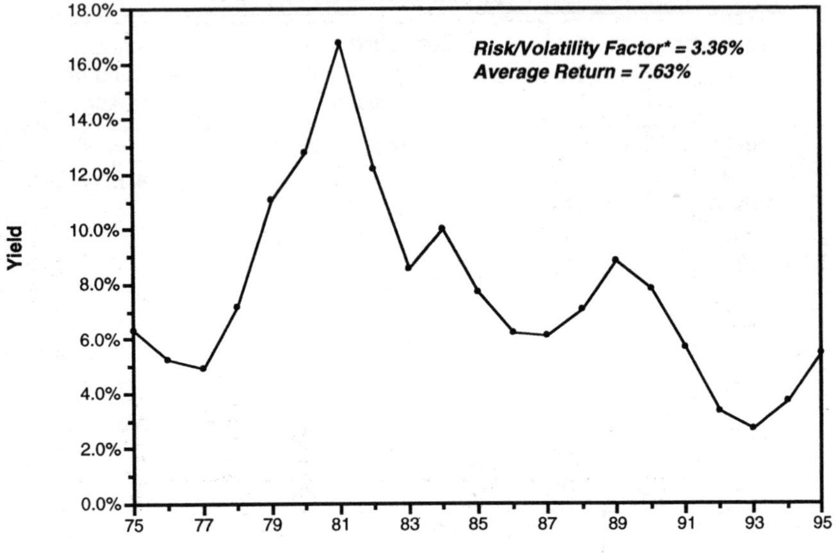


*Standard Deviation

## Taxable Money Market Fund Average vs. 3-Month Certificate of Deposit, 3-Month T-Bill and 3-Year T-Note

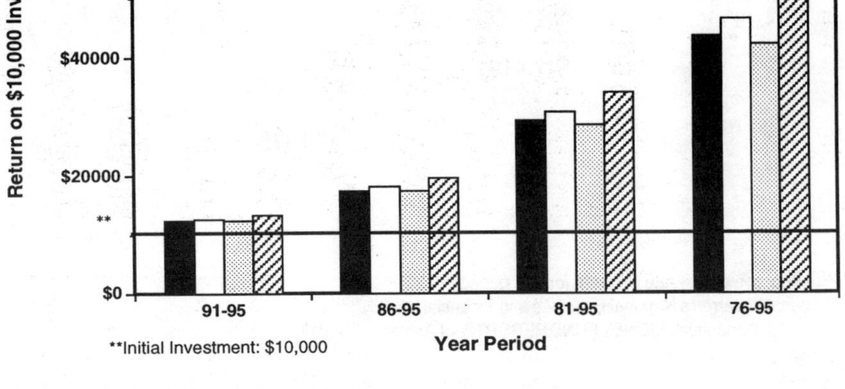


**Initial Investment: $10,000

©1996 Chase Global Data & Research
73 Junction Square, Concord, MA 01742

## Taxable Money Market Fund Average vs. NASDAQ Composite Index, Gold, and REITs

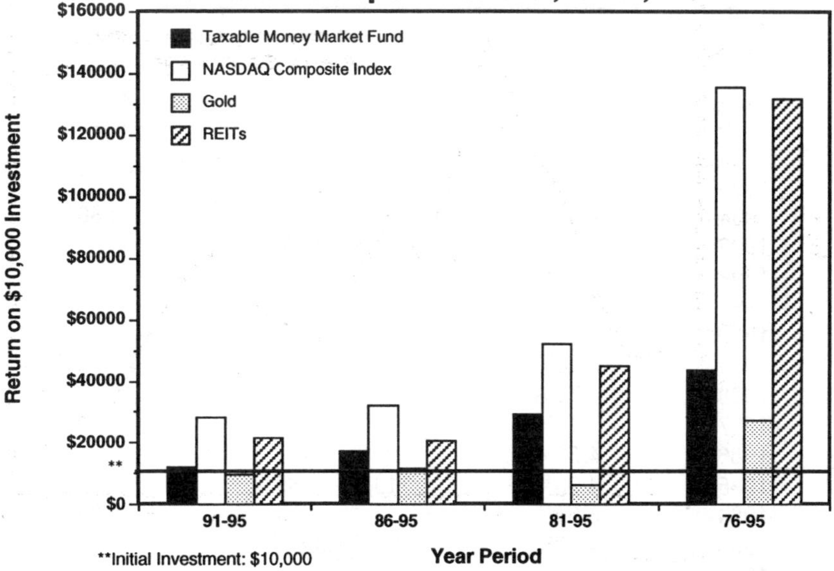


## Taxable Money Market Fund Average vs. Inflation

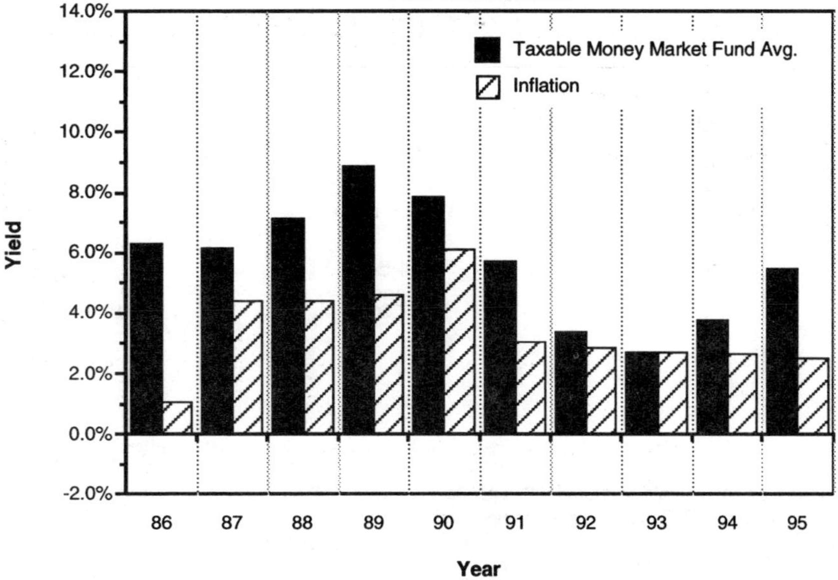


©1996 Chase Global Data & Research
73 Junction Square, Concord, MA 01742

## TAX-FREE MONEY MARKET FUND AVERAGE

[Average annual yield]

| Year | Yield* | Compound return on a five year $10,000 investment | Annual compound rate of return |
|---|---|---|---|
| 1995 | 3.39% | 1991 - 1995 | |
| 1994 | 2.38% | | 2.88% |
| 1993 | 1.97% | ... $11,523 | |
| 1992 | 2.59% | | |
| 1991 | 4.06% | | |
| 1990 | 5.45% | 1986 - 1990 | |
| 1989 | 5.90% | | 4.92% |
| 1988 | 4.79% | ... $12,712 | |
| 1987 | 4.14% | | |
| 1986 | 4.31% | | |
| 1985 | 4.90% | 1981 - 1985 | |
| 1984 | 5.61% | | 5.84% |
| 1983 | 4.82% | ... $13,284 | |
| 1982 | 6.86% | | |
| 1981 | 7.05% | | |

How a $10,000 investment performed over

| 5 years | 10 years | 15 years |
|---|---|---|
| 1991 - 1995<br>$11,523<br>(2.88%)^ | 1986 - 1995<br>$14,647<br>(3.89%) | 1981 - 1995<br>$19,458<br>(4.54%) |

annual compound rate of return for that period

Source: "Barron's National Business and Financial Weekly"; Donoghue's MONEY FUND REPORT® of Ashland, MA 01721.

©1996 Chase Global Data & Research
73 Junction Square, Concord, MA 01742

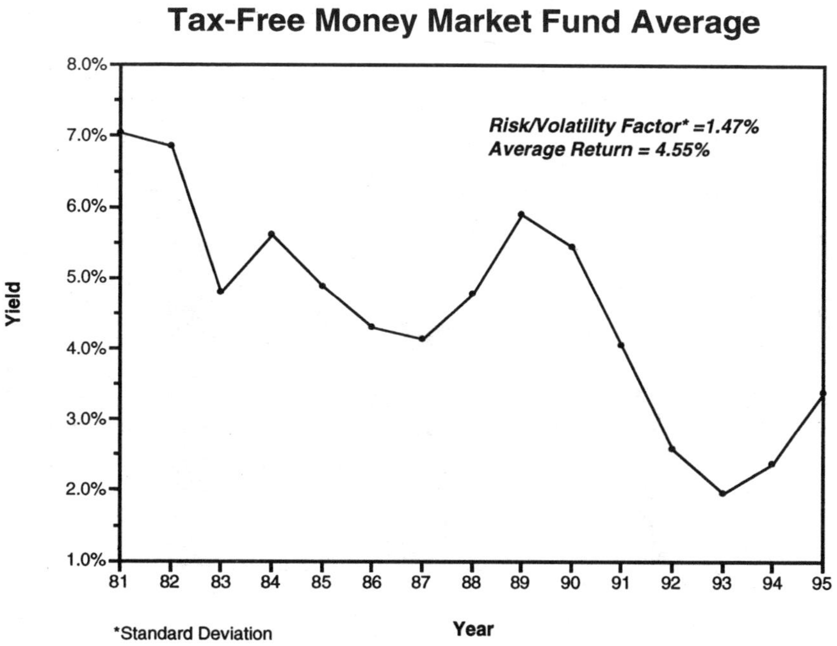


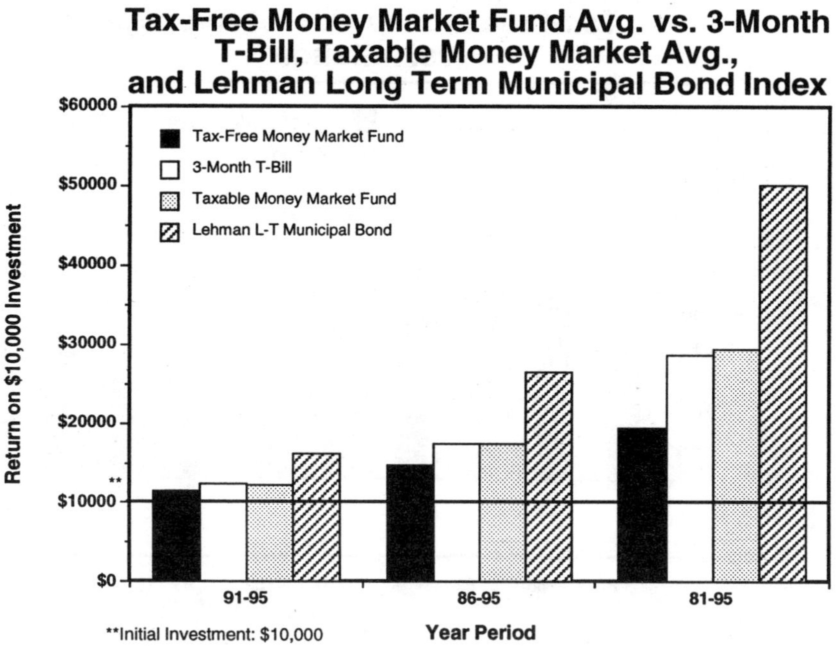


©1996 Chase Global Data & Research
73 Junction Square, Concord, MA 01742

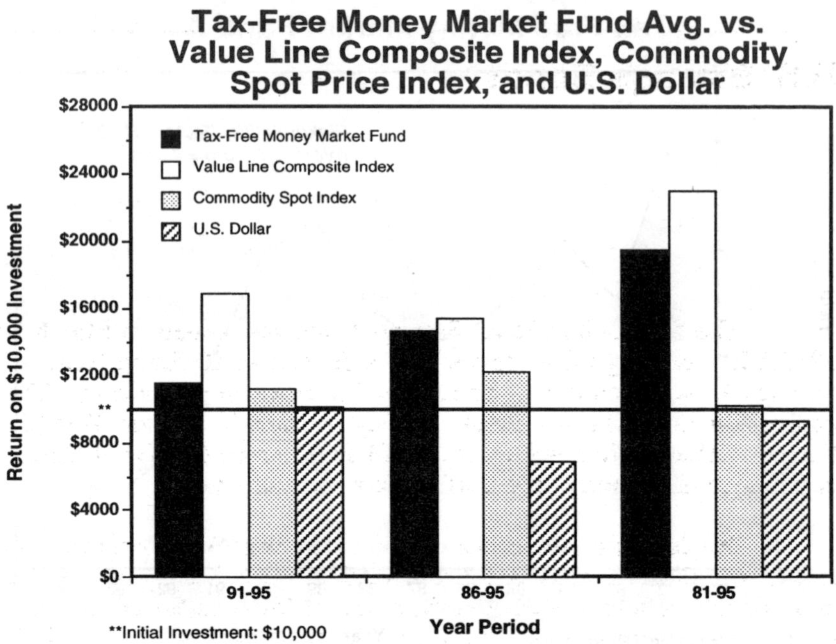


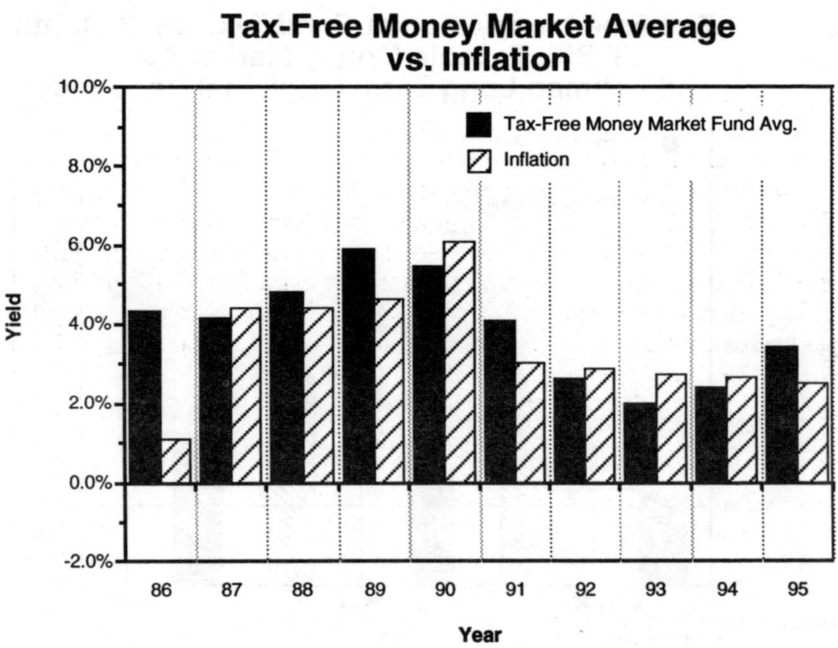


©1996 Chase Global Data & Research
73 Junction Square, Concord, MA 01742

# Chapter Twenty Five

# U.S. Savings Bonds

The first United States Savings Bond was issued on March 1, 1935. It was assigned a "series" label, A, just as all future forms of Savings Bonds would also be assigned a series nomenclature. The concept of U.S. Savings Bonds was the brainchild of then Treasury Secretary Henry Morgenthau, Jr., who had observed that Great Britain and France had similar programs in place for many years.

The basic premise of a government Savings Bond program is to enable an ordinary citizen to invest in the debt of the federal government at a fair rate of return, with no risk, at a cost lower to the government than through normal bond issuance. In all these respects the U.S. Savings Bonds program, now over sixty years old, has been a success.

The positives to the U.S. Government have been many. Perhaps the key reason is that the government has always called on citizens to volunteer in a patriotic as well as fiscal manner to step forward and purchase bonds which were *guaranteed* to be paid back with interest through the full faith and credit standing of the U.S. Government. In fact the symbol of the U.S. Savings Bond program is the volunteer militiaman—the Minute Man of Concord (Massachusetts)—the famous sculpture by Daniel Chester French. Of note, the U.S. Government has a spotless record of repayment, unlike other governments. Even the citizens who purchased $27 million of U.S. government bonds during the Revolutionary War in 1776 were paid in full by the new government, though not without some dissent within the new government.

During World War II, 85 million people purchased U.S. Savings Bonds, raising over $185 billion for the government. 25 million people were part of the Payroll Savings Plan in 1945. After the War in 1947 500,000 people signed up to purchase a "Bond-A-Month". While sales have slowed from peak war year levels, today the program continues to succeed. The total of U.S. Savings bonds held has grown from $10 billion in 1941 to over $200 billion today.

©1996 Chase Global Data & Research
73 Junction Square, Concord, MA 01742

A typical U.S. Savings bond purchase is held for over 10 years—double that of the average Treasury bond, thus enabling the government to avoid frequent and costly re-sale of bond issues. The administration expense of the program is only 1.9% of funds invested, much less than the costs of normal bond issuance. And the government estimates that for every $1 billion in U.S. Savings Bonds sold the U.S. Treasury saves $70 million in debt service costs—or $500 million in 1990 alone.

Today 28% of all American families own U.S. Savings Bonds, with 7.2 million citizens buying them regularly through payroll savings plans. The fiscal reasons for individuals to purchase bonds easily rival patriotic ones. For one, the bonds are easily the safest investment available and are replaced free of charge if lost or stolen. Today Series EE U.S. Savings Bonds (the most popular issue) offer interest rates which are competitive—based on 85% of the yield of 5-Year Treasuries, compounding interest semi-annually. Importantly, Savings Bonds compound interest free of all state and local taxes, and federal taxes are not due until the bonds mature or are cashed in. Thus federal taxes on interest may be postponed for a long period of time while interest continues to compound. Even the federal government tax on interest can be waived if the bonds are purchased and then used to fund college tuition payments (certain restrictions apply). Bonds are easy to purchase and redeem at U.S. Government offices or local banks. There are no fees or commissions involved with buying or redeeming U.S. Savings Bonds.

The first Series A Bonds were issued at a purchase price of $18.75 for a $25 at maturity bond. The interest rate was 2.9% and maturity was in 10 years. Because of its low price it was nicknamed the "baby bond". From 1935 to 1941 18 million Series A, B, C, and D Bonds were issued totaling $4 billion. Ironically the majority of the purchases were in $100, $500, and $1000 denominations. The most popular Savings Bonds ever sold were the Series E, or Defense Bonds. The first series E bond was purchased by Franklin Roosevelt on May 1, 1941. During World War II $10 denomination Savings Bonds were issued to the armed forces, and U.S. Defense Savings Stamps were issued in small denominations of 10¢, 25¢, 50¢, $1, and $5. Schools throughout the U.S. were encouraged to "Buy-a-Jeep" through the Stamp program, with 90,000 Jeeps purchased through Defense Stamps. Post offices and banks (beginning in 1944) would redeem albums of the smaller denominations into Series E Bonds. Thus citizens with even only a dime could help their government with the war effort.

©1996 Chase Global Data & Research
73 Junction Square, Concord, MA 01742

Series E, F, G, and H bonds were introduced and sold at various times from 1940 through 1980 at varying interest rates and with varying maturities (typically 8 to 12 years). Extensions for the most popular Series E and H Bonds were granted on maturity, such that the bonds reached 40 years for maximum maturity. In 1980 Series EE and HH Bonds were introduced. Upon maturity Series E and H bonds could be transferred into their respective cousins with no taxable event regarding interest earned to date.

Over the years the Series E and H Bonds were sold with an initial interest rate guaranteed until maturity, though rates could be raised if the annual new rate formula exceeded the guaranteed rate. Thus eventually as new rates dropped the minimum rate was a strong attraction for buying U.S. Savings Bonds. By 1986 the minimum rate reached 6%, still an attractive floor interest rate given the other benefits of EE Bonds. However, in 1993 the minimum rate was lowered to 4%. In May 1995 the government ended over 50 years of minimum interest rate guarantees and went to a six month floating interest rate based on 85% of the 5-year Treasury Bond interest rate.

Today U.S. Savings Bond denominations available are $25, $50, $75 (newer issue in honor of John F. Kennedy), $100, $200 (newer issue in honor of Franklin Roosevelt), $500, $1000, $5000, and $10,000. A key benefit remains the tax free state and local interest, no federal taxation on interest as the interest compounds before withdrawal, and federally tax free interest upon withdrawal if the Savings Bond proceeds are used for an approved educational institution. One should definitely review the numerous technical provisions which apply to the tax free federal interest status. Among the provisions are the buyer of the U.S. Savings Bond Series EE (issued after 1989) must be age 24 or older upon issuance, tuition and other educational expense must be incurred by the taxpayer and equal or exceed the Savings Bond proceeds (or the benefit will be pro-rated), and the educational expense must be for the taxpayer or the taxpayer's dependent or spouse. Also, the benefit is available only to taxpayers with adjusted gross income (joint return) as of 1995 of under $93,450—and is phased out between $63,450 and $93,450.

The Performance Table which follows outlines the yield to maturity through May 1996 of Series EE U.S. Savings Bonds purchased from each year reviewed. When different yields to maturity were available for a given calendar year, the average for all in the calendar year was detailed. In that Series EE Bonds replaced Series E bonds in 1980, Series E Bond data was used until 1980, and EE Bond data was used thereafter.

©1996 Chase Global Data & Research
73 Junction Square, Concord, MA 01742

**U.S. Savings Bonds**

[Series EE**; Average of initial rates quoted for new issues in calendar year; $100 denomination]

| Year | Yield* | Compound return on a five year $10,000 investment | Annual compound rate of return |
|---|---|---|---|
| 1995 | 4.89% | 1991 - 1995 | |
| 1994 | 4.04% | | 4.84% |
| 1993 | 4.01% | ... $12,664 | |
| 1992 | 5.38% | | |
| 1991 | 5.88% | | |
| 1990 | 6.01% | 1986 - 1990 | |
| 1989 | 6.00% | | 6.23% |
| 1988 | 6.00% | ... $13,528 | |
| 1987 | 6.26% | | |
| 1986 | 6.88% | | |
| 1985 | 7.26% | 1981 - 1985 | |
| 1984 | 6.98% | | 7.25% |
| 1983 | 6.98% | ... $14,191 | |
| 1982 | 7.41% | | |
| 1981 | 7.63% | | |
| 1980 | 7.84% | 1976 - 1980 | |
| 1979 | 7.49% | | 7.56% |
| 1978 | 7.20% | ... $14,394 | |
| 1977 | 7.64% | | |
| 1976 | 7.61% | | |
| 1975 | 7.41% | 1971 - 1975 | |
| 1974 | 7.25% | | 7.10% |
| 1973 | 7.12% | ... $14,094 | |
| 1972 | 6.94% | | |
| 1971 | 6.80% | | |
| 1970 | 7.20% | 1966 - 1970 | |
| 1969 | 7.01% | | 6.83% |
| 1968 | 6.90% | ... $13,913 | |
| 1967 | 6.62% | | |
| 1966 | 6.41% | | |
| 1965 | 6.33% | 1961 -1965 | |
| 1964 | 6.60% | | 6.38% |
| 1963 | 6.45% | ... $13,621 | |
| 1962 | 6.31% | | |
| 1961 | 6.19% | | |
| 1960 | 6.05% | | |

How a $10,000 investment performed over

| 5 years | 10 years | 15 years | 20 years | 25 years | 35 years |
|---|---|---|---|---|---|
| 1991 - 1995 | | | | | |
| $12,664 (4.84%)^ | 1986 - 1995 | | | | |
| | $17,132 (5.53%) | 1981 - 1995 | | | |
| | | $24,312 (6.10%) | 1976 - 1995 | | |
| | | | $34,994 (6.46%) | 1971 - 1995 | |
| | | | | $49,320 (6.59%) | 1961 - 1995 |
| | | | | | $93,466 (6.59%) |

^ annual compound rate of return for that period
* Source: U.S. Bureau of the Public Debt.
**Series E Rates from 1960 to 1980
**Series EE Rates from 1980 to present

©1996 Chase Global Data & Research
73 Junction Square, Concord, MA 01742

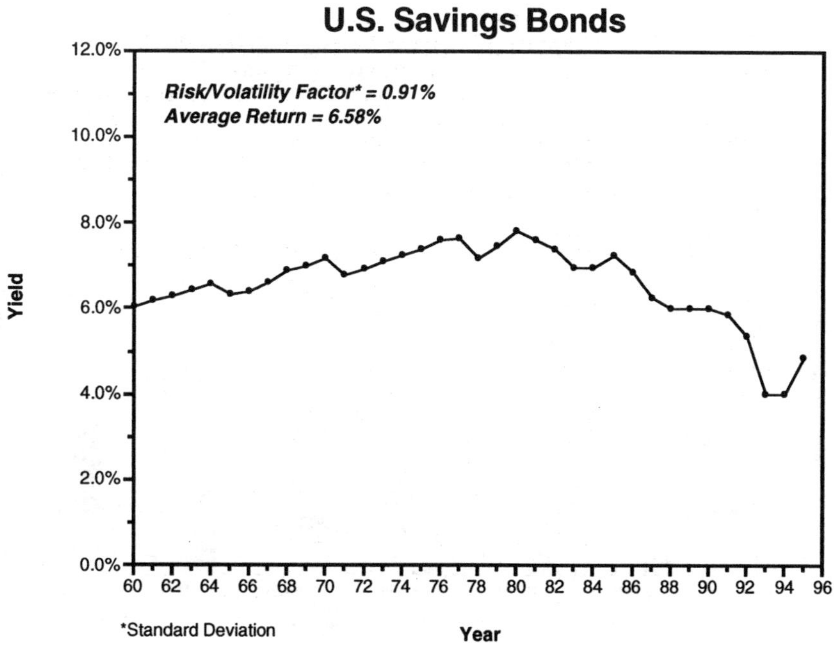


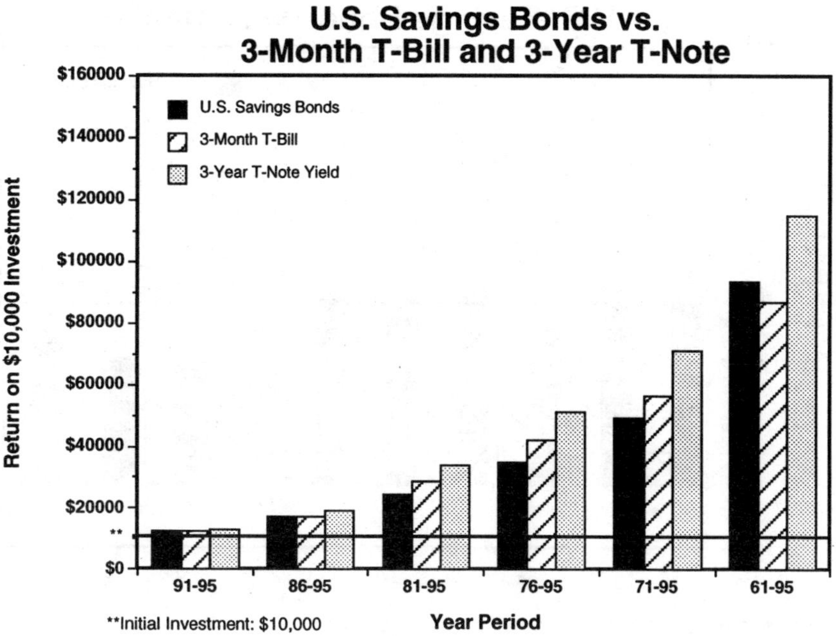


©1996 Chase Global Data & Research
73 Junction Square, Concord, MA 01742

## U.S. Savings Bonds vs. Lipper Income Fund Average^ and House Price Index

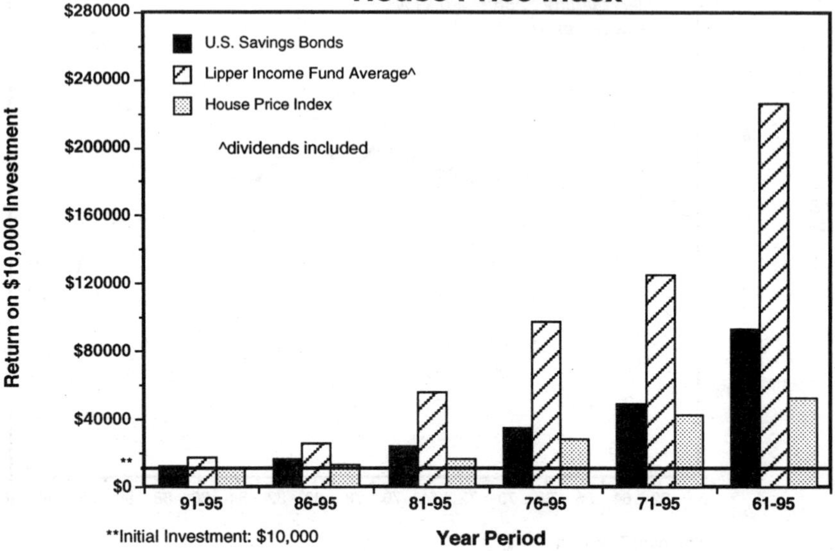


## U.S. Savings Bonds vs. Inflation

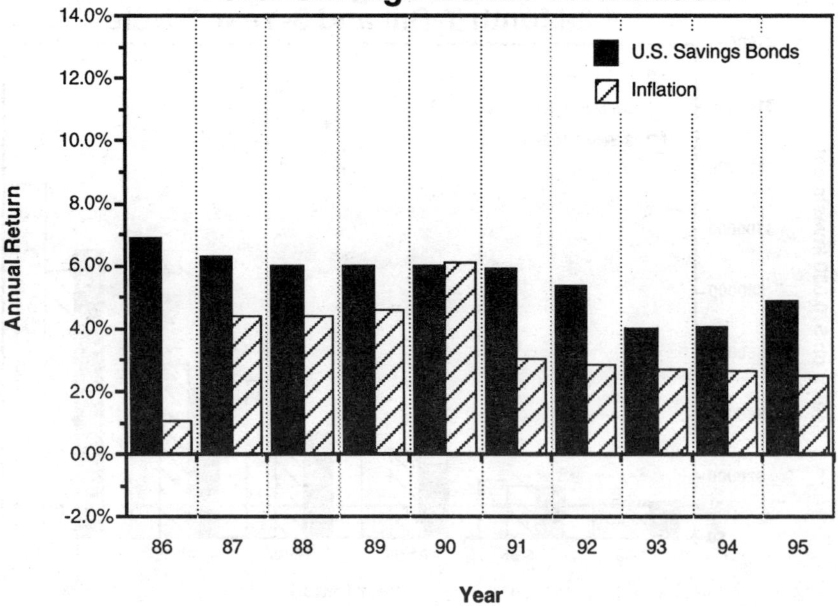


©1996 Chase Global Data & Research
73 Junction Square, Concord, MA 01742

# Chapter Twenty Six

# Guaranteed Investment Contracts (GICs)

Guaranteed Investment Contracts, better known as GICs, were first introduced in the United States in the mid 1970's. A financial cousin to deferred annuities, which were created over 150 years earlier, GICs are issued by insurance companies which guarantee the GIC investor both a given interest rate for a certain period of time and the return of invested principal. With the passing of the Employee Retirement Income Security Act (ERISA) in 1974, and the subsequent introduction of the 401K Plan as an offspring of ERISA, GICs quickly began an explosive growth trend leading to a GIC marketplace now valued at over one half trillion dollars.

Part of the appeal of GICs, especially as a menu item in a 401K Plan's list of investment choices, is their simplicity. Simply put, a GIC guarantees a rate of interest for a set period of time (typically one or more years) and its principal *does not* fluctuate. Thus it is a safe harbor among the several other investment options in a 401K plan that may fluctuate. And GICs normally provide yields/returns significantly higher than short term investment options—such as money market funds.

GICs are as safe as the financial health of the insurance company issuing them. While the insurance company guarantees the return of principal and an interest rate, some insurance companies are safer than others—in the same manner that some banks are safer than other banks. Importantly, GIC buyers become policy holders of the insurer, and in most states policy holders have liens in line ahead of the general creditors of the insurance company. Thus a GIC holder is a well positioned creditor should an insurer fail. Today all GIC/insurance company issuers are rated by major rating agencies such as A.M. Best, Moody's, Standard and Poor's, and Duff and Phelps (see also Chapter 27). Most experts agree that the typical rating for insurers issuing GICs is the very sound level of AA or even AAA.

However, history tells us that even safe investments are not perfect. Just as bank depositors have lost money in bank failures, so

©1996 Chase Global Data & Research
73 Junction Square, Concord, MA 01742

have GIC investors lost assets when an insurance company fails. Famous cases of the recent past where GIC investors lost money, albeit sometimes only slightly, are the 1991 major insurance company failures of Executive Life Insurance Company and Mutual Benefit Life. Together their failures affected insured contracts totaling over $23 billion. Thousands of GIC holders were impacted through lack of liquidity in their investments as the various problems were sorted out by state authorities, and they ultimately suffered some losses. A few years later GIC losses continued when Canadian based Confederation Life Insurance Company failed. Overall, the default rate of contracts issued since GICs were introduced over 20 years ago is 0.2%.

Today GICs remain very popular in 401K programs. 43% of all monies invested in employer-sponsored retirement savings plans which offer GICs have funds invested in them. 59% of all investors in major 401K plans invest in GICs. And the market continues to expand at almost 10% per annum. GICs increase in popularity during interest rate rises, when their yields become more attractive. Also, during times of rising interest rates bond investment's principal is at risk and may produce losses. Stocks also tend to perform worse during times of rising interest rates. Thus GICs and their increasing yields and ever present stability look more attractive than ever as rates rise.

Statistically speaking GICs do provide fair to above average returns, especially in light of their safety attributes. GICs typically yield 2%-3% more than money market funds, and 0.5% or more than similar duration U.S. Government paper. Average maturities of GICs sold to 401K plans are becoming shorter in today's market. In the past average maturities were four to six years, wheras today's average is two to three years.

The Performance Tables which follow outline the returns of two basic maturities of GICs—one year and five year. The five year maturity has solidly outperformed the one year duration over the past five and ten year periods. Five year GIC returns have doubled the rate of inflation, and performed well given interest rates have not been too high during the periods analyzed. Within the confines of 401K portfolios and retirement plans, GICs have provided acceptable returns given their status as an investment alternative providing guaranteed return of principal and returns well in excess of the rate of inflation.

©1996 Chase Global Data & Research
73 Junction Square, Concord, MA 01742

## Guaranteed Investment Contracts (GICs) 1-Year

[Market Average Rate GICs; simple interest maturity; year-end]

| Year | Yield* | Compound return on a five year $10,000 investment | Annual compound rate of return |
|---|---|---|---|
| 1995 | 5.97% | 1991 - 1995 | |
| 1994 | 5.34% | | 4.89% |
| 1993 | 3.43% | ... $12,698 | |
| 1992 | 3.85% | | |
| 1991 | 5.90% | | |
| 1990 | 7.96% | | |
| 1989 | 8.49% | | |
| 1988 | 7.49% | 1986 - 1990 | |
| 1987 | 6.97% | | 7.55% |
| 1986 | 6.86% | ... $14,391 | |
| 1985 | 8.70% | | |
| 1984 | 11.10% | | |
| 1983 | 10.00% | | |
| 1982 | 13.23% | | |

How a $10,000 investment performed over

| 5 years | 10 years |
|---|---|
| 1991 - 1995<br>$12,698<br>(4.89%)^ | |
| | 1986 - 1995<br>$18,274<br>(6.21%) |

^ annual compound rate of return for that period
* Source: ©1983 - 1995 T. Rowe Price
1982 - 1988 The Laughlin Group

©1996 Chase Global Data & Research
73 Junction Square, Concord, MA 01742

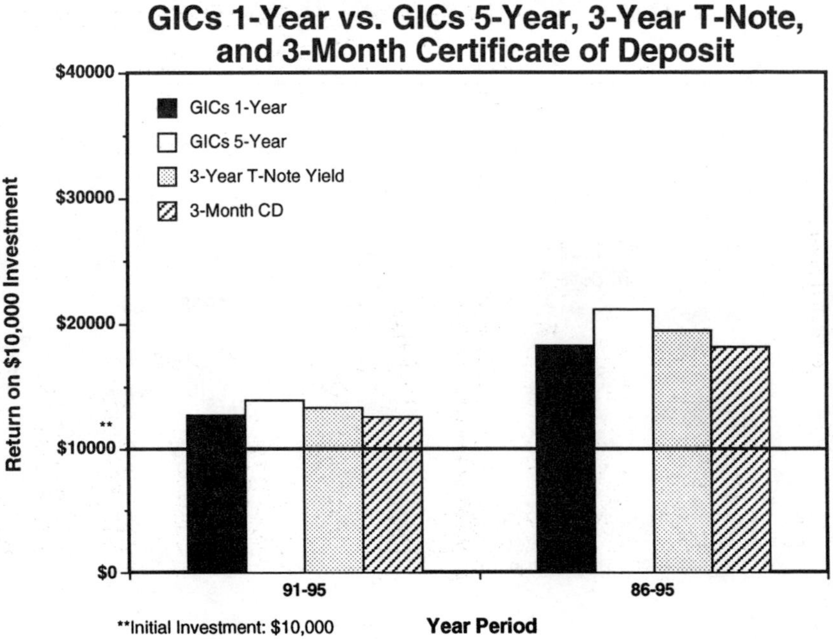


©1996 Chase Global Data & Research
73 Junction Square, Concord, MA 01742

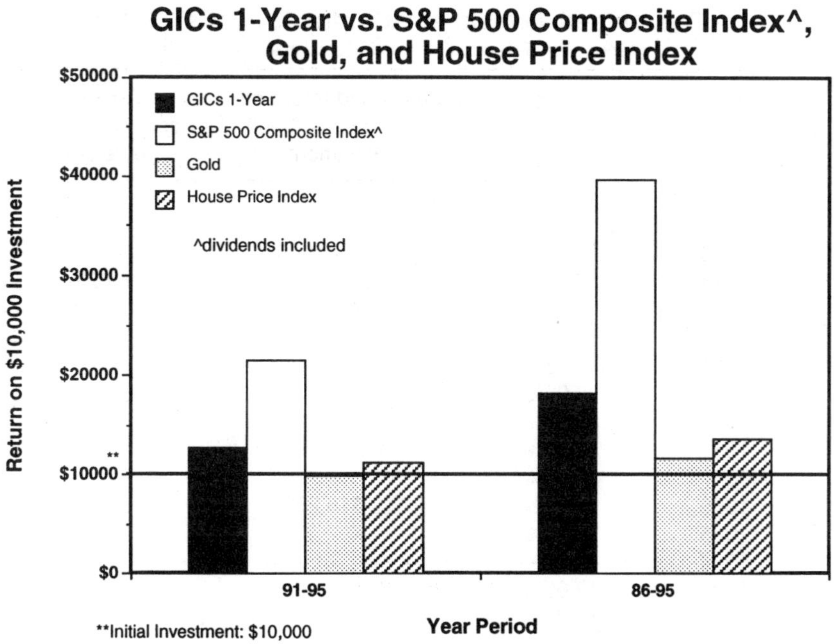


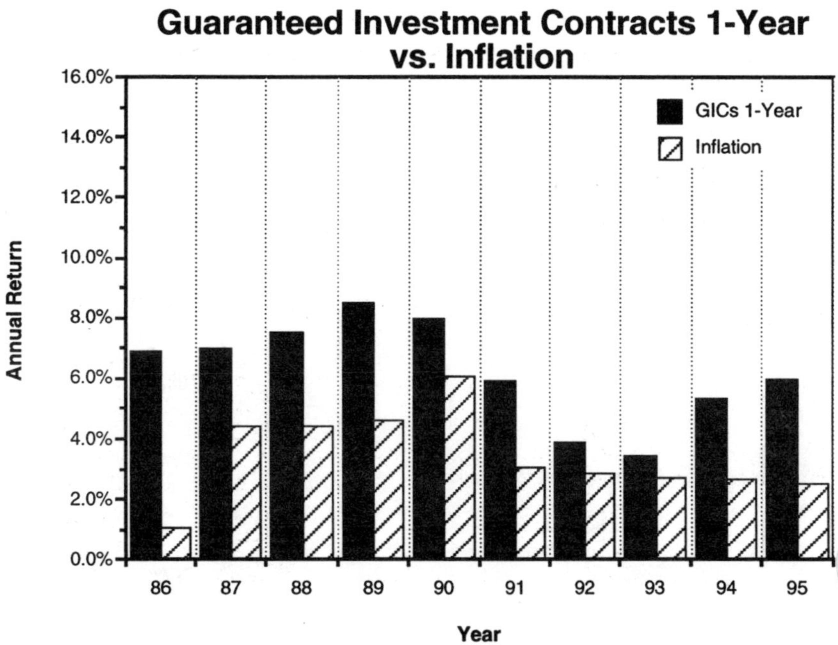


©1996 Chase Global Data & Research
73 Junction Square, Concord, MA 01742

## Guaranteed Investment Contracts (GICs) 5-Year

[Market Average Rate GICs; simple interest maturity; year-end]

| Year | Yield* | Compound return on a five year $10,000 investment | Annual compound rate of return |
|---|---|---|---|
| 1995 | 6.69% | 1991 - 1995 | |
| 1994 | 7.10% | | 6.82% |
| 1993 | 5.62% | ... $13,909 | |
| 1992 | 6.73% | | |
| 1991 | 7.98% | | |
| 1990 | 8.99% | | |
| 1989 | 8.95% | | |
| 1988 | 8.81% | 1986 - 1990 | |
| 1987 | 8.62% | | 8.74% |
| 1986 | 8.32% | ... $15,202 | |
| 1985 | 10.78% | | |
| 1984 | 12.79% | | |
| 1983 | 12.00% | | |
| 1982 | 14.38% | | |

How a $10,000 investment performed over

| 5 years | 10 years |
|---|---|
| 1991 - 1995<br>$13,909<br>(6.82%)^ | 1986 - 1995<br>$21,144<br>(7.78%) |

^ annual compound rate of return for that period
* Source: ©1983 - 1995 T. Rowe Price
1982 - 1988 The Laughlin Group

©1996 Chase Global Data & Research
73 Junction Square, Concord, MA 01742

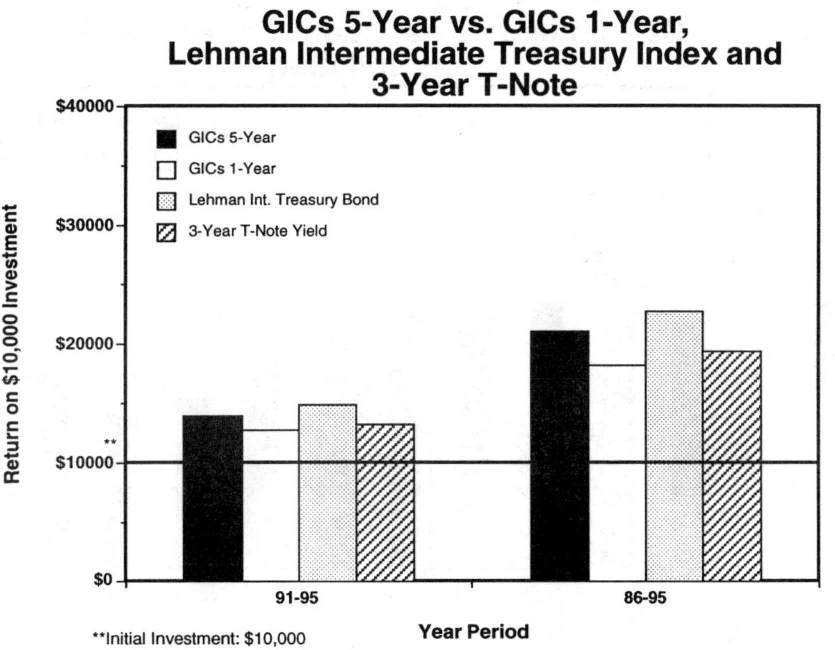


©1996 Chase Global Data & Research
73 Junction Square, Concord, MA 01742

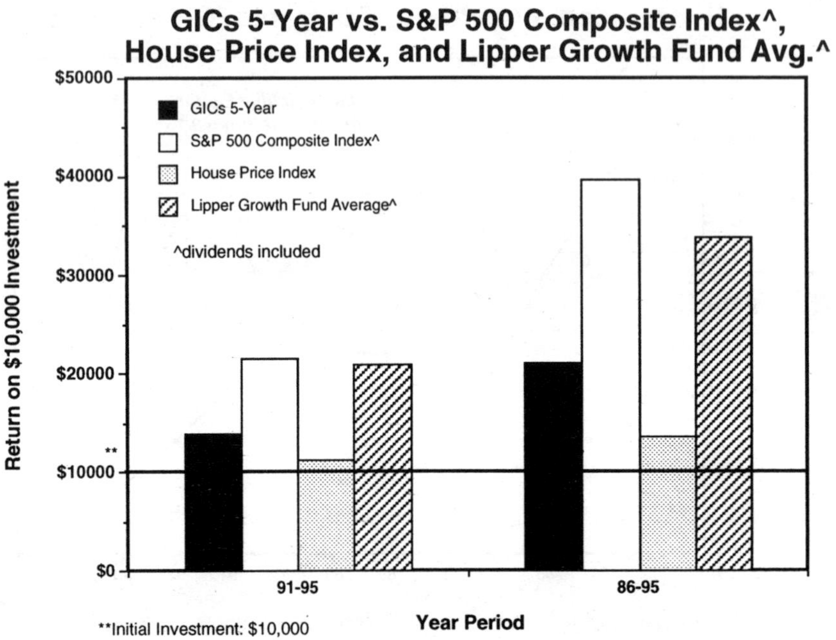


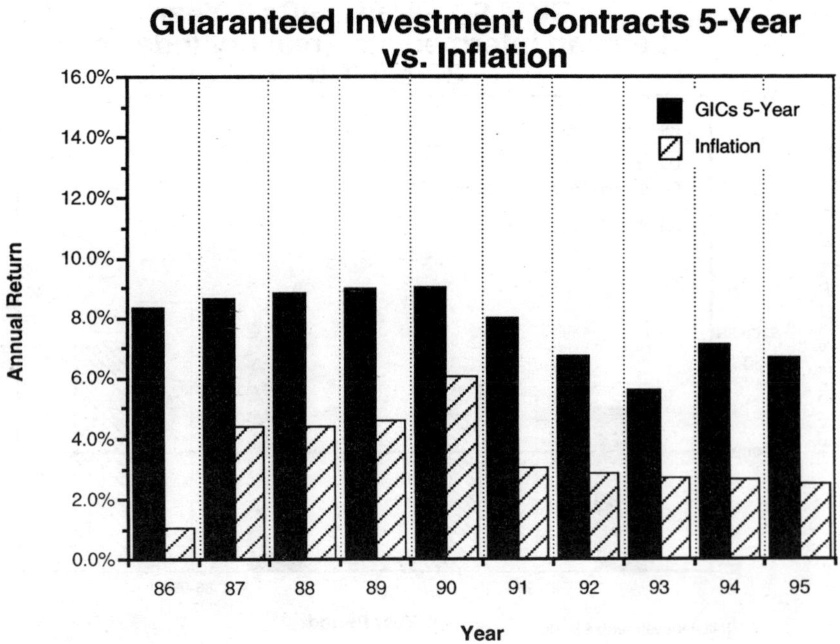


©1996 Chase Global Data & Research
73 Junction Square, Concord, MA 01742

SECTION VII

# Insurance Investments

# Chapter Twenty Seven

# Life Insurance

Life Insurance in the United States, and throughout the world, has evolved into one of the largest of all industries, with unparalleled financial clout. In all major nations of the world the largest domestic corporations are life insurance companies. A key reason for the size and success of these corporations is the fact that the product they sell meets a very basic need required by most people at some point in their lives—no matter where they are from, or what their occupation may be.

In the United States there is over $11 *trillion* of life insurance outstanding today—twice the U.S. GDP—backed by insurance firms with over $1.9 trillion in assets and over $1.5 trillion in statutory surplus reserves. Life insurance is owned by 81% of American households, representing over 160 million people. When reviewing the statistics of the life insurance industry, one is immediately overwhelmed by the sheer size of the numbers. For example, over $1.7 trillion of life insurance was sold in 1994 alone, encompassing 32 million policies. Annual premium payments made to insurance companies are over $325 billion, and represent almost 10% of total GDP. Annual benefit payments made in the U.S. for life, annuity, and health insurance were $150 billion. And with the aging of America's Baby Boom generation these numbers will surely grow—for about half of all sales in 1994 were to that age group alone. Total sales of life insurance has increased 1500 fold since 1900, over 100 fold since 1940, and has over tripled since 1980. Today the average policy size for an insured American household is $152,200.

Life Insurance as we know it has primarily evolved over the past two centuries. However, the first forms of insurance date to over two thousand years ago. The Babylonians began insuring maritime shipments and boats with elaborate contracts as early as 2000 B.C. Hindus in 600 B.C. offered the first commercial insurance covering land operations. Risk, and rates charged for said risk, were not arrived at by scientific means and at best were guesses. Nevertheless, Greek contractual arrangements of the fourth century B.C. were solid enough


©1996 Chase Global Data & Research
73 Junction Square, Concord, MA 01742

that they were closely followed as late as the nineteenth century. The Romans then expanded commercial insurance by insuring loans made to overseas trading partners.

It was the Romans who historians believe initiated the first attempts at insuring lives in about 150 A.D. Roman contracts specified the life insured, the duration of risk, the benefit, the beneficiary, and the contracting parties. A central component of life insurance is the study of death experience in the population, or mortality risk. The first known attempt to compile a mortality table was made by Domitius Ulpanius in 225 A.D. Surprisingly, the table was not improved upon for over 1400 years. Ulpanius estimated that a 40 year old Roman had a life expectancy of an additional 19 years (age 59), while a 50 year old Roman would likely survive but 9 more years, and also die at age 59. Today's actuaries would not appreciate such logic, but at least Ulpanius gave life insurance a basis for risk and associated expense in its early evolutionary phase.

Fourteen hundred years after Ulpanius, Edmund Halley, well known for identifying the orbit of the comet which bears his name, used his mathematical knowledge to study the death records of a town called Breslau in Silesia between 1687-1691. Halley created the first correct, though unsophisticated, mortality tables. By this time life insurance was a flourishing business in England, with several successful major insurers. One can quickly understand why success was so attainable by reviewing the mortality tables by Dr. John Heysham and Joshua Milne, who formulated the Carlisle Mortality Table of 1815. Annual Life Insurance premium expense as outlined in their mortality table was over 15 times more costly than today's rates.

By 1759 the first Life Insurance company was founded in the United States. Now called the Presbyterian Ministers' Fund, it is the oldest life insurance company in continued existence in the world. By 1789 Edward Wigglesworth prepared a modified table of mortality based on Massachusetts experience, the first computation of reserves and premium scientifically calculated in the U.S. During the 1800's much evolved in life insurance. In 1848 the first policy loans were granted. By 1859 the first state insurance department, in New York, was established. War risk insurance began with the Civil War in 1861. Cash surrender values were established by law in Massachusetts. By 1911 the first Group Life insurance contract was issued. In 1918 the American Men Mortality Table was released, reviewing U.S. experience from 1900-1915. More refined major mortality tables were released in 1938, 1941, 1958, and 1980.

©1996 Chase Global Data & Research
73 Junction Square, Concord, MA 01742

Today the United States has evolved into a nation with over 1,800 insurance companies—a dramatic increase from only 84 at the turn of the century. 195 companies in the U.S. are over 50 years old, with 31 over a century old. The century old firms control 44% of all life insurance assets. The majority of the growth in numbers of insurers took place between World War II and 1970, with fewer new companies emerging today because of greater competition, less profitability, and greater capitalization demands. Surprisingly, insurers which are 25 to 50 years old control about 25% of the industry's assets. New companies under 25 years in operation control but 12% of assets. 1,736 companies are stockholder owned, or 94%. The remaining 6% are mutual companies, which are owned by their policyholders who receive dividends on their policies based on the overall operations of their insurer. Despite the shortfall in operating mutual companies, they are generally the older firms with sizeable assets. Mutuals hold over 39% of all assets of life companies, and represent 37% of life insurance in force. Today insurance firms have a combined work force of 2.2 million people, with over 650,000 insurance agents in the field marketing insurance products.

Much has been recently written about the health of major financial industries, such as banking and insurance. While there is FDIC insurance up to $100,000 per account at participating banking institutions, there is no federal "safety net" covering policyholders should insurance firms fail. However, state supervised insurance departments exist in every state, and insurance industry sponsored guaranty funds exist in over 40 states. Contributions by insurers to these state guaranty funds were over $1 billion by 1990, over 20 times more than the average annual payment made a decade earlier. State guaranty funds operate in a variety of ways, but do not cover all forms of insurance. Typical coverage is limited to $100,000 per policy with maximum coverage in some states as high as $300,000. Usually funds cover only claims made by state residents.

While some people feel there may be a parallel between the S&L insolvencies and future problems with insurers, most experts and industry watchdogs feel that assessment is too extreme. There will no doubt be continued problems with insurers during the present era of a weakened economy coupled with softness in real estate. To be sure insolvencies rose to a record 44 failures in 1989. And since 1988 over 100 insurers have failed—but about 1000 S&Ls have been declared insolvent over the same time period. Overall the insurance industry is huge, diversified, and operating with a majority of insurers on a solid foundation. And S&Ls have about 40% of their assets in real estate lending, while insurers have about 15%. Regardless, investors are

©1996 Chase Global Data & Research
73 Junction Square, Concord, MA 01742

encouraged to review the ratings on insurers which are available from several third party sources. A.M. Best Co., Standard and Poor's, Moody's, and Duff & Phelps monitor and rate insurance firms on an ongoing basis.

A.M. Best rates 1,750 life and over 4,000 property casualty insurers with ratings from A++ to F, in addition to various special "NA" (Not Assigned) classifications—which, for example, may occur due to important ongoing changes. As of July 1995 the following reflects the overall results of their ratings analysis and the percentage of firms falling into each category:

| | | |
|---|---|---|
| A++ | (Superior) | = 4% |
| A+ | (Superior) | = 14% |
| A | (Excellent) | = 19% |
| A- | (Excellent) | = 12% |
| B++ | (Very good) | = 6% |
| B+ | (Very good) | = 12% |
| B/B- | (Good) | = 8% |
| C++/C- | (Fair/Marginal) | = 6% |
| D/E | (Below Min. Standards) | = 1% |
| F | (In Liquidation) | = .3% |
| Miscellaneous | | = 17% |

Recent concerns regarding the financial health of insurers primarily involve the decline in value of real estate and junk bonds. However, the average insurance firm has a diversified portfolio of assets which should allow it to survive major financial calamities as well as any fully diversified investor. While insurers, along with banks and mutual funds have in the past been major buyers of junk bonds, it is important to note that by 1995 junk bonds represented 2.1% of general account assets, and bonds in default represented 0.2% of total assets. Mortgages remain a concern due to deterioration of real estate values. But unlike S&Ls, which have approximately half of their assets in real estate loans, mortgages represent about one-sixth of insurers' assets. Property casualty insurers had but 3%. Banks are normally involved with riskier "front-end" real estate financing, such as construction loans, while insurers are less so. In 1990 banks had 60% more in nonperforming commercial real estate as a percentage of assets than insurers.

©1996 Chase Global Data & Research
73 Junction Square, Concord, MA 01742

The distribution of assets of U.S. life insurance companies, as reported by the American Council of Life Insurance as of December 1994 follows:

| | |
|---|---|
| Government Securities | 20.4% |
| Corporate Bonds | 40.7% |
| Stocks | 14.5% |
| Mortgages | 11.1% |
| Real Estate | 2.8% |
| Policy Loans | 4.4% |
| Miscellaneous | 6.2% |

Life insurers have a major asset, not often discussed, which has long term positive implications for their profitability—science, and its ability to allow man to live longer. After all, the longer man lives the better off insurers are. Today the average American will live 60% longer than those living at the turn of the century. In 1900 the average citizen had a life expectancy of 47.3 years. Average life expectancy today is 75.5 years, with women at 78.8 years and men at 72.1. Life expectancy has risen 6.2 years since 1960. Death rates continue to drop as well, to 5.1 per 1000 people per year. In 1900 the death rate was almost three time higher at 14.4 per 1000. The major causes of death are cardiovascular-renal diseases (41%) and cancer (24%), which combined account for two-thirds of all deaths.

Science has also allowed insurance companies to better evaluate risks. Today 97% of all applicants for insurance receive coverage. 93% of applicants are rated as standard risk, 4% are rated extra risk, and 3% are declined insurance. Today insurers are more aware than ever of their financial risk before an application is accepted, which is a far cry from the Roman mortality risk tables and Edmund Halley's mortality pool analyses.

The most popular form of life insurance today continues to be Whole Life insurance (inclusive of Universal Life) with 62% of the market share—although its share has decreased from its peak level of 66% in 1962. Term Life insurance controls 38% of the marketplace. In 1993, 50% of all policies sold were for amounts under $50,000, with 32% of policies sold representing coverage of $100,000 or more. Of note, women are a growing market for life insurance with 30% more women being policyholders today than a decade ago.

©1996 Chase Global Data & Research
73 Junction Square, Concord, MA 01742

Universal Life Insurance (UL), which is reviewed in the following Performance Table, has many strengths over and above providing a death benefit to beneficiaries. UL insurance is a flexible contract which allows for permanent protection and cash value build up. Premiums are not contractual at mandatory fixed amounts, and may be paid in varying amounts based on cash value build up—unlike a whole life policy. All interest accumulation is not taxed as it is earned within the policy—much like an annuity—but unlike a CD or corporate bond. Therein lies a key strength of the Universal Life policy. Cash values accumulated through interest crediting may be borrowed from the policy, effectively providing tax-free withdrawals. Interest charges on the borrowed cash value are normally levied at very attractive "net" expense levels. Interest rate crediting duration varies among issuers, with the normal maximum duration being one year. All contracts provide minimum guaranteed interest rates. As with all insurance contracts the key expense is mortality charges—which vary. Administrative fees may also be levied on some Universal life contracts. Universal Life policies are guaranteed by the issuing insurance company and avoid probate upon death.

The following Universal Life Performance Table and related data shows that UL policy interest rates have proven to be competitive in their overall returns versus alternative safe investment vehicles. UL has been an above average performer, with its volatility less than all subjects tracked by Chase Global Data & Research over the past decade—other than tax-free money market funds. It should be noted, however, that the rates quoted are initial, gross interest rate levels and do not reflect mortality and administrative expenses which will also be charged to the policy over and above the interest credited. The data reflects information supplied by A. M. Best Company, which has been rating insurance companies for over 90 years, regarding over 250 major Universal Life insurance companies. The group was responsible for 98.5% of the face amount of Universal Life insurance policies sold in the U.S. By 1995 there was over $2.1 trillion in Universal life insurance in force, representing 23 million policyholders. Invented in 1977, UL's approximate 18% market share reflects a sharp rise from its meager 2% share in 1981.

©1996 Chase Global Data & Research
73 Junction Square, Concord, MA 01742

## UNIVERSAL LIFE INSURANCE RENEWAL RATES

[Average annual rate]

| Year | Rate* | Compound return on a five year $10,000 investment | Annual compound rate of return |
|---|---|---|---|
| 1995 | 7.00% | 1991 - 1995 | |
| 1994 | 6.60% | | 7.34% |
| 1993 | 7.00% | ... $14,252 | |
| 1992 | 7.70% | | |
| 1991 | 8.43% | | |
| 1990 | 8.75% | 1986 - 1990 | |
| 1989 | 8.94% | | 9.17% |
| 1988 | 8.79% | ... $15,507 | |
| 1987 | 8.88% | | |
| 1986 | 10.50% | | |
| 1985 | 10.50% | 1981 - 1985 | |
| 1984 | 11.25% | | 11.25% |
| 1983 | 11.00% | ... $17,040 | |
| 1982 | 11.50% | | |
| 1981 | 12.00% | | |

How a $10,000 investment performed over

| 5 years | 10 years | 15 years |
|---|---|---|
| 1991 - 1995<br>$14,252<br>(7.34%)^ | 1986 - 1995<br>$22,101<br>(8.25%) | 1981 - 1995<br>$37,660<br>(9.24%) |

^ annual compound rate of return for that period
* Source: A.M. Best Company.

©1996 Chase Global Data & Research
73 Junction Square, Concord, MA 01742

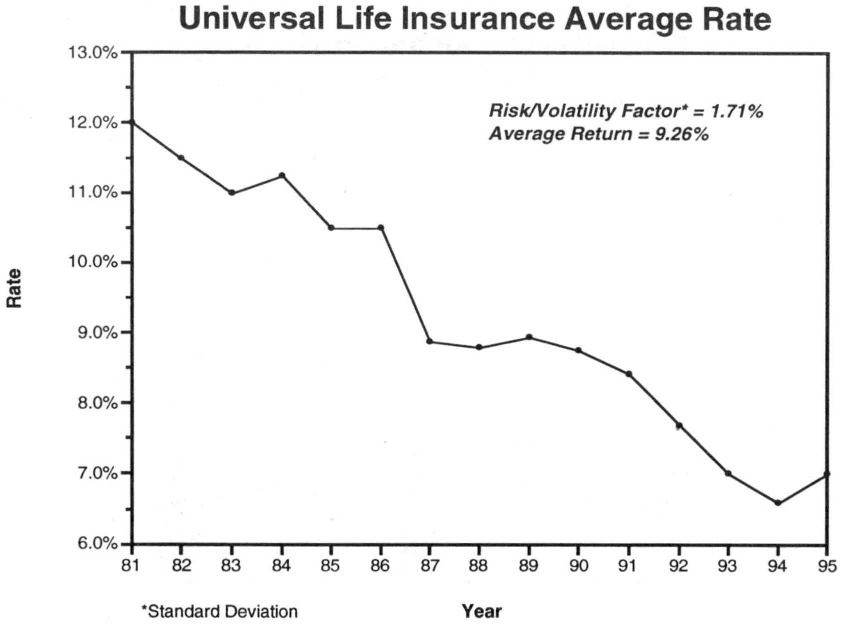


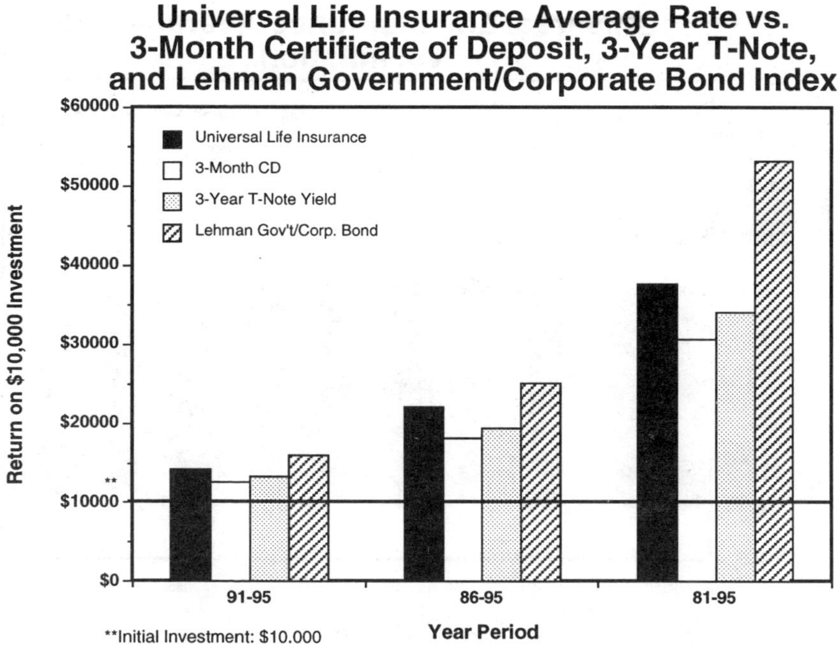


©1996 Chase Global Data & Research
73 Junction Square, Concord, MA 01742

## Universal Life Insurance Average Rate vs. NASDAQ Composite Index, Morgan Stanley EAFE Equity Index^, and Gold

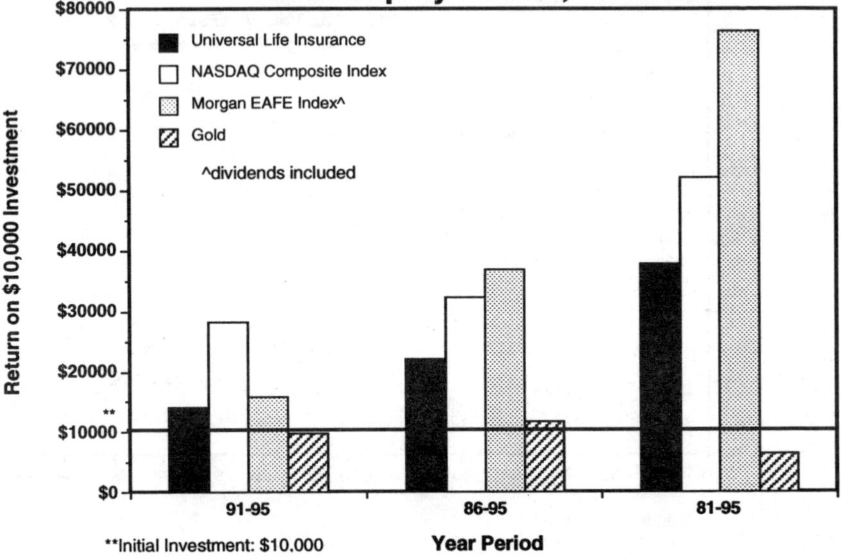


## Universal Life Insurance Average Rate vs. Inflation

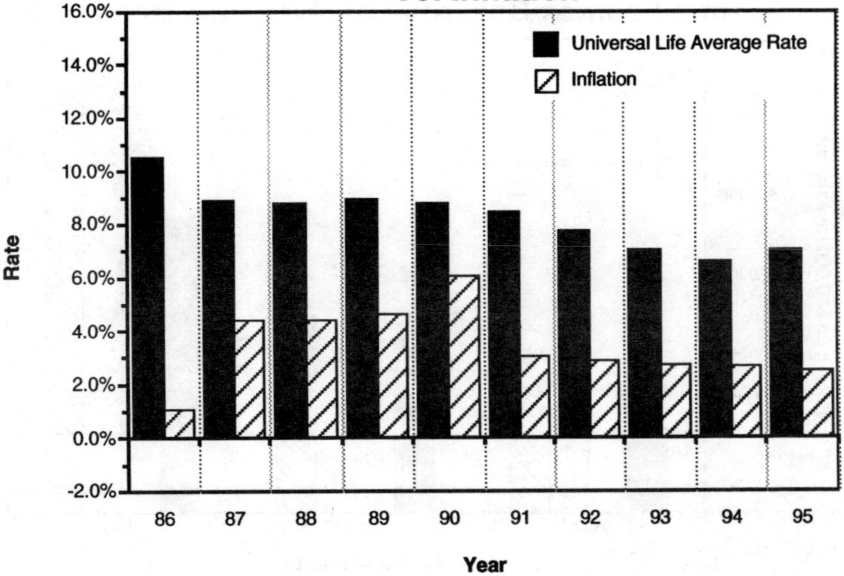


©1996 Chase Global Data & Research
73 Junction Square, Concord, MA 01742

# Chapter Twenty Eight

# Annuities

Annuities have been issued in the United States by insurance companies since 1812. Today they represent one of the most popular investment vehicles used in planning for retirement and other long term needs by investors seeking conservative growth of their assets. There are 22 million individual and supplementary annuity contracts in existence. While annuities have been sold in the U.S. for over 180 years, their popularity has grown dramatically primarily during the past decade.

Income paid through annuities in the U. S. has increased over 200 times since 1940, to $43 billion annually. Due to the highly liquid nature of annuities coupled with the fact that the insurance industry is closely overseen by regulators, there is an unusually large amount of assets set aside by insurers to meet the potential demands of annuity contract holders. Today almost two-thirds of all surplus reserves of U.S. life insurers is put aside for annuity obligations. As of 1995, of the $1.6 trillion in surplus reserves of insurers, $1.1 trillion backs annuity contracts. Reserves for annuities have increased 35 fold since 1960, with twice as much surplus assets backing today's annuity contracts than life insurance policies. Regulators have deemed annuities be backed on a more "immediate demand" basis than long term life insurance contracts, and the insurance industry has complied with the requirements.

The most basic and popular form of annuity is the Single Premium Deferred Annuity. An annuity is a contract between an insurer and a recipient (annuitant) whereby the insurer guarantees to pay a stream of payments to the recipient in exchange for premium payment(s). A Single Premium Deferred Annuity requires but one payment initially, and grows in value through compounding interest payments from the insurer to the contract—until annuity payments begin. The return of principal paid through premium payments is guaranteed by the insurance company. Interest rate levels and time duration guarantees for interest rate payments vary with each contract and insurer but they are also guaranteed.

©1996 Chase Global Data & Research
73 Junction Square, Concord, MA 01742

There are basic and compelling reasons for the popularity of annuities. Safety of principal invested is the primary reason, much like with CDs. While there are questions about some insurers financial health, for the most part insurance companies are respected for their ability to honor long term contracts between themselves and their insured/annuitant contract holders. Generally speaking, the average annuity contract's interest rate level is quite competitive with alternative safe investment vehicles. However, tax benefits applicable to interest accumulation is a major factor differentiating annuities from other similarly safe investments. Simply put, interest earned which is not withdrawn from the contract is *not taxed*—unlike CDs and money market funds. The annuity thus operates much like an IRA account, where taxes are applicable only upon withdrawal. Fixed rate annuities, like CDs, offer time frames from 90 days to ten years where the interest rate is fixed and guaranteed to be paid at a given rate by the insurance company.

Annuities, like many other investments, have negative aspects as well. While taxation applies to all interest earned upon withdrawal, there is an additional 10% penalty on withdrawals made if they occur before the recipient reaches age 59 1/2. And while contracts contain minimum guaranteed interest levels, quoted rates are often higher—yet the higher rate may vary markedly as to its time duration. Withdrawal/surrender penalty charges may apply to withdrawals made in early years, and/or if more than one withdrawal is made per year. Most contracts permit withdrawals of 10% of assets after one year without penalty.

The above complexities and several shortcomings dissipate when the Single Premium Deferred Annuity is "annuitized"—i.e. commencing monthly payments to the annuitant guaranteed for life. There are a variety of ways the annuitization process may be done, based on guaranteed cash payments for life, and/or with guaranteed payments (period certain) made even after death to named surviving beneficiaries. Also, the annuitized payments provide for a return of principal in addition to interest, enabling the annuitized payment to be larger than a standard interest withdrawal payment, as well as partially tax-free through the return of principal. Selecting the manner of annuity payment stream is relatively complex. One should carefully examine the benefits and rates of return for all choices available.

While this Chapter examines the returns of Deferred Annuities, it should be noted there are several types of annuities. Other key forms of annuities include Immediate Annuities—which immediately commence income streams to the annuitant upon premium payment,

©1996 Chase Global Data & Research
73 Junction Square, Concord, MA 01742

and Variable Annuities—which allow for choosing between a variety of, and changing, investment strategies for the premiums dollars placed in the contract. Standard investment choices include stocks, bonds, fixed rate/CDs, and money market funds. Thus the Variable Annuity investor can allocate a portion of his/her funds into risk-oriented or low-risk strategies. While returns are not guaranteed, the Variable Annuity's many options could provide much higher returns than standard Fixed Rate Deferred Annuities. Like all other annuities, growth within the Variable Annuity is not taxed, with only the gains taxed upon withdrawal. Of importance, all annuities—including the more risky Variable Annuity—guarantee that your original deposited sum is payable upon death to your beneficiary. Thus, while an investor's Variable Annuity could conceivably lose money such that it is no longer worth the original deposited sum, it nevertheless is guaranteed to pay the original sum to beneficiaries of the contract owner. (See also Chapter 29.)

Annuity Group Plan contracts are very popular in pension plan management. By 1995 approximately two-thirds of all annuity contracts were issued through Group plans, representing insurers' surplus assets of over $600 billion. The Performance Table of annuity average annual returns which follows reflects qualified (retirement plan) investment asset annuity rates as tracked by A.M. Best Co., the nation's oldest research and information firm on life insurance and related products. A.M. Best has rated life insurance companies for over ninety years. The quoted rates which follow reflect the average Initial Offer Yield as offered by over 100 insurance companies A.M. Best tracks.

Single Premium Deferred Annuities, as evidenced by the Performance Table and Ranking Table comparisons are an above average investment alternative, and consistently outperform other conservative alternatives—such as CDs and money market funds. Annuities averaged more than 8% annually over the past fifteen years—over twice the rate of Inflation. Annuities' performance is even more compelling when their ability to defer taxation is also considered. While U.S. government issues avoid state taxation and municipal bonds can avoid both state and federal taxation, they are also prone to price fluctuation—especially with longer term maturities. Deferred Annuities do not fluctuate, and are guaranteed not to lose value. Deferred Annuities only increase in value—through the process of interest crediting. Like all insurance products, they have the additional benefit of not being subject to probate.

©1996 Chase Global Data & Research
73 Junction Square, Concord, MA 01742

## ANNUITY INTEREST RATES

[initial qualified single premium deferred; median annual values]

| Year | Rate* | Compound return on a five year $10,000 investment | Annual compound rate of return |
|---|---|---|---|
| 1995 | 6.00% | 1991 - 1995 | |
| 1994 | 5.92% | | 6.44% |
| 1993 | 5.75% | ... $13,660 | |
| 1992 | 6.50% | | |
| 1991 | 8.03% | | |
| 1990 | 8.50% | 1986 - 1990 | |
| 1989 | 8.63% | | 8.55% |
| 1988 | 8.50% | ... $15,072 | |
| 1987 | 8.13% | | |
| 1986 | 9.00% | | |
| 1985 | 10.50% | 1981 - 1985 | |
| 1984 | 11.43% | | 11.58% |
| 1983 | 10.88% | ... $17,292 | |
| 1982 | 13.34% | | |
| 1981 | 11.75% | | |

How a $10,000 investment performed over

| 5 years | 10 years | 15 years |
|---|---|---|
| 1991 - 1995<br>$13,660<br>(6.44%)^ | 1986 - 1995<br>$20,589<br>(7.49%) | 1981 - 1995<br>$35,603<br>(8.83%) |

^ annual compound rate of return for that period
* Source: A.M. Best Company.

©1996 Chase Global Data & Research
73 Junction Square, Concord, MA 01742

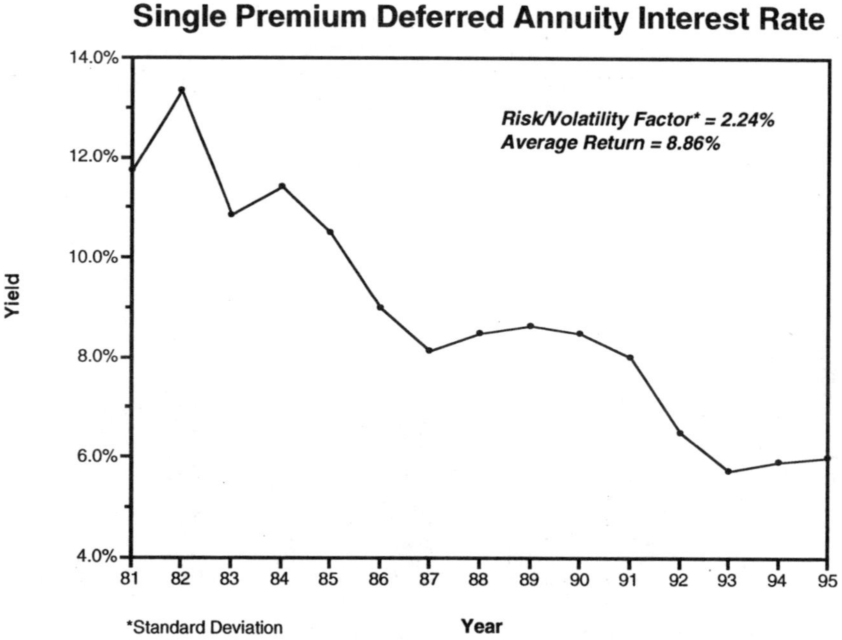


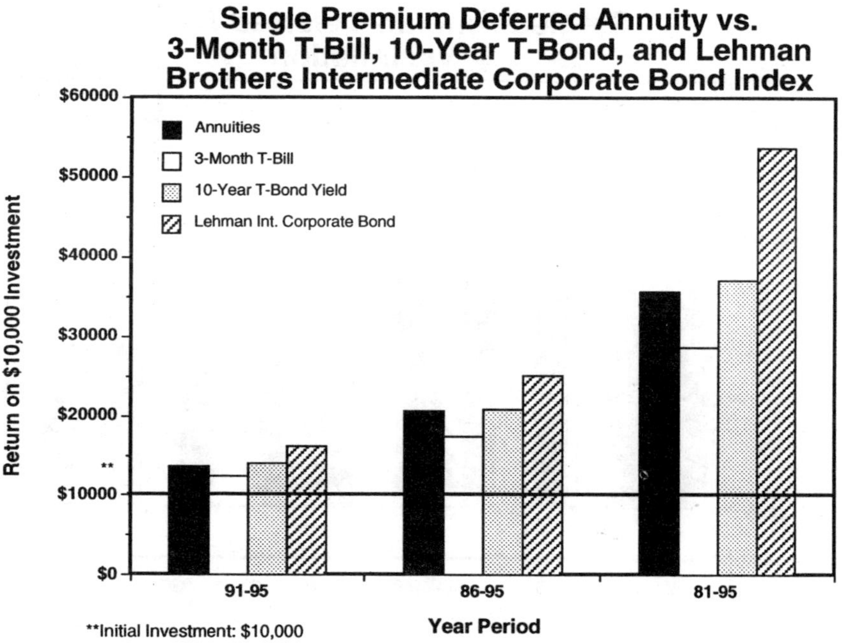


©1996 Chase Global Data & Research
73 Junction Square, Concord, MA 01742

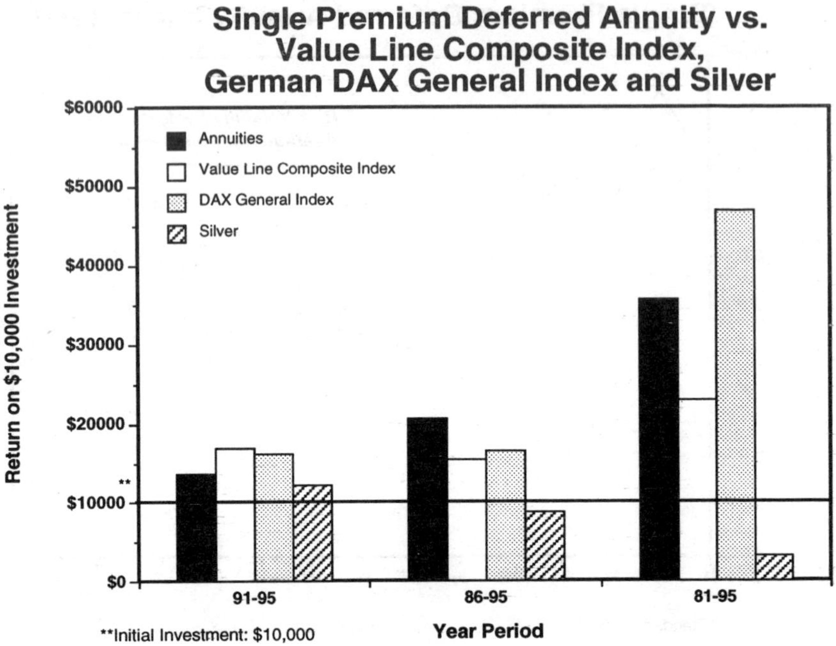


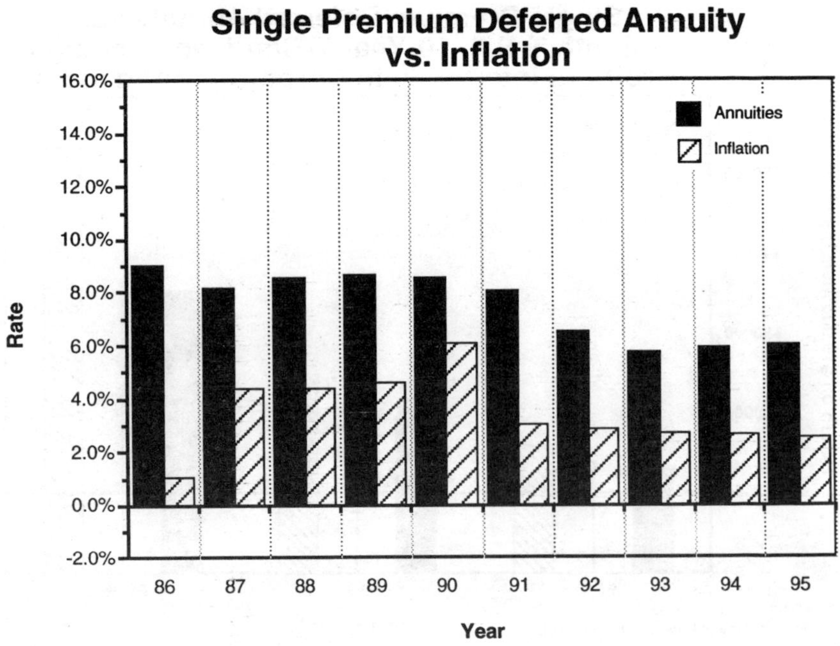


©1996 Chase Global Data & Research
73 Junction Square, Concord, MA 01742

# ORDER FORM

| Product | Quantity | Price |
|---|---|---|
| **1996 Chase Investment Performance Digest**<br>Reviewing over 80 investment subjects covering 1960 thru 1995.<br>400 pages @ **$23.95, plus $4** shipping and handling. | ______ | $ ________ |
| **1996 Chase Guide to Investment Performance**<br>Reviewing over 20 investment subjects covering 1960 thru 1995.<br>160 pages @ **$11.95, plus $4** shipping and handling. | ______ | $ ________ |
| **1996 Chase Page Charts**<br>6 Major Investments. 1960 thru 1995.<br>8.5" x 11", full-color, laminated. @ **$9.95**. Please indicate quantities: | ______ | $ ________ |

_______ Mutual Fund Investing _______ Global Investing

_______ Equity Investing _______ Balanced Investing

_______ Risk: Stocks vs. Bonds _______ Risk: Global Investing

| | | |
|---|---|---|
| **1996 Chase WALL Charts**<br>***Mutual Fund Investing in the Modern Era***<br>6 Major Investments. 1960 thru 1995.<br>37" x 24", full-color, laminated. @ **$23.95.** | ______ | $ ________ |
| ***InvestmentView®* Software**<br>Easy to use, Powerful graphics, with performance and risk data from 1960 to present on 300+ indices. Windows 3.1. 4 MB RAM and 5 MB in hard drive required. Monthly data. | ______ | $ ________ |

**Quarterly Shipments** **$295/year** _______

**Monthly Shipments** **$425/year** _______

| | | |
|---|---|---|
| ***InvestmentView®* Hypothetical Software**<br>All features of ***InvestmentView®*** plus 8,000+ Lipper Mutal Funds with returns and characteristics. College & Retirement Planning (with college tuition database). Disclaimers for printouts, more. Windows 3.1. 4 MB RAM. 60 MB hard disk. Monthly data shipped quarterly. @ **$495** | ______ | $ ________ |
| **SINGLE Edition *InvestmentView®* Version**<br>Indicate Monthly Edition (__________) @ **$129** | ______ | $ ________ |
| **SINGLE Edition *InvestmentView®* Hypothetical Version**<br>Indicate Quarterly Edition (_____Q) @ **$225** | ______ | $ ________ |
| **College and Retirement Planning**<br>(combined programs) @ **$69**<br>(with College Tuition database and Social Security data) | ______ | $ ________ |
| **FREE DEMO DISK** (30 day working copy) @ **FREE** | ______ | $ N/A |

**CALL FOR INFO on 5000+ Stocks, 2,700+ Variable Annuities, and 1200+ Money Managers Databases.**

**Please see continuation of product listing on reverse side ☞**

**Phone – (800) 639-9494 or (508) 371-9100 FAX – (508) 371-9105**

| Product | Quantity | Price |
|---|---|---|
| **Seminar Slide Show Presentation** | _____ | $ ________ |

***Risks and Returns: Investment Options in the Modern Era***
(1960 through 1995) 30 slides with script and audiotape. Please check format(s):

SLIDES @ $295_____ OVERHEADS @ $350 ____

DISK @ $150 ____ (WINDOWS ___ or MAC ___)

Individual Slide @ $35 Please identify: ________________

5 Slides @ $100 Please identify: ______________________________

**Subtotal** $ ____________

(Massachusetts residents include 5% tax) $ ____________

## Method of Payment:

_____Check or money order _____VISA _____MasterCard

Card Account Number ________________________________________

Card Expires ________________________________________

Signature ________________________________________

## Ship To:

Name ________________________________________

Title ________________________________________

Company ________________________________________

Address ________________________________________

________________________________________

City______________________________ State____________ Zip____________

Business Telephone ( ) ____________________

## Shipping and Handling Charges

**Chase Investment Performance Digest and the The Investor's Guide to Investment Performance**

| | |
|---|---|
| 1-3 | $4 each |
| 4-24 | $3 each |
| 25-99 | $2 each |
| 100+ | Call |

Next day shipping – $18 each
UPS 2nd Day – $9 each

**FREE SHIPPING on these products:**

- InvestmentView® Software
- InvestmentView® Hypothetical Software
- College and Retirement Planning Software
- Chase Page and Wall Charts
- Chase Seminar Slide Show and/or Individual Slides

**To order, please call (800) 639-9494 or (508) 371-9100**

**For fastest service, credit card orders may be faxed to us at (508) 371-9105**

**❑ Please send me your catalog!**

Chapter Twenty Nine

# Variable Annuities

Variable Annuities are relatively new to the investment scene, having been first introduced in the 1950s. Today the Variable Annuity is quickly gaining prominence due to its strength as a retirement planning vehicle. As the U.S. population ages, industry experts believe the growth of Variable Annuity sales will dramatically expand as well. Today over 11 million people have variable annuity accounts.

Variable Annuities are insurance based investment products, which like all other forms of annuities allow for growth of invested premiums to be free from taxation until withdrawals are made from the contract. Unique to Variable Annuities are several forms of investment alternatives which vary in both their potential for reward and risk. The typical Variable Annuity contract has six primary choices, but each contract may have more or less choices. The six basic contract account alternatives are:

- equity fund account
- fixed income fund account
- balanced fund account
- money market fund account
- fixed rate ("CD") account
- international equity account

Variable Annuity (VA) choices are broad enough that an investor can employ either an aggressive or conservative approach, or a combination of both, while enjoying the benefits of tax deferred growth. The uniqueness of the VA is obvious when one realizes that losses incurred in the Variable Annuity are insured, such that total premiums invested in the contract are guaranteed to be paid to the beneficiary at the time of death of the owner—even if the account decreases in value below the original invested sum. Growth through capital gains and income derived from dividends or interest crediting are deferred on an equal basis.

Because of the above benefits, Variable Annuity sales today are sharply increasing. In 1990 sales were $12 billion, with 1995 sales at $50 billion. Variable Annuity sales are expected to equal one-fourth of equity mutual fund sales in the near future, with sales more than quadrupling.

Guarantee of principal from loss upon death of the owner is

©1996 Chase Global Data & Research
73 Junction Square, Concord, MA 01742

covered by mortality charges, which are approximately 1.30% per annum. In most other respects Variable Annuities resemble their investment cousins, mutual funds. Like mutual funds, several Variable Annuities have excellent performance results inclusive of all costs associated with the overall contract. Today the Variable Annuities arena is monitored by Lipper Analytical Services, VARDS® (Variable Annuity Research & Data Service), A.M. Best, Tillinghast, and Morningstar. The performance data which follows is supplied by Lipper Analytical, which began tracking this expanding market in 1974. Today Lipper tracks over $250 billion in Variable Annuities invested in 400 different product offerings, representing about 95% of the overall marketplace. The performance data on Variable Annuities supplied by Lipper is net of all expense.

Lipper estimates that 95% of all Variable Annuities have no sales charge, with annual overhead expense for the average equity Variable Annuity being 2.00%. As of December 31, 1995 the average overhead expenses for Variable Annuities is as follows:

| | |
|---|---|
| Mortality expense | 1.30% |
| Equity Manager expense | 0.60% |
| Fixed Income Manager expense | 0.50% |
| Administrative expense | 0.15% |

The above charges are similar to the most costly mutual funds, yet mutual funds lack mortality coverage, and its inherent benefit and expense.

The Variable Annuity market at the end of 1995 was invested as follows:

| | |
|---|---|
| 63% | in Equities accounts |
| 14% | in Flexible accounts |
| 10% | in Special Equity |
| 9% | in Fixed Income accounts |
| 4% | in Money Markets |

An analysis of the management of assets of Variable Annuities reveals that approximately 95% is handled by mutual fund company asset management teams. The other 5% remains with insurance company based investment managers. In 1995 about 90% of all newly issued VAs were managed by major mutual fund organizations.

The Performance Tables which follow outline an investment product dominated by industry money management giants. Given the product's obvious tax advantages, and the exemplary results of many Variable Annuities, experts believe that VAs are an investment alternative which could see annual expansion rates of 20% or more in the 1990s.

©1996 Chase Global Data & Research
73 Junction Square, Concord, MA 01742

## VARIABLE ANNUITIES EQUITY INDEX

[dividends included; year-end]

| Year | Yield* | Compound return on a five year $10,000 investment | Annual compound rate of return |
|---|---|---|---|
| 1995 | 25.50% | 1991 - 1995 | |
| 1994 | -1.90% | | 14.94% |
| 1993 | 12.22% | ... $20,065 | |
| 1992 | 8.05% | | |
| 1991 | 34.41% | | |
| 1990 | -6.54% | | |
| 1989 | 25.73% | | |
| 1988 | 1.72% | 1986 - 1990 | |
| 1987 | 12.94% | | 11.51% |
| 1986 | 27.70% | ... $17,239 | |
| 1985 | 0.13% | | |

How a $10,000 investment performed over

| 5 years | 10 years |
|---|---|
| 1991 - 1995<br>$20,065<br>(14.94%)^ | 1986 - 1995<br>$34,590<br>(13.21%) |

^ annual compound rate of return for that period

* Source: ©1995 Lipper Analytical Services

©1996 Chase Global Data & Research
73 Junction Square, Concord, MA 01742

## Lipper General Equity Variable Annuity Index^

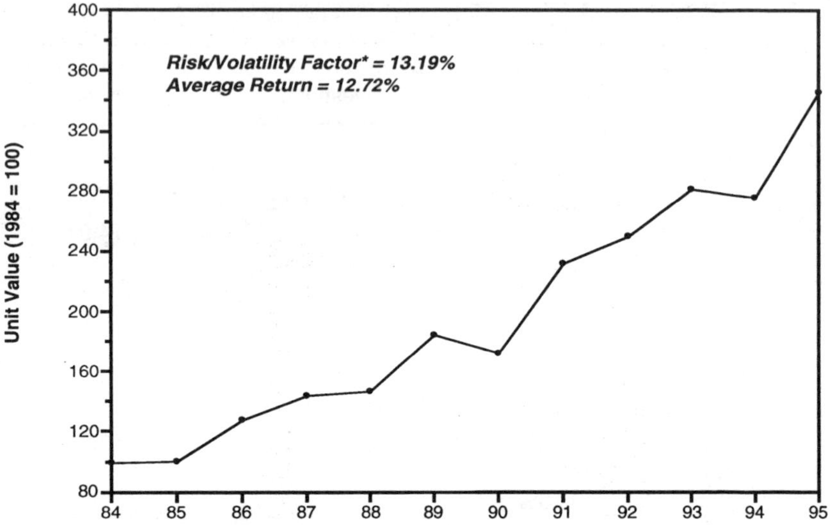


*Standard Deviation
^dividends included

## Lipper General Equity Variable Annuity Index^ vs. Dow Jones 30 Industrials^, Value Line Composite Index, and Lipper Growth Fund Average^

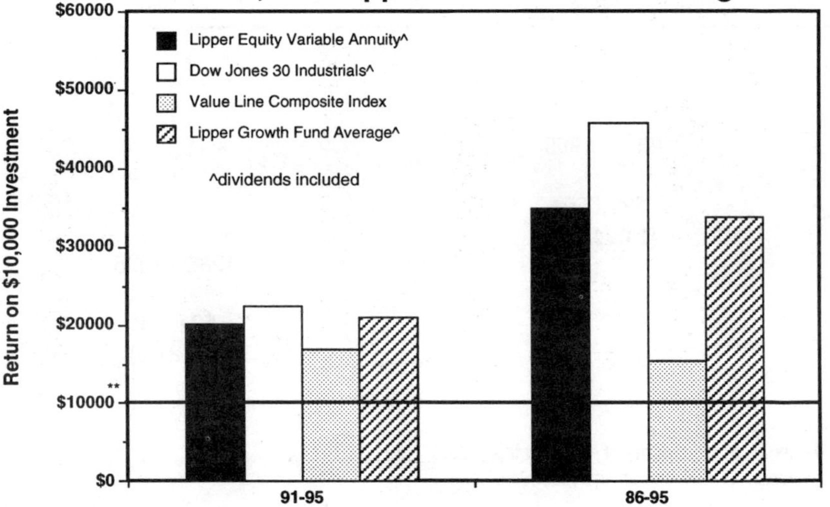


**Initial Investment: $10,000

©1996 Chase Global Data & Research
73 Junction Square, Concord, MA 01742

## Lipper General Equity Variable Annuity Index^ vs. Lehman Mortgage-Backed Securities Index, 3-Month T-Bill, and Merrill Global Government Bond Index

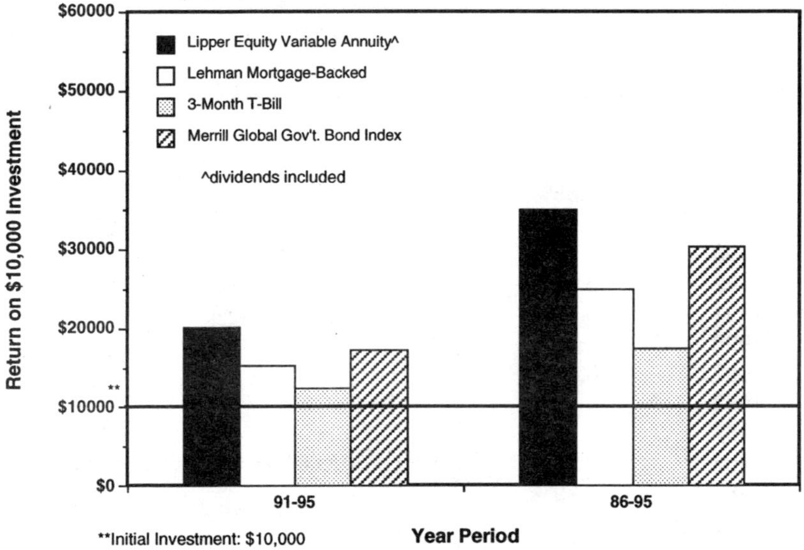


## Lipper General Equity Variable Annuity Index^ vs. Inflation

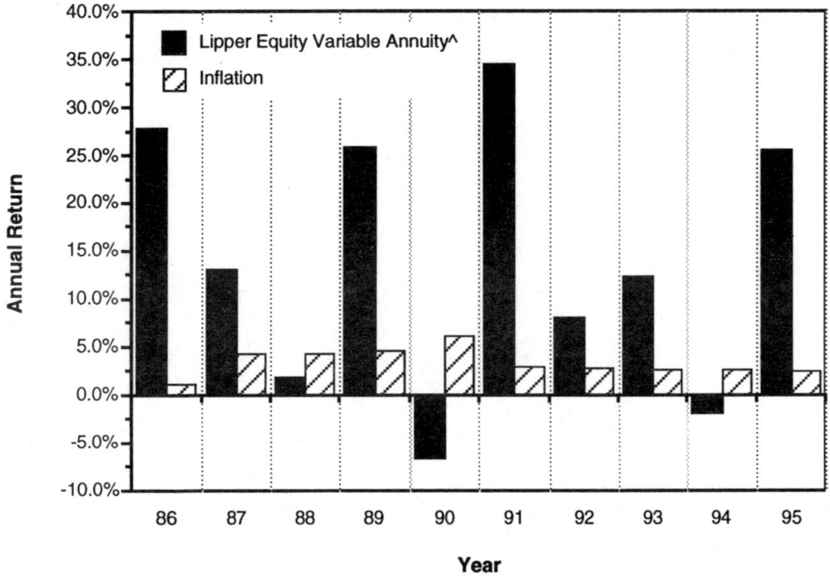


©1996 Chase Global Data & Research
73 Junction Square, Concord, MA 01742

## VARIABLE ANNUITIES FIXED INCOME INDEX

[dividends included; year-end]

| Year | Yield* | Compound return on a five year $10,000 investment | Annual compound rate of return |
|---|---|---|---|
| 1995 | 12.53% | 1991 - 1995 | |
| 1994 | -4.72% | | 9.16% |
| 1993 | 11.18% | ... $15,498 | |
| 1992 | 8.25% | | |
| 1991 | 20.10% | | |
| 1990 | 2.80% | | |
| 1989 | 8.02% | | |
| 1988 | 0.35% | 1986 - 1990 | |
| 1987 | 12.67% | | 8.54% |
| 1986 | 19.98% | ... $15,064 | |
| 1985 | 10.79% | | |

How a $10,000 investment performed over

| 5 years | 10 years |
|---|---|
| 1991 - 1995<br>$15,498<br>(9.16%)^ | 1986 - 1995<br>$23,345<br>(8.85%) |

^ annual compound rate of return for that period
* Source: ©1995 Lipper Analytical Services

©1996 Chase Global Data & Research
73 Junction Square, Concord, MA 01742

## Lipper General Fixed Income Variable Annuity Index^

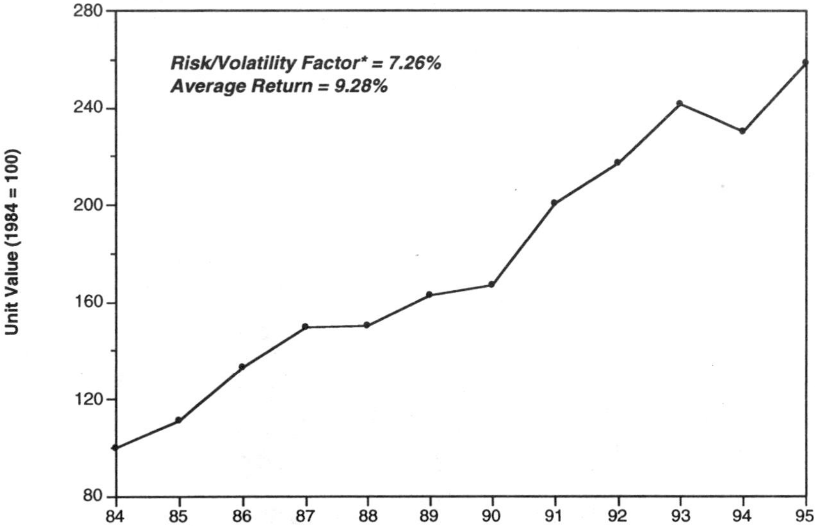


*Standard Deviation
^dividends included

## Lipper General Fixed Income Variable Annuity Index^ vs. 3-Month Certificate of Deposit, Lehman Brothers Government/Corporate Bond Index, and Lipper Fixed Income Fund Average^

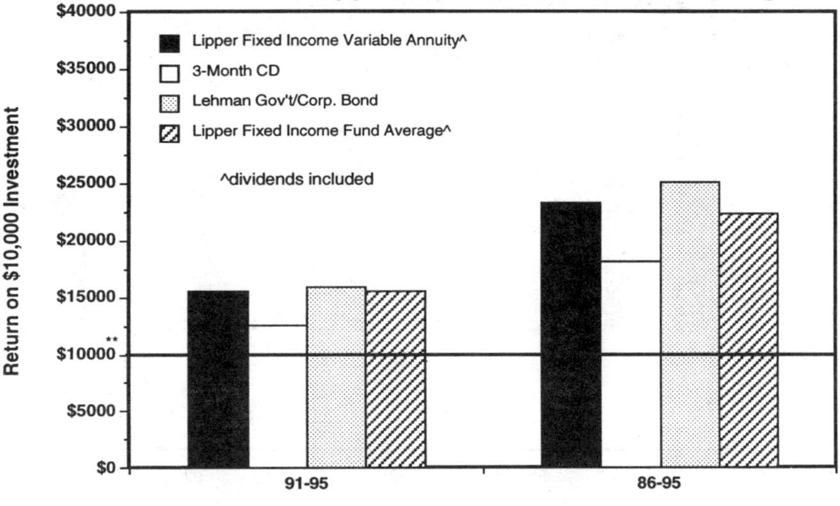


**Initial Investment: $10,000

©1996 Chase Global Data & Research
73 Junction Square, Concord, MA 01742

## Lipper General Fixed Income Variable Annuity Index^ vs. S&P 500 Composite Index^, Morgan Stanley North America Equity Index^, and House Price Index

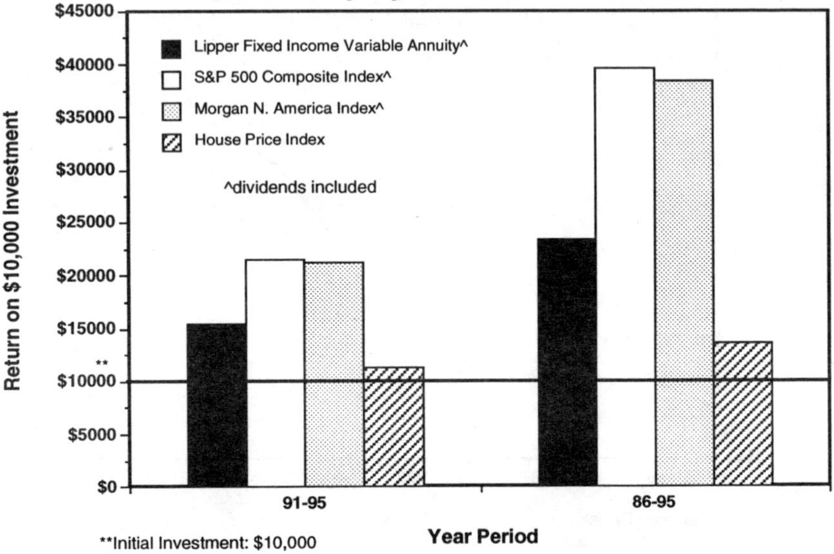


## Lipper General Fixed Income Variable Annuity Index^ vs. Inflation

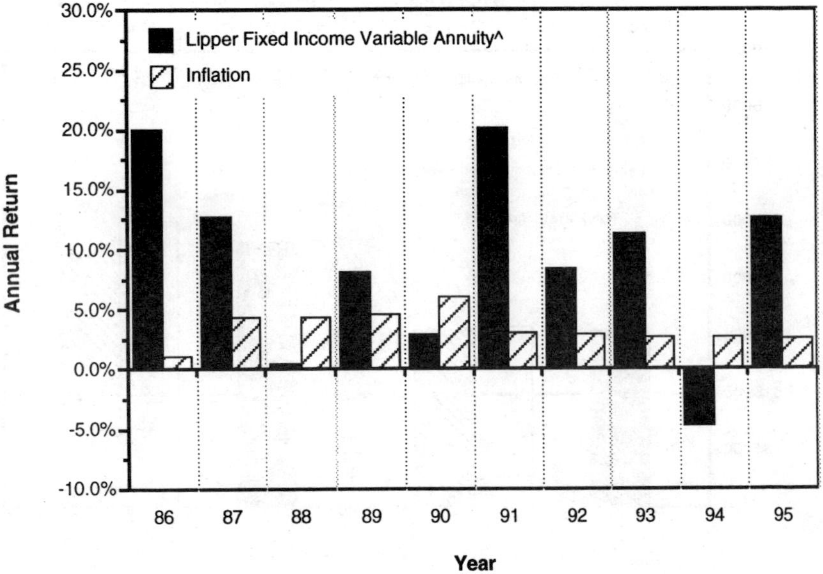


©1996 Chase Global Data & Research
73 Junction Square, Concord, MA 01742

SECTION VIII

# Commodities/Metals/Collectibles

Chapter Thirty

# Commodities

Commodity markets have been in existence for thousands of years—trading raw materials and foodstuffs which are the basis of daily life. The more formalized commodity marketplaces first appeared in the Medieval Ages and helped establish the standardization of bill of trade contracts and purchase and sale agreements. Commodity marketplaces were also the forerunners of all the world's stock exchanges.

Today, commodities are primarily traded in two ways: futures contracts and spot price transactions. Commodity exchanges establish certain forms of lots of standard quantities and agreed upon qualities. These lots, in total, represent a contract. Futures contracts reflect agreements for the receipt or future delivery of a particular asset at a given date in the future—at a predetermined price. Thus, you can lock in today a transaction at a certain price for a given date in the future by using a futures contract. Futures contracts range in duration from one month to two years. The vast majority of commodity exchange transactions are in futures, not in spot price transactions.

A spot price transaction is the equivalent of a normal transaction priced on a given day and completed on the same day. Therefore spot prices are today's market prices. Because the Commodity Spot Price Index does not have the speculative element of future pricing, it reflects fewer mathematical vagaries than futures indexes. Thus spot prices are a better reflection of true commodity pricings necessary for a clear historical review.

Today, more than ever, commodity marketplaces are international marketplaces. Grains and foodstuffs traded in various parts of the world are tied together through the growing capabilities of global communications. Producing countries, often less sophisticated than manufacturing nations, now are able to market their goods in a sophisticated manner through the use of commodity marketplaces. The chain of a commodities marketplace begins with the most basic


©1996 Chase Global Data & Research
73 Junction Square, Concord, MA 01742

element: a collection of the given crop by a local merchant from each farmer in a small area. Some small growers still sell their goods on regular market days in small towns. But on a larger scale, the local merchant collects the goods and then ships them to warehouses where they are sorted to meet requirements of the final customer. For example, cotton is sorted into bales of equal staple length; rubber is separated into various qualities; wool is standardized by grades; and oils and seeds are made up into parcels of commonly accepted grades of quality.

Most of the world's raw materials are sold directly to the final user by a contact who is usually an exporter. In many cases exporters deal with importing agents who arrange for distribution of the goods. Thus only a small percentage of the tonnage of most commodities actually passes through commodity exchanges. Nevertheless, because the commodity exchanges represent a sufficient portion of buyers and sellers, their pricing directly impacts transactions being done throughout the world.

The usage of spot and futures markets declined considerably during World War II. It took almost one decade before their use markedly resumed. Most experts agree that in today's world, futures trading is a valuable function of commodity exchanges in aiding international trade because it reduces risks for both the buyer and the seller. For example, a New York merchant buys a large load of tin to be delivered from Malaysia. The merchant intends to resell the tin to a smelting plant. Under normal circumstances the merchant pays for the metal in Malaysia, but he runs the risk of prices going lower during the month that it takes the shipped metal to arrive at the smelting plant, which is when he sells the tin. To avoid this risk the merchant deals in a future which guarantees a price for the metal through a contract which will expire at the time the metal is expected to arrive at the smelting plant. He has guaranteed himself a price for the tin one month from the time he buys it, without risk. The merchant's transaction is called hedging.

Speculators are also involved in the commodity marketplace. They hope to profit through a rise or decline in the current price of a commodity. Speculators are an important part of commodity trading because they initiate additional trading which in turn creates greater liquidity in the commodity marketplace. They provide an additional dimension to commodity exchange trading that otherwise would be limited to merchants trading among themselves. Speculators also help to iron out price fluctuations because they tend to step in during times of uncertainty as they continually monitor price changes. Without speculators, illiquidity and greater price fluctuation would no doubt occur.

©1996 Chase Global Data & Research
73 Junction Square, Concord, MA 01742

The world's major commodity marketplaces are in New York, London, and Chicago, with Chicago's Board of Trade (CBOT) being the largest. New York and London are the premier exchanges trading metals, with the COMEX being the major metals exchange. Chicago is the key exchange for wheat, corn, and other farm produce, in addition to several financial futures. Other key commodity marketplaces are in Bombay; Antwerp; Amsterdam; Singapore; Colombo (Sri Lanka); Liverpool; Milan; Sydney; New Zealand; South Africa; Roubaix, France; Dundee, Scotland; Pakistan; and Toronto. Key U.S. commodity marketplaces are in Dallas, Houston, New Orleans, Memphis, and Boston, in addition to New York and Chicago.

The Commodity Spot Index was originally tracked and computed by the Bureau of Labor Statistics of the U.S. Government. In May, 1981, the Commodity Research Bureau (CRB) began tracking the Spot Index incorporating data from the Bureau's past statistics. The Commodity Research Bureau Spot Index uses a base of 100, from 1967. The CRB Futures Index is based on 17 commodities. The CRB Spot Index which follows is based on 23 commodities: barley, cattle, cocoa, coffee, copper, corn, cotton, crude oil, flax seed, gold, heating oil, hogs, lumber, oats, orange juice, platinum, pork bellies, potatoes, rye, silver, soybeans, sugar, and wheat.

1991 saw the first decline in futures related commodity trading in the United States in 22 years. The industry had experienced an enviable growth pattern over the past two decades. Total futures volume was over 262 million contracts in 1991, down 4.9% from 1990. Futures Options volume was 62 million contracts, down 3%. International competition and off-exchange trading were the primary reasons for the decline, which has since reversed itself.

The CRB Commodity Spot Index registered its sharpest gain in a decade in 1994 (+16.52%). In fact, it was the #1 performer for 1994 of all subjects followed by Chase Global Data & Research. This strong move reversed recent lackluster trends of the past five years. However, over the past thirty five years the CRB Spot Index has maintained only a 3% average return for most periods, or worse. In fact, the CRB Commodity Spot Index 35 year return of 3.19% is the worst performer in Chase Global Data & Research's rankings when currencies are excluded. It has done well, however, during times of uncertainty and high inflation. Its best performance occurred between 1968 and 1980 when it tripled over a dozen years. It followed that twelve year upward movement with a static change of 0.13% per year over the ensuing 15 years through 1995.

©1996 Chase Global Data & Research
73 Junction Square, Concord, MA 01742

**COMMODITY SPOT MARKET INDEX**
[CRB-BLS; 1967=100; 23 raw materials; year-end]

| Year | Index Value* | Index Growth | Compound return on a five year $10,000 investment | Annual compound rate of return |
|---|---|---|---|---|
| 1995 | 289.10 | 1.09% | 1991 - 1995 | |
| 1994 | 285.98 | 16.52% | | 2.29% |
| 1993 | 245.44 | 4.32% | ... $11,200 | |
| 1992 | 235.27 | -1.25% | | |
| 1991 | 238.24 | -7.71% | | |
| 1990 | 258.13 | -0.95% | 1986 - 1990 | |
| 1989 | 260.60 | -8.35% | | 1.75% |
| 1988 | 284.35 | 10.12% | ... $10,905 | |
| 1987 | 258.21 | 13.10% | | |
| 1986 | 228.30 | -3.55% | | |
| 1985 | 236.70 | -7.97% | 1981 - 1985 | |
| 1984 | 257.20 | -7.42% | | -3.54% |
| 1983 | 277.80 | 22.16% | ... $ 8,349 | |
| 1982 | 227.40 | -9.04% | | |
| 1981 | 250.00 | -11.82% | | |
| 1980 | 283.50 | -1.39% | 1976 - 1980 | |
| 1979 | 287.50 | 14.86% | | 8.53% |
| 1978 | 250.30 | 17.40% | ... $15,056 | |
| 1977 | 213.20 | 5.60% | | |
| 1976 | 201.90 | 7.22% | | |
| 1975 | 188.30 | -9.43% | 1971 - 1975 | |
| 1974 | 207.90 | 0.92% | | 12.14% |
| 1973 | 206.00 | 57.73% | ... $17,731 | |
| 1972 | 130.60 | 21.71% | | |
| 1971 | 107.30 | 1.04% | | |
| 1970 | 106.20 | -7.57% | 1966 - 1970 | |
| 1969 | 114.90 | 13.99% | | -1.06% |
| 1968 | 100.80 | 2.54% | ... $ 9,482 | |
| 1967 | 98.30 | -6.38% | | |
| 1966 | 105.00 | -6.25% | | |
| 1965 | 112.00 | 7.18% | 1961 - 1965 | |
| 1964 | 104.50 | 7.40% | | 3.05% |
| 1963 | 97.30 | 3.18% | ... $11,618 | |
| 1962 | 94.30 | -5.61% | | |
| 1961 | 99.90 | 3.63% | | |
| 1960 | 96.40 | -1.63% | | |

How a $10,000 investment performed over

| 5 years | 10 years | 15 years | 20 years | 25 years | 35 years |
|---|---|---|---|---|---|
| 1991 - 1995 | | | | | |
| $11,200 (2.29%)^ | 1986 - 1995 | | | | |
| | $12,214 (2.02%) | 1981 - 1995 | | | |
| | | $10,198 (0.13%) | 1976 - 1995 | | |
| | | | $15,353 (2.17%) | 1971 - 1995 | |
| | | | | $27,222 (4.09%) | 1961 - 1995 |
| | | | | | $29,990 (3.19%) |

^ annual compound rate of return for that period
* Source: Commodities Research Bureau; Bureau of Labor Statistics.

©1996 Chase Global Data & Research
73 Junction Square, Concord, MA 01742

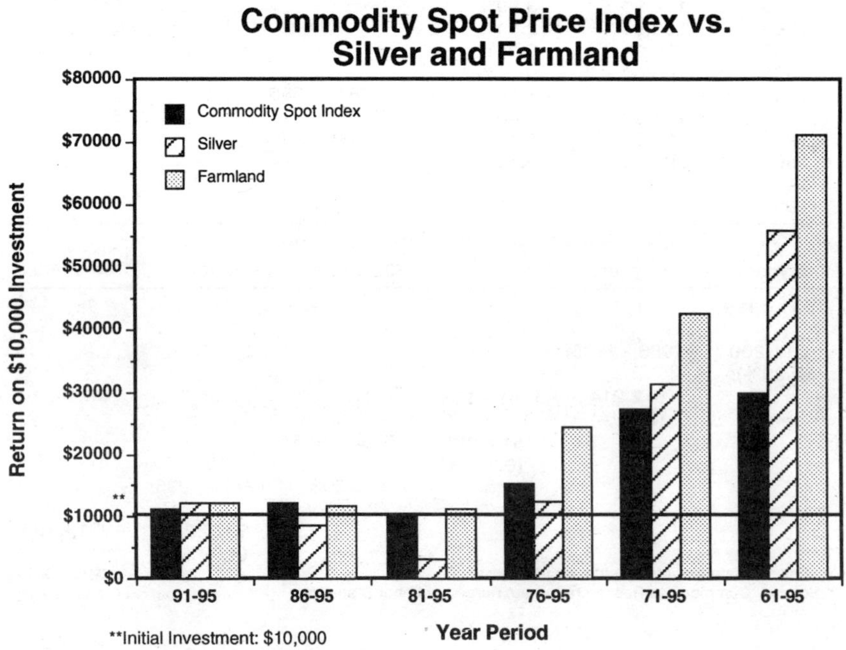


©1996 Chase Global Data & Research
73 Junction Square, Concord, MA 01742

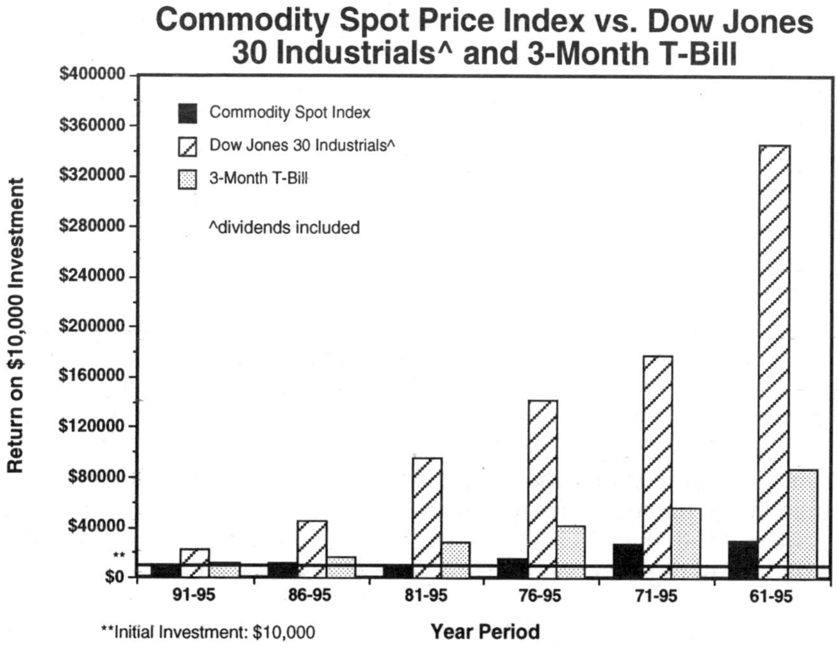


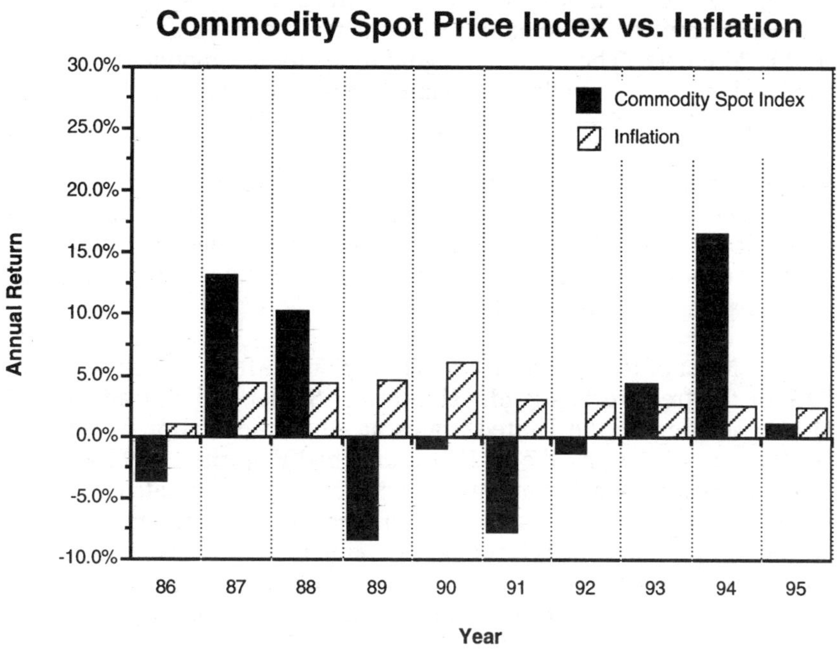


©1996 Chase Global Data & Research
73 Junction Square, Concord, MA 01742

Chapter Thirty One

# Gold

For thousands of years, Gold has been the one metal that could be used as "money" anywhere on the globe. The first official use of gold was in 700 B.C. when King Croesus of Lydia created gold coins that established a unit of monetary value. Since then it has been hoarded by Emperors, Kings, and Czars, crafted into religious artifacts and funeral ornaments by the Pharaohs and the Incas, and plundered and hidden by pirates. Treasure hunters still search for sunken Spanish galleons and the hidden gold of the ransomed Inca King, Atalpha. Miners still dig a ton of ore for a yield of one ounce of gold.

Gold is one of 103 elements of which the world is made and ranks with platinum and diamonds as a precious substance. Gold doesn't rust and most other substances can't harm it. Gold can be beaten to a thickness of 5 one-millionths of an inch. An ounce of gold can be beaten to cover an area of 300 square feet—as is the case with gold leaf. Pure gold is 24 carats. The fineness of gold refers to the amount of parts per thousand of gold in an alloy—a ranking of 1000 is 100% gold; a ranking of 500 is 50% gold and 50% alloys.

Gold has many practical applications because of its excellent ability to conduct electricity and to reflect heat while allowing light to pass through it. Gold is used in computers, telecommunication equipment, the treatment of cancer, to patch damaged blood vessels, help repair nerves, and heal bones.

Most of today's gold is mined in South Africa, which produces 70% of the free world's gold. The former Soviet Union, Canada, and to a lesser degree the United States are the other major world gold producers. (Although the United States had a spirited Gold Rush in 1848, now only a small amount is mined here.) It is estimated that there are .001 parts per million of gold in the earth's crust and .004 parts per billion in the sea. Meteorites have contained gold in concentrations as high as 0.7 parts per million, considerably higher than the earth's crust and seas. Therefore scientists theorize that as we dig deeper into the


©1996 Chase Global Data & Research
73 Junction Square, Concord, MA 01742

earth's surface concentrations of gold may become much higher than previously assumed. To date only 100,000 tons have been mined, which is the amount of steel poured by the world's industries in only one hour.

The United States first assigned a monetary role to gold in 1792 when Congress adopted a bimetallic standard using gold and silver to back the the nation's currency. By 1816 Great Britain had dropped bimetallic standards, exclusively using gold, and by 1900 the United States had followed suit. In the 1930's most nations as a result of the Depression revised their gold policy and severed any relationship of their currencies to gold. The United States banned private ownership and export of gold in 1934, and raised the fixing for the price of gold from $20.67 to $35 an ounce. With the Bretton Woods Agreement in 1944, the world monetary system recognized gold again on a formal basis. At this time, world paper currencies were fixed in relation to the U.S. dollar, which was in turn tied to gold. In 1971, the Bretton Woods Agreement was cancelled when President Nixon ended the dollar convertibility into gold. Nevertheless, today about one-third of the world's reserve of gold is held in U.S. Treasury vaults as a form of backing for its circulating currency.

For thousands of years gold has been a volatile investment—especially in the recent past. However, many people favor gold because its relative value versus other alternative investments has remained quite constant over the course of many years, although its volatility might not be worth the aggravation. Gold reached its highest price ever in 1980 when it sold for $850 per ounce. But if you purchased gold at that level, to merely attain an 8% annual rate of return the metal would have had to reach $2,683 per ounce by the end of 1995. Of note, after inflation, gold was worth less in 1995 than in 1975 when it was priced at $140 per ounce.

Also keep in mind that strange occurrences can happen in the gold marketplace, such as the giant purchase by the Japanese government of 2,000 tons of gold to mint coins commemorating the late Hirohito's 60-year reign. Such purchases send the price of gold skyrocketing, while major selling efforts send it into a nosedive. Politics in gold pricing is also not an unusual event—as in the case of the former Soviet Union choosing to sell some of its large position in gold, or when the United States sells gold from its Fort Knox vault. Regarding Fort Knox and its gold reserves.... those numbers are not well known but they are striking nevertheless. The United States government has approximately $5 trillion in obligations. But U.S. gold reserves backing that enormous figure represent less than 1% of it.

©1996 Chase Global Data & Research
73 Junction Square, Concord, MA 01742

Among its many attributes, gold is famous as an inflation hedge. It is also a common recommendation of the Armageddon soothsayers who periodically predict a debacle in world economies. But today many experts feel that the inflation hedge shine may be a thing of the past, and gold is headed into a new era. Remember, too, that in the modern era gold maintained a fixed price until 1968. The fixed pricing has impacted the return of gold for the *Chase Investment Performance Digest's* 35 year overall return.

When investing in gold, you needn't exclusively buy the metal itself. You can buy gold stocks. But they can be quite risky, with price earnings ratios frequently very high. In addition, many gold companies are not of United States origin and therefore SEC type regulatory overseeing may not apply. Thus in the case of a gold mining security you may not fully know what you are buying. And if you are interested in gold coins, keep in mind that dealers markup gold coins between 2% and 10% or more before selling them to the public.

Recent technological advances in locating and mining gold have increased the search for it. For example, there is an island in the Pacific which is thought to have 12 million ounces of gold—worth over $4 billion. Discovered in 1982, the island of Lihir may contain one of the largest, undeveloped gold deposits in the world. Many high technology gold experts would agree to the possibility of a future glut in gold—which would send prices down. Some even say that low grade gold ore will be mined in the future employing a technological difficulty factor equivalent to today's desalinating salt water into fresh water.

As you will see in the Performance Tables that follow, gold can still boggle the minds of more than kings. It ranked in the top 10% in several past ranking period intervals, but in several other rankings it was in the bottom 10%. In Chase Global Data & Research's Volatility Rankings over the past 20 and 35 years, Gold ranked 3rd. Only Crude Petroleum and Silver were more consistently volatile. Remember, like commodities such as silver and wheat, gold provides no benefit to an investor other than the potential for price appreciation—except for its beauty. It does not pay dividends and you cannot rent out gold as you could your house. These facts alone set apart commodity investments such as gold from many alternatives. If you need cash flow from investments, no matter how small the amount, look elsewhere.

©1996 Chase Global Data & Research
73 Junction Square, Concord, MA 01742

**GOLD**
[1968-1995 New York spot price; $ per troy ounce; year-end]

| Year | Price* ($/troy ounce) | Price Growth | Compound return on a five year $10,000 investment | Annual compound rate of return |
|---|---|---|---|---|
| 1995 | 386.95 | 1.19% | 1991 - 1995 | |
| 1994 | 382.40 | -2.39% | | -0.30% |
| 1993 | 391.75 | 17.54% | ... $ 9,852 | |
| 1992 | 333.30 | -5.63% | | |
| 1991 | 353.20 | -10.07% | | |
| 1990 | 392.75 | -2.52% | 1986 - 1990 | |
| 1989 | 402.90 | -1.95% | | 3.56% |
| 1988 | 410.90 | -15.11% | ... $11,912 | |
| 1987 | 484.05 | 21.93% | | |
| 1986 | 397.00 | 20.41% | | |
| 1985 | 329.70 | 6.94% | 1981 - 1985 | |
| 1984 | 308.30 | -19.19% | | -10.87% |
| 1983 | 381.50 | -16.50% | ... $ 5,626 | |
| 1982 | 456.90 | 13.94% | | |
| 1981 | 401.00 | -31.57% | | |
| 1980 | 586.00 | 14.45% | 1976 - 1980 | |
| 1979 | 512.00 | 126.55% | | 33.09% |
| 1978 | 226.00 | 37.00% | ... $41,753 | |
| 1977 | 164.96 | 22.42% | | |
| 1976 | 134.75 | -3.99% | | |
| 1975 | 140.35 | -24.85% | 1971 - 1975 | |
| 1974 | 186.75 | 66.30% | | 30.10% |
| 1973 | 112.30 | 72.24% | ... $37,278 | |
| 1972 | 65.20 | 48.69% | | |
| 1971 | 43.85 | 16.47% | | |
| 1970 | 37.65 | 6.21% | 1966 - 1970 | |
| 1969 | 35.45 | -15.70% | | 1.47% |
| 1968 | 42.05 | 20.14% | ... $10,757 | |
| 1967 | 35.00 | 0.00% | | |
| 1966 | 35.00 | 0.00% | | |
| 1965 | 35.00 | 0.00% | 1961 -1965 | 0.00% |
| 1964 | 35.00 | 0.00% | | |
| 1963 | 35.00 | 0.00% | ... $10,000 | |
| 1962 | 35.00 | 0.00% | | |
| 1961 | 35.00 | 0.00% | | |
| 1960 | 35.00 | 0.00% | | |

How a $10,000 investment performed over

| 5 years | 10 years | 15 years | 20 years | 25 years | 35 years |
|---|---|---|---|---|---|
| 1991 - 1995 | | | | | |
| $9,852 (-0.30%)^ | 1986 - 1995 | | | | |
| | $11,736 (1.61%) | 1981 - 1995 | | | |
| | | $6,603 (-2.73%) | 1976 - 1995 | | |
| | | | $27,570 (5.20%) | 1971 - 1995 | |
| | | | | $102,776 (9.77%) | 1961 - 1995 |
| | | | | | $110,557 (7.11%) |

^ annual compound rate of return for that period
* Source: American Metal Market, Handy & Harman; U.S. Bureau of Mines.

©1996 Chase Global Data & Research
73 Junction Square, Concord, MA 01742

## Gold

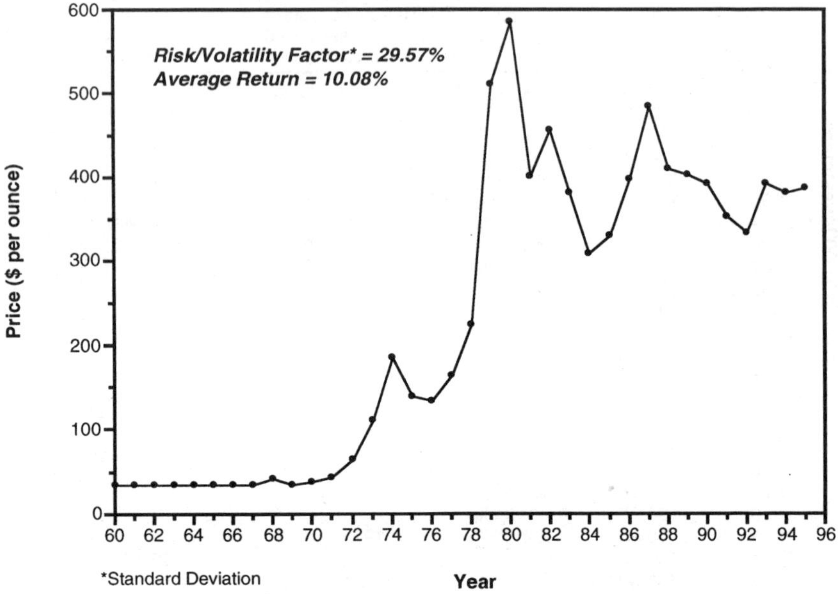


*Standard Deviation

## Gold vs. Commodity Spot Index and Silver

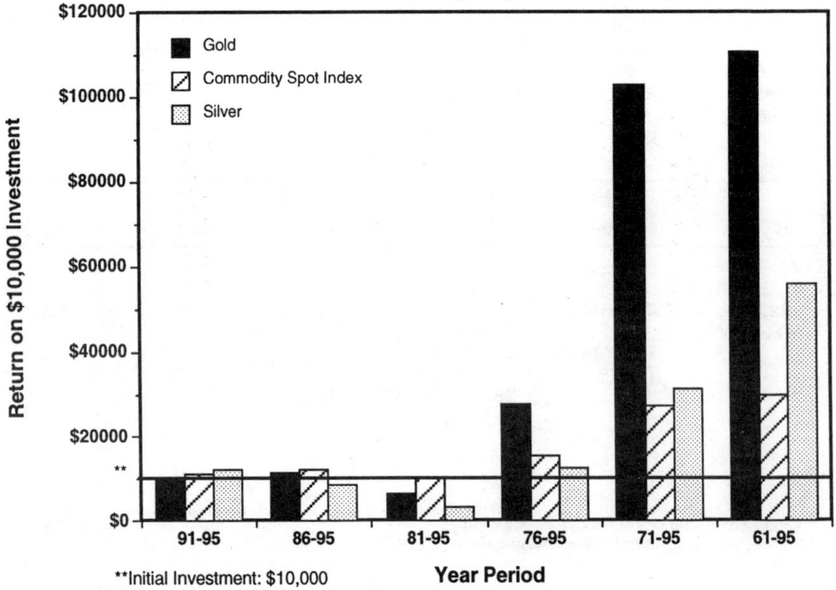


**Initial Investment: $10,000

©1996 Chase Global Data & Research
73 Junction Square, Concord, MA 01742

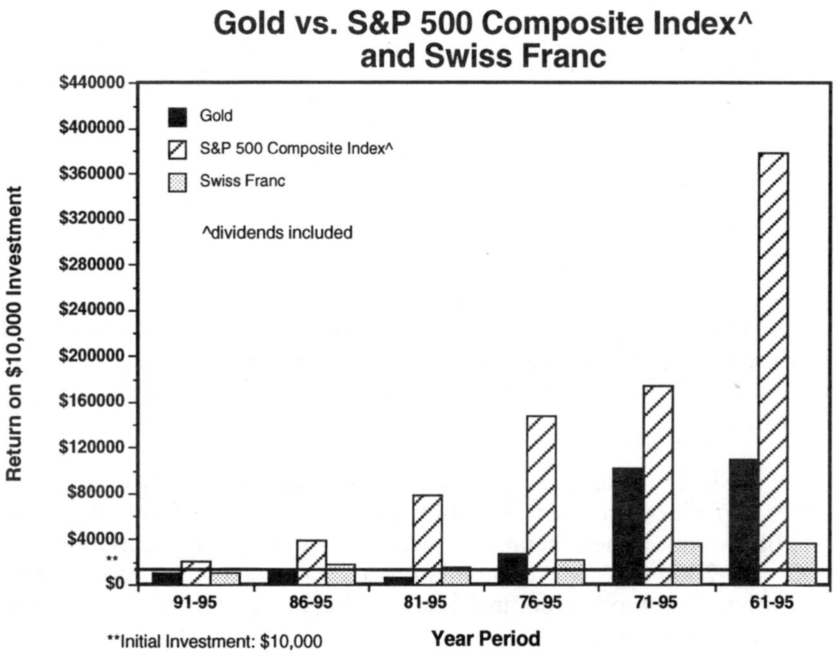


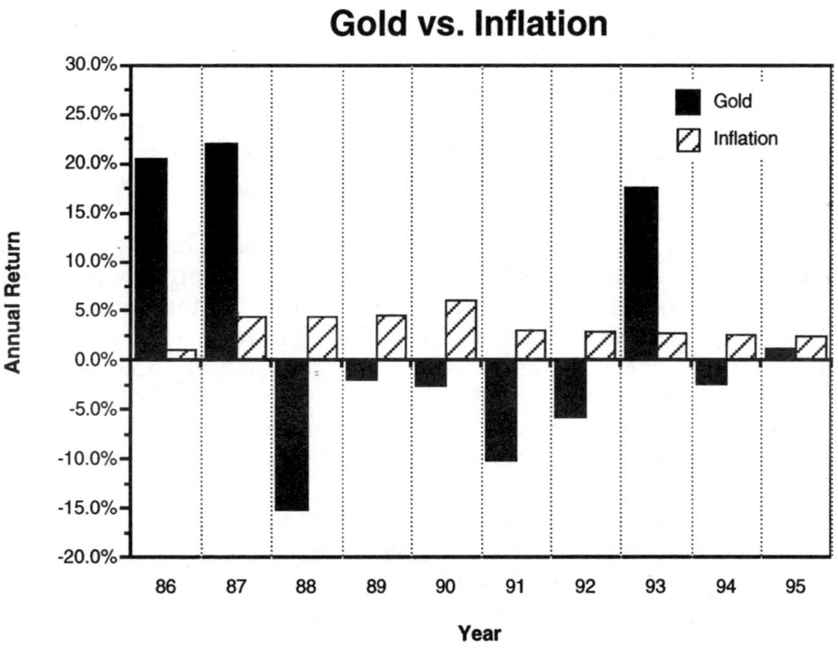


©1996 Chase Global Data & Research
73 Junction Square, Concord, MA 01742

# Chapter Thirty Two

# Silver

Since ancient times silver has played an important role with civilized man, shoring up governments, facilitating commerce, aiding industry, and memorializing the imagination of silversmiths such as Paul Revere.

Silver makes up 1/100 millionth of the earth's crust. Because silver deposits were plentiful on or near the earth's surface, silver was one of the first mined metals and was refined in Egypt as early as 3500 B.C. By 2000 B.C. Mesopotamian merchants used silver as a method of exchange for other commodities. Already silver had become the coin of the merchant class. The very wealthy preferred gold. As early as 1900 B.C., the Babylonians had fixed the value of silver to gold at 1 to 6. By Roman times silver was so plentiful that the ratio increased to 1 to 25. At this time Rome controlled the Spanish silver mines, as spoils of the Punic wars. These mines supplied the major share of the world's silver until the 8th century when the Moors seized and closed the mines. They later reopened and once again, silver, in the form of the Spanish silver dollar, dominated exchange and trade in the 15th and 16th centuries. Mexico, Peru, and Bolivia also became large producers of silver in the 15th century.

Silver in the United States has had a colorful history. In 1792 the Congress of the United States used silver as a currency base and adopted a bimetallic standard of silver and gold. At that time a silver dollar contained 0.77 ounces of silver, making it worth $1.29 per ounce. With the discovery of the Nevada Comstock lode in 1859, the U.S. joined the ranks of the world's major silver producers. From 1871 to 1900 the U.S. led the world in silver production. In 1900 Congress officially adopted a gold monetary standard. In 1965, the silver content of newly minted quarters and dimes was eliminated, and the U.S. Treasury stopped issuing silver certificates of paper money and instead issued Federal Reserve Notes. At the same time the silver content in the half dollar was reduced to 40%, and in 1970 the coin's silver content was eliminated entirely.

 ©1996 Chase Global Data & Research
73 Junction Square, Concord, MA 01742

Silver was price supported by the U.S. government for over 50 years from 1878 to 1933. After supports were pulled, silver's price dropped to as low as $0.25 per ounce during the 1930's. Not until 1960 did the price of silver begin to rise above the earlier values of over $1.00 per ounce. Then, as silver prices began to explode, the U.S. treasury began to liquidate huge silver stocks in order to keep its currency silver based, but it failed. By 1972, the price of silver was over $2.00 an ounce.

Silver has always been an important raw material to industry. It is a superb conductor of both electricity and heat and is a crucial element in film development. The primary industrial use for silver today is in such applications as photography, electronics, sterling ware, jewelry, coins, catalysts, alloys, solders, dentistry and mirror backings. In 1990 industrial demand for silver represented 60% of total usage, investment demand 35%, and coinage 5%. It is estimated that the electronics industry will triple in size over this decade, and thus likely constitutes the primary user of silver in the future. Today Peru and Mexico are the primary producers of silver. Secondary silver sources include coin and scrap metal refinement. Historically silver rides the waves produced by political climates, riding high in less orderly times and declining in periods of political stability. Total annual world output of mined silver is approximately 400 million ounces, produced by the following countries: Peru 14%; Mexico 14%; Russia 13%; Canada 11%; U.S. 11%; other countries 37%.

Today, as in ancient times, silver is considered the poor man's gold. Worldwide demand has edged up slowly since the early 1980's—when silver experienced one of the greatest declines in investment history. Silver dropped from its all time high of over $50 per ounce in January 1980, to $10.80 two months later. By 1986 silver had halved in price to $5 per ounce. Since then silver's pricing has remained relatively unchanged, although in the 1990s it has frequently sold for less than $4 per ounce. Because the second largest demand for silver is by investors, silver trading is maintained in a liquid marketplace. About 40 billion troy ounces are traded annually on the Commodity Exchange Inc. (COMEX)—the world's most liquid silver futures market.

Due to technological changes in the mining of both silver and gold, and the changing demands for each, the old relationship between silver and gold is no longer a reliable basis for investment. However, it is one way to analyze the present value of silver in the marketplace. For example at year end 1995, when gold sold for $387 per ounce and

©1996 Chase Global Data & Research
73 Junction Square, Concord, MA 01742

silver was priced at $5.11 per ounce, the ratio was 76 to 1. Historically this is quite high (in 1816 it was 16 to 1, where it remained until the mid 1800's). 1990's closing ratio of 95 to 1 is thought to be the highest ratio ever. However, investors should remember the many variables: the technological impact on mining gold and silver; changing industrial demands; fickle instincts of investors who seesaw between gold and silver; and the general volatility of silver. In 1993, for example, Xerox annnounced a major new technological variable... development of a photographic process which required no use of silver.

The expense, or commission, for purchasing various forms of silver such as 100-ounce or 10-ounce bars versus coins such as silver American Eagles can greatly vary. Some recent examples of expense levels were the one ounce Eagle premium at 22%; a 10-ounce bar at 14%; and a 100-ounce bar at 6%. Insurance and storage are additional expenses for silver holders. Major brokerage houses and banks charge storage fees for silver of approximately 0.4% annually. All of these risks and expenses must be duly considered to properly evaluate a silver investment, both before and after the dust settles.

Strange things seem to happen in the silver marketplace—like the time the Hunt family between 1979 and 1980 accumulated over 200 million ounces of silver, raising the price from $11 per ounce to over $50 per ounce. The market subsequently crashed. By 1985 the Hunts announced they had sold 90% of their silver holdings, leaving the market in disarray. In 1988 the Hunts filed for bankruptcy, not in the least due to their foray into the silver markets.

Silver, in large part due to the Hunt brothers intervention into the marketplace in 1979-1980, has certainly proven itself an extremely poor performer especially in relation to its volatility. Its performance ranks in the bottom quartile over the past quarter century among all subjects tracked by Chase Global Data & Research. It was #1 in volatility over the past 20 years, and #2 over the past 35 years, second only to Crude Petroleum.

©1996 Chase Global Data & Research
73 Junction Square, Concord, MA 01742

## SILVER

[New York spot price; ¢ per troy ounce; year-end]

| Year | Price* (¢/troy ounce) | Price Growth | Compound return on a five year $10,000 investment | Annual compound rate of return |
|---|---|---|---|---|
| 1995 | 511.0 | 4.93% | 1991 - 1995 | |
| 1994 | 487.0 | -4.13% | | 4.12% |
| 1993 | 508.0 | 38.42% | ... $12,240 | |
| 1992 | 367.0 | -4.68% | | |
| 1991 | 385.0 | -7.78% | | |
| 1990 | 417.5 | -19.40% | 1986 - 1990 | |
| 1989 | 518.0 | -13.95% | | -6.46% |
| 1988 | 602.0 | -10.08% | ... $ 7,161 | |
| 1987 | 669.5 | 24.79% | | |
| 1986 | 536.5 | -7.98% | | |
| 1985 | 583.0 | -8.33% | 1981 - 1985 | |
| 1984 | 636.0 | -28.94% | | -17.66% |
| 1983 | 895.0 | -18.23% | ... $ 3,786 | |
| 1982 | 1094.5 | 32.67% | | |
| 1981 | 825.0 | -46.43% | | |
| 1980 | 1540.0 | -29.33% | 1976 - 1980 | |
| 1979 | 2179.0 | 267.45% | | 30.40% |
| 1978 | 593.0 | 26.01% | ... $37,699 | |
| 1977 | 470.6 | 8.26% | | |
| 1976 | 434.7 | 6.41% | | |
| 1975 | 408.5 | -6.97% | 1971 - 1975 | |
| 1974 | 439.1 | 39.97% | | 20.10% |
| 1973 | 313.7 | 58.76% | ... $24,985 | |
| 1972 | 197.6 | 41.75% | | |
| 1971 | 139.4 | -14.74% | | |
| 1970 | 163.5 | -9.52% | 1966 - 1970 | |
| 1969 | 180.7 | -7.76% | | 4.81% |
| 1968 | 195.9 | -5.18% | ... $12,645 | |
| 1967 | 206.6 | 59.78% | | |
| 1966 | 129.3 | 0.00% | | |
| 1965 | 129.3 | 0.00% | 1961 - 1965 | |
| 1964 | 129.3 | 0.00% | | 7.18% |
| 1963 | 129.3 | 7.84% | ... $14,147 | |
| 1962 | 119.9 | 16.07% | | |
| 1961 | 103.3 | 13.02% | | |
| 1960 | 91.4 | 0.00% | | |

How a $10,000 investment performed over

| 5 years | 10 years | 15 years | 20 years | 25 years | 35 years |
|---|---|---|---|---|---|
| 1991 - 1995 | | | | | |
| $12,240 (4.12%)^ | 1986 - 1995 | | | | |
| | $8,765 (-1.31%) | 1981 - 1995 | | | |
| | | $3,318 (-7.09%) | 1976 - 1995 | | |
| | | | $12,509 (1.13%) | 1971 - 1995 | |
| | | | | $31,254 (4.66%) | 1961 - 1995 |
| | | | | | $55,908 (5.04%) |

^ annual compound rate of return for that period
* Source: American Metal Market, Handy & Harman.

©1996 Chase Global Data & Research
73 Junction Square, Concord, MA 01742

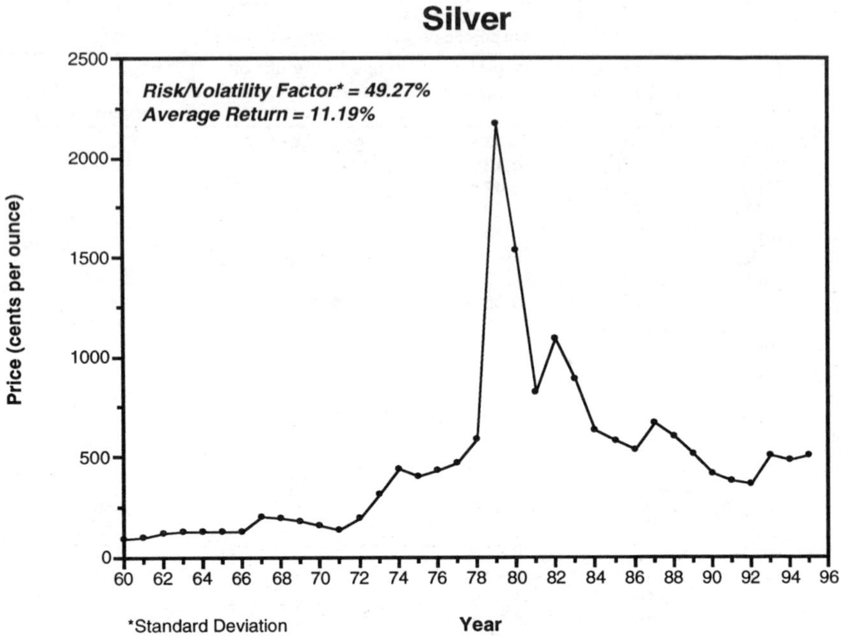


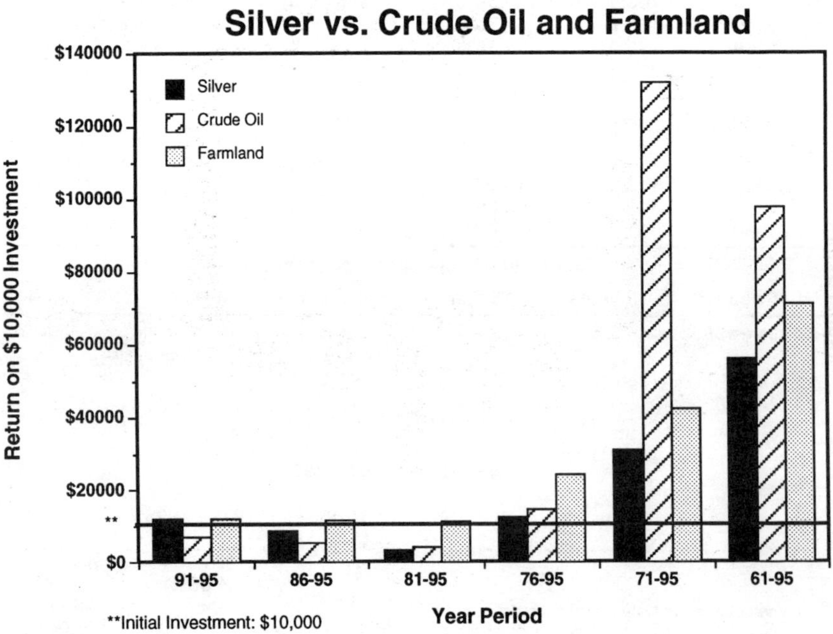


©1996 Chase Global Data & Research
73 Junction Square, Concord, MA 01742

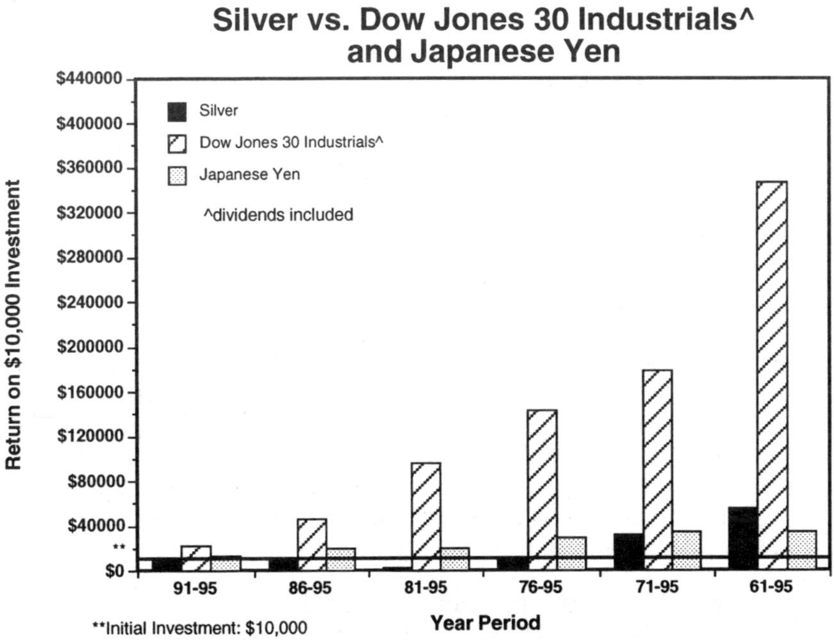


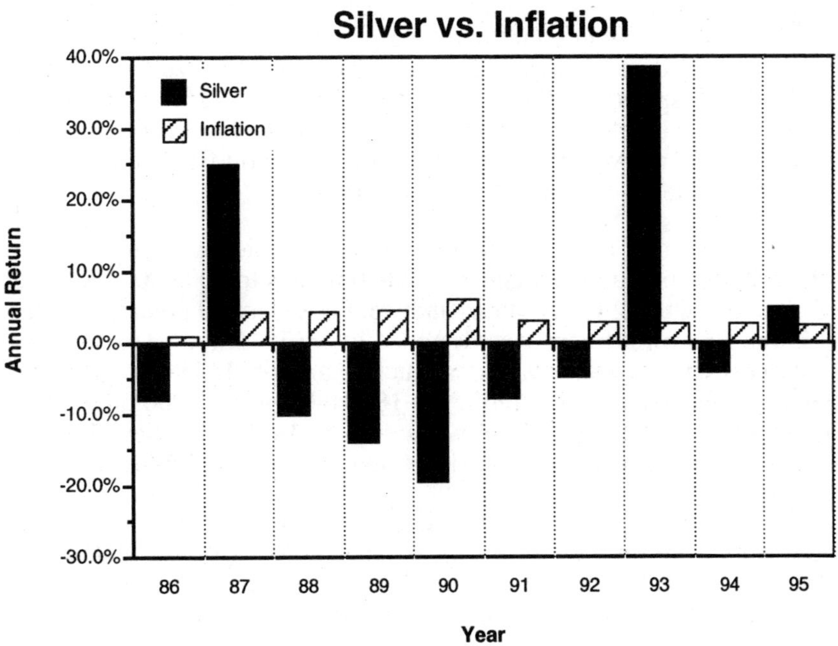


©1996 Chase Global Data & Research
73 Junction Square, Concord, MA 01742

# Chapter Thirty Three

# Crude Petroleum

Oil is one of the most important natural resources on this planet. Yet, if it continues to be consumed at its present pace, experts predict that it will no longer exist sometime in the first quarter of the 21st century. Crude petroleum appears in many forms, but primarily in a liquid state found in subterranean deposits. It can have a pleasant odor or a sour smell depending on the content of sulphur. Today oil is mostly used for fuel, but is also used in medicinal oils, sprays, cosmetics, explosives, detergents, and ointments.

Long before the birth of Christ, oil was seeping out of the ground near the Black and Caspian Seas and used for heating, lubrication, and caulking boat seams. The Persians used incendiary arrows wrapped in oil-soaked cloth during their siege of Athens in 480 B.C. The Chinese are thought to be the first to drill for oil using bamboo shoots as both drilling equipment and pipelines several hundred years before the birth of Christ. The first barrel of Venezuelan oil was exported to Spain in 1539. Peter the Great in 1725 regulated the carriage of oil by boat. However, it wasn't until Colonel E.L. Drake (in Titusville, Pa. on August 27, 1859) found a huge oil field at a depth of 70 feet that the oil and drilling boom started.

From that point on the U.S. was at petroleum's center. From 1859 to 1860 production went from 2,000 barrels to 500,000. (A barrel of oil is equal to 42 U.S. gallons and weighs about 300 pounds.) In the U.S. the first oil refinery was designed in 1861. Three years later the first successful pipeline was constructed, and by 1875 the first steel tanker for carrying oil was built. By 1870 there were 4,000 oil wells in the U.S.; by 1903, 100,000 oil wells; and by 1985 there were 150,000 oil wells ranging in depth from 1,000 feet to over 25,000 feet.

In the early 1900's the U.S. and Russia were the primary producers of oil in the world. In the 1920's, Mexico briefly and later Venezuela were the second largest oil producers. But major discoveries can change rankings very quickly. In 1946 major expansion took place

 ©1996 Chase Global Data & Research
73 Junction Square, Concord, MA 01742

in the Middle East. By 1974 forty percent of the world's oil output came from there. In 1974, Mexico went from 17th to 4th because of major discoveries in the Gulf of Mexico. OPEC, a powerful consortium of 12 major oil producing countries was created during the early 1970's. In 1993 it supplied 60% of the world's oil production. OPEC notwithstanding, the face of global oil production changes continually. Today China, the original explorer of oil, ranks 6th in world production, with the United Kingdom 5th. Over 70 countries presently produce commercial volumes of crude oil.

While the rankings of various countries have changed, world oil production has grown steadily. In 1890 world oil production was estimated to be 73 million barrels per year. By 1900, it was 141 million per year. By 1920 it was 695 million and by the end of WW II it was 2.8 billion barrels per year—more than 150 times the level of 1900. During the two decades between 1954 and 1974 world oil production quadrupled. In 1994 total world oil production was 100 million barrels daily.

Since 1985, trading in oil-related contracts has more than doubled on American futures exchanges. For example, oil futures trading on the New York Mercantile Exchange exceeds ten million contracts, representing over ten billion barrels of oil. (A futures contract represents delivery of 1,000 barrels of oil.) Trading was fever pitched in 1990-1991 during the Kuwait Invasion and Gulf War, with prices more than doubling (from $15/barrel to $41/barrel) and then halving in less than a year. While trading on the exchanges is active, 60% of all oil trading is privately done between major oil companies—firms extremely large in size. In 1981, during oil's heyday, *Fortune* magazine's rankings of the "Top Ten" companies contained six oil companies. Of the top 20, 13 were in oil. Today, with the exception of a few, the largest companies are in banking, computer, and automotive industries.

In 1907 the first gasoline station was established. Gasoline is the most important of all petroleum products and is traded separately on U.S. futures exchanges. Approximately 46% of the end product from crude oil is gasoline. By 1982 more than 100 billion gallons of gasoline were used in U.S. automobile vehicles. Service station expense for gasoline has varied greatly in the past 40 years. In 1947, gas stations sold fuel for 17 cents a gallon. (Prices stated here exclude state and federal taxes.) By 1949, it sold for 20 cents and did not rise above 27 cents until 1973. In 1974 gasoline was 40 cents a gallon. By 1979 it was 74 cents. It climbed over $1.00 a gallon for the first time in the early 1980's. More than a decade later its price is little unchanged.

©1996 Chase Global Data & Research
73 Junction Square, Concord, MA 01742

In 1947 the average wellhead price for crude oil was $1.93 per barrel. It did not rise above $3.25 until over two decades later, in 1971. By 1974 it was $7.00 a barrel; by 1979 it was $12.00 a barrel and rose dramatically from 1980 until 1987. The costs of extracting crude from the earth vary a great deal. In Saudi Arabia the cost is as little as 50 cents per barrel—whereas in the Arctic the expense can run as high as $20 per barrel. Pipeline fees for transporting oil can also add to the overall cost of the delivered product.

One way economists evaluate the relative price of oil is to compare a barrel of oil's cost to that of an ounce of gold. In 1965 it took 13 barrels of oil to purchase an ounce of gold. In 1973 it took 26 barrels. By late 1986, when the price of gold was $393 an ounce, and oil was at $12/barrel, the ratio of gold to oil was 33 to 1—one of the highest ratios in the past 40 years. By year-end 1995 it was 24 to 1. Five major oil price drops have occurred since 1970. By far the 60% drop during a seven month period in 1986—to $9.39/barrel, was the most dramatic. That oil glut came about because the U.S. had failed to increase energy demands for the dozen years between 1973 and 1985—while overall output had increased 34%. But during the late 1980's the demand trend reversed dramatically. U.S. importing of oil had increased 50%, but by the end of the decade imports were reduced about 10%, to 45% overall. Nevertheless, today's level of imported oil is about 20% more than in 1973, when the first oil import shock occurred. And globally since 1983, non-OPEC production has declined from 68 million barrels per day to 60 million.

Ominously, in 1986 more than 23,000 wells were permanently shut-in in the United States, domestic oil production dropped 700,000 barrels a day, and the count of domestic rigs used for drilling wells dropped sharply. Since then over 5,000 small oil companies have gone bankrupt in the U.S. Traditionally, such small operations have accounted for 85% of all drilling in the U.S., and 50% of oil and gas production in the U.S. By 1987 Russia was drilling three times as many wells as the U.S. As a result of generally low prices of the recent past, investment in oil and gas exploration has dropped dramatically. In fact today many major oil companies are now simply purchasing oil reserves rather than drilling for them. U.S. domestic production peaked at 9.6 million barrels per day in 1960—and reached a record low of 7.6 million barrels per day in 1989.

World oil production is analyzed in three tiers—the former Soviet Union bloc's, the Middle East, and Western production. Three-fifths of the world's reserves and production not controlled by the former Soviet bloc states is located in the volatile Persian Gulf.

©1996 Chase Global Data & Research
73 Junction Square, Concord, MA 01742

During the past few years former Soviet countries were net exporters of 400,000 barrels per day. Today the Russians have the same problems as the West, but in some ways even moreso: nuclear power concerns, energy shortages, and sizeable coal usage causing unpopular pollution. Their political instability adds an even greater variable to crude oil supply and demand issues worldwide.

The big question is: what is the future of crude oil? There remains the possibility of another major find in Prudhoe Bay, Alaska which would have a major impact on U.S. domestic oil reserves and thus reduce U.S. demand for imported oil for another decade—if the field is brought along within the next five years. There is also a new unknown in the equation—the recent discovery of super-conductivity—which could someday eliminate the need for most internal combustion engines, most importantly in cars. At present 97% of the energy used for U.S. vehicles derives from oil—with no other substitute on the horizon. Today scientists are predicting that autos will soon run on high powered superconducting batteries—an occurrence which would dramatically affect the oil industry. It can't come soon enough for Americans, who while making up 4% of the world's population, consume 40% of all gasoline. GM unveiled its 120-mile-range battery powered car in 1989, and in 1992 formed a consortium with Ford and Chrysler to pursue aggressively the new technology. The Big Three planned to market 50,000 battery powered vehicles by 1995, but their first introduction is now due in August 1996. Studies predict there will be 3 million electric cars in the Northeast alone by 2015. Perhaps... but California had mandated 2% of its vehicles be electric powered by 1998, but now may push the deadline to 10% of all cars be 100% non-polluting by 2003.

Will oil someday be a part of our past like the horse and buggy today? We'll all know the answer in just a few more decades. But we cannot and should not lose sight of the facts regarding its supply and demand, and that presently those factors are changing dramatically....again. Oil has proven itself a rocky investment medium, but overall it has been a decent performer having increased in value more than ten-fold over the past quarter century. While one may not seek to invest in crude petroleum, we are all affected by its price movements—for as a commodity, and necessity, its price changes impact us all.

In the Chase Global Data and Research universe Crude Petroleum ranked #1 in several Performance Tables, most notably the year 1990. But it managed to go from the top ranking in 1990 to last in 1991. It ranked 16th over the past quarter century. It was by far the #1 most volatile of all investments CGDR follows, ranking first in that category over the past thirty five years.

©1996 Chase Global Data & Research
73 Junction Square, Concord, MA 01742

## CRUDE OIL SPOT PRICE

[Mideast Light-34 API; average annual price]

| Year | Price* ($/barrel) | Price Growth | Compound return on a five year $10,000 investment | Annual compound rate of return |
|---|---|---|---|---|
| 1995 | 15.96 | 9.69% | 1991 - 1995 | |
| 1994 | 14.55 | -0.43% | | -6.10% |
| 1993 | 14.61 | -15.80% | ... $ 7,302 | |
| 1992 | 17.35 | 1.94% | | |
| 1991 | 17.02 | -22.11% | | |
| 1990 | 21.85 | 32.32% | 1986 - 1990 | |
| 1989 | 16.51 | 24.72% | | -4.51% |
| 1988 | 13.24 | -21.05% | ... $ 7,940 | |
| 1987 | 16.77 | 36.34% | | |
| 1986 | 12.30 | -55.31% | | |
| 1985 | 27.52 | -1.99% | 1981 - 1985 | |
| 1984 | 28.08 | -2.23% | | -5.15% |
| 1983 | 28.72 | -9.57% | ... $ 7,676 | |
| 1982 | 31.76 | -7.38% | | |
| 1981 | 34.29 | -4.35% | | |
| 1980 | 35.85 | 20.22% | 1976 - 1980 | |
| 1979 | 29.82 | 130.98% | | 27.33% |
| 1978 | 12.91 | 2.70% | ... $33,473 | |
| 1977 | 12.57 | 8.08% | | |
| 1976 | 11.63 | 8.59% | | |
| 1975 | 10.71 | -2.46% | 1971 - 1975 | |
| 1974 | 10.98 | 290.75% | | 54.67% |
| 1973 | 2.81 | 54.40% | ... $88,512 | |
| 1972 | 1.82 | 7.69% | | |
| 1971 | 1.69 | 39.67% | | |
| 1970 | 1.21 | -4.72% | 1966 - 1970 | |
| 1969 | 1.27 | -3.79% | | -3.15% |
| 1968 | 1.32 | -0.75% | ... $ 8,521 | |
| 1967 | 1.33 | -2.21% | | |
| 1966 | 1.36 | -4.23% | | |
| 1965 | 1.42 | -2.07% | 1961 - 1965 | |
| 1964 | 1.45 | -3.33% | | -2.72% |
| 1963 | 1.50 | -1.32% | ... $ 8,712 | |
| 1962 | 1.52 | -3.18% | | |
| 1961 | 1.57 | -3.68% | | |
| 1960 | 1.63 | -4.12% | | |

How a $10,000 investment performed over

| 5 years | 10 years | 15 years | 20 years | 25 years | 35 years |
|---|---|---|---|---|---|
| 1991 - 1995 | | | | | |
| $7,302 (-6.10%)^ | 1986 - 1995 | | | | |
| | $5,797 (-5.31%) | 1981 - 1995 | | | |
| | | $4,450 (-5.25%) | 1976 - 1995 | | |
| | | | $14,897 (2.01%) | 1971 - 1995 | |
| | | | | $131,855 (10.87%) | 1961 - 1995 |
| | | | | | $97,880 (6.73%) |

^ annual compound rate of return for that period
* Source: U.S. Energy Information Administration; Chase Global Data & Research.

©1996 Chase Global Data & Research
73 Junction Square, Concord, MA 01742

## Crude Oil

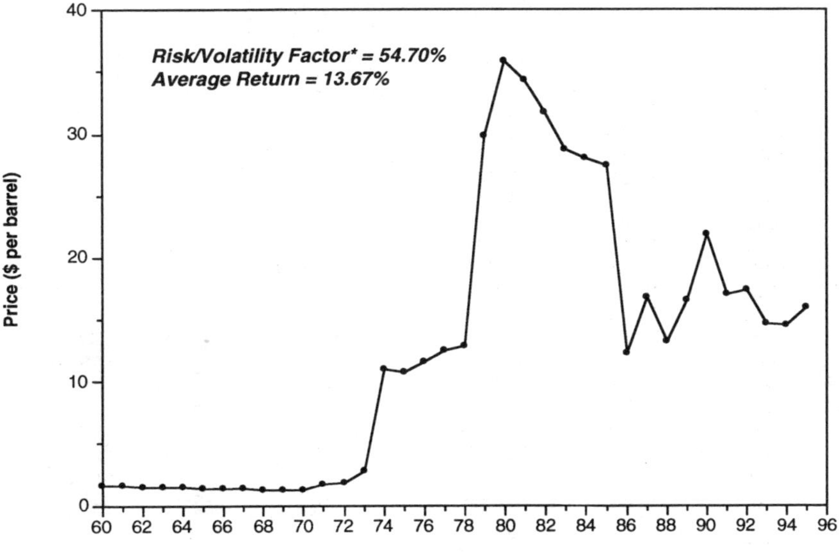


*Standard Deviation

## Crude Oil vs. Commodity Spot Price Index and Gold

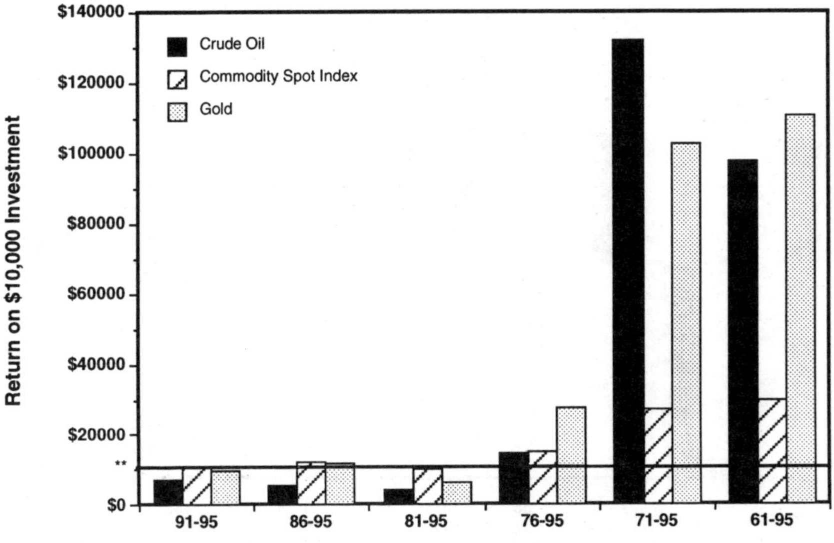


**Initial Investment: $10,000

©1996 Chase Global Data & Research
73 Junction Square, Concord, MA 01742

## Crude Oil vs. Dow Jones 15 Utilities^ and Japanese Yen

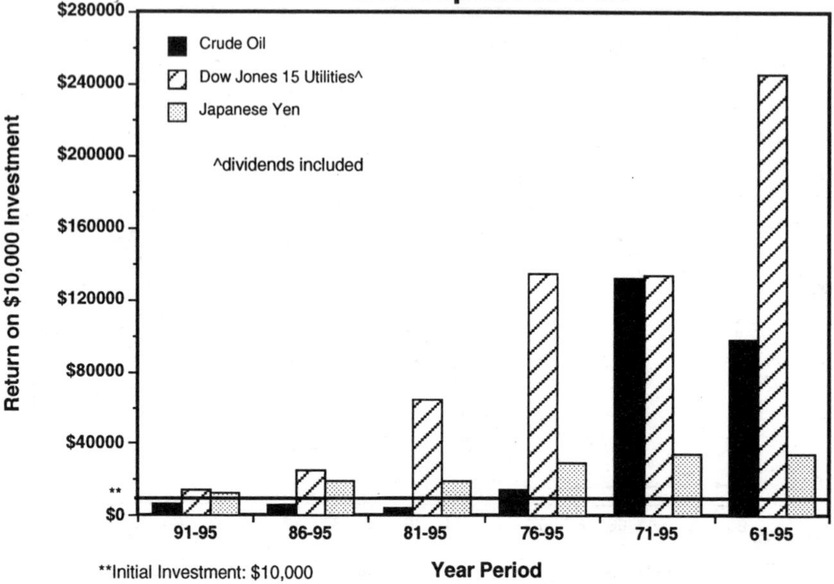


## Crude Oil vs. Inflation

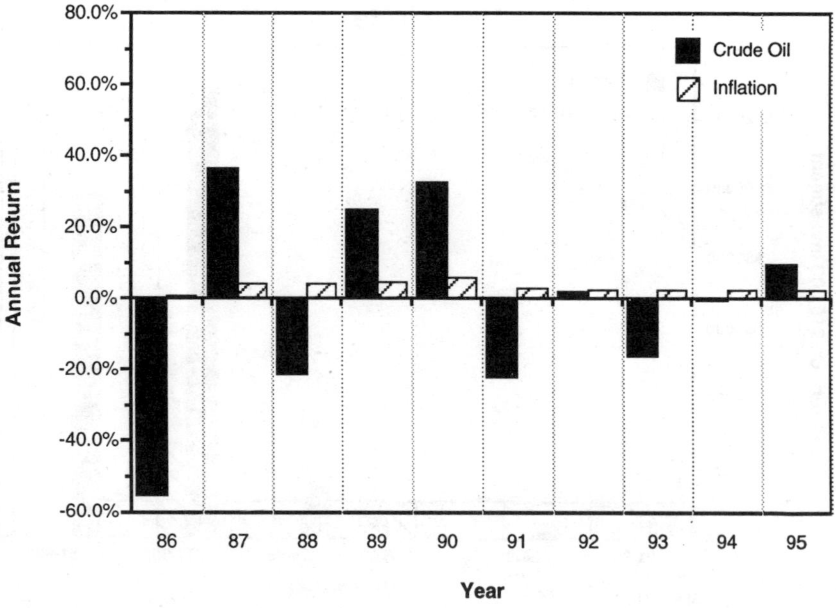


©1996 Chase Global Data & Research
73 Junction Square, Concord, MA 01742

Chapter Thirty Four

# Diamonds

Diamonds are the most famous gemstone, although their historical origin is obscure. It is thought that they were first discovered in India around 500 A.D. Manuscripts dating from that time describe criteria for valuing diamonds. However, some historians believe that diamonds had been used by Hindus in India as early as 400 B.C., as well as by Greeks and Romans several hundred years B.C. The Emperor Augustus and Pliny described diamonds as stones no bigger than a dot with a greater value than gold.

Since then, the use of diamonds has varied from the ordinary to the bizarre. In addition to being appreciated for their beauty and hardness, diamonds have also been the stuff of legends. Throughout history, warriors have worn diamonds into battle because they believed diamonds would protect them. Diamonds were also worn to ward off mental illness and the effects of poisons. In Medieval times, diamonds were ranked in value and popularity below rubies, emeralds and pearls. Later when horseback riding became popular as a sport, diamonds were worn to protect the rider's bones in case of a fall from his horse.

Diamonds have also been ingested for a variety of reasons. In the 16th century, diamonds were used as a cure for stomach disorders. Pope Clement VII died in 1532 despite the 14 spoonfuls of diamonds administered to save his life—instead, they no doubt sealed his fate. Diamonds have also been used as murder weapons. Small sharp pieces of diamonds are capable of cutting open the stomach and intestines of anyone who swallows them. In ancient times people committed suicide by ingesting glass or diamonds, although glass was considered more painful and not as effective. Diamond dust, considered the least painful, most active, and infallible of poisons, was kept as a last resort in times of great danger.

Originally, the world's greatest diamond cutters were in the Far East, but later European and Brazilian diamond cutters gained prominence. Today the chief diamond cutting craftsmen are in

©1996 Chase Global Data & Research
73 Junction Square, Concord, MA 01742

Belgium, Luxemburg, the Netherlands, Israel, India, South Africa, Great Britain, and the United States. The cut diamond the consumer purchases is only a small portion of the stone in which it was originally found. Diamonds originally occur in kimberlite. Any other occurrence is secondary. The proportion of diamonds to kimberlite rock is approximately 1 part per 40 million parts of rock.

The world's predominant diamond producer is South Africa. The first recognized diamond found in South Africa weighed 22 carats and was picked up by children of a farmer in 1867. A second larger diamond was found two years later by a shepherd boy. These discoveries were followed by the diamond rush which spread throughout all of Africa. Today, nearly all African nations have deposits of diamonds, but the major producer is still South Africa. Other countries that mine diamonds are Borneo, Indonesia, Russia, Brazil, India, the U.S., and Switzerland. The first major diamond discovery in Russia was in Siberia in 1954. It is unknown how much diamond mining occurs in Russia each year because it is only a minor exporter of the gems. However, it is possible that Russia is a major producer having more than the 5% of world production they are credited with, because they use most of the diamonds domestically.

In 1987 scientists reported that microscopic diamonds, older than both the earth and the sun, and the oldest minerals ever examined, were found embedded in meteorites. They were thought to be created in the atmosphere of a distant, dying star shortly before it exploded billions of years ago. These diamonds are the first unadulterated minerals from outside the solar system. Scientists were not totally surprised by this discovery because carbon is a basic element in the universe—and all diamonds are formed from carbon. However, previous theory held that diamonds were formed exclusively under tremendous pressure—levels 60,000 to 80,000 greater than the pressure on the surface of the earth. The inter-galactic diamonds were unique—thought to have been created in low pressures in stellar atmospheres.

Today the mining for diamonds is done from depths of 60 feet to over 4,000 feet. The Argyle Diamond Mine in Australia is the world's largest diamond mining operation. Located in the middle of Australia, it mostly produces very low-grade diamonds for industrial use. The mine processes 11,000 tons of rock per day, which produces about 33 pounds of diamonds—an extraordinarily high ratio of 1.5 parts per million of diamond in the ore. The mine's owners admit that the majority of their diamonds are the low grade brown variety, but as one executive said, "We've been looking through our Thesaurus for words meaning brown."

©1996 Chase Global Data & Research
73 Junction Square, Concord, MA 01742

The major consumer of diamonds is industry, which uses 75% of all diamonds mined. The quality of these diamonds is low but they are in continuous demand nevertheless. Diamonds conduct heat better than any known substance and are extremely good electrical insulators as well. Beginning in the 20th century, the diamond became the most important industrial abrasive. Henry Ford was the first to discover that on a large scale, a diamond is the cheapest industrial abrasive for long-term use, despite its initial high cost. As a result, Detroit has more diamond tool dealers than any other city in the world. There are over 15 different uses for diamonds in automobile factories, and they are also a critical component in the manufacturing of airplanes.

The gem diamond marketplace represents 25% of the diamond market and only deals with diamonds of higher quality. Diamonds under 0.2 carats are considered industrial diamonds—especially when their color and clarity are poor. There are four factors used in grading and pricing diamonds, known as the "4 C's": carat, color, cut, and clarity. Yellow and brownish colors are considered undesirable while fancy colors are pink, bluish, violet, green, and white. The clearer the diamond (without color) and the fewer the flaws, the more desirable is the stone.

The color in diamonds is due to lattice defects and not trace elements, as is the case with most other gemstones—except for the pink in diamonds which is attributed to traces of manganese. The Gemological Institute of America rates the color of diamonds through an electronic colorimeter. While jewelers registered with the GIA can rate the color of diamonds by visual review using magnifying glasses, the final say in the actual rating of color, quality, clarity, and weight is by the GIA itself. There are no perfect diamonds, but the term "perfect diamond" is used to describe a stone that reveals no flaws to the trained eye under a 10-power magnification.

The sizing and weighing of diamonds has been debated for hundreds of years. Not until the 19th century was an acceptable level of weighing reached at 205 milligrams per carat. By 1907 another weighing revision was reached through an international agreement. The agreement struck in Paris measured a carat at 200 milligrams, the metric carat, and it is now the standard international unit of weight for diamonds and other gemstones. Sizes of diamonds vary from the low grade (in structure and quality) diamonds called "bortz" which are crushed in steel mortars to produce a powder used to coat saws and other hard materials, to the other extreme of the huge "Cullinan" Diamond which originally weighed 3,000 carats in an uncut state and

©1996 Chase Global Data & Research
73 Junction Square, Concord, MA 01742

was eventually cut to the size of a teacup. Diamonds are cut with a full 58 facets—small, polished plane surfaces that create square, rectangular, or oval shapes.

A major advance in the understanding of diamonds came in the U.S. in 1954. The General Electric Co. succeeded in crystallizing diamonds synthetically. Synthetic diamonds are now produced in the U.S., Ireland, South Africa, the Soviet Union, Czechoslovakia, and Japan. The process applies high temperatures (1700° F) and high pressure (one million pounds) to almost any form of carbon to produce the by-product—synthetic diamonds. Even the carbon in peanut butter has been used to create diamonds in this way. In 1995, Northwestern University scientists announced that a material almost as hard as diamonds had been synthesized, and could be applied at room temperatures. The inexpensive material is expected to have broad applications to industry. Synthetic diamonds are now a $300+ million industry, producing diamonds which are 50% better at conducting heat, and absorb 10 times more light than natural diamonds.

Eighty percent of the world's production of genuine diamonds is controlled by DeBeers Central Selling Organization which covers 3 primary groups dealing in gemstones, industrial stones, and the output of independent producers. This tightly controlled monopoly is encouraged by both miners and governments involved in diamond mining and distribution. In 1990 the Central Selling Organization was responsible for 100 million carats of diamond production. The other 20% of the world supply is represented by approximately 150 individual companies who sell to whomever they please. 1995 sales by DeBeers were a record $4.5 billion worldwide. Thus, while attempts have been made to break DeBeers' six decades old cartel, all attempts to date have failed.

As the diamond marketplace grows, however, DeBeers' expenses to finance weak times have also grown. DeBeers must remain committed to further expand its inventory of diamonds, even though it has doubled in the past decade. In 1992 alone, DeBeers bought a total of $4.8 billion of uncut diamonds from contractors to suport prices, a 20% rise from 1988. In 1994 Russia sold $500 million independent of Debeers, in addition to its $1.2 billion annual quota. Despite its $170 million adverstising budget to sell diamonds, many experts feel that eventually DeBeers will be broken by a major sell off—when the market gets both too volatile and large for even DeBeers to handle. A 1990's style massive downswing would require enormous capital to slow.

©1996 Chase Global Data & Research
73 Junction Square, Concord, MA 01742

An investment in gemstones can be complex as well as volatile. Investors should bear in mind that purchases from jewelers and other retail sources often involves a 100% markup of the gemstone from the wholesale price. While such markups have been diminishing due to the recession in the diamond industry during the 1990's, they are not unusual. The investment also requires storage and the need for insurance to protect against possible theft or loss. After all, you're not dealing with stock certificates or monthly statements when investing in diamonds. And new discoveries of deposits could also cloud the investment outlook. The 1985 diamond discovery made in Australia at the Argyle Diamond Mine alone increased the world's production by 60%. When purchasing a gemstone have it assessed by an independent appraiser who is not associated with either the seller or a competitor to the seller.

In 1983 the American Gem Market System Network (AGMS) began tracking actual wholesale inter-dealer transactions on a variety of gems. Their computer network enabled dealers to shop prices through a grading system which improved diamond price reporting accuracy, for their are 100 levels of gradation. Thousands of actual gem transactions are reflected by their indices. AGMS researched prior years dealer transactions to create a benchmark dating from 1978. Polygon Inc. succeeded AGMS in 1991 in monitoring diamond price valuation. We believe the following Performance Table best represents the pricing history of diamonds, one derived from a less than optimum overall pricing environment.

Diamonds were one of the poorest performing investments in the first half of the 1980's when high quality diamonds depreciated six consecutive years a total of over 80%—an average per annum loss of 17%. However, diamonds stabilized somewhat during the second half of the decade, rising about 3% per annum. Overall during the past ten years diamonds have not even matched the pace of inflation, appreciating 2.48% annually. On the other hand, industrial low-grade diamonds have proven an excellent investment over the long term. In the early 1940's industrial diamonds were priced at $1.50 to $1.75 per carat. Today those diamonds range are valued at $400 and more per carat. Upon a brief review of the Performance Table which follows, one can quickly see that diamonds have not only been volatile, but they have shown a poor performance over the past fifteen years since 1981 (-4.41% annually)—an overall lack of performance unusual among all the investments Chase Global Data & Research follows.

©1996 Chase Global Data & Research
73 Junction Square, Concord, MA 01742

## DIAMOND PRICE INDEX

| Year | Index Growth* | Compound return on a five year $10,000 investment | Annual compound rate of return |
|---|---|---|---|
| 1995 | 1.20% | 1991 - 1995 | |
| 1994 | 0.80% | | 2.22% |
| 1993 | 1.10% | ... $11,163 | |
| 1992 | 2.30% | | |
| 1991 | 5.81% | | |
| 1990 | -2.83% | 1986 - 1990 | |
| 1989 | -2.75% | | 2.74% |
| 1988 | 0.00% | ... $11,444 | |
| 1987 | 6.86% | | |
| 1986 | 13.33% | | |
| 1985 | -2.17% | 1981 - 1985 | |
| 1984 | -6.12% | | -16.83% |
| 1983 | -12.66% | ... $ 3,979 | |
| 1982 | -30.31% | | |
| 1981 | -28.82% | | |
| 1980 | -9.52% | | |
| 1979 | 51.52% | | |

How a $10,000 investment performed over

| 5 years | 10 years | 15 years |
|---|---|---|
| 1991 - 1995<br>$11,163<br>(2.22%)^ | 1986 - 1995<br>$12,776<br>(2.48%) | 1981 - 1995<br>$5,083<br>(-4.41%) |

^ annual compound rate of return for that period
* Source: AGMS Network; Polygon Network.

©1996 Chase Global Data & Research
73 Junction Square, Concord, MA 01742

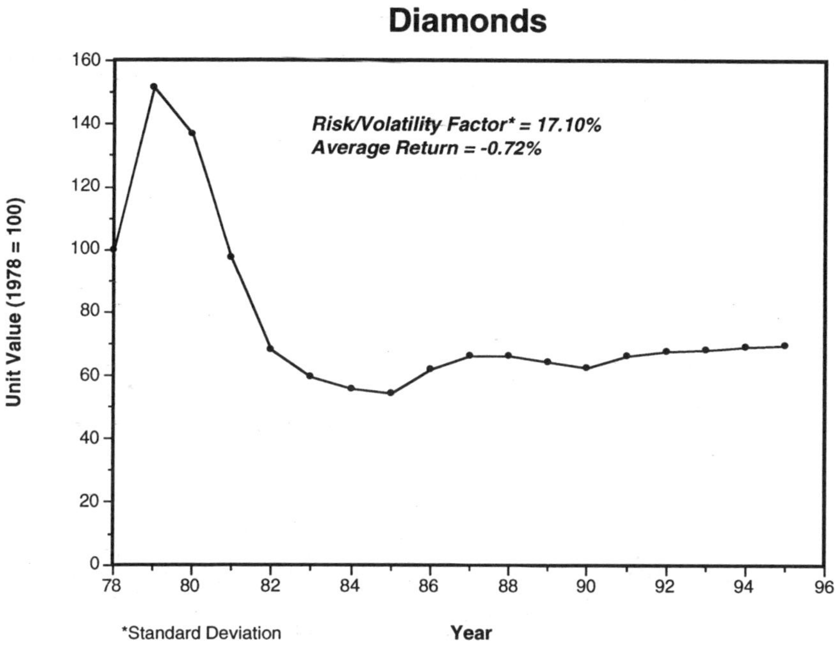


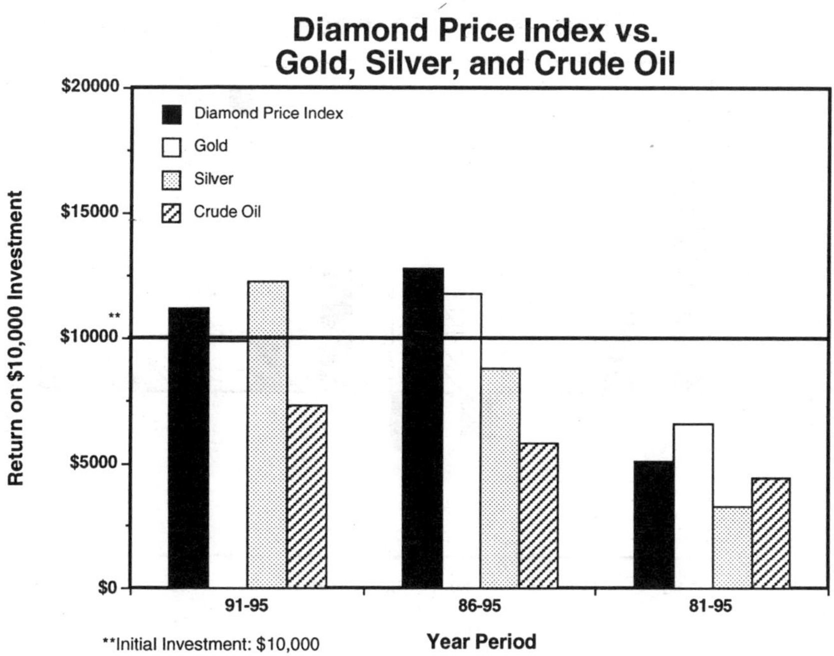


©1996 Chase Global Data & Research
73 Junction Square, Concord, MA 01742

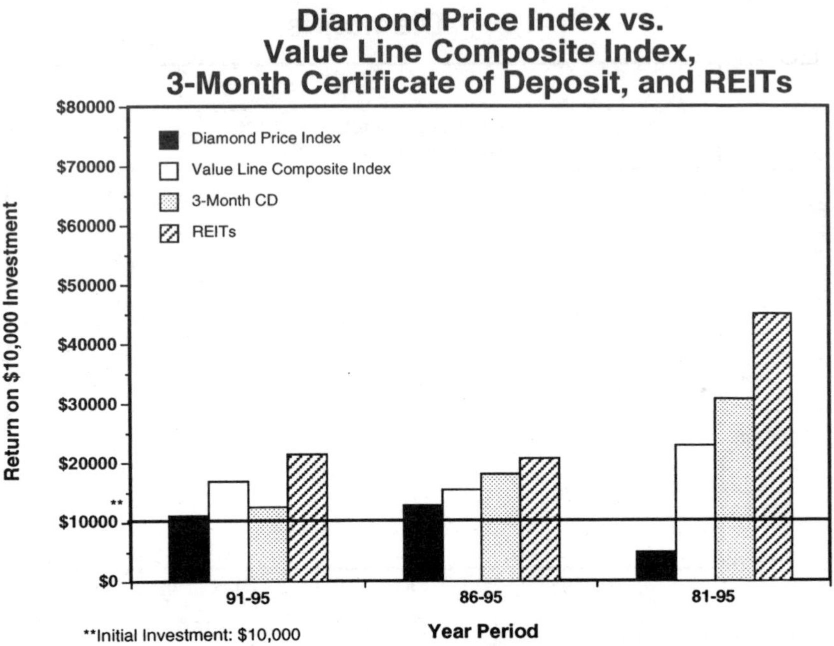


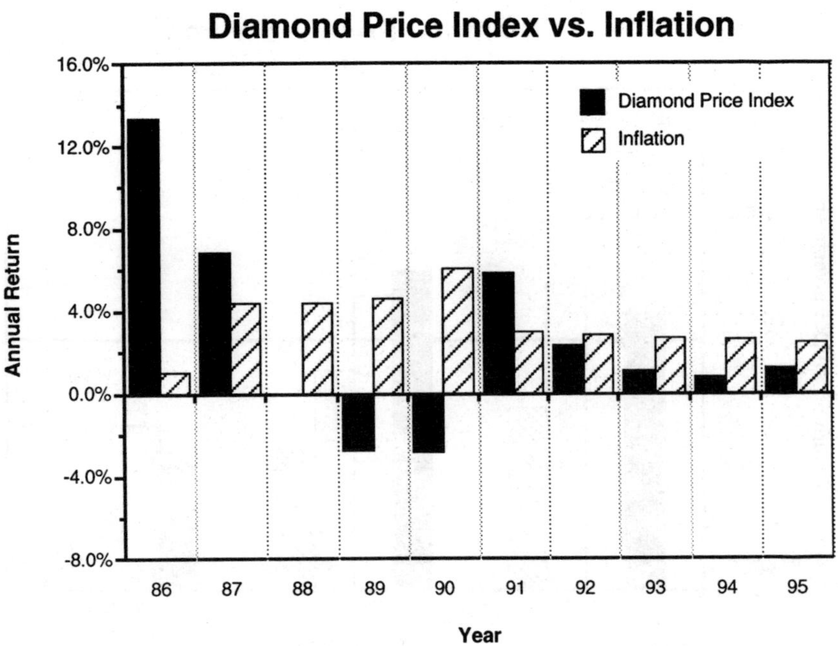


©1996 Chase Global Data & Research
73 Junction Square, Concord, MA 01742

SECTION IX

# Real Estate Investments

# Chapter Thirty Five

# Housing

No sector of the U.S. economy is more sensitive to changing demographic trends than housing. The price for new family housing is based on the rate of population growth, shifts in the population's age and geographic distribution, changes in living arrangements, trends in the characteristics of newly constructed housing and, of course, the stability of the economy in general.

Since the post-war era began, new housing has been primarily dependent upon the growth and number of households in the U.S. Growth in housing took place as a result of new construction, which in turn accommodated household expansion. In a typical year of new housing starts, 90% are to meet new demand, and 10% replace demolished homes. In part due to the specter cast by recessionary times and a slowing population growth, experts anticipate that in the 1990's the U.S. should experience moderate growth of about 1.3 million household formations per year. In 1992 new home units totaled only 1.1 million, with weakness in the marketplace reflecting the fact that almost 3 million homes were on the market at the end of 1991. By year-end 1995 new home unit starts rebounded to 1.3 million.

Non-economic factors can contribute to a decrease in housing. In the early 1980's, when new house formations fell to their lowest levels in thirty years, one of the reasons cited was "sibling squeeze." In the early 1980's, young adults had fewer younger brothers and sisters at home than their counterparts in the 70's and thus received less pressure to leave home, which would have created a need for further housing. Note, too, that several issues that create a demand for housing are discussed in the *Chase Investment Performance Digest's* U.S. Per Capita Disposable Income chapter. And remember that the average number of persons per household has steadily fallen in the post-war era, the number of single-person households has sharply increased, and the average number of children per family has declined. Each of these factors has a different impact on new housing construction. Also, regional expansion comes and goes. For example, although slightly


©1996 Chase Global Data & Research
73 Junction Square, Concord, MA 01742

more than half of the nation lives in the south and the west, from 1979 to 1986 three-fourths of the nation's new dwelling units were built there. Yet in the late 1980's the fastest growing area in the U.S. was the northeast. Then in 1990 that sector collapsed.

The Tax Reform Act of 1986 had a major impact on rental housing, as well as housing in general. Owner-occupied housing still enjoys the deductability of interest and taxes, but rental housing has lost many of its benefits. Additionally, depreciation of rental housing for investment purposes was stretched from 19 to 27.5 years. Housing industry experts estimate that as a result of tax changes, there was a 50% decline in new construction of rental units during 1987. Demand for second-home housing has been reduced because of the continual threat of future tax changes. In general, the aura of boom/bust extremes haunts investments in real estate.

Long term housing demands can be analyzed through various sources. One of these is the U.S. Census Bureau projections, which reported that household formations would gradually decline during 1980's, falling from approximately 1.5 million units annually to approximately 1.3 million in the 1990's. The Bureau projects that both household shrinkage and the downtrend in family size will continue for the foreseeable future. The government also expects that competition for jobs will increase as baby boomers continue to expand in the labor market. This will impact salaries, which obviously impacts housing trends. Another major variable is the growth in the number of households headed by the elderly. Their future special housing needs will play a large role in housing construction during the 1990's and at the turn of the century.

Strict textbook economic theory on demand for housing is based on two major variables: the wealth of the population and the percentage of the population that is wealthy. Given the steady shrinkage of the middle class, housing demand analysis becomes more complex. Another variable in housing demand is the type of housing being constructed—one reason experts feel that the long term marketplace for condominium construction could be strong over the long term, despite periods of softness due to overbuilding. The condominium product's ability to price itself to match demand appears greater than for single dwelling family housing. However, despite the availability of lower priced condominium units and mobile homes, the most popular form of housing in the U.S. remains the moderately priced, single-family detached house.

©1996 Chase Global Data & Research
73 Junction Square, Concord, MA 01742

At the end of 1995, the median price of a new home was approximately $134,800 while the median price for a used home was about $111,600. The average U.S. home was 1,705 square feet of living space, situated on slightly over one-half acre. Housing's attractiveness/affordability has grown in the 1990's principally due to lower rates and minimal price increases. The 1992-1995 Housing Affordability level was the highest (most attractive) since 1976.

The U.S. Government began compiling housing data as early as 1850. Complete censuses of the construction industry were first done by the government in 1929. Since 1967 major census data collection has been done every five years. Today the government performs an update on housing prices annually. The Bureau tracks housing starts and housing completions by structure and by region. Data is collected from over 17,000 permit-issuing jurisdictions in the U.S.

In 1963 the Census Bureau also began surveying and collecting information on the physical characteristics and transaction prices of new one family houses. These national surveys review both the builders and the owners of the houses and reflect over 10,000 observations per year. The Index is intended to measure changes over time in the sale price of new one-family houses and to analyze 10 important characteristics: floor area, number of stories, number of bathrooms, air conditioning, type of parking facility, type of foundation, geographic division within the region or metropolitan area, location, presence of a fireplace, and size of the lot. (Variances cannot reflect standards of workmanship, materials, and mechanical equipment.) The Bureau estimates that these 10 characteristics are present in approximately 60% of all variations in new one-family houses sold in the U.S. Prices are computed from contract sales prices of houses sold and include the value of the developed lot. The total sales price covers the cost of labor, materials, land costs, direct and indirect selling expenses, and the seller's profit. Quality is the major variable. Houses built by the owner for the owner's occupancy, or houses built by an owner for rental purposes are excluded from the Index.

Housing is affected by the volatility of its price changes, especially on a regional basis—a situation not adequately reflected in national average data. Both interest costs and net interest costs after inflation and taxes are major considerations. Most experts feel that mortgage rates under 10% can support reasonable demand, while rates above 10% will deter demand.

©1996 Chase Global Data & Research
73 Junction Square, Concord, MA 01742

If you are considering buying a house—whether it is new construction or an older home for investment purposes—remember the fate of several of the gurus who recommended investing in real estate with "no money down," "cash at closing," or locating the "distressed seller" of the marketplace. In the mid-80's forty real estate investment advisors had TV shows, and hundreds lectured on the subject. Today there are very few left, and likely for good reason. After tax reform, and after the public understood how difficult it was to put guru theories into practice, their businesses shut down.

Overall, the housing marketplace in the U.S. has been a consistently upward performer, especially when you consider that a house gives protection from wind and rain and also can provide rental income and price appreciation. But there are risks involved as a result of population shifts, changes in the economy, changes in household formations, and the up and down aspects of using leverage in purchasing a home. Note, too, that just as with many other investments diversification could be key for successful real estate investment. For that reason a close review of the regional aspects of U.S. housing is a productive exercise—for the national average is not always what it appears.

The Housing Price Index has been a mid-level performer in the universe of investments tracked by Chase Global Data & Research. However, as noted above, an investment in housing provides additional benefits—reflected in its name. Housing Affordability is another key aspect relating to housing as an investment. Be sure to review the National Association of Realtors Housing Affordability Index on page 389. For as that Index rises, housing prices will likely follow—at least on the short-term. Fortunately, because of sharply lower interest rates and accommodating inflation readings Americans have experienced a significant change in housing affordability since the late 80's, with consistent improvement continuing throughout the 1990's.

©1996 Chase Global Data & Research
73 Junction Square, Concord, MA 01742

## NEW ONE-FAMILY HOUSE PRICE INDEX

[U.S. average annual price; 1987=100]

| Year | Index* Growth | Compound return on a five year $10,000 investment | Annual compound rate of return |
|---|---|---|---|
| 1995 | 2.61% | 1991 - 1995 | |
| 1994 | 3.99% | | 2.45% |
| 1993 | 2.94% | ... $11,286 | |
| 1992 | 1.91% | | |
| 1991 | 0.82% | | |
| 1990 | 1.49% | 1986 - 1990 | |
| 1989 | 3.76% | | 3.90% |
| 1988 | 3.60% | ... $12,109 | |
| 1987 | 5.93% | | |
| 1986 | 4.77% | | |
| 1985 | 2.04% | 1981- 1985 | |
| 1984 | 4.37% | | 3.85% |
| 1983 | 2.42% | ... $12,078 | |
| 1982 | 2.48% | | |
| 1981 | 8.04% | | |
| 1980 | 10.36% | 1976 - 1980 | |
| 1979 | 14.97% | | 11.65% |
| 1978 | 14.17% | ... $17,349 | |
| 1977 | 11.23% | | |
| 1976 | 7.67% | | |
| 1975 | 10.26% | 1971 - 1975 | |
| 1974 | 9.55% | | 8.27% |
| 1973 | 8.54% | ... $14,879 | |
| 1972 | 6.84% | | |
| 1971 | 6.23% | | |
| 1970 | 3.21% | 1966 - 1970 | |
| 1969 | 7.28% | | 4.40% |
| 1968 | 4.82% | ... $12,403 | |
| 1967 | 2.89% | | |
| 1966 | 3.86% | | |
| 1965 | 2.19% | | |
| 1964 | 0.00% | | |
| 1963 | n.a. | | |
| 1962 | n.a. | | |
| 1961 | n.a. | | |
| 1960 | n.a. | | |

How a $10,000 investment performed over

| 5 years | 10 years | 15 years | 20 years | 25 years | 30 years |
|---|---|---|---|---|---|
| 1991 - 1995 | | | | | |
| $11,286 (2.45%)^ | 1986 - 1995 | | | | |
| | $13,666 (3.17%) | 1981 - 1995 | | | |
| | | $16,505 (3.40%) | 1976 - 1995 | | |
| | | | $28,635 (5.40%) | 1971 - 1995 | |
| | | | | $42,606 (5.97%) | 1966 - 1995 |
| | | | | | $52,845 (5.71%) |

^ annual compound rate of return for that period
* Source: U.S. Department of Commerce
n.a. = data not available; 1995 4Q estimated by CGDR.

©1996 Chase Global Data & Research
73 Junction Square, Concord, MA 01742

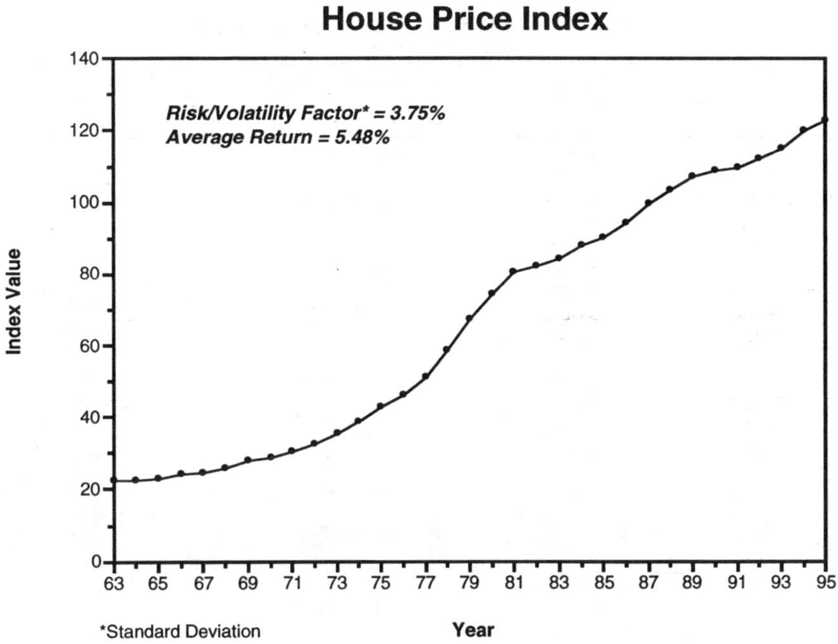


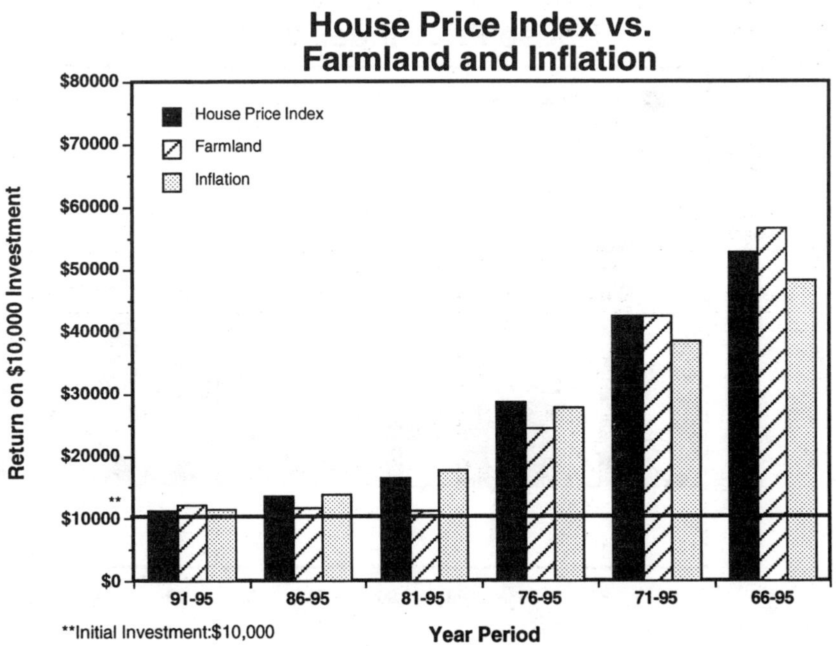


©1996 Chase Global Data & Research
73 Junction Square, Concord, MA 01742

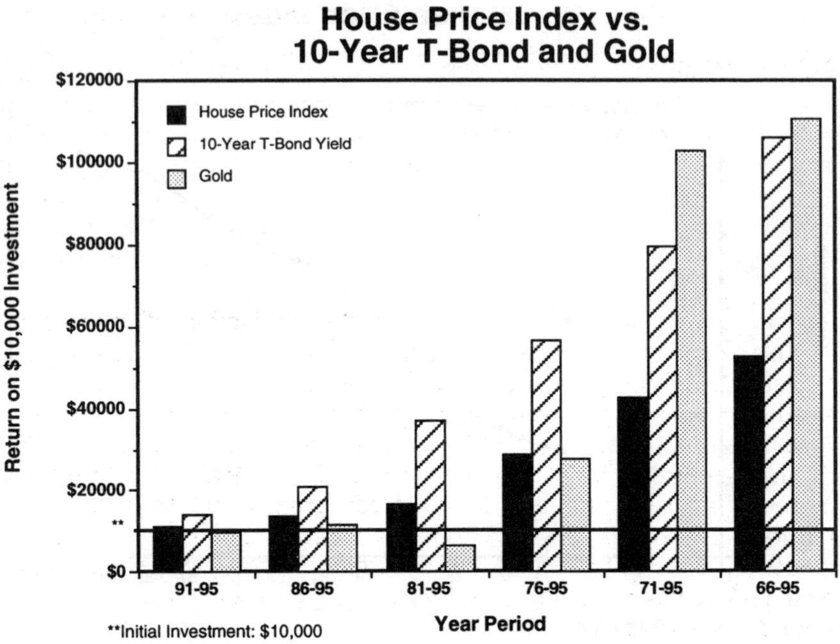


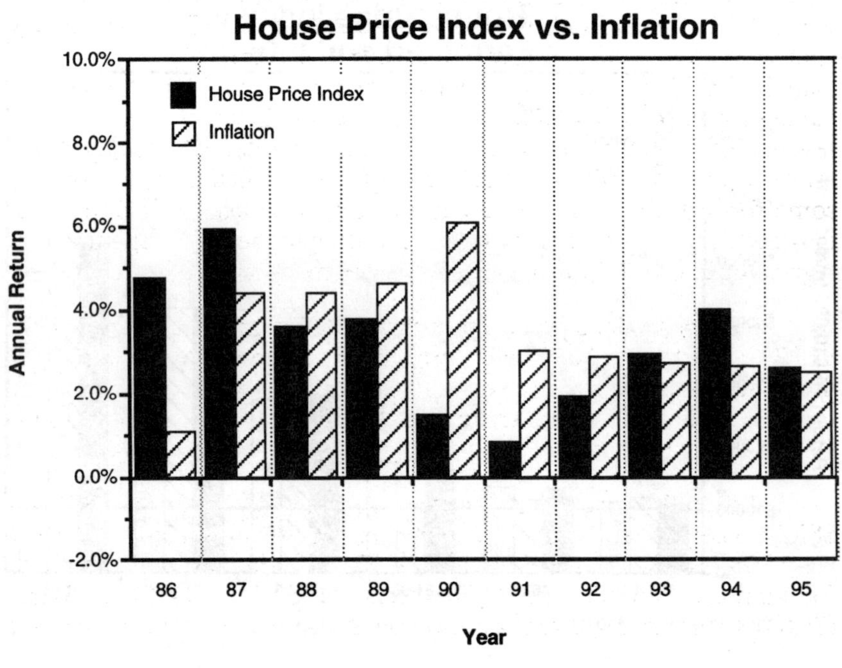


©1996 Chase Global Data & Research
73 Junction Square, Concord, MA 01742

# Chapter Thirty Six

# Farmland

American farming began with the production of tobacco in 1610, and is now in its fourth century. By 1639 American farm exports totaled 1.5 million pounds annually. From those early years, the U.S. steadily developed as a strong agricultural nation capable of supplying foods, grains, and livestock at home and abroad. But finally, in 1935, the number of U.S. farms began to decline. From 1945 to 1992 the total number of farms dropped by two-thirds, from 6 million to about 2 million. Part of the reason is that new farm technology has made the modern farm more efficient and productive. For example, per man hour output has increased five fold and crop production volume has tripled since World War II.

There are primarily two forms of farms in the U.S.—family farms and corporate/industrial farms, with the total farm census ratio being 90% family and 10% corporate/industrial. Today there are approximately 2 million family-run farms of various sizes, and less than one half million large commercial farms. In 1990 the average value of a farm was $240,000. Today the top 10% of farms generate revenue of $250,000 or more per year and the total value of farm real estate is over $1 trillion. About 8% of the population is involved in some form of farming, and about 35 million people work directly or indirectly in the farming industry. According to the U.S. Department of Agriculture, in 1994 the average farmer earned $40,000.

Farm produce prices more than doubled in the U.S. from 1972 to 1979. But that phenomenal growth was followed by 50% to 70% drops in farmland prices in several areas by the 1980's. Prime land in the Corn Belt, which was selling for $3,000 to $4,000 per acre in the 1970's even dropped to under $1,000 per acre during the 1980's.

In 1995 the average value of a farmland acre in the U.S. was $832. The lowest farmland acreage prices are in Wyoming ($192), New Mexico ($225), and Montana ($277). The highest per acre prices for farmland in 1995 were in New Jersey ($8,052) and Rhode Island ($6,947). National and regional prices have shown consistent increases

©1996 Chase Global Data & Research
73 Junction Square, Concord, MA 01742

in recent years, with overall prices up over 30% since 1988.

The Farmland Index is issued by the U.S. Department of Agriculture. It began to price the average value of farmland in the U.S. in 1912—when the original price was $27 per acre. At that time, 33.9% of the total population of the U.S. owned farmland. Today the figure is below 3%. However, it is interesting to note that from the early 1960's to the late 1970's (almost two decades) the Farmland Index outperformed equities by more than 2 to 1.

Recently, overall farmers' debt has begun to drop. By 1994 farmers' total debt fell to less than $150 billion, down from a 1983 peak of $205 billion (which then equaled the total Third World debt). But this decline in debt should be viewed with caution, because today over 20% of farm income (and for some farmers over one-third) comes from U.S. government farm subsidies—which total over $10 billion annually. Farm subsidies reached their peak in 1986 at $25 billion and have gradually decreased, to the $10 billion annual stipend during the 1990's. Today the most common areas of price support are in sugar, dairy products, and peanuts. In 1996 legislation may be enacted which would phase out many federal price support programs over the next seven years.

Farm subsidies are a fact of life globally, despite GATT talks in recent years to reduce in order to even the playing field. The World Bank estimates that farm program subsidies cost consumers and taxpayers about $100 billion worldwide annually. For example, the German government purchases 90% of all butter produced by German dairy farmers. Yet only 10% ends up on store shelves. The government is paying a price 3 to 4 times higher than it receives when it sells butter to Russia. Similarly, U.S. sugar beet farmers receive price supports several times higher than depressed world prices. Recent global trade negotiations have proposed further changes in subsidies and freer farm trade, but only time will tell the true impact of the new guidelines.

The major problem for farming nations with a high standard of living is that they can't compete with some of the lower pay scale nations of the world. One Minnesota farmer stated, "A few years ago I saw the most efficient sugar farmer in the world. He was in Jamaica. He had a donkey and a two-wheeled cart, and a shack on the hill. I can't compete with him." Therefore, as artificial as subsidies may appear to the outsider, they will probably be with us for quite a while. "We've had farm programs for 50 years," one farmland real estate agent said, "and we're going to have them for another 50."

Some experts are very optimistic about the future of farmland

©1996 Chase Global Data & Research
73 Junction Square, Concord, MA 01742

prices, and prices have certainly improved of late. But questions and problems linger on. The Farm Credit System has had to manage one million acres of defaulted property and the Farmers Home Administration also had an inventory of about one million acres of defaulted property. Experts estimate that well over 100,000 farmers have been forced out of business since 1982, and others still face tough times. At the same time, the total planted acreage is now about 50 million less than in 1980.

For investors considering farmland, it can be rented (for cash payment) to other farmers. Depending on the desirability and value of your land the yield on cash rents can vary between approximately 1% to as high as 8%. The primary variable is the land's potential for appreciation, which will likely be the key determinant for the overall return on your investment. There is some good news: Alabama, California, Delaware, Illinois, Indiana, Iowa, Maryland, Massachusetts, New Jersey, Ohio, Oregon, Pennsylvania, Rhode Island, and South Carolina farmland prices have risen over 50% from 1988 through 1995. And for smaller investors the government's $50,000 upside limit (per partner) on subsidy payments (half paid in cash, half in grain surplus credits) still makes investment in farmland a reasonable possibility—when not overdone through buying too much land in one place. If a farmland investment is properly researched, rental payments might well continue into the future and there could be the added benefit of higher land and produce prices. Yet keep in mind the difficulties of renting, managing, and overseeing a working farm, overseeing equipment purchases, avoiding theft of your crops, and conserving the soil. Some experts feel that the best way to invest in farmland is to keep it exclusively as a land investment—and not a farming investment. Recently the Chicago Board of Trade proposed crop option and futures contracts, which were said to assist farmers in hedging their crop price risks.

Farmland as an investment medium has performed in a reasonable manner over the past 25 and 35 year periods, averaging asset growth of almost 6% per annum, excluding potential farm income. By far the worst performance period occurred in the mid-80's. During the past ten years prices have gained 1.56% per year, and from 1994 through 1995 prices have moved up almost 13%. Of note, U.S. Farmland and Housing prices have produced essentially identical returns over the past quarter century and 35 year spans—with the average annual rate of return differnce a mere 0.02% and 0.05% respectively. (Note that neither analysis assumes income, only capital appreciation on the asset.) Farmland, from a long term perspective, may be unusually attractive today. And in that vein, one should always remember Mark Twain's immortal saying about land... "they aren't making it anymore."

©1996 Chase Global Data & Research
73 Junction Square, Concord, MA 01742

## U.S. FARMLAND PRICE INDEX

[average value of land and building per acre, excludes income]

| Year | Price* ($ per acre) | Price Growth | Compound return on a five year $10,000 investment | Annual compound rate of return |
|---|---|---|---|---|
| 1995 | 832 | 6.39% | 1991 - 1995 | |
| 1994 | 782 | 6.25% | | 4.03% |
| 1993 | 736 | 3.23% | ... $12,182 | |
| 1992 | 713 | 1.42% | | |
| 1991 | 703 | 2.93% | | |
| 1990 | 683 | 2.25% | 1986 - 1990 | |
| 1989 | 668 | 5.70% | | -0.86% |
| 1988 | 632 | 5.51% | ... $ 9,579 | |
| 1987 | 599 | -6.41% | | |
| 1986 | 640 | -10.24% | | |
| 1985 | 713 | -10.99% | 1981 - 1985 | |
| 1984 | 801 | 1.65% | | -0.66% |
| 1983 | 788 | -4.25% | ... $ 9,674 | |
| 1982 | 823 | 0.49% | | |
| 1981 | 819 | 11.13% | | |
| 1980 | 737 | 17.36% | 1976 - 1980 | |
| 1979 | 628 | 18.27% | | 16.73% |
| 1978 | 531 | 12.03% | ... $21,676 | |
| 1977 | 474 | 19.40% | | |
| 1976 | 397 | 16.76% | | |
| 1975 | 340 | 12.58% | 1971 - 1975 | |
| 1974 | 302 | 22.76% | | 11.65% |
| 1973 | 246 | 12.33% | ... $17,347 | |
| 1972 | 219 | 7.88% | | |
| 1971 | 203 | 3.57% | | |
| 1970 | 196 | 3.70% | 1966 - 1970 | |
| 1969 | 189 | 5.59% | | 5.92% |
| 1968 | 179 | 6.55% | ... $13,333 | |
| 1967 | 168 | 6.33% | | |
| 1966 | 158 | 7.48% | | |
| 1965 | 147 | 6.52% | 1961 - 1965 | |
| 1964 | 138 | 6.15% | | 4.67% |
| 1963 | 130 | 4.00% | ... $12,564 | |
| 1962 | 125 | 5.04% | | |
| 1961 | 119 | 1.71% | | |
| 1960 | 117 | 5.41% | | |

How a $10,000 investment performed over

| 5 years | 10 years | 15 years | 20 years | 25 years | 35years |
|---|---|---|---|---|---|
| 1991 - 1995 | | | | | |
| $12,182 (4.03%)^ | 1986 - 1995 | | | | |
| | $11,669 (1.56%) | 1981 - 1995 | | | |
| | | $11,289 (0.81%) | 1976 - 1995 | | |
| | | | $24,471 (4.58%) | 1971 - 1995 | |
| | | | | $42,449 (5.95%) | 1961 - 1995 |
| | | | | | $71,111 (5.76%) |

^ annual compound rate of return for that period
* Source: U.S. Department of Agriculture.

©1996 Chase Global Data & Research
73 Junction Square, Concord, MA 01742

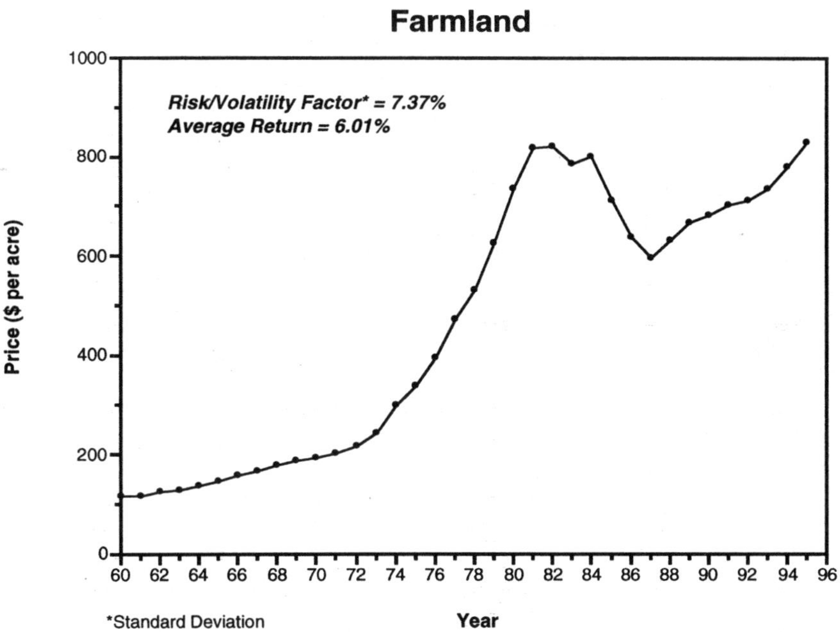


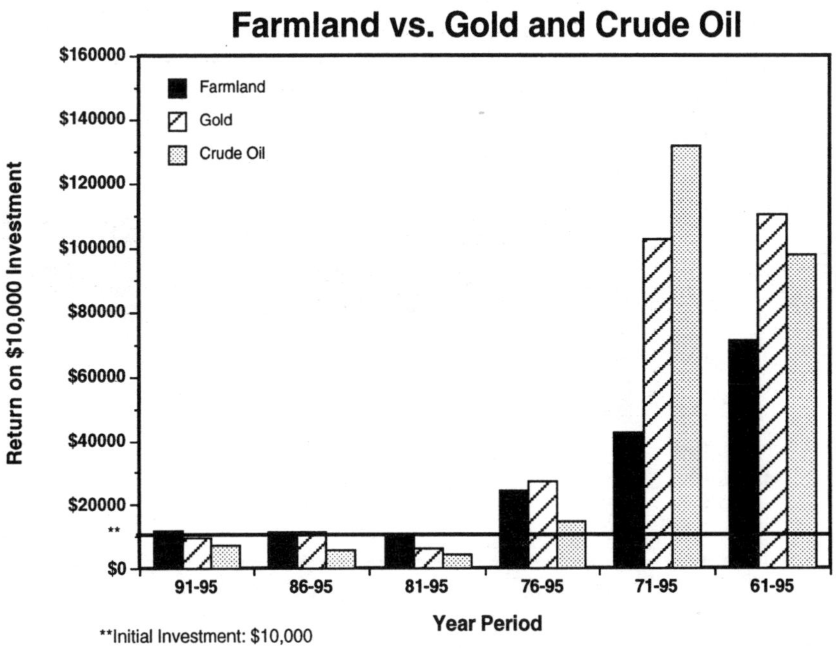


©1996 Chase Global Data & Research
73 Junction Square, Concord, MA 01742

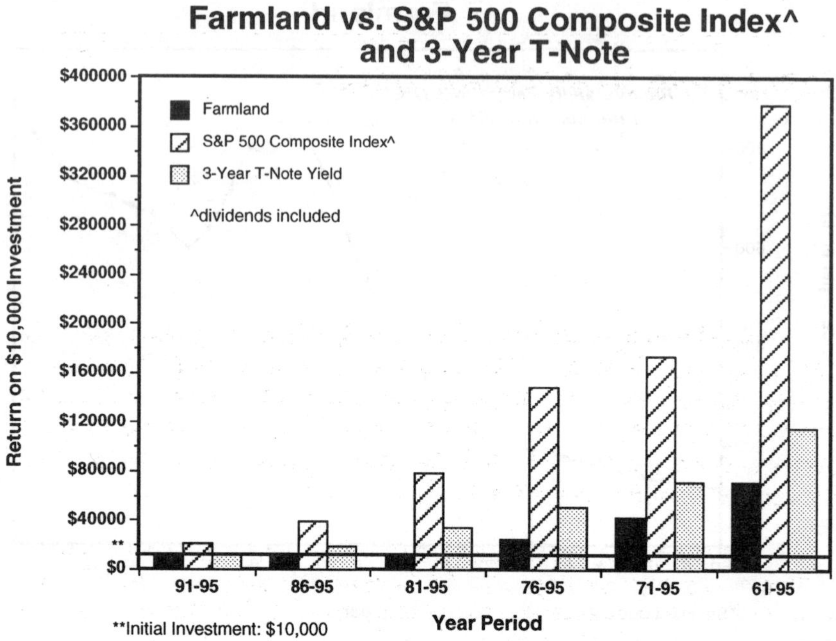


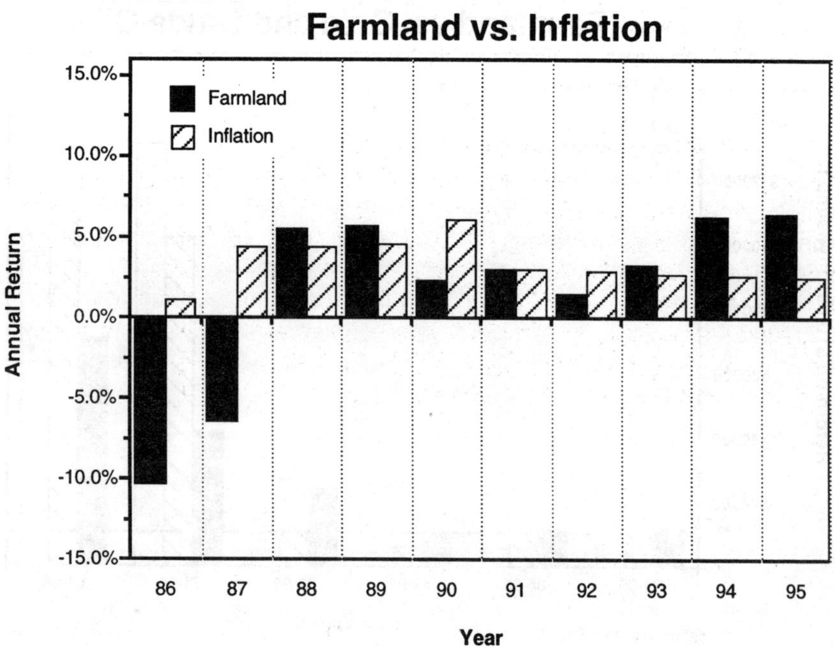


©1996 Chase Global Data & Research
73 Junction Square, Concord, MA 01742

# Chapter Thirty Seven

# Real Estate Investment Trusts

Real Estate Investment Trusts, or REITs, were authorized in the early 1960's by Congress. The goal was to provide small investors an opportunity to invest in large scale real estate and to share in some tax benefits as well. REITs must invest at least 75 percent of their assets in real estate, or derive 75% of their gross income from rent on real property or from interest on mortgages.

REITs are publicly traded securities, sold like stocks on the exchanges. There are over 220 REIT issues on major exchanges and the over-the-counter market with a total market value estimated at more than $55 billion. Eighty percent of REITs trade on national exchanges. Today there are 141 listed on the NYSE, 57 on the AMEX, and 21 on the NASDAQ OTC. Dozens more are not traded on national exchanges. The value of shares of REITs is reflected by property values, rent trends, market perceptions about real estate, and the fluctuating levels of interest rates.

All REITs have trustees which by law are responsible for overseeing the trust's assets and liability management, determining the trust's investment policies, and approving trust loans and investments. Many REITs use an investment advisor to oversee the trust's day to day operations. Typically, the advisor is part of, or a subsidiary of, the original offering group for the REIT. Often the investment advisor is an affiliate of a bank, an insurance company, a real estate organization, or even a mortgage banking firm. Roles and fees for advisors vary from trust to trust and can be an important factor in the overall results of an REIT.

There are several forms of REITs. The EQUITY REIT is the most popular, growth-oriented form. Its shareholders receive reasonable levels of income but primarily expect to benefit through the rise in property values of the real estate investments. According to the Washington, D.C. based National Association of Real Estate Investment Trusts, Inc., the 178 Equity REITs in the U.S. posted an

©1996 Chase Global Data & Research
73 Junction Square, Concord, MA 01742

overall yield of 15.27% in 1995.

The MORTGAGE REIT is a more conservative, income-oriented REIT. They loan money to real estate owners. Their revenue derives primarily from interest on loans made. Some Mortgage REITs also invest in residuals of mortgage-based securities.

HYBRID REITs attempt to combine the qualities of Equity and Mortgage REITs. The following represents the breakdown of REITs forms presently tracked by NAREIT as of December 31, 1995 :

| | |
|---|---|
| Equity | 81% |
| Mortgage | 11% |
| Hybrid | 8% |

By law REITs derive 90% of their income from rents, dividends, interest, and gains from the sale of their real estate holdings. They must pay out 95% of this income to their shareholders. By doing so the companies are exempt from federal taxation at the corporate level, although the dividends are taxable to shareholders. In this regard REIT corporations are different from standard corporations which must pay federal taxes before disbursing dividends.

One difficulty that may be encountered with REITs, as with any form of real estate, is that of appraisals. At times appraisals can be erroneous, and in such cases value that is assumed to be realistic may not be upon actual sale of the asset. In fairness, appraisals can be low as well as high, but conservative investors should be aware of the appraisal being an integral part of owning an REIT. In one case, one expert valued an REIT's shares at $2.80—even though the REIT's appraised value was $13 per share.

Some REITs purchase real estate on a cash basis. Others borrow heavily to purchase real estate in addition to using the initial funds derived from selling shares to the public. Key economic factors influencing the ultimate outcome of an REIT investment are management expertise, property selection, level of diversification, interest expense, real estate taxes, maintenance fees, insurance costs, and inflation.

REITs use several methods to acquire real estate. Sometimes they purchase existing real estate and improve it, or they hire independent contractors and architects and construct new real estate, or they form

©1996 Chase Global Data & Research
73 Junction Square, Concord, MA 01742

joint ventures with developers. Sometimes they acquire property through foreclosure or take over deeds in lieu of foreclosure when they've made loans/mortgages on real estate. Your REIT may enter into a real estate transaction as a co-partner and either control the venture or be just simply an investor within a larger partnership. It is prudent to understand the status of your REIT and its philosophy before you invest in it. Some REITs enter the real estate market one way but as the market changes they modify their philosophy. Such changes can severely impact your investment. Thus REITs should be closely monitored.

From 1972-1974 REITs lost about 70% of their value. After their poor performance at the outset of their introduction to the financial community, REITs, as reflected in NAREIT's All-REIT Index, have performed well with the exception of the late 1980's and 1990. The period from 1976 through 1995 shows an annual gain of over 13%. Over the more recent 5, 10, and 15 year periods the REIT Index has ranged from 7% to 16% overall.

©1996 Chase Global Data & Research
73 Junction Square, Concord, MA 01742

## REAL ESTATE INVESTMENT TRUSTS

[1971=100; year-end]

| Year | Index Growth* | Compound return on a five year $10,000 investment | Annual compound rate of return |
|---|---|---|---|
| 1995 | 18.28% | 1991 - 1995 | |
| 1994 | 0.81% | | 16.56% |
| 1993 | 18.55% | ... $21,515 | |
| 1992 | 12.18% | | |
| 1991 | 35.68% | | |
| 1990 | -17.35% | | |
| 1989 | -1.81% | 1986 - 1990 | |
| 1988 | 11.36% | | -0.77% |
| 1987 | -10.67% | ... $ 9,621 | |
| 1986 | 19.18% | | |
| 1985 | 5.92% | | |
| 1984 | 14.82% | | |
| 1983 | 25.47% | 1981 - 1985 | |
| 1982 | 31.64% | | 16.88% |
| 1981 | 8.58% | ... $21,811 | |
| 1980 | 28.02% | | |
| 1979 | 30.53% | | |
| 1978 | -1.64% | | |
| 1977 | 19.08% | 1976 - 1980 | |
| 1976 | 48.97% | | 23.87% |
| 1975 | 36.34% | ... $29,157 | |
| 1974 | -42.23% | | |
| 1973 | -27.22% | | |
| 1972 | 11.19% | | |
| 1971 | n.a. | | |
| 1970 | n.a. | | |
| 1969 | n.a. | | |
| 1968 | n.a. | | |
| 1967 | n.a. | | |
| 1966 | n.a. | | |
| 1965 | n.a. | | |
| 1964 | n.a. | | |
| 1963 | n.a. | | |
| 1962 | n.a. | | |
| 1961 | n.a. | | |
| 1960 | n.a. | | |

How a $10,000 investment performed over

| 5 years | 10 years | 15 years | 20 years |
|---|---|---|---|
| 1991 - 1995 | | | |
| $21,515 (16.56%)^ | 1986 - 1995 | | |
| | $20,701 (7.55%) | 1981 - 1995 | |
| | | $45,150 (10.57%) | 1976 - 1995 |
| | | | $131,645 (13.75%) |

^ annual compound rate of return for that period
* Source: National Association of Real Estate Investment Trusts®
n.a. = not available

©1996 Chase Global Data & Research
73 Junction Square, Concord, MA 01742

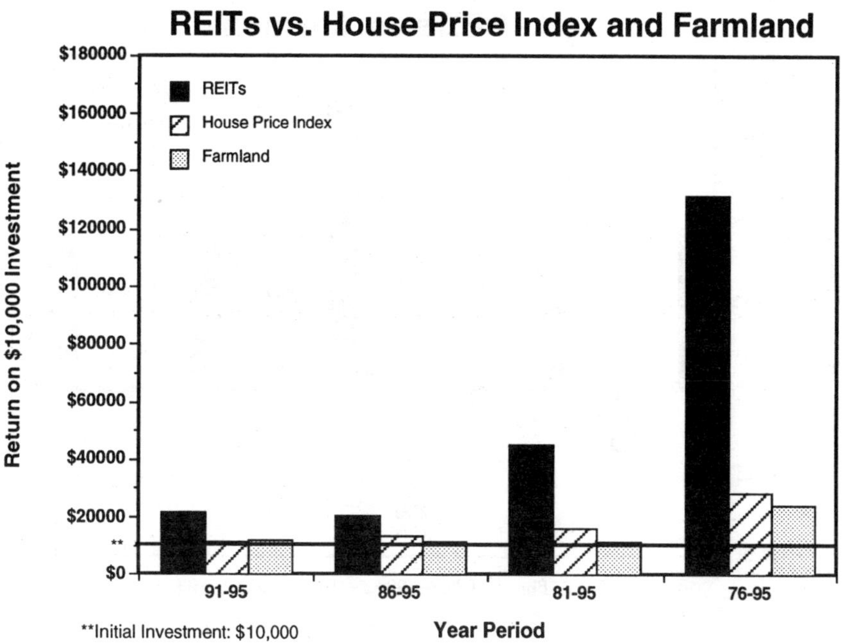


©1996 Chase Global Data & Research
73 Junction Square, Concord, MA 01742

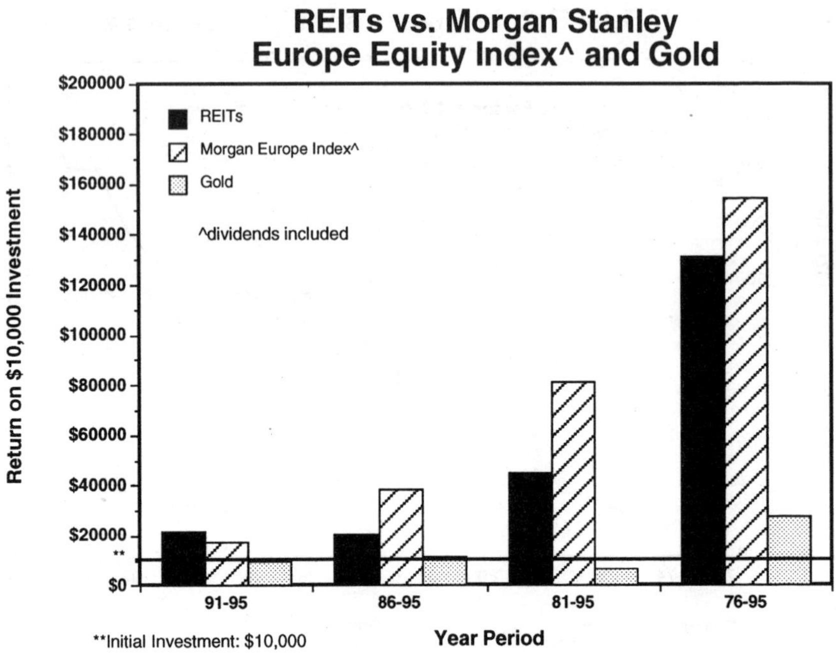


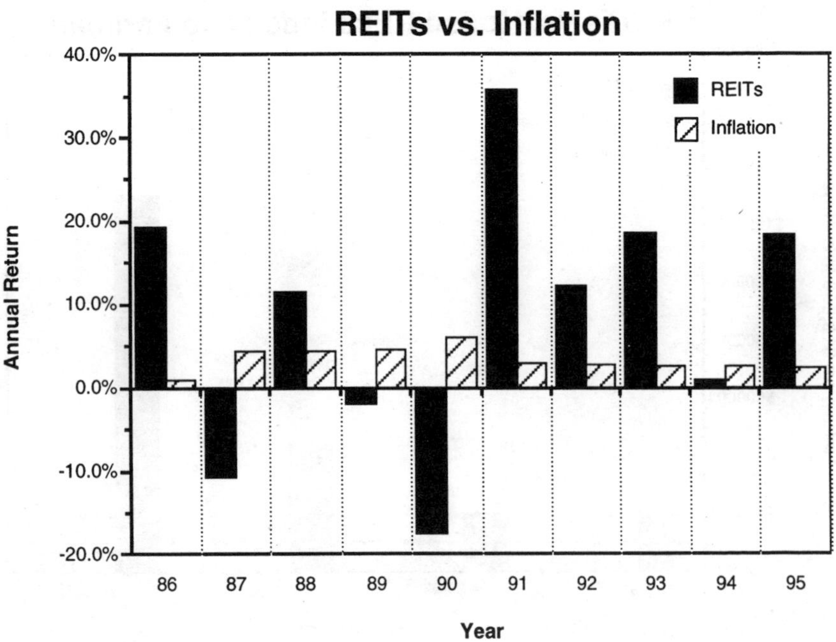


©1996 Chase Global Data & Research
73 Junction Square, Concord, MA 01742

SECTION X

# Major International Currencies

# Chapter Thirty Eight

# Currencies

Currency is a form of money. It is a term usually reserved for paper notes of a nation, but also is understood to reflect coinage as well. Money's key initial use was to allow trade to take place without barter. In ancient times, Indians used wampum (beads made from shells), the Colonists in North America used tobacco, whales' teeth were used in the Fiji Islands, large stones were used in the Pacific Isles, and cigarettes and liquor were sometimes used as money in the 20th century's post-World War II Germany, over 500 years after the first currency exchange booths were established in Frankfurt, Germany.

The word "pecuniary" is derived from the Latin word for cattle—which were also used as money in ancient times. The use of metal as money can be traced back to over 2000 years B.C. Historians place the first standardization of coinage sometime in the 7th century B.C. in Lydia, a Greek state in Asia Minor. The coins were made of a natural mixture of gold and silver and were bean-shaped ingots with punch marks certifying weight and/or fineness. In fact the modern term "being clipped" in a business transaction derives from the clippings which resulted from the ancient practice of shaving tiny slivers from the edges of coins. The first milling of coins in a highly uniform manner began in the late 17th century. Then, as today, coins were composed of copper, silver, gold, and other metals of differing value. Paper money, the more prominent form of currency, found widespread use beginning in the late 18th and 19th centuries, though some historians feel paper money existed in China many centuries earlier.

Money is a financial asset with three primary attributes: a medium of storage; a standard of value; and a store value. When one is accumulating wealth a currency's ability to be a store value, i.e. a means to store and bookkeep one's wealth without deterioration in the medium of storage, is greatly appreciated. To be sure, the concept of money is a complex one. Those pieces of paper are valuable because everyone thinks they are—and everyone thinks they are because in their experience the pieces of paper have always been valuable. This


©1996 Chase Global Data & Research
73 Junction Square, Concord, MA 01742

strength of convention allows governments to issue more and more currencies—and at times, because of over-issuance, to cause inflation.

Almost from the beginning of the issuance of paper currency such notes were issued on a "fiat," or arbitrary basis, by the sovereign. The sovereign or government specified the note was worth so many dollars, or francs, or yen, and as such was legal tender—but did not promise to pay something else in return for the paper money. However, some forms of paper currency did guarantee an exchange for either gold or silver. In fact, after a hundred years or so of issuing paper money and the subsequent over-issuance and drastic drops in the value of money, most major countries during the 19th century backed their paper currency with a metallic standard.

The early 20th century was labelled the era of the international gold standard. Gold coins circulated in most of the world. Paper money —whether issued by private banks or by governments—was deemed convertible into gold or bullion at an official price. Even bank deposits were convertible into gold or paper currency backed by gold. During that time there was a single "world money" called by different names in different countries. There were strict ratios of what pounds were worth in dollars, dollars were worth in yen, etc. Exchange rates differed only by an amount which equalled the cost of shipping gold between countries. Quantities of money in each country were highly reflective of an ability to export and import goods.

The Depression brought an end to managed gold standards internationally. Many experts feel that the Great Depression came about due to poor monetary policy—a policy which permitted the quantity of money to decline by one-third from 1929 to 1933. Part of the reason for the lack of expansion in the money supply was caused by the system being on a gold standard. Britain was the first major country to leave the gold standard, in 1931. The U.S. followed in 1933, and many other nations followed between 1933 and 1934. Between 1934 and 1971 the dollar was officially priced at $35 per ounce of gold, with the U.S. government ready and able to sell gold to foreign countries at that price.

After 1934, currency dealings among nations were primarily done through a fixed exchange rate policy. Using fixed exchange rates, governments coordinated their efforts to keep their currencies' value constant for as long as possible. They believed that fixed exchange rates reduced uncertainty, encouraged international trade and investment, and permitted the world economy to operate more efficiently.

©1996 Chase Global Data & Research
73 Junction Square, Concord, MA 01742

After World War II, fixed exchange rates were written into international financial system and supervised by the newly created International Monetary Fund. In 1971, exchange rates were realigned. By 1973 fixed exchange rates were abandoned by most major currencies, which opted instead for floating rates. Thus beginning in 1973, individual currencies of nations were permitted to rise and fall relative to one another. The fluctuations of the past decade, notably 1985 through 1987, and 1992's upheaval, have had a significant impact on investments and international trade.

Another aspect of currency is that it can also be defined as non-interest bearing notes. Notes are suitable for monetary purposes and payable to the bearer on demand. However, how they are payable as well as if they are payable are questions more readily asked today than in the past when there was a guaranteed direct conversion to other assets such as gold or silver. When specific methods of convertibility are not stated, any effort to convert notes can be refused by a government on grounds of emergency and national interest—as happened in the U.S. in 1933. The government carries the obligation to redeem, but the time of redemption is left for future determination. For example, in the 1860's the Confederate States of America issued currency. Thousands of British and Continental European investors sank $60 million into such notes and bonds but they never received any payment either from the victorious U.S. government or the defeated Confederacy. History is full of such risks with government issued currency and notes.

## U.S. DOLLAR

The history of U.S. currency is complex, and one of slow, but sure, debasement. In fact, the U.S government's first currency, the Continental, was a classic example of a fiat money which became worthless. The famous expression "not worth a Continental" refers to the extreme depreciation of the Continental currency during Revolutionary times. Legend states that it took a wagonload of Continental currency to buy a wagonload of provisions. (The U.S. was not alone, for after World War I German marks, Italian lira, French francs, and other currencies suffered similar fates.) It should be noted that since the early 1800's the U.S. dollar has depreciated 90%.

U.S. currency, until 1914, was issued by privately held banks which had special safety funds in cash or securities. The notes held first lien on all assets of the bank, and government bonds also backed the issuance of the notes. In addition, the U.S. government effectively

©1996 Chase Global Data & Research

issued "warehouse receipts" which showed a deposit of a specific quantity of either gold or silver backed its currency.

Coins have had an even stranger history of issuance in the U.S. Prior to the more formal issuing of coins in the late 19th century, the U.S. was the domain of many private-issue coins. Various gold mining companies in California issued gold pieces in 2.5, 5, 10, 20, and 50 dollar denominations. In fact there were 15 private mints operating in California alone from 1849 to 1855. During the severe economic depression of 1837-1838, there was a major shortage of coins. Tokens (called "hard times" tokens) were created by private companies to relieve the problem. During the Civil War large quantities of private copper coins were minted. Between 1862 and 1864 more than 50 million tokens in 800 varieties were created in 22 states. These coins were issued in addition to the U.S. Indian Head cent coin which was minted from 1859 to 1909. The panic of 1907 showed that our system had many shortcomings. In response to this crisis the Aldrich-Vreeland Act was passed by Congress in 1908 authorizing the issuance of emergency currency by groups of banks organized as national currency associations.

By 1914 the Federal Reserve System was begun. In many ways it reflected the relief bill of 1908. By 1933 the U.S. abandoned the gold standard and by 1935 all national bank notes were eliminated. By 1963 the backing of notes by way of silver was gone, and by 1968 any remaining vestige of the gold standard was removed by the U.S. government. Today, Federal Reserve notes are obligations of the U.S. government and represent first liens on all assets of the issuing Federal Reserve Bank named on each note.

Today about one-fifth of the money outstanding in the U.S. ($725 billion) is represented by coin and currency. The remaining four-fifths is in the form of checking deposits in banking institutions. Of the coin and currency, approximately 10% ($70 billion) stands in coins and about 15% ($100 billion) is in currency, or note form.

The U.S. dollar, based on the G-10 Country Index of the Federal Reserve, has been a weak performer over the past quarter century, losing 30%. Over the twenty-five years, inclusive of the fixed-rate period, it averaged a 1.40% loss per year. Since 1986, as the nation's 219 year old federal deficit tripled, the dollar has fallen 31% in value. Despite its overall weakness the dollar proved a safe haven during the currency crisis in Europe in 1992, rising over 10% in a year where several major currencies fell between 7% and 15%. Its was also a safe haven during the Mexican peso crisis of 1994.

©1996 Chase Global Data & Research
73 Junction Square, Concord, MA 01742

## BRITISH POUND STERLING

The pound sterling has seen much change and volatility throughout the 20th century. However, for hundreds of years the British pound sterling was the world's key currency for international trade. It was the conservative currency to hold both as a means of payment and as a temporary store value. Reflecting the currency's great stability, most of the sterling transfers occurred through London banks rather than the banks of nations where the transactions were taking place. Except for the U.S. dollar in the decades immediately following World War II, no other currency has ever achieved a comparable position in international trade.

The volume of Britain's external trade was a major reason for the use of its pound sterling. British exports quadrupled between 1800 and 1850, and increased eight fold between 1850 and 1913. Britain also became the world's premier lending nation. However, in 1931 Britain took a major step in devaluing its pound sterling. Nevertheless, most of Britain's trading partners pegged their currencies to the pound, even over gold. Following the free floating of world currencies initiated in the early 1970's, the British pound has been a weak performer. In 1971 the pound was as high as $2.55 U.S. dollars, but by 1984 it was as low as $1.10. In the early 1950's and into the mid-1960's the pound fluctuated mildly, usually hovering around U.S. $2.80. Over the past thirty-five years the British Pound has averaged an annual loss over all time periods except 10 years—the 5, 15, 20, 25, and 35 year time frames. Overall it declined 1.68% per annum, or 45% in the past three plus decades. The Pound was in the center of the storm during Europe's tumult of 1992, losing 18.85%—its third worst performance over the past three decades.

## JAPANESE YEN

The Japanese currency, the yen, has shown tremendous resiliency since World War II. But the majority of its history is marred by wars and a general confusion in the currency's evolution, which took place over several hundred years.

Japan's early currency history was chaotic. The first currencies in Japan were introduced in the mid-1600's. By 1870 there were sixteen hundred different forms of paper currency printed in Japan. But by 1879 the yen began to be recognized as the basic unit of currency. After that it took approximately two decades to develop a modern monetary

©1996 Chase Global Data & Research
73 Junction Square, Concord, MA 01742

system, first based on silver and then on gold. By 1914 Japan had formally and completely switched to a gold standard. After World War I, for over three decades Japan's yen floated—unlike much of the rest of the world. It returned to a gold standard only briefly from 1930 to 1931.

Decades later, World War II brought Japan to the brink of economic disaster. But recovery was fast and Japan managed to become a world power in trade, enhancing its currency in the process. After World War II, Japan switched to a dollar exchange standard which was maintained until 1971, when it began to float its yen—a move made in concert with many other world currencies.

The yen has been an exceptionally strong currency. The yen doubled in value from 1985 to 1988 against the U.S. dollar, and has over tripled over the past 35 years. For the twenty year span from 1950 to 1970 the yen was quite stable, trading in the 355 to 360 yen/dollar range. In the past decade it proved to be a powerful currency, and excellent investment overall—appreciating 6.93% annually. In testimony to its popularity, options and futures offering a bet on the yen's movement actively trade in the U.S., along with yen warrants listed on the American Stock Exchange. During the 1992 European currency crisis, the Yen managed to remain unchanged overall, and during the Mexican peso devaluation it proved strong. But the most tumultuous year since World War II occurred in 1995, when it rose over 20% (to an all time high of 79.85 yen/dollar) only to finish 1995 with a loss of 3.77%.

## CANADIAN DOLLAR

Canadian currency has had a brief history—even shorter than the U.S. dollar and certainly less detailed than the Japanese yen or the British pound. Prior to the organization of the Bank of Canada in 1934, Canadian currency was issued by chartered banks and the Treasury. Banks could issue notes up to $120 million against reserves of 25% in gold, or other assets such as securities of railway companies guaranteed by the Canadian government.

At the time of major changes in currency issuance in the U.S., Canadians passed the Finance Act of 1914. The Act allowed the Treasury to issue unlimited amounts of notes to chartered banks and savings banks, but it required a reserve of 100% in gold. In 1934 the Bank of Canada Act rescinded the power of the Treasury to issue notes

©1996 Chase Global Data & Research
73 Junction Square, Concord, MA 01742

and also limited the power of chartered banks to issue them. By 1950 all liability for outstanding notes was transferred to the Bank of Canada through payment of a like amount by the issuing chartered banks. Thus the Bank of Canada became the sole source of Canadian currency issue.

In 1971 the Canadian government abandoned fixed exchange rates along with other nations and allowed its currency to fluctuate in international exchange with limited government intervention. For the most part changes in the value of Canadian currency reflect Canada's ability to trade and expand its economy in relation to its greatest trading partner, the United States. The majority of Canada's exports go to the U.S. and Canada is a significant importer of U.S. goods.

Over the past three decades, the Canadian dollar has lost value versus the U.S. dollar. In the decade of the 1980's it remained unchanged, rising but 0.1% annually. However, from 1975 to 1985 it lost value in nine of eleven years. While annual losses have not been substantial since 1960, the net result has been a 28% devaluation versus the U.S. dollar, or an average depreciation of 0.93% per year. Lately versus the greenback, the Canadian dollar has depreciated four of the past six years. It averaged a 0.25% annual loss over the past decade. 1992's weak currency year was a poor one for the Canadian dollar, when it lost 9%.

## SWISS FRANC

The Swiss franc is famous for its stability and has long been considered a currency to hold in times of crisis. A long political history of constant neutrality is part of the reason for the stability of the Swiss franc.

The Swiss franc was formally initiated in the mid-19th century, and primarily based on the French franc. Although the Swiss franc was originally on a silver standard, by the 1870's it became a bimetallic currency based on silver and gold. By 1930 the Swiss franc was based entirely on gold.

Throughout the 20th century the Swiss franc was exceedingly stable; it was devalued only once (1934-1936). Part of the reason for the strength of the Swiss currency is that as late as 1970, 94% of Swiss bank notes were backed by gold, the highest gold coverage of any currency in the world. The second closest nation of gold-backed currency, the Netherlands, had coverage of 69%.

©1996 Chase Global Data & Research
73 Junction Square, Concord, MA 01742

Despite occasionally weak years, overall the Swiss franc has been a solid performer. Of note, however, 1979 through 1984 the Swiss franc dropped 38% versus the U.S. dollar. Durng the decade of the 1980's it was static versus the U.S. dollar, rising 0.4% per annum. More recently it has been solid, gaining 5.9% annually since 1986. Since 1960 the franc has appreciated over three fold, rising on average versus the dollar every other year. 1992's weak year for European currency affected the Swiss Franc as well, as it lost over 7%. The Franc sharply reversed its most recent losses by climbing over 27% in 1994-95.

**AUSTRALIAN DOLLAR**

Australia has had a volatile economic growth pattern ever since its beginnings in the mid-1800s. The Commonwealth of Australia was formed in 1901. Both before and after that time the country's currency and economic well-being have vacillated due to its close tie to natural resource development. Until recently it has been unable to diversify its economy into other areas.

After a major economic decline from the mid-1970's to the mid-1980's, Australia began a major rebound in 1985. But such recent turnarounds are a far cry from early data that shows that in 1870 Australia's per capita income was the highest in the world, 75% greater than in the United States. By 1929 per capita income had fallen to 25% below U.S. levels, a ratio that remained constant until the mid-1980's.

Australia's reputation as a highly protectionist nation which does not encourage free trade has hurt its currency as well as its economy. Australia's involvement in international trade declined immediately after World War II and failed to increase markedly for several decades. But Australia was one of the countries which immediately benefited from the lifting of fixed exchange rates in 1971. Australia's currency rose over 25% during the first few years of free-floating exchange rates. However, after 1973 its currency dropped over 50% (1973-1986). Then once again its currency began to rebound and was strong in the late 1980's. With the exception of the sharp 14.2% rise is 1994, it has been weak in recent years. Over the past 35 years the Aussie dollar has lost over 30%, or 1.16% annually to the U.S. dollar.

In 1991-1992, Australia's inflation rate halved from early 1990 levels to under 4%. Its bond prices rose sharply due to sharp yield reductions in Australian bonds formerly offering yields above 14%. Foreigners in general have become more attracted to Australian markets, and the Australian dollar has grown in trading volume and value, especially in 1994.

©1996 Chase Global Data & Research
73 Junction Square, Concord, MA 01742

## GERMAN MARK

In the 20th century no major currency has suffered a more catastrophic decline than the German mark. As is the case with so many dramatic declines in a nation's currency, it was caused by a major war. At the outbreak of World War I Germany departed from a gold standard. The government's ensuing printing of paper currency became a classic example of what can go wrong with fiat currencies. Between 1914 and 1923 the German mark devalued by over one trillion-fold. Using an index from 1913 with the base assumption that $1 equalled 1 mark, by 1919 it took 11 marks to buy one U.S. dollar. By December 1922, it took 11,672 marks. One year later, it took one trillion marks to receive one dollar bill. In 1923 the rate of inflation in Germany (and the rate of deflation in the value of its currency) was 5.84% per day, compounded throughout the year. Roughly speaking, that was the increase in the pace of the German government's printing of its paper currency. By the end of 1923 children used German marks as play toys. Both the fall in the German currency and the ensuing economic crisis played a major role in the rise of Adolph Hitler.

Overall, since World War II, the German currency has been a solid performer in relationship to other currencies of the world. Between 1950 and 1970 the German mark depreciated less than 1%. However, from 1960 through 1994 the German mark reversed direction and appreciated solidly against the U.S. dollar—over two fold. It made a substantial move upward over the second half of the 80's, rising over 10% per annum. Overall appreciation of the mark has occurred despite its sharp depreciation against the U.S. dollar for the five consecutive years from 1980 through 1984 and most recently three of the past four years. Over the past 35 years the mark has appreciated 3.09% annually. In 1995 the Mark rose to a post World War II, gyrating almost 20% before closing up 7.82% for the year.

## THE MODERN GLOBAL CURRENCY MARKETPLACE

Today there is no single formal market or exchange where foreign exchange is traded. Much of the $1 trillion marketplace is comprised of the major world banks dealing with one another through direct communication links, foreign exchange brokers, and dealers. The world's biggest marketplaces for currency trading are in London, New York, and Tokyo. Over 100 non-U.S. banks trade currencies in New York City alone. Average daily volume overall is $700 billion, with over $250 billion per day in London, $200 billion in New York, and $100 billion in Tokyo. The major currencies traded by U.S. banks ranked by volume are: German marks, Japanese yen, British pounds,

©1996 Chase Global Data & Research
73 Junction Square, Concord, MA 01742

Swiss francs, Canadian dollars, French francs, and Dutch guilders.

Because of the increasing complexities in currencies, and the obvious risks posed by currencies—as evidenced recently in the European currency crash of 1992 and the Mexican Peso devaluation in 1994, hedging through the use of futures contracts is growing more important. Hedges are carried out via currency futures contracts prominently traded on the International Monetary Market of the Chicago Mercantile Exchange. The contracts are agreements on the price of exchange for a future exchange of U.S. dollars into another currency. Today U.S. exchange listed futures contracts are in U.S. dollars, British pounds, Canadian dollars, Deutsche marks, French francs, Japanese yen, Swiss francs, "European currency units", and Australian dollars.

Despite the aura of sophistication of the currency futures marketplace, remember the lessons of history regarding devaluations and the volatility of currencies. The rising debts of some countries are causing major problems for several nations' currencies both domestically and internationally, and for those who hold the weak currencies. South American nations reporting annual inflation rates of 1000% are one obvious example. Argentina introduced its fifth currency in 22 years in 1991. Its Austral had depreciated 12,500 fold since 1986. Even today vestiges of currency problems that besieged Germany in 1923 remain with us. The Mexican peso's sudden 40% devaluation and subsequent 50% interest rates occured in late 1994. Europe's problems in 1992 should henceforth give everyone cause for perspective and concern.

In 1991 the Exchange Rate Mechanism (ERM) agreement was reached among 10 major European nations to create a single European currency by decade's end. By August 1992 the expanding recession in Europe and the failure for the European nations to proceed smoothly with their union caused turmoil in various currency markets. Sweden devalued its Krona over 20% after raising short term interest rates to 500% in September 1992. Great Britain raised its rates to 15%, and Italy jumped to 18%. The result was the most tumultuous currency trading and price declines since World War II, with $10 billion in losses.

After several major European countries devalued their currencies, Great Britain formally withdrew from the agreement in September, 1992. By August, 1993 the agreement totally collapsed and Europe's major nations allowed their currencies to fluctuate as much as 15% versus the former ERM's 2% maximum. The agreement may be resurrected in a few years, but currency volatility will likely remain nonetheless.

©1996 Chase Global Data & Research
73 Junction Square, Concord, MA 01742

## AUSTRALIAN DOLLAR
[year-end]

| Year | Price* ($ per currency unit) | Price Growth | Compound return on a five year $10,000 investment | Annual compound rate of return |
|---|---|---|---|---|
| 1995 | 0.7435 | -4.10% | 1991 - 1995 | |
| 1994 | 0.7753 | 14.22% | | -0.65% |
| 1993 | 0.6788 | -1.52% | ... $ 9,681 | |
| 1992 | 0.6893 | -9.30% | | |
| 1991 | 0.7600 | -1.04% | | |
| 1990 | 0.7680 | -2.54% | 1986 - 1990 | |
| 1989 | 0.7880 | -7.73% | | 2.40% |
| 1988 | 0.8540 | 18.28% | ... $11,258 | |
| 1987 | 0.7220 | 8.54% | | |
| 1986 | 0.6652 | -2.49% | | |
| 1985 | 0.6822 | -17.31% | 1981 - 1985 | |
| 1984 | 0.8250 | -8.18% | | -10.41% |
| 1983 | 0.8985 | -8.35% | ... $ 5,772 | |
| 1982 | 0.9804 | -13.11% | | |
| 1981 | 1.1283 | -4.54% | | |
| 1980 | 1.1820 | 6.73% | 1976 - 1980 | |
| 1979 | 1.1075 | -2.98% | | -1.17% |
| 1978 | 1.1415 | 0.70% | ... $ 9,427 | |
| 1977 | 1.1336 | 7.66% | | |
| 1976 | 1.0529 | -16.02% | | |
| 1975 | 1.2538 | -4.81% | 1971 - 1975 | |
| 1974 | 1.3172 | -11.20% | | 2.44% |
| 1973 | 1.4833 | 22.85% | ... $11,283 | |
| 1972 | 1.2074 | 2.77% | | |
| 1971 | 1.1748 | 5.72% | | |
| 1970 | 1.1112 | -0.28% | 1966 - 1970 | |
| 1969 | 1.1143 | 0.55% | | -0.09% |
| 1968 | 1.1082 | -0.92% | ... $9,954 | |
| 1967 | 1.1185 | 0.62% | | |
| 1966 | 1.1116 | -0.43% | | |
| 1965 | 1.1164 | 0.41% | 1961 - 1965 | |
| 1964 | 1.1118 | -0.21% | | -0.04% |
| 1963 | 1.1142 | -0.25% | ... $9,981 | |
| 1962 | 1.1169 | -0.22% | | |
| 1961 | 1.1194 | 0.08% | | |
| 1960 | 1.1185 | 0.32% | | |

How a $10,000 investment performed over

| 5 years | 10 years | 15 years | 20 years | 25 years | 35 years |
|---|---|---|---|---|---|
| 1991 - 1995 | | | | | |
| $9,681 (-0.65%)^ | 1986 - 1995 | | | | |
| | $10,899 (0.86%) | 1981 - 1995 | | | |
| | | $6,290 (-3.04%) | 1976 - 1995 | | |
| | | | $5,930 (-2.58%) | 1971 - 1995 | |
| | | | | $6,691 (-1.59%) | 1961 - 1995 |
| | | | | | $6,648 (-1.16%) |

^ annual compound rate of return for that period
* Source: Federal Reserve Bank.

©1996 Chase Global Data & Research
73 Junction Square, Concord, MA 01742

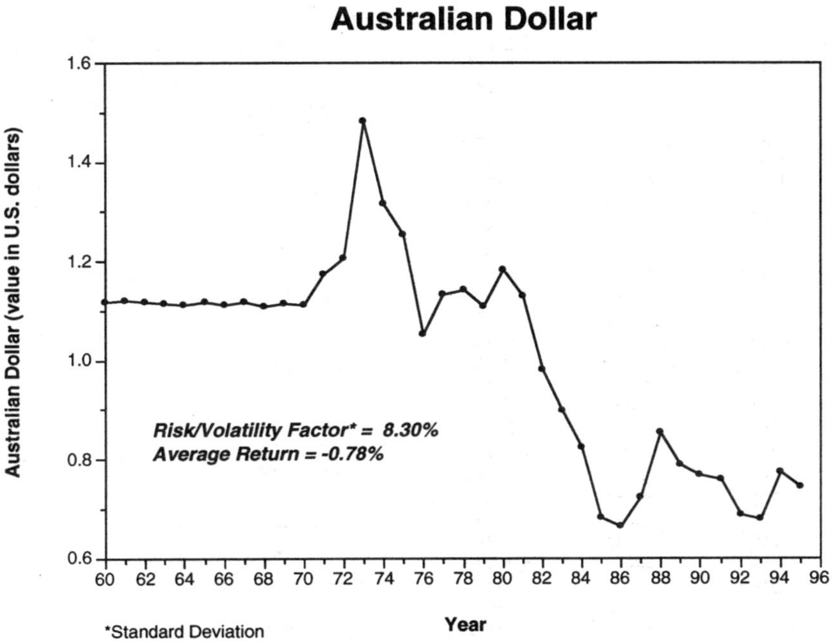


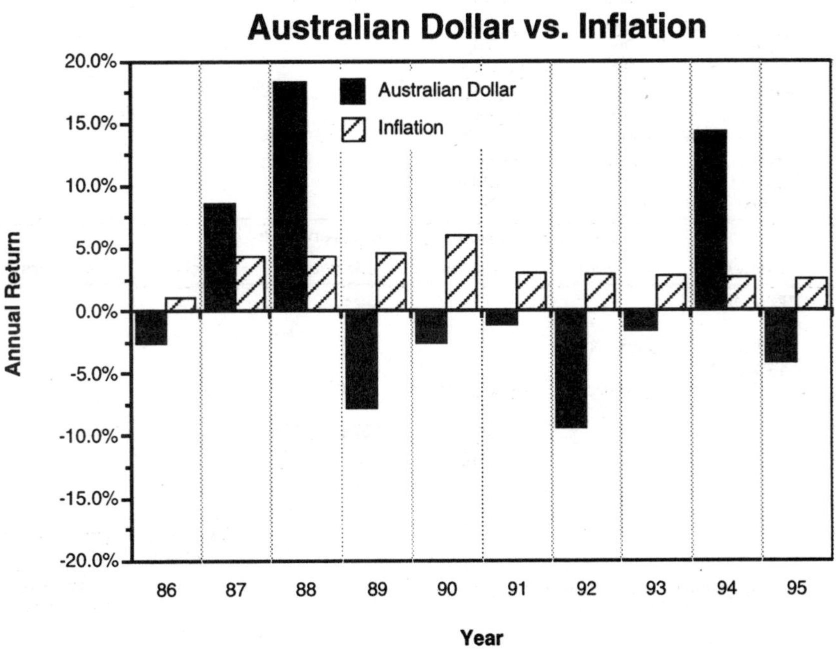


©1996 Chase Global Data & Research
73 Junction Square, Concord, MA 01742

## BRITISH POUND
[year-end]

| Year | Price* ($ per currency unit) | Price Growth | Compound return on a five year $10,000 investment | Annual compound rate of return |
|---|---|---|---|---|
| 1995 | 1.5510 | -0.96% | 1991 - 1995 | |
| 1994 | 1.5660 | 6.06% | | -4.26% |
| 1993 | 1.4765 | -2.54% | ... $ 8,045 | |
| 1992 | 1.5150 | -18.85% | | |
| 1991 | 1.8670 | -3.16% | | |
| 1990 | 1.9280 | 19.64% | 1986 - 1990 | |
| 1989 | 1.6115 | -10.82% | | 5.92% |
| 1988 | 1.8070 | -4.19% | ... $13,329 | |
| 1987 | 1.8860 | 27.26% | | |
| 1986 | 1.4820 | 2.45% | | |
| 1985 | 1.4465 | 25.18% | 1981 - 1985 | |
| 1984 | 1.1555 | -20.56% | | -9.57% |
| 1983 | 1.4545 | -9.94% | ... $ 6,047 | |
| 1982 | 1.6150 | -15.38% | | |
| 1981 | 1.9085 | -20.21% | | |
| 1980 | 2.3920 | 7.51% | 1976 - 1980 | |
| 1979 | 2.2250 | 12.03% | | 3.42% |
| 1978 | 1.9861 | 7.09% | ... $11,829 | |
| 1977 | 1.8546 | 10.50% | | |
| 1976 | 1.6784 | -17.00% | | |
| 1975 | 2.0222 | -13.19% | 1971 - 1975 | |
| 1974 | 2.3294 | 0.52% | | -3.29% |
| 1973 | 2.3174 | -1.17% | ... $ 8,459 | |
| 1972 | 2.3448 | -7.20% | | |
| 1971 | 2.5266 | 5.69% | | |
| 1970 | 2.3906 | -0.28% | 1966 - 1970 | |
| 1969 | 2.3973 | 0.55% | | -3.08% |
| 1968 | 2.3842 | -0.92% | ... $ 8,550 | |
| 1967 | 2.4063 | -13.76% | | |
| 1966 | 2.7901 | -0.21% | | |
| 1965 | 2.7959 | 0.19% | 1961 - 1965 | |
| 1964 | 2.7906 | -0.25% | | -0.08% |
| 1963 | 2.7976 | -0.22% | ... $ 9,959 | |
| 1962 | 2.8039 | -0.20% | | |
| 1961 | 2.8096 | 0.08% | | |
| 1960 | 2.8074 | 0.32% | | |

How a $10,000 investment performed over

| 5 years | 10 years | 15 years | 20 years | 25 years | 35 years |
|---|---|---|---|---|---|
| 1991 - 1995 | | | | | |
| $8,045 (-4.26%)^ | 1986 - 1995 | | | | |
| | $10,722 (0.70%) | 1981 - 1995 | | | |
| | | $6,484 (-2.85%) | 1976 - 1995 | | |
| | | | $7,670 (-1.32%) | 1971 - 1995 | |
| | | | | $6,488 (-1.72%) | 1961 - 1995 |
| | | | | | $5,525 (-1.68%) |

^ annual compound rate of return for that period
* Source: Federal Reserve Bank.

©1996 Chase Global Data & Research
73 Junction Square, Concord, MA 01742

## British Pound

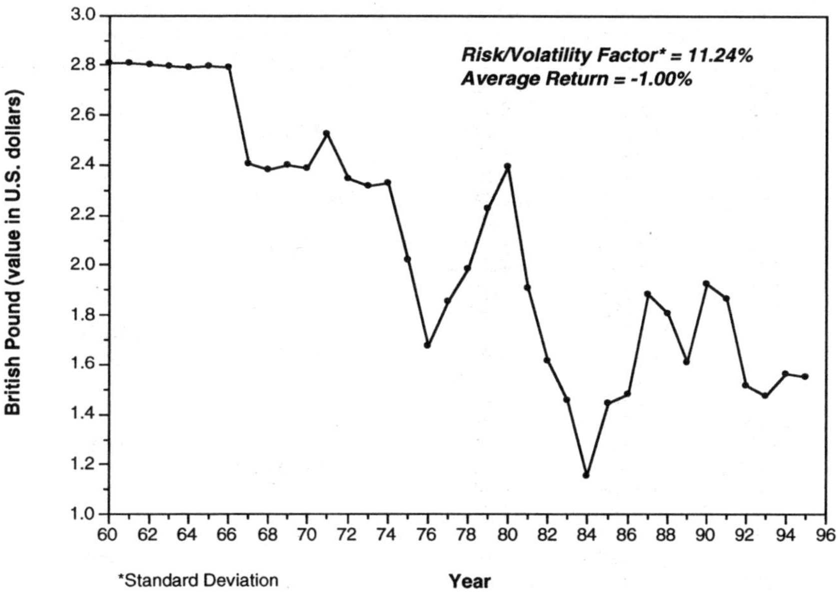


## British Pound vs. Inflation

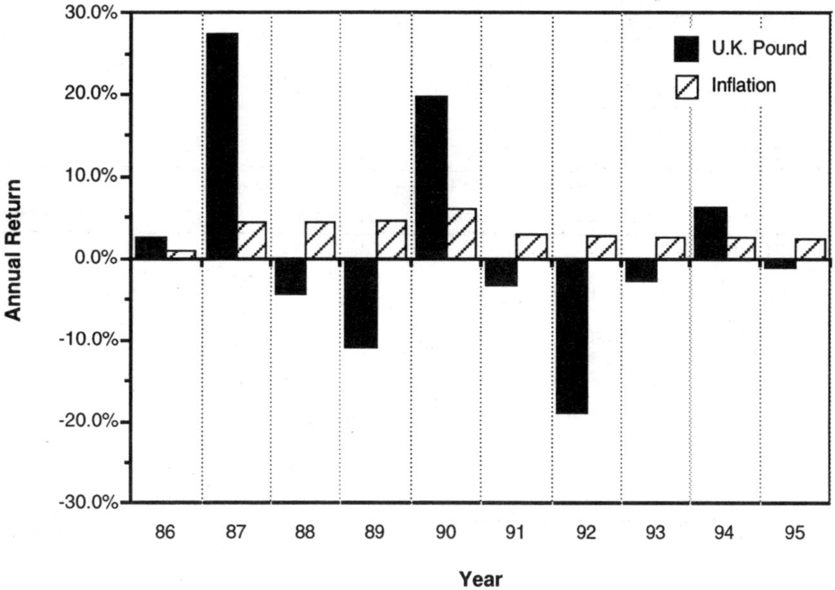


©1996 Chase Global Data & Research
73 Junction Square, Concord, MA 01742

## CANADIAN DOLLAR

[year-end]

| Year | Price* ($ per currency unit) | Price Growth | Compound return on a five year $10,000 investment | Annual compound rate of return |
|---|---|---|---|---|
| 1995 | 0.7334 | 2.79% | 1991 - 1995 | |
| 1994 | 0.7135 | -5.71% | | -3.19% |
| 1993 | 0.7567 | -3.84% | ... $ 8,504 | |
| 1992 | 0.7869 | -9.06% | | |
| 1991 | 0.8653 | 0.34% | | |
| 1990 | 0.8624 | -0.10% | 1986 - 1990 | |
| 1989 | 0.8633 | 2.93% | | 3.82% |
| 1988 | 0.8387 | 9.04% | ... $12,060 | |
| 1987 | 0.7692 | 6.24% | | |
| 1986 | 0.7240 | 1.24% | | |
| 1985 | 0.7151 | -5.54% | 1981 - 1985 | |
| 1984 | 0.7570 | -5.73% | | -3.12% |
| 1983 | 0.8030 | -1.11% | ... $ 8,534 | |
| 1982 | 0.8120 | -3.61% | | |
| 1981 | 0.8424 | 0.54% | | |
| 1980 | 0.8379 | -1.94% | 1976 - 1980 | |
| 1979 | 0.8545 | 0.81% | | -3.21% |
| 1978 | 0.8476 | -6.99% | ... $ 8,496 | |
| 1977 | 0.9113 | -7.20% | | |
| 1976 | 0.9820 | -0.43% | | |
| 1975 | 0.9863 | -2.53% | 1971 - 1975 | |
| 1974 | 1.0119 | 1.13% | | 0.07% |
| 1973 | 1.0006 | -0.27% | ... $10,036 | |
| 1972 | 1.0033 | 0.26% | | |
| 1971 | 1.0007 | 1.82% | | |
| 1970 | 0.9828 | 5.58% | 1966 - 1970 | |
| 1969 | 0.9308 | -0.10% | | 1.12% |
| 1968 | 0.9318 | 0.67% | ... $10,574 | |
| 1967 | 0.9256 | 0.26% | | |
| 1966 | 0.9232 | -0.67% | | |
| 1965 | 0.9294 | -0.11% | 1961 - 1965 | |
| 1964 | 0.9304 | 0.44% | | -1.80% |
| 1963 | 0.9263 | -0.32% | ... $ 9,131 | |
| 1962 | 0.9292 | -3.09% | | |
| 1961 | 0.9589 | -5.79% | | |
| 1960 | 1.0178 | -3.18% | | |

How a $10,000 investment performed over

| 5 years | 10 years | 15 years | 20 years | 25 years | 35 years |
|---|---|---|---|---|---|
| 1991 - 1995 | | | | | |
| $8,504 (-3.19%)^ | 1986 - 1995 | | | | |
| | $10,256 (0.25%) | 1981 - 1995 | | | |
| | | $8,753 (-0.88%) | 1976 - 1995 | | |
| | | | $7,436 (-1.47%) | 1971 - 1995 | |
| | | | | $7,463 (-1.16%) | 1961 - 1995 |
| | | | | | $7,206 (-0.93%) |

^ annual compound rate of return for that period

* Source: Federal Reserve Bank.

©1996 Chase Global Data & Research
73 Junction Square, Concord, MA 01742

## Canadian Dollar

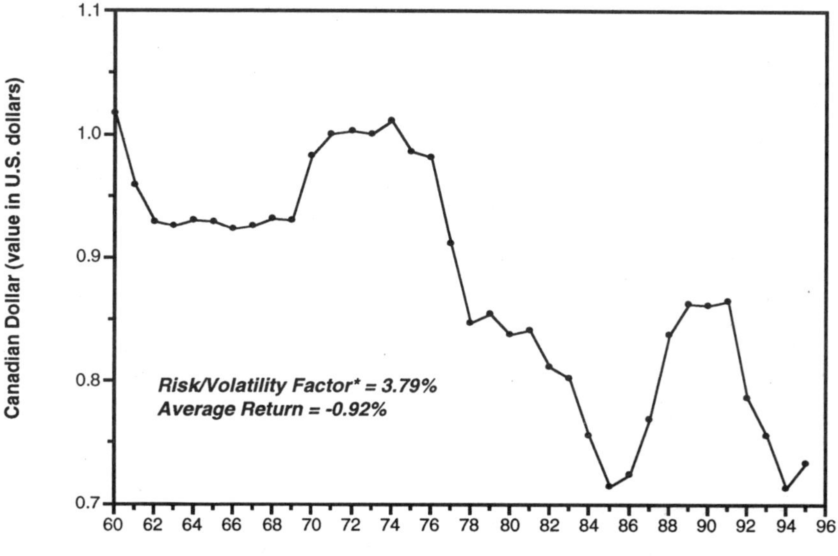


*Standard Deviation

## Canadian Dollar vs. Inflation

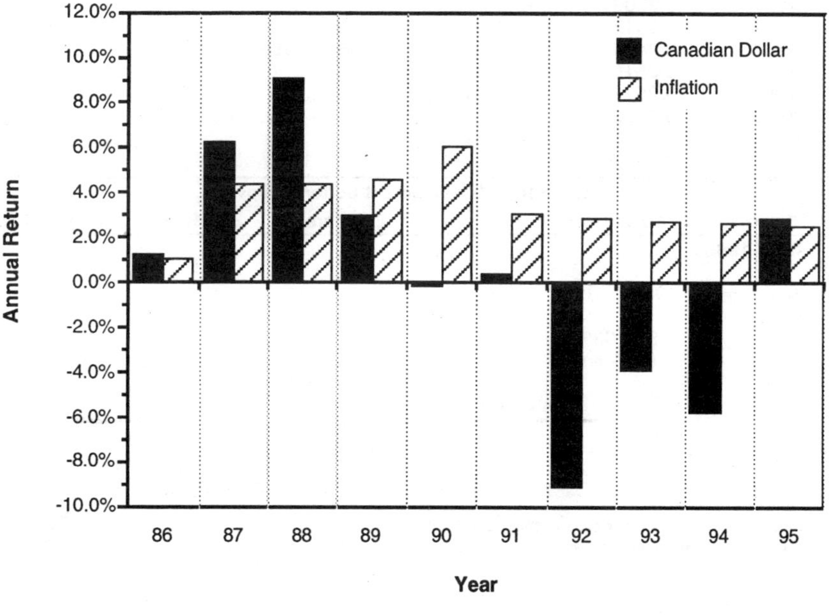


©1996 Chase Global Data & Research
73 Junction Square, Concord, MA 01742

## GERMAN MARK

[year-end]

| Year | Price* ($ per currency unit) | Price Growth | Compound return on a five year $10,000 investment | Annual compound rate of return |
|---|---|---|---|---|
| 1995 | 0.6961 | 7.82% | 1991 - 1995 | |
| 1994 | 0.6456 | 12.22% | | 0.83% |
| 1993 | 0.5753 | -6.89% | ... $10,424 | |
| 1992 | 0.6179 | -6.08% | | |
| 1991 | 0.6579 | -1.48% | | |
| 1990 | 0.6678 | 12.65% | 1986 - 1990 | |
| 1989 | 0.5928 | 5.99% | | 10.32% |
| 1988 | 0.5593 | -12.29% | ... $16,340 | |
| 1987 | 0.6377 | 22.82% | | |
| 1986 | 0.5192 | 27.04% | | |
| 1985 | 0.4087 | 28.93% | 1981 - 1985 | |
| 1984 | 0.3170 | -13.51% | | -4.30% |
| 1983 | 0.3665 | -12.65% | ... $ 8,026 | |
| 1982 | 0.4196 | -5.79% | | |
| 1981 | 0.4454 | -12.53% | | |
| 1980 | 0.5092 | -11.90% | 1976 - 1980 | |
| 1979 | 0.5780 | 8.61% | | 5.95% |
| 1978 | 0.5322 | 28.26% | ... $13,349 | |
| 1977 | 0.4149 | -1.13% | | |
| 1976 | 0.4197 | 10.02% | | |
| 1975 | 0.3814 | -6.55% | 1971 - 1975 | |
| 1974 | 0.4082 | 8.47% | | 6.81% |
| 1973 | 0.3763 | 20.37% | ... $13,902 | |
| 1972 | 0.3126 | 2.19% | | |
| 1971 | 0.3059 | 11.50% | | |
| 1970 | 0.2744 | 1.13% | 1966 - 1970 | |
| 1969 | 0.2713 | 8.39% | | 1.88% |
| 1968 | 0.2503 | -0.25% | ... $10,978 | |
| 1967 | 0.2509 | -0.30% | | |
| 1966 | 0.2517 | 0.71% | | |
| 1965 | 0.2499 | -0.62% | 1961 - 1965 | |
| 1964 | 0.2515 | -0.06% | | 0.84% |
| 1963 | 0.2517 | 0.54% | ... $10,425 | |
| 1962 | 0.2503 | 0.11% | | |
| 1961 | 0.2500 | 4.30% | | |
| 1960 | 0.2397 | 0.00% | | |

How a $10,000 investment performed over

| 5 years | 10 years | 15 years | 20 years | 25 years | 35 years |
|---|---|---|---|---|---|
| 1991 - 1995 | 1986 - 1995 | 1981 - 1995 | 1976 - 1995 | 1971 - 1995 | 1961 - 1995 |
| $10,424 (0.83%)^ | $17,032 (5.47%) | $13,670 (2.11%) | $18,249 (3.05%) | $25,371 (3.79%) | $29,037 (3.09%) |

^ annual compound rate of return for that period

* Source: Federal Reserve Bank.

©1996 Chase Global Data & Research
73 Junction Square, Concord, MA 01742

## German Mark

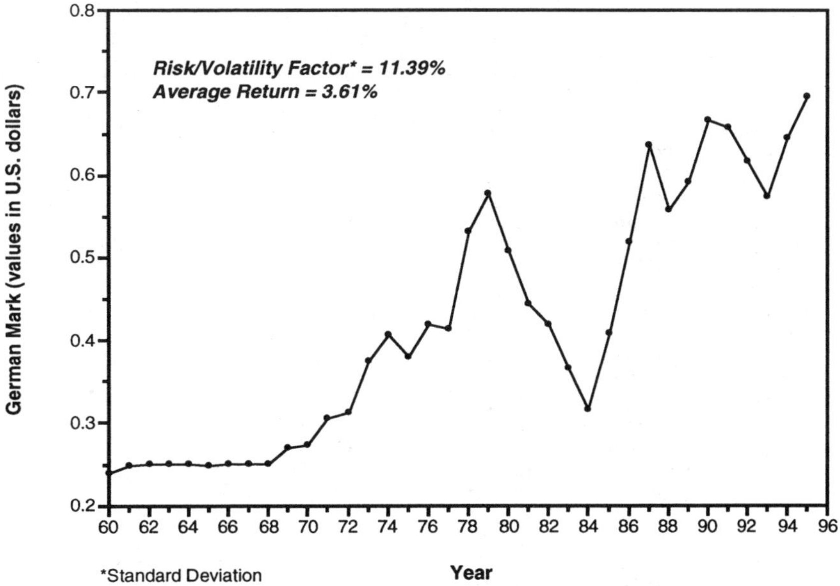


## German Mark vs. Inflation

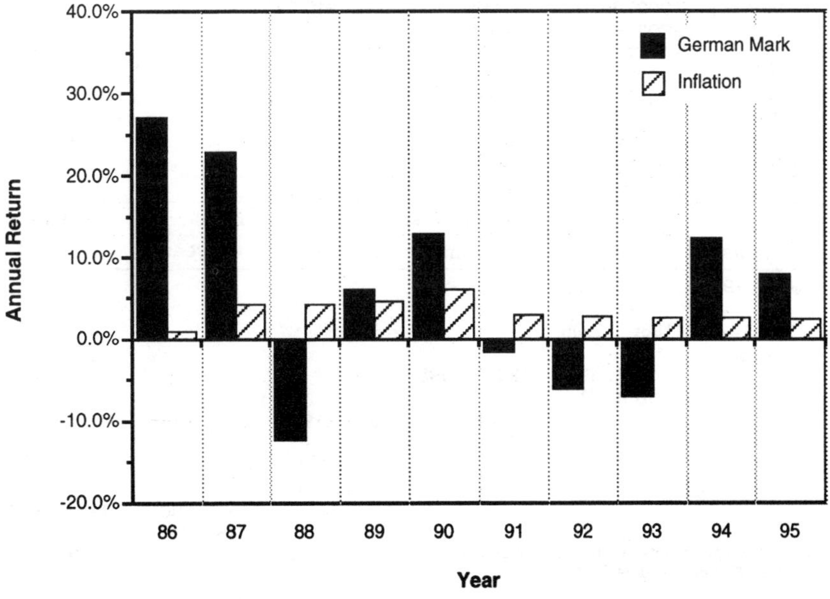


©1996 Chase Global Data & Research
73 Junction Square, Concord, MA 01742

## JAPANESE YEN

[year-end]

| Year | Price* ($ per currency unit) | Price Growth | Compound return on a five year $10,000 investment | Annual compound rate of return |
|---|---|---|---|---|
| 1995 | 0.009671 | -3.77% | 1991 - 1995 | |
| 1994 | 0.010050 | 12.15% | | 5.62% |
| 1993 | 0.008961 | 11.83% | ... $13,144 | |
| 1992 | 0.008013 | 0.00% | | |
| 1991 | 0.008013 | 8.90% | | |
| 1990 | 0.007358 | 5.89% | 1986 - 1990 | |
| 1989 | 0.006949 | -13.14% | | 8.26% |
| 1988 | 0.008000 | -3.19% | ... $14,874 | |
| 1987 | 0.008264 | 30.90% | | |
| 1986 | 0.006313 | 27.61% | | |
| 1985 | 0.004947 | 24.55% | 1981 - 1985 | |
| 1984 | 0.003972 | -7.99% | | 0.04% |
| 1983 | 0.004317 | 1.50% | ... $10,022 | |
| 1982 | 0.004253 | -6.65% | | |
| 1981 | 0.004556 | -7.70% | | |
| 1980 | 0.004936 | 18.23% | 1976 - 1980 | |
| 1979 | 0.004175 | -18.20% | | 8.57% |
| 1978 | 0.005104 | 23.01% | ... $15,088 | |
| 1977 | 0.004149 | 22.27% | | |
| 1976 | 0.003393 | 3.72% | | |
| 1975 | 0.003272 | -1.72% | 1971 - 1975 | |
| 1974 | 0.003329 | -6.74% | | 3.19% |
| 1973 | 0.003569 | 7.52% | ... $11,701 | |
| 1972 | 0.003320 | 6.23% | | |
| 1971 | 0.003125 | 11.77% | | |
| 1970 | 0.002796 | 0.02% | 1966 - 1970 | |
| 1969 | 0.002795 | 0.05% | | 0.19% |
| 1968 | 0.002794 | 1.11% | ... $10,098 | |
| 1967 | 0.002763 | 0.20% | | |
| 1966 | 0.002758 | -0.40% | | |
| 1965 | 0.002769 | -0.53% | 1961 - 1965 | |
| 1964 | 0.002784 | 0.99% | | -0.09% |
| 1963 | 0.002756 | -1.19% | ... $ 9,956 | |
| 1962 | 0.002790 | 0.99% | | |
| 1961 | 0.002762 | -0.67% | | |
| 1960 | 0.002781 | 0.18% | | |

How a $10,000 investment performed over

| 5 years | 10 years | 15 years | 20 years | 25 years | 35 years |
|---|---|---|---|---|---|
| 1991 - 1995 | | | | | |
| $13,144 (5.62%)^ | 1986 - 1995 | | | | |
| | $19,549 (6.93%) | 1981 - 1995 | | | |
| | | $19,593 (4.59%) | 1976 - 1995 | | |
| | | | $29,561 (5.57%) | 1971 - 1995 | |
| | | | | $34,590 (5.09%) | 1961 - 1995 |
| | | | | | $34,775 (3.63%) |

^ annual compound rate of return for that period

* Source: Federal Reserve Bank.

©1996 Chase Global Data & Research
73 Junction Square, Concord, MA 01742

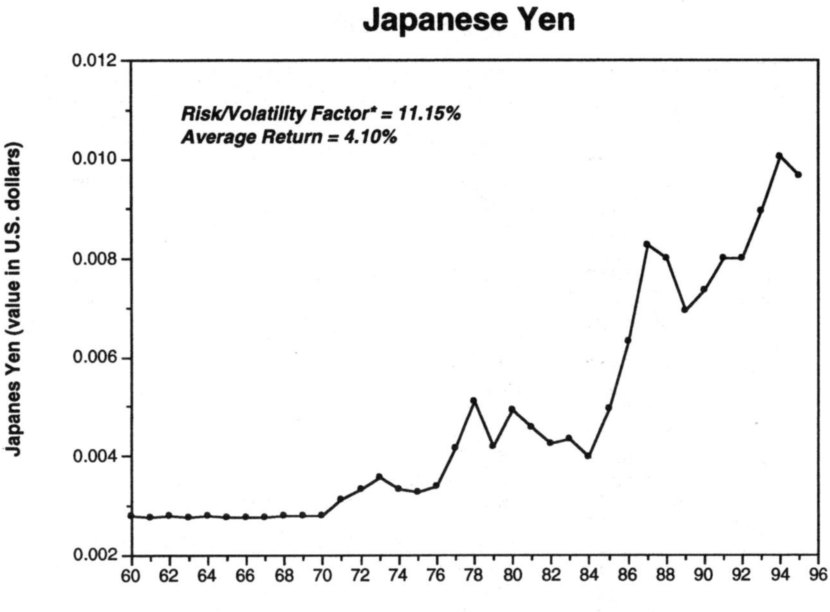


*Standard Deviation

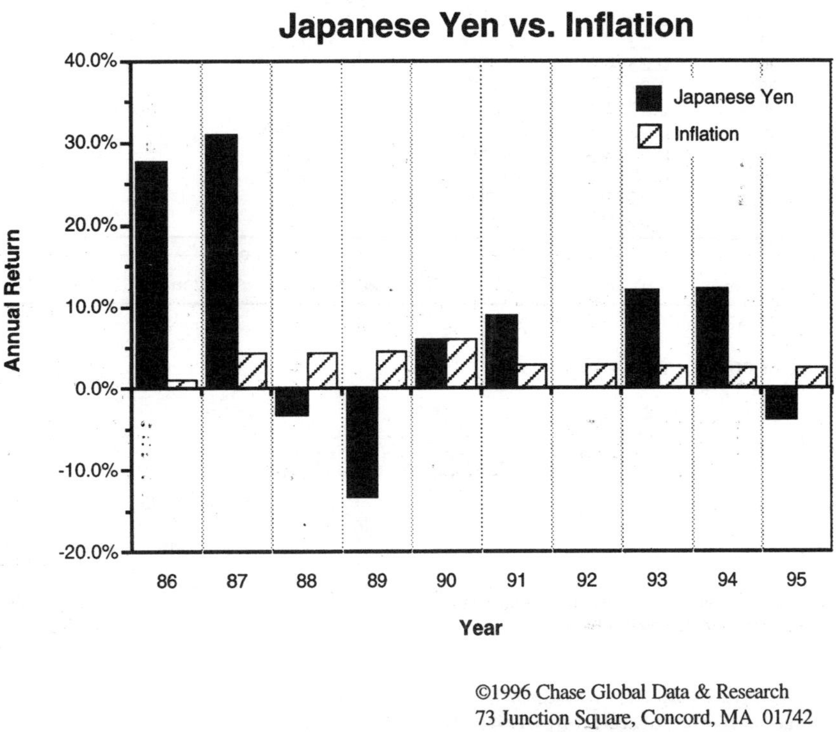


©1996 Chase Global Data & Research
73 Junction Square, Concord, MA 01742

## SWISS FRANC
[year-end]

| Year | Price* ($ per currency unit) | Price Growth | Compound return on a five year $10,000 investment | Annual compound rate of return |
|---|---|---|---|---|
| 1995 | 0.8660 | 13.28% | 1991 - 1995 | |
| 1994 | 0.7645 | 13.76% | | 2.05% |
| 1993 | 0.6720 | -1.48% | ... $11,067 | |
| 1992 | 0.6821 | -7.15% | | |
| 1991 | 0.7346 | -6.12% | | |
| 1990 | 0.7825 | 20.63% | 1986 - 1990 | |
| 1989 | 0.6487 | -2.70% | | 9.91% |
| 1988 | 0.6667 | -15.33% | ... $16,041 | |
| 1987 | 0.7874 | 26.57% | | |
| 1986 | 0.6221 | 27.53% | | |
| 1985 | 0.4878 | 26.83% | 1981 - 1985 | -2.92% |
| 1984 | 0.3846 | -16.15% | | |
| 1983 | 0.4587 | -7.69% | ... $ 8,621 | |
| 1982 | 0.4969 | -10.73% | | |
| 1981 | 0.5566 | -1.63% | | |
| 1980 | 0.5658 | -9.76% | 1976 - 1980 | 8.30% |
| 1979 | 0.6270 | 5.02% | | |
| 1978 | 0.5970 | 23.95% | ... $14,901 | |
| 1977 | 0.4817 | 17.99% | | |
| 1976 | 0.4082 | 7.51% | | |
| 1975 | 0.3797 | -1.23% | 1971 - 1975 | 10.37% |
| 1974 | 0.3844 | 23.01% | | |
| 1973 | 0.3125 | 17.82% | ... $16,376 | |
| 1972 | 0.2653 | 3.56% | | |
| 1971 | 0.2562 | 10.47% | | |
| 1970 | 0.2319 | -0.07% | 1966 - 1970 | 0.02% |
| 1969 | 0.2320 | -0.24% | | |
| 1968 | 0.2326 | 0.44% | ... $10,011 | |
| 1967 | 0.2316 | 0.13% | | |
| 1966 | 0.2313 | -0.14% | | |
| 1965 | 0.2316 | -0.04% | 1961 - 1965 | -0.05% |
| 1964 | 0.2317 | 0.01% | | |
| 1963 | 0.2317 | 0.01% | ... $ 9,973 | |
| 1962 | 0.2317 | -0.01% | | |
| 1961 | 0.2317 | -0.24% | | |
| 1960 | 0.2323 | 0.42% | | |

How a $10,000 investment performed over

| 5 years | 10 years | 15 years | 20 years | 25 years | 35 years |
|---|---|---|---|---|---|
| 1991 - 1995 | | | | | |
| $11,067 (2.05%)^ | 1986 - 1995 | | | | |
| | $17,753 (5.91%) | 1981 - 1995 | | | |
| | | $15,306 (2.88%) | 1976 - 1995 | | |
| | | | $22,807 (4.21%) | 1971 - 1995 | |
| | | | | $37,349 (5.41%) | 1961 - 1995 |
| | | | | | $37,287 (3.83%) |

^ annual compound rate of return for that period
* Source: Federal Reserve Bank.

©1996 Chase Global Data & Research
73 Junction Square, Concord, MA 01742

## Swiss Franc

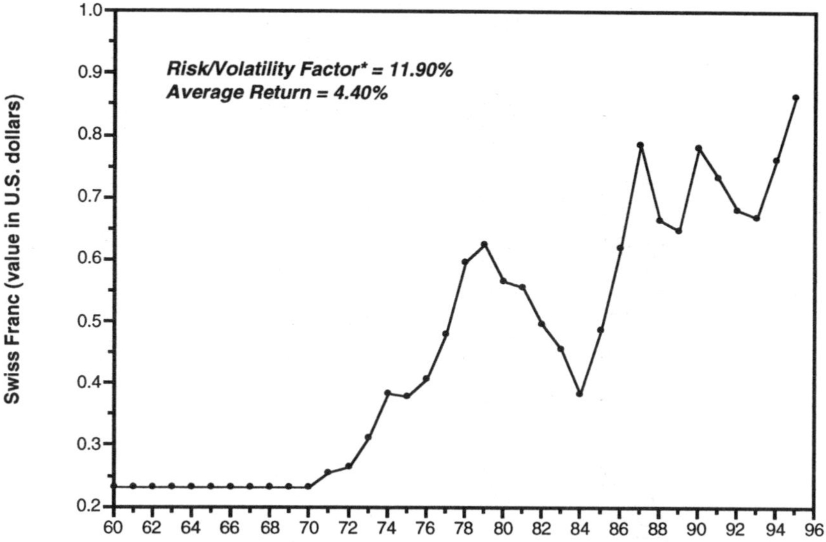


*Standard Deviation

## Swiss Franc vs. Inflation

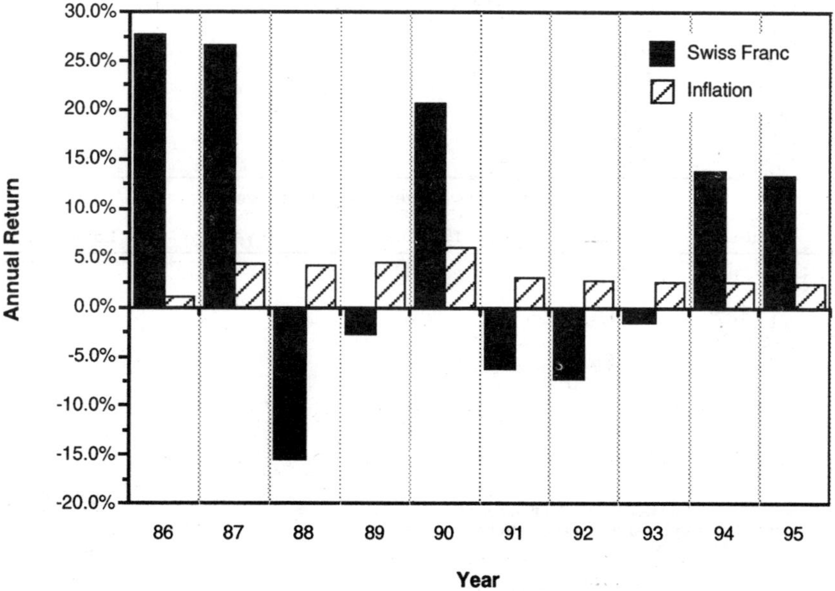


©1996 Chase Global Data & Research
73 Junction Square, Concord, MA 01742

## U.S. DOLLAR INDEX

[avg. against other G-10 countries plus Switzerland; 1973=100; year-end]

| Year | Index Value* | Index Growth | Compound return on a five year $10,000 investment | Annual compound rate of return |
|---|---|---|---|---|
| 1995 | 84.77 | -4.59% | 1991 - 1995 | |
| 1994 | 88.85 | -8.15% | | 0.33% |
| 1993 | 96.73 | 4.73% | ... $10,167 | |
| 1992 | 92.36 | 10.39% | | |
| 1991 | 83.67 | 0.35% | | |
| 1990 | 83.38 | -10.41% | 1986 - 1990 | |
| 1989 | 93.07 | 0.53% | | -7.57% |
| 1988 | 92.58 | 8.26% | ... $ 6,745 | |
| 1987 | 85.52 | -17.60% | | |
| 1986 | 103.79 | -16.04% | | |
| 1985 | 123.62 | -18.39% | 1981 - 1985 | |
| 1984 | 151.47 | 14.93% | | 6.32% |
| 1983 | 131.79 | 10.54% | ... $13,586 | |
| 1982 | 119.22 | 13.32% | | |
| 1981 | 105.21 | 15.63% | | |
| 1980 | 90.99 | 5.41% | 1976 - 1980 | |
| 1979 | 86.32 | -2.49% | | -2.55% |
| 1978 | 88.52 | -10.00% | ... $ 8,790 | |
| 1977 | 98.36 | -6.62% | | |
| 1976 | 105.33 | 1.76% | | |
| 1975 | 103.51 | 4.99% | 1971 - 1975 | |
| 1974 | 98.59 | -2.85% | | -3.02% |
| 1973 | 101.48 | -7.80% | ... $ 8,580 | |
| 1972 | 110.06 | -1.98% | | |
| 1971 | 112.28 | -6.93% | | |
| 1970 | 120.64 | -0.90% | | |
| 1969 | 121.74 | -0.18% | | |
| 1968 | 121.96 | 0.14% | | |
| 1967 | 121.79 | n.a. | | |
| 1966 | n.a. | n.a. | | |
| 1965 | n.a. | n.a. | | |
| 1964 | n.a. | n.a. | | |
| 1963 | n.a. | n.a. | | |
| 1962 | n.a. | n.a. | | |
| 1961 | n.a. | n.a. | | |
| 1960 | n.a. | n.a. | | |

How a $10,000 investment performed over

| 5 years | 10 years | 15 years | 20 years | 25 years |
|---|---|---|---|---|
| 1991 - 1995 | | | | |
| $10,167 (0.33%)^ | 1986 - 1995 | | | |
| | $6,857 (-3.70%) | 1981 - 1995 | | |
| | | $9,316 (-0.47%) | 1976 - 1995 | |
| | | | $8,190 (-0.99%) | 1971 - 1995 |
| | | | | $7,027 (-1.40%) |

^ annual compound rate of return for that period
* Source: Board of Governors, Federal Reserve System.
n.a. = data not available

©1996 Chase Global Data & Research
73 Junction Square, Concord, MA 01742

## U.S. Dollar Index

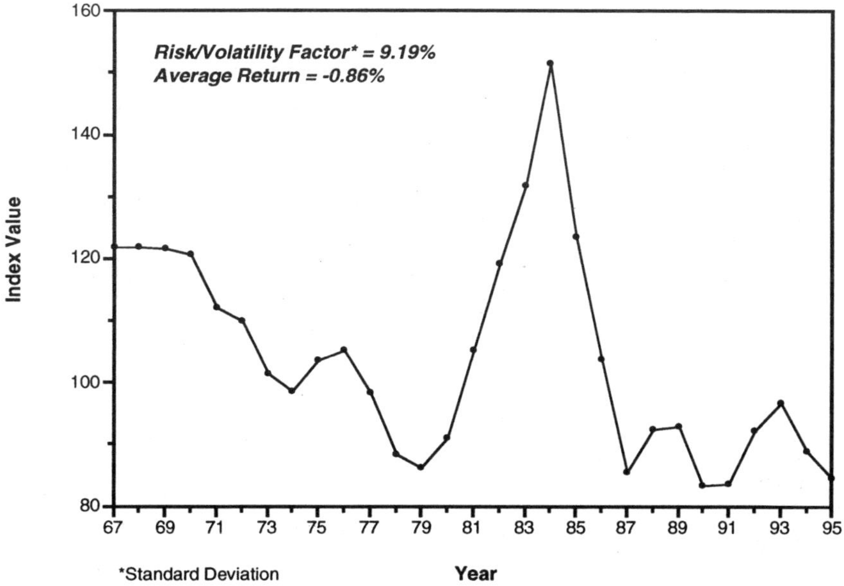


## U.S. Dollar Index vs. Inflation

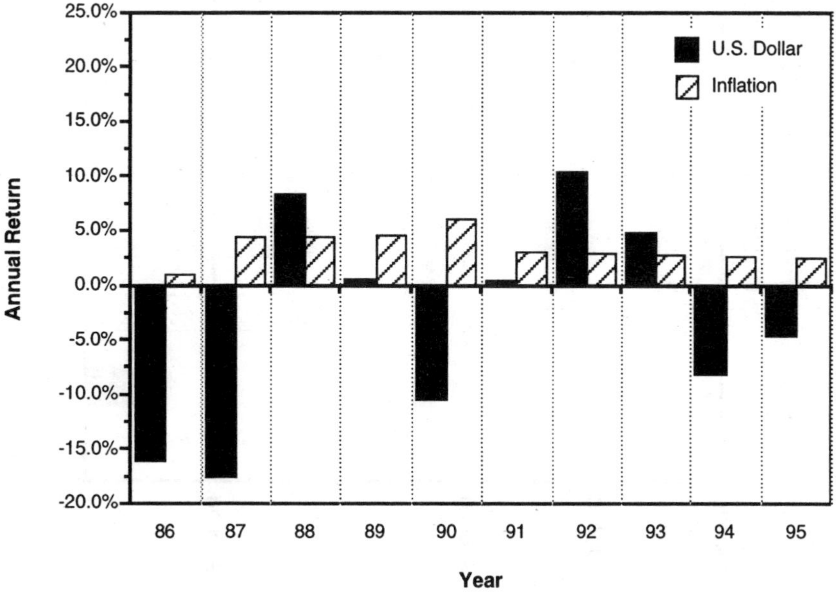


©1996 Chase Global Data & Research
73 Junction Square, Concord, MA 01742

## U.S. Dollar vs. British Pound, Japanese Yen, Canadian Dollar, Swiss Franc, Australian Dollar, and German Mark

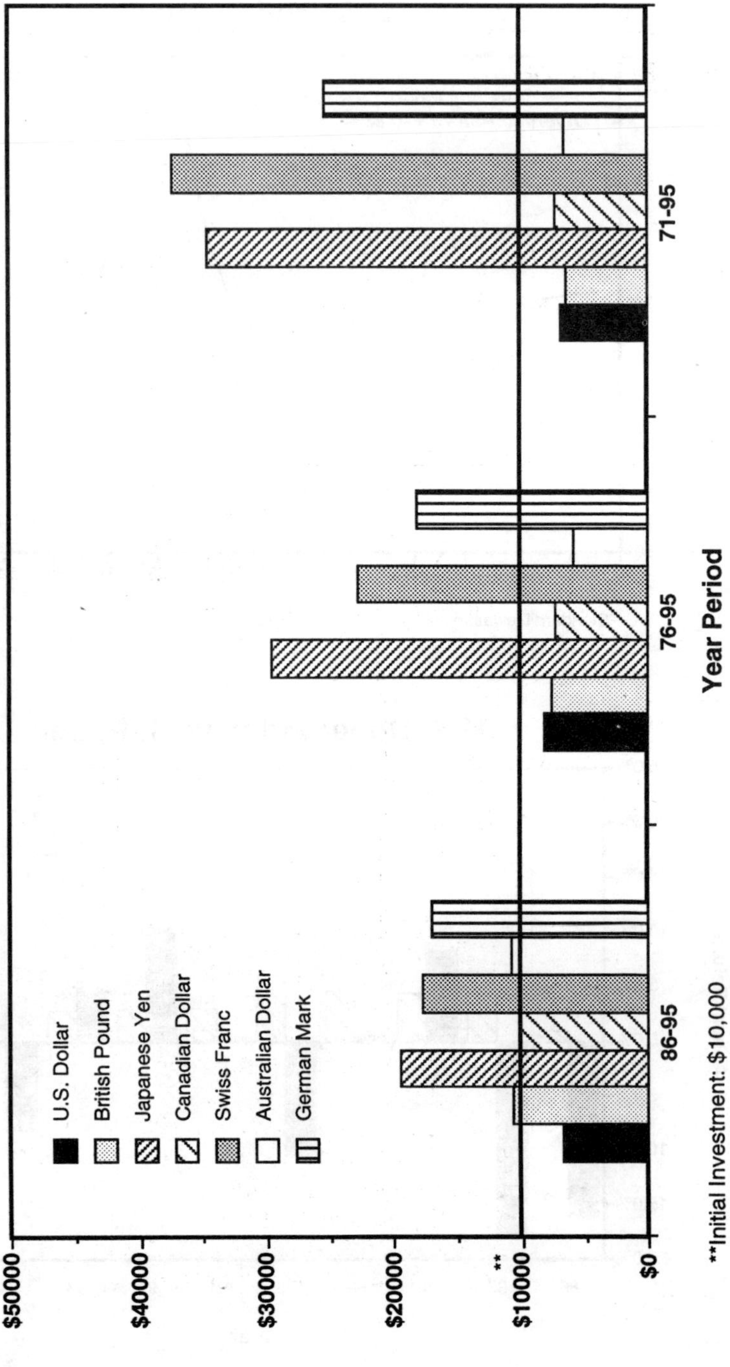


©1996 Chase Global Data & Research
73 Junction Square, Concord, MA 01742

SECTION XI

# Addendum

## STOCK INDEX DIVIDEND YIELDS*

| Year | Dow Jones Industrial | Dow Jones Utility | S&P 500 Composite | U.K. F.T.A. All Share | Tokyo Stock Price Index |
|---|---|---|---|---|---|
| 1995 | 2.27% | 5.76% | 2.24% | 3.80% | 0.85% |
| 1994 | 2.75% | 7.17% | 2.87% | 4.01% | 0.71% |
| 1993 | 2.65% | 5.80% | 2.70% | 3.37% | 0.79% |
| 1992 | 3.05% | 6.09% | 2.84% | 4.34% | 0.88% |
| 1991 | 3.00% | 6.16% | 2.93% | 5.02% | 0.62% |
| 1990 | 3.97% | 6.79% | 3.69% | 5.50% | 0.47% |
| 1989 | 3.74% | 6.29% | 3.29% | 4.24% | 0.45% |
| 1988 | 3.67% | 8.13% | 3.70% | 4.71% | 0.51% |
| 1987 | 3.67% | 9.09% | 3.63% | 4.32% | 0.56% |
| 1986 | 3.54% | 7.42% | 3.47% | 4.04% | 0.74% |
| 1985 | 4.01% | 8.09% | 3.86% | 4.33% | 0.95% |
| 1984 | 5.00% | 9.24% | 4.64% | 4.42% | 1.02% |
| 1983 | 4.47% | 9.83% | 4.29% | 4.62% | 1.31% |
| 1982 | 5.17% | 10.41% | 4.87% | 5.26% | 1.58% |
| 1981 | 6.42% | 10.30% | 5.65% | 5.89% | 1.46% |
| 1980 | 5.64% | 8.94% | 4.67% | 6.10% | 1.48% |
| 1979 | 6.08% | 8.86% | 5.55% | 6.87% | 1.42% |
| 1978 | 6.03% | 8.94% | 5.44% | 5.79% | 1.48% |
| 1977 | 5.51% | 7.40% | 5.08% | 5.28% | 1.68% |
| 1976 | 4.12% | 6.97% | 3.87% | 6.42% | 1.80% |
| 1975 | 4.39% | 8.61% | 4.08% | 5.47% | 2.24% |
| 1974 | 6.12% | 10.05% | 5.37% | 11.71% | 2.41% |
| 1973 | 4.15% | 7.74% | 3.64% | 4.77% | 1.96% |
| 1972 | 3.16% | 5.63% | 2.71% | 3.15% | 2.21% |
| 1971 | 3.47% | 5.57% | 2.99% | 3.25% | 3.37% |
| 1970 | 3.76% | 5.23% | 3.36% | 4.39% | 3.37% |
| 1969 | 4.24% | 5.64% | 3.48% | 3.85% | 3.30% |
| 1968 | 3.32% | 4.45% | 2.99% | 3.24% | 4.26% |
| 1967 | 3.33% | 4.60% | 3.06% | 4.30% | 4.32% |
| 1966 | 4.06% | 4.29% | 3.64% | 5.79% | 3.97% |
| 1965 | 2.95% | 3.40% | 3.04% | 5.23% | 5.13% |
| 1964 | 3.57% | 3.18% | 3.03% | 5.18% | 4.93% |
| 1963 | 3.07% | 3.70% | 3.11% | n.a. | 4.09% |
| 1962 | 3.57% | 3.20% | 3.38% | n.a. | 4.20% |
| 1961 | 3.11% | 3.34% | 2.86% | n.a. | 3.34% |
| 1960 | 3.47% | 3.98% | 3.35% | n.a. | 3.67% |

* Sources cited in their respective chapters.

* Figures reflect year-end values.

©1996 Chase Global Data & Research
73 Junction Square, Concord, MA 01742

## GLOBAL CONSUMER PRICES

[ Percentage changes from previous year ]

| Year | Australia | Canada | Japan | United Kingdom | Germany |
|---|---|---|---|---|---|
| 1995 | 4.5 | 2.1 | -0.2 | 2.9 | 1.8 |
| 1994 | 1.9 | 0.2 | 0.7 | 2.5 | 2.7 |
| 1993 | 1.8 | 1.8 | 1.3 | 1.6 | 4.5 |
| 1992 | 1.0 | 1.5 | 1.7 | 3.7 | 5.1 |
| 1991 | 3.2 | 5.6 | 3.3 | 5.9 | 3.6 |
| 1990 | 7.3 | 4.8 | 3.1 | 9.5 | 2.7 |
| 1989 | 7.5 | 5.0 | 2.3 | 7.8 | 2.8 |
| 1988 | 7.3 | 4.0 | 0.7 | 4.9 | 1.3 |
| 1987 | 8.5 | 4.4 | 0.1 | 4.1 | 0.2 |
| 1986 | 9.1 | 4.2 | 0.6 | 3.4 | -0.1 |
| 1985 | 6.7 | 4.0 | 2.0 | 6.1 | 2.2 |
| 1984 | 3.9 | 4.3 | 2.2 | 5.0 | 2.4 |
| 1983 | 10.1 | 5.8 | 1.9 | 4.6 | 3.3 |
| 1982 | 11.2 | 10.8 | 2.7 | 8.6 | 5.3 |
| 1981 | 9.6 | 12.4 | 4.9 | 11.9 | 6.3 |
| 1980 | 10.2 | 10.2 | 7.8 | 18.0 | 5.5 |
| 1979 | 9.1 | 9.1 | 3.7 | 13.4 | 4.1 |
| 1978 | 7.9 | 8.9 | 4.2 | 8.3 | 2.7 |
| 1977 | 12.3 | 8.0 | 8.2 | 15.8 | 3.7 |
| 1976 | 13.5 | 7.5 | 9.4 | 16.5 | 4.6 |
| 1975 | 15.1 | 10.7 | 11.8 | 24.2 | 5.9 |
| 1974 | 15.1 | 10.9 | 24.5 | 16.0 | 7.0 |
| 1973 | 9.5 | 7.6 | 11.7 | 9.2 | 6.9 |
| 1972 | 5.8 | 4.8 | 4.5 | 7.1 | 5.5 |
| 1971 | 6.1 | 2.8 | 6.1 | 9.4 | 5.3 |
| 1970 | 3.9 | 3.4 | 7.7 | 6.4 | 3.4 |
| 1969 | 2.9 | 4.5 | 5.2 | 5.4 | 1.9 |
| 1968 | 2.7 | 4.0 | 5.3 | 4.7 | 2.9 |
| 1967 | 3.2 | 3.6 | 4.0 | 2.5 | 1.4 |
| 1966 | 2.9 | 3.7 | 5.1 | 3.9 | 3.5 |
| 1965 | 4.0 | 2.4 | 6.6 | 4.8 | 3.4 |
| 1964 | 2.3 | 1.8 | 3.9 | 3.3 | 2.3 |
| 1963 | 0.6 | 1.7 | 8.5 | 2.0 | 3.0 |
| 1962 | -0.3 | 1.2 | 6.8 | 4.3 | 3.0 |
| 1961 | 2.5 | 0.6 | 5.3 | 3.4 | 2.3 |
| 1960 | 3.8 | 1.0 | 3.6 | 1.0 | 1.4 |

* Source: OECD Statistics and International Monetary Fund; 1995 4Q estimated.

©1996 Chase Global Data & Research
73 Junction Square, Concord, MA 01742

## GROWTH OF REAL GNP/GDP

[ Percentage changes from previous period ]

| Year | Australia^ | Canada^ | Germany | Japan | United Kingdom^ | U.S.^ |
|---|---|---|---|---|---|---|
| 1995 | 3.8 | 2.2 | 2.6 | 0.5 | 2.7 | 2.9 |
| 1994 | 5.4 | 4.6 | 2.9 | 0.5 | 3.8 | 3.9 |
| 1993 | 3.9 | 2.2 | -1.2 | -0.2 | 2.2 | 3.1 |
| 1992 | 2.1 | 0.6 | 2.2 | 1.1 | -0.5 | 2.3 |
| 1991 | -1.3 | -1.8 | 5.0 | 4.3 | -2.0 | -0.6 |
| 1990 | 1.3 | -0.2 | 5.7 | 4.8 | 0.4 | 1.2 |
| 1989 | 4.5 | 2.4 | 3.6 | 4.7 | 2.2 | 2.5 |
| 1988 | 4.1 | 5.0 | 3.7 | 6.2 | 5.0 | 3.9 |
| 1987 | 4.7 | 4.2 | 1.5 | 4.1 | 4.8 | 3.1 |
| 1986 | 2.0 | 3.3 | 2.3 | 2.6 | 4.4 | 2.9 |
| 1985 | 4.7 | 4.7 | 2.0 | 5.0 | 3.7 | 3.2 |
| 1984 | 7.5 | 6.3 | 2.8 | 4.3 | 2.3 | 6.2 |
| 1983 | 0.7 | 3.2 | 1.8 | 2.7 | 3.7 | 3.9 |
| 1982 | -0.1 | -3.2 | -0.9 | 3.2 | 1.7 | -2.2 |
| 1981 | 3.4 | 3.7 | 0.1 | 3.6 | -1.3 | 1.8 |
| 1980 | 2.5 | 1.5 | 1.0 | 3.6 | -2.2 | -0.5 |
| 1979 | 4.0 | 3.9 | 4.2 | 5.5 | 2.8 | 2.5 |
| 1978 | 4.0 | 4.6 | 3.0 | 4.9 | 3.5 | 4.8 |
| 1977 | 0.9 | 3.6 | 3.0 | 4.7 | 2.3 | 4.5 |
| 1976 | 4.0 | 6.2 | 4.9 | 4.2 | 2.7 | 4.9 |
| 1975 | 1.8 | 2.6 | -1.4 | 2.9 | -0.7 | -0.8 |
| 1974 | 1.9 | 4.4 | 0.4 | -0.6 | -1.5 | -0.6 |
| 1973 | 5.6 | 7.7 | 4.9 | 7.6 | 7.1 | 5.2 |
| 1972 | 3.4 | 5.7 | 4.3 | 8.2 | 3.5 | 4.8 |
| 1971 | 5.0 | 5.8 | 3.0 | 4.3 | 2.0 | 3.1 |
| 1970 | 5.5 | 2.6 | 5.0 | 10.8 | 2.3 | 0.0 |
| 1969 | -4.2 | 5.4 | 7.5 | 12.1 | 1.8 | 2.7 |
| 1968 | 9.6 | 5.4 | 5.8 | 12.5 | 4.0 | 4.1 |

* Source: OECD Statistics; U.S. Department of Commerce; International Monetary Fund.
1995 4Q estimated.
^ GDP

©1996 Chase Global Data & Research
73 Junction Square, Concord, MA 01742

## HOUSING AFFORDABILITY COMPOSITE INDEX

[annual average]

| Year | Index* Value | Change (%) |
|---|---|---|
| 1995 | 124.7 | -3.78% |
| 1994 | 129.6 | -5.33% |
| 1993 | 136.9 | 9.78% |
| 1992 | 124.7 | 10.45% |
| 1991 | 112.9 | 3.11% |
| 1990 | 109.5 | 3.20% |
| 1989 | 106.1 | -6.52% |
| 1988 | 113.5 | -0.61% |
| 1987 | 114.2 | 4.87% |
| 1986 | 108.9 | 14.87% |
| 1985 | 94.8 | 6.40% |
| 1984 | 89.1 | 7.09% |
| 1983 | 83.2 | 19.71% |
| 1982 | 69.5 | 0.87% |
| 1981 | 68.9 | -13.77% |
| 1980 | 79.9 | -17.80% |
| 1979 | 97.2 | -12.75% |
| 1978 | 111.4 | -7.63% |
| 1977 | 120.6 | -4.13% |
| 1976 | 125.8 | 1.86% |
| 1975 | 123.5 | -5.22% |
| 1974 | 130.3 | -11.90% |
| 1973 | 147.9 | -4.46% |
| 1972 | 154.8 | 1.91% |
| 1971 | 151.9 | 3.12% |
| 1970 | 147.3 | |

* Source: National Association of Realtors.

Editor's note: The Housing Affordability Composite Index reflects the ability of a family earning the U.S. median income to qualify for a mortgage covering 80% of the median existing home price. Interest rates of mortgages, family income, and housing prices are the three key variables addressed in the Index. A higher index value reflects a greater ease in the ability to purchase a median price existing home.

©1996 Chase Global Data & Research
73 Junction Square, Concord, MA 01742

## PRICE TO EARNINGS RATIOS

| Year | S&P 500 Composite Index | Dow Jones 30 Industrial Index | Dow Jones Utility Index |
|---|---|---|---|
| 1995 | 17.5 | 15.6 | 11.7 |
| 1994 | 15.0 | 15.0 | 11.6 |
| 1993 | 21.3 | 25.6 | 20.5 |
| 1992 | 22.8 | 30.5 | 13.7 |
| 1991 | 26.2 | 64.3 | 14.9 |
| 1990 | 15.5 | 15.3 | 16.6 |
| 1989 | 15.5 | 12.4 | 12.7 |
| 1988 | 11.7 | 10.1 | 15.3 |
| 1987 | 14.1 | 14.6 | 9.4 |
| 1986 | 16.7 | 16.4 | 14.7 |
| 1985 | 14.5 | 16.1 | 9.6 |
| 1984 | 10.1 | 10.7 | 7.1 |
| 1983 | 11.8 | 17.4 | 6.7 |
| 1982 | 11.1 | 114.4 | 6.5 |
| 1981 | 8.1 | 7.7 | 5.9 |
| 1980 | 9.2 | 7.9 | 7.3 |
| 1979 | 7.3 | 6.7 | 6.9 |
| 1978 | 7.8 | 7.1 | 6.9 |
| 1977 | 8.7 | 9.3 | 7.8 |
| 1976 | 10.8 | 10.4 | 8.0 |
| 1975 | 11.3 | 11.3 | 7.2 |
| 1974 | 7.7 | 6.2 | 5.9 |
| 1973 | 11.9 | 9.9 | 8.3 |
| 1972 | 18.4 | 15.2 | 10.9 |
| 1971 | 17.9 | 16.2 | 11.6 |
| 1970 | 18.0 | 16.4 | 12.6 |
| 1969 | 15.9 | 14.0 | 11.5 |
| 1968 | 18.0 | 16.3 | 14.9 |
| 1967 | 18.1 | 16.8 | 13.8 |
| 1966 | 14.5 | 13.6 | 15.6 |
| 1965 | 17.8 | 18.1 | 17.9 |
| 1964 | 18.6 | 18.8 | 20.3 |
| 1963 | 18.7 | 18.5 | 19.7 |
| 1962 | 17.2 | 17.9 | 19.9 |
| 1961 | 22.4 | 22.9 | 22.0 |
| 1960 | 17.8 | 19.1 | 17.8 |

* Source: "Barron's National Business and Financial Weekly";
Standard & Poor's Corp.
Figures reflect year-end values.

©1996 Chase Global Data & Research
73 Junction Square, Concord, MA 01742

## MEASURES OF DURATION AND DEPTH OF U.S. RECESSION

[1960 - 1995]*

| Business Cycle | | Duration in months | Constant GNP decline |
|---|---|---|---|
| Peak | Trough | | |
| Apr. 1960 | Feb. 1961 | 10 | -1.2 |
| Dec.1969 | Nov. 1970 | 11 | -1.0 |
| Nov. 1973 | Mar. 1975 | 16 | -4.9 |
| Jan. 1980 | July 1980 | 6 | -2.3 |
| July 1981 | Nov. 1982 | 16 | -3.0 |
| July 1990 | Mar. 1991 | 9 | -1.6 |

Severe recessions: 1973 - 1975, 1981 - 1982

Mild recessions: 1960 - 1961, 1969 - 1970, 1980, 1990 - 1991

*Source: National Bureau of Economic Research; Chase Global Data & Research.

©1996 Chase Global Data & Research
73 Junction Square, Concord, MA 01742

## Federal Individual Income Tax Rate Schedules

[1960 through 1996]

| Taxable Income | Calendar years 1960-63 | Calendar year 1964 | Calendar years 1965-67 | Calendar year 1968 | Calendar year 1969 | Calendar year 1970 | Calendar years 1971-78 | Calendar years 1979-80 | Calendar year 1981 |
|---|---|---|---|---|---|---|---|---|---|
| 10,000 | 26.0% | 23.5% | 22.0% | 23.7% | 24.2% | 22.6% | 22.0% | 18.0% | 17.8% |
| 20,000 | 38.0% | 30.5% | 28.0% | 30.1% | 30.8% | 28.7% | 32.0% | 28.0% | 27.7% |
| 40,000 | 56.0% | 50.5% | 48.0% | 51.6% | 52.8% | 49.2% | 48.0% | 43.0% | 42.5% |
| 76,000 | 69.0% | 61.0% | 58.0% | 62.4% | 63.8% | 59.5% | 58.0% | 54.0% | 53.3% |
| 120,000 | 78.0% | 68.5% | 64.0% | 68.8% | 70.4% | 65.6% | 64.0% | 64.0% | 63.2% |
| 180,000 | 87.0% | 75.0% | 69.0% | 74.2% | 75.9% | 70.7% | 69.0% | 68.0% | 67.2% |

| Taxable Income | Calendar year 1982 | Calendar year 1983 | Calendar years 1984-85 | Calendar year 1986 | Calendar year 1987 | Calendar years 1988-90 | Calendar years 1991-92 | Calendar years 1993-96 |
|---|---|---|---|---|---|---|---|---|
| 10,000 | 16.0% | 15.0% | 14.0% | 14.0% | 15.0% | 15.0% | 15.0% | 15.0% |
| 20,000 | 25.0% | 23.0% | 22.0% | 18.0% | 15.0% | 15.0% | 15.0% | 15.0% |
| 40,000 | 39.0% | 35.0% | 33.0% | 33.0% | 28.0% | 28.0% | 28.0% | 15.0% |
| 76,000 | 49.0% | 44.0% | 42.0% | 42.0% | 35.0% | 28.0% | 28.0% | 28.0% |
| 120,000 | 50.0% | 50.0% | 49.0% | 49.0% | 38.5% | 28.0% | 31.0% | 31.0% |
| 180,000 | 50.0% | 50.0% | 50.0% | 50.0% | 38.5% | 28.0% | 31.0% | 36.0% |

Source: Chase Global Data & Research, Joseph A. Peman "Federal Tax Policy " (The Brookings Institute).

©1996 Chase Global Data & Research
73 Junction Square, Concord, MA 01742

# 1996 Federal Tax Rate Schedule

## Married Individuals Filing Jointly

| Taxable Income | Rate |
|---|---|
| 0 - $40,100 | 15.0% |
| $40,101 - $96,900 | 28.0% |
| $96,901 - $147,700 | 31.0% |
| $147,701 - $263,750 | 36.0% |
| Over $263,750 | 39.6% |

## Single Individuals

| Taxable Income | Rate |
|---|---|
| 0 - $24,000 | 15.0% |
| $24,001 - $58,150 | 28.0% |
| $58,151 - $121,300 | 31.0% |
| $121,301 - $263,750 | 36.0% |
| Over $263,750 | 39.6% |

Source: Chase Global Data & Research.

©1996 Chase Global Data & Research
73 Junction Square, Concord, MA 01742

# MUNICIPAL BOND YIELD TAXABLE EQUIVALENT TABLE

| | ---- Income Tax Bracket ---- | | | | |
|---|---|---|---|---|---|
| | 15% | 28% | 31% | 36% | 39.6% |
| Joint Return Taxable Income* | $0-40,100 | $40,101-96,900 | $96,901-147,700 | $147,701-263,750 | Over $263,750 |
| Single Return Taxable Income* | $0-24,000 | $24,001-58,150 | $58,151-121,300 | $121,301-263,750 | Over $263,750 |
| TAX-EXEMPT YIELD % | TAXABLE EQUIVALENT YIELD % | | | | |
| 2.5 | 2.94 | 3.47 | 3.62 | 3.91 | 4.14 |
| 3.0 | 3.53 | 4.17 | 4.35 | 4.69 | 4.97 |
| 3.5 | 4.12 | 4.86 | 5.07 | 5.47 | 5.79 |
| 4.0 | 4.71 | 5.56 | 5.80 | 6.25 | 6.62 |
| 4.5 | 5.29 | 6.25 | 6.52 | 7.03 | 7.45 |
| 5.0 | 5.88 | 6.94 | 7.25 | 7.81 | 8.28 |
| 5.5 | 6.47 | 7.64 | 7.97 | 8.59 | 9.11 |
| 6.0 | 7.06 | 8.33 | 8.70 | 9.38 | 9.93 |
| 6.5 | 7.65 | 9.03 | 9.42 | 10.16 | 10.76 |
| 7.0 | 8.24 | 9.72 | 10.14 | 10.94 | 11.59 |
| 7.5 | 8.82 | 10.42 | 10.87 | 11.72 | 12.42 |
| 8.0 | 9.41 | 11.11 | 11.59 | 12.50 | 13.24 |
| 8.5 | 10.00 | 11.81 | 12.31 | 13.28 | 14.07 |
| 9.0 | 10.59 | 12.50 | 13.04 | 14.06 | 14.90 |

* Net amount subject to federal income tax after deductions and exemptions. Tax year 1996.

Source: Chase Global Data & Research.

©1996 Chase Global Data & Research
73 Junction Square, Concord, MA 01742

## U.S. UNEMPLOYMENT RATE

[All civilian workers; annual average]

| Year | Rate (%) |
|---|---|
| 1995 | 5.6 |
| 1994 | 6.1 |
| 1993 | 6.8 |
| 1992 | 7.4 |
| 1991 | 6.7 |
| 1990 | 5.5 |
| 1989 | 5.3 |
| 1988 | 5.5 |
| 1987 | 6.2 |
| 1986 | 7.0 |
| 1985 | 7.2 |
| 1984 | 7.5 |
| 1983 | 9.6 |
| 1982 | 9.7 |
| 1981 | 7.6 |
| 1980 | 7.1 |
| 1979 | 5.8 |
| 1978 | 6.1 |
| 1977 | 7.1 |
| 1976 | 7.7 |
| 1975 | 8.5 |
| 1974 | 5.6 |
| 1973 | 4.9 |
| 1972 | 5.6 |
| 1971 | 5.9 |
| 1970 | 4.9 |
| 1969 | 3.5 |
| 1968 | 3.6 |
| 1967 | 3.8 |
| 1966 | 3.8 |
| 1965 | 4.5 |
| 1964 | 5.2 |
| 1963 | 5.7 |
| 1962 | 5.5 |
| 1961 | 6.7 |
| 1960 | 5.5 |

Source: U.S. Department of Labor, Bureau of Labor Statistics.

©1996 Chase Global Data & Research
73 Junction Square, Concord, MA 01742

**ZERO COUPON BOND PRICES***
**(without mark-up)**
**BASED ON YIELD AND MATURITY**

| | $ Value @ | | | | | | | | | |
|---|---|---|---|---|---|---|---|---|---|---|
| Years to Maturity | 3% | 4% | 5% | 6% | 7% | 8% | 9% | 10% | 11% | Years to Maturity |
| 20 | $551 | $ 453 | $ 372 | $ 307 | $ 253 | $ 208 | $ 172 | $ 142 | $ 117 | 20 |
| 19 | 568 | 471 | 391 | 325 | 271 | 225 | 188 | 157 | 131 | 19 |
| 18 | 585 | 490 | 411 | 345 | 290 | 244 | 205 | 173 | 146 | 18 |
| 17 | 603 | 510 | 432 | 366 | 310 | 264 | 224 | 190 | 162 | 17 |
| 16 | 621 | 531 | 454 | 388 | 333 | 285 | 245 | 210 | 180 | 16 |
| 15 | 640 | 552 | 477 | 412 | 356 | 308 | 267 | 231 | 201 | 15 |
| 14 | 659 | 574 | 501 | 437 | 382 | 333 | 292 | 255 | 223 | 14 |
| 13 | 679 | 598 | 526 | 464 | 409 | 361 | 318 | 281 | 249 | 13 |
| 12 | 700 | 622 | 553 | 492 | 438 | 390 | 348 | 310 | 277 | 12 |
| 11 | 721 | 647 | 581 | 522 | 469 | 422 | 380 | 342 | 308 | 11 |
| 10 | 742 | 673 | 610 | 554 | 503 | 456 | 415 | 377 | 343 | 10 |
| 9 | 765 | 700 | 641 | 587 | 538 | 494 | 453 | 416 | 381 | 9 |
| 8 | 788 | 728 | 674 | 623 | 577 | 534 | 494 | 458 | 425 | 8 |
| 7 | 812 | 758 | 708 | 661 | 618 | 577 | 540 | 505 | 473 | 7 |
| 6 | 836 | 788 | 744 | 701 | 662 | 625 | 590 | 557 | 526 | 6 |
| 5 | 862 | 820 | 781 | 744 | 709 | 676 | 644 | 614 | 585 | 5 |
| 4 | 888 | 853 | 821 | 789 | 759 | 731 | 703 | 677 | 652 | 4 |
| 3 | 915 | 888 | 862 | 837 | 814 | 790 | 768 | 746 | 725 | 3 |
| 2 | 942 | 924 | 906 | 888 | 871 | 855 | 839 | 823 | 807 | 2 |
| 1 | 971 | 961 | 952 | 943 | 934 | 925 | 916 | 907 | 899 | 1 |
| 0 | 1,000 | 1,000 | 1,000 | 1,000 | 1,000 | 1,000 | 1,000 | 1,000 | 1,000 | 0 |

The above values are approximate unless ZEROS mature on the same day of the year as purchased. Yields are based on semi-annual compounding of interest.

*Source: "Mugged on Wall Street", copyright © 1987 C. David Chase.

©1996 Chase Global Data & Research
73 Junction Square, Concord, MA 01742

# Acknowledgements

Over the years, thousands and thousands of hours of research has gone into the *Digest* and *Performance Guide's* creation. Associate editor Jennifer Paydos, Jeffrey Kooken, James Worthley, Drago Rajkovic, and Ashby Jennings have worked diligently in helping evolve a great deal of information into a cohesive whole. Without their talent and efforts the *Digest* and *Performance Guide's* release would be a far more burdensome task. Instead it has been, and continues to be, a marvelous learning experience which I have truly enjoyed.

Thank you to my wife, Barbara, who while accepting my curmudgeon habits as I researched and wrote this book, logged untold hours performing a variety of tasks on the project's behalf. Various other research and editorial assistants have helped along the way, too numerous to mention in this space. But Herb Benjamin deserves credit for his help during the initial process of publishing and marketing this book. Special thanks to my mother, Ellen T. Chase, who used her proficiency as a librarian to locate difficult material we sorely needed.

Sean Moynihan continues to be a consummate professional in his ability to explain the strengths and diversity of the *Digest, Performance Guide, InvestmentView® software,* and our various *Page and Wall Charts* as he leads our marketing campaign. Lastly to my most loyal supporter, Alan Stone... and also to George Ruddy, Pat Forster, Mark Kwatcher, and Dan Ewing I owe a fond thank you for all their confidence and comments through the years in which this project was but an idea. The final product is a testimony to their enthusiasm.

Thank you all very much.

# INDEX

## A



## B



## C



©1996 Chase Global Data & Research
73 Junction Square, Concord, MA 01742

## D



## E



©1996 Chase Global Data & Research
73 Junction Square, Concord, MA 01742

## F



©1996 Chase Global Data & Research
73 Junction Square, Concord, MA 01742



## G



## H

# I



# J



# K



# L



©1996 Chase Global Data & Research
73 Junction Square, Concord, MA 01742

©1996 Chase Global Data & Research
73 Junction Square, Concord, MA 01742

## P



## R



## S



©1996 Chase Global Data & Research
73 Junction Square, Concord, MA 01742

## T



## U



## V



## W



## X



## Y



## Z



©1996 Chase Global Data & Research
73 Junction Square, Concord, MA 01742

# ORDER FORM

| Product | Quantity | Price |
|---|---|---|
| **1996 Chase Investment Performance Digest**<br>Reviewing over 80 investment subjects covering 1960 thru 1995.<br>400 pages @ **$23.95, plus $4** shipping and handling. | ______ | $ ________ |
| **1996 Chase Guide to Investment Performance**<br>Reviewing over 20 investment subjects covering 1960 thru 1995.<br>160 pages @ **$11.95, plus $4** shipping and handling. | ______ | $ ________ |
| **1996 Chase Page Charts**<br>6 Major Investments. 1960 thru 1995.<br>8.5" x 11", full-color, laminated. @ **$9.95**. Please indicate quantities: | ______ | $ ________ |

_______ Mutual Fund Investing _______ Global Investing

_______ Equity Investing _______ Balanced Investing

_______ Risk: Stocks vs. Bonds _______ Risk: Global Investing

| | | |
|---|---|---|
| **1996 Chase WALL Charts**<br>***Mutual Fund Investing in the Modern Era***<br>6 Major Investments. 1960 thru 1995.<br>37" x 24", full-color, laminated. @ **$23.95.** | ______ | $ ________ |
| ***InvestmentView®*** **Software**<br>Easy to use, Powerful graphics, with performance and risk data from 1960 to present on 300+ indices. Windows 3.1. 4 MB RAM and 5 MB in hard drive required. Monthly data. | ______ | $ ________ |

**Quarterly Shipments** **$295/year** _______

**Monthly Shipments** **$425/year** _______

| | | |
|---|---|---|
| ***InvestmentView®*** **Hypothetical Software**<br>All features of ***InvestmentView®*** plus 8,000+ Lipper Mutal Funds with returns and characteristics. College & Retirement Planning (with college tuition database). Disclaimers for printouts, more. Windows 3.1. 4 MB RAM. 60 MB hard disk. Monthly data shipped quarterly. @ **$495** | ______ | $ ________ |
| **SINGLE Edition *InvestmentView®* Version**<br>Indicate Monthly Edition (__________) @ **$129** | ______ | $ ________ |
| **SINGLE Edition *InvestmentView®* Hypothetical Version**<br>Indicate Quarterly Edition (_____Q) @ **$225** | ______ | $ ________ |
| **College and Retirement Planning**<br>(combined programs) @ **$69**<br>(with College Tuition database and Social Security data) | ______ | $ ________ |
| **FREE DEMO DISK** (30 day working copy) @ **FREE** | ______ | $ N/A |

**CALL FOR INFO on 5000+ Stocks, 2,700+ Variable Annuities, and 1200+ Money Managers Databases.**

**Please see continuation of product listing on reverse side ☞**

**Phone – (800) 639-9494 or (508) 371-9100 FAX – (508) 371-9105**

| Product | Quantity | Price |
|---|---|---|
| **Seminar Slide Show Presentation** | _____ | $ ________ |

*Risks and Returns: Investment Options in the Modern Era*
(1960 through 1995) 30 slides with script and audiotape. Please check format(s):

SLIDES @ $295_____ OVERHEADS @ $350 ____

DISK @ $150 ____ (WINDOWS ___ or MAC ___)

Individual Slide @ $35 Please identify: ________________

5 Slides @ $100 Please identify:______________________________

______________________________________________________

**Subtotal** $ ____________

(Massachusetts residents include 5% tax) $ ____________

## Method of Payment:

_____Check or money order _____VISA _____MasterCard

Card Account Number ______________________________

Card Expires ______________________________

Signature ______________________________

## Ship To:

Name ______________________________

Title ______________________________

Company ______________________________

Address ______________________________

______________________________

City______________________ State____________ Zip__________

Business Telephone (        ) ______________________

## Shipping and Handling Charges

**Chase Investment Performance Digest and the The Investor's Guide to Investment Performance**

| | |
|---|---|
| 1-3 | $4 each |
| 4-24 | $3 each |
| 25-99 | $2 each |
| 100+ | Call |

Next day shipping – $18 each
UPS 2nd Day – $9 each

**FREE SHIPPING on these products:**

- InvestmentView® Software
- InvestmentView® Hypothetical Software
- College and Retirement Planning Software
- Chase Page and Wall Charts
- Chase Seminar Slide Show and/or Individual Slides

**To order, please call (800) 639-9494 or (508) 371-9100**

**For fastest service, credit card orders may be faxed to us at (508) 371-9105**

**❑ Please send me your catalog!**